Pioneer Women in Texas

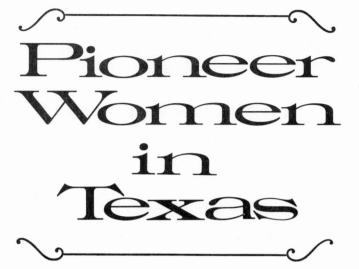

Pioneer Women in Texas

By
ANNIE DOOM PICKRELL

JENKINS PUBLISHING COMPANY
The Pemberton Press
Austin and New York
1970

CONTENTS

PREFACE

These biographical sketches have been prepared in the hope of preserving for future generations a correct idea of the lives and characteristics of the women who lived in Texas prior to 1845. The sketches have been woven from facts contributed by descendants or friends of each woman under discussion, and each sketch has been approved by those who have contributed.

In the name of all Texans, I take this occasion to thank each individual who has thus borne a part in this little bit of historical labor.

THE AUTHOR.

MRS. SAM HOUSTON

BORN

MARGARET LEA

"The woman whom thou gavest to be with me, she gave me of the tree, and I did eat."

These simple words offered in extenuation of Adam's disobedience in the garden of Eden made it plain that Adam was anxious to shift the blame of the apple performance. Natural anxiety under the circumstances, a contemptible anxiety, too, yet the man, Adam, acknowledged, then and there, that man was forevermore to be in some measure under the influence of woman. We know that the influence has lived on in spite of the flaming sword that closed the gates of Eden, that it has withstood all changes incident to growth and development. We are not prepared to say that the men of to-day take refuge as did Adam in the indisputable fact of woman's influence, but we do say, and say it earnestly, that there can be no smallest doubt that each of our grandmothers, living and laboring and suffering in early Texas, influenced each her own particular husband. Whether these women, your grandmothers and mine, exercised a beneficent influence, each upon her own husband, or an influence wide that mark—witness the case of Adam—we must acknowledge the existence of the influence. We may never know how much that grandmother helped or how much she hindered. We may never know whether that husband rose to prominence and power because of her influence or in spite of it. But in extenuation of this ignorance of ours, we would suggest that in the case of the woman under discussion right now circumstances played no small part in the sway of this thing called matrimonial influence, unusual circumstances, abetted by unusual characteristics in the man, her husband. Mrs. Sam Houston was the wife of a brilliant, farsighted, energetic, determined man, a lovable man, too, in the eyes, even of savages. He had come from a state of the United States in which he had risen to prominence and power, only to give it up as if defeated, to take his way on the back of a battered old mule to the wilderness of Texas. In spite of this mule equipage and the attendant poverty, he had made many staunch, loyal friends in Texas. He had made, too, some exceedingly bitter enemies, for he saw the effect the present must have on the future long before other men saw it, and he dared always to speak this vision, even when he knew men about him must fail to see it. These characteristics, worth much in the aggregate to his country, made enemies for the man, and all connected with him were destined to one day realize the venom of those enemies.

Of these connections his wife comes first, of course. She was known as Margaret Lea, and had been born in Marion, Alabama, April 11, 1820. Her father was a man of much literary training, and believed staunchly in the education of the female as well as the male. As soon as Margaret reached a suitable age, she was sent to Pleasant Valley Seminary where she made good records as a student. On her return to the parental abode, her father gave her further instructions, particularly in English, and some poetry from the pen of Margaret is extant to-day. She was a devoted, consistent member of the Baptist church, having taken the vows upon reaching the age required by the church. Her religious idea spread from the house of worship and the hour to her daily life—as some of her intimate associates have testified, and the modest, retiring, young woman could be stern when rebuke of any kind for anybody seemed to her to be in order.

These religious ideas failed in any way to cut Margaret off from the outside world. She came and went among the young people of her day, enjoying their innocent pleasures, urging them on a bit, now and then, if things promised to be dull. She made many visits about over the State and to New Orleans. She lingered often in Mobile, and many there were in those southern cities who could testify to her charm. Strangely enough, the girl remained heart-whole and fancy free until she had reached her twentieth year. Then the inevitable took place. She fell in with a big, strong man who understood her charms, and immediately conceived a passion therefor.

This strong man was none other than Sam Houston. Some authorities claim that she met him first at Mobile while there on a visit with friends. Others claim that this meeting took place in New Orleans whither Houston had gone for medical attention, made necessary by the wound he had received at San Jacinto. Wherever, whenever it happened, it is enough for us to know that in 1840 Margaret's path crossed that of this certain hero of the hour, and that things took on a lively turn from the very hour of the meeting.

Let us visualize for a bit some every-day affairs in the life of General Houston. He had plunged into the fight after the disasters at Alamo and Goliad, and with far-sighted skill in planning, even to the most minute detail, he had routed Santa Anna and had thereby set Texas free. He had served one term as president of the new republic, had been lauded to the skies by some and bitterly blamed by others. Through it all he had maintained a spirit of daring, a spirit of tenderness, had preserved an indescribable charm of manner that made women and children, even Indians, love him with a love surpassing knowledge. He loved life at its brightest, too, the strain of music, the dance, for he felt the ripe, rich blood of youth still aflow in his unclogged veins. He had known sorrow, bitter sorrow, a sorrow that had turned him adrift in a strange world, among strange, uncouth people, but for all that, his commanding form, his manly address, his winning sweetness of manner made each its heavy inroad upon the affections of young Margaret, and she bowed shyly, but none the less happily, before his compelling smile.

That bow held a world of meaning for Houston. He knew that he had reached her heart, but Houston in all dealings, thought, too, of the other fellow. There is evidence that he had fallen in love with the sweet-faced girl at the first meeting, but Houston reflected that he was twice her age, that he was penniless, that his life had held dark days which Margaret could never understand, but days nevertheless for which he, her lover, must pay the price. That price, in Houston's eyes a big one, made him hestitate, no matter how much he had come to love the innocent maiden. He visited her again and again in her home, fighting after each visit a stern, non-committal battle with his own misgivings, but in the end the hero of San Jacinto lost his self-appointed battle and became, before very long, the husband of Margaret Lea.

Now, perhaps, young Margaret had possessed a few misgivings of her own. Perhaps her forty-seven year old lover was not exactly the hero she had worshiped in her girlhood dreams. She was not blind to his faults. She had known of his life among the Indians, but Margaret had seen, alas, how much the Indians had loved him, and had heard how easily and gently he managed, even the deadly Comanches. She had heard the hero swear—he was rather adept at it—and maybe it had been whispered to her a time or two that he had been groggy drunk. She had heard of his inexplicable first marriage and its sudden rupture, but she had felt his hand upon her own arm, and she had heard the music of his voice, and Margaret did as any other woman would have done, Margaret forgot all about any other love affair being laid at the door of her husband-to-be. In that forgetfulness, in full faith in herself, Margaret walked into the marriage with Houston, her eyes wide opened and her heart full of determination to do her best.

Realizing her husband's virtues, Margaret set about, once the marriage was done, to change his vices. From the very first her woman's influence was perceptible. Some

days of course there were disappointments to be met in
this path of endeavor. The San Jacinto hero would forget her admonitions, but respect for the force of his wife's
character, a force hidden under a soft aspect of gentleness, gradually improved the man's habits. Then, too,
Houston was at home, in a real home, one made pleasant
by a Christian woman, and his sweetness of heart responded in a real gratitude toward the individual who had
brought about this beneficent blessing. He became after
a bit an active member in the Baptist church, due largely
again to the influence of Margaret.

On December 16, 1841, Houston took again the office of
President of the Republic. He had been chosen for this
office after the departure of Lamar. Enjoying this confidence of the people, appreciating the problems awaiting
him in the discharge of his new-old office, Houston took
his wife to Austin, the two-year old capital of the Republic,
and there our Margaret assumed full charge of the president's home.

The stormy times of the young Republic drifted on, each
little squall ending as squalls usually end, sometimes in
blessings, sometimes in disaster. Margaret had a fair idea
of the burden her husband carried, and having no help to
offer him, she hit upon the wiser way of maintaining peace
and comfort for him at home. Her children began to
come, eight in all they were finally, and each child she
soon learned presented a different problem in management.
That mother had spent little time in the study of heredity,
but for all her lack of study, she had now to face the
problems offered by the unalterable fact. The same
qualities that had made her husband admirable in her
sight, qualities that had needed her guiding hand from the
first days of their acquaintance, appeared in the youngsters, and as said youngsters hastened on to maturity,
Margaret many times had her hands full. They, too, desired the fun, the frivolity of life, and as they grew older,
they made some effort to obtain it. At one time, a son,
Andrew, during Houston's term as governor of the State
of Texas, announced in his father's presence—and the
presence of many young people in the parlors—that he
was, himself, a "secess." Realizing that Houston was
opposed to secession, Adele Atwood, one of the girls
visiting in the parlor, took it upon herself to avert the
storm that might have followed young Andrew's statement. She, in all earnestness and with much maiden persuasion, begged the tempted father to show them, then and
there, how "to cut the pigeon wing."

Nothing suited the General better. He forgot his son's
foolishness. He forgot the knee wounded at San Jacinto,

the knee that would stiffen at times, and he gave demonstration, full and complete, of the pigeon-wing idea. Fun followed, fast and furious, and from our standpoint said fun was innocent enough. But to Margaret, appearing suddenly on the scene, the fun wore a different aspect. To her such indecorous proceedings must never be tolerated in a Christian household. The Governor's home was to her at the time her own particular domain. The fun quickly subsided, and there was a hint that maybe the General had a bit of a curtain lecture on the side after the children were safe in bed. Later, in this governor's home, our Margaret gave birth to William Roger Houston, and so far this has been the only child born to a governor of Texas while he was in office. (1928.)

The laughing allusion on the part of her son to the idea of secession presaged the next great trial in the life of Margaret. The trial was the war between the States. In addition to the sorrows following naturally in the wake of war, Margaret had to endure the incriminations that inevitably fall the way of these individuals who fail to share the ideas of their friends and neighbors. Her husband had used every means in his power to prevent secession in Texas. His clear-sighted vision had seen in such measures only disaster and ruin for the people of the South. Nevertheless, Houston sent his son to war to fight for the thing he could not approve, sent him because his friends and neighbors believed it to be right, and Margaret gave of her time and strength in any way and every way that she thought might help the pitiful fight. When it was over, Houston must close his lips lest they utter in the ears of his defeated countryman something of the I-told-you-so idea, must close his lips until some fresh spark of that far-seeing wisdom might spring up within him to help a little by the way.

But those closed lips were not to suffer long. The news of the fall of Vicksburg in 1863, no matter his opposition in the beginning to secession, struck a mortal blow, and the gallant soldier of a successful revolution, defeated and bowed down, took to his bed. His wife and children crowded about him, all save his son, young Sam, then wounded and in prison up north of the line. Three weeks later Houston passed away. That passing was preceded by a comatose condition. Across his unconscious lips came many times the cry, "Texas, Texas!" Then with his hand clasped close in his wife's, he whispered tenderly, "Margaret" and spoke no more.

And our Margaret! With her husband gone, with her children about her, Margaret must face privation and loss, must live as best she might through the horrors of reconstruction. She found herself possessed at last of a log-house and a patch of land, and a little while later, the State Legislature appropriated seventeen hundred dollars to pay the salary of her husband's unfinished term of office as governor.

We hear of Margaret again in 1867. An epidemic of yellow fever raged throughout the eastern section of Texas, devastating towns and villages, and among the sick and suffering, Margaret passed, day and night, a blessing wherever she trod. She died, herself, a year later, being but forty-eight years of age, died, because of her service, in the prime of her woman's life, in what should have been the very beginning of her usefulness. Why?

Let him answer who sees in every single event crowding the path of man some spirit of wisdom, some deep, unending sign of the truth of the old saying, "He doeth all things well." Let him answer in the watches in the night when questions run wild and hope fights shy the human heart! Let him express for us the homely, beautiful truth to be seen in a study of this woman's life of sacrifice, for in such expression your scribe has come upon something far beyond her power and her might.

Data obtained from—

> Texas Governor's Wives, by
> Pearl Cashell Jackson.

Additional data from—

> Mrs. Nettie Houston Bringhurst,
> San Antonio, Texas.

MRS. GEORGE W. SMYTH
BORN
FRANCES GRIGSBY

The friends of a certain American individual claimed that said individual was first in war and first in peace and first in the hearts of his countrymen. Kentucky, as a state, has laid claim to this priority idea in horses—almost obsolete, in certain unmentionable liquids as yet by no means obsolete, and in women, beautiful, efficient, gracious women, and may they never become obsolete, God Bless 'em!

Despite Kentucky's claim to priority along these lines, despite the halo or nimbus or whatever mark of priority people might have preferred before horses faced the danger of extinction and pleasant liquids became unmentionable, people, even good people, with no shadow of the law to force departure, such people emigrated from Kentucky, back in the early twenties and settled in the wild, new country called Texas. Joseph Grigsby must plead guilty to this last charge. He turned his back on old Kentucky. He exchanged blue-blooded horses for mustangs. He exchanged ripe old Bourbon for any old liquid chance might throw his way, but to the day of his death, Joseph Grigsby had a quaint way of saying—and believing that when it came to women, he brought with him to Texas, samples, good samples of the very best that had ever been produced in old Kentucky.

There was deep satisfaction in the soul of Joe Grigsby over the thought of the samples of womanhood brought from the land of plenty to the land of promise. Maybe he set an extravagant value on such things, but said valuation failed to influence this gentleman to leave other things behind. Far from it. Along with the beautiful women of his family, he brought money, and plenty of it. He brought slaves, too, and many of them, and he settled his family and his slaves on the league and *labor* of land granted him by the Mexican government and located not far from our Beaumont of to-day, hard by the bank of the Neches River. He built the dwellings, his own big log cabin and its out-houses, the quarters, too, for the slaves, at a point on the river which has ever since been known as Grigsby's Bluff.

Now along with his slaves and his money and his family of representative Kentucky women, Joseph Grigsby brought his daughter, Frances, of whom we are about to say things, and before these things are all said we doubt not that he who reads may say, maybe aloud, that young Frances was a credit, even to old Kentucky. She was winsome and

sweet, a slender dark-eyed girl, weighing a comfortable
number of pounds above the hundred mark and rather a
thing of beauty in the eye of the beholder.   And as usually
happens when one is slender and winsome and sweet, the
eye of the beholder is sure to appear and very soon on the
stage of action.

This last remark is out of time and place.   Some tend-
ency on the part of the scribe to enjoy sentimental things
has caught that scribe in the ridiculous position of placing
the cart before the horse.   We have rushed ahead, suggesting things before other things equally important and
more suitable as to time have ever been mentioned.   We
are supposing that Frances led a life bare of importance
until romance came her way.   Such supposition is far from
the truth.   Save for her own inherent difference in character, Frances lived the life of the ordinary girl of her day
in Texas.   Log-cabin home?   Yes, and bare of the comfort of bath and lights and fans, things considered necessities in the Texas home of to-day.· To Frances, ignorant
of such things, that home lacked nothing in point of comfort.
The rooms were large and airy, shaded and cool in summer,
heated in winter by huge, log-heap fires, the flames leaping
and dancing with the aid of the "lightard" wood deftly
slipped beneath the logs.   Moreover, slaves in plenty
waited to do her bidding, waited to bring the cold spring
water for her bath in summer, waited in winter to bring it
to her heated the right temperature by the addition of
water from Aunt Viney's wash pot out in the yard, which
pot was never allowed to be either cold or empty.   These
slaves cleaned the rooms, they cooked the meals, they
waited at the serving of them, they controlled the little
negroes whose duty it was during meal-time to keep the
flies at bay with a huge bunch of pea-cock feathers.   Easy
to see that Frances, ignorant of plumbing and electric ap-
pliance, suffered no repining because of the things she had
been denied.

A vision of slaves always at hand conveys the idea of an
idle mistress.   It bespeaks a kind of hot-house condition
of life in which the mistress dare not soil her hand with
labor lest so doing she demean herself in the eyes of her de-
pendents.   Descendants of slave-holding people in the
South to-day, served as they are by the descendants of
old-time slaves, must frequently refute the suggestion that
Southern women know little about real work.   The descendants in the case of Frances Grigsby have abundant
proof at hand at such times.   They know that in that home
on the bluff, master and mistress and slaves were all busy,
and that Frances was required with her sisters to do a
certain amount of labor, day by day, and every day as it

came. She carded both wool and cotton. She spun the
carded article into thread, and she wove the thread into
cloth to be used in clothing herself and the family and the
slaves. Six cuts of thread she must card and spin day by
day or its equivalent in value in some other part of the
cloth-making process. She must help, too, with the cutting and sewing of garments for the slaves, for few negro
women could ever be trusted with this precious cloth to
cut it into garments, even for their own children. But
when all this was done, this equivalent of six cuts a day,
Frances was allowed to employ herself as she saw fit.

Can we realize, we who rarely ever even *hem* sheets, can
we make ourselves understand that this dainty little maiden,
just for the love of the thing, put in her spare time weaving
them? Not only sheets, but blankets and cloth for her
own under garments and for the "homespun" dresses to
be worn in this wilderness in the hope of saving the silk
brought from old Kentucky? Maybe not. Maybe the
tax on the imagination is too great. Maybe it seems a bit
beneath the dignity of a woman worth a place in these
records. Maybe, again, we agree with you, but let us tell
you that this carding and spinning and weaving leads us
to the sweetest picture offered in the life of this exemplary
young woman.

Her home, as we have said before, was at Grigsby's Bluff,
sheltered winter and summer by the virgin forest. Beneath the pine and the oak, the magnolia and hickory, that
pioneer home was built. The breeze from the Gulf tempered the Texas sun in summer. The forest, dark and rich
and green, aflame, too, with the holly and the yupon, protected them in winter from the cold north wind. In the
spring, the yellow jessamine and the dogwood added each
its fragrance to that of the glistening pine. On a spring
day—let us hope it was a spring day—Frances sat her down
to work upon her counterpane, a thing she had herself designed, a thing to be made in her own spare time, to be
kept against that glad day when some hero should appear
and take her into a home of her very own, a log cabin one,
maybe, but her very own, one wherein she might use the
sheets and the blankets, the product of her own labor.

Now before we pass on to the picture in the life of young
Frances hitherto classed as sweet, let us pause long enough
to recall a few details of that counterpane. It was woven
in squares about twelve inches each way, each square containing raised places according to design, with flowers afterward embroidered in the plain places, the original of these
flowers being selected from the forest at hand. This arrangement was not always easy for a girl all untutored in
the rules of art. Just how to place a flower to the best

advantage, just how to run it on the stem was sometimes
a puzzle. The sunflower, for instance, seemed most stubborn. Twist and turn and change as she might, the thing
seemed to elude her. She went to bed, still puzzling over
it. She slept soundly throughout the night, but when she
woke she had dreamed the solution of her difficulty, and
the sunflower appeared in all its glory in its own proper
place in the counterpane.

And now for our sentimental picture. One glad day, as
Frances worked over this piece of household vanity, as she
sat demurely in the soft sunshine, apparently absorbed in
her labor, up came the hero necessary to complete the
picture.   The hero, hereinbefore alluded to, not daring to
suggest that she lay by work so important, was content to
watch the little needle fly in and out through the embroidery, just glad to look at her, shy, sweet woman, busy
over her self-appointed task. He even evinced much interest in the design of the affair, his eyes shining a bit with
hers as she explained that the composite cloth was to be
fringed all around, said fringe measured some twelve inches
deep.

This hero seeking Frances out there in her magnolia-
scented bower, was none other than George W. Smyth
whose name is linked forever with all Texas history. He
had come from a line of Smyth's dating back to one Joseph
Smith who had been born in Philadelphia in 1776. They
had emigrated to South Carolina, to Tennessee, and had
finally settled in Texas. He was young and strong and
full of the blessedness of hope and promise, and standing
there in the shadow of the jessamine, watching the little
hands as they plied that needle, young George readily lent
himself to the pleasures of love's young dream, and subsequent events lead us to believe that young George was
not alone in his lending. That dream led young George
to declare many times in after life that Frances always reminded him of a violet. Some there were who came under
her influence in after life who failed to share his opinion.
Modesty and sweetness and gentleness cling persistently
to the violet idea. Frances was all this, but we of to-day
know, for time has proven it, that the weaver of the counterpane had a mind of her own, had as well a will of her own,
and one strong enough to stand by the workings of that
mind, and, remembering all this, one is likely to let the
violet idea slip into the background. But if to young
George, and to old George, too, for that matter, if she was
the violet in all its beauty and its charm, let us rather bow
before the purity of purpose that recognized these qualities
and proceed to concern ourselves with other qualities which

we, falling a little short of the enthusiasm of the lover,
really care more about.

They were married, then, these young people, for some
inexplicable reason at Nacogdoches. Instead of the plantation marriage with its weeks of preparation and the gathering of neighbors from far and near, the bridal pair made the
journey to Nacogdoches on horseback, accompanied by a
slave or two, and then, the ceremony done, rode slowly
and happily back over that deep-sanded road, stretching
beneath the magnolia and the oak and hickory, their wedding music the song of the birds and the chirp of the little
forest-folks and the solemn, holy roar of the pines.

They began life in a log cabin of one room, built near
Indian Creek, the most beautiful creek in the whole world,
and that log cabin, used afterwards for a *smoke-house* (if
this is not plain hunt up a black mammy and ask her),
stood in all its sturdy strength full seventy-five years.
Thither, Frances brought the fruit of her labors, her own
dainty clothes, and her household linens, her counterpane,
and two slaves, a boy and a girl, given her by her father
and her mother. No doubt that father and mother
grieved a bit to see this girl start out in the matrimonial
game. They knew something about it. They knew what it
meant for this girl, shy violet in her husband's eyes, to
leave her girlhood home, to undertake the cares of wife-
hood, cares that must come, no matter the tenderness of
the lover husband, cares augmented a thousand times by
the fact that her bridal home had been reared in the wilderness, still infested with Indians and bears and snakes. In
common with slave-holding people of the South, they felt
as they thought of her in the watches in the night, that no
better thing could they have done for her than to present
her with this boy and girl so that she might train them
while they were still young as she would have them trained
in all matters of daily home-making.

Frances was equal to this task. She began her married
life by accepting the responsibility of these slaves just as
she accepted the responsibility of her husband and his welfare. Many times in after life she told stories of the up-
bringing of the negro children, and all stories illustrated
her interest in the growth and development of the young
scamps.

One of these stories had to do with the duty assigned
these slaves of bringing fresh spring water at convenient
intervals throughout the day for the comfort of those in
the cabin. Easy task, for which one expected to receive
board and clothes, plus a careful up-bringing; easy, yes,
until one remembers the bears that frequented the forest,
bears in no way averse to human flesh as a matter of diet,

and the Indian, eager always to take the life of any new-
comer, white or black. Frances, not unmindful of these
forest dangers, arranged a series of signals to be used while
that water errand was under way. She watched them start
always upon the journey—and temptations to loiter were
close at hand—and when she thought sufficient time had
elapsed for them to reach the spring, she gave one call,
loud and clear, the little pickaninnies answered back, and
then they put out for home. After another wait, timed
according to the slow progress of the son of Ham, Frances
called again, and if there came no answering call she put
forth with her pistol to investigate. Now, we have no
record to prove that Frances ever found the children treed
by a bear or anything that necessitated the use of her
weapon, but one day they gave her a great scare. Being
particularly busy, Frances forgot to give that first call that
was to be answered from the spring. After a bit, remembering her slaves, she began to wonder where they might be.
Investigation showed them nowhere about the cabin.
"Surely," thought Frances, "they cannot be waiting this
long time just to have me call."

Alarmed beyond measure, she slipped to the cabin door
and raised her voice in one long, loud call, a call strengthened by the idea that it had been given in a forlorn hope.
She even grasped her pistol, reached about toward her hat,
but across the soft-scented air the hallo call came back to
her, and the two little blacks soon stood obediently before
their troubled mistress, explaining to her that they were
waiting at the spring to have her call. Surely an individual
so stupid had not been worth the trouble necessary to his
or her up-bringing, but that girl lived to be the "black
mammy" to all Frances Smyth's children, even unto her
grand-children, and as long as that "black mammy"
lived she commanded the love and the respect of those
children and their children.

Let us remember for the time that the husband of this
young Frances was a man worth while. He had come
from a fine family of people. He boasted no mean education, no small amount of polish, and beneath it all he
was a man of sterling character, honest, up-right, God-
fearing. He was accused in his time of being a man of few
words, but when he spoke his words were heard and usually
heeded. While Frances busied herself in the log-cabin, he
went about the more important part of the establishment
of a farm in the wilderness. He had the land cleared, and
it had to be "grubbed," and the work was done by the
slaves brought some of them in the first place from old
Kentucky. He went about the business in all firmness, in
all fairness. His efforts met with success, his broad fields

increasing in acreage and in value, his slaves increasing in
number until overseers became necessary. To these men
was given the task of laying out the work day by day, the
even greater task of seeing that the negroes accomplished
this work, but woe be unto any overseer whoever struck a
negro, no matter how stupid, no matter how vicious, woe
to him who abused any negro after any form. Frances,
sharing her husband's ideas, followed and abetted him in
all this work, and her own children, six in all, growing up
around her, catching a glimpse of the violet idea lingering
still in the father's heart, these children agreed with the
father to some extent in the violet matter, but they realized
many times the value of that mother's mind and her
ability to speak it.

She was a real sympathizer with her husband in his
patriotic work. When the great wilderness of Texas began to stir, began to dream of self-organization, began to
lift its head in the hope of freedom, George W. Smyth, because of his previous training, because of his staunch
character, became a leader among the patriots. He was
eventually a signer of the Texas Declaration of Independence, and that document duly signed, Smyth put forth and
joined the army. Some message delivered somehow
brought him back to the plantation on business for the
week, and he missed thereby the joy of participating in
the battle of San Jacinto, but his thought and his planning
had no doubt aided in bringing about the victory. Smyth
served the young Republic in many ways, in Congress
principally, and later when the Republic became a state,
he represented it in the Congress of the United States for
many years. This popularity was broken by the fact that
he opposed secession. Slave-holder himself, he frowned
upon secession as a method of settling the difficulty, but
when his state seceded, he bowed to the will of the majority
and cast his lot with her, giving freely of his money to the
cause, going even into battle for the thing he could not
respect.

These things said of our men-folks are proud things for
us all, but they take a man away from home and its interests. In Smyth's day and time of slow travel, it took
practically all of a man's time. Did the plantation go to
rack in his absence? Not a bit of it. Frances, his wife,
but took up the farm supervision where he laid it down,
and she carried it to a successful finish. The overseers respected her as she walked out among the negroes at work
in the fields. The slaves in all quarters welcomed "de
missis" with a smile, a smile lacking all thought of the
violet, for "little missis" could still speak her mind when
the occasion demanded it.

The years as they came and went brought an added sweetness of 'soul to the little woman. Out of her abundance, she gave freely to the needy. Sugar, coffee, flour, wine, all laiden in barrels and in sacks made the Smyth store-room a sight to behold, and no man, white or black, ever left the premises without receiving a portion of these precious luxuries, did he so desire them. She ministered tenderly to the people about her, her neighbors and her slaves, and many a fevered patient, because of her devotion and her sound common sense, had occasion to rise and call her blessed.

Records have left us little real information as to the religious attitude of Frances. Churches as we have them to-day were unknown in the community, and the Methodist circuit rider, even he with his gun across his shoulder, made few visits to this section. The Baptist church toward which Frances leaned had few ministers in the country, but there can be small room for doubt that Frances thought and thought often on things of a religious nature. We know, too, that she many times rode ten miles horseback through the leafy woods in order to attend service wherever she might find it, careless of the denomination any such service might represent.

Feeling, perhaps, the privation of this infrequent service, she determined that her slaves, naturally emotional, should not be denied the right to worship God as they saw fit. However foolish their shouts and cries and lamentations had been in her own ears, Frances respected them, for they were to her the outward expression of the negroes' religious idea. She went further, still, than a casual respect for these beliefs. She set apart land for their religious sanctuary, superintended the felling of logs, allowing the slaves their full time in order that they might build this simple house of worship. Some close observer might have claimed that she built this place of worship as a means of keeping the negroes at home at night so that they might be fit for work in the morning. No matter the utilitarian idea clinging about the matter, Frances sat many times on her own front porch listening tolerantly to the shouts of the happy, emotional darkey, *en rapt* in his religious ceremonials.

Frances rounded out her seventy-nine years of age, a neat, trim, erect little woman, her hair still black unto the day of her death. She met all trials in her life bravely, carried all her burdens as best she could, and no man ever heard her complain. She sustained the loss of her distinguished husband and took into her own hands as far as she could the control of things he was thus forced to lay down. She was even denied the pleasure of serving him in his last illness, for while in service in the Reconstruction

Convention in session in Austin, in 1866, Smyth became
ill of a cold brought on by hard work and loss of sleep, and
alone in a strange city, denied the comforts of home and
family life as he had known them, the soldier and statesman
and scholar laid down his life at his country's call, even as
the soldier marching in the line of battle meets the fire of
the enemy's weapon to his own earthly undoing. His
body was interred in the State Cemetery among the noble
dead in Texas, but Frances, shy, sweet violet of her husband's heart, lies in the land of her young love, surrounded
by the jasmine and the dogwood whose fragrance shadowed
her on her bridal morning. And not very far from that
early cabin home, not far as transportation brings things
to us now, another Frances of a third feneration leads her
own efficient, forceful life, sweet as a violet, strong in her
own mind to speak the truth, a blessing wherever she sets
her foot in this journey of life.

By their fruits shall ye know them.

Data contributed by—

> Miss Fannie Smith,
> Beaumont, Texas.

MRS. JOSIAH H. BELL

BORN

EVELYN McKENZIE

A couple of young people answering to the name of McKenzie came from Scotland at some time in the year 1770, making their first home in Iredell County, North Carolina. In 1771 a son, Andrew McKenzie, was born to these young people in this same county of Iredell. He opened his baby eyes into a world seething with talk of freedom and liberty and equality for all, for the Mecklenburg Declaration of Independence had been ardently supported in that neighborhood. Young Andrew grew up in that hornet's nest of independence, took unto himself a wife, and for many years lived on there after the manner of his fathers. During this time a little daughter was born to young Andrew, just a few months before General Washington died, and the little lassie, answering to the name of Evelyn, was proud many times throughout her interesting life to declare herself a contemporary of General Washington. Notwithstanding this fact, this glorious fact of living for three or four months in the same period of time as lived the Father of her Country, this lassie had to feel and know the effect of financial reverses which befell her father and mother while she was yet young herself, but yet old enough to realize after the fashion of youth that her parents were enduring some great trouble. The financial trouble brought about the removal of the McKenzies to Christian County, Kentucky, a newer country then than their own, one beckoning still to people waiting on the eastern border to come on farther toward the glorious West. And there, in that land of promise, Evelyn McKenzie met Josiah H. Bell and married him.

Now Josiah, hereinbefore alluded to, had been born in Missouri, had grown to manhood there, had come on a business trip into that particular part of Kentucky, and one sight of young Evelyn and her beauty, one look into her pretty eyes, and young Josiah decided that he must give a few more days to his trip, for in addition to his business deals, matters of courtship had suddenly bobbed up. With all his ideas of courtship, he was interested in plans that would bring him to Texas, plans in reality that looked toward an ultimate lodging in that special wilderness for him and his. He had signified his intention of coming to Texas with Moses Austin, but since the death of Austin had upset those plans, he waited to see just how far things might develop under Stephen, the talented young son of the would-be colonizer. Weighty matters, these, to be set aside for the sake of love affairs between

man and maiden, but the fact remains that Josiah waited
to court the young Evelyn, and finally married her December 1, 1818.

After that marriage, Bell and his wife sauntered southward, stopping first in Natchitoche Parish in Louisiana.
What their home was there in the land of the jasmine and
the magnolia we do not know. Something temporary of
course, but Josiah occupied himself conducting a small
store, trading for the most part with the peaceful Indians
who lived in this vicinity. Not on any very grand scale
was this mercantile venture conducted, for Josiah but
waited there for Austin to cross the line into Texas, whither
he, himself, waited to follow. This crossing finally took
place about 1821, and there in that part of Texas, so
similar to Louisiana in every way, they lingered until they
had made one crop of corn. Then the Bells came with
Austin to the bank of the Brazos River and set them down,
determined to make them a home. Bell took up his league
and labor of land bordering this same river, and the town
of Columbia was built afterwards upon his own land.

They built them a house there, these young people, after
the most popular plan of the day. Two immense rooms,
the walls built of logs, with a wide hall in between, and the
opening cut for windows were furnished with board shutters
instead of glass. Evelyn had been accustomed to money,
to ease and plenty through a large part of her life, at least
until the time of her father's financial embarrassments in
North Carolina, but the possession of wealth had not made
her lazy, had in no way inclined her to self-indulgence.
The Scotch blood of her ancestors forbade any such contingency. She was a fine house-keeper, a real home-maker.
The stranger who stopped within her gates never lacked
attention. Neither did this stranger ever find anything
awry in the log cabin. He knew, too, in the mysterious
way that such knowledge comes, that Evelyn was master
in that house. Her servants, her slaves, her children waited
her wishes in every matter concerning that home, both
big and little. She, in short, maintained the home, and
she ruled it, ruled everything in it—except Josiah. Evelyn
learned, perhaps through a few bridal tears, that Josiah
was capable of directing his own daily life and habit, and
Evelyn, being a true daughter of Eve, was therefore and
thereafter contented in her married life.

Among other accomplishments, Evelyn was a famous
cook. Many slaves were at hand ready and willing to
cook for her, and possessing, too, no mean knowledge of
the culinary art, but Evelyn liked to give the meal the real
flavor that comes from the touch of the master hand.
Josiah liked to keep "open-house" as the saying was in

Texas in that day, and many men and not a few women could testify to the worth of the "touch." General Houston lived beneath the Bell roof just as long as the capital was in Columbia, and he felt the touch of that comforting hand in many ways. He fell ill, in fact, in that very home, and Evelyn nursed him back to health and strength herself.

Among those guests harbored there from time to time, there came one day a young couple, both utterly strange to Josiah and Evelyn, the wife an attractive little woman, pretty and well-mannered. This man, too, fell ill and died —maybe Evelyn left the nursing to the wife where she thought it belonged—and when the hour for the burial arrived, Evelyn, pitying the young widow, searched the whole house for some black garment in the hope that this same widow might suitably proclaim her grief. The search revealed nothing except a black silk handkerchief that had belonged to the dead man. This Evelyn arranged in folds about the widow's soft, white throat, and then the funeral ceremonies were allowed to proceed.

The young widow married in three weeks time. Evelyn looked on at that marriage a little doubtfully. She felt sure that Josiah's death had not found her willing in three weeks time to promise another man what she had heard this young woman promise. But even Evelyn had to admit that there could be no real objection in her heart to the marriage. The man, her first husband, was dead, women were at a premium in the colony, and surely economical conditions forbade such a pretty little woman going to waste. So argued Evelyn with herself in settling the matter. What Josiah really thought we do not know. We do know that he said that a black silk handkerchief tied about the neck was just about the right amount of mourning for a widow of three weeks. No matter what Josiah had to say about this matrimonial venture on the part of the little widow, it was in itself a success, and the easily consoled widow lived to enjoy her new husband and to bear him sons and daughters.

There were children born in time to Josiah and Evelyn Bell, three of whom lived to maturity. The oldest child died in 1833 in the cholera epidemic that threatened to destroy the country at that time. The third one of these children was connected with the most unpleasant of Evelyn's experiences. It was a babe, six or seven months old, and Evelyn, in her motherly way, set about one afternoon to give him his daily bath. A tub of warm water stood before her, and Evelyn held the little body, guiltless of clothes, in her arms, the arms, themselves, bare to the elbows. A company of Indians stalked in, some two or three in all, and stood there solemnly watching the scene.

Evelyn's heart missed a beat, and then a few more. At last the low, gutteral tone of the elder of the Indians fell on her ear.

Contrary to the Indian's expectations, Evelyn could understand every word the savage had to say. She knew after the first few words that interest centered about the little naked body rather than about herself. She hoped, half-heartedly, that the novelty of the bath for the baby was the cause of the savage interest. That hope was put to flight by one terse sentence from the lips of the only Indian who has as yet spoken. Pointing to the baby, his eyes narrowed in appraisal, his lips twisted with a bit of a smack, this Indian made his comment: "Him make good roast."

Evelyn had never thought of Indians as cannibals. Guilty of atrocious crimes, of stealing and burning, she knew them to be, but this was a new idea. This idea connected with her own precious baby seemed utterly improbable. And yet, an Indian was an Indian, the once proud owner of land they, the white people, had seemed to wrest from him. His savage mind recognized no limit to the idea of retaliation for the white man's interference with his primeval affairs. What could she, the acknowledged wife of one leader in this movement to claim Texas for the white race, what could she hope for at the hands of this, the enemy, who now outnumbered her, who out-measured her weak woman's strength in any defense she might try to set up?

Summoning her courage, calling herself foolish names because she had allowed herself to become excited at all, Evelyn began in their own language to reason quietly with the Indians, to parley as one would parley with a child. The stolid countenances gave no sign that her words had qualified the Indian's opinion as to the quality of the "roast," but after her voice rose a shade—she was doubtless excited—the Indians slunk away. Another time she was surprised alone in the house. Her gun, always handy, was already loaded, but the only extra gunpowder they had for use in the old-fashioned firearms hung in a horn upon the wall. The Indians went toward that gunpowder. Whether he understood that the powder was all she possessed or not, gunpowder was a precious thing to said Indian. Just as his hand touched the coveted horn, he became conscious of a gun levelled on him. The Indian glanced at Evelyn. Something in the defiant, determined eye of the young woman made Mr. Indian decide that other things in this life were of more value than gunpowder, and he acted on that decision.

The three living children born to the Bells were educated in Catholic schools in Kentucky, the boys at a monks

school in Bardstown, the girl, Elizabeth, at the convent
Nazareth, just outside the same place. Josiah Bell and
his wife had joined the Catholic church, had been required
to, in order to obtain their grant of land from the Mexican
government. They educated their children in these schools
because they were at that time the best in the country,
and they were sure of the care the children would receive.
From this school Elizabeth was graduated in 1837.

Elizabeth, this young lady graduate, was married to
James Wilson Copes, a physician who had come from the
Mississippi bottom lands to join the patriot army. He
acted later as Surgeon-General under General Houston.
This wedding, true to the idea of the times, took place at
the plantation home on April 4th, 1839, and was a feast
worthy of the occasion. Josiah had invited the whole
colony to witness the affair. These guests came horseback and in ox wagons and afoot, and they came for many,
many miles, and Josiah knew they must be regaled with
food after the long journey. Chickens and turkeys and
hogs were sacrificed by this patriarch of his times, and
Evelyn had cooked and cooked for days and days, cakes
and pies and bread in order to satisfy the demands of the
hour.

The hour set for the ceremony arrived. The minister
was ready, the pine torches, depended upon for light, flared
about the yard, even the negroes dressed in their best,
waited to see the bride come forth. The groom was at
hand, ready, too. Still the delay. What could it mean?
Surely Miss Elizabeth, daughter of *Miss Evelyn's* well-
ordered household, had long been ready? What could it
mean? Nothing more nor less than the simple fact that
the man who had been sent to the town of Brazoria for the
marriage license had got stuck in the mud, and so far had
not been able to pull himself out. Of course the nasty
little legal matter must be obeyed. Youthful hearts must
wait and so must hostesses, not to mention the host,
wondering just a little as to what he ought to do.

Then a happy thought struck that host, the genial Josiah.
He ordered the feast to begin and the dance, and so with
the prospective bride and groom in the lead, they danced,
and then they feasted, and then they danced some more,
and feasted a great deal more, and so on and on throughout the night. The torches burned out, but the stars came
out to help, and with the first streak of dawn, the bespattered
messenger arrived with the necessary paper. The young
couple were married, and at daylight, they started out for
the *in fair* week. This consisted of visits to the West-
fall plantation, to the Waldecks, the Pattons, and some
other friends scattered about the community.

Less than ten years afterwards, Evelyn had to see her husband die, had to face the necessity of going on alone in the world in which she had once lived so happily with her husband. Prosperity had come to them with the growth of Texas, some losses of course, as the years went by, but there was sufficient improvement made upon the plantation so that it yielded Evelyn a return, far from niggardly, all the twenty remaining years of her life. She continued to manage the plantation, continued her association with her friends and her neighbors, bright, energetic, capable, even unto the time of her death. And in that pioneer home, the home that had witnessed her daughter's marriage, at some time in 1859 Evelyn laid down her work and entered into rest, leaving behind a glowing example for those who must need come after.

Data Contributed by—

Mrs. Lucy M. Carnes,
Austin, Texas.

MRS. EDWARD BURLESON

BORN

SARAH GRIFFIN OWEN

We have now come upon a striking character, one possessing great force and individuality, and there is just a little hesitancy on the part of the writer in beginning the simple story. Said hesitancy is due in a large measure to the fact that the writer is rather puzzled as to the best point of taking hold of the unique character, so we must just fall back at last on the simple statement that Sarah Griffin Owen was born November 3rd, 1796. We can further state that the family of Owen had come to America from Scotland, having at some time in the scheme of things picked up a bit of Irish blood, too. Our Sarah's parents had lived at one time in Owensboro, Kentucky, the town had, in fact, been named for her people, but we cannot say positively that this Sarah had been born there. We know, too, practically nothing of her childhood. Of her youth we are almost as ignorant. Some pictures made later in life proclaim her a beautiful woman, and we do know that she was small and wiry, neat beyond reproach in her dress, and some of the things we shall relate of her proclaim her a woman distinguished in many ways from the common class of people.

Sarah Owen was married to Edward Burleson, he who was afterwards president of the Texas Senate, a man strong in his way as she was in hers. No sentimental happenings of the courtship have been handed down to us—Sarah was not particularly demonstrative—but we know that they came to Texas early in the life of the province, that they settled on the Burleson head-right near the present site of the town of Smithville. They moved before very long to holdings at the head of the San Marcos River. There they built what was then known as a double log house with wide galleries across the entire front, and in this house, Sarah reigned supreme.

That reign was by no means bare of the rough places usually found in the path of the monarch. Remember the place was new. The journey to Texas had been accomplished in ox wagons, and there had been small place for the transportation of luxuries. Before long Sarah realized that all cloth worn by her family and her slaves must be made under her own direction, on her own looms, that her table must be supplied with the fruits of her own efforts. In this work her husband offered little help. He was busy looking after Indian troubles, organizing state affairs for the Republic of Texas, and the day of his return home was ever a matter of uncertainty. All home matters were thus left in Sarah's hands, even to the control of the children. Indeed his work about the republic kept him so much from home that the children stood in awe of him when he did return. Conscious of the awe, Burleson gave it little thought save to laugh over it. He even enjoyed their attitude at times, when they waited to hear his first laughing greeting.

"Old lady, how many hogs you got? What sort of a crop you got?"

Record fails to show that Sarah ever quarrelled with her husband over these prolonged absences. Proud of him in her heart, of course, glad that her own man stood well in the eyes of other folks, Sarah felt sometimes that his home needed a bit more of the master's presence. Maybe Sarah felt a twinge of jealousy that he could thus be contented away from her for so long a time, and nobody claiming to be exactly normal had differed with her in the matter. Women of Sarah's type are slow, however, to speak of their feelings, particularly when they have been slighted, but such women sometimes act and most effectively. There came an Indian alarm on a certain day, and Burleson, always a foe to the red man, collected all the men in the neighborhood, white as well as negroes, and started on the hunt. Sarah, watching the hurried preparations, stopped them long enough to remind her husband that they were without fire wood for either house or kitchen. With some laughing remark as to her skill in emergencies, Burleson mounted his horse and rode away. Sarah, her heart stirred to its depths, laid well her plans. When the wood was gone, she made the negro women climb to the roof of the house built for the family's special use, and made them pull from their places the shingles hauled, some of them, for miles, and always more or less hard to obtain. These shingles, exceedingly easy to split, furnished the fuel for the house through the many weeks of Burleson's absence. When he did return, Mr. Carelessmanofthehouse, he found his dwelling open to the wind and the sun, and maybe Mr. Carelessman wished that he had heeded his wife's suggestion. He realized at least that his wife, just and firm and true, was able to detect the error in the way of her husband and a wee bit stronger than most women in her method of expressing it.

Some of the many children born to Sarah died in infancy, but Sarah found herself much concerned with the rest of them and their up-bringing. She was assisted in this matter of concern by her old cook, Jane. This serving woman boasted Indian and negro blood, half and half, but she was such a successful imitator of her little mistress that no speck of dirt ever appeared about her, either on

her clothes or on her big, bony body. She was so devoted to
her mistress that she made it her duty to be just as much
of a mother to those children as Sarah was herself.   She
believed like her mistress in labor for everybody, and it was
a common thing to hear her say, early in the morning:
"Come on, Davie Crockett, les' go git de greens fur dinner."   David Crockett Burleson and his brother always
obeyed when thus addressed, and after an hour or so in the
woods with Jane, they would return with enough leather
breeches and poke-salad for the family dinner.   Jane's attentions were supplemented by the loving care of an old
Indian, a member of the Tonkeway tribe, answering to the
name of Placedo.   He made periodical visits to the Burleson home, and the younger boys hailed these visits with
delight.   They stole eggs from the mother's barn, they
even stole the young chickens and traded them to Placedo
for bows and arrows and moccasins.   With old Placedo's
help, they relieved a hen of a whole setting of eggs, sub-
stituted buzzard eggs for the comfort of the barnyard fowl
and rejoiced over the hen's dismay when the little buzzards
peeped forth.   Placedo later went with Edward Burleson
as a body servant in the Plum Creek fight, and he did
gallant service in his own Indian way.

But the half-breed woman—*Aunt Jane* they all termed
her—next to the mother, was the outstanding figure in the
lives of the Burleson children.   She nursed them, she petted
them, she scolded them, she helped them marry and she
helped lay them away in death.   Many years after her
days of servitude were over as per the thirteenth amendment, she made herself useful, despite her ninety years, in
many branches of the family.   She visited among them,
and if she found the servant's house occupied, she was
given a clean bed beside the mistress of the mansion.   A
cot of course, for Aunt Jane had never degraded either
herself or any one of her "young missus's" by offering to
sleep with her.   During one of these visits, in the home, in
fact, of David Crockett Burleson, the little boy, long since
grown into a useful citizen, said Burleson sat himself down
by Aunt Jane expecting to enjoy a chat.   After a few de-
sultory remarks, the man asked slyly:

"Do you remember, Aunt Jane, the day you gave me a
sure enough whipping?".

Aunt Jane looked up in scorn, her erstwhile charge continuing his remarks.

"You did lambaize me that time, Aunt Jane, and sometimes I kinder feel myself a tingle from it to this day."

"Lord, God, chile," her tone sunk to that of terrible
warning, "I dun whupped you so menny times I jes' doan

remember no spechul time. 'En, so he' pme, Lord, ye sho'
needed hit.''

But let's not get the idea that might follow all this comment of her serving woman that Sarah's children grew up
without refining influences. Far from it! The wiry,
thrifty little mother had never stood for that. She believed in work, she believed in thrift, in ever phase of
economy. Her Scotch blood mounted high sometimes at
the doings of her few neighbors in these important matters
of life. She was slow, even under the influence of that
mounted blood, to speak her mind to the world, but the
little children about her knee heard her speak many times
her stern belief in thrift and economy. She often quoted
to them the Scotch saying: "If you buy what you do not
need, you will sell what you cannot spare." This thrift
did not rob her of her joy in the sweeter, lighter side of
life. She read much—when the time could be found for
it, and she retained what she read. Some of this reading
was poetry, the best of it, and it remained with her as long
as she lived. Today her descendants quote certain bits
of poetry, and let the hearer know that they do so because
the grandmother before them quoted it.

When we come to discuss the religious side of Sarah's life
we are struck forcibly with the thought that the character
of Sarah was symmetrical. Remember, she managed an
immense plantation with little help from her busy husband.
She looked after the comfort of her home and family, and
she fed many slaves. She carried the keys to the store-
room and the smoke-house, seeing to it that no man went
hungry, but that no waste was allowed in the supplies of
food brought with arduous labor from New Orleans.

She directed the labors of her slaves that they might all
eat of the things the Texas land would produce. She
watched them turn the cotton and the wool into cloth that
they might all be clothed, and as she moved among them,
reproving here and praising there. The negroes, quick to
discern the just in men and women, listened and willingly
to both praise and reproof. They knew without question
that they stood beneath the glance of a woman, just but
firm, exacting, not given particularly to mercy, and they
loved her, even as they feared her in her busy march about
that plantation. But no man among those slaves, no
child born to our Sarah can recall that she ever discussed
religion with anybody. She held to her own views of life
and religion, and they were well-grounded. We acknowledge that she was a good hater, and it is every day history
in Texas that she joined her famous husband in his dislike for General Houston. But she asked no human to
share those views, not even her own children, and she made

no effort to change in any way the religious views of other people about her. She did display, however, a desire to see her children educated. Some of them refused to listen to her advice on this subject, and Sarah learned in bitterness that a mule may be taken to water, but he cannot be made to drink. Mayhap, in that first generation she saw no real scholars as learned men and women are termed to-day, but the fruit of her desire appear in the next generation.

Now your scribe must be pardoned if she turns at this point to consider unreservedly the stories told of this remarkable woman by one grandson. This man has mounted to positions of trust, and has filled them satisfactorily to the people of Texas and the people of the United States. He tells us winning stories of our Sarah. About the time she reached her three score years and ten, this young Albert realized that a grandmother gets a peculiar pleasure out of the association with a grandson. He had met with some kind of an accident and had been sent to his grandmother's home to recuperate. She was by this time a widow, her children married and gone.

In the wilderness she had been forced to prescribe for her children and her slaves when they were ill. She had learned in the famous old school of experience to look after many forms of physical distress, and methinks she rather enjoyed this little attention to the wounded boy. At any rate young Albert came from the experience full of the knowledge of Sarah. He can tell you how she worked, how she—the money not particularly necessary—knitted socks and sold them at the store. He can tell you how she quoted poetry to him.

"And if we do but watch the hour
There never yet was human power
Which could evade, if unforgiven
The patient search and vigil long
Of him who treasures up a wrong."

This bit from Byron fell often from her lips, and remembering her spirit slow to forgive, we may be pardoned for believing that she was trying to administer a bit of self rebuke.

And now in the face of this, we tell you that Sarah Burleson smoked cigarettes. Not the famous Camel nor yet the earlier Duke, but cigarettes rolled by her own hand. Just where she obtained the tobacco we cannot say. We know that she scorned the use of papers. She had corn shucks brought to the house, thoroughly cleaned. She trimmed them to the required size, keeping well at the trimming and rolling until she had a cigar box full of the dainty things. Tiring of this labor, she more than once tried to used a pipe, but went back always to the cigarette of her own manufacture.

Even in this cigarette matter, Sarah remained firm to her belief in thrift. Forced to buy tobacco, she sent week by week enough knitted socks to the store in San Marcos at which her son traded to pay for her own clothes, her personal wants, plus the tobacco. She frequently dwelt during these proceedings on the value of thrift for the benefit of young Albert, and she one day slipped into his hand a twenty-dollar gold piece, explaining its value, and what it might mean if properly invested. Albert listened respectfully to her remarks, but he proceeded without much ado to lose the coin. Judge of his dismay! Judge of his feelings as he thought of appearing before that grandmother to confess his guilt! Right then our Albert learned to value a tender father, a father who understood, for that father slipped another gold piece into his hand and told him to say nothing about it to anybody else.

With the fruits of her own labors and the thrift of her life-long habit combined, Sarah went down into a comfortable old age. She had been some time a widow, had knitted, we fancy, many carloads of sox, when she, the wiry little woman who had cared for the sick, both white and black, fell ill of the measles. Past her three score years and ten, she must fall ill of this children's disease in the city of Austin, at the home of Elizabeth Burleson Sneed, and death finally claimed her after a bitter fight. They stood about her bed, her son and her grandson, thinking each his own thoughts of the woman.

The one saw her flitting about her plantation home, giving orders, a neat wiry, little woman, immaculate in her dress, seeing to it that no man on all that plantation shirked an hour of labor, recalling, too, her religious independence, her desire to let every man live as he, himself, thought best to live. The other, her grandson, knowing her in the gentler time of her life, saw visions, too, of the wiry little woman. For him the stern, upright spirit of the woman longer grown had been tempered with mercy, and he, to-day, proud man before the world, a world grateful for his own achievements, speaks tenderly and reverently of the grandmother gone on before.

Data Contributed by—

> Hon. A. S. Burleson,
> Miss Emma Burleson.

MRS. REBECCA J. FISHER

REBECCA GILLILAND

It seems foolish, to say the least unnecessary, to add one word more to the many things that have been said about this leader among Texas women. Her name has been associated with the history of this same Texas for more than half a century. Her presence has been felt in Austin, the city in which she spent the greater part of her life, for she has borne her part in many of its activities. A staunch Methodist, she has been well known in church circles throughout the entire state. Her fame has gone abroad wherever the society of Daughters of the Republic has been known, for she was for many years its honored president. It might be wise to omit any further mention of this lady, but to collect any accounts however meagre of women in early Texas times and omit this forceful woman would be sacrilegious. So the lenient reader must forgive the scribe, if in telling this story the scribe must be guilty of the sin of repeating what everybody already knows.

Mrs. Fisher was born in the city of Philadelphia, August 31, 1830. Her father, Johnston Gilliland and her mother, Mary Barber, were Quakers, descended of course from those brave spirits, who in the interest of religion, made the pilgrimage to the new world of America, guided and controlled in his inimitable way by the famous William Penn. True in the main to the teachings of the Quakers, these Gillilands had become broad minded in all matters pertaining to religion, and before Rebecca was born, had begun to feel unbounded interest in the growth and development of other forms of religious faith and worship. The mixture of English and French blood, stronger, perhaps, than the Quaker idea, may have been somewhat responsible for this broadness of vision. Certainly we know that one son of this couple was named William McCallah Gilliland, the name William McCallah being the name of a Presbyterian minister of that day, a man highly respected by Gilliland and his wife, Mary. When this same young William Gilliland reached a suitable age, his Presbyterian god-father gave him a pocket Bible, suggesting that he keep it always about him, to read and digest as it were on the run, promising that much wisdom might be obtained if the young man adhered fast to the idea. We have no right to discuss the amount of wisdom so obtained, but we claim the right to testify that young William carried the Bible as per the gentle advice in his vest pocket, and we shall later give proof in substantiating this claim. This brother and young Rebecca with the parents made up that household of William Gilliland in the city of brotherly love.

Now that home hereinbefore alluded to was everything that a home should be. Both master and mistress boasted the beauty of character that should naturally follow on the heels of such religious training. Gilliland was engaged in a big, paying business, one his father had probably founded before him, and that master and mistress lived with their son and their daughter in an elegant home, carefully and tastefully furnished, with many servants to do their bidding. And yet, from this well-nigh perfect Eden, from this scene of business activity, from this world already established on a sure and certain basis, for no reason in the world that may be ascertained to-day, Johnston Gilliland and his wife, Mary, conceived the idea that they must emigrate to Texas. Must exchange ease and comfort for hardship and annoyance! Must exchange the glory of the palatial home, rich in its sober Quaker furnishings, for the log cabin, bare of comforts, endangered day and night by the prowling Indians! Must exchange the music, the laughter of the civilized world for the yell of the coyote and the scream of the panther! Must give up the beauty of the well defined path for the way untried, the way unmarked, and for some reason Johnston Gilliland and his wife remained staunch and true to that conviction despite the persuasive voice of friends who would fain show them the error of their way. Nothing that could be said availed even a feather-weight, and before very long—about 1840—after a long tedious journey by water, Gilliland, his wife and two children passed overland toward Refugio and took up their residence there.

So far as records may be trusted, the yells of the coyote or the scream of the panther may well be classed among those troubles that never happened. The dread of thieving Mexicans failed, too, to materialize, but Indians, pure and simple, unappeased in any way by the idea of Quaker love and kindness, dwelt in great numbers about Refugio. They had shown with little hesitancy their war-like attitude toward the encroaching *pale-face*, and a company of Rangers under Albert Sydney Johnston had been encamped nearby in the hope of protecting the white inhabitants of Refugio. But the Indian, ever watchful, ever alert, picked his chance. He slipped into the home of Gilliland, murdered outright the two grown people, gave Rebecca to the hands of a squaw, trusting young William to the hands of a brave whom they deemed capable of managing him. Forth they started, Rebecca across the saddle in front of the squaw, the boy in a similar position with the brave. They did not travel far. In some miraculous way, word had reached Albert

Sidney Johnston of the disaster, and before any great distance had been travelled by the savages, the troop of cavalry, riding hard, came within ear-shot of the savages, warning them of their own danger. With a certain respect for the prowess of cavalry riding hard in her own direction, the squaw decided that she must herself ride faster. In order to do so she must be rid of her burden, so Rebecca was tossed into a convenient clump of bushes, and the squaw, putting her pony at top speed, put out alone for her own life. The brave, realizing the good, hard sense displayed by the squaw, decided to follow her example, but before parting with his burden, he plunged a knife into the boy's heart. Thinking both boy and girl dead, the brave put his pony at top-speed and was soon out of sight.

Springing from his horse, kneeling beside the unconscious Rebecca, gathering her gently in his arms, Johnson found that Rebecca had been stunned and quickly brought her back to consciousness. He bent then above the boy's inert body, not daring any such hope in his case, for the knife remained just as the Indian had left it, straight up in the young man's breast. Reaching with reverent, tender fingers to remove it, Johnson found that the knife, too, had failed of its deadly mission, because instead of piercing young Gilliland's heart it had stuck fast in the pages of the Bible given him by the Presbyterian minister and worn thereafter as per the minister's command, over young Gilliland's heart. But the Gillilands, both father and mother, were murdered and the log cabin reduced to ashes. To the home of a Presbyterian minister in Refugio, Johnson took the young people thus doubly bereaved, and there they lingered during a rather tedious convalescence. When they finally gained sufficient strength, this minister arranged for their transportation, and they were taken to the home of an aunt, Mrs. Jane Trimble, who had a little while before settled at Galveston.

In this famous old city by the sea, Rebecca grew to womanhood. Recognizing her unusual mental qualifications, Mrs. Trimble gave Rebecca every possible educational advantage. When she reached the required age, she was sent to McKenzie Institute, the school founded by John McKenzie in 1840, her aunt being full of the idea that Rebecca's ambition, plus her unusual ability, might make of her a shining light in the literary world. But right there, in that very Institute, these plans met a sudden and complete setback. An earnest student, apparently immersed in the thirst for knowledge, Rebecca met Orceneth Fisher, a Methodist minister, and that meeting, casual enought in itself, changed the whole course of young Re-

becca's life. Dr. Fisher had been born and reared in
Illinois, had been pastor of a church in that state, and had
numbered among his congregation the afterwards famous
Abraham Lincoln. Fisher had been married, was the
father of one son, but his wife had been dead some time.
Due, perhaps, to her own strength of mind and purpose,
Rebecca found favor in the eyes of this minister, and in 1848
they were married and went soon afterward to Houston
where Dr. Fisher was to take charge of the Methodist
Church. Dr. Fisher was for some years the editor of the
Christian Advocate, the recognized organ of the Methodist
Church in Texas, but in 1855, accompanied by Rebecca
and their children, he made the journey to California and
took charge of a church there. A little later, he went to
Oregon to organize a church, and when this work was
successfully launched, he and Rebecca returned to Texas,
reaching Austin about 1871.

By this time three children had been born to Rebecca,
two daughters and one son. These children were well on
to maturity, the oldest about grown. Dr. Fisher had advanced into a hoary old age, and in this capital of a young
state, they had to face the problem of living and bringing
up these children.

Through the many difficulties that must of necessity beset the minister of the gospel in the discharge of his duty,
Rebecca bore more than her share of the burden. Nor
did she for one moment falter in that strenuous labor when
her husband was taken from her. She but doubled her
efforts, remaining all the while true to the dignity,
the staunch integrity inherited from her Philadelphia-
Quaker people. She showed, too, in a score of ways the
benefits derived from her early life, the life spent in that
Philadelphia home characterized by culture, by ease and
plenty, but if ever in the course of her strenuous life as
the widow of a minister with helpless children dependent
upon her efforts—if ever she sat her down to idle repining
and the fruitless sighs for things of a past day and time, no
human being ever heard her complain. She established a
home for her children, and in that home she fed other
people in order to supply bread for her children. She made
a success of the venture, too, and none seated about the
board, looking into her proud, determined countenance,
listening to her gentle but forceful manner of speech—none
ever dared suggest that in this work she had stepped down
one inch from her high estate. She saw both daughters
grown and married, but remained active in this work just
as long as it was necessary.

These household duties failed to interfere in any way
with her own church activities. Denied the right of speech

—she had no doubt been equal to a sermon and a good one—
she confined her church activities to close attendance on all
public worship, and she was for many years president of
the Ladies Aid Society of the First Methodist Church in
Austin. She presided with ease and dispatch at all meetings of the society, and no branch of the work failed to receive her personal attention. From time to time the
members of this society served dinners and suppers, the
male contingent of the church expected to appear on these
occasions and expected to pay for the meal thus provided.
She rarely took part in the manual labor these occasions demanded, but she maintained a dignified station near the
front door, and she saw to it politely but effectually, that
no man escaped without paying his necessary fifty cents.
During her term of office as president, this society claimed
among its members a very pretty, attractive little widow.
It soon became plain to Mrs. Fisher than more than one
man among the common run of customers had been willing
to pay for two dinners, provided the little widow ate the
second one. And be it known, the little widow, looking
into that kind but determined face, made every effort to
eat with each man as he appeared, for she dared not face
what she felt sure Mrs. Fisher would classify as disloyalty
to the church.

But, perhaps, the crowning glory of Rebecca Gilliland
Fisher's life was reserved for the year 1895. Then was
organized The Daughters of the Republic of Texas, a body
composed entirely of women descended from men who had
in the beginning made Texas. Her father had taken no
active part in the struggle for freedom, but both her father
and her mother had been sacrificed to the cruelty of the
Indians in the days of the Republic. In the course of
organization, Mrs. Anson Jones, widow of the last president
of the Republic of Texas was made president of this new
order of women, but recognizing the infirmities of her many
years, Mrs. Fisher was made Vice-President, and was in
fact president for many years after the death of Mrs.
Jones. She organized in Austin, William B. Travis Chapter,
D. R. T., and was its president as long as she lived. When
Mrs. Sevier came forward to save the Alamo from destruction, Mrs. Fisher became her staunch support in the
battle that followed, never wavering one time from her determination to stand by the plucky little lady in her
patriotic endeavors.

Mrs. Fisher was made, too, a member of the Texas Veteran
Association, and was, perhaps, the sole surviving member
at the time of her death.

Infirmities of age—she lived to be ninety year old—kept
her during the last few years of her life from active par-

ticipation in the affairs of state and of her own beloved chapter, William B. Travis, but she never lost interest in the work. Assisted by her noble daughter, she attended the State meetings of the Daughters of the Republic long after she had been forced to give up every other activity. Upon this daughter she leaned, blind and old and feeble, failing never to sing this daughter's praises in the ear of him who would listen, and in the presence of that daughter, she slipped away into the Beyond, self-contained, upright in heart, true pioneer of a world that owes its being to her and the kindred spirits who shared the wilderness with her.

Data contributed by—

Mrs. Blandford,
Austin, Texas.

MRS. FRANCIS YOAST, JR.

BORN

NANCY OWEN

A keen observer of Virginia people remarked more than thirty years ago that most states included in the United States were surrounded by other states and territories, but that Virginia in the minds of her very own people was surrounded by a halo. In the passing of the thirty years, there has been small evidence of change in the· minds of Virginia people in this halo matter. Neither have Virginia people been slow to speak their minds, and for this reason, people living for many generations in Texas have come to accept the halo idea. Therefore, when the statement is made that Mrs. Francis Yoast, born Nancy Owen, was at the time of her marriage a Virginia *belle*, she immediately assumes in our eyes the customary halo, and any further description of her seems unnecessary. Nevertheless we must proceed with a word or two for the sake of convention, pure and simple.

Nancy Owen was very beautiful. Laughing brown eyes, the laugh hard to subdue, curly brown hair, fair complexion, dainty little form, well-rounded, and a little foot that called always for a number one shoe. Through her father's people she had descended from the Welsh, pure and simple, the line stretching back without a break to Brian Owens, a Welsh king.

The home of this maiden was a fit setting for her beauty. An immense plantation near Bristol, Virginia, her father, this American Owen, being a successful planter, owning many slaves, doing in all a thriving business. For the comfort of himself and his family, he maintained an elegant home, its rosewood and mahogany furniture reflected in the polished floors, its walls hung with tapestries and with paintings, some of the latter rare and well-nigh priceless. In the parlor stood the spinet, the property of our Nancy, and on this she played, sometimes singing to its gentle accompaniment Annie Laurie, Last Rose of Summer, Alice Ben Bolt. From this you gather, and correctly, that this Nancy had been highly cultivated for her day and time, highly educated. She possessed a grandfather who was a Methodist minister, but for some reason this young girl had been sent, with a maid to look after her, to a convent in Paris, France. In this convent she learned something of music, something of painting, and, perhaps, best of all for her in her after life, Nancy learned to use her needle. She was required to make her own underclothes, and the stitches must be infinitesimal. The nuns in charge went a bit further. They taught Nancy's maid to sew, too, for

which said maid thanked them many times afterward in
the course of her checkered career.

This educational regime came to an end, and Nancy began her preparations to return to America. She obtained
many Parisian gowns and much material for future use,
many jewels, all of the approved pattern, and when Nancy
finally dawned upon the horizon of her old home, all the
halo usually ascribed to Virginia seem to have settled about
her pretty little brown head. Young people, one-time
friends, themselves now grown to maturity, flocked to see
this returned princess of a noble house, and Nancy, sweet,
winsome, and unaffected, bade them welcome. There were
parties and dances, there was the riding to hounds, and
when Nancy felt inclined to take the air in a placid manner,
there was the carriage drawn by four blooded horses.

There came the night set for the first real ball since
Nancy's return from France. Said ball was given at the
home of a friend in the community, and Nancy looked forward to the ball with all the eagerness of a young woman
certain of her power. She wore a dress of *buff velvet*, the
skirt measuring yards and yards around the bottom but
escaping the floor by an inch, the bodice plain and tight,
the sleeves puffed to astounding proportions, a lace bertha
of exquisite design encircling her dainty, white shoulders.
About her throat she wore a necklace of amethysts and
pearls, the natural color of the gems enlivened by the tint
of her gown. In her hair there was a high-standing comb,
in her ears there were amethysts with pearl pendants, and
about her slender white arms, there were bracelets that
matched her necklace. In short, our Nancy was a vision,
fair and dainty and sweet, a vision representative of the
daughter of a prosperous man in a prosperous country.

And then fate took a hand. Into that ballroom, his
attire in keeping with the time and place, walked Francis
Yoast, Jr. This gentleman was of English and Dutch
descent, his people having settled first in lower Manhattan
with the Van Wicks and the Van Storms. From this
neighborhood his people had drifted first to Pennsylvania,
then to Virginia. Yoast was as yet a stranger, himself, in
this part of Virginia, a man lacking of that powerful support in the eyes of all Virginians, a well-known family to
fall back upon in case of need. But Yoast was a college
graduate, a man of military training, a man of highly
polished manner, a man possessed of a gentle tongue and a
knowledge of when and how to use it. As he stood before
young Nancy, making in time his best bow, his very garments proclaiming the gentleman, it must have seemed to
every on-looker that a more suitable meeting together of
male and female had never before taken place.

But some things that it were better to know are hidden
sometimes from the eyes of him most interested. With all
his accomplishments, all his education, Yoast fell far short
of finding favor in the eyes of Owen, father of the fair
Nancy. First, Yoast was of Dutch descent, and then, too,
save for his love for Nancy, he failed to bow before the
Virginia halo. Plantations and slaves meant little to
Yoast. He was for opening somewhere in the new land of
America a first class school, a big school, on the order of
English and Dutch schools, and this idea seemed in the
eyes of Owen exceedingly effeminate. For in such desires
and such ambitions on the part of her husband, Owen
could see only one fate for Nancy, once married to this
dreamer. She who had tripped her happy way about her
father's home would in such a marriage find for her portion
tears, labor, and sorrow. And, as if adding sorrow's crown
to sorrows already too heavy to bear, young Yoast drank,
and sometimes to excess.

Perhaps the least said about the storm that followed the
meeting between the two young people the better. Love
was evident on both sides, even to the most casual observer, and no storm, no abuse on the part of Owen abated
in any sense that love's power. Family discussion, prayers
of her maid, who wept with her mistress at times and pleaded with her at others, were of no avail, and Nancy, stubborn daughter of a stubborn man, finally married Francis
Yoast, Jr. No wedding festivity, no feast of reason and
flow of soul, no feast of ham and cake and champagne
characterized the event. The few guests, mostly relatives,
bade the bridal couple a solemn farewell, the ceremony being over, and Nancy Owen Yoast turned about with her
new husband to face another world, one of which she had
read, one which she had little expected to endure.

No record was to be found of the *in fair* or of the first
few weeks of the life of the young bride, thus separated
from her family. We do know that Nancy Owen Yoast
went about her daily affairs, head in air. If she missed
her mother's smile, she only smiled the brighter herself.
If she longed for her father's approving touch, she but
managed to gain a comforting pat from the hand of her
husband. To her husband's plans of school establishment,
she listened, adding ever the encouragement contained in
the fact that she was ready and willing and *able* to help him
in the long-desired undertaking. Her willingness doubtless added fuel to the flame of her dusband's desire. Said
desire included a trip, a removal to some new locality, the
same old story of some other clime, some other place being
of all things the most desirable. This very thing moved
Yoast, this chance for change, for adventure, and our

Nancy, feeding in her woman's gentle way this flame afore mentioned, soon found herself ready for a departure for Texas.

The date of this departure we cannot give. Just how much part her father and her mother took in the farewells, we cannot say, but we can state positively that she left Virginia, even Virginia with its halo, in a carriage drawn by four horses, two of her husband's best beloved cronies having established themselves as outriders. Behind that carriage came the wagons, loaded with some household stuff, some flax, a spinning wheel, some table silver made originally from silver dollars. The slaves they had acquired walked part of the way, riding now and then, turn and turn about on the wagon seat with the driver, but Nancy's maid, she who had endured convents in foreign lands in order to be with the "young missus" probably enjoyed the honor of a seat in the carriage with Nancy.

The journey came to an end in Bibb County, Alabama. Somewhere in the fastnesses of the Tennessee mountains, or in crossing some unbridged, swollen stream, that first elegant carriage had been lost. The Yoasts had managed in the mysterious way peculiar to pioneers to keep ahead until they found themselves in old Alabama. But in its borders they must stop. Money had given out, and Yoast must make a stir about to find some more. With his other accomplishments, Yoast was an expert ginner, and soon found employment. He spent three years with this business, making his wife and slaves comfortable with the proceeds, and saving a bit as well. With these savings in mind, he yielded again to the Texas idea never quite dead in his heart, and before long, our Nancy found herself headed again for Texas. The conveyance used this time was what was known in that day and time as a *hack*, and the young men, the once gay outriders took their places in the wagon.

They made the next stop in Bastrop County in Texas. In the private affairs of the Yoasts there had been many changes since they had left Virginia. Money had given out, and money had been made again—some little bit at least, and the children had begun to come—there were eventually six in all—but to the casual observer the most striking change in affairs with this roving van had been made in their mode of travel. The carriage with its prancing bays and friendly outriders had been lost or sold. The hack taking its place had also gone the way of the earth, and when Mary Owen Yoast reached Bastrop, she rode in a covered wagon drawn by fourteen oxen. The wheels of said wagon were made of wood, seven feet across, guarded round with heavy iron hoops. Inside this wagon were placed beds for the use of

the family, for they dared not camp out for fear of animals
and the even more fearful Indians. They carried in the
wagon an iron pot twelve inches in diameter at its largest
part, measuring about one yard in circumference. (It may
be seen to-day in the Daughters of the Republic Museum
at Austin, Texas). At each stop made by these Yoasts a
fire was made, the kettle swung above the flames, and the
simple meals cooked therein.

Now on reaching Bastrop, the usual proceedings took
place. The kettle swung above the fire and some ears of
green corn boiled away merrily. The children, behind the
curtains of the wagon, waited to hear that the meal was
ready. The smoke of the fire carried its welcome message
to some Indians wandering that way. Scenting food and
fun and plunder, the Indians bore down upon the wagon.
The bubbling pot was the first thing to strike the savage
fancy. Seizing it, careless of the heat, they turned about,
expecting no trouble.

From the covered wagon, between cracks or seams in the
covering, Nancy Owen, one-time Virginia belle—watched
that Indian approach. When they seized the pot,
Nancy's very soul sank. Nancy knew that the stolen pot
represented the whole of her cooking vessels, available
right then for constant use. Reminding her husband of
this fact, she counseled with him hurriedly, watching the
while the Indians, her little heart a pit a pat with fear.
Summoning all his courage, no doubt borrowing some, too,
from little Nancy, Yoast stepped forth and offered to parley
with the savages. In the end the Indians agreed to the
return of the pot, provided Yoast gave them one of the
steers from the wagon train. Yoast complied with this and
bore the pot in triumph back to Nancy, confidently expecting the Indians to pass on as fast as the management of the
slowly moving ox would permit.

But the Indians were of another mind. Within fifty
yards or less of that wagon, they killed the steer, built up
a fire, and proceeded to give a war dance, oblivious of the
spectators behind that wagon sheet. Each one of the six
Indians took in his big ugly hands, a big joint, barely warm,
the blood still dripping in some instances from the flesh
clinging to it, and with his powerful jaws and saw-like
teeth gnawed the meat from the bones, swallowing it in
hunks. During this exceedingly disgusting exhibition, they
kept up a likely motion about the fire, a hop, first on one
foot and then the other, sometimes a double stamp of one
and then the other, all the time maintaining a guttural
sound, hardly grunt, hardly call, a hideous noise, conveying to Nancy a hideous intent on the part of the savages,
once their hunger had been satisfied. Despite that fear,

Nancy gathered her trembling children close in her arms, telling them in her own sweet way that God would take care of them, that the Indians were human beings like themselves, without their advantages, and that they must always try to be kind to them. She promised the children, her own heart heavy as lead, that the Indians would not hurt them, seeing that they had in no way abused the Indians. Over and over she told them this story, wiping the while the cold sweat from her own face. And in the end, Nancy was right. The savages, irresponsible children of another race, another hour, left the fire to smoulder out at will, beside a heap of stripped bones and made off, careless of the fright behind the wagon sheet, feeling no doubt an eminent satisfaction with the day's work. But Yoast and Nancy, dreading a return of the experience, put back to Nacogdoches where the semblance of a fort promised them some protection.

The school idea still lingered in the mind of Yoast, but, seeing that such a thing was not practical, he took up some form of scout work. He was issued his grant of land in 1837, probably for some services at the battle of San Jacinto, and then, seeing that Indian affairs promised to improve, Yoast took Nancy and the children back to Bastrop, and himself put out for Mexico, his love for adventure the only excuse for the deserting of his family. This yielding on the part of Yoast to the call of adventure did not leave Nancy helpless. Her oldest son, Andy Yoast, took upon himself the defense of the family. He had received himself a grant of land. He looked upon said grant as subject to his own disposal. He must help his mother. Such help meant food and clothing. His mother could neither eat nor wear a section or so of land, not even a league. So young Andy traded his land for a staunch, wiry, sure-footed Mexican pony, and on that pony's back, from 1836 to 1845 Andy carried the mail from Austin to Nacogdoches. Tiresome, monotonous for a young boy longing to be at something else! Doubtless, but the danger attached outweighed these privations in the mind of Andy and his mother. Indians lurked along that lonely mail route, and Andy had witnessed with his mother from that covered wagon that hideous war dance. But Andy, inheriting some of his mother's staunch determination, loaded his gun and put forth, week after week on his lonely journey. That gun in the end bore thirty-five notches, each notch representing the life of an Indian taken in order that the mail might be delivered, in order again that the brave little mother might be clothed and fed.

Yoast returned to his home and family, and things brightened a bit in that Bastrop home. The lands, culti-

vated by slaves, contented in their work, yielded abundant-
ly. Nancy, apparently yielding to her husband's opinions
in all matters of importance, really managed the plantation,
dreaming still, that they might some day establish a school,
keeping her own children about her, teaching them as she
would have gladly taught other children the many things
she had learned in her Virginia home and in Paris. A
certain form of social activity came to life in the neighborhood, and Nancy, accepting it with all its crudeness,
brought forth the remains of the buff velvet gown in which
she had made her first bow to Francis Yoast, Jr. Even the
jewels came out on special occasions, and they danced and
they danced, each woman sacrificing a pair of satin slippers,
usually home made, for one night's revel. Thus apparelled
and accompanied by her polished husband, Nancy often
mounted her pony and repaired to the scene of the dance.
At the cabin dance-hall door, the men waited to rush forward, to take Nancy bodily from the horse, lest her little
feet be soiled in the passage to the house. Just what
difference there was between that passage and the floor inside
we fail to see, for Nancy must, perforce, dance upon the dirt
floor, must feel the dust rising from the stamp of the many
happy feet to settle in the wide skirt folds of that buff
velvet gown. But custom was custom, and mayhap, that
tender attention on the part of man in pioneer days was a
way of expressing his gratitude to the woman who soothed
his afflictions, bearing at the same time afflictions of her
own, too heavy for the mind of man to conceive.

In 1846, during the war between Mexico and the United
States, Yoast went with the army to Saltillo. He was
wounded in battle and discharged and undertook the slow
journey back to Nancy. He died of his wounds at Goliad,
the scene of the famous massacre, some ten years before,
and the news travelled slowly to Nancy. Just what she
felt on the receipt of the news, we may never know, but we
are very sure that Nancy feared that life for her as a widow
was to be different from that of a wife. The difference
was, in fact, but slight. In her husband's absence, she had
learned to manage plantation affairs. She had re-lived her
own youth in the up-bringing of her children. Andy, her
staunch defender, had become a comforting companion.
Her daughters had learned at her knee the beauty of life,
and Nancy looked into their faces and saw much hope for
the future. A fortune for her and hers? No, a living
honestly acquired, was the height of her dreams, and
Nancy realized that dizzy height.

The news of her husband's death was carried in some
way, but without Nancy's knowledge to her people in old
Virginia. Said people had not forgotten the light trip of

her feet in her father's house, nor the sound of her voice, nor yet the soft sweet light of her eye, and with Yoast out of the way, it seemed an easy matter to bring Nancy once again into the home of her fathers. So in all assurance they wrote Nancy of the family decision that she might be allowed to come home. They even suggested in so many words that she bring *her Dutch children* home and begin again to live like a *civilized human being*.

Who would dare undertake a description of the mind picture brought before Nancy by that one single letter! Who would dare estimate her longing as memory showed her again the carpeted halls, the polished floors the pictures on the walls, the ease, the luxury, the elegance, the social activity right then the envy of the whole world! This Nancy, knowing how well she might, even yet, with the dust and grime of Texas in her heart and soul, take her place in all that elegance, knowing how beautifully her mother-trained, mother-taught daughters might astonish that Virginia world! Ah, that longing, that struggle! To give it all up, to go back, to float upon the tide as many another woman has floated to her physical comfort—and her moral ruin. Ah! Nancy was by no means blind to these pictures memory placed before her, but she saw the whole matter in a better light. She had been forced by her woman's heart, a foolish one maybe, to lay all that elegance aside, and Nancy had the strength and the force of character that enabled her now to stand by her guns. To the astonishment of every relation in Virginia, Nancy answered the invitation with a happy-hearted, gentle refusal, assuring her people with all courtesy that she was very happy in Texas with her *Dutch husband's children* and that she preferred to *live and die* in Texas.

Soon after this staunch stand on Nancy's part, the maid who had gone to Paris with her, the maid who had stood by Nancy in many trials and vicissitudes, fell ill and died. A colored woman called "Granny" took the maid's place with Nancy so far as service was concerned, but Nancy really grieved for the woman who had served her faithfully through most of her life. Nancy went on about the house and the plantation, attended always by "Granny," and the mistress began to feel after a bit that she had never before rightly appreciated the negro's services. They saw together some thrilling things. They were seated one day, the two of them, mistress and slave, on the porch of the Bastrop home, Nancy busily churning, "Granny" busily shelling peas. The small children played happily about the yard, and a negro man in full sight of all cut wood busily. The sound, unearthly, unmistakable, of Indian approach fell on the evening air. "Granny" grabbed the

children, save the oldest boy, and made her way to a cave
some two hundred feet away, a cave covered with a grape
vine, then in full leaf. The remaining boy took up his gun
and stationed himself for action, just as the negro man made
his way to the house.

Nancy recalled the pot episode and many other experiences of a like nature. She recalled as well that now save
for that young boy and the old slave man she was unpro-
tected. Added to this, Nancy had lost some of the assurance of youth, and as she now watched that Indian approach, her heart died within her. She realized before
many minutes that the Indians wore neither war-paint nor
feathers, that they were in fact naked save for a clout about
the hips and loins. They came closer, and yet closer a
rather unusual determination in each step, all sinister
enough, but Nancy kept on churning.

The Indians reached the step, and the leader paused.
He rubbed his stomach with both hands, and he rubbed
his mouth. He pointed to the churn, and then took the
dasher from Nancy's hand, took off the top of the churn
and laid them both on a convenient shelf. He thrust his
hands into the churn growling and gurgling all the while
like some snarling dog, smeared his own face with butter,
handing the churn then to one of his companions. In this
fashion the Indians finished the buttermilk. The last man
in the line dropped the churn from his butter-smeared
hands, it fell to the gound—O housewives, take notice—
and was shattered. Not another churn nearer than Galveston, and oxen the means of transportation! The
Indians, careless of Galveston or oxen, sprang at once for
the shining brass hoops, quarrelled a bit over them, then
disappeared from the scene.

Now Nancy had no real assurance that the Indians were
gone. So far they had done her no harm. Buttermilk as
a stimulant or an instigator of crime had been voted a
failure, but Indians were Indians and Nancy decided that
"Granny" and the children had best not undertake the
journey to the house. So placing food in a pan, she gave
it to the old colored man and he crawled on his belly,
through weeds and grass to the cave, and satisfied the
hungry mouths waiting him there. Back again to the
"missus," and then he and the one boy took turn and turn
about with the gun through the remainder of the night.
With the morning it became plain that the Indians had no
idea of a return visit, and Nancy went on about her business, making later a churn out of a hollow log.

Then two of her daughters arrived at the marriageable
age. They were duly courted and married at about the

same time.   The idea of a double trousseau in the wilderness of Texas had swamped any other than Nancy.   She
brought forth her amethyst and pearl necklace, sent it to
New Orleans and sold it, and the wedding preparations
went on.   One girl became the wife of a man named Townsend and went to live on his home place near the line between Travis and Bastrop Counties.

In the beginning of the discussion, hot-headed and many
times foolish, that concerned itself with the abolition of
slavery, Nancy Yoast saw a fresh trouble looming high.
Slavery had been an institution in her family for many
generations.   She owned a few slaves still, loving them,
caring for them, reproving them as one would little children,
profiting by their help, seeing in it all no cause for complaint on the part of anybody.   The abolition talk, wax-
ing hotter and hotter, drifted to her in Texas, even to her
own fireside.   Before very long Nancy found herself the
mother of a divided household.   Her sons, Andrew, Frank,
and Peter, shared their mother's Southern sympathy, and
went forth gallantly in the cause of the Confederacy.   John,
her own flesh and blood, brought up with slaves, knowing
all the cares and responsibilities a Southern master felt in
his ownership, knowing the benefits his people had derived from the labor of these dependent people, this John
sided with the United States.   Arguments, prayers, protestations were alike useless.   John left home to don the
blue.   When Nancy realized at last that he was gone, she
turned his picture to the wall according to the custom of
the day, and Nancy never spoke his name again.

Proud little Nancy!   She who had in her youth braved
her father's displeasure for love's sweet sake had apparently held again her own stubborn way.   If she dreamed in
the dead of the night of brother fighting against brother, •
no man ever heard of those dreams.   If she waited, hoping
against hope that John would yet change his mind, nobody ever knew of that wait.   But "Granny," lingering
patiently with her, saw the break in the once erect little
figure, and "Granny" never asked the reason why.

The war raged on to its bitter close, "Granny" still
silent.   Mrs. Yoast undertook to tell "Granny" that she
was free.   She had to tell her twice before "Granny"
understood it.   For answer "Granny" but shook her head
and went on about some simple service for "de missus."
When wages were offered her on the outside for the same
service, she but shook her head.

"I b'longs ter quality.   I'se frum ole Virginny."

And when Nancy Owen Yoast passed away in her
daughter's home near the Bastrop County line, her heart

yearning over the boys still far from home, when they laid the little form away, no single individual in all that company gathered there to do her honor mourned any more than did "Granny," the passing of the "little Missus."

Data contributed by—

Mrs. David Pickle,
Austin, Texas.

MRS. ROBERT KLEBERG

BORN

PHILIPPINE SOPHIE CAROLINE LOUISE ROSALIE von ROEDER

For the scene of the home-life of the maiden possessing the many names we must turn to Oldenburg, a state of the German Empire, having for a small part of its boundary line the River Weser, lying, too, hard by the North sea. For the family domicile we must go into an old monastery known as Marien Muenster, a building comprised in an estate bought by her father many years before she was born. This house was probably like all houses built with the monastic idea in mind. Bare of ornament, walls too thick for heat or cold or sound to penetrate, cold, tesselated floors, a place, in short, that had been designed to protect the religious recluse from contamination with the world. Yet, strange as it may appear, von Roeder, in buying this place for a home had the real comfort of his family in mind. He felt that a blossom here and there, and a shrub or two added to the bleak outside, with pictures and rugs for the inside comfort might be depended upon to turn the religious sanctuary into a home. In this von Roeder was right. The monastic idea fled before the domestic idea, and his children thrived in happiness where lately self-denial had reigned supreme. He provided for these children the best of private tutors, and the industrious German maidens received the best of advantages in music. Our Rosalie, the other names being for the moment forgotten, made the most of these advantages. Of a rather dignified form of maiden, she went her way happily beneath that monastic dome, a lovable girl, pure, sweet, and undefiled.

Just as Rosalie reached her eighteenth year, family trouble began. Through some fraud perpetrated probably in the name of the church or in the name of the emperor, von Roeder lost title to his home. The court process cost probably the larger part of his possessions, and our Rosalie faced the possibility of a great change. Just what she saw in the situation would be hard to say. She suffered, being a true daughter, in every pang that crossed the hearts of her father and her mother. She thought, too, of her brothers, grown up with the idea of inheriting and controlling that vast estate. All these things in mind, Rosalie shook her head.

A wealthy aunt appeared. In Rosalie's sweet womanly beauty, in the straight, clean-cut glance of her determined eye, the aunt saw something worth while. She offered Rosalie a home, she offered unlimited means and inheritance

—Rosalie would become as her very own child. Fine prospects, these! But Rosalie saw it in another light. She preferred life with her own family on a small farm whereon she, too, would be expected to labor to the separation from her parents and her brothers and sisters.

Then, too, there was her lover, Robert Kleberg. Kleberg had been a student at the University at Getting with Rosalie's own brothers. A child, herself, barely ten years of age, Rosalie, at home, waited one day the coming of these brothers, for she had been told that they expected to bring guests with them for a short visit. She had been told, too, the name of the guest, that he was a young lawyer of brilliant prospects, and Rosalie, but ten years of age, mind you, looked forward with interest to the meeting. Kleberg, saturated, maybe, with brotherly yarns concerned with Rosalie and her charms, walked happily into Rosalie's presence, and he declared always afterwards that he fell in love with her on that visit. Maybe so. Maybe Rosalie had believed him in the years that had come and gone since the meeting. But disaster had come upon her family, and Rosalie, now eighteen years of age and somewhat wise, wondered a bit just what her lover might be expected to do. Could he be expected to share his brilliant prospects as a member of the bar with the maiden who loved him, the maiden whose father faced financial ruin? Nay, nay, so thought our Rosalie.

But Robert Kleberg had somewhat of a mind of his own. Conscious of his prospects as a lawyer, Robert had discovered flaws in the governmental ideas then prevalent in Germany. Prussian Autocracy and militarism had seemed especially obnoxious to his well-trained mind, and when Kleberg heard that the father of his sweetheart had determined to lay it all down, had determined upon a new home in Texas for himself and family, Kleberg felt that von Roeder had solved the problem for him, too. He learned that von Roeder expected to sail on a certain date, and a wedding, just before the voyage began, himself and Rosalie the principals, seemed wonderfully fine in the eyes of the young lawyer. He laid his plans before Rosalie, and she, more in love with her lover than ever, shyly agreed. They decided that there must be no festivities, no feast of any kind to mark the wedding. They went to church, paid their vows in the sweet old way, returned to Kleberg's apartment where two faithful old servants had prepared for the couple a simple breakfast. They seated themselves at the table, a little thankful for the simple fare. The first mouthful was interrupted. Friends of Kleberg, sympathizing no doubt with his dislike for governmental policies, appeared on the scene, bringing with them an elegant wedding breakfast, serving it themselves to the newly married couple with many a happy bit of wit and jest.

The voyage, begun almost immediately after that breakfast, lasted nearly nine weeks. They landed finally at New Orleans. At this point the von Roeders and the Klebergs chartered a ship to take them to Brazoria, Texas. This trip ended in a wreck on the coast of Galveston island. The losses attendant upon this event changed affairs materially for the young couple. But they accepted these changes, being of true pioneer spirit, and managed after a bit to make their way inland, probably preferring inland dangers to those offered by the sea.

Nor were they in any way ignorant of the troubles lying ahead. They had heard in Europe of Indians and their jealous objections to the invasion of Europeans, but liberty as they expected to find it in Texas outweighed any little troubles Indians might offer. So much for ignorance on the subject of Indians!

But Kleberg had an idea, an idea shared by his wife's father, that things might be improved. We who have heard all our lives of Indians in Texas, we who have listened to grandmother's yarns and to historian's accounts of depredations, we must acknowledge that Kleberg's idea was not without foundation. Back a century or so for a brief thought of William Penn and his experience in a land given by a grateful king to Penn's illustrious father! Kleberg and Roeder, being well informed men, had known of all this—the story was more than a hundred years old—and some idea in common with that held by William Penn seems to have taken root in their minds. All conjecture aside, we know that Robert Kleberg, with his wife, our womanly Rosalie, made a settlement at Cat Springs in the year 1834, later moving to De Witt County, and that Indians resented it and were expected to act accordingly.

Now for a little backward step! In the homeland, Kleberg and von Roeder had been members of the Adelsverein, which being translated, means for us a Society of German Noblemen. In this body they had known Prince Carl of Sohms-Braunfels, and they esteemed him highly. Prince Carl had established a colony in Comal, Texas, even earlier than the coming of Kleberg and von Roeder. Prince Carl appeared before the provisional government of Texas in 1834 and asked for guns and ammunition in ord er thatt he German settlers might protect themselves from the Indians .Being denied this—the government probably lacked the ammunition—the Prince with von Roeder and Kleberg fell in with men of the Fisher and Miller grant of land, and a discussion of conditions followed. The latter grant of land lay immediately over the territory claimed by the

deadly Comanches—and maybe, they had a right to it—
but the men, denied the ammunition, left the conference determined to deal fairly and squarely and firmly with Indians—and in all loving-kindness, and along with our
Quaker fathers in old Pennsylvania they did report that as
long as this policy was maintained no trouble with Indians
ever occurred.   Miller said afterwards that he expected to
treat them politely—at least until some ammunition appeared—so that the white man might have a chance in the
fight.   He acknowledged afterwards in a kind of naive
simplicity that the sound of the ax and the clatter of the
mills drove the Indian farther back into the mountain
fastness and into the gloom of the forest.   Maybe so.
Maybe the Indian feared he might be put to work.   Nevertheless, the thought of that thrifty valley through which
the Comal winds its sparkling way, a thought of New
Braunfels and its industry and thrift must bring back the
idea of Prince Sohms and von Roeder and Kleberg dealing
with the Indian as he himself would like and of meeting a
similar dealing in return.

    While her husband helped form governmental policies
and Indian policies, while he labored to foster this spirit of
human kindness, our Rosalie, upholding him in every way,
was busy at home.   She was a young woman, but a well-
balanced one.   Her husband, captivated by the womanliness evident in her at ten years of age, availed himself
many times of the wisdom to be gained in a discussion with
her concerning public affairs.   This attitude on the part of
her husband kept Rosalie informed on all public affairs.
She sympathized with the Indians.   She sympathized even
more with the white men determined to live in peace and
harmony with them, but Rosalie, grown a little older and
a good deal wiser, kept always a sharp lookout for Indians.
Along in 1840, in her home at Harrisburg, at that time the
county seat of Harris County, Rosalie found herself at
home alone one day, alone save for her babies.   She was
defenseless, but Rosalie was busy, and the thought of de-
fence takes small root in the mind of a busy woman.
Rosalie did her baking, singing over the kneading of the
bread and the sweetening of the coffee cake, sticking in an
extra raisin or two as she thought of Robert working away
somewhere in forest or field.   Across the sunlight of her
open door a shadow fell.   It proved to be an Indian, and
its owner bore a venison ham across his shoulder.   Frightened?   Ah, even our Rosalie!   No man at home!   No gun
at hand!   Only her helpless babies asleep beneath the one
window of her cabin!   Nearer approched the Indian, every
step conveying a meaning and a purpose, Rosalie's poor
heart sinking down, down, down at every step!   Close be-

side the table, the Indian slammed the ham of venison down on the table, stepped back, stretched himself to his full height, and then he looked Rosalie unflinchingly in the face.

"Me no bad man! Me want bread!"

Relieved beyond measure, remembering, perhaps, in that relief the William Penn covenant, Rosalie stepped forward, thanked the Indian in her best way for the vension, assuring him that she was in every way glad to trade. She made the Indian a bundle of bread, she even slipped in a bit of coffee cake, even again at the risk of denying the princely Robert, and Rosalie had much to say to the Indian of the delight of venison as a table perquisite, and the Indian soon departed, delighted with his bargain.

This idea of trade was fostered afterward in many ways. Rosalie, thanks to her German training, was an expert needle-woman. She could make clothes and many of them, but she could not make shoes. The Indian was a first-class hand at moccasins, so Rosalie gladly exchanged body garments for footwear. Seeing the wisdom thereof, Rosalie afterwards had her young girls take sewing lessons from a Mrs. Swearingen—Rosalie was herself too busy to teach them— and they made clothes for Moore's store.

But the Indian clung to the idea of exchange first hand. Told that garments at Moore's store had been fashioned by Rosalie in her home, the Coshattes, big, strong men, preferred to go in the flesh and trade with Rosalie direct. The same might be said of the Kickapoos, who were small men, and Rosalie humored both tribes, both big and little in this matter of purchase.

The first house in Texas which Rosalie claimed for a home was a log cabin bare both of plank floor and plank ceiling. It was situated some ten miles from San Felipe De Austin, and it served for a shelter in time of wind and rain and sun. As soon as his farming land was in shape, Kleberg set about providing his family with a better shelter. Good of its kind no doubt, but even that home must have brought from our Rosalie a sigh now and then as she thought of the monastic walls, of the tapestries and the rugs, of the flowers on the lawn and the pictures on the walls. Food, even of the coarser kind, was hard to obtain, and it fell heavily many times on the young wife to see to it that her husband was supplied. And the children came rapidly, Clara, Caroline, Otto, Rudolph, Marcellus, Robert and Louise. Educational facilities were lacking, and each child must learn at its mother's knee. Her husband, advancing in his profession day by day, busy, too, with state affairs and farm affairs, must be encouraged and held to the high-

est peak of ability.   All this with no one by but Rosalie to
help.

In this cabin home Rosalie heard of the fall of the Alamo.
Her husband was absent in the army.   The men who
brought the news told Rosalie of disaster, of Mexicans almost at hand, killing as they came.   More messengers appeared telling the same story.   Nothing for our Rosalie to
do but mount her horse, take her two months old daughter
on her lap, and in company with her mother and sister
flee, too, toward the Sabine.   Rosalie bowed before the inevitable and bravely.   They fell in with some forty or
fifty families waiting to cross the Brazos River.   Next
morning, they came to the home of "Cow" Cooper.   Said
Cooper was himself too old for service, but all his sons,
down to the youngest, little more than a boy, were bearing
arms.   Cooper watched from his porch the disordered arrival of the runaways.   Seeing the people were hungry, he
threw open his "smoke-house."

"Help yourselves!" he exclaimed.   "No damned Mexican shall have it."

Maybe they obeyed Cooper's orders.   Certainly they
camped near a farm not far from Clear Creek, and that
night with the stars looking down, Louis von Roeder,
Rosalie's own nephew, was born in a corn-crib.   With that
first wailing cry, came a fresh alarm!

"Santa Anna right behind you!   Mexicans in droves!"

But the credulity of American-born people had been outraged.   This little flock began to think a little bit for themselves, and before the day was over they heard positively
of the victory at San Jacinto.

Prosperity follows always wise endeavor, and Rosalie
and her husband met their just reward.   They saw real advantages come into Texas.   They saw their own home put
on the air of production, and as Kleberg kept his pace with
the rising men of his profession, Rosalie told herself a little
proudly, that the bank account was doing the same thing.
She saw no real trouble ahead for them ever again in all the
world.

The war between the States proved how very blind she
had been.   With her husband and her people Rosalie had
left Germany in the hope of escaping despotism and
militarism.   Thirty years later they found their new country in the horrors of rebellion against a new form of despotism.   They sent their two sons into the service, Otto
and Rudolph, the latter barely seventeen years of age.

The Klebergs lived at this time at Meyersville in De
Witt County.   In common with many other Southern
women, our Rosalie had no idea save that the Confederacy
would triumph.   Her other sons went, then her husband

until she found herself alone at home many times and un-
protected. She suffered little fear. Perhaps the awful
wait for news from the front crowded out the lesser dangers
that might lie about her home. But, remembering pioneer
dangers and the care they called for, Rosalie sometimes
looked about her with some little anxiety. On a certain
murky autumn afternoon she waited the end of the daylight, watching from her window the passing to and fro
in the road. Not much was this passing. War had claimed
all honest, able-bodied men. The presence at times of
Freebooters revelling in the chance, kept women close at
home, even before the coming of the night. Darker and
darker grew this night for Rosalie. The children, already
asleep behind her, made no move, but way off, even beyond the pasture gate, Rosalie described a moving object,
skulking in the gloom, then another, and another—.

War had turned the few Indians left in Texas against
their one-time friends. Tales of atrocities had reached
Rosalie's ears, and Rosalie saw in all this the beginning of
an ugly experience for herself. The idea of killing any
human being was horrible—to her, but, and her heart
leaped, she must protect her children. The skulking object came nearer, and nearer. Snatching up a machete,
Roasalie waited, her aim sure and steady. The sleek head,
black in the coming night, poked its head inquiringly
around the corner. Rosalie, ready, even to the aim, fired
—and killed a calf. Afterwards, Rosalie must bear any
amount of teasing from her husband and her sons, but
Rosalie, to say the least, did her part as she saw it. Later,
at Indianola, there were fifteen women, wives of officers in
the fort. During a battle there the women disappeared,
all save Rosalie. With her baby on one arm, she managed
to hold and fire a carbine saving thus her own life and many
of those around her.

The war between the States came to an end. The Kleberg boys came home from that struggle wiser, perhaps,
certainly sadder, but certainly again a bit steadier, a bit
more determined to wipe out war and militarism from the
face of the earth. The home life of our Rosalie drifted on
then for a little bit in the common run of life.

At this same Indianola, in 1875, our Rosalie had her
most disastrous battle with nature. The tropical storm
that "blew Indianola away"—according to early Texans—
left her family intact but left them penniless. Even their
clothing was lost, and they knew that they must face the
world beginning again at the very bottom. In material
things, nature's battle of less than forty hours had cost the
Klebergs more than the four year's fight of brother against
brother.

But youth and hope, efficiency and courage are hard to down even by storms and war. Kleberg took his family to Meyersville, and on land previously acquired there, he and Rosalie set about making a new home. They built the ordinary ranch house, and Rosalie furnished her house, even to her kitchen, and went busily again about the maintenance of her home. Kleberg brought to bear on the tilling of that soil all the wisdom acquired in years of similar experience in Germany, where efficiency had received due notice in spite of autocracy and war. Meeting some success in his ventures, Kleberg began to feel an interest in new devices that claimed to make life easier for the farmer. He was the owner of the first cultivator and the first planter ever brought to Texas. The men, his neighbors, seeing these implements in the field, looked on in alarm. They gathered in corners and discussed the matter, deciding at last in all solemnity that Kleberg had lost his mind.

Conscious of the attitude of his neighbors, Kleberg held his peace. He was sure of his own mind and of his personal possession thereof, but when Kleberg undertook the management of that cultivator, he found that it took all his mind to run it. Well and good! The cultivator was worth it, maybe, as a time-saver, but the cultivator had to be pulled by a mule, and unless properly guided said mule might stop to clip a dainty bit of niggerhead or bluebonnet blossom by the way. Each mule possesses a hind leg of his own, his very own, and some exceedingly wise somebody reminded us once that there "wuz no derpendince ter be put in de hin' leg uv er mule." Kleberg needed no such reminding. Experience had made all such reminding unnecessary, and even with the glistening new cultivator ready for action, Kleberg decided to go a little slow. But not for long—not for long with Rosalie around. She, too, took her place on that cultivator, and while Kleberg ran the machinery, Rosalie ran the mule. And the mule failed to balk, and we wager he turned seldom to the right or the left for the enticing bit of green. Mules—and some people —know when a master hand holds the reins, and this mule was no exception. He plodded his drab, straightforward way through the day. If the end failed to be that of a perfect day, the mule but went to his corn nubbins a sadder but a wiser mule, and no man ever heard him make a single protesting bray.

Rosalie von Roeder Kleberg lived to be ninety-four years old, passing away at her ranch home in 1907. She had buried her distinguished husband and one of her children. She spent her declining years looking after her home, having as well a voice in the management of the estate she had helped her husband acquire.

And when it is all summed up, this life of our gentle Rosalie, born beyond the sea in a land of thrifty but sometimes mistaken people, resigning affluence to cross the sea with her lover and her family, establishing her household in the wilderness of Cat's Springs and De Witt County, in the Indian-infested nation called Texas—When it is all said, what had been said?

Only he who reads in these simple lines the mother's watch in the night by some bed of pain, no physician within call; only he who sees that mother place coarse food upon her table, the very best she can find, to have her little girl of the delicate palate put it away silently but firmly—and untouched—only he who sees in these privations the gall and wormwood to the mother-heart, he alone sees the glory—the solemn glory of a life well lived, a simple, everyday Texas life, lived to the sweetest and fullest and best, and only he who sees "takes off his shoes."

Data contributed by—

Miss Carol Hoff,
Yorktown, Texas.

MRS. REUBEN HORNSBY

BORN

SARAH MORRISON

Any man or any woman having lived ten years in Travis County, in the State of Texas, and having failed to hear the name of Hornsby has lived the life of a recluse or a hermit or some other form of existence designed to cut men and woman from all association with their fellows. Some Indians, mayhap, roaming beside the Colorado river, camping by night among the purple hills sloping in some places to the river's brink, some such savage might lay claim to some such ignorance, but most white folks living in the aforesaid county have known of the Hornsbys, for Reuben Hornsby, the father of them all, figured prominently in public things, back in the days when Stephen Fuller Austin undertook the fulfillment of his father's desires as to the settlement of Texas. Reuben Hornsby had been born in Georgia, but somewhere, somehow, he, a surveyor by profession, managed to fall in with Stephen F. Austin who hailed from Missouri. From Austin, he caught the pioneer spirit, and in 1830 came with Austin to Texas, came in the capacity of surveyor for Austin's colony and settled then and there on the now famous bit of land, still in the possession of his descendants and boasting at one time a post office known as Hornsby.

Reuben Hornsby, along with children and money and slaves, brought with him to Texas, a wife well suited to his needs and his station in life, a dainty little black-eyed, black-haired woman who had been known in her youth as Sarah Morrison. She was born July 27, 1796 in Mississippi, probably at Vicksburg, her people being of pure Scotch descent. Even as her own bright eyes and raven hair mark to-day the physical appearance of the descendants known to your scribe—the likeness is very much in evidence, even unto the fourth generation—so this Scotch ancestry, with its exactness, and its love of fair dealing, its even greater love of culture and refinement characterized this woman, even in her early life. Born some twenty years after the signing of the famous national Declaration of Independence, and in Vicksburg, the noted social center of the south, with doting parents, able and willing to grant her every wish, with slaves to minister to her many needs, with ease and culture in her own home and in the homes she often visited, Sarah happened to be of a disposition to enjoy the frivolity for a season, but to turn now and then to make a wiser use of her time. Before she reached maturity, she had acquired a liberal education, and had become as well an accomplished young woman. She possessed a sweet so-

prano voice, and her parents had seen to it that she had
been well instructed in its use. She sang, no doubt, most
of the music then in vogue, some classics, too, but, just
because of this inheritance matter, maybe, Sarah loved the
Scotch airs best of all.

> Gin a body meet a body,
>> Comin' thro the rie' "

a lightness, a grace in her every tone.

> "Her brow is like the snow-drift,
>> Her throat is like the swan's."

Somehow, few women to-day would care to be visited in
life with an exact reproduction of the swan's form, particularly the neck business, but as long as she lived, the clear
quality of her notes, the soft sweetness of the tone, colored
by her own tender thought and imagination, made this
little old ballad exceedingly sweet when it fell as it often
did, even unto her death, from Sarah Morrison Hornsby's
sweet red lips.

All these things being true, there must have been many
suitors for the hand of our little black-eyed lady, but from
them all she selected Reuben Hornsby, herein before described. Just when and where they met we do not know,
just how much stratagem was necessary to win the Scotch
lassie we shall never be able to say, but she married Reuben
in her Mississippi home at some time in the fall of the year
1816. For nearly twenty years after this marriage she continued to live with her husband in old Mississippi. Children came to her rapidly in that home, seven boys and one
girl, and Sarah busied herself, world without end, attending to their wants, ministering to their small needs, dreaming of their future, planning how she might give to each
separate child the thing his own individuality craved.

And then, with all these plans buzzing in her brain,
Sarah faced the necessity of a move to a raw, new country.
If this necessity had come about through financial em-
barassments, we have not heard it mentioned. Neither
have we heard of a desire on the part of Reuben Hornsby
for a more healthful climate. Again the pioneer spirit
must shoulder the blame, and we must heave a sigh for the
wife and mother who must perforce follow her husband in
his yielding to the call of the aforesaid spirit. Sarah
cheerfully agreed to the move to Texas—mayhap Sarah
thought it foolish to act otherwise—and still cheerful,
Sarah began her melancholy preparations for departure.
She made her last visits to her friends. She packed her belongings, her household effects, her clothes, her husband's
and those belonging to the children, and then, gently and
a little reverently, she packed with even greater care the

books and the music, precious to her in that she had
gradually acquired them throughout all of her life. With
almost prophetic vision, our Sarah had come to understand
that every bit of knowledge obtained by her children from
henceforth, every bit of culture of any kind, must be at
the mother's knee, and Sarah, faithful and true in everything else, determined that this one mother at least should
not be found wanting in that hour of need.

Straight to his head-right, located near a bend in the
Colorado river which has borne ever since the name of
Hornsby, Reuben brought his wife and children. No
small family, to be sure, for there were eight children besides the father and the mother and a few slaves. Hornsby
built immediately a log cabin, two large rooms and a
hall between, no doubt a faithful reproduction of the many
other log cabins built in that day in Texas. Cramped for
room? Doubtless, and mayhap the stock of provisions
ran low, but before many months had passed, that log
cabin had become famous for its hospitality. Into this
home, Sarah and her slaves placed the few pieces of furniture
brought in the ox-wagon from Mississippi, and, seeing this
furniture insufficient for their needs, Hornsby set about
making whatever else in that line was needed for their
comfort. The trees were felled—by hand, hand-sawed into
lumber, hand-planed, and some of this furniture is existent to-day (1928).

As soon as the cabin home was acceptably clean, and the
scant furniture in place, Sarah put her women to work at
loom and spinning wheel. They had on hand both cotton
and wool, brought, probably with them, and they made
cloth from each, sometimes from a mixture of both, and
this last product was called "jeans." Sarah with her
children and her slaves then searched the woods for certain
herbs and shrubs and barks to make dye-stuffs in the hope
of improving the appearance of the rough, heavy cloth,
which this wise woman knew must before long be depended
upon entirely as clothing for her family and her slaves.
This outward adornment of the body, so very necessary in
Sarah's eyes, suffered only one interruption, and that was
made by the thought of bread. Sarah watched with no
little anxiety while her husband and slaves cleared the
ground close to that cabin door.

She watched them plant and till that virgin soil, watched
them gather in 1832 the harvest of corn and wheat, the
very first harvest ever gathered in Travis County. With
her Scotch thrift she superintended the preparation of the
meal, and being herself thankful for this blessing, Sarah
was not slow to share the fruits of that first harvest with
the stranger within her gates.

Sarah Hornsby was a devout Baptist. Strange, perhaps, remembering that Scotch ancestry, but individuals sometimes have a way of throwing off this ancestral yoke when it comes to religious matters. Being as we have said a devout Baptist, the thought of leaving that church service in Mississippi had played no small part in her grief at the thought of leaving home. Through all that tiresome ox-wagon journey, her children crowded about her, Sarah had wondered just how this privation was to be endured. She possessed sufficient faith in herself and her husband to know of a certainty that they together could bring food from the ground, and clothing, too, for themselves and family. But this matter of religious service required the co-operation of her fellows, and sometimes Sarah's stout heart quailed. Public worship demanded a house and people of one mind and purpose, so thought Sarah, but she soon learned that part of her fancied requirements was not at all necessary. No house of worship at hand, Sarah and her husband summoned to their own home all their friends from far and near who happened to be of Baptist persuasion. These friends came in ox carts and on horses and on mules. The house it was soon seen was far too small, so out under a big tree in the yard, their one table was moved, becoming all in a minute a first-class pulpit. Then these Hornsbys moved out their few chairs and some benches, and there beneath the oak tree was held that simple service, the first Baptist church service ever held in Travis County. And was Sarah happy in listening to that sermon, probably from some travelling minister; was she happy in those simple hymns, unaccompanied by any instrument? Aye, for Sarah heard the voice of God and felt the power of its beauty, recalling, as she many times did the precious promise "Where two or three be gathered together in my name."

While these simple signs of civilization were in the act of growth, what about the Indians, skulking by day and prowling by night? A study of that day and time makes one feel after a bit that early Texas women must have accepted Indians just as our women of to-day accept mosquitoes or fleas—a nuisance to be borne until some smart somebody can evolve a satisfactory disinfectant. Some towns suffered at times from Indian raids, and of course, on isolated farms the danger was three-fold. As long as the men folks remained on the place with a deadly weapon handy, the Indians seemed to divine such a presence and gave a home so guarded a wide berth. But business sometimes called Reuben Hornsby away from home, and his sons, too, and then Sarah but dressed herself in some of her husband's remaining clothes, shouldered a gun and marched oc-

casionally around the house, about the yard, even down to
the field to make the waiting Indian believe that one, maybe more men, had been left at home to guard the apparently helpless women and children. This strategem saved
Sarah and the little children from massacre, but it did not
ward off real sorrow at the hand of the Indian.

In that Hornsby cemetery—a wonderful sight all its
own—the first two graves were made for two young men
who had been sent in 1836 from the Texas army encamped
on the Brazos as a protection for the Hornsby family
against Indians and Mexicans. The young men became
weary of the idleness of watching and took themselves to
the field to hoe corn. A posse of Indians surrounded them
and literally hacked them to pieces. From her cabin door,
Mrs. Hornsby watched the affair, feeling herself perfectly
helpless, the Indians being out of her rifle range, and for
aught she could know, full of plans to descend upon her,
once they had finished the first piece of murder. But the
marauders seemed satisfied with the afternoon's work
and stole away. After dark, Mrs. Hornsby with her
younger sons to help in the lifting, wrapped the poor,
mutilated bodies in linen sheets, brought in the beginning
from the Mississippi home, and had the men buried in all
tenderness, not far from where they fell.

In another Indian trouble, our Sarah was more fortunate.
She, with Josiah Wilbarger figured in this affair, and the
story has been told so many times, and told so well, that
your scribe hesitates a little to tell it again. Josiah
Wilbarger in company with Reuben Hornsby had previously been over much of the Texas land waiting to be occupied
by the Anglo-Saxon. Hornsby selected at last a league
lying on the east bank of the Colorado river, and about
nine miles below the site of Austin. They had carefully
analyzed the different soils, and Hornsby had announced
that the chemical properties of the soil of the league selected were such that the land would sustain at least four
generations of people, and without extra fertilization. All
of which has proven true. Wilbarger selected a tract of
land lying about ten miles above the point where the San
Antonio-Nacogdoches road crossed the river, a spot afterwards occupied by the town of Bastrop. This made
Wilbarger the first and the outside settler in Austin's new
colony until July 1832 when Hornsby came from that two-
year's camp near Bastrop and settled in his first real Texas
home.

At some time during the next year, Wilbarger came up
to the Hornsby home, and then in company with Hornsby
and Christian, Haynie, Strother, and Standifer, rode out
in a north-westerly direction to look over the land. They

met with Indians, and in the fight, Strother was mortally
wounded, and Christian was disabled. Wilbarger had
likewise been wounded and had fallen behind a tree. Thinking Wilbarger dead, too, Haynie and Standifer leaped upon
their horses, and with Hornsby, put out for the latter's
home. There they reported the death of the two men,
claiming to a certainty that Wilbarger was dead, too, because they had seen Indians in the act of scalping him.

But they were mistaken as to Wilbarger's condition.
Recovering from the faint caused by his wounds, he called
for his companions, thinking maybe they waited for him,
but received no answer. Throughout the rest of the day
and far into the night, naked, (the Indians had taken his
clothes as well as his scalp) feeble from loss of blood, suffering with cold and hunger, Wilbarger made more than
one feeble effort to reach Hornsby's home. These efforts
landed him at last beneath the shelter of an oak tree, and
there he fell asleep.

From out the mist of the unseen a vision came to bless
him. "Brother Josiah, you are too weak to go by yourself. Remain here, and friends will come to take care of
you before the setting sun." These words seemed to reach
his tortured ears born by the voice of his sister Margaret
Clifton who had died the day before in St. Louis County,
Mo. Wilbarger, raising one imploring hand, begged her
to remain, but the vision vanished, going in the direction
of the Hornsby home.

Haynie and Standifer had repeated the details of the
tragedy to the Hornsbys, saying they knew that Wilbarger
was dead. No small grief to our Sarah who had known
him and loved him as her husband's friend. No small
grief to any pioneer woman who read in this sinister-
happening just what she might expect for her own husband
and sons! Through her sleep that night this thought
lingered. Later she waked her husband from a sound sleep,
claiming that in her dream she had seen Wilbarger alive,
Pooh-ooh, soothed by her lover husband, patted a time or
two on the shoulder, no doubt, and Sarah dropped again
to sleep.

This time the dream was more vivid. Sarah saw Wilbarger beneath a tree, wounded, scalped, naked but alive.
She sprang from her bed, urged her husband to rise and
dress, had coffee and breakfast ready for him and the other
men on the premises at daybreak, and rested, herself, only
when she saw the men gone on what she believed to be an
errand of mercy.

The men found Wilbarger under the tree as Sarah had
directed, and before the end of the next day as Wilbarger
had been promised in his own vision. They brought the

wounded man, dripping with blood, divested of all clothing save one sock which he had applied to his wounded scalp in the hope of comfort, they brought him thus home to Sarah, and she nursed him there for many days in that cabin hove, no physician near, no antiseptic, no healing drugs same those she concocted from roots and herbs about her.

Wilbarger had been brought to Sarah on the back of a pony, one man, Sarah's oldest son, a boy of 14, riding behind him to serve as a support. When the time for his departure came, it was soon clear that Wilbarger could never ride horse-back because of the pain that answered ever motion of the pony's body. They tried the wagon, piling quilts and pillows about him, but the motion brought unbearable pain. They placed him finally on a sled, drawn by plodding horses. This becoming painful, the men took the ropes in hand and thus Wilbarger was taken to his own cabin home, several miles down the river. The man recovered apparently from his wound. He had a silver plate fitted to the hole left by the scalping, and he lived eleven years in apparent comfort. He struck this spot finally on a low door frame in his own gin-house and died not long afterwards from the inflammation that set in.

Some years later, in 1845 in fact, Sarah's son, Daniel, was killed by the Indians. He had gone fishing in the Colorado River—hunting and fishing formed no small part in the food-getting business in early Texas—and he had with him a friend named William Atkisson. Becoming enthusiastic over the sport—and a little careless, enthusiasm has this effect sometimes—the two men separated, Atkisson going to the other side of the river. A party of Comanches surrounded him. On hearing the noise, Daniel started to swim the river in order to come to his friend's aid. The Indians fired upon him, the arrow bringing instant death. The body sank, but was recovered, several days later, a mile or so farther down the stream. The body of Atkisson was later found buried in the sand. Investigation proved that it had been terribly mutilated with tomahawks and with knives. These, too, were buried in that same cemetery.

At another time, her husband away from home, Sarah sent two boys at milking time to bring in the cows from a nearby pasture. She stood at a small window to watch, gun in hand. Think how the necessity of that constant watch must have preyed upon her mind! This time, sure enough, the boys already in sight behind the cows coming slowly homeward, a band of Indians appeared. The boys began their homeward flight, that mother heart a-leap at every homeward step. The arrows began to whizz, striking now wide the mark, now so close that death seemed inevitable, but those boys, exhausted from fear and flight, staggered into that mother's arms, untouched by the deadly arrow.

But then, this good wife and mother had her share of womanly satisfaction. There came a time when Reuben Hornsby felt that he had prospered in the new country, and his first thought was a home, a nice new home for his cherished Sarah. Men, so argued Reuben, might live always in perfect content in a log hut, he might thus lapse into barbarism, too, but women, particularly such women as Sarah, must have a nice home. So very near the same spot where the first log house stood, the house hallowed by many hours of mother anxiety and mother triumphs, this beautiful new home was built. The lumber was sawed by hand in the same pit in Bastrop County in which the lumber had been sawed for the French Embassy, still standing in Austin. Many rooms, all conveniences known in that day and time, characterized this new dwelling. To us probably, the most interesting place in this new dwelling was the attic. Some housewives at cleaning time deplore the existence of an attic. So much useless stuff can there accumulate—accumulate and lie there to be dusted and dusted until time brings a sentiment to linger about each useless, foolish thing, and then destruction becomes impossible—for this generation. But this attic in the Hornsby home had its most honored part to play in the home life of the builders. No windows in this attic, not one, to attract the attention of the passer-by, but cunningly hidden in its walls there were port-holes on all four sides the building. From these holes, high above the ground, skulking Indians might be detected and successfully routed without disaster to the man firing from the inside. Men and women soon took on the custom of fleeing to this home in the time of Indian raids, and for a while the house was spoken of as Hornsby's Fort.

Into this new house Sarah watched the slaves move her few household possessions, the pieces brought from Mississippi, together with those her husband had made for her. Some pieces of this furniture may be seen to-day in the Daughters of the Republic Museum in Austin, the pieces having been presented by a grand-daughter of Sarah Morrison Hornsby, Sarah Hornsby Smith. Caring little that things of hers could ever have any traditional value, Mrs. Hornsby placed each piece of furniture to advantage, and then our little Sarah brought out the books, so carefully preserved all these years, arranged them, too, so that she and the husband and children might have easy access to them, and then Sarah went on about the business of home-making, joyful in her motherly, wifely duty, for-

getting apparently that she had ever lived any other life
in the world.

Appearances are often deceitful. Through her loving
devotion to her husband and her family, through her intense devotion to Texas, a devotion that echoed in many
another's heart had sent the young nation on to freedom,
through all that absorbing frontier life, Sarah Morrison
Hornsby had dreamed many times of her Mississippi home
and the friends and loved ones left there. The old slaves
abiding with her remembered it too, the land of sugar-
cane, flour and cotton, and they talked many times to
little "missy" of the days that were gone, of the "sugar-
bilins" and the dainty things missing in the frontier life.
And then little "missy"—with some few faithful slaves as
a bodyguard, her son Joseph, too, for company, put out
on horseback in the year 1849 to visit that land of ease and
plenty, that land containing still, it seemed to Sarah, the
greater part of all that she ever held dear. She left her
home in competent hands, giving to all slaves minute
directions as to the care of her husband and sons, and then
with much determination and some tears Sarah began that
long, uncertain journey.

The incidents of that visit home on the part of our Sarah
have not been definitely preserved for us. No doubt
Sarah found a cordial welcome waiting her in that old home.
No doubt she enjoyed without stint the luxury, the ease
and plenty, the meeting with old friends and relations.
No doubt she felt in the first few days of that visit as many
a returned pioneer has felt, that she would never return to
the wilderness, even the wilderness wherein she had left
her husband and sons. But after a bit the luxury of the
old country began to pall. Methinks the tug upon Sarah's
heart-strings as she thought of her husband and sons became too much, for after several months spent in the land
of her birth, she put forth on horseback, to take up again
her life in Texas. No deceiving halo of romance hung
about the second departure. Both the good and the evil
of the life in Texas was fully understood. Sometimes the
evil seemed to far outweigh the good, but in the end Sarah
chose of her own free will to return to her new home, to her
husband and children, even unto Texas, the land that had
seemed all at once to be dear in Sarah's eyes because of the
very struggles that had preceded and attended its colonization. And the welcome she received at that homeward
journey's end! Some things must be left to the imagination. Emotions, deep-seated, stirred by such incidents
as these, fail to form suitable topics for description. Let
us pass it by, save that we must record that her youngest
son, Thomas, had sickened and died in her absence. Can

we imagine this event taking place in any woman's life, we
of the day of telephone and telegraph—without the mother
being notified?   Hardly.

Sarah Morrison Hornsby died April 20, 1862, in that
home at Hornsby's Bend.   She knew of course of the War
raging throughout the United States, knew, too that her
own state had seceded from the Union.   She knew that
slavery had been assigned as the cause of the trouble, but
Sarah had a hard time realizing that such a thing might
find disfavor in anybody's sight.   Previous to this war
Sarah had seen her sons and daughters marry and go into
homes of their own, right there in the old neighborhood,
for as each child had married, the Hornsbys had given it
its own share of land and of slaves.   Unconscious of the
change hanging over them, these slaves continued to serve
the master and the mistress they had loved.   When Mrs.
Hornsby, even our little Sarah, black of eye and limpid of
voice, fell ill, the war between the States was in progress,
but the war made no change in Sarah's attitude toward
her slaves.   Those who remained in her home served her
in all tenderness, in all efficiency, but from time to time,
even upon that bed of pain, Sarah's mind would revert to
the slaves they had given the children.   She knew they
were properly cared for, properly controlled, but Sarah,
the little "missy," had a hankering to see each black man
and each black woman face to face.   Her children, her
friends crowded about her bed to assure her of sympathy,
to lighten, if possible, the hours of their tediousness, and
Sarah saw no real reason why her old slaves should not
come, too.   So sending other slaves to work temporarily
in the homes of Billy and Joe and Reuben, Jr., these darkies,
erstwhile property of our Sarah, would return to little
"missy," to wait on her, to humor her childish whims,
to laugh with her over the joys of life in the first log cabin
home, to weep again over sorrows they had helped each
other bear, and each slave returning to its new owner, the
descendant of little "missy," took up life again, feeling
that the few weeks spent in service to that "missus," so
gentle, so considerate, so capable, always so quick to discern and to correct their childish faults, that these weeks
were weeks worth while.   Then, too, each exchanged slave
visited in the negro quarters of the plantation where they
had grown up, and Sarah listening to their emotional
laughter, sometimes far into the night but smiled herself
in tender sympathy.   She knew that each black man and
each black woman was enjoying every moment and that
each moment would be re-lived in the presence of their own
grandchildren who had never in the world cared to un-

ravel the mystery of the holy relation existing between the Southern mistress and her black slaves.

And so we lay the simple story down. No epoch-making events are to be recorded at any time in the course of this woman's strenuous, energetic, uplifting life. She left behind no bit of music she had written, no books, no records of heroic sacrifice. But her life was one daily sacrifice for Texas, for her husband, for her children, and there be those among us who dare declare and in all reverence that the sacrifice was not made in vain.

Data contributed by—

Miss Irma Robertson,
Hornsby, Texas.

JOANNA TROUTMAN

Texas people have a way of claiming more cotton in a single harvest, and sometimes more cabinet members at a single time than any other state in the Union. Texas leads, too, the whole world in the possession of the sense of self-satisfaction, both as to the past and the future, but being young, as nations have a way of commuting this matter of age, Texas is as yet a little modest in the matter of art. A very large majority of her people lack appreciation of stories done in marble and in bronze, but in the Texas State cemetery, located at Austin, the capital, we come upon convincing evidence of efforts on the part of Texas people to employ this world of art in order that they may do honor to their noble dead. A hillside, sloping gently eastward to a grove of trees, has been selected as the site of this worthy effort. In this cemetery we come upon the remains of Stephen Fuller Austin, the Father of his Country, George W. Smyth, a statesman of renown in the days of the Republic, Albert Sidney Johnston, the brave commander who fell at the battle of Shiloh. At the feet of this commander sleep a number of soldiers who followed the leader in the lost cause, and scattered over this beautiful plot of ground are many other graves of people prominent in public matters in Texas.

Sometimes the monuments in this cemetery fail to mark the real burial place of the hero named upon their gleaming surfaces. Chance and change, sometimes family sentiment, have interfered, but the hearts of a grateful people were not to be outdone. Despite the absence of mouldering bones the monuments have been erected in order that the world might know of the young nation's gratitude. It is of one of these monuments we would speak now. Elevated upon a pedestal made of Texas granite there stands a bronze figure that challenges the admiration of every passer-by, Texan or otherwise. The figure, the work of Copinni, is that of a woman. She holds in one hand a threaded needle, an implement of labor closely associated even yet in the minds of most people with the idea of a womanly woman. From the other hand floats the Texas flag, the very first Texas flag ever made, and even then in the course of construction. The flag wakens at once the interest of every patriotic descendant of Texas heroes, but the charm, the irresistible charm of this artistic conception lies in the form of the woman, the pose of that form, and in the exquisitely beautiful face. From the lettering on the bronze tablet placed on the granite pedestal just beneath the figure, we learn that the monument has been erected in honor of Joanna Troutman.

After an hour or so, after the story told on the bronze tablets has lost for the ordinary mind some of its thrill, the beauty of the face comes stealing back. The lines of the face are perfect, this one thing, of course, making it a thing of beauty. This fact one cheerfully acknowledges at the first glimpse, but the chief characteristic of that beauty stealing irresistibly upon you is the spirit shining in the unseeing eyes, trembling about the rigid mouth. Hours after this first glimpse, one feels the faith, the hope, the unquenchable enthusiasm that guided and guarded and moulded that woman's face, in the artist's own conception at least, and in a leap of patriotic fervor, this woman symbolizes all at once the women, the grandmothers, yours and mine, who helped in the struggle that gave to the world our Texas as she is to-day.

And then, all this being acknowledged, we must make a strange confession. So far as we are able to say Joanna Troutman never lived in Texas at all. She was born in Crawford County, Georgia, Feb. 19, 1818. Of her parents we must remain ignorant, even of her surroundings there in Georgia. It is to be hoped that this last statement may bring forth some objections from somebody who does know these things. In that case we would gladly acknowledge our ignorance and cheerfully accept the information. But some conditions, some surroundings, some educational advantages, some something had fired the soul of Joanna with a love for patriotism rarely ever surpassed. Born nearly fifty years after the Declaration of Independence of the United States was signed, descended, no doubt, from soldiers who represented Georgia in the war that followed that Declaration, she had achieved a broadminded patriotism that spread itself in the interest of any people in any clime who might be struggling to achieve independence.

No telegraphic wires brought the news of conditions in Texas. Even the mails in that day were slow and uncertain, but in some way Joanna obtained definite information concerning Texas and her political situation. Joanna knew vaguely of the vast domain stretching from the Sabine to the Rio Grande, from the Gulf of Mexico to the elevated plateaus that are in reality the beginning of the Rocky mountains. She learned to a certainty that the Anglo-Saxon people inhabiting that territory paid tribute to the Mexican government but were denied the rights and privileges accorded the citizens of other Mexican states.

Her interest in the matter deepened into action. She sent forth an appeal in behalf of the Texans all over her own state of Georgia. The people responded by raising a battalion of volunteers, brave men, all of them, trained and

ready for action in behalf of suffering Texas. Glowing
with the success of her efforts, Joanna went further. She
made with her own hands a beautiful flag, a Lone Star
flag, presented it herself to the battalion, and they landed
with it in Texas, some time late in 1835. The flag was first
unfurled at Velasco, probably the port of entry into Texas,
but it was later carried to Goliad where it proudly waved
over that fortress. It was again unfurled and floated just
as proudly over the doomed fort when Col. Fannin learned
on March 8th, 1836, that the Texas Declaration of Independence had been signed.

A bit of description of that flag might not come amiss.
It had been constructed of white silk, and it bore a single,
five-pointed star of an azure tint in the center. On one
side, heavily embroidered, were the words:

"Give me liberty or give me death."

On the reverse side, Joanna resorted to the Latin words
which liberally translated read:

"Where liberty dwells, there is my country."

The legend on the bronze tablet on the monument erected
in honor of Joanna closes with these words:

"The tattered shreds of that flag silently witnessed the
murder of Fannin and his men at Goliad, Sunday, March
27. Gentle, pure, patriotic, the hands of Joanna Troutman wrought the line of liberty into the beautiful Lone
Star flag which witnessed the sacrifice of the men who
brought it to Texas as an emblem of Independence."

After all—what is a flag? A rag, easily destroyed,
easily replaced. A foreigner, ignorant of its meaning, its
symbolism, might easily use the bunting in the polishing
of his car. He might go further and use it to tie up his
old clothes. Made of cotton, thinly made at that, a thing
any trifling incident might make us despise, but—

Suppose we turn to an incident close at home. Some of
us have heard first hand of the horrors of Civil war and
Reconstruction. An artist, Texas reared if not born,
known throughout the state for his famous painting of
the Surrender of Santa Anna, a genial man named Huddle,
made a visit to Europe—artists must go to Europe occasionally—some twenty years after the close of the Civil
war. Burning still with sectional hate engendered by tales
of the sufferings of his people at the hand of the victorious
United States, he declared to himself that he would shoot
the stars and stripes with the equanimity of boy shooting
robins. But after some months spent in Europe, months
that broadened and deepened his artistic sense, Huddle
boarded an English vessel to return to America. In mid-
ocean, a steamer was sighted. Huddle helped watch its
approach, full steam ahead. Then up that ship's flag-

staff, waving proudly in the salt-ladened air, ran the stars and stripes. And Huddle—he turned a somersault on deck, and broke loose with the Star Spangled Banner, lacking a bit in time and tone, but eminently true to form in the *gusto* from his throbbing old heart.

Joanna Troutman died in August, 1880. She had lived to see Texas become an independent republic—to become later of her own free will and accord a state in the United States of America. She had lived to witness the quarrel of brother against brother over the question of slavery. She had regretted many little things in her life—most women do—but we are safe in saying that as long as she lived, Joanna was spared anything of regret in that she had helped in her woman's way bring about the glad day when Texas had taken her place among "the kingdoms of the earth."

MRS. JOHN WIRTZ CLOUD

BORN

REBECCA JOHNSTON

An adventurous Irishman, blue of eye, perhaps, and comely as well of figure, bearing the name of Andrew Johnston as his father had borne it before him, emigrated as Irishman still have a way of doing from the land of his birth to the newer country of America. He took this step some time near the close of the eighteenth century and drifted from the seaport at which his ship landed into the town of Lancaster in the state of Pennsylvania. There the young Irishman took for his bride Miss Margaret Guy. To this interesting young couple a daughter called Ann was born, and then came another, this Rebecca of whom we write, we think about 1811.

Life passed in that Irishman's home as life is likely to pass under such conditions, a smile here and tear there, with a bit of work and a bit of play thrown in, and then with young Rebecca barely six years of age, the young mother laid her down and died. Grief to the young Irishman? Not a doubt of it, but young Johnston saw fit before very long to take unto himself a second wife. Of this second marriage was born a daughter Margaret, widely known throughout Texas in her own day and time as Mrs. James H. Raymond, and another daughter who married Ben Johnson the name the same in sound, but differing a little in spelling.

Ann Johnston, Rebecca's own sister, and a few years Rebecca's senior, married Elisha Mather who was born somewhere in the state of Ohio. He and his young wife lived some time in Ohio, but on account of the trying climate they decided to move. Mather had become interested, too, in the cotton business, being a buyer on a somewhat extensive scale, and the rich land of Texas whereon it might be grown with little labor appealed to him accordingly. This appeal led Elisha to Greenville, Mississippi, and when the time of departure was at hand, young Rebecca accepted the invitation extended by Elisha and his wife and became one of the family group living there in Greenville.

We know little of the life of these young people in old Mississippi. The climate must have been a vast improvement over that of Ohio. The cotton surely grew to perfection in the grand old state, but even while they lingered there, Elisha Mather was never satisfied. The spirit of adventure seemed to beckon him away from the already well-organized community, and Texas had a way of ringing her call in his willing ears. Young Rebecca, sharing,

perhaps, the adventurous inclinations of her sister's husband, listened to the talk pro and con with never a word to
say.   Her silence was the silence of womanly tact.   Rebecca knew deep down in her own heart that she intended
to act in the matter just as her sister acted, that she intended to make her home with them wherever they went,
just so long as she felt herself welcome.

The departure from Greenville took place in 1833, save
the mark, just after "the stars fell."   I wonder if any
school child of to-day, taught in the beginning the relative
position and importance of the earth in the solar system
would suffer as those people suffered if old Dame Nature
should decide to treat us human folks to such an another
exhibition of the many peculiar things to be found in the
universe?   I wonder if the thing thus designated would
mean anything terrible to him?   We are inclined to pass
the story up with the explanation that the old earth was
simply keeping up the onward march, passing without
hesitation through the tail of some heedless comet that had
returned after a thousand years or so to that particular
part of its own orbit.   But the men and women and
children, the negroes, too, in old Mississippi at that particular time were not possessed of such knowledge. Stars came
out on clear nights, winter and summer, to add to the
pleasure of the beholder.   Stars were at such times but
performing the duty for which God had created them.   On
that night stars forgot their duty.   They rained down upon
folks, great, gilded suns losing their hold in the sky to come
tumbling down on old Mother Earth, and no one dared
prophesy the outcome of such tumbling.   Would they
crush the earth falling about like that?   Would they set
it on fire?   Would there be no more stars?

Foolish, indeed, such questions!   No man might hope
to answer them.   People abroad at that hour of the night
dropped upon their knees in the middle of the streets, confessing their sins and praying long and loud for mercy,
giving to the world about them in each agonized confession
accurate accounts of meanness hitherto hidden from the
outside world.

"I watered the rum" from the lips of the saloon-keeper
mingled with the confessions of the stock broker and the
woman of the street, mingled with the confessions of the
sensitive woman, pure in heart and daily habit, devoted
only to her home and the loving care of its inmates.

In the house next to the one in which Rebecca lived with
the Mathers, a corpse waited for burial on the morrow, and
the miserable watchers envied the dead man, for he had
been denied the agony of thus seeing the world destroyed
by fire, the agony of feeling and knowing the just exhibition

of wrath, the rain of brimstone sure to begin in solemn
proclamation of the end of the world.   Utterly indifferent
to all petitions, all calls for mercy, utterly careless of the
consternation thus brought about in the hearts of those
simple people, the earth maintained its course, and the
comet of floating nebulea passed on its lurid way through
the vastnesses of the Universe, and the people who had
seen it began, after a day or two, to forget their fear, to regret in a way their vows of fervent devotion, to regret very
much their heart-rending confessions, to forget gradually
and before very long all about it.   But our Rebecca, having witnessed that fall of the stars with her sister beside
her, was just a little glad to leave a land that had seemed
to her to thus merit this expression of the wrath of God.

And so some time in 1834 Rebecca, with the Mathers, landed at Galveston Island.   Friends in Mississippi had discouraged this emigration, reminding these people that they
were cultivated, accustomed to the ways of the educated
man and woman, that life as they must find it in the wilds
of Texas among its "common" people would grow exceedingly irksome.   Rebecca and her sister had not dared
deny these possibilities dinned often into their unwilling
ears, but each held her peace in the face of discouraging
advisors.   Forewarned thus, they landed at Galveston
island, expecting naturally to make their home there in this
important gateway to the great promising region of Texas.

The people in Galveston lived in cabins and in tents,
forsooth, discouraging facts in themselves, but after the
first few days, Rebecca and her sister found that said
cabins and tents housed many women in whom the inherent qualities of the lady did shine.   There they met Mrs.
Briscoe, then a young lady, and she and Rebecca grew to
be great friends—a friendship, it proved to be that lasted
through life.   Rebecca knew, too, Anson Jones, then a
young man, and though the idea of romance was lacking, she
had a real liking for this splendid young fellow, and there
were many evidences that he returned the feeling.   She
met on this same footing, young Harris who married afterward into the Masterson family, and many more, their
names met again and again in the history of our state.

The association with these people, living still in their
cabins and their tents, offered a real inducement to Mr.
and Mrs. Mather to make their home permanently on
Galveston island.   The climate was all these people lately
from Ohio might demand.   The soil, according to his untrained eye, might surely be depended upon to raise cotton.
But on a tour of inspection about that island, Mr. and Mrs.
Mather came upon the wreck of a sea-going vessel, tossed
high upon the island, just about where the city of Galveston

now stands. Mrs. Mather argued to herself that said
vessel must needs have been borne thither by the intrepid
force of wind and wave, and her prophetic eye caught a
vision of just what such wind and wave might mean to any
human being caught in its path. Deliberately, Mrs.
Mather weighed the matter, discussing it, too, with Rebecca, to lay the outcome of the discussion finally before
Mr. Mather. This discussion led to the decision that as
a home, Galveston Island in all its beauty and all its charm
was too much of a risk. However, Rebecca and her sister
remained there upon the island among their congenial
friends, and Mr. Mather went abroad on a tour of inspection
of the mainland, determined to find some spot where he
might hope to satisfy his cotton ambitions, both as to sale
and culture.

About this time the battle of San Jacinto took place.
Rebecca and her sister had heard some accounts of the
tragedies of the Alamo and of Goliad, had done their part
in a woman's way toward helping the soldiers, and they
were at home waiting anixously to hear just what Houston
expected to do after taking his stand on the San Jacinto
river. Toward the afternoon of April 21, 1836, Rebecca
and her sister heard the guns in rapid fire, waited at home
as only women can wait for the news of the outcome,
waited there and received the glad news of victory. The
next day, their hearts high in triumph they set out, Rebecca
and her sister, on a barge loaded with friends, and made
their way up Buffalo bayou to the famous battle ground.
There beneath the tree, made familiar to all Texas by the
artist Huddle, there they found General Houston resting
again upon the cot from which he had received the surrender of Santa Anna. The General's wound forbade his
rising to receive his guests, but he made the young women
draw near, made the acquaintance of Rebecca and her
sister, laughed and chatted with them, laying thus the
foundation of a friendship that lasted as long as General
Houston lived.

The battle over, the future of Texas practically settled,
Mr. Mather, influenced by his wife's objections to Galveston
Island as a home, decided to move his family to Brazoria
County, to take up land there for his home, a land that
might satisfy his long cherished dream of raising cotton.
He took his wife and Rebecca to look at this farm, took
them back home,—it was well on into the winter of 1836-37
—and then put out for Houston with the wagon and team,
hoping to get furniture and groceries and some meagre
comforts for their new cabin home. Some distance from
town in an open prairie, a real Texas blizzard swooped
down upon him, a shocking thing, raining ice and snow

from a sky, blue and smiling but an hour before. Mr. Mather, new entirely to this demonstration of nature's fickleness, was easily lost in the suddenness of the thing, and his wife and Rebecca waited and waited in vain his home-coming. The team, frozen stiff, and the wagon blown wide its course were found after a few days, but for years no trace of Mather rewarded the anxious searchers. This search was continued until human bones were found not far from the place once occupied by the wagon, and they concluded that Mather, too, had been frozen to death with the horses.

The shadow of this tragedy was relieved soon after by the coming into Rebecca's life of the great romance. This romance centered about John Wirtz Cloud, born in 1797 in Savannah, Georgia, a graduate of Yale University, educated afterwards for an Episcopal minister. He was a widower, and the father of two children, left behind in Savannah, a man rather frail in health, having come to Texas because he hoped much from the open life he knew he must lead. He was a student, an earnest one, and a scholar, and young Rebecca, believing in her heart in all these things so ably represented by John Cloud, gave unto him unreservedly the whole of her woman's love. The marriage was not delayed, and Rebecca did not rest until her husband's two children of the former marriage were safe beneath their own father's roof. Beneath that roof, too, she established her widowed sister, Mrs. Mather, and she did everything in her power to help that sister forget the crushing sorrow that had ended that sister's marriage. Rebecca succeeded, for before very long, her sister took for a second husband, Asa Brigham, known as the first Treasurer of Texas. Rebecca was glad over this turn of affairs, and went her way about her own household, a busy place as it was, being the home of a minister-planter in a wilderness where ministers were heard of but seldom seen.

The important step in this preparation for cotton-raising was the acquisition of slaves to do the work. There were few implements of labor save the shovel and the hoe, the cotton-gin had not been invented, the labor of raising the cotton plant alone required an individual who could work in the heat. The negro from Africa seemed to meet all these requirements. Slave trading-vessels were busy in old Boston, even though frowned upon by some important citizens. Scenting the fact that slaves might be of real value in a climate more like their own, these slave-traders drifted down to the coast of Texas. They brought their human cargo fresh from the wilds of Africa, and Cloud supplied himself with some of these men and women, barely removed in their customs and habits from the wild animal.

Some of the people bought by Cloud had been in America a few months, long enough to imbibe some few ideas of civilization, but one slave bought by Cloud was a big brawny creature, a woman, too, fresh from Africa, accustomed to running naked in the woods, living as best she might on nuts and berries gathered in the depths of the woods.   Rebecca, a missionary by instinct, took this creature under her personal charge, taught her to talk, gave her with prophetic vision the name of Dorcas, and set about teaching the creature just what she might be expected to do.

She had a set of clothes made for Dorcas, managed in some way to make her understand that she must wear them, gave her in fact her very first idea that certain parts of the human body were best covered from the eyes of the world.   Dorcas rebelled.   It was not cold in Texas, and her own brown body, smooth as the smoothest bronze, could be no offense in the eyes of anybody.   Her mistress insisted, gently but firmly, had the clothes sewed together instead of buttoned upon the body of the unwilling woman, only to have the clothes shredded before her very eyes by fingers grown to gigantic strength in their search beneath the earth for bugs and roots and worms in order that her hunger might be appeased.   Stupendous, thankless task! Not for Rebecca.   She continued her kindness, worming herself little by little into the heart of the bewildered, outraged creature, and in the end Rebecca had in Dorcas a servant-maid, a nurse for her children, a friend, indeed, who would have cheerfully laid down her very life at the command of her patient mistress.   She became in time a fine cook, and owing to travel and the custom of hospitality then prevalent in Texas, her culinary accomplishment became the subject of conversation in more than one home throughout the length and breadth of the land.

At some time in the early forties, Rebecca came with her children from Brazoria County to visit with her sister in Austin, lately made the capital of the Republic, to visit the sister who had on the death of Mr. Mather become the wife of the first Treasurer, Asa Brigham.   We may easily imagine just what this visit meant to Rebecca, how the two sisters chatted over old trials and new, how they laughed and they sighed, how the day of separation drew them close together as it bore down upon them.   Reluctantly, Rebecca made her ready for the homeward journey, a little glad beneath it all at the thought of returning to her husband, but when the driver went in the early dawn to harness the horses, lo! not one horse remained in the log stables.   Investigation proved that Indians had dug beneath the logs, had then pulled them from place, thus forcing an entrance, carrying off the muchly prized animals, among them the two elegant, perfectly matched bays that had served as Rebecca's carriage horses. Perhaps Rebecca, when she thought of her husband, echoed the idea of my kingdom for a horse, even one in place of the spanking bays, but this theft of necessity prolonged her stay in her sister's home. After weeks and weeks of waiting, no obliging mail service being at hand, Cloud set forth from the Brazoria home with another team, and after a week or so spent in the journey took his wife and family back home.

The farm in Brazoria County had justified Cloud's belief in the adaptability of the land to raise cotton. His own acres, rich from a recent overflow of the Brazos River, yielded its many hundred fold. He began to see a realization of his dreams of prosperity, but he saw, too, with the justice of the really educated man, that Rebecca had played well her part in his success. Cloud, himself was a dreamer, a book-worm, devouring the printed page with the avidity of the cotton-caterpillar after a large well-formed boll, a tender-hearted, high-principled man, just such an one as a bright, energetic woman like Rebecca must have loved. Deriving much joy from the association with her husband, learning of him many things in the abstract, Rebecca became, as the years rolled on, the real master of their fortunes. She controlled and directed the slaves, she marketed the cotton and bought the supplies, all the while referring with a sweet deference to her lover-husband who failed to begrudge her the exercise of her power. He never interfered with her plans, and long years after she had laid by all active work, her sons-in-law, some of them lawyers, too, went to her and willingly for advice. She always listened, always replied honestly and candidly, but never a moment did her spirit swell in vanity that she had been thus approached.

Profitable as life had become in Brazoria County, Rebecca decided that it was not the place for their permanent home. Two of the eight children born to her in that county had died, their deaths due, as Rebecca believed, to malarial poisoning. Many slaves died after this same manner, and then the Clouds moved to Washington County. They proceeded after the manner of early Texas folks to establish themselves in their new home. The same regime they had followed in Brazoria County began, Rebecca planning and superintending, her husband helping as best he might, and then with comfort and ease in sight, John Wirtz Cloud fell ill and died.

No need to ask of Rebecca's sorrow over this happening. Too intensely feminine, too deeply rooted in all womanly characteristics, was this woman that she might look upon the death of her husband in any other light than a calamity and Rebecca did indeed look through bitter tears at the future laid out before her. Six sons and one daughter to be reared, to be fed and clothed and trained, and her weak woman's hand the only human help in sight. Seven young children dependent upon her in every way, and to add to her woe, an unborn child who was yet to come into the world, denied from the very beginning the blessing of a father's love and care.

Picture that agony as she awaited her appointed time! Picture the fear of her own pain, the greater fear that she might not be spared because of that pain to properly sustain the little children already crowding her path! Picture the desolation in her woman's heart as she sat bowed in the first deep agony of her grief!

But after the first fierce grief had spent itself, Rebecca rose to meet that hour just as she had met every other trying hour of her life. She went about her simple preparations for motherhood, caring all the while for her household, hiding as far as possible her uneasiness, her fear for her innocent children. With the first feeble cry from those baby lips, Rebecca was told that the baby was a girl. Thinking of her own pain, her own unstable position in the world of business, Rebecca cried out her dismay that God should have sent her this weak woman instead of the man who could make his own way in the world, who could do and die for his country—Rebecca was ever patriotic—who would be spared the sufferings of the ordinary woman of her day and time. Dorcas—she of the African forest, Dorcas who had once torn the clothes from her body in defiance of the command of this very mistress—Dorcas approached that bed, the newly-born babe in her arms, and there Dorcas delivered her telling rebuke:

"Don't you nebber say anyting lak dat ergin. Dis here berry chile may be de gre'test comfut uv yo' life."

Dorcas failed to live long enough to know that she had that day stated a possibility that was destined to develop into a fact. Rebecca Cloud in the declining years of her life thought many times of the black woman's rebuke, and she failed to find any impulse in her heart to deny it.

Rebecca, beautiful woman in her youth, a handsome woman in her more mature years, well-read in all that pertained to her country, watched the coming of the Civil war, her mind fully alive to what it might mean to her. She was living at the time on a farm near Gonzales, surrounded by her children and her slaves. Intensely patriotic, with a patriotism born of sound judgment and strengthened with study, she gave freely of all she had to the Southern cause. Her step-son, dear to her in his own right and twice dear because of the father and husband they had both loved, accompanied by three sons of her own, went forth to battle, encouraged and strengthened by the mother counsel as she bade them a firm good-bye. One of those sons was taken prisoner in battle, and thrown into prison in Chicago. There he lay for weeks and weeks, denied bodily comforts, forced to catch the rats playing about the dungeon in order that he might have food. He returned to his mother, little more than a skeleton of his former self, returned to the home destitute of slaves, the fields in ruins, returned to his mother in his feebleness, and there in that Gonzales home she nursed him back to health and strength.

Rebecca lived to be eighty-six years of age. Lacking the tender beauty of her sister, Mrs. Mather-Bingham, she was yet a handsome woman, a capable, well-informed woman, refined, unassuming, a blessing to those about her throughout her life. As that life sloped down into the sunset, she found herself in the home of her daughter Margaret, the child of whom Dorcas had prophesied much, and in that home, early in 1897, she slipped peacefully away, loved and honored and respected by all who came in contact with her.

Data contributed by—

Mrs. E. T. Moore,
Austin, Texas.

MRS. JOHN W. BUNTON

BORN

MARY HOWELL

In Tennessee, near the town of Gallatin, on February 22, 1816, a rather daring invasion in the matter of birthdays—seeing that we are all Americans—a daughter was born to Thomas Howell and his wife, and soon thereafter given the sweet name of Mary. The wee lassie, honored in her name and the date of her birth, found as time passed on that she was fortunate in many other things besides names and birthdays. Fate had indeed been kind. It had placed her in a pleasant place, a home characterized by culture, by refinement, by ease and by plenty. More than this, her home held the indefinable, unchanging air of the domicile presided over by Christian men and women.

Looking back from the high ground of a generation or two removed from the day and time, we say a little proudly that these advantages had been worth nothing to Mary save for the fact that Mary understood the value of her surroundings and possessed as well the ability to make the most of the advantages such surroundings offered her. She became as time went on a cultivated, intelligent young woman, accomplished, too, far beyond the average woman of her day. And then, according to family tradition and daguerreotypes, Mary possessed no small share of beauty. Of a form designated as statuesque, she was possessed of beautiful brown eyes, wavy, nut-brown hair, soft complexion, an oval face of delicate lines, her very features alight with the beauty of mind and soul within.

Such conditions usually suggest the idea of a lover, and these conditions ran this time true to form. Somewhere there in old Tennessee Mary fell in with one, John Bunton by name, and the old love drama was duly enacted. There were doubtless moon-light trysts and lovers' quarrels and lovers' reconcilliations, but for some reason, with this engagement in full swing, John Bunton conceived the idea of *going to Texas*. Just what his sweetheart thought of the venture, just what her parents *said* of the same venture, we may never know, but in some way, probably on horseback, John Burton made the journey from Tennessee to Texas, being numbered at last in Austin's first colony. This entry into Texas on the part of Bunton seems to have been made along about 1833, and it is plainly evident from facts at hand that he bore a good part in those early struggles of the young republic. He had a share in the Indian troubles along the frontier, serving under Zachary Taylor, experiencing at close range all the horrors such as warfare may bring. He listened to political arguments of

Houston and Smyth and Everitt. He mingled with Sterling C. Robertson, Lorenzo de Zavala and other brave, determined men, and in the end, he, too, signed the Declaration of Independence, and, as Col. John Bunton bore his own good part in the battle of San Jacinto. And then, these things being accomplished to his satisfaction, Col. Bunton put him back to Tennessee for the sake, no doubt, of a glimpse of his lady-love.

It is not difficult to imagine the satisfaction of that glimpse. Through his sleeping hours the face and form of his loved one had mingled in his dreams. By camp-fire and in battle, in convention and in caucus, her beauty had haunted him, her beauty and her loving kindness. When he came again into her presence, his heart leapt anew, for in the years he had spent in Texas, his Mary had developed mentally and physically, even beyond his happiest dreams. With that love-light ashine in his eyes, with his own heart high and light and happy over the victory at San Jacinto, with his own military bearing making its appeal, Bunton soon had his own way with Mary, and the wedding took place in short order.

Family records fail to give the reason, but we know that the young couple remained in Tennessee for more than a year after their marriage. Just what occupation John Bunton followed in those days spent in Tennessee we cannot say. We do know that Texas as a country, that Houston and Austin and Lamar were never very far from his thought. We do know that he went about his old home discussing here and there the delights of Texas, plus her glorious possibilities, for when Bunton and his wife finally decided to move to Texas, they had gathered together a company of one hundred and forty persons, all ready and anxious to accompany them. There was Desha Bunton with his wife, Elizabeth Hudspeth Bunton, and their baby John. John Kendall who had married Polly, a sister of John Bunton, accompanied them too, and there were as well about one hundred slaves included in the company. They took passage before long in a boat, slipped easily down the Mississippi River to New Orleans. They boarded another steamer at this point, and feeling that they were nearly home, they settled down for a trip across the Gulf of Mexico.

The victory at San Jacinto as told Mary by her enthusiastic lover had been a decisive affair. In his eyes Mexico had suffered a crushing, silencing defeat. Henceforth the Anglo-Saxon might wander at will over the proud domain of Texas—so far as Mexico was concerned. So thought John Bunton. But out on the rolling wave, at some distance yet from the Texas port of Galveston, a Mexican man-of-war rejoicing in the name of Julius Caesar, bore down upon the smaller vessel, siezed it by the power of might, carrying crew and passengers captive to the city of Vera Cruz. The horror of the Alamo and of Goliad, the tales of Mexican butchery in isolated cases, must have come with alarming force to the mind of Mary, the young wife and mother. She must have lost a bit of her faith in Houston and Lamar and her husband's many other heroes. When they were later transferred to the City of Mexico and actually thrown into prison, Mary Howell Bunton must have felt that her husband had vastly over-rated the power of his wonderful, new-found friends.

No matter what Mary throught, Mary must submit to the power of Santa Anna. She who had lately tripped her happy, religious way through her father's elegant Tennessee home, must pine in prison and for no fault of her own. She must see her husband languishing there, his face growing pallid in the inactivity forced upon him. Old Uncle Rance, faithful slave and true, cared for her child and the other children of the colony, and no mother suffered any anxiety on account of her child. But when three months had come and gone, and release seemed no whit nearer, Mary Bunton, quiet, efficient, determined, beautiful, too, despite her anxiety, made her way to General Bravo, demanded an audience, and stood at last before him and made her plea.

Mary had known all her life, for she had seen it manifested, that women possess a subtle influence over men. She had probably never discussed sex-appeal with anybody, but Mary knew that her beauty, aided by her woman's helplessness, was likely to cause a stir in the heart of that tribunal. But Mary had no idea of resorting to such methods. Her education, her religious training, her experience in wordly affairs offered in her eyes an idea that seemed to her more noble, more certain in the power of its appeal. Calling to her aid her knowledge of treaty law, her knowledge of international affairs, Mary began her defense. She represented that in spite of her husband's part in the defeat of Mexico, she and her relatives were as yet citizens of the United States, expecting to enter Texas under the colonization law granted by Mexico to Stephen F. Austin. Perhaps, the mention of the United States, the nation that had even then come out victorious in two fair fights with England, both on land and on sea, perhaps this carried a bit of weight with Gen. Bravo, for after three more days of prison life, the party was released, and returned by way of Vera Cruz to New Orleans. The party, including the Buntons, then made their way back

to Tennessee as if they were forever disgusted with Texas
and her affairs, Mexican or otherwise.

But, despite these experiences, despite months in prison
and all the attendant horrors, Col. and Mrs. Bunton returned, and before very long, to Texas. This time they
were accompanied by Col. and Mrs. William McCreary,
the latter being a sister of Col. Bunton. They tried the
same manner of travel, we suppose, for they entered Texas
at Indianola on Matagorda Bay and went almost immediately to San Felipe de Austin. In 1840, Col. Bunton .
took up agricultural pursuits, cattle-raising, farming, and
all things connected therewith. This business led Bunton
to establish a home on Cedar Creek, Bastrop County, and
here our Mary experienced some thrilling things.

No matter how carefully men may plan for the protection
of those dependent on them, there invariably comes a
time, an unexpected time when women must be left to
protect themselves. Actual contact with dangerous things,
even with Indians, dulls the individual apprehension, and
Mary, herself, grew less afraid of these primeval creatures
as the days came and went. On one occasion, Mary was
left alone in the house save for two little children and an
old colored woman. Perfectly contented, Mary went
about her work, seeing in the situation no smallest cause
for worry. But for all her assurance, there came a morning when Mary noticed Indians coming from all directions,
their plan, evidently the surrounding of the house. The
danger stared her full in the face. She knew, too, that she
must depend entirely upon her own efforts, her own
ingenuity in the matter. So she loaded her rifle, she was
an expert shot, and sat her down at the opened front door
and kept her solemn vigil. The Indians, realizing her
bravery and her determination, kept a safe distance between them. They even suffered the old negro woman to
come in and out of the cabin, allowed her to attend her
chores, even to the family wash, and then deciding that
Mary meant business in the management of her strange,
uncanny weapon, they took themselves off, having done
no harm. At another time Mary had fallen sick, was, in
fact, confined to her bed, when into her presence rushed
the negro woman, declaring that Indians were beginning
to surround the house. Mary had the affrighted woman
close the door, had her move the bed against the door so
that it might act as a barricade, and then through a hole,
left by a knot having fallen from the wood of which it had
been made, she placed the barrel of her shot-gun, and there
Mary kept her watch throughout the live-long day.

But these days of anxious watching came to an end.
Texas was received as a state into the United States, and

then more ample protection for her people against the Indians was afforded. Civilization made its certain and sure approach. In 1857, Mary and her husband moved to Hays County, Texas, settling near Mountain City, a point between Buda and Kyle. They built at this point a comfortable house, and then Mary went about the inexplicable, intangible business of making a home. She was by this time the mother of six children, one daughter and five sons, and Mary found as many another woman has found, that no business in the world required such a variety and such a depth of training as does this business of being a mother. All her religious experience, all her intellectual activity, all her musical ability, all these were brought to bear upon the stupendous task. Did her son become interested in worthwhile literature, Mary was ready to discuss it with him. Did her one daughter require assistance in the study of music, Mary was ready and able and willing to help. She was herself possessed of an unusual voice, a voice that had been trained, and the music she left us is a witness that she sang songs of the highest type. She had memorized stanza after stanza of poetry as well as quotations from the best of prose, and about her cabin home and in that better home in Hays County, she, busy as the wife of a frontiersman must be busy, let fall those solemn bits of beauty, the work of men feeling as she felt and possessed of the power to put such feeling into words. For her own self-gratification, perhaps, she made the effort to store into her mind these literary and musical gems, but their recital on that mother's part left lasting impressions on the children lingering about her in the home. Even her sons, grown into stern, sturdy manhood, long after the mother had passed away, repeated that poetry and sang those songs, adding always at the close: "This is the song my mother sang," or quoting a tender poem with the even more tender addition at its close, "Mother taught me this." Her letters, still in possession of her descendants, were couched in good English, written in a fine Spencerian hand and on the nicest of stationery. With all these accomplishments calling, as accomplishments have a way of calling, for the individual's time and thought, Mary neglected no smallest affair of her plantation home. She superintended the spinning and the weaving, the cooking, the garden-planting, having always many slaves at hand to do her bidding. She abhorred even in men the use of tobacco and snuff, and the most inveterate user of either article was likely to abstain in her presence.

On September 16, 1862, in the forty-sixth year of her age, in the early prime of her useful life, Mary Howell Bunton passed away. The home over which she had labored was the scene of her going, and her body was laid tenderly away in the burying ground on the place. In regretting that early passing, let us remember that she went down with her faithful slaves about her, ministering to her every need, saving the distressed children every possible labor about that bed of pain. She had but to raise her hand, and a slave hastened to obey the mute signal. Even then war was raging, war that was in the end to set the slaves free, but in her early passing Mary Bunton was spared reconstruction and its attendant horrors. And we doubt not as her loyal sons and her one daughter lived through that war and those same horrors they many times felt a certain wave of thanksgiving that mother, tender, brave, faithful and true, had been spared.

Data contributed by—

Miss Brewye Bunton,
Kyle, Texas.

MRS. JOHN RABB

BORN

MARY CROWNOVER

Austin, the capital of Texas, lies for the most part on the north bank of the Colorado river, just about two hundred miles from the sea. The capitol, itself, sits on one of the seventy hills included in the limits of the city, and Congress avenue, a street one hundred and twenty feet wide and about one mile in length, slopes gently and in a southerly direction from the capitol grounds to the bank of this Colorado river. Strangers hailing from Michigan or Illinois and reaching this river in the month of August, or even in September, may find it shrunken to an insignificant stream, red and muddy, the dried mud stretching to the water edge suggesting, but rather helplessly, that its cracked and blistered surface had once been covered with water. This stranger, to his surprise, maybe, finds this Congress avenue hereinbefore alluded to, ending in a bridge of no mean proportions and of no mean quality of design and construction. It stretches out before him for no mean distance as bridges are expected to stretch, and the stranger, being from an economical land asks why all this waste of time and energy and money in order to bridge a stream so insignificant. The same stranger returning most any time, April preferred, but even another August might do, may find the same little stream swoolen to a raging torrent, covering every vestige of blackened mud, reaching well up the piers, some of which had seemed so useless. And the stranger carries in his mind the idea that Texas rivers, even in flood tide, are rather disappointing as to color.

But after the stranger in his journey southward leaves the bridge across the Colorado, he finds a well-kept road branching west, lying in a way close to the river's bank. He follows the road beneath trees, beside a precipice of rock, mostly limestone, some straggling pebbles, some daring, defying trees growing in the crevices, a precipice rising many feet high to the south of him. Then about a mile from the river bridge, the road, just before it makes a turn to the south, crosses another bridge. The stranger glances down looking for some more baked mud, some more muddy water, and said stranger experiences a surprise. The stream flowing beneath this second bridge is bold and daring, seeming to say with its every gurgle that drouth and wind and sun had never affected it, and marvel upon marvel, it is a limpid, greenish blue, white sand and pebbles glistening through, an unmistakable tribute to the water's purity. Even in August, with corn and oats already gathered, their remaining stalks dried to a crisp, with some few shrubs already speaking of autumn, the stranger happening that way finds Barton creek near its mouth, the stream having rolled and tumbled and complained its way among rocks and hills and fallen trees from a group of bold ever-flowing, dashing springs, some eighteen miles farther back in the mountains.

But the springs in the mountains are not the only source of supply for Barton creek. A little beyond the bridge spanning the creek, the well-kept road makes a turn to the south. Some few hundred yards from the turn, there comes to view a grove of pecan trees, some of them ages old, the ground beneath speaking of their long subsistence on such fare. Across this low-lying land and the stranger is at the creek's very edge. This edge slopes a little gently to the water, but the eastern bank, lying in full view before him, is formed of immense limestone ledges and boulders and from beneath those ledges and boulders, water, clear as crystal and cold as ice gurgles winter and summer, filling a large pool to the depth of fourteen feet, still limpid, still gurgling, and as thousands of bathers can testify, still sparklingly cold. The adjacent property was years ago presented by Mr. A. J. Zilker to the city for the benefit of the school children of Austin. Improvements have been made, bath-houses built, the residents of the county have made good use of it, for the automobile has placed it in easy reach of all people, but we are especially interested right now in another feature of the landscape immediately about the spring.

East of this bathing pool, a hundred yards, maybe, stands a solid, substantial, well-planned, two-storied rock house. Its very lines suggest comfort and ease and elegance. The house was built in 1867 by Mrs. John Rabb for her son, Gail Texas Rabb, just exactly as it stands to-day, and the family of this son still occupy it.

It is of this Mrs. John Rabb that we would think for a little while right now. The daughter of John Crownover, she was born in Buncom County, North Carolina, April 8, 1805. Contrary to Southern people of his day, John Crownover was a manufacturer, his product being the tall black silk hat, very much in evidence in that day. For each finished article he received twenty dollars, and there must have been some demand for the hats, for there seems to have been money in plenty in the Crownover home. The man, himself, was of Scotch-Irish ancestry, was a great believer in education, and saw to it that his children received all the benefits possible in that line. Miss Mary Crownover became the wife of John Rabb in Arkansas and then she came with her husband to Texas in 1822. She

found the new land suffering all the privations of a new
land under ordinary conditions, but added to the vicissitudes natural to life in any wilderness, she found Texas
still a province of Mexico. Fully fourteen years she lived
under Mexican rule, her heart burning with the neglect her
country must suffer, her heart beating high at the thought
of the indignity thrust upon Texas, every now and then,
when Mexico happened to need funds. She saw Texas
throw off that yoke, saw her maintain her own independent
government for nine years. She saw Texas go voluntarily
into the United States, grateful in her heart for the protection thus offered. She saw Texas leave the Union to
throw her help and strength with the Confederacy. She
saw Texas go back into the Union, making in all five changes
and four different governments under which this lady had
lived. A life this was, rich in experience, a life, perhaps,
worth studying.

Naturally we like a little help in visualizing our heroines,
a word now and then to convince us that our mind picture
may be correct. This Mary, even as girl, was tall, well-
formed, well-developed. Her eyes were dark, her hair
black, and not particularly grey at seventy-eight years of
age. She possessed the majestic mould of woman, the
type that carries its graces through the changes of any life,
no matter how vigorous, straight to the grave. And men
in her day were not slow to recognize her charms. Accordingly, our Miss Mary fell in with Mr. John Rabb during the family sojourn in Arkansas, and being d u l y
courted as seemed suitable for the winning of this rather
remarkable maiden, she soon became his bride. John
Rabb, a man of no mean education, a thrifty man in every
respect, decided some two years after this marriage that
he and his Mary must go to Texas.

The young wife, accustomed to ease and plenty, silk
hats were still in much demand—to move to Texas! To
her family the idea was appalling. Not so to Mary! She
had every confidence in her husband's judgment. Then,
too, she loved him, and to her any thought of remaining
at the home of her parents for the sake of bodily ease was
contemptible. She felt a sense of wifely duty toward that
husband, a sense of duty that made her desire above everything else to do all in her power to add to his comfort.
And then, above all, Mary possessed a truly religious
nature, a nature that could find joy where other woman
saw only privation. As we would put it to-day, she was a
jolly woman, depending on the Unseen to guard and guide
her through difficulties that to other women would have
seemed unbearable. So Mrs. Rabb, bride of a year or
two, as yet denied the joys of motherhood, mounted her

old horse, Nickitypoli, took another woman's baby in her arms in order to help out, and thus came all the way to Texas.

The Rabbs settled first in Fayette County, Texas. Seeing that John Rabb, himself, had emigrated from Fayette County, Pennsylvania, we naturally suppose that Rabb had some say in the naming of the new county, and that a little love for his old home influenced him in the matter. We know that in this Fayette County, the Rabbs joined in with Stephen F. Austin, and that the Rabbs thereafter played well their part in the happenings of that colony, for Rabb eventually took part in the government, serving in the army at the battle of San Jacinto. They built there in Fayette County a little frame house—not logs—of two rooms, with a lean-to, for John Rabb having erected the first saw-mill in Texas, had no trouble procuring the lumber. For this daring enterprise, Rabb was granted by the government a full league of land in addition to his other grant. From this same mill Rabb afterwards gave the lumber for the first Methodist church ever built in San Antonio. In this little cabin home, redolent with the freshness of the lumber, a thing wonderful in the eyes of Indians and the like, Mary Rabb went about her woman's work, cooking, spinning, weaving, and when the day's work was done for other folks, she sat her down to piecing quilts. She gave birth to nine children, saw to their comfort and their up-bringing, and they repaid her for her time and care. There was the first son, Montgomery Rabb, who served in the Mexican war of 1846. There was Melissa Rabb, a daughter, who possessed along with other womanly qualifications, a beautiful soprano voice. A son, V. S. Rabb, was a captain in the Confederate army, another son Wesley, occupying some position of honor and trust at the same time. A daughter, Betty, married a Mr. Croft and went to live on a big plantation near Winchester. Gail Texas Rabb, the baby, was named for Gail Borden of condensed milk fame, a fine, up-standing man of his day and a close, personal friend of John Rabb. Marion, another son, died at ten years of age, and Lorenzo, about three years of age at the time, had to be taken from a sick-bed to take his part in the famous run-away scrape, and died soon after from the exposure. The seven children left them were educated at Reutersville College, of which their father was an officer. This college, spoken of by many of our forefathers and, therefore, appearing often in these pages, was the first college in Texas. Gail Texas Rabb is probably the only ex-student of that college alive to-day (1928) but even for us who must count ourselves more fortunate, there were many worthwhile happenings in Texas traceable to the influence of that college. Gail Texas Rabb afterward attended a military school in company with John Crownover, his cousin, Joseph D. Sayers, afterwards Governor, and Seth Shepherd, for years our Congressman. Major Allen was president of the school, and it was located at Bastrop.

But through all these duties, through all the many things demanded of a mother, Mary Rabb found time for intellectual things, for political things, above all, for things pertaining to her church and its hopes. She was even more deeply interested in the intellectual side of life when it had some bearing upon things of a religious nature. She had become a member of the Methodist Church before coming to Texas, and her husband, John Rabb, was the first man to join the Methodist Church after it was established in Texas. Thrall in his history of early Methodism, had much to say of John Rabb and his wife and the work they did in church circles. Mary Rabb held a life membership in the Foreign Missionary Society of the church, and her husband gave at one time eleven hundred acres of land to this society that they might use the proceeds in the furtherance of the work. Her oldest daughter, the musician, married a gentleman named Reese. He had taught languages at Reutersville College, and was a man of much culture. Mary's own son, Washington Rabb, had been trained for the ministry, but his death while yet young, put an end to Mary's joy in his achievements. This, perhaps, gave her an even keener joy in the association with her son-in-law. With him she discussed the things of the world as they appeared to her, and from a scientific, as well as a religious standpoint, and this was to Mary Rabb a joy deep and true and undefiled.

At some time in the year 1860 it became plain to Mrs. Rabb that her husband's health was failing. After much discussion they decided that a change of climate might be beneficial. Financial affairs made it possible for Rabb to retire from business, and to Mary, the life in the little capital of the state, replete with social and religious advantages, made a mighty appeal. They made the trip from Fayette County to Austin in wagons, unmolested, so far as we know by Indians. Rabb looked out over the land at his disposal, and following the custom of the day, selected a site removed several miles from the city limits. He bought fifty acres of the land originally granted to William Barton. He built on this land a log house—his sawmill days were over—the exact site of the house now included in the tourist park, just west of Barton Springs.

In this new home, hopeful for her husband's health, hopeful in the beautiful surroundings for the future of her

children, Mrs. Rabb saw her household wares set up. She
settled her slaves about her, and joined with her husband
in their control. They were taught to work with the
children and for the children, and in that home, every
night of the world, the slaves and the children and the
"stranger within the gates" met for family prayers. No
drop of liquor was tolerated on the premises, and there was
in the manner of John Rabb a certain mark of superiority
that made individuals respect his wishes. To enforce his
ideas against intoxicants of all kinds, John Rabb frequently
related an incident that had been told him by Major Allen,
president of the Military school at Bastrop. In a talk before the students of his school, Maj. Allen showed them the
skull of a man who had all his life been a drunkard, dying
finally in delirium tremens. The body had been turned
over after death to Major Allen and the doctor, seeing that
the man had no friends, and the two of them proceeded to
hold a post mortem. Part of the skull was removed in
order to examine the brain, and as soon as a lighted match
was applied to the brain it took fire, the blue flame circling
the entire brain. One student under Major Allen had
caught the idea, and mayhap many folks for just and honest
reason rose up many times thereafter and called him
blessed.

The home of Mary Rabb seems to have been spared all
Indian invasion, but her eldest son, Montgomery Rabb,
was not so fortunate. He had settled in Blanco County,
and along in the early sixties, Montgomery and his son,
William, were returning late one afternoon from a cattle
drive. They had yet several miles to go when Indians
appeared, ready for fight. The Rabbs, being mounted on
the fastest horses, escaped without injury. The following night, however, a band of Indians came to Montgomery
Rabb's home, his wife being there alone save for his older
son William and two small children. William happened
to look out of the window in time to see a number of Indians dancing round some pots of meat that had been left
to cook in the open air, only a few yards from the house.
Frightened beyond measure, the mother cautioned them
all to be still, and finally the Indians stole away, as if
perfectly satisfied with the day's pleasures.

In spite of the benefits hoped for in the new home, John
Rabb died there in 1861. Mary lived on, for some twenty
afterwards. Her son Gail Texas Rabb made his home with
her, but Mary was the ruling influence in all matters. She
endured the four years torture of the Civil war, sending her
sons to battle, waiting and watching for their return. One
made his way home to her, his wounds all but causing his
death, and in her lonely home, Mary nursed him back to

health and strength.   She remained active, almost until
the day of her death.

This account of Mrs. John Rabb cannot be closed with
any sense of satisfaction on the part of your scribe without
a word or two about Uncle Kit.   Back in Fayette County,
not very long after John Rabb came to Texas, he bought
a young negro woman.   In the course of time she gave
birth to a boy, and she named him Kit, he assuming as
did other slaves the name of his master.   Old Kit grew up
in the Rabb home, a playmate for the boys near his own
age, a faithful nurse to the young ones, a faithful attendant
always at the family prayers held by his master.   Kit
listened respectfully to all that was said,   He showed the
same respect when his master dwelt on the horror of
whiskey.   "Yes, massa, yes, massa," bowing politely before the would-be advisor, but old Kit kept on drinking.
With the abolition of slavery, and the many changes it
brought, old Kit lingered on with "massa," working just
the same—and drinking when he could manage it.   He
married a woman who had been a slave of the De Cordova
family, but he kept on living on the plantation owned and
operated by "massa."   But he did drift finally into the
city, and there he was employed as porter in the Bank of
James H. Raymond and Co.   Old Kit was very much at
home in this institution, for Hamilton and Myrick, and the
Raymonds themselves had been frequent guests in the
Rabb home.   After his strength left him, and he had to
give up his porter's duties, old Kit provided himself with
a blacking-brush and started out to shine shoes.   Shuffling
down the street, hitching his suspenders into place, assuming his most engaging "quality" smile, Kit would
manage to fall in with Frank Hamilton.

"Massa Frank," his smile most alluring, "want dem
shoes shined dis mownin'?"

Conscious that his shoes had already been brought to a
state of perfection past anything old Kit had ever been
able to produce, his mind full of financial matters, sometimes large, sometimes small, Frank Hamilton would give
a glance at old Kit, slip his hand in his pocket, pull forth a
dollar and escape down the street, thinking it cheap at
the price.   That same day, likely that same hour, old Kit
would meet D. W. Doom down the street and make his
same plea.   Judge Doom, hurrying to court, would slip
his dollar to old Kit, and to both gifts old Kit would bow
and smile and scrape, his lips forming always the same
reply, "Thank ye kindly, Sir.   Thank ye kindly!"

Perhaps old Kit spent the dollars for things John Rabb
had denied him.   We go even further.   We state broadly
that the money went for the most part for the despised

liquor, but even in his wanderings thus produced old Kit never forgot "massa" and "de missus," never forgot to speak of them in the highest praise. He could dwell on stories of San Jacinto in which that loved "massa" took part. He could tell of the runaway scrape because he with his beloved "missus" had been among the frightened refugees. He could tell tales of the hours spent beside the bed of the soldier-son who had come home from the Confederate army sick unto death. And perhaps the individual interested in the doings of another day and time could do no better than to listen to such a man.

"Out of the mouth of Babes and sucklings—"

Data contributed by—

Miss Mamie Rabb,
Austin, Texas.

MRS. ASA MITCHELL

BORN

EMILY BRISBANE

According to a proud descendant of this certain Emily, she was born some time in the year 1818 in St. Louis, Missouri, the Christian name of her father being uncertain, but that of her mother being known as Mary. Little has been said anyway of these same parents, but from some source young Emily inherited an independent streak, for we find her some fifteen years after her birth, drifting from that St. Louis home down to Brenham, Texas, where she followed the noble and enthusiastic profession of teaching school. Subsequent events in her life lead us to believe that she was a success at this venture. Certainly, we know that she proved herself goodly in the eyes of men, for in 1835 she became the wife of Asa Mitchell, hailing himself from Somerset County in the grand old state of Pennsylvania.

In order to really understand young Emily it might be well to glance at this man who had thus early in her life put an everlasting end to all pedagogical endeavors so far as young Emily was concerned. He had been born in 1795, some twenty-three years before young Emily came into the world, had married Charlotte Woodmancy, and his son, the first-born of that first marriage, had come into the world on the same day with young Emily. Two other children came in swift succession, and then Asa Mitchell moved his family and his slaves to New Orleans. In this quaint old city of the South, Mitchell fell in with Stephen F. Austin. Something in Austin's manner, something more, perhaps, in the call of the new and the untried country had it sweight with Mitchell, and he soon found himself among the famous three hundred persons who composed Austin's first colony. He left his slaves in New Orleans, and accompanied by his wife and children, put out for Texas, settling first at Velasco. In this wild new country, Mitchell buried his first wife, Charlotte Woodmancy, with her last baby in her arms, and then turned him about to face what seemed to him a desolate future.

Thinking of the slaves left in New Orleans, realizing their possible worth in the rich lands of Texas, Mitchell put out for New Orleans, intent upon bringing the slaves to settle in this new land. He hired a boat in New Orleans for the return trip, and then Asa Mitchell put forth a master stroke of finance. He loaded that same boat with pictures, images, pottery, all of a type more or less sacred in the eyes of Catholics, and it is recorded that Mitchell realized a nice profit from this venture. He moved his family to

Washington-on-the-Brazos, where he helped draw up the first Constitution of Texas. He and his elder son, Nat, were in the battle of San Jacinto, and his second son, William, was one of the Mier prisoners who drew a black bean.

Into the home of this man, thoroughly in sympathy with Texas in all her hopes and all her fears, came this young girl, this Emily Brisbane, ready at her tender age to assume the cares and responsibilities of the wife and step-mother. As before stated, Emily, following the death of her father and mother in St. Louis, had come to Texas to teach school. She came with a sister, Mary, who was married to a physician, and in accordance with surgical ideas of this day and time, Mary rode her hobby of cleanliness and rode it hard. Her family no doubt profited by her industry in this line, but the masculine element grumbled now and then to find the feather beds on the fence in the sunshine, and all the chairs out in the yard at the same time while Mary cleaned the house to her liking. One member of this family, her own brother in fact, said to his children after Mary's death, a little reverently, a little lovingly, that he felt very sure that Aunt Mary was cleaning up Heaven.

Now Emily may have shared in some degree her sister's fondness for an immaculate home, but we are inclined to believe that Emily placed an even greater value on some other things that go to make life worth while. Realizing the unpleasant possibilities of a home life that must rest on the basis offered to the average step-mother, thinking of the children of an equal age with herself, Emily studied that life from every angle. She respected her husband's love for his first wife, and she made herself big enough and broad enough to see in every individual circumstance the side of the children of that first marriage in the same just light that she saw her own. She made herself, in short, a real mother to them. And those efforts met their just reward. Emily and that eldest son of her husband kept their birthdays together as long as Emily lived, and we feel very sure that he did many times rise up and call her blessed. She became in the fullness of time the mother of nine children of her own, the first one born March 2, 1836, and twin daughters later came into the world on Christmas day, 1842.

In 1846, after Texas had been admitted into the Union, Mitchell moved his family from Washington-on-the-Brazos, to Bexar County. He built a home for them near the bank of the Medina River, not far from San Antonio.

This home is still standing. The present owner, a descendant of Mitchell and Emily, says the home has been

changed since first built, and she confesses that the few
additions and substractions thereto have robbed the house
of some of its picturesque features.   In the beginning, this
ranch house contained twelve rooms, and most of them
(architects please take notice) measured eighteen by
twenty feet with ceilings ten feet high.   The kitchen—ye
who would live in delicatessen fashion—was the largest
room in the house, with a chimney big and broad, with a
fireplace, big enough, no doubt, to roast a whole pig at
once, and a Dutch oven, forerunner of the fireless cooker
of to-day, in which delicious cakes were baked.   A large
under-ground cistern, connected by pipes with the kitchen,
kept them supplied winter and summer with icecold water.

The front room—so were parlors called in that day and
time—was furnished with mahogany overstuffed chairs,
the color being green, and a davenport to match, and this
latter piece is in existence to-day in the home of a descendant in Tucson, Arizona.   In the front bedroom upstairs a four-poster bed proclaimed the time of real elegance,
but a sleepy little youngster rolled from its majestic height
in the dead of the night, and one of Emily's sons calmly
sawed the legs off lest the incident be repeated and the
next time fall short of a real accident.   And she who gave
these words for record states calmly that after the Civil
war, when she would visit her one-time slaves in their
cabin homes she would find them sleeping on spool beds—
which had fallen slightly out of repair and had been given
to the faithful darkies.

When the twins, the Christmas presents of 1842, were
old enough to appreciate it, their father presented them
with a piano, one of the very first ever brought to Texas.
This piano was of the type called "square" not quite so
large as the one afterwards in use in that home, but many
children banged upon it and used it and doubtless came to
love it as a precious part of that home life.   There was,
indeed, joy and gladness in that home maintained by Asa
Mitchell and his wife.   Mitchell engaged a "Professor" as
such teachers were dubbed in those days to instruct the
young lassies in the noble Cecilian art.   No doubt they
made good progress under this man's instructions.

Each tune in its turn was wafted by the gentle
south wind to the negro quarters, and there those
tunes fell on willing and apt ears.   The "missis" soon
learned that the negroes, both big and little, had learned to
play these tunes themselves, using Jew's-harps, French-
harps, bones, and many instruments of their own manufacture.   They danced, too, to this music, these irresponsible children of another race, in the soft, southern twilight
of that Bexar County home, and Asa Mitchell and his

wife, Emily, never found it in their hearts to say them "Nay."

But for all this leniency toward the slaves dependent upon them, the home of Asa Mitchell was a Christian home. Such a home in that day had a little different meaning from one so described to-day. His children were trained to obey, and without question. They were trained to be reverent of holy things as their father saw them, and they never forgot his training. Did this training rob life of its gladness? For example:—

One daughter among the older children was married and went to live in the home her father gave her close by the old ranch home, close, a mile or so. Emily went for a visitation one summer day with his daughter, and the two of them remarked more than once as the day advanced that there was a smell of burnt feathers in the air. As Emily approached her own home in the late afternoon, she was met by Aunt Ann, the negro mammy, cook, and general "boss" of the house and yard. Said Ann wore a sorrowful face, and her mistress prepared to listen to a tale of deepest woe. And old Ann told the tale, slowly, deliberately, and it was none other than that two little boys aged respectively eleven and nine had been playing Indians with the little negroes about the same age, using in true imitation the deadly bow and arrow. The result: Said boys had killed two of "Mis' Emily's" finest turkeys. Ann further declared that when she found the scamps, the turkeys had been picked and a fire built around them to roast them.

"Den I roasted de whole endurin' bunch, Mis' Emily, deed I did, en I tuk dem tukeys home. De's mos' ready now fur supper."

Records fail to show that Emily rebelled at Aunt Ann's usurpation of parental authority in the matter of "roasting" when it came to her own particular children, but we do know that Emily, her liege lord and master being away from home, sent for her daughter, lately visited, for another daughter, Carrie, also living near by, and that a feast followed the tragic ending of the small boy's play.

Feasts of this nature were not uncommon in the Mitchell home. Respect for their stern, religious father kept the many children subdued in his presence, but his many trips abroad on business, his own and that of the newly-forming nation, left ample time for the frolic. The big kitchen, always warm in winter and cool in summer was often turned into a dance-hall, and the boys and girls came from San Antonio and danced and frolicked just as long as their breath held out. Then the negroes waiting by to watch "de quality" would take a hand, amusing themselves and the company, too, turning hand-springs, doing a "cake-

walk"—anything a darkie might choose to do in the hope
of bringing a ringing laugh from his dear "missis." These
dancers then, both black and white, would eat of the delicious cake, baked in that Dutch oven, or had the bee hives
been robbed on that particular day, they would be served
with pan-cakes floating in delicious honey. They rode
horseback, these Mitchell boys and girls, they fished and
they hunted, they laughed and they chatted as do the young
men and women of to-day, but when Sunday morning
came, when they met that father's eye at breakfast-table,
knowing that it took in the wearing apparel selected for the
day, they knew, too, that they would eventually go to
service with that father whether they wanted to or not.

Not a sign of deprivation in all that account of home-
life, despite the attendance upon church. His children respected his desire in the church-going matter as they respected him in everything else. They knew as well as his
wife, that Asa Mitchell was a man of stern integrity, for
they saw him fill many places of trust in the wild new
country. During his sojourn on the Brazos, he headed the
Committee of Safety designed to protect Austin's first
colony from the Indians, and he held a similar position
during the Civil war. He was as well a stern member of
the Methodist church. In his own Bible, written by his
own hand this statement occurs: "It pleased God to
convert my soul the 18th day of November, 1840."

These things had their unconscious influence on the type
of men who made free to visit in Mitchell's home. Wharton
was a life-long friend, and spent many hours in the famous
old ranch house. Mitchell loved Stephen F. Austin with
the love of a brother, and Austin most duly returned his
regard. The Father of his Country visited Mitchell often,
and it is easy to imagine that to a man denied the joys of
home and real home ties, those frequent visits to Mitchell's
home must have a little short of a real blessing. Mirabeau
B. Lamar and Anson Jones were frequent visitors in that
home. Upon the death of Emily, one of the Wharton
brothers took her daughter, Carrie, home to live with them,
and some memory of the hours passed in Asa Mitchell's
home made them willing, nay anxious, to serve in some
way this little daughter so bitterly bereft.

And to-day in that home built hard by the bank of the
Medina river, near the famous city of San Antonio, under
the shadow of the Missions and beneath the benediction
of the Alamo, a descendant of Asa Mitchell still lives and
speaks to us thus of Emily. She tells of her wifely duty
well sustained, of her parental cares and responsibilities
met in every way, of her pains-taking care of her home, and
then she adds feelingly:

"She was bright and she was witty until she lost her two sons, but her own death came soon after."

Tender-hearted little woman, drifting into the great Southwest in the hour of its birth, making a happy home in the wilderness for her husband, his first children and her own, bright, happy, cheerful in the face of all calamities! God keep her memory ever before us an inspiration, "an ever-present help in time of trouble."

Data contributed by—

Mrs. Maurmann,
San Antonio, Texas.

MRS. JOEL COFFEY-JONES
BORN
MARY KNOX

In Somerset County, Kentucky, in 1818, Mary Knox became the bride of Joel Coffey. This safe-same Mary, the child of Scotch parents, as her name would indicate, was born August 5, 1798, her father being Lieut. John Knox and her mother Elizabeth Eoff. The parents of Joel Coffey, Mathan Coffey and Mary Saunders Coffey, had emigrated just after the Revolutionary war from Wilkes County, North Carolina, to this particular part of Kentucky. They had made them a home there, and young Joel had fallen into the snare set, unconsciously of course, by this certain Mary Knox. Joel had gone, however, no matter the pangs of love, to do his part in the war of 1812, a gallant part no doubt, and some six years after his return, according, of course, to Scotch methods, the marriage had taken place. The marriage being duly solemnized, Joel received a grant of land in Alabama in recognition of his services in the war of 1812, and hither he moved some ten years after his marriage, he and many of his kinsman.

The duties, the cares, the problems came fast into the life of Mary. She had become the mother of three children before they left Kentucky, and in that new settlement of Alabama she kept herself busy considering from every angle the proper method by which these youngsters must be brought to maturity. She had herself been taught little more than the average woman of her day, had been trained, along with this meagre knowledge, in the ways of Presbyterian faith as seen through the eyes of the Scotch, the faith to which she had been born. Many lasting beneficent traits of her character might be laid at the door of the good old faith. The first church established in her neighborhood in old Alabama came, alas, from the Baptist persuasion. To add to this complication, the father of Mary's husband, James Coffey, by name, helped establish that church. A Baptist church, close at hand and the only church, and established by her husband's people, and good old Presbyterian blood flowing full and free through Mary Coffey's veins. That woman faced a problem.

Conscious of her problem, Mary watched that church grow, thinking all the while of her own children growing up from the communion of religious people. Honorable and upright like herself she might make them, those boys and girls entrusted by God to her care, but Mary began to realize her own limitations, began to see, did Mary, that if she would bring up those children in the fear and admonition of the Lord she must have the help of some organized

Christian association. The Baptist church being the only one at hand, Mary sought its fellowship, signifying to the pastor her willingness to accept its rites and ceremonies and to abide by any promise it might see fit to exact of her.

Her old father heard of her intentions. Seething with disgust beneath his ponderous Presbyterian faith, his belief in predestination and foreordination, that old father, daring not to try his daughter's patience too far, attended that baptismal service in which it seemed to him his daughter had parted with her woman's crown of glory, the faith of her fathers. As Mary made her way from the baptismal pool, the hurt in her father's heart demanded expression.

"Daughter," his voice stern beyond belief, "what are you going to do with your infant baptism?"

A strange, harsh note this, sweeping as it did upon her in her moment of exaltation! Daunted, upset? Mary Knox Coffey? Not a bit of it. Through the midst of her tender feeling, through her mother determination to do the best for her children, the exaltation of the moment became supreme. She looked that stern old man proudly in the eye and answered:

"Leave it in the church of Rome where it originated."

A world of significance clusters about that reply. Trembling a bit, maybe, from force of habit before that father's displeasure, she dared mention to the Presbyterian Scotchman, strong in his own established faith, that one precious tenet had come bodily from the Catholic church. There is no record that she suffered from this daring reply, but we know what the reply must have cost her. Martyrs are not made of sterner stuff.

Joel and Mary Coffey lived on their busy lives in old Alabama. That stern old father and Mary's mother, too, died there, but they were never lonely. Kinsfolks had emigrated with them from Kentucky, and they, too, had followed the command to be fruitful and multiply. Mary, herself, was the mother of a flock of ten children, varying naturally from grown men to a babe in arms. Joel Coffey, half-Irish and therefore voluble, enjoyed this circle of kinsfolks, but in 1842 his sons came before him with another story. These two sons had already attained their majority, and they had inherited much from their purely Scotch mother. They stood before the half-Irish father, his eyes fastened on them in amusement, and they made a strange demand. They said they were young and strong and willing to work, but not in that community. With the self-same calmness of spirit they declared separately to their astonished father that it had become futile to try to make a living where one was surrounded with kins-folks,

who each and every one expected these young Scots to
spend their time working for the comfort of these same
relatives who never thought to offer any pay for such
services. A little disturbed, the father, probably remembering a like experience in his own youth, caught a
gleam of the truth of the position maintained by his
sturdy sons, and before very long he and his wife and
children had made the trip by boat from Alabama to Texas,
landing in Paschal County, and settling themselves far
from the annoying kinfolks in the neighborhood of Mt.
Pleasant.

Now Joel Coffey had been a feeble man when he left
Alabama, and he died about six years after they reached
Texas. This left Mary the full burden of the bringing up
of her brood, and subsequent events proved Mary fully
equal to the task. Be it remembered, that upbringing
meant the providing of food and raiment, and every other
thing needful to the sustaining of human life. It meant
clearing the land of the Mt. Pleasant farm, the planting of
crops, the even more difficult task of harvesting, the disposal of such produce as remained when her own family
had been fed, the laying in of supplies, the control and the
care of slaves, all this it took that she might feed and clothe
these children. Just as she had demanded in old Alabama
some religious association for her children, so was she
equally determined in her new home that her children must
be educated. She carried her point, and her children went
forth from that home well equipped for life. One son,
William Coffey, accumulated a fortune in the California
gold-fever of 1849, returned to Texas about 1853, and
settled at Sherman, his brother, Nathan, going into business with him there. Her daughters as they grew to
maturity seemed goodly in the eyes of men—and most
women enjoy this—and these daughters were in due season
taken to wife. One of these daughters married a physician,
and Mary spent her small quota of spare time reading his
medical books, and be it known digesting them. There is
nothing extant to show whether these books treated the
noble art of medicine from the allopathic standpoint or
from that of the homeopath, but there is a blessed certainty
that Mary Knox Coffey's knowledge thus obtained brought
a sense of healing to many a bed of pain. This knowledge
came too late for the comfort of her own family, but said
knowledge was by no means thrown away.

Far from it. A radical change came into the life of
Mary. For some reason, she left her cheerful home in
Mt. Pleasant for the rough, rugged country of San Saba.
Snakes lived in the rocks, wild beasts roamed the hills and
the valleys, and the Indian had not yet made up his mind

that the pale-face was entitled to his country. Then, too, Mary had reached her three score years and ten. She had labored long and labored hard at the up-bringing of her family. By every law of justice, Mary should have sat her down in ease and plenty, waited upon by those children and the many others she had served. Gladly had those children rendered this service, but life had been too full, too active for Mary to enjoy even the prospect of idleness. She maintained control of her home, her business affairs, and she kept up her study of those medical books, and put that study into practice. The calls came from far and near for her help. After a bit, she provided herself with a shaggy little pony, and no call for her ever met a denial.

To the expectant mother of to-day, sitting in ease in your love-guarded home, your physician strong in the might of scientific research, your nurse, herself highly educated, serene in her own efficiency, both physician and nurse waiting the call of your hour of pain, to the father waiting, too, his own heart beating high lest he let some little thing slip by that might add to your comfort, to you I speak and ask you to look back with me just for an instant, to the figure of that wiry, little Scotch woman, guiltless of germ theories, possessing few instruments, most of her knowledge obtained from her own keen experience, look at her I say, and wonder and adore. Some of the cases she attended were young wives who had followed the young lover into the wilderness and must, perforce, give birth to the first child without a mother's hand to give courage, without the comforts and conveniences known in a city home. Think what it meant to a young husband to leave the young wife in her agony, and she must be left while he made his way to Grandma Coffey, for in her little hand lay his only chance for help. No telephone to warn her to be ready as the young father reached her cabin home! No assurance under Heaven that he would not return to his cabin home and find that Indians had prowled about waiting just this chance to catch the pale-faced squaw unaware, had prowled and done his dirty work, leaving for that returning husband only the ashes of the home he had struggled to build!

Just such a man came to Mary Knox Coffey one day late in her life. He stood before her in anguish, and Mary Coffey read the signs in his drawn, white face. His silence meant nothing to her. She knew just what he wanted, and Mary made herself ready, without so much as a single question. As she settled at last in her saddle on that shaggy pony, he turned apologetically to her and asked: "Grandma, how fast can you ride."

"Set your own pace," she replied, gathering the reins in her hands, and those who stood by to watch them off saw them later pass over the rugged mountain path, each horse in a hard lope.

But there came a more quiet time for Mary, a happier time if the truth must be told. Mary had loved her husband, had stood by him through joy and sorrow, but, with that man many years in his grave, Mary began to think that woman's life alone was a rather trying thing. Many of the ten children were married and gone. Her youngest daughter was a student in McKenzie Institute, and her one unmarried daughter made her home with her mother. Old maids are not exactly the company such a woman as Mary would choose for companionship, even be they her own daughter, so Mary turned herself about and married the Rev. Mr. Jones. Said Mr. Jones was the Baptist minister who frequently supplied the church Mary had helped organize and build. The old maid daughter objected very much when the idea of her mother's marriage was suggested to her—such objection was natural for the old maid—but the woman who had in her youth gone contrary to her stern old father's ideas in religious matters, was not likely to care much for her daughter's objection. In vain that daughter voiced her opposition, voiced as well her disgust to other people. In vain she alluded to the minister as "that old man Jones." Her mother went on about her own business in her own sweet way, and that marriage brought to her probably the happiest time of her whole life.

Mary had within herself the practical ability necessary to a materially successful life, but Mary had as well a deep desire to worship God, and to worship Him as she saw and understood Him. She saw in the association with Mr. Jones a help along such matters, and Mary was not disappointed. Deeper in mind, perhaps, than her preacher husband, she found rare pleasure in studying with him. She read her Bible with his help, and she read it alone, and Mary soon became able to discuss it intelligently and pleasantly for those less fortunate in the matter of speech than herself. She did discuss it many times for the benefit of the entire congregation gathered in the Union Church she had helped build in San Saba, and the men and women listened to her as she spoke as they might have listened to one "having great authority." And yet, when her own teeth became too frail to eat the crust of the biscuit, she made her grand-daughter eat them, promising as a reward for this bit of frugality on the part of the grand-daughter that eating biscuit crusts was sure to make the hair curl.

Did Mary Knox Coffey-Jones believe this little bit of sophistry?

Could she who rode so fearlessly the uncertain mountain path, her shaggy pony and her own body tempting targets for the straying Indians, could she, standing staunch and firm and true by many a bed of pain believe this as she said it? Maybe she did—maybe she didn't. What boots it either way it may prove? We know that Mary Knox Coffey-Jones lived and breathed and died. We know that she blessed the world about her every day of her simple little life, and we thankfully acknowledge that the blessed influence of that life plays its part in making men and women just what they are to-day.

Data contributed by—

Mrs. J. A. Walker,
Brownwood, Texas.

MRS. E. H. WINFIELD

BORN

ANN HALL GRAY

In the close study of the life of Ann Hall Gray, particularly if the student happens to live in Texas, he must begin with the same old idea of emigration and the reasons why, for some deep form of experience was necessary in the old days to start people to Texas. Some, of course, came from choice, answering all too eagerly the call of the new and the wild, but when the life of a cultivated, refined, intelligent woman is under consideration, one is likely to find that some unpleasant form of experience provoked the move to the Southwest. Ann Hall Gray, being cultivated and refined and intelligent, must have been influenced by some powerful, all-compelling circumstance to come to Texas, a circumstance she could neither control nor yet overcome. An intimate glance into the details of her life must surely reveal it.

She was born, this lovely Ann, in Charleston, S. C., on January 16, 1796. Her father, Captain Peter Gray, had served with honor to himself in the revolutionary war which had closed some twelve years before Ann was born. While Ann was yet a school-girl, this gallant captain moved himself and family to the Spartanburg district, and it was there that Ann met and loved and married Alexander Vernon. In the course of a rather extensive business, Vernon went on the bond of a friend, only to find his friend unworthy and himself bankrupt. The extent of the financial trouble realized, and young Vernon and his wife put out, some time in 1835, for Texas. So much for the particular experience that sent this troubled couple into the new country! So much for the spirit of hopefulness that started the young people again in the path of fortune, but just what particular form of optimism led Vernon to this particular section of the wilderness may never be known. Neither are we particularly interested in the man's optimism or the effect thereof, but there are some high spots in the life of Ann Hall Gray, his wife, that make it seem well to pause a bit so that we may learn something of how she fared and what she did as the wife of that young pioneer.

Vernon and his wife took the steamer at New Orleans and landed at Velasco at the mouth of the Brazos, for Galveston island at that time boasted only a few fishermen's huts. They set up their home in the little historic town of Washington-on-the-Brazos. They prospered in the new country in that strange form of prosperity peculiar to a new country, a prosperity so bound up in its dreams of the future that it finds contentment in crude comforts, in the plain, every-day substantial necessities of life. Ann played well her part in the new environment. Beautiful in the rich type of beauty peculiar to Charleston, that asset in her favor was overshadowed by the more important characteristic that make up the real woman. Energetic, efficient, she looked well to the ways of her household. Her woman's wit planned the first Texas home. It consisted of two large rooms in the center built of sturdy logs, with two frame rooms attached front and back, thus forming six rooms in all. A log cabin after all, and Ann had known better things.

Mayhap Ann grieved for other things as many a Texas woman had grieved, but no man ever heard of that grief, and what is more to the point, few, if any, ever saw her idle. She superintended the clearing of the land about that cabin, the planting and the harvesting. With the cotton and wool ginned by hand-picked had been the better word— she had it spun into thread and woven into cloth that was later made into clothing for her family and her slaves. She had log cabins built for these slaves, all of them five or six hundred yards from her own home, and to them she went her busy round, caring for the sick, reproving the idle, teaching the "teachable," in short, a typical Southern "missis" on a typical Southern plantation.

In her South Carolina home, previous to her departure for Texas, Ann had given birth to four children. Another child was born in Alabama after they had begun the journey to Texas. She raised three of these children. Hearing no mention of a school in her immediate neighborhood, we suppose that Ann, along with her other manifold duties, superintended the instruction of these children. Ann no doubt felt the importance of the pioneer woman in this matter of education for her children, no doubt took it seriously. She had thought of course for the education that must come to fit the child for financial independence, and Ann thought, too, in the rough newness of the wilderness of what might be said and what should be said to those same children of a spiritual nature. She had no fast-set, fanatical rules for the conduct of life for herself. She thought at times and deeply, of her relation to the Unseen Power that had led her thither. Born into the Episcopal church, married in the Presbyterian church, Ann, through the inexorable force of circumstances in a new country, became a member of the Baptist church in Texas. That she ever ascribed wholly to its ideas of Christian faith is exceedingly doubtful, but in her broad view of life, a broadness of vision that granted to every other individual the privileges she claimed as her own, she felt very sure that

she many times found helpful strength in the communion
offered by this Baptist idea of Christian fellowship. But
when people differing from her in belief undertook to over-
step these liberal bounds, undertook as it were to lay down
the laws of religious belief for herself and her children,
trouble was sure to come. In her broadness of vision, Ann
was sure to object to some of the primitive ideas of religion
carried hither and thither by the travelling preachers of
the day.

The ministers travelling thus through the country, upright, devoted, devout men as they were, failed very often
to grasp this side of Ann's character. A Baptist minister,
more zealous than wise, accosted Nancy Jane, one of Ann's
young daughters, a bright-eyed girl who had inherited much
of her mother's individuality, one who had followed that
mother as she went about the discharge of her duties until
she had herself become efficient, and in this young girl's
presence, this minister asked Ann with all solemnity if
"Nancy Jane had yet had a 'change of heart.'" Seeing
the young girl's embarrassment, quick to resent the flush
rising to the young check, Ann replied gently, but O, how
firmly, "I would not have her heart changed for anything
in the world." Routed by the determined quality of that
mother's tone, the minister had nothing further to say.
The little daughter's heart was forevermore left in sin so
far as that one minister was ever able to testify.

No matter the lack of testimony from that one source,
there had been much said of young Nancy Jane Vernon,
and the heart of the maiden seemed to be ever satisfactory
to her many admirers. Her brillant mother, this Ann of
whom we write, may have over-shadowed her—mothers
sometimes do—but here is written evidence extant to-day
to show that young Nancy was much admired. None
other than Mirabeau B. Lamar indited poems to her fairness, poems written in the hand-writing of the author and
in the possession of Ann's descendants to-day.

> "The richest rose, the rarest flowers in Texas
>   valley shining,
> Can never match the absent one for whom
>   my heart is pining.
> My thoughts are with her day and night, nor
>   can I from her turn 'em,
> Go where I will I still behold the smiles of
>   Nancy Vernon."

Nancy always declared that these lines betokened no
real love for her, and she claimed the same thing for the
other poem written after hearing her sing.

"O, where is the soul who's so dead to all
      feeling,
As not to be moved when thy voice
      sweetly flows,
When music's soft notes from thy bright
      lips are stealing,
To lull all my sorrows and cares to repose."

So there we have it. How much allowance we must
make for gallantry, just how much, indeed, young Nancy
resembled her mother in such things, we cannot say. She
may never have resembled the rose at all—few maidens
do—but young Nancy's daughter has a very convincing
way of telling you to-day that the voice was one of rare
sweetness, rare power, and rare beauty. The poetry as
poetry lays small claim to that standard of excellence that
might class it to-day among the things worth while. In
fact, the sixteen lines composing the whole of the effusion
will not bear the sharp criticisms, the exacting adherence
to meter demanded by critics, but somehow, the idea of the
gentle Lamar sitting down to this form of expression carries
a charm all its very own, and the picture thus produced of
the life in Ann's home is very sweet and very soothing to
him who would smooth over the rough places of frontier
life with a dash of sentiment and its deep regard for beauty.

With her children Ann raised a nephew of her own, Mayberry B. Gray. The orphaned youth received every care and
attention in her home, and was no doubt just as interesting
in his way as young Nancy. Limitations of sex forbade
the idea of poetry, even from the facile pen of a Lamar, but
Ann loved him, and the boy had his share in the vivid
dreams she had for her own children.

The family thus composed lived under the shadow of the
Texas Revolution. It is easy to picture those young people
listening to the stories told of the doings of Houston and
Austin and Lamar. These men, not always in a poetic
frame of mind, stopped frequently in the home, and the
stirring, distressing news of war was thus handed back and
forth. They heard, too, of Bowie and Crockett and Travis,
sometimes a word of praise for the rough scouts, sometimes
blame.

The stories thus told them were sometimes misleading.
The news of the fall of the Alamo was accompanied in this
particular region with the false alarm that led to what is
now known as the run-a-way scrape. With all her wit,
all her penetration, Ann, full of the thought of the tragedy
at Goliad and the tragedy at the Alamo, believed with all
her heart that the Mexicans were coming and that safety
lay in immediate flight to the Sabine. She was at home

alone save for her children, even her nephew, Mayberry
Gray, being absent in the army. Ann took her three
children with her on her own good horse, an animal left
at home for just such a contingency and put out for
safety.

This run-a-way soon found herself in the company of
other women and children—and a few men, for the consternation was general. She took her place among the
leaders of the expedition, urging, encouraging the women
thus met on the way, women who had fled as she had fled
before the dreaded Mexicans, their hearts full of fear for
the men, the few who happened to be at home at the time
having put out hastily on receipt of the message in the
hope of helping Houston in the stand they felt sure he
would make as soon as his army might be under proper
control. They met in their hasty flight a few soldiers
bent upon this very purpose.

One of these soldiers, a general in fact at home on business for the army, spied Ann's horse and recognized the unusual quality of the animal. In true soldier fashion, accustomed to the sacrifice of the stay-at-homes this general
demanded of Ann her steed, explaining that it was impera-
tive that he join Houston at once.

Now Ann had been loyal and true to her country. She
had up to this point made every sacrifice that partiotism
demanded, but with her children's lives in danger—and her
own, Ann began to suffer a full-grown attack of the law of
self-preservation. At the behest of this law, Ann refused the
horse, at first gently. Even a second time, but when the
general approached to take the horse whether or no, he
met a pistol in the firm steady hand of this fleeing mother,
and the officer decided and immediately that he had better
undertake to find some other mode of travel. When the
run-a-way ended in its ludicrous fashion, Ann safely
housed at Nacogdoches and half-way ashamed of herself,
sent the horse to the general in the army only to have it
returned with a letter of thanks.

With the end of the war and the fear of the Mexicans
abated, Ann returned easily to her round of home-making.
She felt the quickening of the new country in its process of
building, and her interest in such things together with her
household and her plantation affairs made the world move
for Ann at a pleasant pace. Her husband, her children,
her slaves, and the many things incident to the care of them
gave her ample employment and she was therefore happy.

In July of 1836 there came a real change for her. Her
husband, Alexander Vernon died. Little has ever been
said as to what this meant to Ann. She had done well her
part by her pioneer husband. Failing sometimes to agree

with him in important matters—individuals of strong mind
are likely to do this—there is yet no ground for other belief than that the death of her husband was a cruel blow to
her.   But men and women are mutually dependent in a
new country.   The woman with little children must have
help and protection.   The man, left alone, must have his
home and fireside.   According to this idea, in the city of
Houston, on June 25, 1837, Ann Gray Vernon became the
wife of E. H. Winfield.   This gentleman had come from
St. Petersburg, Va., and was the first tax assessor of
Harris County.   Governor Lubbock defeated Winfield in
the race for the second term.

In about 1840, Winfield with Ann and her children moved
to Mexico, living a little while in Carmago.   They came
back to Texas shortly, settling this time at Brownsville.
From this place Winfield was sent as a member of Congress
of the young republic, and Ann was again in her element.
She took her family and followed her new husband to
Washington-on-the-Brazos.   Her husband's position there
in that little capital brought men of note to her home, and
Ann entertained them with the joy of the efficient.   That
home became in a little while a place of rest, a place of inspiration.   Business men, statesmen, the hopeful, the down-
cast came to her for advice.   Houston, Austin, Lamar
spent many happy hours there.   Lockhart, later speaking
of the first Congress of the Republic held in Washington-
on-the-Brazos, declared that Ann as a conversationalist,
was unrivalled by any man of her time.   And the daughter,
even Miss Nancy whose heart was claimed to be satisfactory to her mother, this same Nancy whose singing
drove the gracious Lamar to poetry, this daughter held her
own little court, played her own little part in this happy,
helpful life maintained there in old Washington-on-the-
Brazos.

There seems little doubt that Winfield derived a peculiar
pleasure in the society of Ann's children.   There remains,
indeed, some touching accounts of his tenderness toward
young Nancy.   His regard for young children extended beyond his own family.   During his term of office in the Congress of the Republic, he became interested in the young
daughter of Dickinson who had been killed in the Alamo.
This child, with her mother had been in the Alamo at the
time of the fight but afterwards allowed to go free by the
Mexicans.   A glorious thing it seemed to Winfield, to
adopt the "Child of the Alamo," but Ann saw the matter
in another light.   Ann had brought up her own children
in the wilderness without the aid of physicians, and Ann
knew what it meant.   She declined to take this burden
upon her shoulders, and Winfield had to content himself

with speeches before Congress in which he begged that the
state adopt the child, but this was never done. It might
be well to state here that the child of the Alamo lived to
maturity, and that her descendants are living in the state
to-day.

In spite of the gaiety, in spite of the satisfactory relations between Winfield and his step-children, this second
marraige on the part of Ann brought its note of pathos.
Mayberry Gray, Ann's own nephew, brought up in her
home as one of her own children, older by some years than
her oldest child, this nephew bitterly resented Ann's second marriage. No effort on the part of Ann or Mr. Winfield could ever make him see anything in the marriage except the repudiation of the ideals of life to which Ann had
led him to subscribe. Young as he was, close as he was to
Ann through long association, bound to her by ties of
blood, this youth displayed no small amount of the disposition of man to claim for his own comfort the women
who happen to make up his household. In all his jealous
anger, he failed to fabricate any real reason for his opposition to the marriage, no one single objection that he
could justly bring against Winfield as the husband of the
adored auntie. At last in a fit of anger, the result doubtless of long brooding over the matter, young Gray left
home and joined the Rangers.

The story of Gray's dissatisfaction spread among the
neighbors, and some highly romantic individuals built up
many thrilling anecdotes with young Gray's escapades for
a background. Marberry Gray lived to full maturity,
and we know, too, that he served his country well, so well,
in fact that an Alabama senator thought it right and proper
to write his biography for the sake of generations yet to
come. This biography is said to be inaccurate, but the
spirit of romance was allowed some sway.

The beautiful, unknown Mexican girl is even brought in,
the becoming mantillo, the dark southern beauty demanding place in the imagination. The picture is further
heightened by the suggestion that this beauty was troubled
by insidious foes, and that young Gray died from wounds
received in striking at these foes in her defense. The truth
was, in fact, quite prosaic. Gray served his country for
many years in the Ranger service, and was stricken with
some fatal disease in Carmago, Mexico, where he died and
was buried. No dusky senorita tended that last illness.
His faithful nurse and friend was none other than Nancy
Vernon, his cousin, and the daughter of the dearly beloved
auntie.

Ann, herself, lived long enough to see Texas under many
conditions. She had helped in her woman's way to wrest

it from the despotic power of Mexico. She lived through the nine years of the Republic, through the early statehood and the four years following secession. She held her own through the horrible, blasting days of Southern recontruction. She died in Houston, Texas, August 11, 1883, old and full of years, sweet and firm and true, even unto the end.

Data contributed by—

Mrs. Maggie L. Haynes, Austin,
Mrs. Maurice Turner, Dallas.

MRS. ALLAN CARTER JONES-CARTER

BORN

MARIS DAVIS

After a careful study of the data presented for this sketch, with perhaps, an intruding thought of the individual who gave it, with full recognition of valor and bravery and service, there is a lingering kind of an impulse to declare that the leading characteristic of this certain lady, born Maris Davis, was a gentleness, or maybe, we mean a sweetness of manner, a sweetness grown out of a heart that could harbor no evil thought of anything or anybody. A great thing this to say of any individual, male or female, a rare thing to be able to say this of a woman grown to maturity and living her married life in family mix-ups that are, to say the least, very trying to ordinary heart and soul. Perhaps, and then perhaps again, your scribe had best let the reader have an unbiased view of these conditions in order that each may form an opinion all his own.

Maris Davis was born somewhere in old Mississippi on May 17, 1805. We like to think that the magnolia and the jessamine smiled that May morning as a welcome to the tender little thing. We like to picture that home one of ease and plenty—we know there were slaves at hand ready for service—and we love to imagine the stamp of the horses in the stalls and any other sign of prosperity common to that day and time. Ignorant at last of circumstances surrounding that hour of birth, no matter how much we may dream, we do know that previous to 1830 her parents moved to Texas, locating in Grimes County, seven miles from the town of Bedias. The life of young Maris was characterized thereafter with the usual things that feature the life of a pioneer maiden. A touch of privation here, and a touch of adventure there, work all the time, nearly, and then we know to a certainty that at some time in the year 1830 she married a gentleman named Stone. One son was born of this marriage and given the name of William. Mr Stone died shortly afterwards, leaving Maris with this tiny baby, a young widow alone in a strange new land. The child grew and thrived, and then along about 1832, Maris Davis Stone became the wife of Allan Carter Jones.

This certain Allan Carter Jones was twenty years older than his bride, his birth having taken place in 1785. His own father had been a commissioned officer in the Fifth Maryland regiment in the Revolutionary War. Jones himself, had emigrated to Texas in 1826. He had settled near Nacogdoches, his head-right being located later in

Grimes County. Jones, an adherent to the Catholic faith, had been married in his early youth to a woman whose given name was Mary Jane. Keeton, Charles, James, Theresa, A. C. Jones, Clarissa and Delilah were the children born of this marriage. So this marriage between our Maris and Allan Carter Jones brought together a ready-made family. Four sons and three daughters on one side and a son of the sweet hopeful bride came thus to live beneath the same roof, and the burden of that arrangement fell heaviest of course on the wife's shoulders.

The home these people set up in Texas was in no way a reproduction of the home Maris had left in old Mississippi. It stood no doubt on that head-right in Grimes County, and there were fields rich and rolling lying about, waiting still the first stroke of the white man's plow. There was some brush along the creek bottoms, all of which must be cleared, there were a few rolling stones to be gathered up. This was all plain to Jones at a glance, but there was something far more important. He must have a home for his wife and children. He set the slaves to work on a log house intended for his family shelter, but as soon as this was complete—their few neighbors helped, no doubt, in the building—Jones put all able-bodied negro men in the field, each negro being held responsible for a mule and a full day's labor in the ploughing. No whit behind her husband in this matter of energy, Maris—her child and his to manage—put the women slaves to work in the house-spinning and weaving, carding, all the work, in short, incident to the manufacture of the ugly cotton and woolen cloth. A black silk dress in existence to-day speaks a world of meaning for the elegance of the clothing worn in old Mississippi, but Maris, with real thrift and econony, saw a day coming when silk could not be had, either with money or with persuasion, and Maris preferred to use the cotton cloth in the hope of preserving the precious silk. Against some great day? Not exactly. To take the silk out occasionally and let her slender fingers wander down the folds, just a few minutes at a time, a time snatched from her labor, to Maris this seemed a re-inforcement of the desire in her heart to think always that she was a lady, no matter the circumstances surrounding that pioneer home. She carried this matter of economy even further. When her daughters were of an age to sew, when they desired sometimes a bit of the precious linen brought from the old home, or some bought from an unexpected peddler, they must slip it out of the precious chest without their mother's knowledge trusting to get it cut up ready for the needle before her inquisitive eyes rested upon it. They made some beautiful garments, were brave enough to wear them before that mother, hugging themselves in the folds of the linen chemise, thinking how smart they had been. We risk a guess that the deception was not of long duration. Children rarely deceive a mother, a good mother, in these little matters of dress, and Maris, who was herself a painstaking needle-woman, must have been aware of the theft of cloth sewed into dainty underwear, sometimes under her very eyes.

We are a little bit ahead of things in this stolen linen matter. Let us return to the log-cabin before the children were old enough for the needle. The family life within those walls was pretty near ideal. The children brought together by the marriage agreed about as well as children agree who must see each other every single day. Then as the years came and went, there were four children born of this second marriage, David, George, Tom and Fannie Ann, all in quick succession, the last daughter being born about 1842. Then, crowding about the cabins built for the negroes, were the *pickaninnies*, born in rapid succession, too, great playmates for the white children, the promise in themselves of great help at some future time for the master. Sometimes that promise seemed vain. Little *pickaninnies* would fall ill, particularly likely to in "hog-killin' time" or in the time of the "sugar-bilin's." Fearful to trust an ignorant negro woman with the care, even of her own child, Maris had the ailing children brought to her own house, and from pallets on the long porch and through the length and breadth of the wide hall the little scamps received every attention from the hand of a stern but devoted mistress.

There were pleasures, too, for our Maris, midst all this toil and responsibility. There was no carriage at her disposal, but her husband was a believer in good horse-flesh, and possessed many fine specimens. Maris was an expert horse-woman, sat her horse with a courage and a dash not to be denied. Her maternal cares diminished in no slightest way her natural interest in this form of sport, and as each daughter grew old enough she was taught to be at home in the saddle.

With Texas almost ready to be taken into the United States, this particular section of Grimes County suffered a raid from the Indians. The details are exceedingly meagre, but we know that Delilah Jones, the step-daughter of our Mavis, was stolen by these Indians and carried away, captive. The pursuit of the Indians began immediately upon discovering the loss, but diligent search day and night, through dangers and terrors hard to imagine in this day, brought no knowledge of the girl's whereabouts. The parents offered bribes and rewards. Between each offer they felt a little swell of hope, only to have it sink as they reflected that the girl might even then be bringing wood and water for some squaw busy over the meal expected by her lord and master. Said reflection ended and often in the thought that she lay prostrate beneath the lash of some irate Indian chief, but think and feel, act and plan as they would, no single solitary trace of that girl ever came to her bereaved parents.

In the providence of the Almighty we learn somehow to bear the inexplicable burdens thus imposed upon us. This mixed-up family growing up under the sweetness of our Maris, a sweetness tempered by a firmness unbelievable, maintained always a tender regard for each other. They grew into men and women, married and set up homes of their own, most of them in the same neighborhood with their parents. Occasionally, a marriage would move a boy or girl to another county, and there was neither railroad nor overland bus to lend a hand. Small matter to these young people! Good horses were ever at hand, and both men and women were equally at home in the saddle.

One son, Allan Carter Jones, took for a bride Margaret Whitby, living herself at the time in the historic old town of Goliad. Maris may have felt the pangs all mothers feel at the thought of marriage for their sons, but remembering her good sense and judgment, we fancy she had little complaint to make of this son's selection in the matter of a wife. We have very little at hand about this young lady's father, but we do know that the mother, Mrs. William Whitby, was one of those staunch characters among women on whom the foundations of our civilization rest to-day. Intimate friends claim for her that she was known in her day throughout the country, known and loved because of her unselfish service, her deeds of helpfulness. Known for her bravery at a time in the Indian infested Texas when women had to be brave if they would live, she bore her own good part in many Indian fights. She had labored, too, at home, never forgetting the sweeter, gentler arts of the real mother in the up-bringing of her children. Small wonder, indeed, that Allan Carter Jones, Jr., should have selected for his wife the daughter of such a woman. He had heard doubtless of the old saying concerning the foolishness of going to a hawk's nest to find a dove. He must have felt if he had ever heard at all of the value of heredity that in choosing his wife he had obeyed all heredity's laws and paid, as well, due heed to the old adage against hawks' nests.

And then, with this very propitious marriage in full swing, with three little children, all little more than babies, Allan Carter Jones, Jr., must see his wife die, leaving him the

care of the three little children.   Did those children suffer?
Not a bit. Their grandmother, Whitby, along with her
household cares, along with the thousand duties falling to
the lot of the pioneer woman, raised those children, Martha
and William and Clara. She made worthwhile folks of
them, too, and we haven't a doubt in the world but what
Mrs. Whitby frequently discussed with their paternal
grandmother, our Maris, the intricate duties of child-
rearing.

Mrs. Whitby found time to help other folks as well as
her own grandchildren. There is in existence to-day a
letter bearing the date of January 21st, 1843, written to
Mrs. Whitby by a certain Miss Oceana Hughes who was
then attending Clifton Ridge school. The penmanship is
legible though the paper has browned and has become very
brittle. The contents show that Mrs. Whitby has rendered
this young woman some valuable service, that she has in
some way reached the young woman's heart, a difficult
thing in all ages and in all climes. The letter includes an
acrostic the girl had made on the name of Mr. Whitby,
saying that her father had once given it to her as a lesson
in composition. It is too long for insertion here, but it
speaks along with its literary achievement a beauty of
thought and feeling not to be denied. The letter itself
contains one very beautiful passage. After referring to
some kindness rendered by Mrs. Whitby, this young lady
writes: "I beg you will accept my sincere thanks and may
He that said, 'Whoso giveth to the poor lendeth to the
Lord' add to your stores a thousand fold in the present life
and crown you with immortal joy in that world which is
eternal and full of beauty."

The death of Allan Carter Jones brought a change in the
current of the family life for Maris. She could not claim
that she had been the man's only love, but she missed him,
missed his gentle presence, missed the reinforcement of his
approval of her household labors. She continued to
maintain her home, a happy meeting place for *his* children
and *our* children, but before very long, Maris fell in with
another gentleman named Carter and married him. This
man was in no way related to the husband she had lost.
His family had lived in Bee County, but it seems that Maris
had known him some time. We base the assumption of
this previous acquaintance on the fact that soon after the
marriage, Fannie Ann Jones, Maris' daughter, made a
horse-back journey with her new father into Bee County
in order to renew her acquaintance with her step-father's
family. There is something so sweet, so wholesome in the
attitude of this young woman toward the man who had
taken her own father's place that we feel sure the family of

the new father fell very much in love with her. Were we
in the happy habit of romancing we might picture al lkinds
of relationships growing out of that visit, but historians
must beware lest they enter into temptation.

Then came secession and the war. Far removed from
any Yankee influence, in the very heart of Texas, a Texas
that had won out single-handed in her own battle for freedom, surrounded by her slaves who had never to her knowledge grumbled at any single thing ever demanded of them,
listening the while to their happy, care-free laughter, Maris
must send her sons, one by one, to do battle for the Confederacy. Perhaps she sent them in high hope, expecting
them to return in all the glory of victory. Perhaps she
waited, many times alone in the dead of the night, denied
sleep, denied hope, waited thus alone for the familiar step
upon the stair, for the ringing voice of youth, the only real
comfort that can ever come to bowed old age. With the
fall of Vicksburg, she knew that her country's hope had
been in vain. She knew that she must give up the care,
the control of the simple black people dependent on her
bounty. She knew that she must learn to do the menial
tasks these slaves had done for her in return for that bounty.
She faced these changes soberly we admit, but in her heart
these changes seemed insignificant in comparison with her
anxiety about her absent sons. She yearned for the return
of these gallant boys who had donned the grey and marched
so proudly from her, seeing naught but victory beyond that
cloud of war. And one of them, George, came home to his
mother and his family, came home in the ignominy of defeat and in the wretchedness of poverty, a poverty brought
about by the change in economical conditions and labor
conditions, a poverty he felt that he could not endure.
His brothers, David and Tom, failed to return at all.

In 1867, at the age of sixty-one years, Maris Davis Carter
Jones-Carter passed away. She was buried in Grimes County
near Bedia, probably in the family cemetery established
there when the land was first settled. We know nothing of
the circumstances surrounding her death-bed, but with the
thought of these triumphs and these defeats beating about
in our consciousness some few fancies demand expression.
They are probable, too, these fancies, and they must be
allowed. Through Indian raids and pioneer hardships
Maris had borne her gallant part. Through the intricacies
of pioneer life she had managed to hold her own, had
managed to lay by a bit here and there of the fruits of her
incessant labors. Self-denial and stern discipline had each
played a part in the every-day life, and each had taken its
toll of her strength and of her endurance. This last
struggle of brother against brother, the last struggle to

retain the right to property as she saw it had been too much. So thinks your scribe, and in the passing of this woman in the prime of her life she sees a useless sacrifice on the altar of human misunderstanding, and her heart swells anew with the old pain.

Data contributed by—

Mrs. M. Jones,
Austin, Texas.

MRS. SAMUEL McMAHON

BORN

PHOEBE YOUNG

Your scribe can remember hearing a wild story way back
in her youth of a day and a community in which women,
like children, were supposed to be seen and not heard.
Such a day and such a community according to that story
received some extravagant praise from a few folks—mostly
of masculine persuasion we think—and, maybe, the few
folks were right. Maybe the dead and gone past held a
sanctified atmosphere in which women were content to
labor incessantly, the only recompense desired for that
labor the voice of their own inner consciousness, telling
them gently that they had done well. We say, maybe so,
but we add in the next breath a bit of bitter denial. In
our minds, there never could have been a time and a place
in which women, beautiful, winsome and sweet, conscious,
too, of admiring masculine glances, when women, real
women, could be content with said glances and through
that content remain dumb. Women, glad always—when
properly clothed—to be seen, have a way, too, of demanding full right to exercise the power of speech, and so far, if
your scribe knows anything at all, man has never yet been
able to deny that demand.

But when it comes to finding some definite facts concerning the daily lives of our Texas pioneer women, the
inaudible idea bobs up. Any amount of things may be
learned and with little research as to the habits and doings
of men, your Texas forebears and mine, but the women,
their wives and daughters were kept in the background,
at least so far as any authentic record was concerned. We
argue from this that they, like children were supposed to
be seen and not heard.

The fact as deduced from that argument annoys us a
little. We know that the women in question were fine
women, and the public must excuse us if we openly announce a belief in the fact that they furnished the world
with some mighty fine folks. When it comes to proving
all this to a skeptical world, American people think as they
will, when it comes to proving that our grandmothers were
truly noble and fine, we wish that the grandmothers had
taken sufficient interest in public things to place themselves
where some record of such doing had been made. When
your scribe recalls on the heels of that thought or that wish
that this inaudible idea for women of two generations gone
produced in our own time descendants who did us honor in
Congress as well as in State activities, then your scribe
changes her mind. She begins to dream of a log-cabin

somewhere in the wilderness with all kinds of struggles
necessary to provide food and even greater struggles to
outwit Indians and snakes and panthers, not to mention
the burden of sewing—by hand—and spinning and weaving. Aye, your scribe dreams of all this, wondering as she
dreams if said conditions brought again to her particular
part of the earth might make of her such a specimen of this
inaudible type of woman who has so blest our own great
nation, even our Texas.

These dreams read well on paper. No sane member of
this generation had willingly exchanged present-day circumstances for pioneer circumstances, even in the hope of
attaining unto the possession of the characteristics of these
pioneer women. We know this, and we here acknowledge
it. We console ourselves for this apparent lack of righteous desire on our own part to the oft-stated fact that each
generation, like each age has its own peculiar charm for
those who dwell therein, but when we pause to think for a
bit of such women as Phoebe Young McMahon we are
likely to find some qualities of mind and heart and soul
that make us feel for the time that we would like to gain
them for ourselves, no matter the sacrifice required.

Now for these real facts. Phoebe Young, the daughter
of Merlin Young and his wife Tabitha Witcher Young, was
born on October 2, 1792. Her parents were then living in
Tennessee, and two more years were to elapse before this
Tennessee could be called a distinct territory, all to itself.
Her parents had lived previously in Virginia. Her father,
Merlin Young, had served in the Revolutionry War, and
her uncle on her mother's side of the house deserves mention
for the same thing. Merlin Young and his wife, Tabitha,
had been accompanied in this emigration to Tennessee by
Milton Young, his brother, who had previously married
Nancy Witcher, a sister of Tabitha. These young people
set up pioneer homes in the same neighborhood there in
Tennessee, and there on the date mentioned, little Phoebe
had been born to Merlin and Tabitha.

Of the childhood of Phoebe, we know little. Various
family relics prove her to have been a gentle, refined individual in her old age, and old age of this type exists only
where youth has been well spent. Old daguerrotypes prove
her beauty, and we know as a matter of family truth
handed down from one generation to another that she was
possessed of womanly charm in proportion to her beauty.
As a matter of family record, we know that she married
Samuel Doak McMahon on April 26, 1811.

The young couple went immediately after this marriage
to live in a house built on the spot where Alabama, Tennessee and Georgia join in a pronounced corner. Each

state and territory interested in this family domicile had a
room all its own. The foothills of the Cumberland mountains looked down upon the valley, and through the valley
the winding Tennessee river made its way after many a
turn to join the Ohio river at last, some three hundred
miles and more to the west of them. Many years they
lived in that smiling fertile valley, sheltered by mountains
from the cold north wind, catching even at that distance,
the cooling summer breezes, fresh from the sea. In this
house nine children were born to the McMahons, Elizabeth
Moore, James B., Merlin Young, Susan, Nancy, Hardin,
Diana, Margaret, Tabitha, and Louisa H. The work of
our Phoebe in that pioneer home, the usual run of cooking
and spinning and weaving, was doubtless interrupted with
many a maternal care.

Phoebe had married a good man, a pious man, a man with
no small influence over people about him. This husband
and father gave no small amount of help in the care of
those children, but even the best of fathers must acknowledge that the work, the sacrifice demanded of the
father in rearing a large family of children is infinitesimal
compared with the labor and sacrifice demanded of the
mother. In this case the wife's duties were augmented
by the fact that her husband was a minister of the gospel.
Family troubles, social troubles, heart affairs were laid before the minister, and many times, failing to find the minister handy, these pioneers let our Phoebe take his place.
None of these delicate duties were ever neglected. None
were too trivial, provided they troubled somebody else,
for Phoebe to give them her thought. Busy, therefore, as
they could be, McMahon and Phoebe watched their own
little flock grow, watched the boys develop toward manhood, laying plans the while for a life of service for each
sturdy fellow. The daughters were taught to *look well to
the ways of the household* and we have no doubt they became
polished as with the similitude of a palace.

One of these daughters was particularly attractive.
Possessed of luminious brown eyes, hair of the same color,
she moved among the young people, a sweet, shy queen in
her own right and to this daughter we are indebted for
these facts. A beautiful character herself, she spoke always in veneration of her mother. She felt rather than
saw her piety, her beauty of life and character, and she was
not slow to speak to others of the beauty of the thing that
had been so largely instrumental in the moulding of her
own life. She felt, too, that the beauty of her mother's
character had been strengthened by the association with
her husband, Samuel McMahon. She told proudly that
two men, sons-in-law of her father, had been converted

under this father's preaching, speaking a world of commendation for the man thus honored in his own household. These converted men afterwards became ministers of the gospel, due largely to the influence of McMahon, and each man was successful in his chosen field. One of Phoebe's own sons became a local preacher, being licensed to preach at a Texas Quarterly Conference, held by a man named Alexander at some time in 1837.

This statement makes plain that the McMahons had left that Tennessee home to take up a new life in Texas. The missionary spirit must have played some part in that move. They settled, we believe, in the neighborhood of Nacogdoches, for we are told that Samuel McMahon, preacher of the gospel, commanded a battalion in a fight with the Piedras Indians near Nacogdoches.

As a rule there is little to record in the life of the man or the woman of missionary spirit. Viewed in the light of the world, their work falls short, sometimes of even bare interest. In the solemn records of the church they serve there is usually little said of the men thus employed, and nothing at all ever of their faithful wives, bearing every burden each with her own husband, and many more burdens which though willing can never share. But such men— and such women know that they have walked the earth in power and in truth, and to their glad descendants we can to-day say that the earth holds no richer inheritance.

Data contributed by—

Mrs. W. P. Hobby,
Mrs. Margaret Cooper Jacoway.

MRS. JOSEPH MANSON McCORMICK

BORN

AGNES LOUISA McKENZIE

"Change your name and not your letter,
Change for worse and not for better."

This old saying had been dunned into the ears of all prospective brides for a dozen centuries, more or less, and many a gay young miss, deep down in her heart, has believed it. Not quite strong enough, maybe, has been that belief to turn a lassie, Scotch or otherwise, from the importunate pleading of a canny lover, but safe to say, any lassie, face to face with this condition had given most anything had she loved and been loved by a John whose name began with some other letter than her own. Now, we have before us here, a young couple who had to face in the beginning the fact that they wanted to be married, but that each surname gloried in the good old Scotch way in the possession of the aristocratic Mc. Agnes Louisa McKenzie, sister to Evelyn McKenzie Bell, had been sought in marriage by Joseph Manson McCormick, a man true in every way to every trait suggested by his name. Said Joseph, owing again to that Scotch character, gave little heed to the woe of a bride's failure to change her letter, and he overcame Louisa's objections, if she had any, for she became his bride in January of 1832 in Christian County, Kentucky.

McCormick had an uncle in Texas, and Louisa a sister, Mrs. Josiah H. Bell, so this young couple conceived the idea of a bridal trip to Texas, a visit, in short, to his uncle and her sister. McCormick had been adopted by this uncle and made his sole heir. We know little of the visit they made to this uncle, but McCormick afterwards inherited his uncle's league and labor of land with all its improvements. We know, too, that Louisa enjoyed being with her sister, that she enjoyed with her husband the famous hospitality of the Bell's log house, but after a little while of greeting, a longer while, perhaps, of the exchanging of bridal woes and wifely disappointments, this wedding trip became a trip to a permanent home. McCormick was careful to receive the league and *labor* of land to which he himself was entitled, and then he passed on, he and Louisa, from the Bell home to the San Bernard river, some eight miles away, and began life there in the home built by McCormick's uncle. No tent for them! They entered at once into their house, a log one to be sure, but it was rainproof, and it was McCormick's by inheritance.

Joseph McCormick, as became the husband of a woman more timid than her sister, took a large share in the main-

taining of the family regime.   While Louisa cooked breakfast, probably corn-pone and bacon, Joseph, by the aid of
a hand-mill, ground the corn into sufficient meal to feed the
family and slaves for one day.   Think of the deliciousness
of that meal, smell the fragrance of that corn-pone baking
in the Dutch oven piled with coals!   Maybe the pioneer
woman, barring a few Indians and a few Mexicans, had a
pretty good time after all.   But, before we decide that
matter, let's look a little bit into the lasting effects of that
delicious breakfast.

You see an Indian is constitutionally opposed to labor.
So is a Mexican, and some few white men—and women.
These particular Mexicans living in the neighborhood of
the McCormicks learned that McCormick thus thriftily
labored in the morning hours—probably before they were
astir, and said Mexicans determined to profit thereby.
Why work, when the product of another man's labor lay
at hand?   So waiting until McCormick was in the field for
the morning, they betook themselves to the house, fully
determined to demand that the follish little wife turn over
the product of her husband's labor of that morning.   They
had probably heard that Louisa was afraid of them, and
they waxed confident in the outcome of this simple game.

The Mexicans were doomed to disappointment.   Louisa
could not speak their language, but despair lent power to
her flashing eye, to her frail, little hands, to the shake of
her determined head, and the Mexican, for some reason
took himself off.   This was no uncommon occurrence in
the life of Louisa.   Where other pioneer women suffered
from fear of Indians, Louisa suffered from fear of Mexicans.
They were new things to her, born as she had been in old
North Carolina, and a Mexican of the lower type is, after
all, not very far removed from his half-brother, the Indian.   They prowled, these half-breeds, throughout Texas,
eyeing the white man in his settlement activities with
some of the same animosity with which the Indians surveyed the white man and his coming.   The Mexican failed
to see that his own government had encouraged the white
man to settle in Texas, and that he should loyally stand
by his government.   Maybe again the ordinary Mexican
failed to care a whit just what his government had seen
fit to do.   Said Mexican looked upon the elemental theft
as opposed to labor as the better way to procure property,
and cared little where he took it, or when or how.   Be that
as it may, the appearance of the ordinary Mexican was
against him with young Louisa, and she conceived a deadly
fear of him, a fear that made her desperately unhappy at
times, but for all that, a fear that failed to make her give
up in the face of fancied danger.   There were likewise

snakes coiled in the bushes, in the house, too, climbing sometimes into her shoes, big, hissing rattlers, the like of which Louisa had never seen before, and wild animals, resenting, too, the encroachments of the white man, and Louisa felt sometimes that her very life was a burden of fear with little to compensate her for her misery.

But even this fear of Mexicans and wild things brought a comical turn of affairs—sometimes. One day, Louisa was busy hanging out clothes that had been newly washed, using a rope that had been stretched for the purpose. A sound made her turn about in fearful questioning. A Mexican, clad in the usual red flannel shirt, the usual pointed hat, and the tucked-in breeches stood before her. Pertrified with fear, she waited. The Mexican approached, and to Louisa a threat accompanied every step. He raised his hand—to strike, so thought Louisa, and then she screamed, and Louisa's scream was not a thing to be denied. Her husband ran to the scene, expecting all manner of things, to find two people, man and woman, staring each other in the face, the Mexican praying to the blessed Virgin to be protected from one suddenly gone made, one who had misconstrued his attempts to be polite in such a horrible light, the other, the woman, seeing in everything the man did a threat against her very life.

In 1833 the stars fell, so we have been told,   The wonderful sight was viewed in Louisa's vicinity in the early morning, just a little before day. Her husband had already risen, had dressed and had filled the hopper of his little mill with corn to be ground into the daily meal. At the first strange, unearthly sight, the first wild, running-about of scorching suns, the first awful, blinding glare, Louisa shrieked out her fear, her pain. It is not recorded that she made any confessions of past sins, or even of any evil thoughts. She did run to her husband, her help in time of trouble, and in her fear-mad voice inquired of him just what it all might mean.

Joseph gave one look at the outside world, removed his hand one instant from the handle of that mill. Then, in answer to his wife's tragic demand, he made slow, solemn answer:

"O, it's nothing" he said, "It's nothing. Just a new country!" and went on calmly, grinding corn.

This wonderful calm pervaded the spirit of McCormick, even in the army. The soldiers were in camp on the night of April 20, 1836, on the famous San Jacinto battle field, the small cannon in place, and all soldiers had been ordered to retire. McCormick picked a spot for his slumber hard by one cannon. He proceeded after the most approved Scotch method to make himself comfortable for the night.

Part of this preparation consisted in tying the mosquito bar to the cannon and then tucking it in tight around as he stretched out for slumber. Now this whole matter became ludicrous in the eyes of some soldiers close at hand, and after McCormick was well into the land of Nod, one man slipped up to the cannon and fired it. The noise really did arouse McCormick, but it did not startle him. The cannon had been fired. With ammunition precious in the eyes of the struggling army, McCormick could see but one reason for using any of it. The Mexicans had surprised them.

Excited? McCormick? Not a bit of it! He but turned about beneath his mosquito netting and inquired soberly: "Boys, have they got here yet?" The joke turned upon the perpertrators. The ammunition had been wasted, and McCormick was as calm as a June day.

Louisa, strong in the face of any real danger, afraid of her own shadow in ordinary times, spent thirty-three years of her life with this man and his imperturable calm. Three children were born to them, a son, Andrew, and two daughters. The younger of the two daughters died when she was but five years old. By the time the other two children were well on toward maturity these young parents had prospered in their new home, and the children were accordingly sent back to Kentucky to be educated, the boy at Center College and the girl at Shelbyville. Returning home, to that same place eight miles from the home of Mrs. Bell, Louisa's sister, the home near the bank of the San Bernard river, the young folks belonging to the two families held high carnival in the good old fashioned way. No automobiles were at hand to route the intervening eight miles, but there were trusty horses and youthful hearts, and the journey back and forth became many times the occasion of much innocent enjoyment.

The McCormick's lived to bury both of their daughters, but they lived, too, to feel and to know a justifiable pride in their only son. They saw the Civil war almost through, lived together through its hopes and its disasters, but Joseph died early in 1865, happily unconscious that General Lee had surrendered. And then Louisa went to make her home with her son Andrew in the little town of Brazoria.

They gave her a room of her own in this son's house. A glimpse therein had been worthwhile for some wordly women of her own day, for that room, controlled alone by that grandmother, was typical of what any good woman might be in the home of another. Her easy chair, her big comfortable bed, her sewing-table, all these clustered about her, and on its own special table, her Bible which she, being a Presbyterian from her youth, read regularly every day of her life.   There she sewed for her six grandchildren. There they played about her, their toys remaining always in her room.   There she settled their little disputes, there she gave her gentle warnings.

In 1875, Andrew McCormick took his family consisting of his wife, his mother, his children, and his governess for a summer's visit on the coast.   They stopped at Quintana on the coast, near the mouth of the Brazos, and the young folks had a great time in and out of the water, boating, fishing, swimming, playing in the sand. Louisa fell ill there, and her family's attentions seemed of little avail.   About the second week in September a hurricane swept into the Gulf of Mexico, and not satisfied with that broad expanse of water, it lashed its fury upon the coast towns, sending most of them to destruction.   With the storm at its height, with a mother sick unto death, with a wife and children and a governess depending upon him for safety, Andrew McCormick listened to the whistle, the roar, the tumult of the wind outside.   He heard the sheets of rain crash against the windows, the walls, the roof of the house, wondering how long that house might stand.   And in that tumult, the mother, Louisa McCormick passed away, her peaceful face, white and still upon the pillow, careless of the world, careless of the elements, her life's journey ended.

And they who do come after speak her name yet in all tenderness.   Gentle, little woman, brave in spite of her timidity, loving, faithful and true!

Data contributed by—

Mrs. Lucy M. Carnes,
Austin, Texas.

MRS. HEZEKIAH JOHNSON
BORN
MARY E. HAMPTON

There is a peculiar pleasure in planning the sketch of an individual one had personally known. It brings back beautiful memories of tender things. These beautiful memories are mingled sometimes with memories of a sharp rebuke, uttered now and then for, children must be rebuked. Otherwise there had been no reason for parents looking after the welfare of offsprings. Circumstances, some sweet, a very few bitter, brought me into intimate association with Mrs. Hezekiah Johnson, and as I write, the vision of her white, white hair, her bright, bright eyes peering with interest into my own, makes any other picture of the lady a little tame, but just the same, there shall be an honest effort made to show you this dear old lady as she was from her youth up.

She was born in North Carolina in 1810, to a couple answering to the name of Hampton. She was married in Jonesville, North Carolina, in 1843 to Hezekiah Johnson. We know little of the courtship that preceded that marriage. Little was said of matters of the heart in that day in old North Carolina. Whether Johnson had been a childhood sweetheart, or whether or not he had come across her path in the glamour of a soldier we cannot say. But we do know that he had been a soldier. Seven years of civilian life may have robbed him of the soldiery carriage and the sheen of brass buttons, but Johnson had been at the battle of San Jacinto, had probably borne his own good part in the famous battle-yell anent the Alamo and Goliad. Nothwithstanding this glory, young Johnson had decided about 1842 that life in Texas was unsatisfactory. He returned to North Carolina, married the gentle Mary Hampton, and settled down in apparent forgetfulness of San Jacinto and battle-cries and everything else that pertained to Texas.

Four children were born to them in the natural run of things, one son and three daughters. To one daughter he gave the name of Mary Houston, because of the gentle mother who had given her being and because of his great love for the hero of San Jacinto. Mary controlled these children and ministered unto them and unto Hezekiah Johnson as all good women have a way of doing, and found boundless joy in her efficient service.

In 1885, Hezekiah Johnson died. Whether from sudden illness or not we cannot say. We do know that he had talked much to his wife of Texas. He had told his children of the Alamo and of Goliad. He had lived over the stirring

thirty minutes glory of San Jacinto. He had spoken in
all enthusiasm, all reverence of General Houston and his
plans of Texas. These things had made a promised land
of Texas, even then, a state in the United States. And to
add to the seductive, beckoning hand of the new country,
there came to Mary the news that San Jacinto heroes and
their widows were to receive grants of land, to be held for
life, and unto their heirs forever.

Mary had never, for one moment, entertained the idea
of raising her family at the expense of her relatives. No
desire in her heart to wrest the right of suffrage from man,
her brother, no desire to quarrel over the conditions of
things political, national or domestic, none of these things
crossed her mind. Mary but felt in her heart that her
children were her own, that they had only the mother to
look to, and to Mary the land donated her in Texas seemed
a solution of her difficulties. Thrilling with the memory
of San Jacinto as her husband had described it, longing to
see the land abloom with blue-bonnets and fire-wheels and
butter-cups, drawn, too, no doubt, by the invincible spirit
of the pioneer, Mary decided that she would take her four
children, her one son and her three daughters and start to
Texas.

She went about her preparations in a manner worthy a
financier of long standing. Her diary, extant to-day, tells
us this. Not a maidenly diary, full of slush and foolishness, but a bona fide record of things worth while as they
were done day by day. Under the date of September 10,
1856, we find this entry:

"Leaving to-morrow for Texas with Bynum, Mary,
Julia, Alveda in four wagons driven by Bill,
Amanda, Phoebe and Solomon. I am to ride
Solomon's wagon (a negro), the three girls in
Almedas (another negro) and Bynum with Bill.
Am taking all my feather-beds and quilts. Fifty
bushels of corn, five hundred pounds of hog-meat,
two barrels of flour, and some furniture and
clothing. Hope to reach Weatherford, Texas in
about four weeks."

September 12:
"Crossed the mountains at the Indian Graves."

So on these entries continue, this woman with four small
children, four slaves and four wagons made this trip across
an almost unknown country, finding few roads to guide,
no bridges to help at the streams, and no ferries. These
things seemed of little weight in her mind, but at some time
in September she makes this entry in her diary: "My expenses so far have been $6.25. This is awful."

She reached Weatherford, and nearby this little city she took up her claim, as her husband's headright granted. There she undertook the struggle to subdue the land in order that she might make "both ends meet." Fields needed fencing, the jealous Indians watching every post-hole as it was dug—and maybe he had a right to watch it —and proceeding to rifle barns, once they had anything within to reward such rifling. Among these savage folks were numbered the Tonkeways, a friendly band of fellows, and Mary soon learned that she might profit by a little consideration for her neighbors. She found some glass beads, some other little worthless trifles, too, among her things, and Mary cheerfully propitiated the child of the forest and the plain with their glitter. Of course the Tonkeway saw no real wrong in stealing from this new-comer, her meat and her chickens—if he could, but his friendship was a defense against the deadly Comanches. Indeed, with the fruit of her spring's labor gathered into her cheaply-built barns, with young chickens crowding her hen-house, Mary many times heard the Indians prowling about, and she knew they were after her chickens. She was afraid for the sake of her little children to rouse the ire, even of these Tonkeways—she knew they, too, stole from her when the occasion demanded—but she did occasionally fire her husband's trusty rifle, just to let them know that there was a fire arm on the place and a woman who knew how to use it, and what was more to the point, a woman who dared.

Then, even with the money at hand, there was trouble in that Western country in procuring even the bare necessities of life. Immense distance from the railroad, and it necessary to procure sugar, tea, coffee, flour, molasses from some outside source, and children and slaves in a new country at work and hard work must eat and eat in plenty! A stupendous job this, but Mary Hampton Johnson managed it. Mayhap, she dreamed of the comforts left in old North Carolina. Mayhap, she many times called herself a fool that she did not give up this venture and return to her childhood's home. With wolves howling about at night, with Indians, some friendly, some otherwise prowling the line of her fences, with her little children and sometimes her slave women to bear her company, Mary sat many a lonely night by that cabin fire in the land obtained itself after much difficulty, sat there listening to the roar of the wind, wondering if the meal would hold out until harvest, wondering what she might do should the bacon and lard become rancid before the first howling norther made it advisable to begin hog-killing in earnest.

Managed it?   Aye, that and more, too.   She raised her four children, clothed and fed them, and nursed them through their little ailments.   She taught them at her knee, and she lived before them the convincing example of an industrious, honorable, upright life.   She sent the children one by one as they came of suitable age through college, sent them all the way back to Davidson college in North Carolina.   Through all this she was a devoted member of the Baptist church.   She attended services in Weatherford, and the journey there and back from her home on that head-right of land was a long one.   She gave the church there the first organ it had ever possessed, and throughout her life, under many changes of many kinds, she remained a consistent member of this church she had chosen in her youth.

Mary saw her children married, saw them settled one by one in comfortable homes of their own, helped in the birth of her grandchildren, helped by her tender, clear-cut advice in their up-bringing.   She came after a time to live in the home of one daughter, Mrs. D. T. Iglehart of Austin. In that home she saw one great-grandson born, a frail little fellow who passed all too soon.   She lived to bury all her own children, but her grandchildren, particularly one noble man, walked the earth, a blessing wherever he trod. A grand-daughter has spent much time encouraging and promoting the study of music, and what they are to-day must rest in a way on the foundations offered by the life of this noble woman.

There are some left in Texas to-day, some few who recall Mary Hampton Johnson in her old age.   They believe with little trouble the stories of her youth.   They can believe that she was beautiful, that her blue eyes flashed a challenge not to be denied.   They can believe that she was a tower of strength in her home, in her church, in any sphere, in fact, in which life found her.   They can believe all this, for they recall the figure in its old age, the figure patient in the shadow, her white, white hair glistening above eyes still bright, still alive to daily happenings, a strong, determined character speaking to another generation the valuable truths of pioneer life.

Data contributed by

> Mrs. Robert G. Crosby,
> Austin, Texas.

MRS. CLAIBORNE KYLE

BORN

LUCY BUGG

Back in old Tennessee we go to find the beginning of things for the lady under discussion right now, for in Williamson County of that state, on the tenth day of May, 1801, a little daughter was born to one Bugg and his wife, a couple descended from good, old English stock, and she was given the name of Lucy. This Lucy must have lived in that home the life of any ordinary, happily situated woman of her day. No record exists to the contrary, and records have a way of being explicit when life is filled with shadows and forebodings. We know that she sat at the feet of her mother or her grand-mother or the mother of somebody else who had become adept in household arts, for Lucy could sew, and she could spin, and she could weave. All her life Lucy had been accustomed to slaves, to their cheerful ministrations, to the attention paid by the mistress to the welfare of each individual black. She had felt many times the beauty of the devotion of her serving men and women, but it had never robbed Lucy of her own rights to useful womanhood. She even learned how to cook, and she was not averse to a morning in the kitchen where those same serving women looked upon her, not as a hindrance but an inspiration. Had she real educational advantages such as our women of to-day demand, such advantages have not been mentioned in the stories told of her life, but subsequent events lead us to believe that somewhere, somehow Lucy had been led along the narrow path of learning, and that she had imbibed some little bit of its value, enough to make her a gentle, shining light among the women of her time.

We do know that a little late in life for a woman of her day, romance came into the life of Lucy. She had, in fact, reached the age of twenty-six years before any mention was ever made of a sweetheart. When the sweetheart came at last, he proved to be one Claiborne Kyle, a man about one year older than herself, a Tennesseean, too, but hailing from an adjoining county called Hawkins. All accounts of young Kyle's peculiar qualifications have been lost, all stories of his youthful comeliness and his youthful prowess, or whatever it was that led Lucy to bow before his charm, and we of to-day in our prosaic fashion have a way of looking back and wondering at Lucy, since she was, herself, ever the better manager of the two. But however we feel about it, Lucy loved him, and Lucy married him, and these simple facts shed a halo about said Claiborne, and there we shall be forced to let it rest.

But halos as rest-producers are not always successful.
The outside world may have easily recognized the superiority of Kyle's wife when it came to the management idea,
but Kyle, himself, being a natural male, was never quite
ready to admit it. He lacked, in short, the sagacity to
allow his wife the whole of the management, home, business
or otherwise. With all these matters in fairly good shape,
with children drifting into the home as children will drift
into the home of the young and the brave, Claiborne Kyle
went the bond of a certain Dr. Graves back there in old
Tennessee, and along about 1844, this Dr. Graves defaulted,
disappeared, and left young Kyle to meet his obligations.
There was nothing for young Kyle to do but to meet these
obligations, and this meant the giving up of property, the
crippling of his own operations, the financial ruin that few
men have ever been known to overcome.

On all these matters, family records are most explicit.
There is one item of property that has been overlooked.
No mention was made of the sale of his slaves, the money
thus acquired to be used in settling the difficulties. They
were considered property, and valuable property in certain
localities where the soil and the climate made agricultural
success possible. In meeting his debts and obligations, it
would seem plausible that Kyle had but followed the
regime usually ascribed to slave-holding people, and had
proceeded to sell husbands away from wives, and mothers
from daughters and so on through the list of family tragedies
usually laid at the door of slave-holding people. But to be
perfectly accurate, Kyle, even he who had been forced to
allow that his wife's business judgment outranked his
own, this Kyle, steeped in debt, had never entertained any
such notion, even though such notion had immediately can-
celled his debts and, mayhap, provided his family with
luxuries. No! Face to face with failure, Kyle realized as
many another man has realized, that emigration to a new
country was all that was left to him. His wife, made of
real pioneer stuff, agreed with him. They had heard of
Texas, had heard of San Jacinto and the royal gift of land
to all new-comers. They decided to follow on into the
new nation that they might test its glories first-hand.

Then what of the negroes, happy, go-lucky creatures, dependent upon "Massa" for their very bread! This thing
weighed heavily on the heart of Kyle as he went about his
preparations for departure. Mayhap the negro wondered
a little, too, just what "Massa" intended to do with him.
It is a safe bet that he had no fear that "Massa" would desert him. It is a safer bet that he cared not a whit that
"Massa's" desertion meant his own freedom. He helped
load the wagons made ready for the long journey, he

helped, this happy slave, pile up the bacon, the meal, the
flour, the corn, the household things, singing as he worked,
trusting as he sang, happy, care-free dependent on another's
bounty.

With every note from the dusky throats, the heart of
"Massa" grew heavier. He knew the black man's weak-
nesses, he knew his faults. He knew that even the men
and women trained under his watchful eye were helpless
if denied his supervision, but beneath all this there lurked
the horrible thought that in the new land he might not be
able to feed his own family. Then, too, if he left these
slaves behind, he virtually gave each man and each woman
his or her freedom, and he or she might put out for the
North where the growing bitterness against slavery might
be trusted to give each black a splendid chance.

The day of departure dawned. With every wagon in
readiness, with every detail arranged, with Kyle finally
won over to the idea that his slaves would take advantage
of the freedom idea thus offered them, Kyle made a last
pilgrimage about that place. Then with the sun high in
the heavens, with those slaves in hearing distance, Kyle
raised his voice for one last farewell. The farewell took on
a strange turn. Strictly speaking, it lacked the fundamental
idea of a farewell. Instead of any advice, any kindly
spoken words of hope for the future, the stentorian tones
of "Massa" made one sharp, clean-cut announcement:
"Every nigger at the Mississippi river to-night when I
cross goes with me to Texas."

Surprised at himself, relieved in a way that he had thus
put matters in their own hands, Kyle gave the order to
start. Throughout the day, filled to the brim with emotions,
Kyle thought occasionally of his negroes and his last sharp
command. When he reached the ferry, in the solemn dusk
of the February day in 1845, one hundred and fifty negroes
waited him there, waited to do his bidding, and followed
"Massa" without complaint, sometimes footsore and
nearly always weary, into the promised land of Texas.

And there they began life anew. They took up land on
the Blanco river, Kyle and his wife, Lucy, and they built
a log cabin in a chosen spot, and saw to it that the negroes
built themselves quarters, using in the construction the
same logs, felled and trimmed by hand to a state of usefulness. They thrived and prospered there in the new
land, for the soil was rich and new, and no question of
labor shortage ever troubled the "Massa" who had lacked
the courage to leave his negroes behind. Kyle became a
man of prominence in the community, and the little city
springing up, probably on his land, bears the name of Kyle

to this day, now some seventy-five years since this family entered Texas.

In all this new home-building, Lucy Bugg Kyle was as before the center of things. To her the children and the slaves came when real advice was needed. Her husband, too, profiting, perhaps, by his earlier defeats, was wont to ask her opinion on any fresh step, anything that bore any slightest chance of a risk. Under her direction and with her own help, her serving women carded the cotton, spun it into thread, wove it into cloth, and then her own dainty fingers fashioned the cloth into garments for her household, including her slaves. She made it her personal business to see that the colored women were taught—taught to cook, to sew, to spin, and she many times taught them herself as they clustered about her the deeper lessons of life, just as she taught her own children at her knee.

Neither did she ever forget that she was a mother. No faintest shadow of a desire displayed by any youngster to deviate from the straight and narrow path escaped that motherly eye. She trained them to live as she lived in the fear and admonition of the Lord, and there can be small doubt that her piety helped her over many hard places.

The Civil war broke into her prosperity. Five noble sons left her one by one to join the Confederate army. What she felt at the time of their departure, we have no right to say. Just how her heart bled over each "good-bye" must be forever a matter of conjecture, but we do know that every day she made her way alone to a cave on the bank of the Blanco river, one not far from her own home, and there she offered up her prayer for the safe return of her sons.

Lucy Bugg Kyle died, herself, in Hays County, June 2, 1863. Perhaps as she slipped away, the thought of the absent sons weighed heavily on her heart. Perhaps the faith that keeps men serene in the face of certain danger kept ever before her the idea that the "effectual fervent prayer of the righteous man availeth much." We know, we who were left behind, as she went down the Valley of the Shadow of Death, that each stalwart son returned from that futile conflict, that each man did his part afterwards in the upbuilding of his trampled nation.

Some among us may doubt the efficacy of prayer. Some may feel that the hour spent in meditation in that lonely cave had best been spent in organized, determined effort. There may be some who would decry the waste, the loss of energy necessitated by that hour given over to the play of the emotions. Others walking the earth, declaring at every step the power of truth that must rest at last on simple, clear-cut, clearly stated facts of life as they come and go would surely meet all this with a derisive shrug of the confident shoulders.   But even this man in this instance, for all his confidence, all his cleaving to facts pure and simple, would be slow in his condemnation.   He knows, and he must acknowledge with your humble scribe, prayer or no prayer, that there are few, indeed, among honorable men and women of to-day who would dare question for one instant the power for righteousness that dwelt in the olden days in this simple woman's honest, upright, God-fearing life.

Data contributed by—

Miss Emma Burleson,
Austin, Texas.

MRS. JESSE L. McCROCKLIN

BORN

ISABELLA HARRIS

To call this woman, this Isabella McCrocklin, a Kentucky girl is even in this day equivalent to placing her upon a pedestal. Beauty and grace and charm linger about the women of old Kentucky. So much so, in fact, that the faintest mention of the name of this old blue grass state bids us remember that women thrived there as well as horses, thrived and budded and blossomed into a state of rare perfection. And the woman we are to discuss right now is a splendid specimen, a rare sample of the thing we expect to find in a woman born in her day in old Kentucky.

Isabella began life August 12, 1814, near Owensboro, Kentucky, the fourth child of eight born to W. W. Harris and his wife whose name has been lost in family annals. The father was a physician, and his four sons followed hard in his footsteps. Isabella and her three sisters lived with these sons on the immense plantation owned by her father, lived the life of the average Kentucky girl of her day. Waited on by many slaves, courted and *feted*, she was yet strong of heart and will, a strength which stood her well in hand in the difficult life that was to follow that care-free youth.

If there were any touching incidents in the courtship that preceded Isabella's marriage to Jesse L. McCrocklin, they have been withheld from her descendants. The marriage took place in Owensboro, Kentucky, 1830, probably in that plantation home. McCrocklin was some fourteen years older than this bride, a man of adventurous spirit, a man who dreamed of making a fortune, always in some other place than that in which fate had placed him. When Stephen F. Austin, the intrepid colonizer, appealed for men to make up the company, then nearly ready to start to Texas, McCrocklin read in the appeal the promise of his dreams. Isabella, lately of the Kentucky plantation, reeking with its ease and plenty, Isabella, brave, determined, efficient, followed him, and willingly.

The details of that journey's beginning are somewhat in doubt. Some craft must have borne them down the Mississippi river, for we do know that they came in a small schooner to Powder Horn near Port Lavaca, some time in 1832. McCrocklin took up his head-right in what is now Washington county, and his farm land stretched over land now occupied by the cities of Independence, Brenham, Washington-on-the-Brazos, and Chappell Hill. There was a house on the land, a cedar house, my lady, you who prize your cedar chest take notice—built of logs to be sure, and possessing, O, ye who would smile, small window-panes of bona fide glass to allow the light of day to penetrate the fragrant interior. This house had been built in 1828, and is still standing (1927), just outside the city of Independence and is occupied at present by Judge Coles, a friend of Isabella's and a relative by marriage.

Isabella led a busy life in that cedar-log house. In the course of time she became the mother of five children, two sons and three daughters. In addition to the bringing-up of this little flock, supplying both spiritual and physical wants, Isabella faced the problem of conducting this home in the raw, new country just as her somewhat erratic husband demanded that it be kept. Generous, optimistic, hospitality was with McCrocklin a ruling passion. "Come right in. Make yourself at home. Peace and plenty reign here."

These words greeted the new-comer and the old, and many a man and his family thus greeted took McCrocklin at his word and stayed on there in the home month after month. It was no unusual thing to find thirty-five people seated about that dinner-table, and none prouder at the feast than McCrocklin whose provisions these people thus casually devoured. His friends, his Masonic brothers (he had founded the first Masonic lodge in that part of the country) came from time to time, uninvited, unexpected, but no matter for that, when they did so appear, McCrocklin's cup of joy was full.

Now methinks this might have brought a drop o'er much in the cup of joy belonging by right to his young wife, for though slaves had been brought to the wild country to help with the work, cooking appliances were crude, and dishes of any kind were hard to obtain. In that first Texas home, all cooking was done on an open fireplace with the aid of a Dutch oven and a spit. Said oven in keeping with McCrocklin's ideas of life was large enough for this young woman to roast a whole pig at once, and many pigs must have been needed to gratify her husband's ideas of hospitality. In addition, Isabella dried fruits and preserved them, put away dried beans from her own garden, amused herself in spare moments spinning the thread and weaving the cloth that was to clothe her family and her slaves, and if she ever complained, even in her heart, of her husband's company-loving inclination, nobody ever heard of it.

When the Texas Revolution took on form and shape, the McCrocklin home became a center of interest. Houston and Austin, Asa and Nat Mitchell, Taso Clay, Lamar, Anson Jones, Dr. Asa Hoxey, Nester Seward and Jerome Robertson were frequent visitors in this home. From the stirring conversation of these mighty spirits, McCrocklin knew that the time was ripe for his great adventure. Isabella, her own patriotism aroused, abetted her husband in these activities, and herself moulded bullets that were used in the first skirmish at Nacogdoches. She knew as the battle of San Jacinto was in progress, that her husband was taking part therein, and when the news of victory came she began to dream of his home-coming, expecting to share this great joy with one who had done his own good part toward bringing it about.

She heard at some time during the summer following the battle that he had been retained in the army as a colonel of volunteers, and she was further told that this regiment was being kept pretty busy proving to the Mexicans that they must let Texas alone. The summer waned. Fall came on but brought no word from her husband. With heavy heart, Isabella went on about her work, her planning, her ceaseless watch lest Indians surprise her, telling herself sometimes that her husband was dead, reproving herself at others for her want of faith. Finally, in the dead of that winter of 1836-37, McCrocklin returned to his wife, so old, so worn, so broken, that she who had watched for his coming day and night failed to recognize him when he at last stood before her. A Colonel in the army! Aye, but he was bare-footed and sore, and his clothes were in tatters. For days he had existed with no food save a piece of mule-meat tied in his mouth to keep his lips from parching, its putrid juices slipping down his throat to keep him from starving. And he carried deep in one arm a bullet that had struck him at San Jacinto.

There was nothing of importance now for Isabella to do save help the worn, world-weary man take up his life again on the happy footing of home, a home in the new country growing up around them, a country peopled and controlled by men and women of determined spirit and dauntless courage. A country bought with the blood of heroes, a priceless heritage, but one yet to be brought to its full perfection! Right there, McCrocklin took up his old line of work, farming, raising sheep and cattle, showing his Kentucky blood in his fondness for blooded horses, imported, many of them, from the old home stock.

And this love for fine horses brought to Jesse and Isabella the next vital step in their lives. There were horse races scheduled to take place in the community and one man, Rigdin Quinney by name, a lawyer by profession, closed in a bet with McCrocklin, a bet in which McCrocklin had staked his whole league and *labor* of land. One time at least in this horse racing day, McCrocklin's judgment was at fault, and he lost the bet. Simple thing this losing seems to us to-day with horses heading straight for the Museum, but Quinney appeared in due time and demanded his ounce of flesh, and no young judge stood by to help him out.

To Isabella this demand must have been bitter. She was as yet a young woman, comparatively, and changes are not hard for young people, but she had spent twenty-three years of her life in that cedar-log house, her children had been born there, her whole woman's life had centered about it, but when her husband suggested that he *must* keep his word, that he must give up the place, when he further suggested that they move to Blanco County, Isabella agreed and apparently in all cheerfulness.

The first home of the McCrocklin's in Blanco County, built some time in 1853, was built of cedar logs, too, but mud and sand filled the cracks outside, and the whole of the inside was plastered, thus making it cozy and warm in winter and cool in summer. It had small glass windows in the bed-rooms, but the living-room was lighted by the use of glass in the upper part of the doors. This new home boasted an orchard surrounded by a fence built entirely of honey-combed rocks, the negro slaves brought from the old home supplying the labor that built it. The flower garden and the vegetable gardens were each enclosed with a white picket fence, but the farm, proper, including acres upon acres, was enclosed with this same honey-combed rocks. The same old Dutch oven was installed in this new house, and there Isabella took up her life again.

In 1861, the Dutch oven had to give way. Among the many house-guests who had shared the fruits of Isabella's culinary labor, one man, William Haviland, viewed her efforts with an appreciative eye, taking in the difficulties, the stooping above that Dutch oven. Being of an executive turn of mind, said William set himself to relieve the situation. The result was a cook-stove and all its utensils, brought with great difficulty from some remote eastern point and established in Isabella's kitchen.

"Cheap board!" we of to-day would exclaim, remembering that every meal has its price, but Isabella looked upon the gift of that stove as an evidence of real feeling, real appreciation on the part of the donor, and her little heart glowed because of the thought, perhaps, just a little more than the bare fact of possessing the stove had been able to make it glow, O ye women of to-day, with your thoughts economic and otherwise.

A step backward now to 1853. Before they were well established in Blanco County, it dawned upon Isabella that they had come to a country even more wild than had been that first settlement on the Brazos. Wolves and coyotes, fearless of men, ignorant for the most part of the effects of the shotgun,—preyed upon all livestock. Chickens, hogs, penned beneath the dwelling house for safe-keeping, were taken by these wild animals while the family slept above them.   No single night did they fail, some one of them, in this visitation, and at different times in the year the roaring of mountain beasts could be heard in their nightly serenade.   Snakes coiled in the rocks, owls hooted from the trees, sombre in their dense leaves, each hoot making life miserable for him who could not keep from listening.

None of these, however, compared in point of real danger with the Indian.   Eyeing the horses, proud descendants of old Kentucky stock, the Indians came by the light of the moon to help themselves to the beautiful animals.   Expecting the raids at such times, men sat up all night, for a horse in early Texas times was a horse, not worth a kingdom, perhaps, but a very precious thing in the daily life of a man or woman.   And no man in the settlement was free from the raids of the Indians.   Neither kindness nor firmness, nor even harshness in dealing made any man in the eyes of the Indian any different from any other man. They were not particular as to whose horses they took. Provided the horse was a good one, he was looked on as the just right of the Indian plucky enough to steal him.

Sometimes white men took advantage of this reputation of the Indian, fostering thereby their own ends, letting the blame rest where it was so likely to fall.   Kentucky horses were goodly in the white man's eyes, too, and alas! they were sometimes hard to obtain honestly.   On one particularly bright night, the men of the neighborhood gathered at the McCrocklin home and put their horses in the corral, each man taking his turn in the watch that was to be maintained throughout the night.   In his turn, McCrocklin at the watch, heard a stealthy tread toward one of his particularly fine horses.   He made his way carefully toward the animal, depending entirely upon his ear, believing of course the worst of the stealthy tread.   As he reached forth in the darkness of the corral to put his hand upon the horse's halter, he met the touch of another hand, intent upon the same purpose, but coming from the other side of the animal.   Indians, of course, so though McCrocklin, and he drew his knife and struck the fatal blow. When a light was brought, McCrocklin found that he had killed a white man, one always counted among his own best friends.   It was afterwards supposed that this man had come into the corral guard while McCrocklin slept, and that McCrocklin was thus unaware of his presence on the premises.   The man, too, had heard the stealthy tread and had started out to intercept the Indian as he had supposed McCrocklin to be.   The natural mistake under the circumstance resulted in death of one of the men. Unfortunate circumstance, regrettable incident, but one common enough in the settlement of a new country. Isabella recognized the truth of this matter, recognized the possibility that he who guarded the horses, man or woman, stood just this chance to be mistaken in the dead of the night, but she took her own turn at the watch just the same, and had it been necessary, had shot the Indian down who dared the theft of their property.

So she stands out, this Kentucky girl, a striking figure in our pioneer days. Weighing her stingy ninety pounds, suffering all her life with asthma, her house was as well-ordered as that of our modern, well educated woman to to-day. She carded and spun and wove the materials for clothing, searched the woods for materials to dye the thread before it was woven, keeping her eye open, her progressive mind always willing to take on new methods. And the blood of her father cried out in her, making of her a doctor, a nurse, a mid-wife, and ever present help in any physical predicament. In the absence of physicians, she brought most of the white children of her community into the world, her frail little hands showing unusual skill in the bringing, and she rendered the same service many a time to her own slaves and the colored women in her community. Outliving her husband by many years, Isabella attained unto a ripe old age, maintaining always her well-ordered household. Trouble, aye, plenty of it, real trouble that always greets the pioneer woman, but faith and hope and perseverance guarded round about with love and truth made of her an unusual figure, a real inspiration to us, the children of another day.

"When the labor of an undertaking appalls me, when one after another of many obstacles arises in the path of endeavor, when the heart-breaking certainty of failure stares me in the face, somehow I recall the life in that cedar-log house, the boom of the loom, the grind of the grain in mill, the call in the night of the fierce animals, the fear of Indians waiting always their chance, and when that busy, intrepid life comes before me, my own cares grow small. The spirit of conquest rises. No trouble in my life of to-day can ever approach what she suffered, and proud of her blood in my veins, I go forth nerved afresh for battle."

So writes a descendant of Isabella Harris McCrocklin to-day, and we who read of her join in a solemn "Amen!"

Data contributed by—

Mrs. H. H. Ueckert,
1102 Hyde Park,
Houston, Texas.

MRS. R. C. DOOM

BORN

ALTA ZERAH WILLIAMS

A half-wit, long past his first fifty years of life, met rather
suddendly an old friend and neighbor, one long since become
a successful lawyer in his own native state.   Even the half-
wit grasped the idea of success radiating from the lawyer's
appearance.   In the light of that idea the half-wit's own
condition became niggardly by contrast: He sidled up to
the lawyer after the passing of the first embarrassing moment
and whispered:
"Ye see I never had no book-larnin'."
Education, and the common acceptation of the term is
"book-larnin'," is a large factor in the success of the individual of to-day.   Even the man endowed with the full
measure of wit seems lost in the struggle for livelihood
without a certain amount of this same "book-larnin'," and
young men and women seem content to spend many
otherwise easy years in "book-larnin's" ardent pursuit.
And no man ever says them, "Nay."
Most of the men who formed and shaped and governed
the new republic called Texas, had received a good education.   In many places, the women, their wives and particularly their daughters, had not been so fortunate.   They
had come at an early age to the wilderness where there was
none to teach them save their fathers and grand-fathers,
and said antecedents were too busy subduing the soil and
quelling the red man to care particularly about the intellectual achievements of females.   In these sections of
the state "book-larnin' " was not common as a feminine
adornment.
The absence of mental training has ever been a loss.   In
the case of the early Texas woman, the loss made itself
felt unto the next generation, but once in a while in those
early years of Texas history, the young mind thus left to
itself developed a rare keenness of perception, a rare
strength of reasoning that set it a little apart, a little above
some of the men and women found in the more fortunate
class; even in the class addicted to "book-larnin'."   This
was the case with Alta Zerah Williams.   She was born
January 19, 1813, in some flower-scented nook in Louisiana.
Her father, William Williams, and his wife, Sittine Southern, had emigrated thither from North Carolina.   In this
same company had come Alta's grand-father, Stephen
Williams, a doughty old warrior who had followed Col.
Morgan through the battles of Camden, Brier Creek and
Eutaw Springs in the Revolutionary war.   He buried his
wife in Louisiana, the land of Alta's birth, the land of the

jasmine and the fragrant magnolia, and, following his son on into Texas, the old soldier found a peculiar comfort in watching Alta, in waiting upon her, in humoring her. Alta responded to his clumsily expressed preference, herself half-conscious of the response, and there can be no doubt that Alta gained much strength both in mind and heart from her association with the brave old man.

Alta led the life of the normal girl of her day, born thus and coming thus early to the wilderness of Texas. She spun, and she wove, and she plied her needle diligently, and a daughter of hers, years after Alta had passed away, declared that every thread was counted when that steel needle was in action. She made her own garden, and there were slaves at hand who might have done it for her. She made her garden, half an acre at a time, made it with a hoe in that soft, deep white-sanded soil of the Walnut Run country, and every row was straight, and every single vegetable in the row stood at its proper angle. This precision did not hold in her care of the house. Things might strew about a bit now and then, but she was particular to a degree about the character and the quantity of food appearing upon her table, and she saw to it all her life that said table was well supplied.

Romance was slow in its approach toward this independent damsel. She was fully twenty years of age before her girlish heart had missed a beat because, perchance, some man had looked upon her with favor. Men had looked thus upon her, for efficient women are ever at a premium in a new country, but Alta had remained perversely, stupidly blind to all impassioned glances. But— when Stephen H. Everitt, hailing lately from New York, a physician by profession, possessing in himself all that culture and education might lend an already strong mentality, when *he* came into the presence of the independent, fearless maiden, all the tenderness stored through the years welled up in her heart, and Alta loved with a love passing knowledge.

Everitt was worthy of her adoration. He had come to the wilderness, leaving culture and ease behind him. He had left as well a domestic shadow that clung about him, a shadow none ever dared discuss with him. He took his place at once among the makers of Texas. Family tradition claims that he made the pen draft of the Declaration of Independence of Texas on a little table in the hands of a descendant of Alta Williams to-day (1929). Certainly, his name is signed to that document, and various other state papers of importance. But all this was to come later. To Alta Williams, fearless, herself, exact an dmethodical, Stephen Everitt, polished, cultivated man of the world, was a

present reality, the sum and substance of all life and its
dreams. She listened proudly when he talked with her of
his plans for Texas, proud because of Everitt's place therein, caring little for things political. When he suggested
marriage they were married, and Alta took up life in the
typical home of the day, a little cabin not far removed from
the big, comfortable home in which she afterwards passed
the greater part of her life.

This cabin was deep in the heart of the woods on a hill
some three miles or more east from the Angelina river and
about seven miles west from the town of Jasper. There,
in 1834, with the first flush of married joy upon her, she
took up her garden work, her sewing, her spinning, her
weaving. She many times passed the day alone, her
husband away on business. There her first child, William
Everitt, was born. There the Indians came to see her,
bringing baskets woven of split cane, expecting to exchange
each basket for as much as it would hold of meal or corn.
And be it recorded of Alta, she was not above haggling with
the dirty, hungry savages as to the price paid per basket.

With the business of state in mind, foreseeing even then
the fact that he might be called from home for a long period
of time, Everitt, with an ox team as his means of tran-
portation, put out some time in the fall of 1835 for New
Orleans where he expected to buy a stock of goods. He insisted that Alta's grandfather stay with her while he was
gone for protection, and Alta agreed readily enough, not
that she was afraid, but because she liked to have the old
man pottering about. She laughed deep down in her
heart at her husband's solicitude—but she liked it.

Alta and her grandfather whiled away the hours while
Everitt was gone, working, fishing, playing, each busy in
mind over the few political truths Everitt had let fall just
before he left. When the happy communion was interrupted by a call for Stephen Williams to go to a sick son,
Alta sent him on with a light heart, and passed the nights
as well as the days alone in her cabin, no sound save the
noise of the forest or the yelp of a dog lost in the forest to
fall upon her ear. Afraid? Never a thought of it!

One afternoon she placed her sleeping babe in his crib
and turned about gently to take up her sewing. She
caught sight as she turned of two Indians *sneaking* up to
her door. An Indian sneaking augued trouble. The
trouble was more than likely whiskey. The same Indian
sober who would haggle with her back and forth about the
price of a basket was quite another matter under the influence of the long-sought whiskey. Close behind him
another Indian, and, save the mark, Alta saw him stumble

as he, too, *sneaked* toward her. What must she do?   What *could* she do?

Any other than Alta had screamed out her helplessness. Alone, deep in the heart of the forest, two drunken redskins heading for her cabin door! What could she do, save watch them come?   What could she do save yield her life and her babe's at the Indian's pleasure?

Some of this passed quickly through her mind, some of it slowly. Not fear exactly. Rather the grim acknowledgment of a startling situation. She stepped, still bewildered, toward the open cabin door. Then she closed the door instinctively upon the intruders.

Her action outraged the drunken brutes. She had virtually slapped each man in the face. There was in the savage mind no thought but to avenge the slap.

Alta sensed all this. She knew that she had given them all incentive for battle. She felt, however, that barricaded in her home she held a chance against them. As long as the door remained tight she was safe unless—and then her heart did miss a beat—they set fire to the cabin.

Shaking her heart back to its normal rhythm, she determined to keep that door closed. A barrel of flour—and how precious it was in those days—stood in the corner. With that strength so often born of necessity, she rolled it against that inward closing door, and a half-forgotten, rusty, flintlock musket fell clattering to the puncheon floor. She grasped the rusty thing in a forlorn hope.

Failing to understand the quiet, the cessation in battle, Alta glanced through a knot-hole in the door. She saw the two Indians standing shoulder to shoulder, saw them start in a run toward her, coming thus together as one man. She felt the impact of the two bodies against the door, felt the door give way, watched the barrel burst, watched the precious contents spreading about over the floor.

Flushed with victory, the two Indians stepped over the threshold. Then they paused. They had met a determined little woman, an unflinching piece of audacity, but more audacious still, that little woman held a gun levelled straight at the head of the first-comer.

The Indians paused. As a pause producer a gun has few equals. In this case the pause lengthened into a wait. Seeing no waver in the face behind the gun, they waited some more. Then with slinking step, and a slow Indian smile, the taller of the two Indians approached a step nearer.

"Gimme gun," he said. "You 'fraid. I" pointing to his parner, "I shoot de damn rascal."

The long, bony fingers reached the butt of her gun. Alta shrank back a step, her fingers dangerously near the trigger.

Then her face lit with the magnanimity of the conqueror—so thought the Indian—for she pointed toward her husband's demijohn and asked them quietly to leave the house. They backed out, that gun still persuasive—and Alta passed out the portion of whiskey. The offering was gladly accepted. They gulped it down and reeled off in drunken anticipation. Alta turned back to her baby. Then she smiled a slow, contemptuous smile. The gun had not been loaded.

Alta Everitt bore her part in the runaway scrape. No need to recall the circumstances here, save to state that she, too, believed that Houston had been defeated and killed at San Jacinto and that there was nothing left to do but to get beyond the Sabine. Dr. Everitt was away, so was her grand-father, the doughty old warrior gone with his grown grand-sons to take part in the battle of San Antonio and this same San Jacinto so disastrously reported to them. Alta believed with the rest of the stay-at-homes that the Mexicans were coming in droves and butchering as they came. So she bade the cripped old uncle who bore her company at that time get out the wagon and mules, and gathering a few clothes and household articles—mostly skillets and pots with a few fat feather-beds—they set out to join the run-aways. They had to make their way by a road little wider than the wagon tread, a road cut deep in the soft sand and overlaced with boughs and vines that swung low, almost to the wagon-top. They drove two stout mules, stolid creatures, unmoved by any thought of the invaders.

After a few turns in this tunnel-like road, Alta spied the Pamplins, husband and wife, in a wagon ahead of them, said wagon packed with household goods, bearing as well one slave named Judy and drawn by two good mules, driven feverishly by a colored boy named Jake. The presence of friends lent encouragement, helped them all to hurry on a bit faster in the race against the deadly foe.

But there came a sudden upheavel in the path of this flight. The obstacle was none other than the household wares of one named Jehu Bevil, wares piled high on a carrylog, the vehicle drawn by two huge oxen. The ten-foot wheel of this inconvenient carriage had straddled an overhanging limb. No amount of *Gee-ing* or *Haw-ing* or *Buck-ing* could persuade the team to move in such a fashion as to release the limb. To sever the limb from the tree would take time, and might blockade the road.

In the eyes of those coming behind the blockade had already occurred. Mrs. Pamplin had been brought to a stand, so had Alta and others coming up from time to time. With perfect realization of this blockade and what it meant, a man, a stranger to them, rushed up on horseback, declaring that the Mexicans were close behind and butchering as they came, tearing off through the under-brush, apparently intent upon warning others.

The departing horseman gave the Pamplins an idea. They cut out the mules and each appropriated one. They had the boy pile feather-beds and pillows behind Mrs. Pamplin, and Jake, without so much as begging leave, sprang up behind Mr. Pamplin. No such hope for Judy. The pillows and feather-beds left no room on the other mule's broad back. The negro saw no hope save to die of fright before the Mexicans might reach her. Her face grew ashey, and her lips trembled in their agony. Alta, already mounted a la Pamplin, caught the tremor of the ashen lips. With a quick surge of pity, she motioned to Judy to get up behind her, and Judy did so in a hurry, grabbing the baby from Alta's arms, and saying low, "Fur God's sake, Mis' Alta, hurry."

A courier overtook the company a half mile farther on, and he brought to them the astonishing news of Houston's victory at San Jacinto. In the silence that followed the announcement, Mrs. Pamplin approached Jake, hastily slidden from his perch behind Mr. Pamplin, and began a solemn command.

"Here, Jake," she said, "you kin ride faster'n we kin. You git right back on this here mule, en don't never stop till you gits home and waters my goslins. Ay! God, I know they're all dead."

The days of the Republic of Texas were great days in the life of Alta Williams Everitt. She adored her husband as only a shrewd, capable woman can adore the man who manages in some way to catch her fancy. His intellectual brilliancy continued to charm, continued to stimulate her own eager mind. His manner continued to please, and Alta, happy and loving, managed his household, his slaves, planned with him the fields retrenched from the heavy forest, and in the fullness of time and amid the hardships of a new country, she bore him another son and one daughter, all the while the outwardly calm, efficient woman despite the tide of feeling welling deep in her heart. Things prospered with the Everitts. Land claims were settled, and political affairs became well grounded. Everitt laid the foundation for a big mercantile business, for the profession of medicine—he was a physician of no mean ability —brought little return in the new country and consumed little of a man's time. His business was located in what is now Jasper County, Texas, and he hauled the goods by ox teams through the forest from New Orleans. He brought Alta dainty articles of wearing apparel from the markets of

New Orleans, some of them in the possession of her descendants to-day, and Alta, always ready to do her part, kept up plantation affairs in his absence, managed the slaves, looked after all affairs of that Everitt head-right, already growing into a handsome estate, and managed it all with that same efficiency that had characterized her work in her own home garden.

Everitt had an associate in these business trips to New Orleans, one who shall here be nameless. He, too, was suave of manner, cultivated, a fit companion in that regard for Alta's beloved husband. But beneath the polish, differing from the polish of Everitt, at least in Alta's eyes, there seemed to her to lurk a dishonest streak. Everitt was never able to dislodge Alta's belief in the dishonest streak. Respect for her husband whom all Texas respected, kept her silent on the matter, but Everitt sensed her suspicion. About ready to depart on a trip with this partner, Everitt dared ask Alta to try to subdue her prejudice for his partner and friend. She smiled back at him, but made no further reply. She watched her husband depart, knowing that down the road a bit he would join this companion, but she maintained her silence.

Days became weeks, each week stretching further into a nameless dread, and then that companion returned and reported to Alta in his suave, easy way that her husband had died in New Orleans and had been buried there. Along with her heart-breaking grief leaped into her mind the old suspicion, that same companion the object. She waited the slow return of her husband's effects, hoping for some detail of her husband's last illness. When the things did arrive, Everitt's fine watch was missing.

Alta made no outcry. The loss seemed so trivial in the face of her greater one, but that suspicion never left her. It made her watchful ever afterward of the man who came to deal with the widow and the orphan.

Alta did not remain a widow very long. Associated with Everitt in another branch of his business had been a man, a lawyer, who had managed to escape her suspicion. Col. R. C. Doom had buried his wife in Austin about the time of Dr. Everitt's own death, had sold his lands there, now some of the most valuable property in the city, and with two little children had gone back to Jasper County to make a new home. A third daughter, the oldest, he left in Austin with her mother's people. He and Alta met soon after his arrival in Jasper County. The idea of mutual helpfulness drew the two together, and they were married some time early in 1847. Col. Doom assumed control of the estate as well as the children, Alta reserving always the right to her own opinion in all matters, both business and social. Col. Doom soon won the love and the respect of the Everitt children, and the idea of the cruel step-father was ever far from their minds. After the birth of their own children, for there were three born after this second marriage, Col. Doom built a commodious home in a grove of magnolias, oaks and beeches down nearer the Angelina river, and in that new house Alta Williams lived the longest part of her life, lived it broadly, energetically, efficiently. From that home she sent forth two sons. One, James H. Everitt became a gallant soldier in the Confederate army, losing one arm at the battle of Arkansas Post. The other son, a courageous man in his own humbler sphere of life, inherited his mother's exactness, her appreciation of the details of life, her efficiency, her steadfast purpose, and that man, Judge D. W. Doom, lived to bless the world as it lay about him. Another child, a daughter, lingered on in the home with Alta, a woman blessed with her father's sweetness of thought and feeling, endued as well with her mother's tenacity of purpose, her insight into life and its matters of real worth. She, the daughter, left behind her a son, Robert Velasco Shelby, and he lives with his own father to-day in the home hallowed by the presence of Alta Everitt-Doom. Brave, keen, energetic, untiring in her devotion to her family, ready to maintain that home that her husband might do battle for his country, Alta played well her part on that early stage of Texas history, and no man will deny that to such women as Alta we owe in part the civilization of Texas to-day.

Data contributed by—

 Mrs. R. P. Shelby,
 Jasper, Texas.

MRS. JAMES CUNNINGHAM

BORN

SUSANNAH TATE

One hears a great deal said to-day of woman and her place in the world. Some enthusiasts, politically inclined, declare that something really worthwhile has been gained for individual women in the attainment of this place, and some others, smiling complacently, make bold to declare that this place has been attained by consistent and united effort on the part of the few real leaders in the feminine world. It is not advisable to enter into argument over the matter, either pro or con, but a student of history must once in a while be granted the privilege of stating that many a pioneer woman of Texas evinced, even in the old days, certain inherent qualities of leadership that gave her in her own day her own good place in the world. It may be—as has been suggested before in these pages—it may be that woman's blessed inquisitiveness, her blessed search for something a little better led her to suggest the apple to her partner in Eden, but the record fails to show that the woman in question ever grumbled over the punishment or ever failed in any way to do her part in that ignominious flight that was, after all, the very beginning of life for old Adam. At that time, no other woman shared the world with Eve, and this deprives us of the right or the power to make comparisons, but there are some women of our day able to hold their own if suddenly transplanted to a more difficult walk of life, and to lead other women successfully in the battle it takes. We like to think of Eve as just such a woman, had there been any followers handy, for there are many women to-day standing out in the story of the world's progress, just as there were many of our grand-mother's day who thus stood out in that same story. Could they come back to-day and mingle with us now in this civilization of another day and time, they would doubtless become leaders by the very inherent qualifications that made them leaders in the early days of Texas.

Susannah Tate Cunningham is a brilliant example of this type of woman. She was born December 22, 1817, in Warren County, Tennessee; her father being Aaron Tate and her mother Elizabeth Connolly. Arriving at her eighteenth year, she became the bride of James Cunningham, choosing in the good old way, February 14, of that year 1835 as her wedding day. Twelve children were born to this couple, nine boys and three girls, all of this dozen of young Cunninghams attaining their majority. Family records pass lightly over the first four years of that married life, and we know only that it was spent in Alabama, and

that at the end of that time Cunningham and his wife,
Susannah, moved from Alabama to Titus County, Texas.

The mother of many children under any circumstances
has small chance to eat the bread of idleness. There might
be situations where slaves or servants relieved the mother
of all manual labor, but that part, after all, is a very small
part in the bringing up of a child. And deep in these
maternal cares, helped in a way by well-trained slaves for
her servants, Susannah found it necessary to move with
her husband and children about over this great wilderness
of Texas, living in some half-dozen counties before settling
in her permanent home in Comanche.

When this couple did finally settle to the building of a
permanent home, they built a house that was in every way
worth while. It is standing to-day, most of it, (1927) in a
fine state of preservation. Both stone and lumber were
used in its construction, the lumber being brought from
Georgetown, Texas, the nearest railroad point to Comanche.
The people of the community gathered there in early days,
and this stone part of the house became a fort. Indians of
that vicinity had a way of showing their animosity by
means of raids, and when news of the raids travelled about—
how, Heaven only knows—the white women and children
sought refuge behind stone walls, because, forsooth, they
could neither be torn down, nor yet destroyed by fire.
Welcome to the shelter? Aye, the home of the early
Texas woman was her own castle, her very own, but it was
open on all occasions to him who needed help and comfort.
And in this particular home, the mistress deserves unusual
credit, for the brunt of that home-making fell upon Susannah. Her husband, never very robust, became practically
an invalid, not long after the house was built, and he remained so during the last half of their married life.

But that home suffered little because of the weakness of
Cunningham. Fully determined to make a permanent
home in Comanche County, Susannah superintended the
clearing of land, the building of fences, the planting and
gathering of crops, working with her own hands if need
were at such labor. On rainy days, the farm laborer's
paradise, she wove cloth for her neighbors on her home
loom or on the loom of her patron, taking many times in
payment for such labor just as much corn as she could herself carry home. She moulded bullets when the weaving
grew scarce, for the ever-present Indian and the beasts of
the forests, sneaking by night and by day to rob them of
their cattle, made bullets just as much a necessity as bread
and meat.

Through it all she was brave beyond belief. Indians
sneaking upon her met a gun pointed with aim level and

sure.   When the Indians came in crowds to raid the white
man's home, the home of the selfish usurper of his happy
hunting ground, and maybe, the Indian had a right to
raid these homes, most women agreed to the indignity of
being shut up in a fort for safe-keeping while their husbands went out to meet the infuriated foe.   Not Susannah.   When her husband suggested the danger for her if
left at home while he joined the company of white men determined to avenge the raid, she made the reply that she
preferred to stay at home and look after her "stuff."   She
reminded her husband that chickens must be fed, and cows
must be milked, and garden must be planted and tended.
And she carried her point.   She went on about her housework, her cooking, singing happily, a determined, defiant
little woman.   Speaking years afterwards of one particularly long stay her neighbors saw fit to make in the
fort, she said she stayed at home so that next year she
would have seed for her neighbors.

Sometimes, her spirit failed her a bit.   Sometimes she
had a kind of haunting fear that Indians might get the
best of her and then the women in the fort would return
smiling and happy because they would have the eternal,
the damnable right to say "I told you so."   One day not
long after an alarm had been given—and ignored—by
Susannah, she went about her house-cleaning, a farce in
itself, for no dirt ever dared enter her doors, and she put
her feather-beds out to sun on frames or chairs or anything handy—remember she had a big family—and left
them all day.   Toward afternoon, her children happily at
play near these feather-beds, Susannah and her mother
made a jaunt of a few hundred yards down toward the
creek in order to obtain sand for the already spotless
kitchen floor.   Glancing back on the way—she was ap-
prehensive of course, Susuannah saw feathers flying in the
air.   It could mean but one thing.   Indians had come to
destroy, to torture.

"Mother," exclaimed Susannah, "the Indians have come
and have most likely killed the children."

If Indians had killed the children, making havoc the
while of the feather beds, these same Indians might surely
be depended upon to murder Susannah when she appeared
on the scene.   Perhaps that thought came to Susannah.
Self-preservation is a strong law of nature.   The human
thought can never be accurately read by an outsider.   But
history tells us that Susannah rushed head-long toward the
spot, ready to lay her feeble all on that sacrificial altar.
Arriving at the scene, her mother panting behind her,
Susannah found some enterprising hogs, escaped somehow
from their pens and leaping rampant in the middle of her

feather beds. We would fain draw the curtain. A
definite description of the conflict between house-wifely
thrift thus outraged and maternal solicitude thus quieted
is far beyond the power of this feeble pen.

In some branch of the family established by Susannah
Cunningham there is still a walnut quilt chest. Beneath
those smoothly folded quilts bags of gold and silver were
frequently kept. Indians in some way divined the truth
concerning the contents of that famous "chist" and decided that gold and silver might be nice things to have.
Susannah and one daughter, busy in the milking-pen toward the close of day, observed several Indians approaching the pen from the house. Thinking of the lost gold, for
of course, argued these women, the "chist" had already
been robbed, regretting it with a heavy heart, no doubt,
recalling in the instant the fact that guns (they always
went armed) in the hands of two women were worth little
in the fight with five or six Indians, Susannah and her
daughter crept on their hands and knees, hoping thus to
remain unobserved, nearer still to a place where the
rails were pulled to one side, crawled beneath the pile thus
made and waited. A noise from the house gave an alarm,
and the Indians in their haste to get away stepped right
over the two prostrate women, failing to suspect their
presence in the gloom of the departing day. So you see
for all her independence, all her bravery of spirit, Susannah did sometimes falter in the face of the enemy. And it
might be well, right here, to add a little account of one
experience with Indians that fell to the share of her husband.

James Cunningham, and now maybe, just maybe, Susannah obtained some of her bravery from constant association with this husband, took part in what is known in
this country as Brown's Creek fight. In telling of the
event afterwards, Cunningham said the men were separated
into bunches, each bunch being detailed to wait behind
bushes and trees, or any other convenient objects that
might form an ambush. Each man was to single out his
own Indian, wait to be sure of his aim and then fire to kill
instantly. One man whose given name was Arthur,
followed these instructions to the letter. He singled out
his Indian, aimed his very best, waited that suggested
moment, and then his voice rose solemnly in prayer:

"O, Lord, place this bullet right between his God
damned eyes!"

Now there is nothing extant to show that the Giver of
every good and perfect gift objects to use of phrases
commonly classed as "cussing." Moreover it has been
said "that the fervent prayer of the righteous man availeth

much." However we may construe this effort, whether it could be called prayer or just plain "cussing," the fact remains that Arthur's Indian with his "God damned eyes" got away, and we who read can only draw conclusions.

There were many of these fights in which the sons and relatives of Susannah bore their part, and bore it bravely.

One son, scarcely more than a child, begged to go at the time of one threatened raid. His elder brother, struck with the absurdity of the demand, taunted the little fellow with the fact that he had neither the size nor the strength to manage a gun. Rising in the might of his inheritance from that plucky mother, the boy replied that he could put the gun in the fork of a tree and shoot. Let us hope that the young scamp got his chance some time, for there was the Dove Creek fight in 1864 and another Comanche raid in 1867, and the Hog Creek fight down as late as 1870.

This last named fight holds a peculiar interest for us because of the part Susannah played in it. Frank Brown and a friend, both men of that community, started one day to San Saba mills. They were attacked by forty or fifty Indians at Mustang Water Hole on Big Mountain Creek. Captain Roach, coming from San Saba, had just met Brown and his companion. The captain drew the wagons together, cut the harness from the mules, mounted Brown, the other man and himself on a mule apiece, and then the three men put out to escape. They were not cowards, but each recognized this as one of the occasions that sometimes come to a brave man when there is nothing left to do but take to his heels. Roach, telling of the episode afterwards, declared that at that particular time he ran twenty-five brave warriors and at a furious rate, but that he had sense enough to keep always in the lead.

But however lightly Roach might speak of the fight afterwards, it was generally known that he failed to keep sufficient distance between himself and his enemy, and said failure might have been due to a trembling of the knees, for we cannot believe the staunch mule he rode failed to do his part. An arrow, maybe the Indian's pony was noted for its speed, struck Roach ignominiously in the back, pierced one lung, and pushed the skin up in his breast. On and on he rode, clapping his feet against the belly of his mule, and desperation had driven every vestige of a tremble from his knees, reaching at last Watson Ranch Springs. Leaping down for one drink of water for his famished lips, that arrow still at work in his breast, and then Roach turned to see his mule lie down and die without so much as asking leave or stating beforehand his desperate intentions. Afoot now, his arrow-pierced breast throbbing at every step he made, Roach walked on toward the Cunningham home. He knew that within that home, help waited his call. In his distorted vision he saw the nimble fingers of the mistress of that home at work on his breast. Just to get there, just to let her see his troubles, needless at all for him to speak, but alas! Roach but staggered into old negro Bill's cabin, and there he laid him down before the astonished darkey in a swoon. Ever on the alert for just such emergencies, old Bill knew immediately just what to do. He carried that suffering man in his arms, as one would carry a suffering child, and laid him down at the feet of his mistress.

Susannah removed the arrow, gently but firmly, soothing as best she could the well-nigh mortal pain of the removal, and then she sent for Dr. Montgomery. The doctor was slow in arriving, and Susannah dressed the wound, and by dint of nursing and careful feeding, she pulled Roach through to perfect health and strength.

As one would naturally expect from the account of such a character, Susannah was a Christian woman, a member of the Baptist church, and a staunch one. She helped organize the first Baptist church in her country, and the ministers were entertained, and most royally, in her home.

Susannah died June 8, 1899, a little past eighty-two years of age at the time of her death. Many changes had taken place in that once wild country, in which she had lived and labored, and she deservedly felt that she had done her part in bringing about those changes. It was no longer necessary for her or for her daughters to stand before the loom weaving the cloth needful to the every-day garments. It was no longer necessary for any woman to mould bullets for the defense of her home and children, no longer necessary to watch for the Indian in his uncanny approach. Civilization had rendered all these things unnecessary, but the same spirit that held her far in the night before that loom, her little body already weary and worn with the day's labor, the same spirit that made her bold in defense of her household wares, lingered ever with her, making her voice a shade gentler, a shade sweeter, a shade yet more firm when the occasion demanded it. One descendant, a man of wide experience in a world not very unlike the one in which she lived, speaks of her as the best woman he ever knew, and what more could any man say at any time in defense of any woman?

Data contributed by—

> Mrs. Howard B. Cox,
> Ozona, Texas.

MRS. ROBERT HENRY

BORN

ELIZABETH DOWNING

"Teach her to be brave;
No coward mother ever bears a valiant son."

We live in a Democratic country. Most of us Texas
folks swear allegiance to a political party that calls itself
Democratic, even in its formal name. Through, this Democratic idea, we have come to care little for kings and queens
and lords and ladies. We Democratic people know in our
own happy minds, in our own happy country that each
individual has a right to sing with the Psalmist of old, "We
are His people, and the sheep of His pasture." Our men
in high authority hold those positions because we, the
people, have placed them in that authority, and by virtue
of the same power we may recall any dignitary whenever
we may see fit. Nevertherless, when we foolishly leave
America, even in our reading, when we must look among
Englishmen and their history for the doings of our forefathers, even among Englishmen who have claimed always
to be free, when we find that our folks have lived among
these Englishmen and have been honored by them, there
comes a satisfaction of soul decidedly *un-democratic.*
Learning that said folks had been numbered among the
lords and ladies, we smile a bit broader, for it follows, so
we tell ourselves, that when such enumeration has been
possible, somebody, somewhere in that line of descent must
have been worth while. So when we introduce to you Mrs.
Robert Henry, we are nothing loth to say to you that she
was an English girl, born in the city of London, an uncle of
hers bearing the title of Lord Downing.

A word or two at this point about the Downings. Their
position in England was old, reaching back into the fifteenth
century. They had borne a part in that stormy time, had
seen many changes, some to make things better, some
otherwise. One of the many Lord Downings had felt no
small interest in the excitement in England grown out of
the growth and development of the religious idea of his
country, an excitement that held sway in part of the
fifteenth century and the next one. A member of Parliament, this certain Lord Downing had been absent with his
regiment—many wars were at hand—when he learned in
some mysterious way that a vote was to be taken in Parliament to settle matters between Catholic and Protestant
people. An enthusiastic Protestant, this Downing leaped
upon his black charger, put spurs to its sides, and rode pell-
mell to Parliament House. Fearing that he might be a

moment too late, the man urged that charger, white with foam and quivering with action, up the steps of the building, on down the hall, to clatter at last into that dignified English body and there cast his vote against all papal authority. A certain Dr. Johnson, an ornament of the Presbyterian church in Texas, related this incident a few years ago to a descendant of Mr. Robert Henry, closing the recital with these words: "Downings as a people allus raised er fuss, en Henry," pausing a bit for solemn emphasis, "they're raisin' hell yit."

We allow the reader to settle this matter for himself.

We have little to say of the youth of this niece of Lord Downing, but her after-life has been so replete with incidents that we are willing to pass by the youth with this simple statement of inheritance. We know that she had received a good education in London, better far, in fact, than the average woman of her day. She was rather talented in the gentle arts pursued by maidens of her day, was sweet, true and fine. She was pretty, too, with some aptitude in the matter of dress. At the pschological moment a good looking Irishman appeared on the scene, Robert Henry by name, a nephew of Lord O'Hara of Ireland, and courtship and marriage intervened as was natural and altogether agreeable to all concerned.

Nothing remarkable in all this. Many charming London girls marry gallant, whole-hearted Irishmen and fail ever after to regret it. Th s marriage was, however, the first step in a wild new venture, an unheard of venture—among their friends—a foolishness in everybody's eyes, not to be denied. Henry, happy lover and newly-wed, interested in crops and soils and horses and cattle, accustomed all his life to sixty or seventy acres of land in old Ireland, had heard of Texas, wild, boundless and free, Texas, where land—thousands of acres of it, rich, virgin soil, a-hungered for the plow of just some such determined Irishman as Henry—such land was to be had in this Texas and for the asking. These facts had been communicated in short order to his cherished Elizabeth, and as that lady stood before the altar beside her bonny Irishman, she knew that the voyage to the new world, across rough waters and in the face of rough winds waited her as a bridal journey. Hesitating? Fearful? Not Elizabeth. With all the assurance of a bride crossing the gang-way of a trans-Atlantic steamer of to-day, she took her place in the sail-boat provided for that voyage, and no distruct of the future lingered anywhere in her valiant soul.

Perhaps she was sea-sick? If so she suffered it without aid from stewardess or cabin boy. Maybe her very soul sickened before the nausea, augmented with every fresh burst of wind and wave, but no word of complaint fell from her ashen lips. A storm arose, brutual in its might, every mountain-high wave seeming to demand a reason for the invasion by so small a craft of the stronghold of the mighty deep. The storm blew the boat back, back to the starting point—such a good chance for Elizabeth to demand that her husband give the whole thing up as foolish! They but waited again the wind that must fill the powerful sail and put forth once more. They landed this time on the coast of South Carolina.

The Henrys lingered for a little while in that region. The man, no whit less interested in Texas, gathered together some farming implements, possessed himself of some horses, some oxen and some slaves, and along in 1832 began the last lap of the journey to Texas. They settled upon reaching the country, then a province of Mexico, on the Brazos river, They found a colony of people already settled in this region, but despite these people and their holdings, Henry, his heart full of hope and courage, realized his dream. He owned his land, a full grant of a league and a labor of it, more land it seemed to his happy Irish eyes than any one nation, even, in all the world ought to own, let alone one individual. And of that land so proudly accepted as a gift from the Mexican government, many acres remain after nearly one hundred years in the hands of his descendants.

So much for Henry's joy in the new possessions! Let's think a little bit now of our Elizabeth, the bride venturing thus with her land-hungry husband! She found herself before very long settled in a log cabin, bare of ordinary comforts, but the love in her heart and the hope and the determination covered all such bareness with a mantle of promise. Some day that home, or a better one, was to be replete with everything her woman's life craved. Well, perhaps, for our gallant lady that she could not look into the future! Well for her that she did not know save by hearsay of Indians and animals, ferocious, determined, totally unlike anything she had ever known in old Londontown!

The Indians were not slow to proclaim their interest in the new-comers. The little colony formed of families widely separated—each man, remember, claimed his league of land—offered them opportunities in plenty for the display of their savage ability. Elizabeth soon realized that for her own safety, she had best remain always within her cabin walls. But Elizabeth preferred to do always just as she pleased. She believed, too, what people had to say of Indians, but traits of her character stood in the way of her willing to suit her life, day by day, to the whims of this primitive man of the forest. Her staunch Presbyterian faith, her husband's faith, too, as it so happened, was opposed to any such servile obedience to the savage demand. Their cabin home completed, with thought of Indians in mind, they summond their friends and neighbors avowedly for a bit of public worship. Those neighbors gathered in quick obedience, tethering their ponies where they hoped no Indians might see them.

Now Elizabeth was brave as her Irish husband was brave, but they took no fool-hardy risks. With that little company of people gathered beneath their pioneer roof, hungry all of them for a simple religious meeting—together of folks of a common mind, Elizabeth saw the danger. Indians might fail to understand the religious service, but Indians could easily grasp the idea that attention thereto on the part of the white man made said man an easy prey for the savage watching from without. The idea once grasped by the Indian, and the white man was likely to suffer. So Elizabeth divided the group of people attending each service into those who *watched* and those who *prayed*. Two services thus necessary at each meeting-time, but no man or woman in either division grumbled at that. The prayers, the simple hymns swelled above the rafters of that log cabin, each bringing its comfort to those taking part. A little moment for change, and the other half the company, they who had watched from the door and between the logs of the rude home, took their turn at the swelling hymn and the word of prayer. God help all men and women who must face such difficulties in the path of their search for religious expression!

So far as we know the Indians failed to interrupt those services. Not from any preconceived idea of reverence for the white man's God. More than likely, if they possessed any reverence for anything, it was for the white man's powder and shot which they had learned had a convincing way all its own. How be it, these services continued, and the Henrys began to prosper in the new land. Henry's dreams of unlimited acreage were realized, and the man soon found that, with conscientious work and material aid from his slaves, food a-plenty could be brought from the ground. The years came and went, easily, naturally, bringing to our Elizabeth her children, four in all, each child an added care in itself, in Elizabeth's tender mother heart, an added blessing.

With the second child three months old, the trouble with Indians increased. Elizabeth, yielding to her natural bravery, found herself one day alone in her home, her husband having gone to the field and having taken all slaves with him. A runner on horseback passed the door, announcing the uprising of Indians and warning all settlers to get beyond the Navasota river. Elizabeth knew that this river was the boundary line of safety. She had frequently been told this by her now absent husband. Quick as a flash she ran to the barn, hitched two horses to the wagon, horses strangely left at home, put her children in the wagon, and with them a bag of gold, gold that must be kept in the house because there were no banks in all that vast territory. Thus encumbered, she put forth to obey her husband's commands anent the Navasota, trusting that he would somehow hear of the flight and overtake her.

When Elizabeth reached the Navasota river, the boundary beyond which no Indian dared peep his head, she found it swollen beyond belief, and the ford impassable. A crowd of refugees, alarmed, some of them paralyzed with fear, waited there, expecting torture and death. Elizabeth listened to their outcries, looked again at that raging water smothering the ford, and for the one hundred millionth part of a second, Elizabeth lamented with them. It seemed to her that right there in spite of all her past effort, she, with her little children, was to meet death at the hand of the savage, all because the stream was without its banks—

Not Elizabeth! Not by many million-million parts of a second! All the bravery of a thousand ancestors rose in its might. Downings of all descriptions demanded of this young mother one last supreme effort. She tied her wagon securely to a tree, tied one horse to the wagon, took one of the two children, wrapped it in a blanket, took up the bag of gold, and thus burdened, mounted the loose horse, forced him into the raging river and made him swim to the other side. There she found some more refugees, warned as she had been warned, and to one of the number, a woman who had come to meet her, she confided the child, still wrapped in his blanket, and to some man, rushing down to her, too, she handed the bag of gold. Back into the raging flood, this time without her horse! She swam back to the other side, she picked up the remaining child, wrapped her in another blanket, mounted the other horse and put out for her second brave crossing.

Well and good! What had once been done can be done again. Any coward can remind a hero of this fact. Weakening a bit, she urged her horse, onward, onward. Then a slipping, a sliding of that precious bundle in her arms. Her baby, God help her! her helpless little bundle was slipping from her! Onward, urging the horse, praising his weakening stroke, that bundle slipping, this time beyond her reach, to slip at the water's edge from the horse's back, to stagger up that bank, her heart one wild burst of pain!

And then, when she sobbed out her story, when quick hands unwrapped the blanket from her body, the little baby girl, the wee, sweet sample of human frailty and beauty, lifted its feeble cry for food, each cry a triumphant burst of assurance in the heart of that agonized mother. Her husband and slaves came up a little while later. To him she told the story of the crossing. They learned a few days later that every white man, woman and child, that had failed to make that crossing had been brutally murdered by the Indians.

When things quited down a bit, when the company of people began to make their way back to their once-threatened homes, Elizabeth thought of her bag of gold. To whom had she handed it? Friend or foe? She had heard that Indian raids had been sometimes announced in the hope of robbing people, already crazed with fear. This time the danger had been genuine, but the chance to rob in the confusion of the flight was none the less apparent. There was the chance that some desperate character had slipped in among that band of refugees waiting just such a chance as that presented by Elizabeth and her precious bag. She worried no little over the loss, blaming herself for her folly, losing in her blame all sight of the good she had accomplished in that one night's terrible adventure. Two years later, a man rode up to her door, a stranger. He looked intently at Elizabeth to be sure of her identity, explained that in the confusion following that hasty retreat to the Navasota river he had never been able to find her. He then returned to Elizabeth the bag of gold, every coin in number as it had been when Elizabeth last saw it when she had yielded it up that night in her moment of extremity.

At another time horses played no small part in Elizabeth's trouble with Indians. Of these animals her husband always had plenty, and very fine ones. Having been trained in Ireland to care for them and to look to the matter of breeding, Henry had selected good stock only for his Texas stables. The Indians eyed these animals in all covetousness, and Indians lacked the power, usually, to curb so dangerous a vice as covetousness. At a time well selected —when white men were busy—a crowd of Indians led by a rather noble-looking chief appeared at the outer gate. Elizabeth saw the Indians nearly a mile away. She immediately sent word to the men at work near the pasture to hide the horses in the brush. The young child thus sent misconstrued the message, failed to convey the idea of Indians at all—they were still half a mile away—and the men sensing no danger, turned the horses loose so that, according to the child, they might come up to the house to please Elizabeth.

Realizing the mistake, hearing, too, the coming of the enemy, Elizabeth ran to the lot, turned all the horses inside, drove them into the big stable, a substantial stable that boasted a genuine lock and a key some eight inches in length and probably more than a pound in weight. She heard the chief's step, even the step of the Indian who knows how to step light, as he came toward her, followed by his braves. She went on about her business. She urged horses to pass in, pushing the last one in with an energy impossible under other circumstances. She turned deliberately, coolly locked the door, then turning to face the old chief standing by this time near enough to touch her, she looked him coolly, calmly in the eye—and put the key in her pocket.

Nothing has ever appealed to an Indian like bravery. He sings of it in his natural, unearthly idea of music. He preaches it about his campfire. He instills it by hard means and by gentle into the heart and soul of his own offspring. This chief, seeing the bravery writ large on the face of this woman, looked long into the determined countenance, took in the poise, the carriage of her head and shoulders, and then he approached her gently, step by step —a little as a proud father might approach a gifted son— patted her gently on the shoulder exclaiming: "Bravey heap! Bravey heap!" Then a signal to his men, and the chief turned and rode away, followed by an astonished band, leaving a woman before her stable door, struggling, herself, with astonishment, wondering just a bit if it had not all been a dream.

But they had their joys, too, these pioneer women in their homes on the Brazos. They possessed fine horses, particularly was this true of Elizabeth, and they galloped in their few leisure hours across the wild, free plains, beneath the hanging oaks, sucking in the wind fresh from the Gulf, free, happy-hearted, in spite of Indians. They had their simple religious services. They had their "quiltin' bees," and they cackled happily about the broad square of the framed-in quilt, and they tried to out-rival each other in the daintiness of the stitches they let sink into the padded mass. They helped each other in every way, counting distance as naught, if some trusty horse waited their pleasure near the door.

They helped each other. Perhaps this thought justifies the whole of pioneer woman's suffering. To feel in your heart that, no matter the pain, somebody stands by to help! To feel that you have within yourself the ability to stand by another in just such an hour of need! This sense of mutual helpfulness crowds from the soul of men and women all thought of danger, all thought of fear. Certainly we know that the man wrecked on the desolate island, his own the first foot to press the sod, surrounded by nature's most lavish gifts, this man had gladly exchanged the greater part of those gifts for some human soul to help him, some human soul, and be this underlined—*that he might help in return*. Out of· this spirit of mutual helpfulness grew some of the deepest experiences in the life of Elizabeth Downing Henry. She had all her life been interested in the study of medicine—a youthful descendant promises to ornament the profession to-day (1928)—and she had read somewhat along that line in London. With the coming of her own children, she had made practical use of knowledge thus acquired. Denied the advice of physicians, she had been forced to experiment, and some of her experiments had proven to be worth while.

Real ability, another phase of the shining light, cannot be hid under a bushel. Her fame spread among her neighbors, and she soon found that some of her time must be given to this work.

Why not? Her home was well organized. Her husband, true to his early training, was the owner of much good horse-flesh. He had bred for Elizabeth's own particular use a black mare named Kitty. True in color to the gallant charger urged by Lord Downing up those Parliament House steps, Kitty was brave and daring, fleet of foot, quick of eye, and Elizabeth rode her on a side-saddle, enjoying the motion produced by any one of her springing, rhythmic gaits. On the back of this mare, Elizabeth answered every call of distress that came her way, day or night, refusing only when some of her own children were ill.

On one particular morning, before daylight, a man rode up to her door and told Elizabeth that a neighbor was desperately ill and needed her attention. Elizabeth had no thought of refusing, but right then there were points concerned to be considered. In its crib lay her three months old baby, dependent on her breast for its nourishment, and woe upon woe, out in the stable, Kitty, the faithful mare nourished her own colt in the same fashion. What must be done? Sending the messenger back to the sufferer, Kitty looked about her nonplussed. Then she did the only logical thing under the circumstances. Elizabeth called for her horse and mounted in time her saddle. Receiving into her arms her baby, she bade the slave-woman who held it up for her to take, to look after the other children, to prepare breakfast for her husband, giving that husband some special orders about one of the children who was not quite well. Then Miss Kitty's colt, black and sleek as his own famous mother, was turned loose that he for the sake of his own nourishment, might trot skittishly at his mother's heels.

Through lanes skirting fields barely visible in the morning light, on into the forest, the messenger sent on ahead already out of sight before her, her baby, her mount and its colt, her only real companions, Elizabeth made her way. A pistol in her pocket, to be sure, and Elizabeth's aim was sure and steady, but faith in Kitty's trusty heels seemed in Elizabeth's eyes to render that pistol of small use as a protection.

On now into the depth of the forest, the road barely showing beneath overhanging trees and shrubs crowding close either side. On and on, and then on an overhanging limb, Elizabeth saw a panther.

This animal in North America is usually classed as a cougar. In the South of the United States before the war between the States, the animal was classed by negroes as a "painter," a darkey corruption, probably of the word *panther*. The panther is no small animal as the cat tribe go, for his body is frequently four and one half feet long, and his tail, slender and black-tipped, measures another two and one half feet. He is an active climber as well as a prowler, and he has a scream that brings terror to any human heart within reach of the sound. Vicious, too, the animal hunts, not merely for food, but to destroy, sometimes killing an entire heard of deer, leaving each carcass as he kills it, no flesh having been taken from the bones. Elizabeth knew all this, for Elizabeth had been many times warned. She knew that the long, spotted body waited above her on that limb in order to take the life of any animal within reach. She could plainly see the greyish-white face, the snow-white of the breast. She could even see the long black whiskers and the shining eyes above them, now bent full upon her.

The panther, giving one scream, dropped from that limb upon black Kitty's colt. Cursed with a certain form of cowardice, the panther calculated on less resistance from the colt. The panther had not counted on Kitty. With the maternal instinct surging high, with some thought we are sure for her gentle mistress, Kitty sprang forward, then gave a backward leap toward the colt in danger. Keeping her seat in the saddle, holding her baby in one arm, making still some frantic effort to guide the infuriated mare, Elizabeth felt the mare leap upon the panther, heard her front feet, turned now into weapons of defense, beat hard upon the animal's head, heard the white, even teeth tear in the flesh of the panther just above his white breast, felt the mare bound again beneath her in one mighty leap, kept her seat, fearful to use her pistol with no chance for aim, kept her seat until the panther, cowed in the fight with Kitty, slunk off in the grass and disappeared in the coming of the light.

Business continued to prosper with the Henrys. The tyranny of Mexico became more and more unbearable to the Anglo-Saxon man. The same old love of freedom gave rise to the Declaration of Independence, and some men saw the light. The massacre at the Alamo, the result of disobedience to the commands of Houston, roused their little world. The massacre at Goliad added fresh cause for fury. When the story of this last sacrifice reached Robert Henry, he made his way to the scene of the butchery, helped wrap the body of poor, mistaken Fannin in a flag and with his own hands helped to bury him. He felt, too, the glory of San Jacinto. A gallant Irish soldier in his youth, he stood with Houston's men in that masterly-planned battle. He returned to Elizabeth, himself unharmed, but his soldier hat shot full of holes by the retreating Mexicans.

After these thrilling adventures, the Henrys settled for a time to the establishment of a permanent home on that league and labor of land. Two more children were born to them, their slaves increased in number, their horses and cattle keeping up the increase in no mean proportion. They built a nice house, a real house with windows and doors, with wide chimneys and open fires at a point in Brazos County known as Red Top. The children grew to maturity there, married and went into homes of their own —all on that league and labor of land granted Robert Henry by the Mexican government and given in turn to each child as marriage made it necessary or convenient. To-day the land remains in the family, not one acre ever having been sold (1928). Some of it is fine, some of it rough. On the rough stuff there has been talk of oil. One sharp descendant has exclaimed: "The Lord must have put something under it, for He knows nothin'll ever grow on it."

Elizabeth died on this plantation, surrounded by her children, her years having reached the full four score and five. She had lived under Mexican rule, under the Texas Republic, under the United States, under the Confederacy, to return again to loyalty to the stars and stripes. Through it all, she had been loyal to her own best self. She has left behind the property she accumulated. She has left behind the glory of her bravery and her daring, but, perhaps, of it all the sweetest and best, she has proven in this record made of her simple life the chief glory of the pioneer spirit—*"We helped each other."*

Data contributed by—

Mrs. H. B. Granberry,
Austin, Texas.

MRS. J. PICKNEY HENDERSON

BORN

FRANCES COX

We come now to think for a little while of a woman connected with pioneer times in Texas whose life at a cursory
glance seems wonderfully free from the usual run of ills
that befell other pioneer women. This certain Frances
was born July 21, 1820, in the beautiful old city of Philadelphia, and she was the second daughter of John Cox, her
mother being Martha Lyman of Northampton, Massachusetts. A fine combination, all things considered, a
mixture of Puritan and Quaker with a strong chance of inheriting the best in both, and in addition to this unusual
mix-up, her lineage on one side the house could be traced
without a break to a certain King Alfred of old England.
We have no disposition to shout aloud for this lady, to
boast as a disgusted schoolteacher once boasted that she
had "the blood of kings in her veins," a boast brought
about by the fact that certain young American hopefuls
under her immediate charge had refused her implicit
obedience. Neither do we entirely approve the answer this
boast received from another pedagogue, a crusty old maid,
long enured to the ways of the said American youth. That
reply was an earnest plea that the young teacher refrain
from putting always her worst foot foremost, reminding
the three or four assembled pedagogues that kings were the
most dissolute people in the world, and that it was poor
policy for any young woman to claim such blood as a filler
for her own young veins. No matter the justice or the
truth to be found in the old maid's advice, no matter how
much that vein filler had been diluted and divided and
parceled out, Frances felt the advantage of having come
from people who had kept *intact* precious family records,
and that influence moved her always to deport herself as
really and truly became the daughter of a scion of a noble
house.

Many beautiful things are told of this young Frances.
Among other accomplishments she seems to have possessed
a wonderful ability when it came to the study of foreign
languages. She knew many of them. She read her Bible
in French at six years of age, and then, as if to turn rapidly
about, she excelled all her young companions in the study
of mathematics.

Recognizing the unusual abilty of the child, her father
and sister decided that she must have better education than
America then afforded, that she must be taken where men
had studied for generations before Columbus performed
his wonderful feat, and so along about 1829, the young

Frances, guarded by her father and sister, found herself established in Paris, France, beginning what was to prove to be a ten year's struggle for knowledge. We do not know that Frances in any way rebelled at the exile from native land and country. A strong tie existed then between France and the United States—a tie that should be even stronger now (1928), and the enlightenment to be found in the older country was made a lot more precious for Frances by the thought of this tie between the more fortunate country than her own. Then, too, Frances was young. She was intellectually eager, she was musically inclined. Possessing a scant knowledge of the rudiments of music, she learned in France to play both the piano and the harp, and to play them both well. These with a few social diversions leave small room for discontent in the mind of any young woman.

Now in that French capital, some faint whispers of the stories of Texas and her independence had reached Frances. Glowing under a rather ardent allegiance to the United States, the republic then over fifty years of age, the heart of Frances had kindled, no doubt, at the thought of a handful of English-speaking people throwing off the Mexican yoke in order that they might establish, way down in the sunny, southern land, a republic like unto her own. Some little desire, perhaps, to see first-hand the glories of Texas mingled in her dreams, but Frances, busy with her music and her studies, put it all away.

And then, right there, in that gay French capital, attended by her father and her sister, at some brilliant function, no doubt, Frances met J. Pinckney Henderson, the distingusihed young minister from the Republic of Texas to the court of Louis Phillipe, the king appointed "king of the French" by its own chamber of deputies. Henderson wore the quiet, subdued dress of his country. He deported himself after the manner of a people free from affectation and deceit. He answered the young woman's witty remarks with deference and with courtesy, but with a wit that outrivalled her own. He was, to her, the American man. A step further, he was the Texas man, and he met the attractive young woman, satiated with French gallantry, on a basis of deferential equality that appealed mightily to her Puritan-Quaker blood. And Miss Frances, true to form, listened to the call of blood and accepted the wooings of the young minister.

With all her French up-bringing, Frances had retained a lasting affection for the Church of England. Moreover she was of English blood, and when the idea of marriage presented itself, Frances and her lover crossed over to England, and their marriage took place in St. George's Chapel in

Hanover Square. Shortly after the ceremony. the young
couple set forth for the New World—using as a means of
transportation one of the tiny little ocean-going steamers
at that time looked upon as marvels of invention. They
landed at Galveston, the port of the young republic, in
January, 1840. Of course young Henderson was glad to
be at home. He had so deported himself in the struggle
for freedom that his country had entrusted him as a
minister in a foreign land. He was glad to be back among
his own folks, to tell them first-hand of Paris and its glitter,
to have them slap him on the back and tell him that he had
done himself proud.

But what of Frances? The ten years spent abroad had
been the formative years of her life. The friends that
might have slapped her upon the shoulder were three
thousand miles of salt water removed from her. She,
accustomed to ease and gaiety and study and art, was
brought suddenly into the wild, new country, boasting an
acreage many times larger than France, all as yet a wilderness. Her very accomplishments set her a little apart
from the women of the young republic—so one must
think—but to be strictly truthful, Frances saw no room for
any such thought in the most careful survey of the situation.
Her ambassador-husband had brought her proudly home
to his own country. He had planned a home for them at
San Augustine in the eastern part of the Republic, and
thither she went, gladly, gaily, no shadow of a repining
in her happy young heart.

Somebody in describing this home failed to say that it
was a log house. That somebody seemed a bit reluctant
to set my lady from Paris down in such a place of abode.
That somebody "side-stepped" the issue by speaking of
the house as "the equal of any in the community at the
time." But Mrs. J. Pinckney Henderson, much in love
with her brilliant husband, seemed to care little that the
house was built of logs. She was so concerned with the
soft, fragrant breath of the pines surrounding that home,
so full of inquiry regarding every flower abloom in that
virgin forest, so happy in her own sweet woman's way, so
eager to do her part in making her husband's life a success,
that she gave little thought to the character of the walls
that protected them from summer's heat and from winter's
cold. With her husband's few slaves to help, she adopted
her household policies, dreamed over as every young woman
dreams over them, and colored now in their actual existence by many things learned during her stay abroad.
This being accomplished to her liking and her young
husband's delight, no doubt, she began a systematic study
of languages and mathematics, a carrying-on as it were of

the work done in Europe. She went even further. She studied law with her husband, studied it in earnest, and she mastered it sufficiently to do her husband's office work with no small efficiency after he had become established as an attorney, there in their new home. Henderson's partners in the business were K. L. Anderson and T. J. Rusk. When away at court, Henderson felt no uneasiness as to the conduct of business in his office. He knew that even if his partners were both called away that matters in his office would receive every attention, for he knew that his wife would be able to hold any case of any kind in hand until some member of the firm should appear.

Frances, with all this, had no idea of neglecting the religious needs of her nature. The young girl who had braved the English Channel in order to be married by an English clergyman must have possessed strong convictions in all matters pertaining to church association. The form and ceremony, the ritual in her church was a sacred thing in her eyes, but when she found such a thing beyond the range of possibility in this new home, she joined in with other people of other convictions to find as best she could some comfort in the exchange of religious ideas. She worked in what was known as a Union School. Thither came men and women of all cults, all persuasions, perhaps seventy-five in all, driving in several miles from distant points in the county. Of the corps of teachers in this Sunday school, only two were women. Most women in that day lacked Bible knowledge, or possessing the Bible knowledge, lacked the self-assurance that made them willing to speak in any gathering concerning sacred things. Mrs. Henderson and Mrs. Fowler, her warm personal friend, did not hesitate to teach in this Sunday school. Becoming acquainted with the young people of San Augustine and the community through this religious teaching, Mrs. Henderson conceived the idea of training them in some other matters as well. She brought to bear all the knowledge gained in France, all that pertained to things musical and things dramatic, and with no little effort persuaded the young people to give musical and literary entertainments. To her the results of the efforts of these young people must have seemed exceedingly crude, but the fact that the young folks continued to work with her proves that she kept all thought of crudeness locked deep in her heart as she went about this branch of the Master's business.

Some years after the beginning of this community Sunday school, an Episcopal church was established in San Augustine. You may be sure that our little lady was happy over this. She gave free rein in this new venture to her own enthusiasm. She had a church built for the con-

gregation out of her own private funds, the edifice costing
her about seven thousand dollars. She furnished the altar
with suitable silver and linen, placed a small reed organ
in the church, and then culling some of the best singers
from among her young friends, she trained them in the
music of the Episcopal service. The glitter, the form, the
pageantry, above all, perhaps, the music, attracted people
from a great distance. Some went no further, perhaps,
than a casual look-in. Some, being of Quaker or Puritan
ancestry—and remember our Frances was both—scorned
even the look-in, claiming that the whole matter was the
work of the "devil." But there were doubtless many men
and women who owed much at times to the hour spent in
that formal service, and whatsoever comforts or rests or
strengthens a weary soul must have its place in God's
eternal scheme. The church building, hallowed by this
woman's loyalty to truth as she saw it, soon fell to decay,
being rather faulty in construction, but the silver and
linen used in those services are still intact.

With all this work on hand, Mrs. Henderson was serving her family wisely and well. Her first two babies failed
to survive babyhood, but she brought up in her own
inimitable way three lovely daughters, born later in her
life, said daughters answering to the names of Frances,
Julia and Martha. Her husband, a foreign minister to
France when she first met him, back yonder in 1839, was
sent in 1844 as special minister to the United States. In
1845, after Texas had become a state of the Union, Henderson was elected governor of the state by the Legislature.
This brought our Frances of course to abide in Austin, the
young capital. From this proud office, Frances saw him
appointed Major-General of Volunteers in the war with
Mexico that followed the annexation of Texas to the
United States, and she was to learn later with many a
proud flutter of her heart, that the Congress of the United
States had voted a sword to her lawyer-governor-soldier
husband as a recognition of his gallantry at Monterrey. In
1857, this husband was elected to the United States Senate,
elected to fill the unexpired term of his one-time partner,
T. J. Rusk. In all hope and pride, Mrs. Henderson, early
in 1858, accompanied her husband to Washington, but her
hopes political were ended in the death of her husband in
Washington, a death which occurred before he had even
taken his seat.

In the death of this man, Frances Henderson had lost
more than is sometimes implied by the word husband.
When two individuals, male and female, maintain a home
together, bringing up together the children that come into
that home, there must come about a certain blessedness of

mutual trust and confidence that cleanses life of anything like real sorrow. But this marriage of Frances Cox Henderson had been even more than that. Through her own unusual mental ability, through her unusual training, she had been an intellectual help-mate for her young husband. She had mounted with him, step by step, her advice many times saving him endless worry and annoyance. When such annoyance did come, he had for his comfort the womanly hand, eloquent with feeling, twined about his own. She had for her comfort in such a moment the thought that he recognized the little hand and was grateful. But he was gone. The children, three helpless little girls, must be trained to meet the world as their father had met it, and hers the only hand to guide their untried feet.

With her own grief at last under control, the thought of the little girls became absorbing. She was possessed of some means. To actually work for her daily bread would never be necessary for our Frances. What more natural than the desire to take her own little girls back to the land where she, herself, had been educated, back to France where she first met and loved her gallant, distinguished husband? And what more natural as the shores of America faded from her sight that she should think of that lonely grave in Washington, that she should think of Texas and promise her troubled heart that before very long she would return and take up her life again in the land she had come to love because her husband had first loved it, and because he had served it with his whole heart and soul.

But human plans suffer changes—sometimes. The war between the States intervened in this instance. When the first wild news of secession reached Frances, her heart stood still. She had heard the rumble of trouble, even in her Texas home, and she had sufficient information on the subject to know that men had grown excited, that feeling— bitter beyond compare—had been given full reign. Remember, she, herself, had come of a mixture of peoples. The blood of the New England abolitionist mingled with the blood of the Quaker must have had some influence on her own feelings. Trained through those very ancestors to abhor slavery, she must have maintained yet a bit of that training. Leaning, as every woman leans, toward her own people, believing in them, upholding them, she was yet bound to confess that in her soft, Southern, Texas home, waited on by the very slaves the Puritans and the Quakers would liberate, listening to their laughter, catching glimpses of that slave life, free from worry for the morrow—*Massa* carried all that on his own shoulders— she was yet bound to confess that slavery as she had seen it had lacked most of the horrors pictured thereof by her own people. Remembering this difference of opinion, feeling it keenly, even across the broad Atlantic, Frances Henderson decided that it must be very much better that she and her daughters remain in Europe until the struggle was over. Cowardly? Perhaps—

During that long absence abroad, one of her daughters married a European. Afterwards, her daughter Julia married Edward White Adams, a sugar planter of Louisiana. He had met this captivating young lady in Europe. Some sweet southern sympathy had helped out his wooing, no doubt, for Julia, even as her mother had done before her, married her lover and turned her back on France, for the glory she seemed to expect in that sugar plantation in old Louisiana.

With this bride happily settled in her new home, Frances, she who had lately struggled with many contending emotions, decided that she must visit the bride, just to see, maybe, if that bride conducted herself as Frances would have her. Little record has been left of her opinion of the young wife's house-keeping ability, or, indeed, of the impression made on the mind of Frances by that vast expanse of cultivation included in her new son's premises. The fields in their beauty, their culture, their very cleanliness must have impressed her, but if so she failed to leave any note of it behind. She did find there, however, in old Louisiana, the Southern negro, just beginning to know he was free, and Frances set her down to study this new individual. Sometimes as a negro man, working now be it remembered, on "wage" for "massa" approached this boss, laid a tale of woe before him, begged and received bread for himself and family which he, under the new scheme of things, had not been able to earn, sometimes at such time, Frances and her Puritan-Abolitionist streak had a battle. The study, however, led her to write a sketch entitled "Prissell Baker, Freed-woman." Just what the nature of this sketch proved to be, we do not know. We do know that it was bound with other sketches from the pen of our Frances, and that Frances, remembering her youthful study, sat her down and translated the whole volume into seventeen different languages.

Frances drifted gracefully with the tide of life, busy in her own quiet way, helping all who needed help, her religious life in keeping with the pre-nuptial voyage in order that she might be married in the Church of England. She felt and cherished always the romance of her love's young dream. She fulfilled her vows in that she trained as their father would have had them trained, the children he must leave behind. Then having reached the seventy-seventh year of her age, without any previous illness to annoy either herself or anybody else, Frances Cox Henderson died suddenly January 25, 1897.

Data obtained from article by—

Dora Fowler Arthur.

MRS. JAMES SCOTT

BORN

SARAH LANE

A little daughter born in Hickmann County, Tennessee, to Garrett Lane and Nancy Hale, his wife, on May 25, 1803, was given the name of Sarah. In this same home in the course of time, Sarah met and loved a canny young fellow, James Scott by name, and history bears gallant testimony to the fact that he was just as much Scotch by nature as he was Scott by name. He was a little peppery, just to show that he was a Scotchman, but he was wise, too, and loving, and, according to Sarah, just and true. They were married in Tennessee but moved shortly after the wedding into Mississippi.

In the natural course of young Scott's life, aided by the wife of his bosom, he acquired many tracts of land, many houses and many slaves. He attained, supported again by the gentle Sarah, unto the proud position of Judge of the Supreme Court of Mississippi. A royal couple they made, he shrewd, honest, upright, walking fearlessly before the world; she gentle, accomplished, highly trained in every side of woman's life—a princess of young womanhood mated with the prince of her own choosing. Her apparel, costly as her purse might buy, was ever becoming, ever dainty. A peep into her mahogony-framed mirror brought a picture passing sweet, a picture not unlike those made by her own artistic efforts, for there were laughing, happy eyes, flowing curls, cheeks too rich in color to allow rouge with a tender strength of feeling spread over those features that presaged even then the glory of her woman's life that was to come after. Through the halls of her husband's Mississippi home, her light voice rang out, sometimes in song, sometimes in happy laughter. There her feet tripped their innocent way to the strains of music, and her soft white hand bade many a passing stranger "Godspeed" upon his journey.

But changes came into that life so rich in promise. When her husband's term of office was over and he began to look about him to take stock of his business, he found, as many a public servant has found at the end of his service, that his own individual business had suffered much. In Scott's case, it was all too plain that a fresh start must be made. To make that start complete in every way, a new country must provide the setting. Therefore in 1838 this cherished Sarah came with her husband to Texas. They took up a grant of land in Grimes County, joining old Washington-on-the-Brazos, hard by the Sante Fe Trail.

And what did Sarah Lane Scott find; she the tender-voiced, accomplished young woman? What did she find her position to be in this home in the new land they had chosen?

Dirt floors! She whose foot had lately trod the festal hall! Walls of rude logs for her, and no pictures, no tapestry to hide their ugliness. And scattered far and wide, yet ever near, a deadly foe, the ever treacherous Mexican mingled with the far more treacherous Indian.

What did she do, this young wife and mother? Sit her down to weep and sigh for past glories, past ease, past comfort? Not a bit of it! She gathered together the slaves they had brought with them. She answered the frown that seemed to ask why "Massa" had subjected them—and her to all this privation with a glance—a glance born of her proud position as director of individuals less capable than herself—a glance born of her loyalty to her young husband who had considered this move best for them. She pulled from the things they had brought with them from Mississippi the looms and spinning-wheels. She, the dainty lady of the mahogony-floored hall, super-intended the setting-up of the wheels and loom. She produced the cotton also brought with them, had it spun and then set the loom to work. And the first thing she ordered was wagon sheets and many of them, Why?

The journey from Mississippi had been long and hard. Wind had flapped and briars had scratched the wagon sheets to pieces. But why new ones? Surely the tilling of the soil, the supplying of food and clothing for her family and slaves had been a more worthy object! Well enough said in peaceful times in the ears of dwellers in the land of ease and plenty, but young Sarah Scott had come to Texas in 1838. No matter the determined spirit, the energy of pioneer women in early Texas, she must be ever ready to fly before the face of the on-coming Indian or the more deadly Mexican. The victory at San Jacinto had fired the world to believe in Houston and Burleson and Stephen F. Austin and the future they visualized for Texas. But the Mexicans had not all fled across the Rio Grande when it became known that Santa Anna had been captured. Those left behind the fleeing army plundered and killed according to previous custom. The Indians, surveying the poorly equipped army, sensing with little difficulty the frontier troubles of the new Republic, wandered at will from border to border. The wanderings of Indians has ever boded ill for the white man. In this particular region, the Bedias Indians stole cattle, sheep, horses, provisions, anything that might be handy. The Pontiac Indians came with baskets offering each basket in exchange for what it might hold of groceries. While the filling of that basket went on with meal or potatoes, the roving eye of the red man located any article he thought worth while, and the owner of said eye usually returned by night to avail himself of what he had discovered during the day. Was it not a matter of real foresight that made this young woman keep the wagon ready for flight for herself and family?

As time passed and children came into the home of Sarah, this fear of the Indians assumed tragic proportions. There was always the chance that some little child might unwittingly stray beyond the limit of rifle range. If the men followed the plow with rifles strapped to their shoulders, the women stood at the loom or the spinning-wheel, or bent to do the simple cooking over the hearth of the fireplace with another rifle just as handy. When it became necessary to take the corn to the water-mill some thirty miles away to have it ground into meal—and this was necessary about every two months—the men in one community made up a company carrying all the corn at once so that no man might be over taken alone and killed. Ten miles from the Scott home stood Ft. Comanche, and to this retreat, the men took the women and children and shut them up to wait their return from the mill. Imagine three or four families—maybe ten—thus quartered, each woman with her little children crowded about her at night, lying down cheerfully upon pallets on the dirt floor, dropping off anxiously to sleep night after night, wondering if the sentry—a woman, too, might be able to keep awake, wondering if, perchance, the men, gone together on the necessary errand, had been able to outwit the ever-present foe. Seeing the anxiety of mind in the faces of those women about her, shuddering herself at the thought of what this journey for the men might mean to them, Sarah Scott, led on by the spirit of the true pioneer, threw all her wonderful reserve power into the brightening of the long-drawn-out days. Under her leadership the women gradually began to laugh and to chatter. They exchanged cooking recipes and gardening ideas, and they told stories of days gone by. They indulged a bit in political discussions, all the while a quick glance around for the foe.

One day just as the trouble seemed farther from the countenance of them all, the sentry announced the approach of Indians in war paint and full battle array. They sprang at once to the defense, the defense that had long been planned. Each woman knew her part. Some moulded bullets, some loaded guns, and some, the nervier ones, shot them. On this one occasion, the aim, too, was true, for the second shot fired brought a

lusty Indian to the ground. His companions, deciding
that there were men in the fort for other shots had followed
close behind this deadly one, took their departure, and the
women settled down again to the old attitude of waiting
for the return of the absent husbands.

The advancing years brought some help. The nine
children grew, became able year by year to watch for the
Indians themselves, became in time grown men, able to
bear a sure rifle in defense of home and country. They
lived with their parents the normal life of the frontier
country. They hunted and they fished, they helped in the
field and with the stock. John Scott, the oldest son, had
as a special favorite among the animals an old white mule.
The Indians appropriated the mule from the pasture, much
to young John's dismay. Months afterwards, young John,
lounging around the one little store that had grown up in
the settlement, saw a strange man ride up on his old mule.
The man cheerfully returned the mule to John, confessing
that he had bought the animal from an Indian. The mule
was glad to come home. No matter how kind his recent
master may have been, the mule retained some knowledge
of Indians and their methods, for as long as he lived thereafter, no matter when a Pontiac Indian appeared within
a half-mile of the premises, the mule quickly gave the
alarm. Many a life was saved by the snort of the old
fellow, and he went to his just reward rejoicing in the name
of old Pontiac.

They prospered in the wilderness, these young Scotts.
They raised cotton and corn and hogs, Merino sheep and
cattle. The slaves brought with them to the new country
multiplied, and they bought others. Weary at last of the
responsibility of slavery, James Scott offered his men their
freedom. He went further. He offered each man with a
family a goodly piece of land and a mule and a plow. The
slaves saw nothing worthwhile in such an offer. They had
boasted too long they were aristocrats. They, according
to their own loudly voiced comments, were "Scott Niggers,"
and this left absolutely nothing more to be said. This
aristocrat laughed in his dear master's face at the thought
of freedom and land and a mule. The master, stung with
the thought of the negroes and their shiftlessness, would
declare in return that they were worrying him to death,
that he would set them all free and then they might shift
for themselves. Then the happy, care-free slave, son of
Ham, knew there was one way and one way only to solve
that difficulty. Tears and prayers were no longer of avail.
There was nothing left for them, lazy rascals, but the
"shovel an' de hoe," and, remembering the set tone of that

dear master's voice, they would turn to with a mighty will lest "Marse James might sure 'nuff sot 'em free."

While her husband struggled with slaves and the problems of barter and cotton-raising and corn and hogs, Sarah Scott was bearing her children, suiting her wants and theirs to the wilderness in which fate had placed her. Doctors were practically unknown, but from the store of things brought from her old home, she produced volumes of chemistry and works on herbs. Then her previous knowledge of botany came into play—not the kind of botany that consists largely in gathering and pressing flowers. The saying of an uncle who had been thought of as an herb doctor came to her mind. When two of her little children died from what she believed to be calomel poisoning, she planted medicinal herbs and used them according to her uncle's directions. Afterwards with herbs and compresses she saved her husband's life when the doctors, lately come into the country, had given him up to die. From this one success, her fame spread. She became an ever-present help in time of illness. She found it occasionally necessary to make a trip of ten miles horseback—Aye! twenty miles —to relieve some sufferer, but for all this she took no money. She looked after her slaves in the same way. She influenced her husband to build a big two-roomed log cabin, and she furnished it for a hospital for the use of the slaves. She picked a few of the more intelligent among the slaves, both men and women, and trained them to care for the sick, and no thought ever entered her mind but that she was doing the thing demanded of her by her position as James Scott's wife and the mother of his children.

James Scott was one of the sixty-one men who made up the Constitutional Convention held in Austin in 1845, the convention that had as its object the voluntary entrance of Texas into the United States. Previous to this, many of the politicians thus interested held caucuses in Scott's home. This home was a big, roomy, log house with puncheon floors with huge fireplaces at either end. Rude enough, but the furniture was good, most of it brought from old Mississippi, and the mahogony bureau vied with the hand carved horse-hair covered chairs in the question of real beauty. Colonel Wallace and Pinckney Henderson were among the many distinguished guests in that home. David Crockett had given up his life for his country before the Scotts came to Texas, but they had known him intimately in Tennessee. Crockett had made the race for Congress in his native state, and James Scott had financed the campaign. The race being lost, Crockett left for Texas. When Scott afterward suffered financial losses, the memory of his quizzical old friend, reinforced by the call of the new country, led Scott to come to Texas, too, gave him and his wife a tender consideration for all people interested in the formation of the new republic. So they gathered there, those Texas statesmen, in the big old log house and held their political discussions and formulated many of their plans, and Sarah Scott mingled with them and held her own end in the talk with little effort. She loved this company and the other company that came their way, for she loved light and laughter, and she provided always for these guests of the very best her garden and larder afforded.

But how she longed for the luxuries, the beauties, the graces of the "old house at home." In her dreams the rough-hewn walls became white as alabaster, the coarse, homespun muslin draping her shutterless windows became the flowing lace of old Brussels. The tallow "dips," the smoking pine chunk became the lamp of alabaster, and the puncheon floor the polished boards o'er which she had once tripped so lightly. These dreams, foolish phantoms of a longing heart, could never become a truth, but other dreams promised somewhat of a glad fruition. When the silk and velvet and laces she had brought with her became exhausted, when she was confronted with the necessity of wearing homespun dresses and russet shoes, her spirit rebelled. The loads of goods brought from time to time in ox-wagons from New Orleans were slow in coming. She watched, therefore, for caravans of movers into the new country. She begged from these people seeds for her flower gardens, new books and a bit of new music.

After a business trip to the East, after selling his slaves—such as would agree to the transaction, James Scott, with thirty thousand dollars in his pocket, was lost in the Gulf of Mexico in the equinoxial storm of 1856, he being one of those who went down in the steamer Nautilus. Denied forever afterward the companionship of her husband and lover, the longings for the days of a past glory grew ever more intense. They went with her down to her grave, there in old Grimes County, Texas, but in all her life she kept her face resolutely toward the light, and no man ever heard her complain.

Data contributed by—

    Mrs. L. N. Throop,
    Austin, Texas.

MRS. JAMES DUNCAN WILLIAMS

BORN

MARY SCOTT HILL

Young Mary Scott Hill, daughter of Middleton Hill and Julia Foster Walker Hill, his wife, according to her own accurately given account, was born twelve miles from the town of Bastrop, July 25, 1844. The spot of this pioneer woman's birth is still called Hill's Prairie, though the house once built there by her father was burned to the ground many years ago.

Middleton Hill first came to Texas in 1835. He overlooked the land and found that it was good. He obtained a land grant from the Spanish government, the ususal league and *labor*. Then he put back to his old home for his family, leaving his brother, Wiley Hill, and a negro slave named Beryl to hold the land while he was gone. Wiley Hill took part in the battle of San Jacinto, but Middleton Hill did not return until 1837, thus missing the joy and the satisfaction of helping in the fight that freed Texas from Mexican rule.

But escaping as he did the horror of the Alamo and Goliad, the joy of participating in the battle of San Jacinto, Middleton Hill and his family suffered the full measure of anxiety meted to the pioneer. This daughter, Mrs. Williams, after eighty-five years had passed, recounted scenes in the life of her mother as told her by her elder sisters that placed plainly and forever that mother's name on the honor roll of the brave. The oldest of Mrs. William's sisters, Sarah by name, a happy urchin, for children are happy, no matter the danger, longed as a child to play in the outside world. The substantial house that later made Hill's Prairie famous was not then built, and the four walls of the temporary cabin home were much of a restraint to young Martha. The mother understood the child's desire, but she understood something else better.

She knew the danger surrounding that liberty. So young Sarah was tied to a convenient table-leg with a hank of thread just spun by the negroes so that she might inhale the fragrant prairie air without straying off where the Indians might pick her up. To the practical, fresh-air mother of to-day this seems a little foolish, this fear of a human being, but fear of Indians in those days in this particular part of Texas was justified. The red man resented, and bitterly, the invasion of the white man, and he did not hesitate to show his resentment. Every few days, according to the account of this pioneer woman, a band of red-skins would sneak up in the absence of the white men and steal horses, calves, mules—everything in sight. The white men, the loss discovered, would trail them. Some of the live-stock would be brought in, but not until the women at home had suffered all the agony of fear—the fear that some white man among them would be brought home with an arrow in his heart. Then some bright day, the potatoes and corn-pone smoking on the fire-place, the coffee-pot ready beside them, the bacon or venison fried to a turn placed there, too, the savory odor penetrating far through the pure prairie air—Ah! Who could fail to recognize that odor? And who of all men could fail to appreciate it? Young Mary and her sister were not men, but they recognized the odor and its savor. Alas for such powers of recognition! They had many times to go hungry until a second batch might be cooked in the long, drawn-out, old-time way of cooking, for Indians, too, cared for the savory odor, and would step aside from the chase to wrest from the "white-face" the dainty morsel while her frightened children stood by fearful that the meal might not be the only thing the Indian would care to appropriate. Pioneer days! Ask of the angels what women suffered at the hands of such foes!

A question as to education brings a twinkle to the eye of Mary Hill Williams. She will tell you easily that she went to school in a little log cabin about a quarter of a mile from her father's house. This log-cabin had a puncheon floor. Can any young miss in our schools of to-day grasp just what a puncheon floor was? Logs split in half, and laid on the ground, flat side up and jammed together in the hope of closing the cracks. For desks? The same logs, sawed a convenient length, split in half and pegs inserted in the rounding sides to leave the flat surfaces to serve as reading-tables! Funny? Yes.

Well, young Mary attended such a school, but she could not at this date give the name of the teacher. When she was fourteen she went to a fine school in Bastrop conducted by Mr. and Mrs. Carmer. Middleton Hill later helped found Ruetersville College, and Mary's older sisters, Martha and Sarah, were among the first students at that college. Afterwards, young Mary was enrolled there, too, and she was taught there by the well-known Chauncey Richardson, a Methodist minister. The historian, Homer S. Thrall, taught a school at Bastrop before this which Mary attended.

"Mr. Thrall wore a wig," commented this Mary a little longer grown, "and we girls planned and planned to pull it off some night when he was kneeling at family prayers, but somehow, talk all we might, we never did get up the courage."

Approached unto the estate of young womanhood, young Mary Scott Hill, afterwards Williams, seems to have lived a rather interesting life. By that time her father had prospered in the wilderness, and had built up a fine business. Part of this business was a sawmill. With lumber brought from the neighboring forest and stones also found near by, Hill built his own colonial mansion, differing very little in outline and arrangement from the Governor's Mansion as it stands to-day. There were spacious rooms and cedar-lined closets, and there were negroes in plenty to keep it in order. There were many guests there from time to time, friends of Middleton Hill, himself, friends of the sons and of the daughters. In addition there was always the guest travelling to and fro, more than willing to pay for the kind of comfort they received there.

Many famous Texans were enrolled among these guests. Three-legged Willie and the genial Tom Ochiltree! Monsieur Saligny, the French minister to the Republic, was a warm friend of Middleton Hill and a frequent guest in that home at Hill's Prairie. He brought young Mary her first real doll, a pert, young thing, fresh from Paris. He presented her brother with some tin soldiers, also brought across the water. A nephew of Saligny, his brother's son, sick with tuberculosis, stayed in that house until he was well. General Sam Houston stopped there many times, just to have negro Henry parch corn to his liking. This same General found a gay crowd of young people on one visit to Hill's Prairie, and in a spirit of fun, the General made a wager with a certain young lady there, claiming that if she would make him a shirt, he would wear it tail out. She made the shirt, O nimble fingered young lady, and General Houston lived up to his bargain.

Perhaps no woman in all Texas felt the horror of the Civil war any more than did our Mary. With the Declaration of War, she was just seventeen years old. She was a student at Reutersville College. Her five brothers were enrolled in the famous Terry Rangers, and when the last one was called to battle, Mary came home to assume charge of the Hill plantation. Remember, that farm was worked by slaves, by negroes right then the bone of contention, the occasion of strife of brother against brother.

Mary must superintend their efforts in the hope that they might bring food from the ground for both white and black. She must go among them, conscious that meddlers from the North had already sown seeds of discontent in the hearts of the one-time happy, carefree people. Nothing daunted, she mounted her pony, day by day, her pistol strapped to the horn of her saddle. With head high, she went her way, saw to it that the slaves collected and branded the cattle, marked hogs, and sheep, and goats. She watched them plough and plant, and gather the crops. The war over, but Mary's brothers still away, Mary saw Union soldiers and *carpet-baggers* camp about the plantation. They drew all the water from the wells on the place and killed all stock within reach. Not satisfied with this, the *carpet-baggers* formed a plot by which the negroes were instigated to crime. They were instructed to kill all the old women they could find and promised in return that they should then select a white girl as a wife, a wife to follow him on into Mexico where he might have lands and silver and gold for the asking.

Among the Hill negroes, one man answered to the name of Henry. Led on by this new white friend, Henry conceived the idea of capturing his "young missus" our Mary in order that he might have her for his own. He knew that she was sick in bed, that she was alone, and too weak to raise the alarm. Steadily, yet in all confidence, he approached her room, lust shining in his big black eyes. Divining his purpose, she the helpless seventeen year old woman, lying on her bed, rose to a sitting posture. She answered the purposeful light in his eye with light just as purposeful. She raised her young voice in the tone of command, quiet, gentle but firm, the tone she had ever used with her father's negroes:

"Henry," and the room grew deadly quiet, "go back to your quarters."

A sudden stop, a sudden change in that purposeful eye, and Henry obeyed her. Obeyed the *young missus* because he must? Because he feared abuse? Not Henry. He bowed before that authority, because he knew that it was just and right.

In July of 1869, this young daughter of Middleton Hill became the wife of James Duncan Williams. They moved to Giddings, and one daughter, Mary, was born of this marriage. James Duncan Williams died there in 1885. Just about this time the wife of another man named Williams died in Giddings, and our Mary had the bereaved husband and father move his nine children into her own commodious home, and there she cared for them as their mother would have cared. The youngest son of that family, a man now crowding fifty years of age, speaks of her lovingly to-day as "mamma" and carries her tenderly in his heart. In addition to this work, she brought up and really educated sixteen children beside her own.

"Yes, we had some good times, too. We worked. We spun thread both cotton and wool, and we wove it into cloth. Sometimes the Indians would bother as I told you, but then we'd forget even Indians when we got together."

A smile between the two grand-daughters sitting near. "I must tell you," ignorant of the smile, "of this one time. Lou Caldwell, Sue Trigg and I went to spend the night with the Morgans, some young married people in Bastrop. The front room had a bed in it—all front rooms had beds in them days—and we had to entertain our company in this room. We didn't look for the boys that night, so after supper, just for fun, we got hold of some of Mr. Morgan's clothes and dressed up. We were prancing round right lively when up walked Bob Hill and Ike Jones to call on us. The other girls got out of the room, but I was cornered and had to hide under the bed. Mrs. Morgan went out and told the boys something and they went away."

Here an interested grand-daughter broke in.

"Did the boys get mad, grandma?"

"No! Bon and Lou were engaged fourteen years. They were married heap longer than that, and if Bob ever got mad at anything Lou ever did I never heard of it. I don't believe he ever did."

The deep quality of the old voice grew a shade gentler. The old lady had slipped into a description of the inauguration of General Houston as Governor of the state of Texas in 1859. She told of their coming from Hill's Prairie to Austin to attend the ceremony. Houston, according to this young witness, rode in a carriage with glass doors (it was called a "glass front" in those days) drawn by two satiny-black horses, boasting red plumes in their bridles, each horse covered with a netting whose tasselled edges reached almost to the ground. Some turn of events on that day had put young Mary into another carriage in the procession, and she declares that she felt mighty fine, riding along between lines of folks crowded thick on either side the "gulley" as Congress Avenue was then called.

"Yes," the voice gentler still, "it was a great time, a great way to live. Work, but we had comfort and peace and prosperity. None of your new-fangled things" looking about her, "but we had our slaves to wait on us, and so far as I can remember, they all liked to do it. I wish I had one right now to help me get to bed."

There was a chance, just a chance, that the lady meant nothing personal in her allusions to bed. There was another chance that she was tired of her questioner. At any rate the questioner took her grateful departure so that the old lady might have a chance to dream her own sweet dreams of life as it used to be on Hill's Prairie.

Data contributed by—

Mrs. Scottie Williams,
Austin, Texas.

MRS. TACITUS KENNERLY

BORN

MARY PALMER

In the country, the real country, in the vicinty of Montgomery, Alabama, and at a time when that place fell far short of being a city, Mary Palmer, a dainty, black-haired girlie, was born to John Palmer and his wife, some time in the year 1832. In that same country home she lived through the experiences common to normal childhood, reaching at last her ninth year, a keen, quick-witted child, her beauty increasing as the years flew by, her keen wit recognizing that beauty, and making, even at that tender age, the most of it.

In that ninth year of her life came the first real change for Mary. Talk of Texas and its glowing possibilities had penetrated even to that secluded part of old Alabama, and young Mary, listening always whenever the conversation held any remotest chance of interest for herself, drew in her mind a graphic picture of Texas and what it might mean. When it became settled that the family intended to emigrate to this new nation forming on the Rio Grande, her heart leaped, for Mary believed that great things lay in store for her in this marvelous new world.

The Palmers made the overland trip from Montgomery to Mobile, slow-going ox-wagons the mode of travel. This proved rather dampening to one of Mary's spirit, this mode of travel, and in this instance, Mary was true to her spirit, and her expectations suffered a distressing cloud. Her expectations, however, lived on, beneath the cloud, and when they reached Mobile, the very last shred of a cloud vanished from her horizon. The reason? Mary had had her first glimpse of real water.

When told that this water, sparkling in the sunshine, rippling in beauty beneath the more tender moonlight, when told that it stretched on and on until the sight of land would be denied, she stood and looked at each rolling wave, each driving current with a fascination beyond belief. Something of interest crept into her childish face, some of her fascination shone in her eyes, and the Captain of the steamer that was to bear them to New Orleans was not slow to read it aright. He singled her out from all that company of people—remember, even at nine years of age Mary was beautiful—and appreciating her inquiring mind, this Captain took time to conduct Mary all over the boat and to explain to her all the details of the vessel's working. The child's unusual thirst for knowledge on any and all subjects had appealed to that Captain with an appeal not to be denied.

At New Orleans at last where there were more boats even larger and finer than the one that had brought them hither, boats loaded with bananas, the first sight ever vouchsafed Mary of the rich yellow fruit, boats loaded with other foreign fruits, and Mary seeing and tasting and believing all such joys was gladder at every step that she had come, telling herself all the while that the journey brought them always to something better, telling herself that in Texas she must surely find the new Heaven and the new earth.

Alas for young Mary and her optimistic dreams! Their vessel brought them into port at Galveston, and her parents, persuaded by friends to do so, journeyed on to the little city of Washington-on-the-Brazos, and there set them down to make a home. One glance about that rough country, one short hour spent with the people of the vicinity, and Mary realized that her dreams of a great new world had ended in a condition far more uncomfortable than any she had ever known in old Alabama. Texas, shorn of its halo of romance, was at last the frontier country, and she, loving the light and laughter and noise of the great city, was here in Texas to stay. God help any woman face to face with such a cruel disappointment!

Some of Mary's anticipations and some of her disappointments may have lingered in the heart of Mary's mother. She, too, had looked upon Texas as the promised land, the land flowing with milk and honey. She found that the bees had departed for more promising fields, and that the cows, big, broad-horned things, had all gone dry. And she grieved, as Mary grieved in her childish disappointment, but she, being older and wiser, soon settled down to the drudgery of the life of the ordinary pioneer woman. She cooked—men and women and children must eat—on an open fire-place, aided by a Dutch oven, cornpone, she who had eaten nothing all her life but wheatbread—and she cooked potatoes in that first fireless cooker, the Dutch oven covered over with red hot coals. She spun the thread that they wove into cloth, she cut and sewed the cloth into clothes for her family—just as all pioneer women did—and young Mary, disappointed young Mary, must do her share. No school to attend, had happy, go-lucky Mary, conscious of her beauty, cared for such a tiresome thing as school. No church association to break the monotony of work. Hard? Aye, ask any young thing glowing with health and strength; ask any young thing cursed with the ambition that springs from that very health and strength if Mary suffered, and risk your last dime on the affirmative quality of her answer!

But along with the troubling ambition, Mary was young, and she grew up in a family of nine children, the girls, all of them more or less beautiful. The presence of such individuals, even in the wilderness, naturally attracts life and color and light. In the natural course of events, with Mary in her sixteenth year, life and light and color drifted into that pioneer home.

That home was a log house on a small farm, purchased with the remnant of Palmer's money, for he had reached Texas too late to receive a grant of land. The house had two large rooms, divided by a hall, this hall so wide that an ox-team and wagon could be driven through it. Dirt floors throughout the hall, but the rooms boasted puncheon floors, logs split in halves, the rounded side placed in the dirt, leaving the smooth surface, rather the flat surface up. A very good floor, provided the logs had been smoothly split, but it is a recorded fact that pioneer mothers became expert at locating and expelling splinters from the bare feet of their children. This floor necessitated a step-up from the hall of six or eight inches, but, tiresome as this may seem to my lady housewife of to-day, that puncheon floor with its step-up was a welcome change from being forced to live eternally in the dirt. Beds were built into the rooms, slats, but no springs to hold the mattresses, with a feather-bed if the house-keeper were thrifty—to make it comfortable. All furniture was home-made from hand-sawed lumber. Add to this the meagre equipment for cooking, and one sees the outline of that home in which Mary, her eyes all the while growing blacker and her hair growing more shiny, grew to womanhood.

With Mary in her sixteenth year, there came into her life the big romance. It took the form of Tacitus Kennerly, himself only sixteen years of age, big, bonny, blue of eye and masterly of spirit. He had come of good old Tennessee stock, his ancestral line counting senators and judges and governors among its members. His parents had come to Texas in 1828, settling at Washington-on-the-Brazos, receiving the usual grant of a league and *labor* of land. In 1832, the same year in which Mary had been born back in old Alabama, in this Texas wilderness, Tacitus Kennerly began his own earthly career, his parents and his brother, Josiah, born previously in Tennessee, forming the family. In 1836, both parents died, leaving these Kennerly children alone in the world, save when friends and neighbors interfered in their behalf. But they both grew and thrived, human kindness is a great characteristic of pioneer people, and the neighbors of these children were shining examples of this fact, and the boys managed always to maintain a hold on that league and *labor* of land. Something, perhaps the blood of statesmen flowing in their veins, kept them straight-forward, honest and clean, and showing all these characteristics in his young face, Tacitus walked unwarned in to the presence of young Mary Palmer.

He walked into a snare from which he was never able afterwards to extricate himself. Inured to poverty, young Mary had but to cast her eyes upon this Tacitus, had but to cast them once and to let them fall becomingly, and from that day forward as long as Kennerly lived, she held the upper hand, and, be it known, Mary never scorned to use it. They were engaged almost at once, but the wedding for some reason was deferred until they had each reached the mature age of nineteen.

That wedding was an event in the community. Throughout the three years of waiting, Mary and her sisters had been busy providing household stuffs. Homespun sheets, pillow-cases, towels, blankets, too, for the wool was at hand, and the cloth from which her wedding dress was made came from the loom in her mother's own house. Even the women who made that homespun cloth failed to lay any claim to beauty for this product of their tiresome labor, but when young Kennerly beheld his bride, dressed for that wedding ceremony, that dress was perfect in his eyes. Or, mayhap, he had no thought for the dress at all. As long as he lived, however, he described her appearance on that wedding eve in glowing terms, dwelling on the beauty of her black eyes and her blacker hair, ending always proudly with the statement that his wife's waist measured that night but twenty inches, and that he could easily span it with his big, loving hands.

They were married at six p. m. under the big oak trees near the house, and after the ceremony they sat them down to a wedding supper, the table set for one hundred people. They devoured roast pig and roast turkey, pies and cakes and preserves, corn-pone with a bit of flour bread, precious beyond compare, thrown in by way of elegance. Coffee —remember at that time in Texas the coffee-pot rarely ever got cold—and maybe a glass or two of something stronger as the daylight faded, as the stars went down.

The days fading had little effect on the revelry. Pine torches, that is rich slivers of pine, taken from some specially rich log at its very heart, had been nailed to the oak trees on that spacious lawn, and with the coming of night they were lighted, and the one hundred and more people, come some of them a distance of fifty miles in ox-wagons and on horseback, danced all night to the tunes furnished by the negro fiddler, danced in the house on the puncheon floor, and in the yard in the dust, danced on in happy abandon, Mary's beautiful young sisters sharing the revelry, setting snares for the brave young gallants waiting a chance to follow young Kennerly's footsteps a-down the apparently flowery path of matrimony. The old folks, too, took a hand, they whose feet were many times weary of the saddle and of the house work, they whose every hour bore some fear of Indians or animals that might molest them unaware, and when the long journey back home had been accomplished for these wedding guests, they rested their tired bodies, and relived the fun and the frolic many and many a day afterwards when the heat of battle or the stress of work made the present for them a little tiresome, a little discouraging to the men and women determined to do each his very best.

The months passed on, Mary going with her husband into her own home, probably similar to the one she had left. By and by children began to creep in as children should do under such circumstances, and at some time while her first child was a baby, the young couple went to live in Blanco County. Another unwelcome change was this for Mary. A certain type of civilization had drifted into the community surrounding old Washington-on-the-Brazos. The foremost men of Texas congregated in that little capital, and Mary was thrown with them and enjoyed them. Indians had grown weary of the little settlement, and wild animals gave it a wide berth. This was not true in Blanco County. Indians prowled, ready to kill and destroy, and Mary soon learned to keep her trusty gun handy, hanging in close reach upon the cabin wall. Wolves howled by night in the mountain fastnesses, and the real mountain lions were no uncommon sight. The latter animals sometimes made their slinking way to the very doors of that mountain home, and woe be it to the individual, man or woman, whose shot missed the mark.

The Civil war brought new responsibilities to Mary. Early in the strife, her husband and four of her brothers joined a company of volunteers in support of the Confederacy. Despite her motherhood, despite the hardships and disappointments, Mary was at this time, still enthusiastic, still in the lead of any enterprise coming her way. When that company of soldiers, including her husband and her brothers, was ready to leave for the front, Mary led a group of women in the making of a flag and then marched the women down to camp and there, despite her lack of education, Mary, of all that group, was chosen to make the presentation speech. The women, recognizing her fitness, were firm in their demand, and Mary complied with that demand to her own credit and to the everlasting delight of that lover-husband who was wont to span her twenty-inch waist with his loving hands.

The excitement over, Mary went back to her lonely home, to the care of her children, there were two by this

time, to the management of the big wild ranch, stocked
with common cattle, threatened day and night with wolves
and bears and mountain lions, with Indians, too, grown
bold, no doubt, over the thought that the white man was
away. Busy all day struggling to provide food for herself and her babies from that wild stretch of land, oversee-
ing the activities common to a ranch, fencing, branding,
driving the cattle, all these strenuous matters requiring
her personal attention, and yet Mary fared very well.
Alone many times with her children throughout the solemn
watches of the night, alone save for her old father, her ears
startled now and then with the howl of the wolf or the cry
of the mountain lion. Alone, thus, this Mary who had in
her youth looked upon Texas as a haven of delight! Alone,
too far from the scene of battle to know just what had be-
fallen her husband and her brothers, wondering many
times in the dead of the night if she, alone there in that
cabin home with her helpless babies, was not destined to
live thus alone the balance of her changing life. Cowardly
in her wondering? Not exactly.

Her trusty gun always on the wall behind her, two fine
dogs, both well trained to protect her, made of her home a
very tower of defense. Nothing could ever harm her under
such conditions, so she told herself when nervous over the
cry in the still of the night.

A pitiful incident proved to her how futile, indeed, that
defense might be. In the uncertain light of an early
morning, a mountain lion approached her cabin, intent on
fresh meat for his breakfast. One dog immediately gave
fight, and the noise of the battle awakened Mary. She
siezed her gun, gave a glance through a crevice of the door,
grasped the cause of the noise and waited. The first dog
to show fight in her defense was already down, practically
dead, but the other brave fellow, going to the help of his
loyal companion was still unhurt. A shot from her rifle
might save the life of the second dog. Dared she risk her
uncertain aim in the uncertainty of the dawn? Would it
do for her to shoot and miss the mark thus calling the
attention of the wild animal to her and her helpless children? Would it do, could she stand there and see the faithful dogs torn to bits, her fingers at rest upon that powerful
trigger? In that moment, Mary realized that discretion
is sometimes the better part of valor. Mary realized that
to save herself and her children she must stand there and
let the wild animal do his worst. And as that animal
slunk away in the coming of the day, Mary glanced at the
heap of shining bones shredded of their meat, and somehow Mary grew old with the very horror of the thought
that life might hold such things for those of her kind.

With this trouble still fresh in her mind, Mary was called
to her front gate one morning, and there a mounted man
demanded of her her entire drove of cattle, claiming that
the Confederate army had issued orders that everything
available must be sent to the front for the comfort of the
soldiers.   Now, Mary had done her part towards the boys
at the front.   She had seen her husband and her brothers
depart for the scene of battle, and she had cheerfully done
her part toward keeping up their neglected work.   She
had heard in a round-about way that the war was drawing
to a close, and as Mary looked into the face of the man who
had demanded her stuff, there came into her quick mind
the idea that the cattle entrusted to this man for the army
would never reach any such destination.   Her eyes fixed
upon that man's face, she thought of her little children dependent upon the milk of that herd for their very lives,
and right then Mary's patriotism, coming into conflict with
her motherhood, received a hard blow.   With head erect,
with eyes deadly quiet, Mary explained the conditions to
him who would make this demand.   The reply received
lacked a little of the deference Mary had come to believe
her just due at the hands of men, and then before the man
realized her intentions, the trusty gun was again in her
hands, and this time no qualm of conscience, no fear of
consequences, stilled the finger upon that trigger.   The
man again made the demand, but this time the tone was a
little less rough.   Mary saw the gain she had made, and
in a voice deadly quiet, she went on: "Come inside that
fence, and I'll shoot."

The man read her purpose in her cold flashing eye, and
the gun looked every bit a gun, even if a woman did hold
it, and the would-be marauders quietly slunk away, leaving the cattle grazing quietly in the yard.

Tacitus Kennerly returned from the Civil war soon after
this affair, returned as all Southern soldiers returned, lean
of purse and rather broken in heart, and together he and
Mary patched up the home, fallen to waste during his
long absence, then took up life again as the brave must take
it up when they have met and borne defeat.   They continued to live there on the Blanco ranch with their two
children for several years, moving first to Creedmoor, then
finally to Austin where they took up their residence with
one or another of their proud descendants.

Times changed and then changed again, and the lovers
married in their nineteenth year, beneath the flare of the
pine torches in that home near Washington-on-the-Brazos,
began to be looked upon as among the ancient people of
the earth.   They had been born in the same year, Mary
back in old Alabama, but Tacitus had come into the world

in 1832 in Texas, and the seething, boiling condition that prevailed prior to March the 2, 1836, had colored the whole of his childhood. They had married, had brought their two children through the troubles of childhood, troubles increased a thousand fold by the demands of a frontier life, and in their old age they found themselves, these young lovers, again under the shadow of war.

The World war claimed two grandsons, and Mary saw them march away, not quite so patriotic over their going as she had been when her husband and brothers had left her in defense of their country. Tacitus, perhaps, shared a little the boyish satisfaction of the real soldier when he felt himself thus becoming a part of the great adventure, but Mary, soon after the grandson's departure, fell ill, lingered for three months or more an invalid, then passed away some time in February, 1918.

That lover of her youth lingered a little longer. Interest in the boy "overseas" gave him strength in his old age. The boy, himself, felt the old grandfather's interest, felt it enough to write him long letters, between battles, between long marches, telling him many interesting bits of the foreign land where he fought beneath the flag of his own country. Toward the close of the war, the boy wrote that he was soon to come home, and that he looked forward to many happy hours with his grandfather, for they would be old "vets" together.

Tacitus, apparently still hale and hearty, carried that letter about with him, showing it to any who cared to read it, bragging of his plans when the young "vet" should reach home to make merry with the old.

After one particularly happy afternoon thus spent, his throat being a little raw and tender, he went to the City Hospital for a little treatment, and later asked them to put him to bed for the night, just to save him the trouble of going home. In that bed he was found dead the next morning, a smile upon his patient, old face.

One significant fact remains. They were buried, these young lovers grown old, side by side, in the beautiful cemetery of Oakwood, just east of the city of Austin. In the old State School for the Blind, back in 1918, the University School of Military Aeronautics, preparing men for the World war, was close at hand. In a newer part of the cemetery, but recently purchased, and still a level field, the soldiers were drilled every afternoon. At each funeral of the two people, Kennerly and his wife, the commands of the officers, the tramp of the feet, the blare of musical instruments made a noise of sufficient volume to drown the voice of the minister who vainly tried to speak his words of comfort.

Brave young souls, meeting and bearing together life's joys and life's sorrows, bound together with an unfaltering trust, and unfailing love, and in their very death they were not long divided.

Data contributed by—

Mrs. Fred Cloud,
Austin, Texas.

MRS. JOHN CHAFFIN

BORN

SARAH LIVONIA CRIST

A little more than two years after the battle of San Jacinto, with Texas still unsettled, still haunted by Indians, her colonists still wondering a bit just how far Mexico might go in her efforts to make trouble for the young republic, with all these things to annoy, the Indians must needs make a raid upon the white people living then in Anderson County. Stephen Crist, in company with other men in his neighborhood had gone to avenge the raid, to bring back if possible some of the stolen horses. He had left his wife, Annie Parker Crist, in Fort Houston. The fort was at that time located in Houston County, the territory is now known as Anderson County, and the women were often left there as a matter of protection during the enforced absence of the men.

During one of these seasons spent in the fort, on May 25, 1838, denied the help of doctors and the sustaining presence of her husband, Annie Parker Crist gave birth to a little daughter. No white-capped nurse in attendance, no antiseptic walls to ward off germs, but when that little girl, later given the name of Sarah Livonia came into the world, the arms of Annie Parker Crist's own black mammy were ready to receive her, ready to do for the young miss just as she had already done for two generations of her mother's people.

She grew and she thrived, the little Sarah Livonia, controlled and petted and spoiled and unspoiled again by this same black mammy. Perhaps she wore neither lace nor satin in her pioneer home, and this, of course, was a sorrow to her "black mammy." We know that she had small chance of education there, but as the years went by, Sarah Livonia learned to read and to write as well as to card and to spin and to weave, even to cook when her "black mammy" failed to be around to prevent it. She had no need to waste time acquiring the arts incident to the chase, the man of her choice, the object. She had been endowed in the hour of her birth with the indefinite, intangible something which makes men turn from the beaten track, and in 1854, this being the fifteenth year of her life, Sarah Livonia became the bride of John Chaffin, himself a resident of Anderson County. She went with her husband shortly after the marriage to Limestone County. They settled there upon a five hundred acre tract, built a home there, and Sarah Livonia lived in that house full fifty-eight years.

The house, viewed from the standpoint of the pioneer woman, was rather pretentious. Built of logs, of course, but it had four large rooms down stairs, and yet another upstairs, and reached by a bona fide stairway. Afterwards the house was covered on the outside with clapboards, and is to-day standing (1929).

There are many things to be done in the establishment of a new home in a new country. John Chaffin must needs ride after stock and look after fences. He had brought fine horses to Texas, some of it registered stock, and fences must be in order lest such animals stray. This left to Sarah Livonia the management of the farm. She watched the negroes as they cleared the land. She superintended the gardening, the dairying, and she dispatched all this business thoroughly, satisfying, even herself. The Indians left the little white woman alone in her work—to them such work was ever the work of squaws—but the horses, kept ever near the house, were to them a temptation.

An Indian has little idea of the resistance to temptation under any circumstances, and when a fine horse is the object to be obtained by the simple little matter of theft, the Indian forgets that there is such a thing as sin in the matter of theft. Knowing, too, that the only white man on the place was often away from home, Mr. Red Man, in this instance called together a goodly number of his fellows, and they planned a raid upon Chaffin's usually well-protected horse lot.

Sarah Livonia's quick eye saw the Indians coming. Contrary to Indian expectation, she had a few slaves close at hand, and these men went with guns and rifles to protect the horses. Sarah Livonia, satisfied that this part of the business had been duly managed, remembered with a pang her beautiful silver. Most of the silver had been the property of her own mother in her own youth, and with heart thumping hard, Sarah grabbed it up, tea-pot and spoons and forks, all thrown together, pell-mell into her apron, and then she rushed to the smoke-house. Beneath the slabs of bacon hanging from the rafters, aye, beneath the very fire that furnished smoke necessary to the curing of that bacon, Sarah Livonia hid the precious silver. She had on the way closed the precious box—the silver had been kept always in a box to be ready for just such an emergency—and she dug a hole, making the dirt fly like some industrious squirrel, laid the box within the hole, covered it first with earth, and then she spread the coals back and coaxed them into a blaze, never leaving the spot until satisfied that its appearance was perfectly natural. Indians loved silver, almost as much as they loved horses, but no Indian in that bunch thought to look beneath the fire for the coveted article.

During the Civil war, Sarah Livonia found herself set some heavy tasks. She raised flax on her own premises and spun and wove it into fine linen. She had her sheep sheared and spun the wool into thread, then wove it into cloth, the cloth being used for uniforms for the Confederate soldiers. Then with news that her husband was stationed on Galveston island, Sarah Livonia put out to see him.

There was no hysterical idea connected with this proposed visit. Sarah Livonia had no desire to fall upon her husband's breast and there sob out her woman's griefs. She was impelled by the wifely desire to see her husband supplied with bodily comforts, and she made her plans accordingly. She took two ox-wagons, personally selected the oxen that were to pull them, loaded them with sides of bacon, a whole barrel of molasses with clothes including socks she had knit, and other things, designed to comfort men in camp. There were bits of sweet things, surely, and with one negro man for company, aye, one negro man to drive the second team, she put out from Limestone County through a lonely country to see that husband stationed on Galveston island. The trip, successful in every way, consumed in all about eight weeks. And a colored man her only escort!

And what did she do, when she left for this trip, with the little boys and her baby girl that had been born to her there in the Limestone County home? Easy enough! She left them with that same black mammy whose arms had first enfolded her, left them with implicit confidence while she went to help her husband, to help the man who right then did battle to keep this same black mammy in her so-called chains. Chains! Maybe they were, but that black mammy never knew it. She gave to her mistress and the children that service that grows out of unbounded love and trust, and if she had ever been shackled, her own loving heart had never realized it. And,—when Sarah Livonia returned from that visit to her husband, did she demand a detailed account of a daily happenings among her little flock? No need for it. The log house was in apple-pie order, the children a bit gentler in spirit than usual, and Sarah Livonia had but to take up her life again just where she had put it down to take command of her ox-wagon. And the negro man, her solid companion on that long journey! Had she no fear of him? Nay, for carpet-bag rule had not then been experienced.

Sarah Livonia belonged to the Primitive Baptist church. Upon her own land in Limestone County before the Civil war, she erected a church building. It is standing to-day

(1927), still functioning, the association from time to time being held there. She was an earnest member of her church, a hard worker, a deep thinker, and whenever she rose to speak, she received the respect of the entire congregation, for they knew she always had something to say worth while.

When it became known in her neighborhood that Sarah Livonia Crist Chaffin was ill unto death, the neighbors gathered in great companies, longing to help, trying to show some appreciation, most of them for her services she had rendered before her own strength had failed. They lingered, waiting, hoping, some of them for some miracle that might spare the precious life. Such miracles fail to happen. The spark of life, fanned to a persistent flame by her indominitable spirit was fading, was passing on as God in His eternal wisdom ordained, and in that home sanctified by a thousand tender memories, she passed away in December of 1912.

She walked in and out before the Lord, blameless, and those who lived about her felt it.

Data contributed by—

Mr. Araminta McClellan Taulman,
Fort Worth, Texas.

MRS. BEN HUBERT

BORN

ANNA MARIA SIMPSON

On the tombstone erected in honor of this woman, these few, simple words are carved:

"She came to Texas with her husband in 1836."

A whole volume might be written of any woman of whom this could be said. Such coming meant that somebody had looked ahead. Somebody had visioned the future of the great wilderness lying between the Sabine and the Rio Grande, and somebody had sufficient faith to give up home and friends and ease, in some instances, luxury, that they might come on ahead to lay the foundation broad and deep for the millions of souls who were to come after. This simple statement carved on that block of stone meant, too, that somebody in this day and time possessed sufficient appreciation, sufficient gratitude to realize that the fact contained in that simple statement placed the woman, Anna Maria Simpson, high on the roster of our Texas women.

And suppose we append to that statement a few more statements just as true, just as significant. She had been born, this Anna Maria on May 20, 1818, at *Handyside*, Baltimore, Md., her father being Walter Simpson, Jr., a prominent hardware merchant, and her mother, Annie Russell Handy. Her mother died in 1832, and her father in 1835, thus leaving the seventeen-year-old Anna and her sister Bessie alone in the world. There must have been considerable property accumulated by these parents before they died, for we are told that John Eger Howard, Joseph Barling, an uncle by marriage, and Charles Carroll of Carrolltown, a cousin, had been appointed guardians of these lassies.

We wish we might have known a little more right here of young Anna Maria and her disposition. Her guardians were all men of prominence in their day. Her parents had possessed unbounded faith in their integrity, their judgment, else they had never been asked to assume this trying obligation. Carroll, the intrepid signer of the Declaration of Independence, with his partners in this new duty must have feared a little of the unmanageable in the beautiful wards, for it is stated calmly in family history that upon the death of their parents, Anna and her sister, Bessie, were sent to live with a brother in Tescumsia, Alabama.

No doubt the young ladies made that brother's home resound with music and with mirth. Not much doubt is there, either, that said brother came to understand the reason for the guardian's attitude in the matter, for he, too, saw that flocking beaux and sighing swains could become a nuisance. But most annoyances grown out of youth and its follies have a way of passing, and Anna Maria, tripping away to Mobile for a visit with friends, met Ben Hubert, a man just a little older than herself, met him and loved him and married him—and came to Texas with him in 1836.

Love in a cottage or love in a palace had a way, after all, of being just love, pure and simple. No man has ever dared estimate its power, either for good or for evil. In this instance, it led young Anna Maria to give up much in the way of material comfort, led her to undertake a journey that must have seemed to her friends the very tip-top of foolishness. She came with her husband by boat from Mobile, across the Gulf, landing on Galveston island. She was glad to put her foot upon ground again, this seventeen-year-old bride of a few weeks, glad to stroll a little about that island, wondering as she strolled just how much the island resembled the mainland, her future home. She found there a few huts, weather-beaten and rude, and men stared at her through windows, their wooden shutters thrown wide that they might the better view this woman, this strange phenomenon on the island. She realized as she looked about her, this seventeen-year-old bride accustomed all her life to luxury, she realized that she faced the duty of home-making for her young husband somewhere in that land stretching out to the westward, a home based on the same fundamental principles that had characterized her home and his ever since they were born, and she must have felt, as she looked about her, gay, happy, sweet-spirited sprite that she had been set the thankless job of making bricks without straw.

Her first home failed to be the well-nigh proverbial home of the early Texan—the log cabin. She found herself housed in one room above what was known in early Texas times as a saloon. Meagre furnishings, no doubt, and through the cracks in the floor of that room the young wife could see plainly everything that happened about that bar below her. The rough gamester of his time came here for his libations of whiskey and wine. The few polished men of the day did the same thing. They swapped lies and horses, they made and lost bets, they told ribald stories there as they drank, alluding to a side of life hitherto unknown to young Maria. Sometimes they fought, usually when men had there indulged not wisely but too well, and a pistol shot, its ball penetrating that floor between them, was no uncommon occurrence in the life of young Maria. From this home, a trifle precarious we must admit, Maria went to that of her husband's brother, Matt Hubert, for

her own man had been summoned early in the fight to
join the Texas army.   This home was in the Nacogdoches
district, peopled even then, with the very cream of Texas
people, and young Maria enjoyed a short respite in this
settlement of men and women who were a little more of
her own kind.

Not long after this happy change, Ben Hubert became
what was known in early days as an Indian agent.   It was
his business to establish trading posts between white men
and Indians, to use his influence to see that the Indians
met the white man squarely, to settle matters of dispute,
to help if need were in the matter of trade, the barter of
skins, buffalo meat, the white man cheerfully paying for
these necessities with beads and gew-gaws, so dear to the
heart of the Indian.   In this business, Hubert took his
wife and family—they had a baby by this time—to the
very outposts of civilization, for methinks young Maria
refused to be left behind, took them in the hope of establishing a home for them and himself, and this spot, remember,
on the very outskirts of civilization was no other than the
land facing the Brazos river, reaching up the sides of that
river as far as Gainsville.   In that wild region they lived
as best they might on venison, wild turkey, buffalo meat,
and this last in plenty, and the plain cornbread made of
meal ground every day on a hand mill.   Sometimes they
woke in the morning to find Indians camped thick around
them, looked at those Indians, wondering whether they came
peacefully for the business of trade, or if, because of this
coming, the life of every white man and every white woman
was in danger.   Sometimes the Indians had with them
pack mules loaded with the skins of wild animals, hides
already dried, moccasins and strangely woven blankets.
The trading of these articles accomplished, the children of
the forest then wended their way back home, leaving no
heartaches behind, leaving a little hope that the future was
to be brighter on that score.

But—when the Comanches put in an appearance, usually
by the light of the moon, the situation was far different.
They came from Ft. Sill on the reservation, and they came
on the war-path, greatly outnumbering the whites, and
there was nothing left for the white man to do but scamper
for safety, his women and children, his household goods
piled helter skelter on his good old trusty wagon.   One
caravan of people attacked by the Comanche Indians, said
Indians bent on the theft of cattle and horses, found itself
outnumbered two to one, but gun powder proved to be a
wonderful force against the bow and arrow.   Then, too,
this tribe of Indians would sacrifice five men in battle
rather than leave one dead body where it might fall into

the hands of the enemy, for they firmly believed that the
soul of the man whose body was left at the mercy of the
white man was forever denied admission to the happy
hunting ground. A nice belief, perhaps, surely nice in this
instance for the white man, for each Indian sallying forth
to reclaim a fallen body was shot by the white men, and
the enemy thus put to flight.

Maria and her husband later established themselves in a
real home in Bryan, Texas, close by that same Brazos
river. The place was then called Booneville, and the advance of civilization had already appeared. Hubert established himself in the real estate business, proving a
genuine pioneer in the honorable trade, being, in fact, one
of the first men in all Texas to take up the business. He
became right-of-way agent for the Houston and Texas
Central railroad being built right then between Houston
and Bryan. In the city of Bryan, Hubert erected a large
colonial home, a long step upward from that room above the
saloon. There Maria gratified her home instincts to the
limit. The blood of her ancestors rose to her assistance,
and the men of Texas, gathering about her table, must have
thought a bit of old Maryland, of the Carrolls of Carrolltown, and the other choice spirits who had surrounded
Maria in her youth. They must have made some allowance for the inheritance and what it had done for this
daughter. Hubert had, in fact, built there in Bryan a
genuine Southern mansion, and the hospitality, superintended by Maria, encouraged and abetted at every turn
by her husband, was in evey way the old Southern hospitality.

Maria took particular pride in this hostess idea, and her
friends were frequently summoned to "supper," and those
friends knew when the summons came that they would
find upon that table a sample of every variety of food to be
found in the country, and a sample cooked under Maria's
directions, and therefore "to the queen's taste." Maria
had many slaves to do her bidding, and preserves and
pickles and jellies were made in abundance in the fruit
season. Cordials and brandy, all home-made, divided
honors on the sideboard with bottles of old Rye or old
Bourbon, and he who entered that dining room drank his
full in the good, old way. Maria, not a teetotaler herself,
frowned upon him who would imbibe too freely, and was
not slow to let him who slipped feel her disapproval.

Ben Hubert, bearing his part bravely in the struggles
for independence of Texas, giving of his time and talent to
help shape and form permanent policies for the young republic, living long enough to see some of these hopes
realized, died in Bryan of yellow fever, in the year 1867.

Needless to say this death brought its sorrow, and with the sorrow borne until the first ragged edge was worn a bit down, this death brought about for Maria many changes. Maria had lived in that colonial home in Bryan some thirteen years, had enjoyed home and all it can mean to a home loving woman. She was to find, even Maria with her eleven children to think about, to help, to call upon, was to learn that a home without the partner who helped establish it has lost a beauty that can never come again. So she sold the home whence the children one by one had fled and followed some of these birds of passage to Rockdale. She made herself comfortable in the homes of these children, kept herself always well in hand, so that she was a blessing wherever she went. She had been a great reader, even when she managed that hospitable home in Bryan, and she kept abreast of the times in every branch of human progress. She died in 1911, aged ninety-four years. Through the association with every kind of people, the highest, and sometimes the lowest, the riff-raff that will gather about in a new country, she maintained the inherent ideas of behavior due her station in life. She stated that she never learned to dip snuff, but through her broadness of vision she never failed to add that she knew some very nice ladies who did use the despised article. She likewise never failed to maintain that the early settlements of Texas boasted men and women of education and of culture, and when we study this life with all its hardships, all its disappointments, its triumphs and its glorious attainments, we are inclined more and more to believe implicity just what this woman has had to say of the early pioneer.

Data contributed by—

Mrs. E. B. Phillips,
Rockdale, Texas.

MRS. JOHN HOUSTON

BORN

ANN GORDON WHITE

On the famous old battlefield of Blenheim, on August 13, 1704, in grateful token of swift messenger service, a Duke of Marlborough knighted one John Houston, giving him as his coat-of-arms an hour-glass with a slender greyhound reared upon his hind feet at either side, his front paws resting the while upon the rim of the glass. The widow of that John Houston came from Ireland to America in about 1740, bringing her son, John, with her and settling in old Virginia. Many Houstons sprang in time from that swift messenger, and one of them, his name John, too, was born in Tennessee, and there married Ann Gordon White. This same Ann had never been able to convey messages in time of battle, but she lived her simple, forceful woman's life according to her day and environment, and there are a few things worth remembering in the course of her existence.

The young couple first made a home in Savannah, Tennessee. They lived there in ease and comfort, Houston being employed in a kind of general business, buying and selling live-stock, farming on a small scale, making a home according to the ways of the time. Three children were born to them in time, three daughters, and Ann White Houston, gentle, tender lady of high degree, watched them grow in grace and fear of the Lord as became the mother of Presbyterian faith. Business reverses came to them, the failure to make a paying business of the manufacture of staves, and John Houston and his wife found themselves facing bankruptcy. News had come to them in Tennessee of Texas and of the work done there by a cousin, Sam Houston, and John Houston conceived the idea of moving to Texas to *recoup* his fortunes. The idea struck terror to the heart of his wife. She loved the refinements, the daintiness of the life in Tennessee, loved it for herself and for the sake of the daughters growing up around her. She dreaded the hardships necessary for herself in the wild country, but when her husband announced his determination to emigrate, she stifled her personal objections and began her solemn preparations.

Her first thought was for her children. Not particularly well educated herself, she yet had ambitions in that line for her little girls. Knowing her own inability to teach the girls as she would have them taught, she shrank from the idea of taking them into the wilderness during the formative years of their lives. She looked into the face of her oldest daughter, Martha, into her thoughful eyes, thought of her habits of study even then at seven years of age, and Ann White Houston experienced her first pang of renunciation. She determined to leave that daughter for her own good in the home of her bachelor brother, John White, a home then presided over by a spinster sister. And the daughter agreed, for obedience to parental authority was a strong element of the Presbyterian idea. Ann Houston's own father sensed something of his daughter's reluctance. He pondered a long time as to what he might do to render her going more cheerful. The result of that pondering was the gift to Ann of a man slave who had made the gardens in old Tennessee, who would thus serve Ann in the new country.

So the journey was begun, Houston and his wife and the black man and the two little girls. After a time they took boat at some point on the Mississippi river, on a small craft compared with boats of to-day and ladened with supplies of the people seeking homes in the new Southwest. The boat took fire in the hold, and there was a wild scramble for deck and cabin. The fire was soon under control, but in the confusion the colored man, belonging to the Houstons, was washed overboard and drowned. To Ann, accustomed to slaves and their unfailing care and attention, the event assumed disastrous proportions.

The Houstons reached Texas in 1838. After a short stay in Shelby County, they settled near Nacogdoches, but moved shortly afterwards to Hardin County, then known as Jefferson County, and made a home a few miles from Villiage Creek. In this home, John Houston farmed, raising everything necessary for his table save flour, sugar, tea, and coffee. He had herds of cattle and a tannery that prepared the skins of animals for use. Ann Houston superintended the garden about her log-cabin home, and she planted a flower now and then in the hope of bringing some of the natural beauty of the woods to her own door-step. Seeing this enjoyment of flowers on his wife's part, John Houston began, too, to watch for flowers of unusual beauty in his passing to and fro about the country. On a necessary trip to Beaumont, a small town in that day, he saw for the first time a cape jessamine in bloom. Struck with its beauty, he cut one carefully, placed it for safe keeping in his hat, and bore it home—a distance of sixteen miles and made on horseback. From that one cutting there came in time many immense bushes. She planted roses to run about the log cabin, and when the two plants bloomed together it formed a beauty even more pronounced because it existed in a land where few people thought of beauty.

The Houstons had no trouble with Indians. They came in small companies to the house bringing split baskets for sale, hoping in the Indian fashion to exchange said baskets for the amount of meal or potatoes each basket might contain. They eyed the big log cabin Houston had built with favor, catching glimpses of hens' eggs laid along those walls inside the cabin for safe-keeping, noting the comforts the white man's squaw had been able to draw about her. They came one cold, rainy day, seven or eight of them, to interview this same squaw on business of barter, and as the dark came down before they were quite through, the white man's squaw bade them spend the night in her big comfortable kitchen. Seeking her own bed a little later, she wondered just how foolish she might have been in her tender-hearted consent to such strange guests. To her surprise the Indians were grateful for her kindness when ready to leave the next morning, and more surprising than all, these Indians always designated as a silent people had talked with each other the whole night through.

Into this same home, about 1843 came one Reuben Pusey. He hailed from Pennsylvania, and he had come to Texas for his health, then sadly impaired by the long, cruel, northern winter. He paid nothing for his board in that Texas home, but to the Houstons, particularly to Ann Houston, his presence was a great blessing. Trained in the ways of Northern men, Pusey could help about the house and yard without serious hurt to his sense of manly dignity. He gathered plums from the nearby thicket, he gave advice to the little girls, taught them some little bit, and in a manner so gentle that the little girls paid full heed always to anything he might say. He gave Ann Houston herself some wholesome advice as to the daily life of the little girls, and she harkened unto what he said, remembering his wider experience in the world. Another little daughter was born to the Houstons while Pusey made his home with them, and he in a quaint, refined way all his own, claimed the privilege of naming her Esther Pusey in memory of his wife who had died some years earlier. Pusey stayed in the Houston home until his health seemed to be completely restored. He contracted a cold, however, a little while after returning to Pennsylvania and failed to have the strength to endure it. Ann Houston grieved sincerely when she heard of his death. Part of the original Pusey head-right, bought in at a tax sale by a devoted husband, stands to-day in the name of Esther Pusey Houston, the little girl named by Pusey for his dead wife.

But even this association failed to cure Ann White Houston of her longing for old Tennessee, and the comforts and luxuries, the social and religious refinements that be-

long always to an older country. Thinking constantly of
that daughter left with her brother, paying sometimes as
high as a dollar for the transportation of a letter from the
daughter, Ann persuaded her husband that they must put
back overland after the ten years had passed in order to
bring the young lady daughter to her parents' home. John
Houston finally agreed to the journey, and in 1848 they
started. Anne saw to it that an old white woman was left
in charge of her log-cabin home. She even arranged things
to suit the comfort of the woman, but she packed all her
little keepsakes, all her silver and linen among the clothes
they were to take with them. Ann was determined never
to see Texas again. She was going to take her little
daughters just as far from the rough, uncouth frontier as
possible.

That homecoming, after ten long years of separation,
must be left to the imagination. Back and forth through
all that portion of the state in which they had lived, seeing
old friends and relatives, attending service in a real house
of worship, listening to refined conversation, Anne revelled
in the things her soul had longed for in her pioneer home.
Nor was she in any way disappointed in that daughter left
behind. Ten years had developed her beauty. Ten years
of ease and culture and plenty had given her the manner of
the princess of the blood royal, and Ann Houston, looking
at her, thanked God that she had been wise enough to leave
that daughter in old Tennessee.

But—after a few months of uninterrupted delight, John
and Anne Houston became restless. They hid it at first
from themselves and then from each other. Finally the
truth had to be acknowledged. They were homesick for
Texas, homesick for the wilderness and the Indians and the
new republic that had of its own free will become a state
of the Union. And back to Texas they went, accompanied
this time by the elegant young lady-daughter.

Ann Houston took up her life in the new state with a
lighter heart. She went straight back to the old home on
Village Creek. Her few neighbors had much to tell her
of the Alamo and Goliad, of San Jacinto and Houston and
his victory. She in turn had much to tell of old Tennessee,
but she gathered her children about her and together they
scattered the comforts they had brought with them about
the cabin home. That eldest daughter, Martha, highly
educated for her day, opened a little school in order to
teach the neighbors' children and her own sisters. The
travelling Methodist ministers stopped many times in that
Presbyterian home, and more than once they held a religious
service in the Houston home, a service attended by the few
neighbors, Indians and slaves. All this owing to Ann's

determination to throw the best of influences about her children.

But, her lighter heart notwithstanding, Ann's difficulties were by no means over. The country was still infested with rough men, with dangerous characters, and there was little law to keep them in order. With her grown daughter at home, with the little girls fast growing toward womanhood, Ann bethought her many times of Reuben Pusey's solicitude for the little girls. The law of hospitality, the only real law of that time in Texas, demanded the open door to indiscriminate guests. She had kept her children out of sight when such guests happened in, and had managed to maintain her own personal dignity so as to prevent anything approaching the free and easy behavior toward herself. But one evening, her husband gone for the night, two men appeared begging for shelter. She laid out supper for these visitors, a supper of cornbread, venison, coffee and a little touch of green from her own garden, and then she sat her down to serve it as best she could. No matter her efforts, the ruffians sighting her homespun dress and her coarse shoes, taking in the rude furniture of the rude cabin home, these bullies began to make remarks—to each other—but the weight of those remarks set Ann Houston's cheeks a tingle.

With the men asleep finally in the one spare room of the cabin, with her children—even the baby, her only son, asleep in the lean-to, she sat long before that dying fire pondering the situation, struggling between her pride and her fear of her guests, but when she rose to go to her own bed, her head was held high, and her lips usually placid and sweet, were drawn in a line, determined and stern.

When the two men, hastily dressed (they had removed little of their clothing for the night's rest) appeared next morning for breakfast, Ann read in the eye of each a plan for fresh assault upon her ideas of the consideration due woman. The color rose in her cheeks, but she stepped lightly toward the lean-to and summoned her daughter, even Martha, the child so tenderly guarded the night before. Martha answered the summons.

"My daughter, Miss Houston, gentlemen."

There may have been an emphasis on the word *gentlemen*. There was more than emphasis in the vision confronting those ruffians looking toward "My daughter, Miss Houston." Melting brown eyes, curling auburn hair, alight in the soft morning air; soft, dainty cheeks, a little rosy now under the masculine scrutiny! A manner a princess might have envied, a dainty woman wearing a dress of bombazine, fitting to perfection a form well-nigh perfect in itself.

Nothing was said. The men sank back into their chairs silently, and then moved said chairs without scraping over the puncheon floor, so as to be a little nearer the table. Ann Houston served the simple meal in prim decorum, but with heart alight. She was conscious of victory, the victory of beauty over the uncouth and the rough.

Shortly after this episode, Houston moved his family to the town of Jasper, now the county seat of Jasper County. Mr. and Mrs. Montrose taught a school there, and finding the curriculum of her liking, Martha Houston entered this school and was the first young lady in that county to receive a diploma.

Ann Houston lived long enough to bury her husband and all her children save one. This one, named for Reuben Pusey's wife, married David Williams Doom, a son of Alta Williams Everitt-Doom, and they moved from Jasper to Austin in 1875. Ann Houston went with them, taking up the hard position of mother-in-law in the home of a struggling young lawyer with a wife, three children and two nieces to support. No unpleasant feeling ever existed between that young lawyer and his mother-in-law. He once walked more than a mile on a warm Sunday afternoon to spend an hour with her just, forsooth, because she had left his home to spend a week with Martha Houston Mattingley's children. Her grandchildren have tender memories of her voice, her manner. Never physically strong, she remained young in that youth that sees the other fellow's side, and she died peacefully in the presence of that one daughter left to her and the son-in-law of whom she had never spoken, save to bless him.

Data contributed by—

Mrs. D. W. Doom,
Austin, Texas.

MRS. JOHN DUFF BROWN

BORN

SARAH HARRINGTON WADE

On a big farm near Nashville, Tennessee, on February 11, 1808, a little daughter, Sarah Harrington, was born to Austin Wade and his wife, who more than likely bore the same name, Sarah. Fate had placed this little girl in a Christian home, a home wherein the Baptist church ranked supreme, and throughout her life, Sarah was true in the main to its counsels and its teachings. What other advantages in addition to this church relation came to Sarah from living in that certain neighborhood, we are not now prepared to state. We do know that Columbia College was afterwards built on the site of that Tennessee home, and this would lead one to believe that the Tennessee home had been maintained among people who cared for culture and knowledge, else the next generation had never sacrificed itself in order that a college might spring to life on the old familiar spot.

In that same farm house, about 1823, with young Sarah barely fifteen years of age, one John Duff Brown appeared in the family home, and we of another day and time are not loth to believe that the customs, the beauties, the aches, the pains of courtship were carried on in that old farm house. This John Duff Brown had been born in North Carolina, not far from the Tennessee line, on January 6, 1806, had lived, we suppose, the life of the normal young man of his times, and his marriage to Sarah took place July 13 (brides of to-day take notice) in the year 1826. Simple annals of two simple young souls obeying in the beginning of life the promptings of nature.

Sarah began her married life in a large stone, two-storied house, standing to-day (1903) on South College street in Nashville, Tenn. It was a country house in those days, the confines of the city still far, far removed, and every luxury, every convenience possible, including the service of many slaves, was at hand to render Sarah's life comfortable. Four children were born to her there in that home, three girls and one boy, Franklyn T. Brown, known afterwards throughout Texas as Frank Brown.

Early in the year 1830, Sterling C. Robertson began the move that was to bring the company of people known to-day as his colony to settle upon the upper Brazos. Some personal admiration for the brave colonizer, influenced largely no doubt by the spirit of the times, maybe, some inherent desire for life in the new country among things wild and free induced John Brown to join with Robertson in this venture, and Sarah, being a true wife, went about her preparations for departure, just as many other women did, without complaint, but a bit solemn over the whole thing.

Solemn! To leave home and kindred, to leave luxury even of the poorer kind as we might term it to-day, to go to make a home in places, perchance, where no white man's foot had ever trod! Dare you in your ease and comfort of to-day suggest any hilarity on the part of any woman face to face with the thing that lay right then before Sarah! But she went on about it, packing a few things precious for their association, packing many more she felt sure would be wanted in the wilderness. Medicines, linens, flannels, for Sarah knew that the move meant for her the breaking of all hope to supply herself with these things.

But all was at last ready. The canvas-covered wagon, packed to the limit with the things Sarah had collected, with provisions, with seed for the planting in the new coun- try, the two horses chosen for the pulling of the wagon, and Sarah gathering her four children about her, took her seat in the wagon beside her husband, and they turned their faces toward Texas.

The trip consumed the better part of a month. Through Mississippi, West Tennessee, Arkansas, and North Louis- iana, they found the road infested with highwaymen. These outlaws were under the leadership of the celebrated J. A. Murrill, and much caution had to be used to escape their robbery. They encountered, too, a few streams swollen by recent rains, learned from first-hand experience that forest mud can stick, but there were some redeeming features to the long journey. They camped at night, and Sarah was forced to cook their meals on an open fire built of crooked wood that had an ugly way of burning out in spots and tilting the skillet and the coffee-pot, but she managed them through it all, managed the hoe-cake over the glowing bed of coals, and sometime—nay many times, they had squirrels and birds shot while on the way, and fish, too, caught from some deep, dark stream to add a tasty bit to the supper. When the weather permitted, the children looked upon the journey as a lark, but it is safe to say that Sarah Brown crossed the line into Texas that November day in 1835 with a feeling of thanksgiving that she was near her journey's end.

This first stopping-point was a hamlet named Wheelock, but before the end of the winter Sarah and her family had gone on to Nashville, Texas, and had there established her first permanent Texas home. The house was palatial, in keeping in every respect with the buildings that housed the leading men of the settlement. It consisted of three big log cabins, the largest eighteen by twenty feet, the others just a bit smaller, and all three rooms were joined under one roof. There were puncheon floors, welcome change from the dirt beneath one's feet, no matter how splintery they might become. In this home Sarah heard the false alarm of Houston's defeat, and from its roof she took her part with many prominent people about her in the famous run-away scrape. A little daughter, Mary Louisa, was born there May 5, 1836.

This palatial log-house, surrounded by other homes just as palatial, occupied by people just as interesting from every standpoint as Sarah, was raided many times by the Indians. The alarm would come sometimes when Sarah was alone in the house save for the children, and there was nothing for her to do but gather the little brood about her and flee to the woods, hoping to find a hiding-place. She managed thus to save her own children, but during one of these raids, she saw one baby thrown by the Indians into a bunch of prickly-pear, saw the frantic mother dash in to save it, saw the Indians snatch it from her arms again and again until the swollen little body, suffering a thousand pricks from poisoned spines, was hardly recognizable, saw the savages laugh—an Indian laugh is rarely audible—in their fiendish glee, to ride on leaving the mother alone with her grief but otherwise unharmed.

Brown moved his family in the winter of 1839-40 to Washington-on-the-Brazos, and there he erected another home similar to the one the family had enjoyed at Nashville. The idea of associating with men of standing, men of culture, had probably influenced Brown to make this move, but he failed to enjoy it. He died November 18, 1840 of pneumonia.

No matter how many times Sarah had differed with her husband as to the best method of procedure for them and their little flock, no matter the dozens of times she had been impatient with her husband, when she stood beside that dead body, she knew that the real hardships of life had but begun. She knew, for Sarah was no fool, that it takes a good round sum of money to equal one good active man when it comes to the providing of even the bare necessities for a family of growing children. She knew that the burden of all this must fall straight upon her own frail shoulders. In addition to this, Sarah felt in her heart that she faced a desolation, the like of which had never before come into her life. Brown had been a brave man. He had been characterized as a brave soldier, a crack shot, a fearless scout. He had been, too, a tender husband, and death had taken him.

To use a very expressive Texas phrase, Sarah had to rustle. She continued her residence there in her log house, planting gardens, raising chickens, looking after things, doing a bit of work here and there for a neighbor. She learned, as every woman of strong character learns if the opportunity demands it, to stand alone. The girls, her little daughters, grew to womanhood and followed in the footsteps of old Mother Eve in that they took unto themselves husbands. The oldest daughter, Martha Ann, married Francis Dietrich in that home at old Washington-on-the-Brazos, some time in 1845. Be it remembered, Sarah was a staunch Baptist, had received the rite of baptism by immersion in the Brazos river, but at this daughter's marriage they made gay according to custom, dancing all night by the light of the moon or the pine torch or the bon-fire, whichever mode of illumination was most convenient. The young couple went to Austin, and being in no wise selfish, they took a sister of the bride along for company. This young woman, answering to the name of Lydia Jane, soon married William H. Cushney, and then Sarah decided that she and the rest of her little flock would find life more pleasant in Austin with these daughters close by.

So some time in January of 1846, into another wagon, twelve big oxen the motive power this time, Sarah placed her household wares and her three children and began her journey. James Deitrich, a neighbor but in no way related, a colored woman and a colored driver completed the little company. The weather was cold in the beginning, and the camp-fire at night was a luxury. They made at first as high as fifteen miles a day with the ox team, but bad roads slackened this pace materially at times. In the western part of Washington County, Sarah, sick and tired of the sight of mud, began to feel that the journey must be given up, that to pull and strain against the bog was not only useless but foolish. All day the rain fell, sometimes in gentle patter for hour upon hour, then again in showers that blinded one in the face. Once or twice this rain turned to sleet, but just as she decided that she had made a mistake to undertake such a journey, the sun came out, smiled as a January sun can sometimes smile in Texas, and one day of the glory of its warmth and light put to flight Sarah's forebodings. She reflected that no Indians had bothered them, no outlaws of anykind had tried to molest them, she told herself that wood and water had been handy all along the way, but when the ox-team pulled in at Well's Prairie, just twenty miles from Austin, when they found there a cordial welcome and a real house to sleep in, Sarah gladly accepted the invitation. Glad to stretch her weary bones between sheets, clean and fresh, above mattress and feather bed, glad to feel once more the tender beauty of a real welcome from one of her kind!

They were up and off again the next morning, but mud, deep and sticky, restricted their pace that memorable day to five miles per day. However, they reached Austin before very long, and Sarah set herself again about the business of making a home, of bringing up the remnant of her little family.

Among the new things to be met in Austin, Sarah found that her hitherto unknown son-in-law, William H. Cushney, was a writer of no mean ability, and that he was at that time the editor of the Southern Intelligencer. Cushney took Sarah's only son, Frank, and made a printer's devil out of him. Later in life, this same Frank Brown passed the honor on to John Dignon, and said John retaliated by marrying Frank Brown's daughter, the gentle Effie, looking in her youth like a ray of the morning. Another grand-daughter of Sarah's and a daughter, too, of Frank Brown, married Henry Hutchings, a printer, who in turn trained two young brothers of his own wife.

But before all this could be, Sarah must needs bring up that little flock, and to do this well must establish a home for them. Selecting the house as best she could, she set up her wares, and there she maintained her family life with precision, with neatness, with law and order. Her skilful needle became her chief weapon against the wolf that threatened her very door. Before very long, however, she realized that she had established a trade, for in connection with her ability to make the little steel instrument ply in and out, she possessed a certain creative ability, had an eye for design, and what was more to the purpose, could suit the design to the individual wearer. Such ability rarely fails of success.

Busy as she was in all this, Sarah did not fail to help others about her who were less fortunate, The beggar rarely left her door empty-handed. The sick were nourished from her own scanty, but otherwise perfect kitchen. She moved from her first home, down where Congress Avenue crosses first street, to the home of her son at the corner of Twelfth and Lavaca Streets, but the beggars soon found her there. Indians, still prowling about Austin, came frequently to see her in her son's home, just west to-day of the State capitol, came for help, too, and they were never turned away. Any little gew-gaw that attracted the fancy of these Tonkeway Indians was given them. One grand-daughter tells of seeing the hall of this home filled with Indians, come, (ye who would remember only tomahawks and arrows) to bid Sarah farewell, before they were moved to the reservation. They told her there that they were going to the reservation to fight the Sioux and the Comanches in order to keep them from coming down to Austin to kill Sarah and her little flock.

As she drifted down into middle life, Sarah's health failed her. Already an inmate of her son's home in Austin, she continued there until her death, some time in 1876. She maintained always her youthful carriage, straight as an arrow, her bright blue eyes and her black hair. She maintained, too, the love and respect of the children in her son's home, and one of her grand-daughters in giving us these facts has made a somewhat striking statement about it.

"I remember her, sweet and gentle, a smile that was always ready, but I never heard her laugh a real happy laugh. It always seemed to me that her early life in Texas, her early struggles, had taken the laugh from her."

And who knows? Who can say just what inroads into that woman's soul were plowed deep by that experience? Again we bow reverently and thankfully at the memory of one gone before, the memory of one whose sacrifice of another day made possible our present comfort, our present security. And again we add our fervent "God bless her!"

Data contributed by—

Mrs. Stark Washington,
Austin, Texas.

MRS. WILLIAM JOSEPH RENNY-HAMILTON

BORN

ELIZABETH ISABELLA VIRGINIA STANSBURY

In the heroine of this sketch we come upon a little lady whose descendants of to-day cheerfully confess that she was the 13th child of fourteen born to Thomas Stansbury and his wife, Phoebe Skelton Stansbury. In addition to the chance attendant upon the idea of thirteen, Elizabeth Isabella Virginia was a kind of a mix-up from the very beginning, for her father was a staunch Presbyterian and her mother a Quaker, hailing from old England. Now we are not prepared to state the effect of this thirteenth position in the matter of birth, but we are bound to believe that this mixture of religious idea must have borne certain fruits in the children born from time to time to Stansbury and this same Phoebe. We know that one son studied medicine, and became a successful physician in Cincinnati. Another son, full of the spirit of adventure, went to Central America, and took unto himself a Spanish wife. In due course of time a son was born to this additional mix-up in blood, and he, grand-son of the little Quakeress, became a Catholic priest. Another grandson, son of another son, became a Baptist minister. This latter descendant was bright, entertaining to a degree, but a certain grand-daughter, remembering all these accomplishments, declared that nothing could ever reconcile this man in her mind with the ministery, for she knew to a certainty that he was the grandest prevaricator that ever talked. Now, maybe she used a stronger word then the lengthy one just employed, stronger and shorter, and maybe, she being a cousin, had rather over-estimated the ability of the young minister—family pride is a great thing. At any rate, it rather seems right now that we had better say no more about this one characteristic of the young Baptist minister, for words have a way of living on and roving, too, where no ordinary man or woman would expect the pesky little things to rove. He had come to Texas, this young minister, had projected about as the saying is, and all young men like to do so to this day, had enjoyed camp fire and military life, and had been rather a success in this mode of life. He later lent material aid in the capture of the Harriet Lane, that brilliant, daring, unbelievable venture on the part of a few Southern soldiers against a trained army of Northern men. And then all this being over and done, this gay, debonair, (let's omit the next adjective) young fellow entered the ministry, and be it recorded, to the everlasting benefit of the cause he championed.

With this little digression dealing with the future of, and the characteristics abounding in the make-up of this particular one of Elizabeth's grandsons, let us return to the lady herself. As if to palliate the idea of being thirteen in the family group, we are told to remember that Elizabeth came into the world into a home that lacked none of the comforts which money could buy. Her older brothers, as we have already seen, enjoyed the blessings of education and at a time when *schooling* was not as free as air. We may infer from this that life in the city of Cincinnati was easy and cheerful, that no necessity presented itself that demanded a change from civilization to the wilderness then known as Texas. And it comes to us in accents not to be denied that the spirit of adventure, the call of the wild, the new, and the undeveloped brought Thomas Stansbury and his family to Texas.

Elizabeth was about ten years old when this move was made. The first home in the new country was in the city of Houston on Rusk street between Milam and Louisiana streets as the streets are called to-day. Not far from this home, or at least between the home of Elizabeth and the school attended by this young lady, there was a large stockade which was used to confine captured Indians until some decision could be reached as to punishment for their various crimes. On the way from school Elizabeth stopped many times, and climbed the stockade for a long study of the captives. She had listened to tales of murder and fire and torture inflicted by these brutes, and her curiosity was natural, rather commendable in fact, and if the climb on her part revealed athletic tendencies unbecoming the female of her day and time, let's remember that all ages have their bold spirits that look prophetically toward the future. The climb, resulting from that curiosity, was commendable then, even as the athletic swim and tramp of her descendants is to-day considered worthy of every honor in the curriculum of our woman's colleges. According to the stories young Isabella told of the Indians enclosed in that stockade, she saw little of the noble red man, little of the traits that did shine in the heroes of leather-stocking tales. She saw a bunch of lazy, dirty human beings, divested of every shred of romance, and she had in those stolen glimpses her first proof that parasites live upon the human body, in this instance, upon the skull covered with straight, coarse, stringy hair.

Thomas Stansbury, as becomes the father of an interesting woman, had found much to interest him in the new world, had enjoyed a bout or two with the Indians himself, maybe, but he had looked with something like alarm on the condition of the new country, even then looking in a way toward the glad day of independence. He wrote back to Cincinnati to the men and women he had known there, telling them something of the needs of the new country, and the women of his old church, the Presbyterian in Cincinnati, began a campaign of work, and there is little work in the world that can surpass that done by organized church women, and the result was a nice little sum of money. This money was used to purchase the Twin Sisters, the two small cannon placed upon the rising ground before Houston's famous camp on the San Jacinto. The roar of these cannon mingled with the cry: "Remember the Alamo! Remember Golaid!" and methinks, when he sat him down in that solemn hour of victory, Stansbury must have felt a justifiable pride in the result of one or two letters written to his old home town.

But we must return to Elizabeth. Not long after the Stansbury family came to Texas, William Renny made his appearance in the home in Houston, struck the fancy of Elizabeth's parents, and there he remained in the bosom of that family. He became an Indian fighter of no mean ability, straying from that Houston home to give aid wherever he was called. He fought Indians all over Texas. On the hills about Austin, he led a party of men who rescued a young lady her name lost to us now, who had been stolen by the Indians. After effecting this young lady's release, the rescue party became surrounded by Indians on a hill east of the city, in all probability Robertson Hill, the place chosen for a home by our French minister during the days of the Republic, becoming afterwards the property of Dr. Robertson. This rescue party consisted of white men and a few friendly Indians, and they were vastly outnumbered by the savages. This fact forced them to throw up a temporary fort, to wait there for a chance to escape. They became very hungry. Some delicious-looking red berries grew close at hand, and the men began to partake. A friendly Indian advised them to endure the pangs of hunger rather than eat the berries. Renny took the savage advice. Some men who refused to obey, died after great suffering.

Renny displayed rather good sense in the matter of land in Texas, too. Of course he had received his own league and *labor* of land, but to Renny, this was not enough. As he went to and fro in his Indian warfare, he met many different kinds of people. Here a disgusted man, anxious to return home, would offer his entire head-right for a pair of water-tight boots. Again a saddle would outweigh the head-right in some man's eyes, and Renny always took the chance to obtain the land. He bought some with ready money, too, for Renny was an industrious man, capable of turning his hand here and there and always to advantage, a thrifty, enterprising individual, born of good new England stock and forsaking not the ways of his fathers. So this man, brave beyond compare, far-sighted in land matters, had but to return to the Stansbury home between fights to find a glad welcome. The little Elizabeth finally reached the age of fourteen, becoming all the while more comely in the eyes of men, and though Renny was years older than the child-bride, the marriage took place to the satisfaction of all concerned. To all appearances the courtship had been bare of incident, but we doubt if any courtship is ever perfectly bare to the participants, even though these participants are aided and abetted and urged on by the delighted parents of the bride watching by.

She was a strange contradiction in herself, this Elizabeth, so soon a wife and mother, for the first baby came within the year. Her father had helped organize the First Presbyterian church in Houston, had taken a big share in the building of the Presbyterian church building, a building erected then on the same lot used by the same congregation to-day (1927). Elizabeth was deeply interested in all this, and in all other matters pertaining to religion. Even the Quaker blood of her mother put in its plea, mostly in the matter of dress designed to be worn in the place of worship. Gay, laughing, happy sprite, she disdained bright colors for any occasion, and on the Sabbath day, she went to those Presbyterian services clad in a black silk skirt with a long white sacque above, reaching well below the hips, with a demure, dainty, black-silk bonnet above her smoothly combed hair and black lace mitts upon her hands. The service done, and Elizabeth back again in her home, and she became at once the life, the light, the ever-present power in everything that took place. She enjoyed nothing more in all the world than a real practical joke, pulled off at the expense of somebody else. She would go great lengths to carry out these jokes, revealing often no mean ability as an actress. One memorable day, she disguised herself as a beggar and plead for food at her neighbor's back door, repeated the process many times, and each time had to reveal herself before her pitying and astonished friends. She was, as well, a perfect mimic, and woe be to him who appeared ridiculous in her quick eye.

The first home in Houston in which Elizabeth lived as wife and mother failed to receive much attention from her. There were a few slaves and many servants to look after such affairs, and forgetting that slaves and servants are prone to take on the habits of the mistress, Elizabeth gave them full rein. In extenuation of this shortcoming, Elizabeth was known as an artist. Her sketches were well done, considering the absence of teachers. She did as well exquisite embroidery, and all patterns used were her own original ideas and were all drawn free-hand. She had a beautiful voice, could carry any one of the four parts according to note, could improvise if need were. In short, lacking the skill and technique of to-day, she was a real musician in mind and heart.

This life of ease and plenty was interrupted by the death of her husband, some time in 1853, her third child little more than a baby. With all her wit, all her ability with the needle, all her artistic ability, Elizabeth proved herself to be a poor business manager. Her father, too, had become old and well-nigh helpless, and there was none by to advise her. She allowed lands accumulated by her father and Renny to slip through her fingers. She held on to some rent property there in the city, and she had a few roomers in her own home, but it soon became plain that she and her babies must depend largely on the fruit of her own endeavors. She fell back upon the needle as a means of livelihood, and it served her well.

Fine hand-hemmed ruffles for my lady's things, daintily tucked bosoms for the gentlemen's shirts, dresses elaborate and plain, stretched in some cases over immense hoop-skirts, none of these appalled her if so be it they offered in return the money her children needed.

During all this labor, Elizabeth maintained her sprightliness, her sense of humor, her love of a joke. If she toiled all day, her eyelids were never red, nor her fingers weary and worn. She was always ready when the opportunity arrived to bring into her poverty-cursed life a bit of her own bright sunshine. She was busy once upon a finely-tucked shirt, ordered by a lady for her husband, and in the conversation necessary to this enterprise, she discovered that the lady was inordinately jealous of her husband. Accordingly, Elizabeth laid her plans. She disguised herself, appeared in all solemnity before this woman and then told her in agonized whispers that her husband was false to her. Just as the outraged wife had swallowed the story, the whole of it, too, just as that wife rose to declare her vengeance forever on her faithless lord and master, Elizabeth dropped her idisguise. Methinks she must have dropped this woman's friendship in the same instant she dropped the disguise, but record fails to verify any such thoughts on the subject.

After thirteen years of widowhood, at some time in 1866, Elizabeth became the wife of William Morgan Hamilton. Her own children were grown and married, and one little grand-daughter, answering to the name of Deane Robinson, was the go-between in this second courtship. Hamilton, a printer by trade, had come from Missouri, was a man a little older than Elizabeth had been married and was the father of three children. Young Deane, with the peculiar instinct of childhood, soon recognized that in some peculiar way she was making her grandmother happy in accepting and loving Hamilton, and before long she began to use many little wiles peculiar to the eternal feminine that went far to strengthen Hamilton's courtship of her young grandmother. These efforts on the part of little Deane helped to bring about a very happy marriage. Hamilton's children came to live with them, and these children and Elizabeth's three grew to be brothers in heart if not in blood. "Grandpa Hamilton" became a real live, happy fact to all the members of the third generation, and Elizabeth, taking in this idea, began to thank little Deane for her intervention in the matter of courtship. Certainly, she many times declared this second married life to be the happiest time of her life. Married at first too young to appreciate, to understand the joys of life as women should feel and know them, married, too, to please her parents only, she frequently declared that she in reality grew up with her own children. Small wonder that in the companionship of Hamilton she found a real pleasure, a deep joy that lasted as long as she lived.

After her marriage to Hamilton, Elizabeth moved to Belton, leaving her home, her friends, the last being particularly dear to her. She spoke of those friends years afterwards and with real affection. She numbered among these friends Mrs. T. W. House, Mrs. Bagby, Mrs. Bachelder and Mrs. Zabo. She longed for them in her new home, realizing as time went by that real friendships are likely to be those made in the glad hey-dey of youth. To her grand-daughter she gave accurate accounts of real neighborly service, the service that reaches its highest state of perfection only in a new country. She made more plain than ever the fact that what one pioneer woman had, all had, all that could be reached. She was however devoid of that quality of mind that would disparage the present in comparison with the past. She kept up with progress. She enjoyed the very fact that her children and her children's children found life easier than she had found it.

This enjoyment slipped from her dear old lips many times, and never with more genuine thankfulness than when she could be enticed to give an account of her yellow fever experience. To those who sit to-day safely guarded from the pesky mosquito in that same city of Houston this mention of yellow fever can mean but little. The advance of scientific methods in all matters pertaining to the human body has about wiped that one scourge from the Texas coast. I repeat we know nothing about it, and so far as I am able to judge, we are not eager to obtain any knowledge that must demand the price of that experience. Doctors went about their work day and night, sleeping in the buggy between calls, some faithful negro man guiding the horse. Nurses learned to hold the blanket over a man with fever, threatened with the chill that brought the black vomit and death, learned to hold it there and catch a few minutes sleep. The question of previous experience in nursing soon disappeared. Every man, every woman who could hold an aching head, who could quiet a fractious patient was called into nurse's service, and they, too, slept only between screams and cries on the part of the patient.

Elizabeth soon attested her superiority in this matter of nursing. From one friend's house to another she went, there to obey the doctor's orders, there to use the knowledge picked up in her quick fashion as each new experience came her way. Her fame travelled throughout the length and breadth of the city, and many blessings fell from suffering lips as the wiry little figure flitted to and fro. This she modestly left for other people to state, but she did say always when speaking of her friends that she went through two epidemics of the fever in Houston, saw many a friend die, eased as well as she could the pain of both friend and stranger, never suggesting either by word or tone or glance that in doing this she had done anything outside the line of duty as she saw it.

In the new home in Belton, her husband died, the well-beloved companion, and from the day of his death, she began to slip away, being from that time forward an invalid. She died about 1902, brave, tender and true, and the flower of her memory sheds its sweet fragrance about the lives of her many descendants.

Data contributed by—

Mrs. J. J. Brydson,
Austin, Texas.

MRS. JOHN M. KIMBELL

BORN

SARAH ELLIOTT

In the city of Nashville, Tennessee, about the year 1826, a little daughter was born to R. M. D. J. Elliott and his wife, Sarah McCullough Elliott. With peculiar insight into the future, with peculiar appreciation of that little baby's inherent characteristics, the child was given her mother's name, was designated, in other words, as the Princess, the light of the house and the joy thereof, and subsequent events in her life proved how fitting, indeed, had been the name chosen for her christening. She had opened her eyes, this lassie, in a cultured home, a home of wealth, and Tennessee, even in that early day, boasted many of them. There were pictures on the walls, and there were carpets for her feet, and many slaves to do her bidding. Morover, there were instructors to see that Sarah received an education. In addition to her literary studies, there was music and a bit of work on canvas. To-day samples exist to display her marvelous skill with the needle, and stories still float about in DeKalb, Texas that proclaim her beauty and her charm.

Sarah had to thank the blood of many worthwhile men in the ancestry behind her for these certain delightful traits of character. Her grandfather, David McCullough, was a noted privateer during the Revolutionary war. He originated the flag that bore the coiled rattlesnake with the subtle warning: "Don't tread on me!" This flag was afterwards adopted by Paul Jones as the ensign of the United States Navy. David McCullough had amassed great wealth, and during the war of 1812, he lent the state of Georgia one-half million dollars, a debt which the state afterward repudiated. Then in her own immediate family, there was David Chissolm, a half-brother, the son of her mother by a previous marriage. He was from all accounts a brother worthy of admiration, but about the time Sarah was eight years old, this David was inveigled into a duel with some man, his name lost to us now, and David killed his opponent. Duelling, even then, was falling into disrepute, and it soon became plain to David that he must seek another home. No matter his talents, no matter the life of promise once opening out before him in Nashville, David knew that friends of the dead man and men violently opposed to duelling in the abstract would combine against him in this, the land of his fathers. So David swallowed his regret, settled all business affairs and formed a company of men to make the trip to Texas. His step-father, R. M. D. J. Elliott and Mr. Titus were in that company, Elliott holding for many years the office of county judge of Bowie County.   Mr. Elliott located his head-right, the customary league and labor of land between the little towns of De-Kalb and Old Boston.   In that same county, David Chissolm, still a young man, made his mark, wiped out the stain of his Tennessee experience, and years afterwards, when Runnels was governor, he held the office of Secretary of State.

Back in old Tennessee, John M. Kimbell had read of Indians and their atrocities, and however much he may have deplored the sufferings of the white people exposed to the savages, his young mind, fired by the spirit of adventure, conceived the idea that it would be a great thing to fight Indians first hand, if for nothing else but to see just how it was done.   When Col. Fannin, hunting throughout Tennessee for soldiers who would be willing to help free Texas from Mexican rule, when the intrepid Fannin came across this sixteen-year-old boy, he had but to suggest that said boy was needed where Indians roamed in plenty, and young John fled from home and kindred, covering as best he could his tracks, for he was determined, in spite of family opposition, to take up his life in far-off Texas.   He became in time a noted Indian fighter, the thing he had longed to be.   He took part in after years in many battles, many skirmishes in the dark, as he must skirmish who would fight Indians, and he learned thoroughly the tactics necessary in such warfare.

Kimbell had been one of the brave party of men who dared bury the body of John Denton.   Denton was a Methodist minister hailing from Arkansas and had preached probably the first sermon ever heard in Grayson County. When the Indians came on a raid, Denton, failing to hide behind the sanctity of his pulpit, shouldered his gun with the other men and sallied forth.   As they neared a creek in what is now called Denton County this intrepid soldier of the gospel called a halt and advised his men not to ride through bushes near the crossing, for he feared that said bushes had been used by the Indians as a hiding place. Some of the men accepted his warning.   Others accused Denton of being afraid and wanting to turn back.   Denton replied that he would go as far as any man and started ahead.   Indians arose from the very bushes Denton had viewed with suspicion, and the whole company of men began a hasty retreat.   A halt at a safe distance proved that Denton's horse had no rider.

To return meant that they must face the arrow and the tomahawk, but these even counted for little if there remained a chance, even the slighest, that John Denton, the brave, earnest, Christian soldier, might be suffering the tortures of Indian captivity. So the little company of men, including Kimbell, put back into the danger, found the body of Denton undisturbed, the Indians probably unaware that they had killed him, and braving the chance return of the foe, these men buried Denton, digging the grave with knives and hatchets, and lining it with slate rock. They laid him away, covered him with another slate slab, smoothed and levelled the grave lest the Indians return and exhume the body.

In 1842, some three years after the rescue of that body, this adventurous lad, John Kimbell, came into the life of Sarah Elliott. She had reached the mature age of sixteen years. Her family had prospered in Bowie County, her father and her brother obtaining honors at the hands of men, and young Sarah had developed into something of the promise vouchsafed at her christening. She had known little of Indians save by hearsay. Her parents had brought many slaves with them to Texas, had influenced other families to join them on the way, and this had made such a large company of people that the Indians had not dared attack them. Small wonder that John Kimbell, brave, adventurous lad, should appeal to this young Sarah with the race-old appeal. They were duly married.

The young couple soon set up their own home at De-Kalb in Bowie County in a two-room log house, part of which is still standing (in 1927). Thither Sarah moved her few belongings, her sampler, we hope, and that house soon became a social center. Men of many kinds visited the young couple there, and the place gradually became a hotel in all save name. There were many slaves to relieve Sarah of the work, had this pioneer woman been so minded, but no single detail of her household management failed to receive her personal supervision. Her garden, her yard, everything about the premises interested her. She had a peculiar knack of growing roses and flowering shrubs, apple trees and peach trees, and many of these thus grown are still standing (1927), still bearing fruit and blossoms for the comfort of those about them.

And through all this labor, all the planning necessary to the establishment of a home, Sarah gave birth to four children, all daughters. There may have been some disposition on the part of John Kimbell to complain that the Lord had thus dealt harshly with him in that his sons were all daughters, but the house sheltering the young people resounded many times with laughter, felt many times the tap of dancing feet, for these girls were full of life and health and strength, full of energy and the joy of youth, and inheritance had given each her full share of beauty.

Other girls, similarly endowed, joined them from time to time, and the *beaux* flocked as *beaux* will under such circumstances, and the hotel—the home had come to be so designated by this time—afforded ample space for all these amusements.

Mrs. Laura Johnson, a grand-daughter of Mr. Titus, was a frequent guest in the Kimbell home. Mr. Titus had come to Texas with Sarah's father, had settled in DeKalb though an adjoining county had been named for him, and in this Laura, Sarah's own daughters found a dear and highly valued friend. She was present at all social functions in the Kimbell home if possible, and she proved to be just as fascinating, just as interesting as Sarah's own daughters. She with these aforesaid young ladies probably wore hoop-skirts, their dress-skirts measuring yards and yards around the bottom. They wore big, puffy sleeves, and they looked up at the young men with eyes of blue or brown or grey from beneath hugh poke-bonnets that defied the wind and the sun. But the allure was in the eyes, despite the poke-bonnets, and the Texas swain was caught in the snare, just as he is caught to-day, and he was made to answer in the very same fashion for his credulity.

When the men-folks were absent, these girls held high carnival, choosing usually their own bed-rooms for the scene of festivity. Those of us who have drifted a bit with the times are not so charitable as we might be *sometimes* with our present day miss, and we have a way of speaking of the days gone by to the everlasting disparagement of the "flapper" as we term her. If fun and a love of finery, if a certain speed in grasping the situation characterizes the "flapper" to-day, then she is an old article, never to be classed strictly as a twentieth century product. Neither is the athletic girl entirely new, for horses and dogs and tennis played each a part in the lives of grandmothers, both yours and mine. The athletic idea may have yielded over much to the dance in the eyes of the females of that day. We know by hearsay that many a belle of that day claimed to be able to dance all night, provided the music and the floor were suitable, and the partner agreeable in every way. They grew agile and efficient in the use of their nether limbs—this is the result of practice—and a never-to-be-denied witness speaks to-day in Sarah's old home, and that witness says that Sarah and her happy playmates of eighteen or so could kick and kick high whenever the occasion demanded.

This witness, though dumb, yet speaketh. On one particular evening, the girls were gathered together in a room in Sarah's home making merry, all to please themselves.

The room had been newly papered or repaired in some way, and up beneath the high mantel—mantels were set in those days on a level with a six-foot man's shoulder—it had become necessary to use some cement or plaster. Said cement had not dried, it was slow to dry in those days, but small heed paid these gay young sprites to this deficiency. Laura Johnson, suitably clad, stepped to the center of the room, and Laura gave a *ballet*, the cheers and laughter of the girls furnishing the music. Laura kicked high, and then a little higher, and still the shrieks of laughter furnished their encouragement. One more kick, she told herself, one higher than ever before, just to show what she might do. A little higher this time, and Laura's dainty foot landed in the cement, nearly as high as her own dainty head. She drew that foot back with a screech, but she left forever its tender imprint upon the hardening wall. Sarah, busy about her household matters, heard the shrieks of laughter, and of course Sarah proceeded to investigate, but there is small doubt but that Sarah joined in the laughs, for her heart was yet young, and she had kept these lassies well in her heart, in her strong, loving hands.

There came little radical change in the life of Sarah. She continued to live as became the wife and mother of her day and time, doing a bit here and a bit there. She saw the oldest of her girls married to Dr. R. W. Reed, a graduate of the Medical School of the University at Philadelphia, saw the bride go into her own home, and was later present in that new home at the birth of her first grandchild. This birth took place during the Civil war, and we who know first-hand of war conditions sympathize even to-day with that young grandmother. She saw this same daughter grow a little sadder, a little wiser in the cares of wifehood and motherhood, but Sarah cared little for this. She knew that this girl was but living life as it must be lived, was but filling in her own day and time her own destiny on earth.

Then when Sarah was thirty-six years of age, she knew that another child was coming to her, even to her the anxious grandmother of the year before. Perhaps the dreams of a son to carry on his father's name, to cure the heart of that father of his previous disappointments mingled a bit in her simple preparations. Whether or no, when the young son was presented to Kimbell he soon realized that the long looked for joy had brought the bitterest sorrow. The little mother, already a grandmother herself, yielded up her life in that fierce conflict.

That son lived to be grown. Perhaps, as the years went by, John Kimbell read something of the blessedness of the Divine Providence in this strange answer to his prayer.

Perhaps that child of sacrifice went in and out before his father, a precious blessing as the days flew by. We can never know, we who read of Sarah to-day, just how much of this was true. We can but hold her in tender memory, brave, loving, happy-hearted woman of her day.

Peace be to her in her narrow house of death!

Data contributed by—

Mrs. R. L. Penn,
Austin, Texas.

MRS. HENRY RUNGE

BORN

JULIA HORNUNG

Most people know that the desire for political and religious freedom brought many men and women in the old, old days from Europe to America. Prominent among these seekers for political and religious freedom are the Quakers and the Puritans, the one settling in Pennsylvania, the other in New England. There may be people in these United States who believe that none but the Pilgrim and the Quaker dared make this serious change in life for this high and holy reason, but when we come to look into the life of Julia Hornung Runge we are brought face to face with another set of people, not quite so stern in their ideas of God and religion as the Puritan, not quite so distinctive, maybe, as the Quaker, peopling Pennsylvania under the leadership of William Penn, but a people for all that who had emigrated from Germany to Texas in order that they might maintain their own ideas and ideals of religion and of government. Just what those ideas and ideals were, we shall not discuss here. We shall tell you simply that these people were bound together under the name of Adelsverein. Let us state for the comfort of English-speaking people that this name meant that the leading members of the order were German noblemen who had forsaken the land of their birth in the hope that they might, in the new country called Texas work out their ideals of a perfect government.

Any plans for the maintaining of a government supposed to be perfect must soon fall short and then die of their own accord. Governments grow as the people to be governed grow. The rule of to-day must be changed to meet the needs of tomorrow. Failing to realize this in their attempts to bring about that perfect form of control, this company soon came to grief, bringing about great money losses to its founders, but it brought to Texas such people as Prince Carl Solms, the Landas, the Runges, the Hornungs, and maybe, in the eternal scheme of things, this end justified the means.

In this company of German noblemen hailing from Hildesheim, Germany, we find one Hornung and his wife. Among the six children born to this couple, there was one among five very beautiful daughters who was given the name of Julia. She had been born on some day of April, 1834. In a Protestant family, a family concerned much with education and the refining influences of life, this Julia grew to womanhood. If she ever attended any big school, we can find no record of it. She could write perfect English and German. She read everything worth while which came her way. She was, in fact, a fitting illustration of the child allowed to tumble up in a library stored with good books, a child allowed to read the books at will until he finds himself possessed of an education above reproach. But this little German maiden loving music, enjoying even the opera, must forego any real knowledge of the Cecilian art because she was denied the opportunity for study.

With this attractive family about him, Hornung settled with a number of his noble friends at a point on the Texas coast called Indianola.

About 1844, with Texas still an independent country, Hornung fell ill, and, after four years of suffering, passed away. He left his widow to face the world alone in the new world, her six children dependent on her for money, for advice. The widowed mother, eyeing the five beautiful daughters and the manly son, must have felt a helplessness at the thought of their upbringing, an upbringing that must be in keeping with her own and that of their carefully reared father. She turned in her extremity to her sister, Mrs. Pearce. The Pearces had a fine home on the Navidad river, near the town of Victoria. The recently bereft children found in this ranch home the culture, the elegance that had surrounded them from birth, and life for the children, particularly for our Julia, moved on at practically the same pace.

When asked about the attitude of the masculine element toward this certain Julia, her descendant declares that had she possessed scores of lovers she had remained too modest throughout life to make any statement to that effect. But we remember her beauty and her modesty, her loving kindness and her tender mercy, and we hazard a guess that our Julia did not lack attention from this masculine element, even in her early life. We do know that when she was barely seventeen years of age, Henry Runge, himself an emigrant from Germany, crossed her path and that things were never again quite the same for Julia.

Now for a word about Mr. Henry Runge. He was born in Bremen, Germany, April 11, 1816. He had been carefully educated for a business career, and he had followed some form of shipping business, shipping things, even unto the end of the earth. He had acquired a knowledge of many people and many countries, and he spoke many languages, all to perfection. He had come from Germany to Baltimore, Maryland, in 1836, but he moved in 1841 to New Orleans. In 1845 he joined the German Emigration Company which had Texas as its promised land. He, too, settled at Indianola. He established there a fine shipping and banking business. This was the beginning of the firm of H. Runge and Company. Later Mr. Runge established a bank, housing it in one of the two stone houses built in Indianola at that time, and it was known always afterwards as the first real bank in Texas.

A glance back at the uncompromising dates of birth brings to mind the fact that Henry Runge was eighteen years older than our gentle Julia. But Henry was a good-looking man, straight and true and fine. He was energetic, and he was public-spirited. He had been educated as we have just said for his work, and to our Julia, so modest herself that she might be called shy, so tender, so sweet and so true, he became at once the hero of her dreams, sleeping and waking. Love laughs at the years between, just as he laughs at locksmiths, and Julia, a happy bride, became the wife of Henry Runge.

Now we must remember that this one branch of pioneer folks in Texas had suffered few hardships. They lived on the coast. Runge's business made it possible for him to secure many luxuries denied people living in the interior. They suffered no raids from Indians, no trouble from Mexicans, and the business prospered, so that no privations of any kind were necessary in the home. Some nine years after this marriage, Mr. Runge took his wife and children back to Europe, to Germany and to France to see the grandparents and other relatives waiting there to hear about Texas and the wonders beyond the sea.

The news of secession and the war following reached Mr. Runge in Germany. He knew as did Julia that it meant disaster, public and private. They both knew that it meant peculiar trouble for them, because, during the outburst of feeling, they must find themselves in a land at war in the hope of maintaining an institution in which they had never believed. They had used colored servants, but they had never owned slaves, because they had never believed it to be right. The young men employed in the business at Indianola had not shared Mr. Runge's opinions in the slave matter. They had been required to join the army—those who had not done so voluntarily—and Runge must hasten home to look after his business interests.

He found Indianola blockaded. He found conditions there to be far from pleasant for his family. He, too, felt keenly the hurt that must come to a man who sees a bit ahead of his fellows, but has no power to make them see their own error. He decided to move his family away from these conditions, to take them, in short, to New Braunfels, for he felt sure that in that settlement he would find himself in more congenial surroundings. He and Julia had their clothing packed, some of their finest china and glass and the household linens, and then they made their way in a fine carriage drawn by a pair of dashing horses. Runge, ever a great admirer of good horse flesh, spared no pains that his wife's carriage might always be drawn by the best. Incidentally, this trip from Victoria to New Braunfels consumed four days, the nights being spent in homes along the way.

The life in New Braunfels was most nearly like that of the ordinary pioneer of any life Julia had ever known. She found many German people there who held the same feelings toward the war and slavery as did the Runges. They felt keenly the privations of war, for, owing to the blockade, they must give up the sale of their ranch and farm products. Having depended, too, upon foreign markets for some of their food supplies, for potatoes, coffee and flour, etc., things began to look serious. Mr. Runge finally made trips into Mexico, returning nearly always with a nice line of eatables. Some of these he disposed of to the New Braunfels folks at actual cost, thus relieving the situation of some of its sting. Our Julia, sensing the lack of things in the home of her neighbors, would have her women cook up potatoes in many ways and then invite the women in to eat them. She went even further in her attitude of loving kindness toward her neighbors. She allowed her elegant clothes to hang in the closet. She dressed herself simply as her neighbors were forced to dress in order that she might be one of them.

None of the luxuries surrounding Julia had ever succeeded in making of her an idle woman. She had always looked after her home. She had done her own very fine needle work, and had demanded of her serving women that her own clothes and those made for her children must be well made. Her strained position during the war rather added to her efforts in this line. She helped make soap, she helped make candles. She turned her hand, in short, to any labor life seemed to demand of her.

The war being over, the young men employed by Mr. Runge having returned in the sorrow of defeat, Julia had a fine chance to exclaim, "I told you so!" Did she yield to this idea? Not a bit of it. She sympathized with her husband in his feelings in the matter. She was glad to know that each returning soldier of the Confederate army was to be reinstated in his old position in her husband's business, glad to feel that people who had once differed in opinion on vital things were yet broad enough to settle back into business relations with the same confidence that had existed between them before the difference arose. Mr. Runge took his family shortly after the close of the war to Galveston to live, and he, himself, went into the firm of Kaufmann and Runge in the famous old island city.

In taking this step, Mr. Runge made it possible for his family to escape the horrors of the storm that threatened Indianola in 1875.   Newspapers of an early date made it plain that the fine harbor offered by the little penninsula on which this town of seven thousand people had been builded had its drawbacks.   Slow to accept the idea of danger, determined men continued to make their homes there for the sake of the shipping.   The storms of 1875 and 1886 convinced even the most determined fellow that the sea was hungry for the little point of land, and the place was abandoned.   But before either disaster had taken place, Mr. Runge had moved his family to Galveston. More significant still, he, himself, had passed on.   An old newspaper, dated March 18, 1873, contains a notice of his death and a tribute to his sterling worth as a citizen of that community.

"The loss of such a man is a public calamity."   He had led "a life of spotless integrity."   At his death he had been able "to leave to his children the noble inheritance of an unblemished character and an honorable name."

There is little left to tell of our Julia.   Crushed by her sorrow, she turned in time to her children, born to her of her happy marriage.   Two of her daughters, previous to the death of their father, had gone with that father's sister, even unto Bremen, and had enjoyed three years study in the place that had once been the training ground of their father.   At the end of that three-year period, Mr. and Mrs. Runge had gone to Europe, had brought the girls home, but had left two sons to study in Germany.   At the death of her husband, Julia took her children in America back to Europe and settled in a home in Hanover, Germany. Her life there was the life of any wise mother.   She lived to see her girls married, and she frequently declared that they brought her the nicest sons-in-law in Germany.

I wonder just how much one is influenced in the estimate of these women of the past by the manner and thought and habits of the descendants telling the simple stories of their lives.   That the influence exists there can be no faintest doubt.   That it is colored by inheritance, there can again be no doubt, inheritance on the part of the descendant and the scribe, but however that may be, your scribe right now, with a certain descendant in mind, relates in all tenderness that Julia Hornung Runge was a religious woman.   A Protestant in training, a true supporter of the church and its many activities, she made it plain to those about her that her own inner light was her guide.   She lived at home and abroad a true disciple of the Golden Rule.   No needy man or woman, no helpless little child ever failed to receive her gentle consideration.   In reproving the little

children crowded about her knee, she would say simply:
"Would you like to have anybody do that to you?"

Beautiful illustration of the thought of the Master, falling thus from the lips of one of our pioneer women, and
then sitting before your scribe, listening to a story tinged
a bit now and then with discouragement, this descendant of
Julia can lay her hand gently on your arm, even as Julia
had laid hers, and say to you in tones sweet and fine, tones
that crowd out all thought of annoyance," God will take
care of you."

Julia Hornung Runge, the personification of these types
of beauty in life and in character died in Germany in 1893,
some twenty years after the death of her husband. She
was buried there, probably in the land of her birth, but in
America, even in Texas her memory lingers yet in all its
power and its beauty.

Data contributed by—

Mrs. Johanna Runge,
Austin, Texas.

MRS. WILEY MARSHALL-FLACK

BORN

LAURA ANN ELVIRA METZ

There is a peculiar pleasure in obtaining facts connected with a woman's life when her only son must be the source of information. The leading facts, the more important details are likely to be the same had a daughter related them, but an only son, grown up in intimate association with his mother is very apt to give a touch of reality, a touch of quaint humor to these details, as if he saw in it all the frailty of woman's ways and her whims. This touch of reality in the opinion of your scribe adds no small degree of interest. Now for a few facts.

Back in the young state of South Carolina we find a young man, Henry Metz by name, whose forefathers had emigrated from Alsace-Lorraine. Metz had made an effort to establish himself in the dry goods business, had fallen into the snare set by Miss Nancy Sulton, a daughter of a wealthy, slave-holding planter, and Metz had married her. Of this marriage, on October 1, 1826 was born a daughter. She was given in all tenderness the name, Laura Ann Elvira, and as the baby grew and thrived there were many willing to prophesy that the mantle of an attractive mother had fallen in this instance upon her daughter. They could see in each gracious act of courtesy, each tender, soul-winning smile, an attribute of the mother intensified in another generation. And there are people willing to-day to testify that such prophesy was fulfilled. Asked as to this girl's beauty, her son will tell you to-day with a sly smile that she claimed to be beautiful. Unable to make a statement to this effect, we do say that outsiders have agreed with her own claims, saying that she was beautiful in a queenly kind of beauty, and we are prone to believe both the outsider and the girl, herself, now ninety years and more of age, in her own statement. We know positively that as she grew in beauty, she grew in grace and accomplishments. She was taught at an early age to play the piano, and save the mark, she was able to play the Jew's harp to the delight of the young folks, old folks, too. She was well read for her day, and she could sew and knit, spin and weave, could do, in short, anything that a girl of her day and circumstances was required to do.

We go back a step or two. When Laura was eight years old, her parents decided to change Newberry District, South Carolina for Texas. Metz had not been successful in his business ventures in South Carolina. A merchant, the owner of many acres seemingly adapted to the raising of cotton and corn, he had for some intangible reason failed to make it pay as he would have it pay. His older brother had at that time been in Texas some few years, and to Texas Henry Metz must come, too, bringing with him his family, including our Laura. They went first in a wagon drawn by horses down to Memphis, the boat center of Tennessee, and there embarked at some time in 1844 for Galveston. The remainder of that year was spent in Galveston, but early in 1845, they took boat again, finally reaching Houston via Buffalo Bayou. At Houston, Metz procured the services of an ox team owned by a man named White, and then the Metz family with their possessions reached Austin, the six-year-old capital of the Republic, on July 4, 1845.

For his family residence, Metz selected the southeast corner of the square made by Congress Avenue crossing Sixth Street. This house was a two-storied, frame affair, and was the family domicile as well as the store. The ordinary line of goods was found in this store and sold at pioneer prices. One bolt of bright red calico received a generous wetting during its progress toward this place of business, but Metz retailed the calico at one dollar per yard, and the hardy pioneer women were glad to pay the price. Metz moved afterwards to a point on Congress Avenue between Seventh and Eighth streets. This property is still in the hands of the family, occupied at present by the Chamber of Commerce and the C and S Sporting Goods Co., and is under a lease to a New York store for no small amount for full fifty years.

These things give us some idea of the home conditions in our Laura's life. Before she reached her fifteenth year, beaux began to flock about her. Heart whole, herself, she, being a normal woman, enjoyed the flocking, but she remained for some time untouched. Then appeared Mr. Wiley Marshall, and things began to change. This Marshall was a smooth talker, a handsome man, some twelve years older than Laura. He dealt in race horses, a profitable business in his day, was a good judge of horse flesh, able to make it pay and pay well. He had descended from Captain John Marshall, an officer in the Royal Army of England under King Charles the First. Captivated by our Laura, he appeared before her parents, stated conditions, ending his statements with some solemn advice.

"You might as well let me have her," he said, "for I'll steal her anyway."

Needless to say, our Laura became in a short time the bride of this man who had threatened her parents with the stealing of her.

Laura did not lose her beauty or her charm in assuming the cares of wifehood. She maintained, too, her stately, beautiful poise, but there came a gradual change in the thought of the woman. The reality of life impressed her, the demand, and she became active in many lines. She had given birth to one son, to whom they gave the name of Benjamin. The Marshalls continued to live on in the home established by her parents. As time passed on, as Laura developed in womanly power, she took her part in the labor of store-keeping. She still owns the property on which this business was conducted, a building leased at present to one of the leading banks of Austin. In this business, conducted there in the olden time, according to her son's statement, "she laid the foundation for everything we have to-day."

Indians formed no small part of the store's customers. Expecting this, Metz and Marshall had bought trinkets in New Orleans, glass beads, brass ornaments, a bright ribbon now and then, and a feather, and these savages began after a time to think Metz a great man. They traded unrestrainedly with this *pale-face*, betraying sometimes choice secrets of the unknown forest. They came in one day proudly displaying bridle ornaments hammered out of silver. Keenly on the watch for such opportunities, Metz asked where the white metal had been obtained. Delighted with his friend's interest, the chief announced that on the *next moon* he would take Metz to the place. The Indian kept his part of the bargain. When he reached the store he went in and inquired in steady tones for the "good man." The mother of our Laura, lately bereaved widow, pointed solemnly upward. A look into her face, a sudden appreciation of the sorrow written large in her beautiful countenance, and the Chief and his followers went out under a big oak tree and there held a solemn burial service in honor of Metz, who had been their friend.

In 1856, Marshall died, and in 1858, our Laura married again, her choice this time being James A. Flack. She had retained through marriage and widowhood most of her youthful charm, but to this second marriage she brought as well the poise of a woman whose eyes had been wide open down her short journey of life. She went into the store with Flack, and she studied the business from every angle. She thought carefully over each step. She weighed and measured all articles for sale, looking out always to the idea of profit. As the years passed she developed into a shrewd buyer, particularly of real estate, having always a careful eye to the chance of increase in value. She grew, perhaps a little too particular in her demands, a little fussy as behooves most women who accomplish things in this world. At one time she felt that her Austin attorney, Judge Doom, had become careless or to say the least a little slow in managing a law suit involving the title to some land. She proceeded to expostulate with her attorney as to the matter of delay, and said expostulations were forcibly expressed. The attorney, a man noted for his patience in his dealings with woman-kind, made an unexpected reply. Said reply took on the form of a question.

"Who is the attorney in this case?"

Laura read something new in the tone, and Laura heeded what she read. Long business training had brought a sense of balance to her wise head. She backed away from the table, a bit of an apology in her manner, and from that day forward, as long as the attorney lived, Laura remained one of his clients who signed papers he suggested signing without asking the sum and substance contained therein.

That common sense, weighted with justice and mercy, characterizes our Laura of to-day. From the height of her ninety-three years she looks back on the past, but she keeps well her own part in the present. In her own home, she maintains as yet her proud position as mistress, and her son, his wife and daughter render her the loving care and consideration, the watchful tenderness such a woman deserves.

Data contributed by—

    Mr. Ben Marshall,
    Austin, Texas.

MRS. THOMAS PRATT WASHINGTON

BORN

ELIZABETH TATE HARRIS

Texas raises more cotton than any other state included in the United States. She raises her own wheat with some to spare. The same may be said of her corn. She brings her own oil and gas from her own under world, with some to spare for other states less fortunate. And then, Texas raises Washingtons, all her very own, and lots of them.

We would in no way belittle the Father of His Country. We even like to believe the story of the cherry tree and the hatchet, and the sight of his face on a greenback brings a glow of pride not to be denied. We sympathize with every Virginian who would claim kin with the noble man. Just because we feel this sympathy and this reverence, we gladly undertake right now to show a skeptical world just what Texas can do in the way of producing Washingtons.

In the city of Austin, the capital of Texas, lives a Washington, a man who tills vast acres of Texas land with unusual success, a man whose word is equal to his bond. His son, Colonel William Claude Washington, a graduate of Texas Agricultural and Mechanical College, an officer in the United States Army during the World war, stands out bravely, tenderly, a man worth while among young men of to-day. And we, professedly interested in Texas women, particularly pioneer women, turn proudly back to the elder Washington's mother to trace her life from the beginning, sure in our own minds that we shall find in the story of her simple life some things worthy the name of Washington, some things that are in themselves the foundation for the two lives that have been alluded to in these opening pages.

Back yonder in Albemarle County in the state of Alabama there stood in a state of perfect preservation as late as 1874 a fine, old colonial mansion. All evidence pointed to the fact that it had once been the property of John Harris and his wife who was born Frances Rouzee. It was surrounded by many acres of rich land, tilled in those days by slaves who served willingly an efficient master. Around that house, a comfortable distance removed from sight and sound, the negro quarters had been established; said quarters furnishing many times a place of amusement for the little folks growing up in "de big house." Within the walls of the mansion there was furniture of the most elegant design and material, there were pictures on the walls, and books upon the shelves and silver and china in the dining room. In this home, perfect in its day and time, surrounded by peace and plenty, during February of

1818, another little girl was added to the big family of
Harrises, and she was named for some of her forebears,
Elizabeth Tate Harris. And of this young lady we are
now about to say things.

Memory does some strange things to folks sometimes.
Your scribe in thinking of this baby girl must be troubled
with visions of Elizabeth as she knew her. She must see
in her mind's eye a delicately formed, aristocratic old lady,
the mistress of her home and all about her, even then in
her ninetieth year. But said sight, given a little time,
leads one finally along the path of imagination to picture
the beautiful girl growing up in that home of ease and
plenty, a home characterized by culture and things worth
while. She can see the flash of her eye, the ripple of her
hair, the delicate bloom of her cheek. Seeing these, she
can lend herself to the stories told by a devoted son of
to-day. He acknowledges his mother's beauty, and her
charm, but he dwells more on the fact that she was "quick
as a whip at school" in her rather limited opportunities in
that direction, a fine musician, and so in visualizing the dear
lady we come to see her flitting about that colonial mansion,
a joy to herself, her family, a dearly beloved "young
missus" to the slaves, sharing those broad acres with the
Harris family. It is easy to imagine that she held her own
part, she who had bloomed like a flower into her womanhood, in the gaiety infesting that mansion. It is easy to
imagine the dance, the dinings in which the masculine
element bore no unwilling part. It is easy to scent romance and a few heart-breaking episodes and all the other
foolish little things that go to make up the life of the young.

When it comes to heart-breaking episodes, these imagin-
ings are wide the mark. Across the road from her own
elegant home, in another home just as elegant, surrounded
by acres just as rich, just as bountiful, lived her only
sweetheart, Thomas Pratt Washington. He had been born
in Virginia, had lived a year or so in Kentucky, but at
some time in his childhood his people had acquired this
property lying thus handy to the Harris estate. But a few
years her senior, this Thomas had grown up with Elizabeth, the circumstances being practically the same. He,
too, had played with negro children. He, too, had been
reproved by Uncle Junus, slave on the Harris plantation,
had listened to old Junus's yarns and had believed them.
He had laid aside some of these joys for the more serious
things in life, had acquired a fine education, had returned
to Alabama to settled down into active life of a Southern
planter. If this young fellow and Elizabeth ever quarrelled, if any other swain ever succeeded in arousing the
sparks of jealousy in the heart of young Thomas, we can

never know of it. We do know that Elizabeth was married in her elegant home to this only sweetheart, at some time in the year 1836, she being then just eighteen years of age, her husband a little older.

We know, too, that the celebration of those nuptials was in keeping with the plantation customs of old Alabama. The feast was lacking in nothing. The bridal array was all one might desire. The guests came for miles around, arrayed, too, in *wedding garments*, and they probably danced all night as was the custom. The mother of our former governor, Joseph D. Sayers, was one of the bridesmaids. Picture that ceremony! The bridesmaids of course entered the room first, then the bride, her rich dress stretched above a hoop-skirt barely able to squeeze through the wide door, then the pause before the minister and the solemn words, and then after a suitable time, the wedding journey, a walk arm in arm to the home of the groom, just across the road.

We have no doubt the negroes enjoyed that wedding and its preparations, the young men and maidens, the old negroes, knowing the young people their whole lives through. Uncle Junus no doubt wasted one whole evening listening to the festal music, but we have no doubt that he sat himself down the very next afternoon at his own cabin door and drew from its nail on his cabin wall his own trusty fiddle and after a twist or two proceeded as of old to ease his soul with the weird strains.

It might be well to tell of a little experience that fell into the life of Junus. He happened to witness the phenomenon that made a certain evening known forever afterwards as "de nite whin de stahrs fell." The earth must have passed through the tail of some comet or some nebular stuff afloat in the great universe, but the negro mind saw in it another meaning. To him the end of the world had come, and the illuminated heavens could be nothing less than a sign. Uncle Junus could think of no real evil in his own life save his proneness to "fiddle." Some old negro preacher had once declared in the hearing of Junus that the "fiddle had *druv* menny er soul ter tohmint." Uncle Junus now rose to the moment. He laid his beloved "fiddle" on his sacrificial altar. He promised the Lord in the presence of that falling universe that if he might be spared he would never again touch the bow or tighten the cat-gut strings. Junus kept that promise—for two years, resisting the pleas of young folks, both white and black, but after a bit the solemn warning—and his promise lost its hold on the old fellow, and he went back to his fiddle, careless of how many young folks might t h e r e b y b e "brought ter tohment."

In that beautiful home, just across the road, Elizabeth lived with her childhood sweetheart until five children had been born to them. Washington had become a colonel in the militia of Alabama, and they had prospered financially. Then Washington went on the note of a friend, the friend failed, and left his bondman to pay the debt. Ten thousand dollars covered the whole matter, but people living in ease and plenty at that time found it hard to raise that much ready money. Washington found himself confronted with two evils. He must sell his land, or he must sell his negroes. The man, influenced no doubt by Elizabeth, decided to sell the land, and with the money thus acquired—no small amount for that day—Washington and his family and his slaves at some time in the year 1845 put out for Texas.

The family rode in a carryall drawn by a *spanking* team of horses, and the black driver occupied his accustomed seat for all the world like he had been taking "de missus" for her afternoon airing from "de ol' house et home." They packed in wagons the elegant clothes worn in the mansion, the silver, the glassware, the books, the many thousand little things people of culture have a way of gathering about them. In addition to these Elizabeth placed in safekeeping the book of notes and references she had obtained from her family physician, Dr. Minor, a book used extensively in that new home. Beneath that furniture strong bags were placed, bags containing the money received for the plantation, Washington having kept out what he deemed sufficient for the journey.

Most folks' money has a way of giving out. Washington's pocket money ran true to form. At the end of a week or so, he saw nothing to do but unpack the wagons, which meant stupendous labor and a waste of time. Then, just as he reached his decision, one of the wagons got fixed in a rut, and turned over of its own free will, thereby lessening the labor by half.

The journey once more resumed, Washington began to fear that both slaves and children might be ill for want of exercise. So ahead of the procession on his own stout horse, Washington rode briskly, letting it be known that he scattered money by the way and that whoever found it might have it. Some children, white and black, eagerly took advantage of this bonanza. One daughter, Mildred Pratt Washington, wanted to walk all the way, and her father frequently declared afterwards that if the journey had been one hundred miles longer the thrifty Mildred had broken him up a second time. Incidentally, this Mildred is alive to-day (1929) hearing perfect, if her own statement is to be taken, free always from aches and pains, and we wonder just how much her idea of thrift may have assisted in prolonging her life. Surely the walk is a fine exercise for folks, particularly when the shining coin may turn up at most any old place.

Into Texas at last, just in the closing days of the Republic, Washington settled his family near the mouth of Onion creek, just twelve miles from Austin. Too late for the land grant, he bought land from Col. Caldwell who owned seven leagues in all. Before the deed was signed, Washington asked Wallace, the surveyor, if he must have the land measured. Wallace but shook his head, advising Washington "to stick to the Caldwell lines." Washington heeded the advice to his own everlasting advantage.

So here they were at home, these Washingtons, on Texas land, no sign of a house, no place to lay the head, even our Elizabeth brought up in ease and plenty. She slept with her husband in the wagon-bed, helping the slaves prepare their meals on the fire built in the open, moving at last into the log cabin as soon as the walls were up and the roof on. Into this rude home Elizabeth had them move her piano, the mahogany legs resting on the dirt floor. O, ye who would recall its old home of brussels and tapestry, lace curtains and the like! When the simple Indians paid them a visit, the piano was to them a sight worth seeing. To hear it tinkle beneath the fingers of Elizabeth filled them with awe. Elizabeth granted their requests cheerfully, watched them leave after each performance with a lightening heart, and if company came that night, she cheerfully resigned her bed for her old place in the wagon and cared little so the Indians let her piano alone.

But the new home in the wilderness rapidly assumed proportions. Fine lumber was ordered from Houston, taking sometimes three weeks in the hauling, sometimes three months. The rough lumber came from Bastrop. The house was two stories in height, four rooms downstairs and three above. They built nice quarters for the slaves, and said slaves went to work on the broad fields with a willing mind. Mr. Washington, astride his favorite mount, "Steamboat," rode about the vast plantation, a kind word here and there for each black worker. Then in this new land there were plenty of eels to be found, and the negroes lost no time acquainting "massa" of the fact, for he already knew that nothing could excell eel-skin strings in "de wropping uv de h'ar." They made shoes of goat skins, the negroes, the more apt ones, spun and wove, glad all to take on once more the run of life as they had known it in old Alabama.

Before very long it became plain that Mrs. Washington must take over the management of the farm. Distances were so great that it took most of her husband's time to see to the outside management. In all this work, Uncle Junus, the fiddler of old Alabama, was Mrs. Washington's right hand man. She trusted him implicitly in all matters. When the cotton-picking time came about, she placed the old man at the scales. Remember he could neither read nor write. He had scorned to work a simple "sum" in arithmetic, but Elizabeth managed in some way to teach him to weigh cotton. Every day during the season, with some seventy-five negroes at work in the field, Uncle Junus sat by and weighed the day's "pickin's." The negro children not old enough for work—and the white children, too, clustered about the old man listening to his stories between calls for weight of that cotton, but when night came on, Uncle Junus repaired to the house and there gave "de missus" and account, accurate and full.

"Clem, he dun picked er hundrid pounds, Jack eighty-five, Mary er hundrid en' tin."

On and on throughout the list, and so far as it was possible to find out, Uncle Junus never made a mistake. One young master tried his best to catch the old fellow in a mistake as to the number of pounds, but he was forced to acknowledge defeat in the matter. Elizabeth established what she called a "Depot," a place at which the negro women might leave their children while they worked in the field. The elder women there cared for the children, and Elizabeth left her own babies there many times when the work grew pressing, so strong was her faith in the black women in charge. Her own children and the slave children wore the same kind of clothes on week-days. She even saw to it that a patch of sorghum cane was planted on the place for the joy of the little negroes who loved to chew it. She kept a couple of little quirts, one red and the other green, and white children and black were alike tickled upon the legs for any misdemeanor they might produce, punished solemnly, tenderly as one might punish who had the real good at heart.

Later on in life, Elizabeth gave Uncle Junus permission to make little cakes and pies and to sell them to the other negroes. Having been trained in the ways of Elizabeth, old Junus was in a fair way to do a rushing business. The negroes had little money of their own save what was carelessly thrown by "massa" or some stranger visiting the plantation, but what little they did have, old Junus was about to take unto himself. Possessing a correct idea of the *morale* of the negro children, the sweets were kept under lock and key. The young "massas" and two young pickaninnies, sons of Junus, being of corresponding age, decided to rob Junus of his wares. They succeeded to the last detail. As long as the taste of the sweets lingered, the children felt fully justified in their theft. By and by conscience got the upper hand, and the sweets turned to gall and wormwood. Fear of the little mother began to wrankle in the white boy's soul and so they resorted to the race-old expedient. They decided, white boys and negroes, to run away.

They slipped off before night, the two white boys and the son of old Junus, the other negro boys refusing at the last minute to take part. All night the other boys lingered in the forest, picturing the dismay pervading the hearts of the parents thus left behind. After a bit they realized that they were hungry and that they were not as yet capable of supplying themselves with food. Toward sun-up the pangs of hunger were not to be stifled. They must go home. Did they dare?

Mrs. Washington, not the least disturbed, waited at home the outcome of the rebellion. In the early spring morning she walked out to the gate, to see the boys standing some feet away. Old Junus had reported the return of his prodigal Paul some time earlier. Now the mother called out: "Why don't you come in?"

" 'Fraid!"

"Uncle Junus didn't whip Paul." (She had whipped him herself.)

On came the boys in their blessed ignorance only to be taken solemnly to the dining room where the mother behind closed doors proceeded to administer the necessary rebuke. A sister, Theresa by name, stole in to watch the fun. The chastisement of the two boys complete, Mrs. Washington turned to Theresa. Scenting danger for herself, Theresa exclaimed hastily: "I ain't done nothin'."

"That's just it," the little quirt descending accurately, "go get to doing something."

With this discipline in sway, Mrs. Washington taught her children many of the things she had learned in the old plantation home of ease and plenty. She managed as well the plantation, and made it pay. One year her cotton rotted. In any other hands it had been thrown away. Elizabeth but put it in with the three hundred bales shipped to Galveston, and the buyers, thinking it Sea Island cotton, paid her five cents more per pound than they paid for the pure white.

About 1869, Elizabeth went to live with her family in Austin. She chose the corner of 13th and Trinity streets for her residence. She left the management of the farm in the hands of one of the little truant boys now grown to manhood. Elizabeth took to Austin her piano, her negro driver and her carriage, her books, her old furnishings, and there she enjoyed city life to the full. She affiliated with the Methodist church. She entertained her friends. She lived through the horrors of Civil war, made clothes for the soldiers, watched the pathetic figure of her own husband, one time a soldier, now incapacitated for service by the streaks of yellow fever left in his body. In 1873, she buried this husband, this lover of her youth, but with her son Stark's help, she continued the management of her her farm full twenty years. The land yielded her perfect obedience. She planted once thirty acres in turnip seed, to have every seed produce "two" turnips according to her idea, and young Stark never al lowed his mother to plant turnips again.

Elizabeth came into trouble with the Freedman's bureau soon after the close of the Civil war. An order had been issued that farmers must sell crops at once in order that the negro might have his share, ignoring the possible good if one waited for a rise in price. Mrs. Washington appeared before the bureau, stating that she had advanced money to feed the negroes and that she had a right to wait for the advanced price. In the argument that followed, the irate lady asked what she must do with her cotton seed.

"Let the negroes eat it."

The heart of Elizabeth fired. Cotton seed then was considered unfit food even for cattle.

"Negroes are human, same as we," she exclaimed.

A little while afterwards the negroes on the plantation became unruly and Elizabeth sent her son, Stark, for help from this bureau. A risky thing on her part, seeing that these men were anxious to catch an erstwhile slave owner in the act of cruelty to a negro. Elizabeth met the "carpetbagger" with her best smile. She served him her best dinner, in her best style. When the time came for the man to talk to the negroes on the error of their way, the man said to them just exactly what Elizabeth's sons told him to say, and there was never any more trouble with negroes in the plantation. At another time, Mrs. Washington and her son were in her buggy en route to Austin, five hundred dollars in gold in their pockets. Desperados, knowing perhaps of the spoil, stopped them. Showing not one trace of fear, Elizabeth smiled at the men riding for miles beside her buggy, smiled and talked until the men forgot the money and left her in peace.

And so she lived her life, dying at seventy-five years of age, having reared ten children. Talented, cultivated woman, capable, energetic in all matters of business, absolutely free from fear, she lives to-day in the hearts of her children's children, a remarkable example of a remarkable woman wherever she may be found.

Data contributed by—

Mr. Stark Washington,
Austin, Texas.

MRS. THOMAS COKE THOMSON

BORN

MARY JANE CHREISMAN

A certain mother, born and brought up in Texas, has been many times heard to say that her thirty-six year old son has never given her a heart-ache. Other mothers look at her quizzically as she says it, wondering as they look if she be guilty of the sin of prevarication, or if such a mother must be classed with the plain, everyday fools. We are not prepared to say that Mrs. Thomas Coke Thomson ever made this statement about all or about even one of her three sons, but a careful interview with any one of that trio of trusty men gives one the idea that the little mother, a real pioneer among pioneers, had managed in some way to win the undying love and devotion of her sons, had managed to impress them with a deep reverence for the gentle, efficient woman who had given them being.

In the famous colony brought by Stephen F. Austin to Texas back yonder in 1822, there was a competent surveyor named Horatio Chriesman. He was at the date of his coming a widower, but he married shortly afterwards a woman named Augusta Hope. Chreisman lived with his wife in the Austin colony, and there in that home on August 11, 1830, a little girl was born and given the sweet old name of Mary Jane.

A question as to the events of her life directed toward one of her sons brings the fact first and foremost that she professed religion and joined the Methodist church when she was ten years old. When asked as to her education, he replies that it was of necessity limited. When asked about her work, he replied that she had slaves to work for her. Then as if some magic of another day and time had settled about him, this son began to tell us stories of Uncle Jacob and Aunt Isabella, stories so true to life, so full of tender, beautiful meaning that his hearers could think for the time of little else. After a bit of maneuvering we turned this son from thoughts of Jacob and Isabella. We learn in the turning that Horatio Chreisman had settled on the league and labor of land granted him by the Mexican government. He had there built a double log house, one story and a half high, a large hall in between the two main rooms, with wide galleries both front and back of the house. The floors of the house and the woodwork were made of boards, hand-sawed from cedar logs, some of the boards measuring from eight to ten inches wide. The dining-room was another log cabin, thirty feet from the house, and the kitchen was built still another thirty feet further on, there being no covered passages to protect one from sun or rain. In that kitchen the cooking was done on a fire-place, a crane to hold the pots, a stout piece of hickory bark always at hand to support the hoe-cake. Ash-cakes were baked there at all hours for the children, and we who have known corn-bread at its sweet-est, before the civilized mill had ground the meal so fine, we feel a suspicious watering of the mouth at the mere mention.

And now about Uncle Jacob and Aunt Isabella. We hope sincerely that no reader of this article may evolve the idea that Jacob and Isabella enjoyed blood relationship with the Chreismans. Far from it! They represented in them-selves, particularly in their titles, a certain blessed human relationship now about banished from the earth. They were slaves belonging to the Chreismans, and they repre-sented in themselves no mean example of the slaves of that time in Texas. Uncle Jacob had never demeaned himself by work in the kitchen. He managed the stables and the yard for "massa," but, just the same when the day's work was done, when twilight had descended upon the earth, Uncle Jacob did not fail to make his way to Aunt Isabella's kitchen, to establish himself comfortably before Aunt Isabella's roaring fire. Then from "outen de big house" would steal Horace, Rector, and Thaddeus Thomson, all little boys, sons of our Mary Jane on a visit then to grand-pa, and close by Uncle Jacob they would settle for the evenings entertainment. Encouraged by a few questions from the boys, Uncle Jacob would begin his yarns.

Uncle Jacob had never heard of sequence or introductory sentences. He had never heard of paragraphs or climaxes or anti-climaxes, but he managed to hold the attention of his audience. He told of bears and wild-cats and snakes and some miraculous escapes. As the fire burned a little low he told of "hants" and "sperrits," the grown negroes drifting in, listening with interest almost as deep as that of the children. Then, influenced by some in-born soul-sav-ing desire, Uncle Jacob would drift to stories of demons walking the earth, bent on tempting men and little chil-dren from the straight and narrow path. Then, if the rain fell dismally, Uncle Jacob would reach the height of dramatic ferver, describing in tones slow and solemn some special occasion when the very "Debbil, hisself" had walked the earth, eager to snatch men and boys from their evil way in order that he might "thust 'em inter eberlastin' toh-meant." Believe it? Those boys had to make a distance of fifty yards before they might hope to reach the security of their mother's presence—and in the dark. They made the distance, and at a speed not to be denied even in this day and time, sure that the devil's own hand reached out at every step to grab. A stumble on the way over a sleepy dog or a prowling cat brought from each boy a yell of terror, but back to Uncle Jacob's cabin they went the very next night, anxious for some more stories of "hants" and "sperrits," even anxious a bit, deep down in their hearts, for some more tales of the devil.

Even in his conversation with the grown-up folks, Uncle Jacob was religiously inclined, an inclination that increased with his years. He could quote "de scripture" on all occasions, remembering in part what he had heard read and quoted, manufacturing, too, many sayings never before heard upon the face of the earth. When questioned by folks, some young, some old, either white or black as to his authority for some specially wild combination of words, he would reply with a solemn shake of the head that "hit wuz bertween de *leads* uv de Bible."

Then there was Jack, son of Uncle Jacob, a "duck-legged nigger" according to plantation classification, not fit to work in the field and so kept at home to help in the kitchen. This Jack had some experiences of his own that might be recalled in the hope of preserving a correct idea of everyday life in that early Texas home, even in the life colored and guarded by slavery at its height. Jack was then about thirty years of age, but Jack had by no means laid by childish things. He considered himself great with the ladies of his own tribe and color, and Jack lost no opportunity or spared no pains to strengthen his position. While Jack sat about that Chreisman fire listening to stories his daddy told, stories that harassed the soul of the Thomson boys, he busily "wropped" his "ha'r." This meant a separating of the kinky stuff into locks of a certain size, each lock to be "wropped" in time with strings of buck-skin. When the day's work was done, particularly on Saturdays, Jack removed the strings and then combined his locks to a state of inky-black, kinky perfection.

His coiffure satisfactory in every way, Jack then proceeded to his master's stables. There he selected one of the best horses and immediately put forth to make "a night of it." Summoned before his master the next morning, his hair as yet in all its kinky glory, Jack would deliver a long story, free from any thought of "sperrits" or of "hants" but—hardly as reasonable, for Jack would there claim that he had been *kidnapped* and kept out all "de endurin' nite." Struck with the stupenduous foolishness of the negro's lie, averse always to the punishment of his slaves, *Massa*, surveying that kinky, inky-black hair, made a hasty decision. He had old Jack's head shaved as a stroke at his manly pride. The master entertained a vain hope that Jack might remember thereafter to remain at home at night and to leave his master's horses in the stable where they belonged. But Jack, emulating the example of the children who went back night after night for ghost stories, continued to steal out "massa's" horses, trusting that the gentleness of the female negro heart might look over the indignity of his poor shaved head.

Losing hope of any reform in the horse-stealing matter, somewhat disturbed over Jack's delinquencies, Chreisman, on Jack's next offense evolved another mode of punishment. He had Jack, black man as he was and full thirty years of age at the time, put to *bed* in one of the rooms in "de big house." and beside that bed, Chreisman installed two of Jack's own young "missus," two sisters of our Mary Jane, to wait on Jack, to keep the flies and mosquitoes at bay with a huge bunch of peacoack feathers.

"God er Mighty!" exclaimed Jack afterwards, all but humiliated to death, "I'd er ruther hed two whuppin's den dat!"

During the years spent by Jack in acquiring his duck-legged manhood, Mrs. Chreisman would occasionally gather up stale medicines from her chest and ask Uncle Jacob to see that they were buried in the garden. Usually obedient to "de missus," old Jacob rebelled at this extravagance. He collected bottle after bottle of blue mass and quinine, some paregoric, some prescriptions made up in the hope of keeping off chills and fever, and then Uncle Jacob made duck-legged Jack, perfectly rebust, healthy even from a stand-point of chills—Uncle Jacob made Jack take all the medicine to keep it from being wasted. And then Jacob, doubtless, in his frequent talkings "wid de Lord," wondered that his own son could be so nearly akin to "de debbil" in point of behaviour.

Blessed picture of another day and hour! No man or woman in the South to-day would willingly have it returned, but there comes to us ever and anon some blessed reminiscence of the past that speaks a beauty of mutual love and helpfulness between white and black denied us to-day. Perhaps slavery as an institution was a mistake. Perhaps, on the other hand, slavery civilized the negro as no other institution had ever been able to do.

Mary Jane Chreisman, the idolized young mistress of these slaves took a hand in their control, in their entertainment, in their general welfare, and Mary Jane was equal to the task. Then along with these worth while qualities, she possessed the intangible, inexplicable capacity of appeal to the male sex. They gathered about her, those early Texas men, coming of course to see Chreisman on some matter of business, winding up with a lingering visit to Mary Jane in the *front room* of the big log house. From among these admirers, Mary Jane soon singled out Thomas Coke Thomson, a man some eight years her senior, one in every way worthy of her, though he, himself, failed to think so. This Thomas had a twin brother named Frank, and save for a slight difference in size, the older they grew the more the men seemed to look alike. Enjoying a bit of a joke now and then, the two men exchanged places in the social game. Thomas even went so far as to prostrate himself at the feet of Frank's dearly beloved, vowing eternal fealty—and Thomas carried the joke through. More than once he played his prank, and with more than one damsel. No small amount of trouble when the fraud was discovered, and more than one love affair met thus an early end. Shaking his head over the success of his brother Thomas, Frank declared, in some humility that he had never been able to fool our Mary Jane.

From this study of slavery as our Mary Jane knew it, from this talk of beaux and the like, we turn now to one of the first remarks made by one son in a short interview. This was the simple statement that Mary Jane professed religion and joined the Methodist church when she was ten years old. This in itself calls for another bit of picturing. This woman had been born in Texas under Mexican rule. The Catholic church presumably held sway in all matters of religion. We like to feel that the Catholic priest made a few visits to this early Texas home. We have no desire to detract in anyway from the widening, broadening influence of the teachings of those devoted sons of the Catholic church who left us the Alamo, the mission at San Jose, the beautiful structure of Concepcion. We know that they left in the making of those structures a better thought of life for Indians and the like, a better idea of how to live, a happier idea than any of these strange people had ever known before. But our Mary Jane would have none of it in her own religious life. The Methodist minister, pioneer representative of the Protestant church, had made his way, too, into the wilderness. He constructed no missions, left no monuments to mark the path of his endeavor, but he played his part, nevertheless, in the civilization our Mary was destined to see. They helped to establish houses of worship, bare of picture or of ornament, houses used on week-days for schools, but the touch of the gentle hand, and the sound of the ringing voice left each its own influence on the daily lives of the determined men and women who listened as they talked.

The first church our Mary Jane attended in Burleson County was some four miles from her home, but in her second home in the same county, the church, to Mary Jane's great delight, was only one-half mile from her own

door.   Crude building in the eyes of present-day worship-
ers, the church building was great in the eyes of Mary
Jane.   It was furnished with *benches*—so they were called
in early Texas times—made of cottonwood logs split in
half, pegs being placed in the rounding side to raise the log
a comfortable distance from the floor, leaving thus the
straight side free to support the body.   They were placed
in two rows, leaving an aisle between.   There were benches
reserved in the back of the church for the slaves of the
community, and—they were plainly marked, "Negro
Seats," and no white man dared invade their sacred
precincts.

In this church—and school-house, too, be it remembered,
Mary Jane listened many times to Thrall and DeVilbliss
who expounded the gospel as they understood it.   Jim
Ferguson, father of a former governor of Texas, preached
there, too.   He was not an educated man, according to all
accounts, but he read everything that came his way, and
forgot nothing he ever read.   About that Thomson fire in
the winter time, he sat with the family proving himself to
be an interesting conversationalist, as well as a forceful
preacher.   Morse and Alexander were frequent guests in
the Thomson home and preached in the church.   Another
Methodist minister, answering to the name of Sneed, made
frequent visits to the Thomson home.   He looked at the
negroes in the congregation with no objection, but he had
a way of asking for a chance to preach to the negroes alone.
Perhaps he knew in his heart that the negro in his simple
understanding must be reached in another way.   Perhaps,
again, the rude church with its separate services, had laid
in all wisdom the foundation for the *Jim Crow* law as it
exists in Texas to-day.

Then there was the camp-meeting.   In some well selected
grove, shady and well watered, those Methodist people
would construct a tabernacle, its coverings, mayhap, the
boughs of trees at hand, the seats, chairs or split logs
brought from home.   About this structure the families,
living in some instances many miles from the shady spot,
would build little log camps and then for two long weeks
enjoy the simple outdoor life, flavored with the religious
ideas of the men who preached to them day by day.   They
sang together the sweet old hymns, and they discussed
religion and nothing else.   You may be sure that our
Mary Jane entered into this camp-meeting life with all
enthusiasm.   For days before the opening she saw to it
that suitable things were provided for her own table, and
then with the help of the slaves, she put forth with her
whole family to enjoy the camp-meeting.

And how shall we sum up this woman's simple, forceful life? Born of pioneer parents in the dawn of the new Republic, entering the church in her tenth year, holding sway in her father's house over slaves, rejoicing in the approbation of the other sex, married in her sixteenth year to her best beloved sweetheart, a man some eight years older than herself, and thereby all the more able to appreciate her at her true worth! A notable house-keeper, looking after her family and her slaves, attending to the physical infirmities of all about her, even unto the doses of blue mass and calomel! Milking in her girlhood in that famous Chreisman home some twelve cows a day, superintending on her own plantation during the Civil war the making of cloth for soldiers and for home use, feeding and clothing and training her sons in the way she would have them go, entertaining the man of God about her own hearth, sustaining him and invigorating him by her sweet counsel, slipping at last away on February 7, 1877, not yet forty-seven years of age. Simple, yes, but every endeavor in her life has blossomed and borne fruit upon the earth. Among the individuals come under her immediate care, some have doubtless failed to heed her warnings or to hearken to her words of encouragement, but there be those among Texas folks of to-day who can read in the faces of her descendants the power of that simple life at its best.

Data contributed by—

Mr. Horace Thomson,
Austin, Texas.

MRS. T. H. DUGGAN

BORN

ELIZABETH BERRY

If any human individual should be foolish enought to suggest that he or she might lay down any definite law of inheritance or environment or any thing else that could explain the superhuman strength of character to be met in the lives of men and women, the other individual listening to that suggestion has but to turn to the lives of the women of early Texas times, and there he will find solemn refutation of things claimed by the first individual. The woman, inured to hardship from her youth, sometimes fails now, as she did in the early days of Texas, when confronted with the cares and duties of middle life, fails to perform even her simple duty as the world sees it. The woman brought up where ease and plenty must have encouraged idleness and a love of luxury, sometimes rises in the might of her strength to meet unexpected and well-nigh appalling situations, carrying the burden of such situations with the same grace, the same ease with which she had drifted through her hitherto care-free existence. And the daughter, indulged to the limit of her desires in her father's house, has proven herself a tower of strength in the wilderness whither she has followed her husband.

This was true of Elizabeth Berry, born early in the nineteenth century, at the home of her parents in Fort Gibson, Mississippi. Her father owned three large plantations fronting the Mississippi river, and the cotton and the sugar-cane grew to perfection in that land, fanned by the soft breeze, fresh from the Gulf of Mexico, the breeze fragrant with the magnolia and the jessamine, bearing no hint of frost to distress the ease-loving inhabitants. Slaves in large numbers lived upon these farms, lived a happy, rollicky life, compelled to labor just enough to keep them in physical trim, the fruits of that labor bringing many comforts and luxuries to the family of "massa" and "ole miss." Boats, luxuriously equipped, went to and fro upon the bosom of the river, bringing from northern factories dainties of every description to the wives and daughters of those Mississippi planters. From neighboring plantations there came other daughters just as care-free, just as happy as Elizabeth, herself, and there were some sons, too, and many a couple tripped lightly in the moon-light upon the deck of those river-steamers. Safe to say, too, that many a courtship thus begun ended in matrimony, just as they have a way of doing to-day.

Without any enlightening details, we are told that one, T. H. Duggan, came into the life of Elizabeth Berry. We know little of his home, his antecedents, his condition in life, but we safely surmise that he was comely of person and pleasing in manner, for before very long it became apparent that Elizabeth had decided to cast her lot with young Duggan and to follow him if need were to the end of the earth.

Now when a young woman arrives at such a conclusion, no earning, no threat, no advice has ever been known to turn her back. No limit has ever been set to the foolhardy length a young woman will go when thus intent on following the lover of her youth, and mayhap, the destiny of the world rests in a large measure on this same peculiarity in woman. When Elizabeth Berry informed her parents that she had decided to marry Mr. Duggan, and had further agreed to go with him to Texas to make their new home, consternation, bordering on despair, siezed the hearts of that father and mother. They warned her that she would thus meet rough, wild conditions in life to which she had never been accustomed. They told her of Indians, and they told her of snakes and animals abounding in the new country. Elizabeth but smiled back at them. They told her of ruffians prowling to do her harm. She but reminded them that she would have her husband as a guard and a protection against all evil. Then her father shook his head and went on about his own business as one utterly routed in battle.

The wedding day hovering near, the family physician made bold to appear before the bride, and with some tender concern for the child he had brought into the world, some tender misgiving for one going thus ignorantly to face "an untried pain," the gentle old man presented Elizabeth with a volume dealing in a simple way with the practice of medicine, particularly the bearing of children and the care of them, the care of the sick, some first aid suggestions, and the physician further suggested to Elizabeth that she begin at once to study it. Young Elizabeth flared. The old man had dared invade her maiden modesty, and she gave him to understand in no unmistakable fashion that he had better keep his medical knowledge to himself. The father, standing by during the interview, waited a suitable moment, and then he broke through the storm of his daughter's wrath with a solemn warning that she had best thank the doctor and resolve to follow his advice to the letter. We have no record of Elizabeth's reply. She may have left the doctor's presence in outraged silence, but we do know that she brought that very book to Texas with her, and that she many times thereafter thanked the old doctor in her heart, and most humbly.

Elizabeth and her young husband settled first at Goliad, but moved before very long into what is now Travis County. She found many strange things in the wild, new country, some of them far from pleasant, and Elizabeth began to see the why and the wherefore of the solicitude on the part of her people concerning her welfare. Things were decidedly novel. Indians prowled, and wild beasts followed their example. The latter howled through the night, and Elizabeth, lying awake, grew a little sober over the situation. After a bit she realized that she was soon to be a mother, that she was to go through her first maternal trial in the wilderness and practically alone. Aye! for that doting young husband was as ignorant as she in all such matters. She did not rebel at the thought. Elizabeth was a real woman, but she pulled forth the despised book given her by the family physician, and Elizabeth, sober and determined, set her down to study.

The knowledge thus gained helped her through her own struggles, helped her with the care of the baby after it came. The few people scattered throughout the county heard in some way of her ability, and she was called upon almost before she was strong enough herself, to minister to another woman in her hour of travail. Again, on a dark night and far into the night, a negro man appeared at the door and declared that a young white woman, living farther up the country, was very much in need of Elizabeth's services. Elizabeth got on her good horse, took her own baby in her arms, bade her husband farewell and put out for the scene of trouble. The negro man who had come for her afoot, took the horse's reins in his own hands, and walked ahead of her, his rifle cocked, ready for the Indians, always expected to interfere in anything the white man sought to do. They reached the cabin in safety, and putting her own baby to bed, Elizabeth proceeded to help this woman, a stranger to her, and right then apparently alone in the cabin.

After a few turns about the cabin, Elizabeth found that the woman was not entirely alone. A half-grown girl sat within the shadows of the fire-light, but she had nothing to say. Elizabeth, busy over the work at hand, paid small heed to her silence. She applied herself to the needs of the woman, following the advice gained in her study of the once despised volume, soothing, helping, wondering all the while if she might not be mistaken in her method of procedure. When at last the child was born, when the long battle seemed about over, the young mother went immediately into hysterics of the most violent form.

Now this was a new procedure on the part of a human being, new as far as Elizabeth was concerned. She had seen women weep for anger, and she had seen them weep for joy. She had herself indulged in a few tears and lamentations when disappointed in some feminine desire, but the conduct of this young woman was to Elizabeth an astonishing revelation of what a young woman might do. Just as she was about to administer a rebuke as one would rebuke an excited child, the stolid girl from the other side the bed of pain made solemn answer:

"Her husban' wuz killed by Indins las' week. She hain't got no body."

Not long after this last episode, Mr. Duggan moved his family to Guadalupe County. He built them a house there of logs. He had the negro men, slaves probably, cut these logs from the woods close by, selecting elm because of its evident strength and toughness. The first rain that came swelled said logs in a most enticing fashion, rendering the walls peculiarly tight and the rooms nice and cozy. When the sun came out and delivered his say in the matter, the logs shrank to an astonishing degree, leaving cracks through which heat and cold and wind had easy access to the inhabitants within. Nothing daunted, Duggan filled the cracks with clay and stones and sand, and the result was most satisfactory, a cozy home in winter, a cool one for the hot summer months. They made furniture for the new house from the native woods, and some of it was worth while. At San Marcos about this time there lived a German cabinet maker named Ezelle. He made for Mrs. Malone whose daughter afterwards married a son of Elizabeth Duggan, some very elegant pieces of furniture. He felled the walnut trees growing in abundance beside the beautiful San Marcos river, polished the wood by hand, and formed a dresser or bureau that was a work of art. This same man made Elizabeth a wardrobe of the same kind of wood, simple in line, perfectly plain, polished by hand to a state of glossy beauty, and so perfectly joined that it could be taken apart and set up again, no screws, no nails of any kind being used in its construction.

The negroes cleared the land about the house for planting, and through part of the head-right, but Duggan's farming endeavors were frequently interrupted by the call of the new-comer for help. This call meant that Duggan's slaves must leave the shovel and the hoe and go into the woods and fell logs for another cabin home destined to rise in the new country. Then, too, men from the northern part of the United States, already agitated over the slavery question, came frequently among the slaves disguised as Indians, spreading dissatisfaction and discontent among the trifling negroes numbered among Duggan's slaves.

But, despite these facts, things prospered with these young people. In that log-cabin home, gradually filling with many comforts and a few luxuries, Elizabeth lived, perhaps, the happiest time of her life. Her husband went in and out, a man of honor among his fellows. He had the distinction of being the first county clerk of Guadalupe County. Civilization crowded them close, and with slaves to do most of the hard work life became brighter and easier. Elizabeth bore her husband several sons and daughters, and to the bringing-up of these children, she devoted all her love, all her sympathy, plus the knowledge gained in the early experience in the wilderness.

Just before the birth of her last child, Elizabeth commissioned her husband, going to New Orleans to buy goods for his store, to bring her something nice. Remembering his wife's beauty, remembering her love of dainty things, Dugan resolved that the *something nice* must be designed to further adorn her beautiful self. Further remembering her crown of snow-white hair—this hair had been white since early in her youth—Duggan decided upon a bonnet for the adored, one of the latest style and handsomest of materials. The thing was acquired and brought home carefully lest some untoward thing mar its beauty, and Elizabeth was delighted. A friend standing by as she opened the box, continued her stand until the bonnet was in place above the snow-white hair. Then she began to sympathize with Elizabeth that so soon in her life she had been forced to wear this sign of old age. Elizabeth replied that she thought her white hair perfectly beautiful and that she was very glad it was white, so glad that she would not change it for any other hair in the world.

She turned then to Mrs. Pitts, another friend at hand, and holding the bonnet strings beneath her chin, demanded Mrs. Pitt's opinion. Now whatever Mrs. Pitts thought of the bonnet and the snow-white hair, she made a peculiar answer to Mrs. Duggan. That answer conveyed the idea that a bonnet brought to an expectant mother was a sure sign of twins and of the death of the mother. Two months later twins arrived to share the home of Elizabeth, and Mrs. Pitts hearing of the arrival, realizing in a flash that the first part of her prophecy had been fulfilled, fearing that the death of Elizabeth was sure to follow, fainted dead away, sure in her own mind that the gift of her husband had demanded the life of Elizabeth in exchange.

Elizabeth attached no such importance to the gift of the bonnet. She was too very much alive, too much interested in everyday happenings at home and abroad to be appalled by so small a thing as bearing and rearing a pair of twins. She brought up these last children as she had brought up the others with due regard to mental, moral, and physical welfare. She brought up, as well, most of her daughter's children, for she spent her last days in that daughter's home in Seguin, her husband having been dead many years. She died herself at the age of eighty-three, full of life and its glory, just such a woman as God had planned when Elizabeth Berry first opened her eyes in that luxurious home in old Mississippi. And as we leave this little white-haired woman, thrilled with the thought of her courage, her daring, her devotion, your historian for some inexplicable reason, is reminded of the saying of an old darky:

"Ole Mississippi mought be 'er li'le slow, but she git dar, jes de same."

Data contributed by—

Mrs. Medie Duggan,
Ft. Worth, Texas.

MRS. MASON G. COLE

BORN

HARRIET DUKE

At some time in the year 1800, in the now famous town of Durham, North Carolina, a daughter was born to one Duke and his wife, and she was given, after a bit, the name of Harriet. The new republic in America of which North Carolina was no small part, was but a quarter of a century old, and it had yet to go through the second war before England must finally acknowledge that her one-time colonies, bound by solemn oath into a nation, had taken a certain place among the acknowledged powers of the world and that those colonies must thereafter be treated with respect. There were, perhaps, even then some men and women among the citizens of the new nation who doubted the wisdom of the break from the mother country, and young Harriet, no doubt, heard much talk for and against all matters pertaining to a republican form of government. However she may have felt about matters pertaining to government, young Harriet took on the ways of her people, took on the refinements, the culture, for until the day of her death she maintained her dainty, lady-like appearance, her white lace caps, which she contrived to make herself, representing always the daintiness of habit that was one of her strong characteristics.

Now there was one thing in which young Harriet's people were interested that might at first notice seem out of place in the life of one so professedly dainty. She had been born a Duke, and many men and many women, alas, of the present day have occasion to bless the day on which the Duke's began business on an extensive scale. Now we have no intention of entering upon any anti crusade of any kind. However objectionable the pungent brown weed may be to any of us personally, we shall confine ourselves as far as possible to facts in the course of these simple naratives, and we all know that tobacco is tobacco, a blessing or a curse just as any individual reader may see fit to class it. When a good strong man sits him down beside his own comfortable fireside and proceeds to light his preferred brand of cigar, there is something a little touching in his enjoyment. Mayhap, after all is said and done, after all tobacco wrecks have been inspected and forgotten, maybe that one good man's enjoyment of the weed justifies the time and the labor necessary to raise the tobacco, makes honorable the fortunes amassed in the cigar's manufacture. Then, too, remembering that good man and his sense of satisfaction, it is easy for us to recall that *Nicotiana tabacum*, the common form of tobacco, is an

American product, the plant generally believed to be indigenous to this western country, and it had been poor business to let such a valuable product go to waste.

The Dukes did not let it go to waste. They raised it in old North Carolina, and they raised it in islands adjacent. They prepared it into the famous mixture bearing the name, and they made it into cigars and cigarettes. They gathered in the shekels from these preparations, and they founded Duke University for the everlasting joy and satisfaction of the many youths who cared to avail themselves of its rights and privileges.

Now Harriet had enjoyed the many advantages accrueing from the tobacco, and like the youth of her college-yet-to-be she had profitted thereby. About 1817, with the war of 1812 about forgotten, with the tobacco business in pretty good swing, a certain young man, Mason G. Cole by name, appeared in the life of young Harriet. This young man had descended from soldier Cole, a man who had rendered his country valued service in the Revolutionary war, and in Harriet's eyes at least the young man had inherited the virtues of his fathers. In the same loving eyes, young Mason was everything desirable, but Harriet's family could not be blinded to the fact that young Cole indulged a bit too much in wine and in cards and the other excesses of the day which did right then seem so very attractive to the young men. Her family doubtless remonstrated with Harriet, endeavoring as parents will do to show their daughter the error of her way, but all endeavors were in vain. Harriet but slipped across the border with her wild young man, and in the state of South Carolina became the bride of her beloved Mason Cole.

This action on the part of Harriet speaks at least a certain determination that makes for success, a trait her mother, no doubt, had many times deplored. It bespeaks, too, a loyalty to the man of her choice, a bit rash, perhaps, for any woman, remembering the fickle heart of man in general, but however it speaks, it brings us face to face with the unforgettable fact that all the world loves a lover. We look into her individual life as she lived it day by day, finding sweet, tender characteristics displayed by young Harriet, and somehow we find ourselves sighing about it, but forgiving young Harriet this flagrant disobedience of parental authority.

For instance: We know that Harriet was industrious. Some great man, somewhere, sometime, gave utterance to the idea that each individual was worth just as much in the world as the things were worth about which he busied himself. Viewed in this day of feminine achievement in the world at large, Harriet did little. She made no speeches, made, in fact, no money, but she plied her needle assidously in order that her family might be clothed. She went farther than that. She spun the thread, and she wove the thread into cloth, all at home on a loom set up for the purpose. She wove counterpanes of rare design and made bed-quilts of the most approved style and pattern. She could cook, too, and was not afraid to depend entirely upon her own efforts along that line.

So when Harriet took matters in her own hands in the matrimonial game, she knew that discretion rather demanded that she seek with her unwelcome husband some other place of residence. Conjugal discussion resulted in Texas as the best choice for a home, and Harriet packed her clothes and her household linens including one of those counterpanes existent to-day (1927), and the newly married couple put out for Texas. This must have been about the year 1817, for the marriage took place in that year, and we cannot imagine young Harriet lingering long where parental approval of her marriage had been denied.

This young couple reached their destination as soon as might be expected with the slow-going ox-wagon the means of motion, and they settled at Nacogdoches. They soon found themselves at home in a log cabin, found plenty of real work at hand, and young Cole probably forgot all his wild tendencies in his effort to clear the forest, to plant the fields, to keep himself and his bride free from Indians and the thousand and one things that do so easily beset the pioneer. Children were born to them there, some in the log house, some in the better house they built as prosperity appeared, and life passed on evenly, smoothly until this couple had grown middle-aged, until they had to acknowledge to themselves that they had spent almost two decades in Texas.

Then came the Texas revolution. In Nacogdoches feeling ran high, though there were few Mexicans at hand to show just what Mexicans might do. Men went to the front eagerly and determined. Women stayed at home and did their own work and the work of the absent men, and waited as usual the result of battle. Sometimes a word drifted to them across the wide frontier, and they shivered, those lonely women, over the accounts of Goliad and the massacre at the Alamo. They heard, too, but faintly, that General Houston was preparing to make a stand somewhere near the eastern coast, but they were then fearful of heart, ready to believe any story of disaster.

Into the ready ears of those Nacogdoches folks was poured the famous lie concerning Houston and his defeat. and those same Nacogdoches folks put out to join the runaway folks in their certain indecent haste to find

themselves beyond the Sabine. They packed their few
household goods on any vehicle at hand—ox-carts being
most common—and they took up the egress just as rapidly
as ox-flesh would permit. The bunch of runaways which
included Harriet must have travelled at a goodly rate of
speed oxen or no oxen, for we are told that they stopped
only when they had reached the state of Mississippi.

Now when Hariett and her family had so eagerly joined
the runaways, her oldest son, true to his mother's strength
of mind and purpose, uninfluenced at that moment as she
had been by other folks needless alarm, this youngster,
eyeing all that indecent haste to reach the Sabine, had been
of another mind. His family might dread Mexicans,
might see nothing in the future for themselves but ready
obeisance to this despotic rule, dared they stay in Texas,
but young Cole saw matters in a far different light. Barely
grown, he was just able to shoulder a musket, but what was
greatly to the point right then, he possessed to an astonishing degree the desire to bear that weapon. Accordingly,
the ignominious flight of his people was staged without the
assistance of young Cole, and he took himself, despite his
youth, to the camp of the Texan army, and thereafter took
his own glorious part in the victory at San Jacinto. The
glory thoroughly enjoyed, young Cole probably wrote his
mother of the change in affairs for the young republic, but
she was never again persuaded to take up her life in Texas.

Harriet remained in Mississippi, reared her family there,
giving them every advantage she could. Her oldest
daughter, Nancy Cole, married Alfred Townsend and went
to live at Monroe, Louisiana. Harriet followed her
daughter, Mrs. Townsend, to Louissiana, and she made her
home with this daughter until her own death. Not long
after this death, in about 1870, Alfred Townsend conceived the idea that the climate of Louisiana was detri-
mental to his health, and this Mary Cole, persuaded her
husband to come back to Texas to live. And so, despite
the change of residence, despite the up-heavel that sent
Harriet to the land of old Mississippi, Texas counts among
her people to-day the descendants of Mrs. Mason G. Cole,
and if any individual one among them has brought the
blush to any citizen of this big common-wealth, said
blushes have been carefully hidden from the old lady who
now writes these annals down.

Data contributed by—

Mrs. W. P. Webb,
Austin, Texas.

MRS. E. B. NICHOLS

BORN

MARGARET STONE

When the good women of Texas realized that two men bearing their own good part in the Revolutionary war had found graves in Texas soil, they proceeded with commendable haste to mark those graves so that the world might know that the new country honored the old. These markers have a way of settling in the mind of the general public the link in point of time between the glorious July 4, 1776, and the glorious March 2, 1836. They even make plain and permanent the fact that one man saw service in both of these successful revolutions, but right here in the history of Mrs. E. B. Nichols and her sister, Mrs. Henry DeLespine, we are come upon two women who lived in Texas in her revolutionary days, women whose father, George Stone, signed the famous document now known to all good Americans as the Declaration of Independence. This George Stone was a straight-line descendant of William Stone, Governor of Maryland, appointed to serve by Lord Baltimore, and serving in that capacity from 1648 to 1665.

With these forefathers to their credit, Margaret and Jane Stone opened their eyes in old Virginia. The plantation home was all that could be asked of any home. There were books and carpets, pictures on the walls, slaves to anticipate their every want, horses—the very finest of racing stock—waiting the command of these girls from their immaculate stalls. Margaret and Jane with their parents, Mr. and Mrs. George Stone, formed the entire personnel of the family, save for the many guests that from day to day availed themselves of the hospitality of that well-kept mansion.

Without warning almost, George Stone and his wife died within a little while of each other. No near relatives were at hand in old Virginia to offer a home to the two little girls thus bereft, and Margaret, a little older than Jane, stood beside her father's grave, her arms laid protectingly about the shoulders of her young sister, wondering just what she might do. She wondered on into the night, poor child, when they were once returned to that mansion, once so gay, but her young mind could see no solution of her difficulty.

At last a friend appeared, no other than Judge Gray, a man of wisdom and foresight, a man of gentle heart and tender feeling. He was already full of the idea of Texas and the advantages to be gained by taking up a permanent residence in the new nation, and the judge decided that he would take Margaret with him to Texas. He had, perhaps, known little of her, but he saw in the person of that fourteen-year-old girl an agreeable companion for his wife, and then again, perhaps, he was moved by altruistic feelings alone in this idea of taking Margaret to Texas. We do know that Judge Gray went to that Virginia home, declared his intention of taking Margaret to Texas, more determined than ever to do so after he had seen her, but Judge Gray found himself face to face with an unsurmountable obstacle. Little Jane, winsome lassie, some years younger than Margaret, stood there beside her sister as she appeared before her new protector, and Jane's tears flowed freely, and her sobs mingled with the sobs of Margaret, just as much distressed at the thought of separation. The genuineness of that grief struck a chord in the heart of Judge Gray, and he, boldy declaring that two sisters should never be separated, bade Jane wipe her tears away and pack her baggage, and so the two sisters put out to Texas together.

Margaret, older than Jane, soon reached woman's estate and was married in time to Gen. E. B. Nichols. Gen. Nicholas was a West Point graduate, and was the commanding officer on Gen. McGruder's staff. He was connected in business with Mr. Rice, was in fact a full partner in all Mr. Rice's early business ventures in Houston, and as Jane began to blossom into womanhood, it struck Mr Rice that she might easily become the one woman of the world—for him. Margaret and her husband viewed the situation with delight, and they managed to let Jane know just how they felt about it. Differences in age counted for so little where so much of worldy advantage was to be gained by a step so simple.

Now Jane was beautiful. No man and few women ever thought to deny her that. She possessed as well the charm of wit, and a mind quick to see and to feel any intimation of beauty in anything. Small wonder then, that Jane, in the imperious demand of a woman conscious of her own beauty, saw things in another light. Being, so to speak, the prisoner at the bar, Jane saw in her elderly lover none of the qualifications that did so recommend him to the mind of her sister. Morever, Jane had fallen in love with a Frenchman, Henry DeLespine, a man in whom youth and comeliness and gay good humour had been happily combined. Her heart full of the allure of youth and comeliness and joy and light, Jane made bold to hold up her elderly lover in all manner of ridicule, and the result—between the two sisters, even, whose devotion had swayed Judge Gray in spite of himself, between them and the in-laws and all connections there sprang to life a first-class family row.

The result?   Jane eloped with her lover, Henry DeLespine.
This heart-breaking settlement of the family difference
took Jane to Palestine, Texas, to live.   If she ever regretted her ove for the young Frenchman, she never told
it.   She went on about her life in her own happy-hearted
way, but alas! she died at nineteen, little more than a child
in years, but she left behind two little baby girls.

There can be small doubt that this separation from her
sister, ending as it did in the young woman's death, was a
great blow to Mrs. Nichols.   She was living then at
Galveston where her husband had long since established a
paying business.   Boats from all over the world supplied
their needs, and there was no occasion for the labor done
by the women of the interior.   No spinning, no weaving
was ever necessary, for the cloth purchased in New England and in Europe was always at hand ready for my lady's
needle.   Gen. Nichols built a broad rambling house there
in that city by the sea, a one-storied affair, but it covered
almost one entire square of city property.   He built a
school house in one corner of his city property, employed a
teacher for his seven sons (they had no daughters) and
other children, paying tuition to the teacher, were made
welcome at this fount of knowledge.   The slaves were
housed in little houses, sometimes two rooms in each house,
all houses scattered about this low, rambling residence of
the "Massa."   These houses were not log houses, for the
lumber had been cut on the mainland and brought to the
island ready for service.   One unusually long building
among these slave houses had two floors, the lower of con-
crete, the upper of wood.   After slavery had been abolished,
the sons of Gen. Nichols took this house for a bowling alley.

Margaret Nichols superintended the care of this home
and the gardens about it with characteristic good sense and
enthusiasm.   Slaves in plenty to do her will, but hers to
do the planning, the supervising, and she did it well.   Her
husband liked to entertain on a lavish scale, and Margaret
met his desires at every turn.   She greeted his friends with
a hand-shake that was sincere and a smile none doubted as
genuine.   She smiled back at her husband across his table,
many times surrounded by prominent men of the day,
conscious that her own direction in the matter of preparation had rendered each viand perfect.   She kept her
place with each guest, male and female, as it came and
went.   She considered it her woman's privilege to minister
in a sensible way to the unfortunate people on the island.
She had advice for the servant out of employment and for
the city belle out of sorts with her lover. She is remembered

to this day on Galveston island as a queen among women.

General Nichols died about 1872 following a long and tedious illness. Margaret, thus watching him slip away, felt little of the shock of her husband's death. Her children then took up the management of her estate, and she lived on her quiet, peaceful, beneficent life surrounded by those seven sons and by their own children, come to gladden the later years of their grandmother. To the end of her days she was a blessing, rich and rare, to those about her.

Data contaibuted by—

Mrs. Reba Gaines.

MRS. JAMES M. BROWN

BORN

REBECCA STODDART

In the character of Mrs. James M. Brown we have met the product of an inter-racial marriage and a mixture of German and American blood. Environment, of course, has lent a hand, but it may be at least interesting to set down here the plain facts of Rebecca's inheritance. Rebecca's father, John Stoddart of Philadelphia, had met and loved and married Sarah Moses, her mother being a Gentile by birth and a Christian by training, her father being designated by the rather misty title of "a reformed Jew." It is hardly clear to your scribe in just what manner a descendant of God's chosen people had so conducted himself that this matter of reformation became necessary, but the term has been found in family annals, and for the sake of family peace your scribe is disposed to let the term stand. Then, too, in this one instance in question, the great-grandfather on this same Jewish side, even the side bearing the name of Moses, was none other than the Baron Rhinestein who lived in Castle Rheinstein on the Rhine river, a man of importance in his day in Germany. Now the Gentile father of this Rebecca in whose veins the Hebrew blood was flowing had been considered by many people the very handsomest man of his time in all the old city of Philadelphia, and many people made bold to declare that his young wife was the prettiest woman. A strange statement this to make in a city infested with relatives both male and female of this same John Stoddart. It awakened of course the slumbering jealousy and envy in all hearts of both sexes, and it came to the ears of Rebecca that some of her husband's people had spoken lightly of her in that they had called her a Jewess.

Failing to recall the stories of Sarah, of Rebecca, of Rachel, of the host of beautiful women walking in and out before the Lord, this certain Rebecca lost her poise, burst in fact into vindictive anger, and finally traced the remark to some member of her husband's family. Reminding these despised in-laws of her own mother's race and religion, Rebecca answered her in-laws not wisely, perhaps, but too well, and there was to say the least considerable coolness from that time forward in the manner of each when they were forced to meet. Children came to this Rebecca, some two or three of them, and they were brought up no doubt according to orthodox Christian faith. They were allowed to visit their people, allowed to do so fully and freely, but they went to the mansion of their fathers unattended by their mother. Rebecca had felt the sting of insinuation, and Rebecca never forgot it.

When Rebecca had been married some eight or ten years, her husband, John Stoddart, died. We have no record to show just what this death meant to Rebecca. We cannot say how she treated his family when death had appeared with its softening influence. We do know that very soon Rebecca began to grow restless in her Philadelphia home. She had property of her own, enough to make life pleasant for her there in that Quaker City, but try as she might to amuse herself, Rebecca grew more restless as the days went by. Some warm friends of hers emigrated to Texas, all the friends left behind prophesying that they would return before the year was out. The friends did not return from Texas, and this proved to Rebecca that they had found Texas a far better country than the one they had forsaken. So Rebecca, being her own master, disposed of her affairs to her own advantage— thanks to her self-denied Hebrew blood—gathered her little flock about her, and boarded a south-bound boat, headed straight for Texas.

We know little of that boat. Luxurious appointments in our steamers of to-day may have been evolved since that day. We care little about it. We do care that on that boat Rebecca Moses Stoddart met one C. K. Rhodes, looked him in the eye and decided to look again. She learned that he was a hardware merchant bound for Texas, coming on a venture, knowing no more of the real state of affairs in Texas than did the restless Rebecca, and before the voyage was done these young people met thus accidentally, had decided to be married as soon as they landed in order that they might face the wilderness together.

Rebecca Stoddart-Rhodes began life in the city of Galveston under most pleasing circumstances. The despised in-laws were not present to suggest aught to the world but that Rebecca was a beautiful woman entitled to the admiration of friend and neighbor. Her own Stoddard children were liberally cared for, her own funds and those of Mr. Rhodes being at their disposal. They established a home on Galveston island, and though Mr. Rhodes lived to be an old man, he died at last, leaving Rebecca again a widow. She lived on in her Galveston home, watching her Stoddard children grow to maturity. The same cares, the same joys incident to motherhood came her way. One daughter, Rebecca by name, developed an astonishing beauty. She was as well a great companion for and a great comfort to her mother. Due in some measure, maybe, to her quarrel with the Stoddard family over the Jewish question, Rebecca became most devout in her church work, most regular in her attendance on church services. To most of these services she took her daughter with her.

At one of these services in old Trinity church in that same Galveston, one James M. Brown watched Rebecca as she followed the services. He knew the young woman beside her was her daughter, but a thin scarf thrown across Rebecca's shoulders revealed some of the beauty of the dainty flesh beneath, and Brown decided to look further into the matter. He found Rebecca to be a woman after his own heart, and before long Rebecca found herself mistress of the Brown home.

This home was a nice one, the equal in its time of any home in the state. Texas was beginning to dream, too, of an independent, individual life, and many of her foremost men gathered in the Brown home from time to time, sometimes on business, more often on pleasure. General Houston, a warm personal friend of Mr. Brown, was a frequent guest. Through the association with Houston, Brown contributed liberally toward the war fund in 1836, but he took no active part as a soldier in any of the battles. And Rebecca, looking always well to the ways of her household, found joy always in the association. For twenty consecutive years, a New Year's ball was held in her home to which all influential people of the day were bidden. Supper, so called in early Texas days, was always provided and ample in every way, and the wine flowed freely.

At the close of the Civil war, Federal troops took charge of the Brown residence as well as that belonging to Mrs. Nichols, for the proud owners had fled at the first notice of Lee's surrender to the interior of the state. The soldiers occupied these homes for many weeks, and the housekeepers, the mistresses of these mansions, thought of them and their furnishings with vain regret. Rebecca could see in her dreams the destruction of her fine linens, her carpets, her bric-a-brac but when the home was returned to her finally she found it to be in nice order. And in that home Rebecca Stoddard-Rhodes-Brown lived out the remnant of her days, five generations of her people many times assembled about her.

Data contributed by—

Mrs. Reba Gaines,
Austin, Texas.

MRS. JOHN LITTON

BORN

SARAH STANDIFER

Most things worthwhile in this world come from a tiny thing which we call a seed. When seeds are gathered together and sown in suitable soil, something worth while is almost sure to happen. When that something worthwhile has really happened, we are likely to look back proudly to that little bunch of seeds. If any human being connected in any little way with our own line of folks happens to possess just claim that he be numbered with any one bunch of seeds, we are likely to become a bit puffed up over the connection. To-day, Texas, with her three millions of people looks proudly back to the illustrious three hundred, and many of her people, following the instinct to puff up, state with pardonable pride that his or her forebears were among the people thus numbered. Now, some newcomer into the land may ask for particulars concerning this certain three hundred. Some few descendants of old-timers may need a little information on the subject. They were the three hundred men and women who came to Texas back yonder in 1824 with Stephen Fuller Austin and his first colony.

History, particularly any good history of Texas, will tell you all about the men in that first colony. Volumes concerned with the life of Stephen F. Austin are being written all over our own state to-day. This writing entails much labor and much research, and no man or woman of to-day would disparage in any way the work of those thus interested in the intrepid colonizer. Spanish grants and ancient land titles, dating back a couple of centuries will show the gift of the league and *labor* of land to each man who came thus with Austin. Any lawyer, proficient in his business, can trace a land title back to the men among the three hundred who received it first. We are proud of those men, just as we are proud of Austin and his far-reaching vision, but we want right now to call your attention to two women who started out to do that very same thing.

Elizabeth Standifer, a widow, came from Missouri with that first colony brought by Austin to Texas. Why she took this step, we cannot say. Were it a matter of financial troubles, or disappointment in social matters, it must ever remain a mystery. Moreover her daughter, Sarah, a young woman, unmarried, elected to come with her, and the two women with five other children, no grown man in any way connected with them to act as a protector, undertook the long perilous journey to Texas in order that they might make for themselves a home in the wilderness.

But before our Sarah could reach Texas, before the young lady, in fact, had reached the number of years commonly ascribed to discretion, at some place in the wilderness, she fell in with John Litton. Said John, the son of Lem Litton and Anne Forrester Litton, had been born in South Carolina in 1812, had gone with his parents to Missouri, had run away from that Missouri home in 1830 to take up his home in Texas with an uncle named Leman Barker. Leman Barker later had married Elizabeth, the mother of our Sarah. One year later, our Sarah became the wife of this John Litton, lately decamped from old Missouri.

And that marriage, true in every way to the characteristics of the bride, had been an outstanding event, even in our own day and time. Sarah was married five times, but each time, save the mark, to her own dear John. Neither was Sarah particular as to Protestant or Catholic form. In fact her trouble lay in the fact that neither form of church worship furnished right then in her locality the necessary man to administer the marriage sacrament. The laws of her country changed, too, with every one of its boasted six flags. Determined to obey those laws in every respect, Sarah, therefore, married her John many times. She jumped the broomstick with him, she took a lick of salt another time, and John, believing intensely in Sarah, did each time as he was bidden.

Some years after this marriage was first celebrated, Sarah took part in the runaway scrape. Back of a trusty mule, perhaps, or then, perhaps again, in an ox-wagon, but this we do know. During that hysterical flight from a mistaken sense of danger, Sarah's baby, the first of fourteen children, was born and died.

Along in 1841, on February 6, John Litton received a grant of land from the Republic of Texas, the papers being signed by David G. Burnet, and Thomas William Ward, Commissioner of the General Land Office. On this land, Sarah and her John finally took up their residence, the place being known far and wide as Hog-Eye.

The title is, to say the least, lacking in beauty, both as to sound and suggestion, but as time went on, that settlement became one of importance to the people in that vicinity, a place now known as Elgin. There is a legend connected with its name, true, maybe, false more than likely, but we are told that as time went by young people—and a few old ones—began to dance at this home, the music being furnished by a travelling fiddler, and he knew, alas! but one tune. He could play said tune on most any two strings of his little red fiddle, if so happen the others were missing. He might have, for all we know, antedated the famous violinist who delighted his vast audiences with his own composition played entirely on one string. It is pretty nearly certain now that the immortal tune that stimulated the young people in the frolic had been dubbed "Hog-Eye," and the home where the traveller first played it, soon took on the name of the tuneful bit of harmony.

On another spot of ground Litton found an ever-flowing spring. He found as well that deer abounded in the region, so Litton built a platform above the spring, and from this platform the venison was *killed*, there being many testimonials extant to-day as to the venison's tastiness. The place is to-day known as Litton Springs.

But the settlement at Hog-Eye, on the Brenham and Austin road, was a type far different from the lodge established at Litton Springs. A house had been builded there, of logs, to be sure, but a woman presided over this place of habitation, and it was not slow to show the effect of such presiding. It was furnished as well as one might expect it to be in a new country, some few things therein reminding Sarah of the old home in Missouri. Slaves, brought from across the border, had multiplied, and had rendered their services. Wild lands had been turned into fields and gardens, furnishing both vegetables and flowers suitable for our Sarah's table. Being near the public highway between Houston and San Antonio, the place became after a time to be known as a "Stage Stand," for the travel was becoming heavy as the dawn of Texas advances. There the stage horses were changed, there men and women came to wait the arrival of the stage, as little as one would wait the arrival of a railway train in our own day and time. They had there, too, what was known as a family grocery. This emporium was supplied with the necessities of life, all brought in by ox-teams, plying back and forth over that same road. One corner of the store held the *bar*, over which was dispensed without question the now widely tabooed liquor. And be it said in tone of warning to him who would doubt the widsom of the eighteenth amendment. no matter how earnestly Sarah might speak her woman's warning, many killings took place in that same family grocery, a pint or so of liquor clearly to blame. Before that same bar, Bowie and Crockett and Travis paused many times on their way about the new country, and there is little reason to believe that they failed to enjoy the libation provided for the asking. Bowie stopped there on his way to enter the Alamo, stopped and chatted with Sarah and her husband as men so often chat with no thought of the tragedy that may be lying in wait for them.

In the work incident to maintaining such an establishment, Sarah bore well her part. She managed the slaves that cared for the travellers' comfort. She gradually took entire charge of fields and gardens. The cattle collected from year to year through her husband's efforts covered apparently the whole face of the earth. They brought the Standifer's gold, too, these cattle, and it was kept in its precious beauty by this thrifty Sarah in a secret locker in the big, old fireplace.

Through all this hard, stirring, active life, Sarah Standifer Litton gave birth to fourteen children. The black mammy was present to help of course, but the real burden of parenthood must always fall upon the mother. If Sarah, and we know she recognized this duty, if she ever rebelled against this part of her life, it has been kept from the public eye and ear. We even believed that she went about the task joyfully, happy, contented wife that she was. Her children appreciated her efforts, unfolding like so many little blossoms, snuggling close to the parent stem.

Her love for her children brought Sarah one distressing experience. While she was yet a young woman, when her oldest boy had reached the proud estate of ten years of age, when they were still a little new to the Indian infested country, that oldest lad was stolen by the Indians. Sarah, realizing the situation, raised the alarm, using clouds of smoke, blasts from a horn, and her husband in the fields and her friends and neighbors answered the call. All day they scoured the woods, the banks of the streams, keeping a sharp lookout over the prairie stretching in between. A thousand visions floated through that mother's mind. Mindful of tales of Indian atrocities and Indian outrages, those visions were visions of torture. That boy's face, usually bright and merry, wore in that mother's eyes the pinched, white agony of suffering, and the other children, crowded tearfully about her, were but ready in her tortured mind to be carried off when the brutes should appear on the morrow. And then with the sun sinking in its unfeeling glory, with aching eyes still scanting that prairie stretching in golden light before her, Sarah saw two Indians coming toward her door, two of them, and between them they bore her son. Tortured! Not a bit of it. His eyes alight with the spirit of adventure, his smile beaming upon her, his mother, he made his low bow before her, dressed, if you please, in a suit of deerskin, to all appearances made new for him in a day, and dotted before and behind with beads as only Indians know how to dot things! Friendly Indians, a whole tribe of them living near her, and Sarah had not known of it!

In 1857, John Litton was stricken with what is now commonly called appendicitis. The doctor called in proceeded after the manner of the day to bleed his patient, and the patient lost his life as the result. The blow fell heavily upon Sarah. She had come with her mother to Texas, had braved the trials of a new country alone, but for twenty-eight years she had been the wife of a good man and true. She had learned the value of real companionship, and Sarah's heart rebelled at the thought of thus giving it up with life still young for them both. Distressed, well-nigh broken-hearted, Sarah but doubled her efforts for the sake of her family, and she, a lone woman in this still raw, unsettled country, raised all of her fourteen children.

The life of this rather remarkable woman may be summed up thus. She was a matter-of-fact, plain-spoken woman. Her education had been limited as many another woman's has been limited by the want of advantages in the environment in which life had placed her. She possessed, however, a keen mind, a quick mind. She took a matter as it was laid before her and studied it and sifted it until she reached conclusions satisfactory to herself. Through these conclusions she was able to gather about her no mean amount of property, and continued as long as she lived to manage this property and that acquired in connection with her husband. She escaped the snuff-stick, but she sat her down once a day and smoked her clay-pipe, deriving, apparently, the same comfort therefrom that one sees to-day on the face of the lord of creation when similarly employed.

She knew little, perhaps, of the dainty ways of the women drifted hither from the cultured parts of old Virginia. Her life had never known the ease, the manner that follows the possession of wealth from generation unto generation. She had spent little time in the dance, in the frolic, in the gay, light-heartedness to which youth should be justly heir, but her stern integrity, her dauntless courage, her undying loyalty to her family and her country have left their enduring mark upon her children and her children's children.

Data contributed by—

Mrs. S. J. Smith,
Austin, Texas.

MRS. LAFAYETTE HEMPHILL

BORN

MARY ROGERS

In glancing over the lives of pioneer women in Texas, one is struck with the fact that Texas is in no small measure indebted to Tennessee for the men and women who came first to live within her borders, the first save the Indians so far as history knows anything about it. Stephen F. Austin's colony, formed in Missouri in 1829, had many recruits from Tennessee, and among them we find one, Joe Rogers, who had some years before that year of emigration married Nancy Burleson, a sister, by the way, of Gen. Edward Burleson, who was afterward to play his own good part in the history of Texas. Children were born to Joe Rogers and his wife Nancy, back there in Tennessee, the youngest among them being this Mary of whom we write, and she, save the mark, had reached the mature age of four years when the Rogers family reached Texas.

Search as we may among the private affairs of Mr. Joe Rogers, we can find no excuse for this emigration, no business failure, no political disappointment, no entanglement with wine or women. We find just the plain, unvarnished desire to see a new country, to move as the birds of the air and the beasts of the field move to a newer and, as they hope, a better place. A yielding to Greely's trenchant advice, "Go west, young man," and that is the most one can say for the reason why, at least in this instance. Rogers took up his headright in Bastrop County, built him a log house near Wilbarger creek, and there he and his wife, Nancy Burleson that was, set them down to make a home. And our Mary, being a young and dutiful daughter, sat her down to help with all her might.

Now Mary was probably too young by many years to be able to contrast conditions in Texas at that time with conditions in old Tennessee. Childhood's desire, usually, is met within the bounds of home, and outward environment counts for little. Young Mary, then, in this home of love, should have been perfectly content to live out her little life, but Mary wasn't. When her daughter of to-day was asked the reason of this discontent, a daughter crowding eighty-three years of age, she made a definite and a comprehensive answer.

"Mary wanted to go to school."

We wonder if Mary understood exactly just why her heart overflowed with this desire. Did she realize that going to school was supposed to be an aid in the process of mental exercise necessary to the development of a forceful character, or did young Mary see in that school idea the

enforced gathering together of other children, and did she
know that friendship grown out of this association is in
itself one of the important benefits of this same school
idea?   Mayhap, we may never have a satisfactory answer to
these questions, but we do know that Mary went willingly
and glady to school whenever the chance permitted. Sometimes a teacher, travelling through the country in search of
health, would be prevailed upon to stop there in that part
of Bastrop County and open up a school.

At one time a school thus maintained was situated about
two miles from the Rogers home, but this distance made
little difference.   The Rogers children went back and forth
regularly as long as the school lasted.

But if the distance failed to be a stumbling block in the
path of learning, there was an ever-present condition that
made that path dangerous for young Mary, and that
condition was Indians.   Before we enter into this particular evidence of the treachery of the red man, let us look a
little dispassionately into the matter.   More than one descendant of pioneer women has been heard to express a
certain sympathy for the Indian, and to wonder a little bit
if the white man had behaved any better, had the Indians
invaded the white man's territory with the avowed purpose
of claiming it.   He who would thus take the part of the
red man has a convincing way of referring to William
Penn and the fact that no Quaker blood was ever spilt by
an Indian.   But it remained for the daughter of this very
Mary under discussion to give another exceedingly plausible excuse for the white man's desire to enter Texas.   Says
she, "There was land in plenty, both for Indian and white
man. The Indian needed very little land, for he wanted
only to hunt and fish, and he didn't want to work in the
fields."   Maybe so, but we must return to young Mary on
her way to school, her eyes stretched wide lest some Indian
slip up upon the little company of people bent with Mary
on going to school, for Mary knew that such slipping meant
instant death to them all.   Fortunately the Indians in
Bastrop County adhered to their custom of raiding in the
light of the moon, and staying well at home even in the
day time of this period, and thus young Mary had a breath-
ing space while the moon was dark.

But Mary remembered all her life one particularly trying episode with Indians.   In the dead of the night, at a
time when all things seemed safe, Mary, still a little child,
awoke in the night and felt very much the need of a drink
of water.   Now the water bucket hung in the good old
way from the eaves of the front porch, but young Mary,
being of good pioneer stock did not hesitate to go after the
desired drink.   Just as she opened the door, some horses,

some very fine ones driven up at dark and turned into the
yard for safety, gave a snort and a peculiar neigh, and
young Mary looked out upon a yard full of Indians. They
had pulled the fence down and were riding in solemn,
silent file about the house, planning, so thought Mary, the
best manner of attack. Mary slipped within doors, whispered the alarm to her father, and the family sleeping beside
him was quietly aroused. The house was then barricaded,
the means of barricade was always at hand, and Mr.
Rogers got his gun ready. The Indians were a bit surprised and slowly dispersed. There was a horse or two
missing, but at that time no man lost his life.

Such Indian episodes were frequent enough. The famous
Wilbarger case occurred in 1833. The story of the dream
has been told and retold until all Texas people know it by
heart. Mary told the story, herself, to her children and
her children's children, for she saw the men gathering to
go in answer to Mrs. Hornsby's demand, that they go to
the rescue of Wilbarger whom she had been told in a dream
was still alive, and waiting their deliverance. It was
Mary's own father, the gentle Joe Rogers, who brought
Wilbarger, still alive, across the front of his own saddle
back to the Hornsby home, wrapped in the sheet Mrs.
Hornsby had sent for his comfort, so sure was she of his
return alive.

Despite all this, Mary grew to womanhood, developing
like a flower in that raw country. Her cheeks were none
the less soft and fair because the Texas breeze fanned
them, and her eyes, lingering under blue, blue skies took
on the beauty of that hue, took on as well a certain light
that spoke the character of the woman within. She was
industrious, she could sew and cook and weave and spin,
but more than all these, young Mary possessed the elusive,
indefinable, something that rendered her desirable in the
eyes of men. Many men, their names well known in our
history, were nothing loth to ride ten miles out of the way
for an hour's chat with Mary, but Mary in all modesty
saw nothing in all this save the thing that fell in her simple
eyes into the lot of all women.

Now Mary's desire to go to school was not the whole of
her desire. As she grew older, Mary began to long to take
part in the dance. Joe Rogers, being a fond father, saw
no harm in this simple desire, and with Mary and her
sisters ripening into rare beauty, Joe took them
to dancing school, and maybe old Joe enjoyed it a little bit
himself.

The family conveyance, a real carriage, closed in, and
not unlike the *glass front* of the late eighties, drawn by a
pair of fine-hundred dollar dappled-grey mules, was used

to transport these young ladies back and forth to these dancing lessons, and it was no mean way of transportation. Even to this day we must admit the worth of the colored man's philosophy when he declared that "dere ain't no dependunce ter be placed in de hin' leg uv er mule," but it is safe to proclaim that the Rogers carriage never bogged hopelessly in the prairie mud, nor did it fail to reach home in time to be just a little bit ahead of any Indian raid that tried to swoop down upon it. At any rate, we feel sure that Joe Rogers, Indians or no Indians, mules or no mules, watched his pretty, modest daughters float through the quadrille and the Virginia reel, saw them taught to drop the proper curtsy and to cut the pigeon wing, and Joe at least showed no inclination to interfere in the harmless pastime. They danced there, according to Mary's own daughter, with "Joe and Billy Sayers," and we feel sure had they been so inclined, these girls could have told their descendants of many other members of that dancing class who afterwards became famous in Texas.

Mary and her sisters enjoyed, too, the home of an uncle, Jack Nance. He kept the stage stand near Bastrop, and there, from time to time, many prominent people gathered. General Houston was a frequent and welcome visitor, and so was Gen. Chambers. These men of note, perchance, were attended by young lieutenants, and said youngsters formed acceptable partners for the dance. Gen. Chambers was a warm, personal friend of Joe Rogers, and it was said that they two, together, once owned the land on which the city of Austin now stands. Years afterwards, acting on this belief, the Chambers heirs entered suit, and received $21,000 for their holdings.

About 1836, from out of the land of Alabama, one LaFayette Hemphill, in company with his cousin, Judge Hemphill, made his way to Texas and settled about six miles from Bastrop, the place of the settlement being known thereafter as Hemphill's Prairie. LaFayette, drifting about between Indian fights and efforts to subdue the soil, came into the presence of young Mary Rogers, came quite casually, so their daughter now declares, and love and courtship and marriage all followed in the natural course of things, the only reason for his success being that Mary preferred young Hemphill above her other admirers.

The Hemphills, the marriage duly celebrated, began the always beautiful work of home-building on Hemphill's own prairie in a log house daubed with mud. Mary received a negro woman as a gift from her father, and Hemphill's father gave another one. With these slaves to help, the new home started under the most favorable conditions.

Hemphill, ten years older than his pretty little wife, was much in love with her. In addition they were both thrifty, both determined to succeed in the battle for existence, and that home soon showed the effect of that determination and that thrift. As the family increased in number, a larger log house was built, and the slaves, also increasing in number were then housed in the old. Ten children in all were born to the Hemphills. One of them died with scarlet fever, and just exactly a year from the date of his death another child was drowned. The accident occurred in the Colorado river. The nurse, a devoted slave, slipped in a hole, the hole hidden in the red water, slipped to her knees and she and the child, riding high upon her shoulders, were both drowned.

Save for these sorrows, life slipped on pleasantly in the Hemphill home. Thrifty people, they prospered in every way, and by the time the two oldest girls were grown, Hemphill built a real house for the comfort of his family. It was well planned and the materials were carefully selected. The work of building it occupied more than a year.

Many interesting things occurred from time to time in that home. The girls made home merry with their noise and their chatter, and the boys brought to it the news from the outside world. The deadly Comanche Indians had been moved to the Indian Territory, and the Tonkeways, more afraid of the Comanches than they were of white folks, came into the settlements to work for a little food or a little bodily raiment as payment for any form of labor the white man might desire at his hands. Pioneer days were passing, but Mary still found plenty to do. Her house required and received her attention. Her slaves, already increased in great numbers, required her supervision. Her family physician, the father of her old friends, Joe and Billy Sayers, lived some distance away, and Mary learned many valuable truths concerning the care of the sick while waiting for him to answer the call. In this capacity of nurse, without antiseptic aid, without mechanical appliances so necessary in the treatment of the throat, Mary brought one little negro boy through three attacks of diphtheria, her skill aided only by the cast iron constitution of the child.

The Hemphills lived in that home the rest of their lives. They saw the Civil war wrest from their neighbors and friends the slaves they had valued and cared for. They saw the little boy, tenderly nursed through dihptheria, turned loose upon the world to shift for himself incompetent, untrained, inadvised. They felt the shock of the money loss following so hard upon the days of reconstruction, but they lived the natural life of the thrifty, their old age comfortable because of a provident youth, and they died the same year, Mary in February of 1872, and her husband in October of the same year.

This delving into the past for the incidents of women's lives in any one century brings a peculiar knowledge to the individual who delves. Maybe it brings knowledge of many things, and maybe some of it were better forgotten. But after all is considered, there is one fact that your scribe would like to state right now. This world is a beautiful place. From generation unto generation man has struggled to make his own handiwork a fitting complement of the work of the Creator. As she looked, this same scribe, into the face of the dear old lady giving these details lingering as she did on the efficiency, the beauty, the gentleness of her own mother long gone, as she turned for a glimpse of the face of the daughter sitting patiently by lest the mother grow weary in giving these details, somehow the scribe saw in the daughter's face recalling in detail the beauty of that other Mary long gone, the beautiful spirit of devotion between a good mother and a good daughter, and she told herself that that devotion at its height was the most beautiful thing in all the beautiful world. And she dares anybody to deny it.

Data contributed by—

Mrs. S. C. Granberry,
Austin, Texas.

MRS. ROBERT SELLERS

BORN

NANCY STUART SELLARS

Nancy Stuart Sellars was born somewhere in Tennessee, during the month of September, 1812, her father being Lard Sellars, a man who had served with dictinction as a captain in the war of 1812, but who died soon after Nancy was born. Her mother's name has been lost in the devious ways of history, and there seems to be none able to supply the deficiency.

Young Nancy soon arrived at years of discretion as children and puppies have a way of doing, and then in 1830, being considered fully grown, Nancy became the bride of Sam Wallace. Wallace brought two little daughters to the new home, daughters by a previous marriage, and in the course of time three children were born to Wallace and Nancy, two sons and one daughter. While these children were all still young, Sam Wallace died, leaving Nancy a widow with a helpless little flock dependent entirely upon her endeavors for their support. Nancy no doubt proved herself equal to the task, but there has been little mention made of her struggles during her widowhood. In September of 1842, Nancy married Robert Sellers, the name the same in spelling as her own maiden name, save the change of one letter. The father of her new husband and her own father were cousins, and the change of spelling had come about in some haphazard way which nobody understood and nobody bothered very much about.

In 1846, Nancy Sellars Wallace-Sellers started with her husband, his two daughters, her Sellers child, and the three Wallace children, on the long journey that must bring them to Texas. They journeyed from Gibson County, Tennessee, to Mills Point on the Mississippi river in a big old wagon drawn by two horses and two oxen. At this place they found a steamboat waiting their pleasure, the gangplank down, and Nancy passed over said gang-plank into a hitherto unknown world. Her sensations may have differed a bit from those of her son, for Nancy was grown, and Nancy had come of stock, stout, firm and true, but after a lapse of eighty-one years, that little boy declares that when a man took his hand to guide his own feet up the untried way of that gang-plank, the boat towered so high above him, that he had a sudden feeling that he was being carried into the sky. They established themselves in the boat for the trip down the river, its furnishings making it a palace to Nancy, its workings, its crew, its passengers forming items of interest to the six children, leaving everlasting impressions upon their childish minds, new entirely to this kind of world. At New Orleans, these Tennessee folks saw a bunch of boys licking molasses from the outside of a barrel. One of the little boys inquired of a deck hand just what the boys on shore might be doing. He received the astonishing reply that he had better speak low, for the boys licking that barrel were all Indians. Eighty-one years later, one of the boys on board the boat declared that the Tennessee children were the victims of a joke, but at that time the answer was sufficient to keep the children quiet and out of the way until they passed New Orleans, until they were safely out of reach of the deadly red men. Nancy Sellers cared little for the boys who enjoyed licking the molasses barrel, for just about that time a woman appeared on deck with a pug dog in her arms, a pet, a lap-dog of the deepest dye.

Now Nancy had been accustomed to dogs in old Tennessee. She had heard them baying throughout the night while on a camp-hunt with the men. She had depended upon them herself a little bit in the pursuit of a chicken selected for the family dinner, but on that boat, that floating palace, Nancy had come upon her first lap-dog, had been compelled to associate for the first time with a woman who cared for such animals. When this woman, in her presence, called the dog "Sweetie," when she kissed it on the slobbery mouth, Nancy left the woman's presence in silence, but Nancy voiced her disgust in the ears of her family in accents strong and to the point, and the children crowded about her never forgot it.

With the dog matter settled as far as Nancy was concerned, the boat passed from New Orleans down the Mississippi river delta out into the Gulf of Mexico. Somewhat accustomed by this time to the boat and the flow of the big river, the entrance into the Gulf made little impression on Nancy. Water was water, a thing to help them on their journey to Texas, and to Nancy a thing of charm, a thing of beauty. But a storm arose, a big storm, the like of which Tennessee folks had never dreamed, and the cry of the wind, the roll of the wave, the crack of thunder brought many a shiver. Time after time, the waves met across the boat's deck, washing every loose thing into the sea, and methinks this Nancy was glad to change even her palace—like surroundings for dry land, willing to endure any hardship if she might once more feel something stable beneath her feet.

Part of the luggage brought from old Tennessee was a farm wagon, and in the city of Houston, Nancy's husband bought three yokes of steers. With this equipment they began the journey to Reutersville, Fayette County, Texas, it taking Mr. Sellers, the oldest son and a negro man to do the driving. The road, guiltless of engineers and their levels, was shoe-mouth deep in mud all the time save when it was waist-deep for the men driving, and the water lying freely along the road sometimes assumed the same astonishing proportions. Frequently, rather frequently, the axles of the wagon found themselves dragging on the ground. No need of that journey for traffic cops and speed laws! No need for signs to warn these passengers of dangerous turns in the road. They made with this big team over this road, the astonishing pace of a quarter of a mile in a day. At the Brazos river crossing, another yoke of oxen was bargained for, said oxen answering to the names of Let and Lion. The trade arranged to suit both parties, young Sellers, already attained to the great age of four years, was asked to rise from the horse-hair trunk which had formed his only seat on that long journey, and from the till of that trunk Sellers drew forth the money and paid for the oxen. No banker's check, no money-draft, nothing but the pure coin and green-backs carried thus through the wilderness, every cent Sellers possessed in the world, and at the mercy of Indians and free-booters, anybody, in fact who might come along in a mood to rob. There is no record of theft on that journey, however, no record, either, to show that the new purchase increased the rate of speed by which they travelled. It is safe to say the purchase did not, at least until they were safely without the confines of the Brazos bottom.

They reached Reutersville at last, and Nancy and her household took up the task of home-making. They selected a spot about a quarter of a mile from town, for they found a log house already built there, and in that house they lived until 1849. In January of that year they moved into a house that fronted the main street of Reutersville, and stages between La Grange and Brenham passed before their front door. Over this same road passed many men on their way to the gold fields of California, many an enthusiastic "forty-niner," and the excitement of the venture made many a break for people in the otherwise monotonous round of life.

This break in family life was not always pleasant. In this thoroughfare, two men from La Grange indulged in a quarrel. Words followed words, and pistols were drawn, and one man was killed. The real reason of the quarrel was right then a mystery, but when the office of the dead man was opened by a committee of ten citizens, they found among his papers a plan whereby a band of men had been thoroughly organized for the purpose of stealing horses and slaves from the Sabine to the Rio Grande. The news spread, of course, and this company of ten, known as regulators, arrested a man whose name was on the list found in the dead man's papers. They found the man sitting under a tree eating watermelon—probably stolen— arrested him, took him to Reutersville, tried him before regulators, convicted him and hung him. His companion was cleared, but some strange want of confidence in him gave him three days to leave the country. Before forty-eight hours had passed, the regulators had sufficient evidence at hand to convict him, too, but he had realized the wisdom of flight and had not stood on the order of his going. Of a similar nature was the affair known as Dawson's defeat. Some years before, maybe only months, Dawson's men had been shot to death by some Mexicans. Citizens went as soon as it was safe, gathered up the dry bones of these victims and brought them back to Reutersville for burial. They dug one big square hole, built the side up high with rocks and poured the bones into the receptacle thus made. Nancy and her husband attended this funeral, riding six miles on horseback to do so.

The church came in, perhaps, for the largest share of attention paid by Nancy to any one thing outside her own home. A member, herself, of the Cumberland Presbyterian church, her house was yet the home of all preachers happening to come her way. Brother P. B. Chandler, a Baptist missionary to Texas, had been present at the burial of the bones of the victims of Dawson's defeat, and he and his wife went home with Nancy. While on this visit, the Reverend Chandler invaded the folds of the Cumberland Presbyterian minister and administered the rite of baptism by immersion to Nancy's seventeen-year-old son. Allan Walker, a Cumberland Presbyterian minister, retaliated by immersing a number of young people in the neighborhood. With the democracy of the true Christian, Walker baptized the negroes as well as the whites. This is a strange thing to us in the South to-day with our separate schools and churches for white and black, but your scribe recalls more than one church in East Texas whose balconies were occupied on Sundays with negroes, slaves of men and women who sat below. Another Cumberland minister, Rev. A. J. Atkisson, bought the farm adjoining the Sellers place, and he went fifteen miles for eighteen years once a month to preach in Nancy's church.

Nancy's husband sympathized with her in her religious work. He felt sometimes that he lacked the subtle fire of his wife in the conduct of religious discussion, but when it came to the doing of the word of the Lord, Sellers showed up in the front rank. At one time a minister named Walker appeared at their home for an all-night stay, and Sellers observed that his visitor's coat was shabby. Now Seller's own coat may have been shabby, even threadbare or ill-fitting, but in Seller's eyes that counted for little. Sellers did not stand before the people in the pulpit to tell them of the better way. Most any coat would do for Sellers, so long as Sellers was conscious of an upright heart, and in the end Sellers pressed upon Walker his own last remnant of elegance, his wedding coat of black broadcloth, and Walker took it. Sellers loved Allen Walker, loved as men sometimes love each other, and they never met in after years that Sellers did not feel a suspicious moisture running down his own cheek, a moisture that found a ready counterpart in the eyes of Walker bent lovingly upon him.

Then Sellers was ever broad in his religious view. At one time his neighbor, this same Atkisson, a Cumberland Presbyterian member, and Sellers a staunch Baptist, took their respective families fifteen miles in a farm wagon pulled by oxen to a Cumberland Presbyterian camp-meeting, and the two women, Nancy and Mrs. Atkisson, with a negro to help cooked three meals a day for two or three weeks for a crowd varying from ten to one hundred.

At Shiloh, twelve miles from La Grange and not far from Nancy's home, the Cumberland Presbyterians and Baptists built, about 1855, a combined church. This brought the crowd of Sundays to Nancy's table, and she, feeling that she was but doing her part, prepared on Saturday after Saturday, lest she desecrate the Sabbath, turkeys, hams, pies, cakes, bread and beans for the enjoyment of her guests. She maintained this custom long after she was an invalid, directing her servants and slaves from her bed of pain. This invalidism resulted from four attacks of pneumonia in twelve months time, brought on no doubt by overwork, the result of her loyalty to her family and her friends.

Prior to 1849, the business of Nancy's husband had consisted largely in the management of big teams that hauled cotton from their vicinity to Houston and brought back supplies to towns along the way, La Grange, Bastrop, even as far west as Austin. He one time went farther still in that he moved a lot of emigrants from Houston to New Braunfels and Fredericksburg. He sold his first big farm in the spring of 1853 and improved a much larger plantation in Colorado County. In 1881, the Colorado County farm was sold, and Nancy took her family to Luling to live. In the home established there, even though Nancy was an invalid, the same neatness, the same careful preparation of food was maintained. In all that work hers was the guiding influence, the law by which it moved. Two daughters, brought up in her own careful ways, her own exquisite neatness, supplied the strength she lacked and supplied it well, for they had been brought up in the fear and admonition of the Lord.

That new home, once destroyed by fire and rebuilt, stands to-day (1927) still presided over by two of those daughters—old maids we call them—and the home exhibits the same exquisite neatness, the same regularity demanded by this same Nancy.   As one stands within its walls, one feels anew the veneration for the pioneer woman, the woman who did her part, who blessed her husband and her home and her church with her bright presence, who strengthened them ever with her own strength, who did them good and not evil all the days of her life.   In this sanctified home Nancy died in 1883, leaving her husband to linger without her ten long years.   He, too, in time passed on, but to-day the power of Nancy and her upright life shines forth in the heart and soul of the noble son who has given us these few words for record.

Data contributed by—

Rev. Issac Sellers,
Austin, Texas.

MRS. WILLIAM BUCK BILLINGSLEY

BORN

ELIZA PINCKNEY WILSON

Samuel Wilson was a Kentucky gentleman of the old school—only the aforesaid Wilson failed to be a colonel, and then, too, he failed to live in Kentucky. Notwithstanding these trifling deficiencies, we stand firm in the decision first stated, for, viewed in the light of refinement, the light of occupation, of customs, even of habits, Wilson had passed for a Kentucky colonel in any court of any nation ever conceived by the mind of man.

Maybe this statement needs a bit of justification. Some folks criticize other folks when they give to Tennessee men, born and bred, the title of Kentucky colonel. Sometimes this criticism becomes irritating. The irritation thus produced is no doubt strengthened by the thought that these other folks may be right. It may be a bit far-fetched to call a man from Tennessee a Kentucky colonel, but the circumstances surrounding the case in hand will at least stand a bit of investigation. First of all this man Wilson owned a big plantation. We must admit that the land stretched along the banks of the Stone river in Gibson County in Tennessee, and that the farm was not very far from Murfreesboro. But on this farm, Wilson raised slaves and tobacco and some corn and some cotton. On this place he collected, no doubt, some good old Bourbon, meaning extinct—or should be—and then (spirit of old Kentucky take notice) he raised horses, fine horses, big horses, little horses, fast horses, and slow. He sold all these articles, save his slaves, at a fair profit, and then— Kentucky again,—he raised a pair of horses, called Shapespeare and Conqueror, said horses according to tales told, failing always when it came to the matter of taking anybody's dust. Wilson dressed as became a Kentucky colonel. Clean but careless, a big hat to shade his eyes when Caesar and Conqueror came in facing the sun in the last length, a drooping mustache, big boots, no diamonds, no flashiness, all in all the habiliments adapted to the subjugation of the soil and the care of slaves and the proud ownership of Ceasar and Conqueror. And then, too, Wilson was a Whig.

Some splendid stuff from which to develop a real heroine, and as usual, the law of evolution has not failed. This Tennessee Whig was blessed with a daughter, Eliza Pinckney Wilson, and she, enjoying the receipts from her father's various activities as most daughters have a way of doing, enjoying the care and attention of a very faithful black mammy and a few other slaves just as faithful, grew up among the well-kept fields and the carefully groomed horses, grew up in her father's big house on Stone river, a thing of beauty, a joy in her ownself, but, as her father later learned, not according to his idea, a joy in an uninterrupted forever. She was sent to college as it was called in that day, the Sharpe school it would now be called, and there she speedily became a leader in her classes—even as Ceasar and Conqueror had ever led all other equine productions. There she learned to really spell the words of the English language, using as a text-book the "Blue-Backed Speller." More than this she learned to parse the English sentence, learned to know when and where to use the personal pronoun and how to adjust the little matter of case, old Kirkham's grammar being her authority in this last little matter. She obtained a quickness in the manipulation of figures, all these things, because of her keen interest therein, remaining with her until the day of her death. Under the careful tutelage of her mother, Eliza became an expert needle-woman, some of that work in existence to-day and exhibited from time to time to the humiliation of all spectators, including her descendants. She could make an elegant pound cake and other cakes not designated by weight, and this latter attribute she transmitted to her daughters and her grand-daughters after her. And she could laugh, and she could dance. She could even sing a song or two to the twang of a jeweled guitar, and maybe as Wilson looked upon her, this girl often proclaimed the most beautiful woman in Gibson County, maybe he forgot for a moment or two to rejoice in the possession of Caesar and Conqueror.

But into that home, placed by mistake in Tennessee near the bank of the famous old Stone river, into that very home trouble made its hateful appearance. Whether by day or night, we cannot say, but it came in the form of William Buck Billingsley. Billingsley had roamed afar, and every word he spoke at any time or any place was tinged with the flavor of romance. He had been to Texas, had galloped madly across her prairies in front of determined Indians. He had managed always to keep ahead of the savages, and he had borne, too, his own good part in the Texas struggle for freedom. He was full of the glory of victory, and fired with an uncontrolable admiration for San Jacinto's glorified commander. He was a soldier, guiltless, perhaps, of brass buttons—the Texas army had no time to acquire outward adornment—but Billingsley was erect in his bearings, a comely man, a forceful man, and a very few glances of his bright eye satisfied him forever of young Eliza's charm. Eliza, herself, was adept in the glance of the eye, and old man Cupid and his troupe staged another performance right in the presence of her astonished father and mother, the old back mammy and old Daddy Clem.

All well enough. Some folks *say* they believe that all the world loves a lover. Some folks are sometimes mistaken. In this instance Wilson failed to feel any throbs of anything like love for the male participant in this affair. He saw in the man, so captivating in his daughter's eyes, an object of aversion. To him the man hailing from a *town*, even from Trenton, dressed according to city requirements, deporting himself as a city man—such a man, to Wilson was the living embodiment of the most contemptible thing on earth, *a city dude*. Moreover, Wilson made no attempt to hide his aversion in the matter, and people round about, knowing Wilson and keeping in mind the flash of Billingsley's eye, began to look for some happenings of interest.

There was no doubt an instance or so of real interest. The courtship proceeded, despite the attitude of the father. Billingsley, struggling with his love and conscious of his own ability, had no thought of drawing back. Eliza, just as conscious of her own feeling, aided, mayhap, by some Wilson stubborness, all honestly acquired, was just as determined. Paternal orders were as naught. Denied the house that sheltered his lady-love, Billingsley received from the black hand of Clem, Eliza's slave boy, a tender billet-doux, and Billingsley did not scorn to trust his reply to the same black hand. Matters continued in this way for some weeks, maybe months, but in the end, Wilson had to give in half-way, and preparations for the marriage began in earnest. The bride's dainty household linens, all handmade, hand-woven, her own wearing apparel, the cakes, the meats, the sweets, all in readiness for the feast, and then Billingsley and the fair Eliza stood before the minister at nine a. m. in that home on Stone river and were solemnly married. Witnesses in plenty, friends and relatives, even the proud, determined, outwitted old father, but the latter sat in a corner during the ceremony and read his newspaper.

Apparently indifferent to her father and his newspaper, Eliza tripped her happy, subdued way among her wedding guests, hiding beneath a smile the tears that seem to come to every good woman with her wedding ring. And then the time having arrived, the bride, according to stories often told by old Clem, this happy bride got into a buggy with her new husband and allowed her over-taxed nerves to relax during the long drive to Trenton.

Sometimes a bit of parental objection is an aid in working out a marriage venture. If the man thus opposed

happens to be a real man, if he happens to love the woman
he has married against her father's will, the thought of that
objection must bring a sting like unto that inflicted by a
lash. It must forever afterward exercise a certain invincible incentive to labor and to labor hard to bring into
this certain woman's life, even the woman who had voluntarily given up her home for him, to bring to this woman
every comfort, every luxury within his humble reach.
Remember, according to the old slave's letter, written in
1902, the Wilson home teemed with luxury. The grandmother, Mrs. Samuel Wilson, Sr., made her home with her
son.

"The old lady was vast rich," so the ex-slave wrote of
the elder Mrs. Wilson. "She pulled de money out'n her
pocket and had her two sets of silver spoons made. She
was vast rich, the bent over old lady was."

These things must have floated through Billingsley's
mind during that sweetly, tenderly solemn wedding journey,
must have mingled in his thoughts and his dreams throughout those first glowing days and nights of married life.
Something, perhaps, of course, some inherent worth in the
"dude" he had despised, or maybe, the birth of the first
grandchild, Samuel Wilson Billingsley, dissipated after a
bit some of the colonel's wrath, and things slowly but surely began to move with a better pace. It might be possible
for even a Kentucky colonel, born and bred, to remain
impatient always with a daughter like Eliza. It had been
well nigh impossible for a man like Billingsley to fail to
remember the sting of the lash of his father-in-law's objections.

Then, mid all these home delights, Billingsley one day
made to his wife, Eliza, a startling statement. *He must go
back to Texas!* To Eliza the idea was appalling. Told by
her lover-husband, even, these stories of Texas meant little
to Eliza. She could not grasp the enchantment to be
found in the Texas prairie, in the Texas forest, in the wild,
wide sweep of the cooling Gulf breeze. To Eliza, Texas
was as yet a thing apart, a dreary, desolate scene located
the other side of the world, inhabited by Mexicans and by
Indians and infested by snakes and bears and centipedes.
When Billingsley's eyes snapped with the memory of San
Jacinto, and his tongue reeled off his praise of Houston
and Austin and Lamar, Eliza thought only of Bowie and
Crockett and Fannin and the death-dealing enemy who
had failed to spare them.

But the determined lover was the determined man.
Eliza soon found that the same thing that had withstood
her old father was now about to overrule her own desires
and her own prejudices. She knew she must go to Texas,

knew that she must go back with that lover husband to
the land he had helped redeem, and Eliza finally agreed
openly to the plan. The wagons were made ready, their
household effects packed, and the day set for their departure. Col. Wilson watched those preparations for departure with real anxiety. Since his daughter's marriage he
had suffered a thousand pangs of regret that he had been
forced to part with her. Those pangs had been augmented
a thousand times by the look of resigned determination on
his daughter's once beaming countenance. Under the spell
of that regret, Wilson gave to Eliza the boy Clem, the go-
between in that courtship, and suggested that she take him
with her to Texas.

Fine! The presence of the slave would save Eliza from
many a menial task. Clem was a real character. To
Eliza's son who loved old Clem, we are indebted for this
vivid description. "His teeth were as white as snow, and
this skin as black as the ace of spades, yet spotlessly truthful and honest to the core. I know he was for no other
reason than that my mother often said so." Such an individual would be worth taking to a wild new country.
So thought Billingsley, quivering a little under the idea of
his father-in-law's magnanimity.

Then Clem came forward to express his own ideas in the
matter. Clem claimed to be in love with a dusky maiden
who belonged to the owner of the adjoining plantation.
Clem saw no real reason for separation from his dearly beloved. Did Wilson resort to the whip and the lash? Not
one bit! There was no need for it. Already tender under
this parting business, feeling himself, perhaps, much to
blame in the whole matter, Billingsley stepped forward
with the necessary amount of money, purchased outright
the damsel so necessary in Clem's eyes, and the two negroes,
man and maid, began the long journey to Texas in all
confidence in the new master and mistress thus romanti-
cally acquired.

There seems to have been some money in the pockets of
Buck Billingsley, the so-called *city dude*, for immediately
upon his arrival in Texas this second time, along about
1854, he settled rather substantially in the town of Bastrop.
He built there a big, white house, four rooms and a hall
above, and five rooms and a hall below. He opened a
general mercantile business, his partner being Frank
Glover. He made considerable money hauling freight
from Houston to Bastrop and to other Central Texas communities. In all these undertakings, Eliza did her part.
She even unbent a little as her old father had been forced
to unbend, and began to feel at last some little bit of
enthusiasm for some of Billingsley's Texas heroes. The

big white house began to seem like home to her—it was a nice house in itself—but Eliza let it be known that to her it seemed woefully bare of furnishings. She felt keenly the want of the mahogany and rosewood of her Tennessee home, but she learned after a while that an educated woman can exist in comfort in a wilderness. She learned that her mind worked just as well where things were new. She even found partners now and then in her intellectual gymnastics, a joy unto her soul. A gallant descendant testifies that Eliza and Dr. McCall of Austin, a frequent guest in the Billingsley home, held many parsing tournaments and spelling bees, the battle lasting sometimes far into the night, each side claiming the victory when the late bed-time finally arrived. She learned that her delicious cakes and pies, her dainty custards found willing consumers in the wilderness, and this sense of importance added to her woman's happiness. She attended the inaugural ball given in honor of General Sam Houston when he became governor of the state. For this occasion she was gowned in a navy blue silk, lined throughout with linen and furnished with innumerable whale-bones. Now the son who told us of old Clem—the son whose heart was always full of love for his mother—tells us that this dress worn to that ball was a *black* silk, the skirt trailing the floor according to custom, her ears supporting dangling ear-bobs of no mean proportions, her beautiful black hair, thick and long, allowed on this occasion to flow freely. The son dwells long on the beauty of the hair, reminding us that it "is God's greatest heritage to woman." On a hot summer day women of this day might be inclined to refuse such a heritage, but for the time we are living in another day, another time when such thoughts had been a little less than sacrilegious. But while this man speaks tenderly of that mother he unconsciously brings before us a picture of a grand-daughter which your scribe has one time seen so attired, and she must confess that the whole costume, even the hair, brought a sweet picture, one not to be denied. Eliza enjoyed that ball, for she basked in the reflected light of her ex-soldier, hero-husband, and during the simple gaiety she caught a gleam of Houston's own personal charm, and understood a little better why her husband *would* come back to Texas. And she stayed her time without maternal misgivings. A baby at home to be sure, a little girl baby, but Aunt Jenny, the wife of old Clem, sat beside that cradle, her black hand at rest on the rail, nodding a bit now and then, her head erect at the first little sound. That same baby, years afterwards, hearing the story retold, added triumphantly: "Mamma never would have left me with no white woman." O, ye who would belittle the devotion between the Southern slave and her mistress!

But, beneath her enjoyment of that frivolity,—frivolity has its place in the best of lives—beneath her mother love, her devotion to her lover-husband, beneath her cake baking and her exquisite sewing, there lurked always a determination, sweetened a bit by her womanliness, but none the less firm for all its sweetening. On one occasion her husband bought for her what was called then a dress pattern. Silk, the gown dark blue, spread with gaudy white flowers, bought perhaps with some sacrifice to himself—remember he had been classed as a *city dude*—a piece of loving kindness that should have been met with womanly tenderness and smiles of appreciation. But in that day, silk was silk, everlasting—sometimes, but *always* bought at a price. No doubt Eliza longed to feel its soft richness beneath her fingers. She longed to hear its soft rustle behind her as she trailed it about. But—Eliza possessed a sense of the eternal fitness of things. She looked about her home, bare of pictures, of furniture, of carpets, and to Eliza her husband's silk purchase became a wicked thing. Worse than that, it appeared to be a wicked thing likely to be repeated, for it came to her that this lover of her youth was exhibiting some of the qualities of the *city dude*, so despised by her old father. Maybe after all, the gallant Texas soldier cared too much for personal adornment at the expense of other things!

Eliza made no complaints. Complaints were not included in her methods. But Eliza made a resolve and formed her plans. The day following that silk purchase, her devoted son sat at her knee as was his custom, and toying with the delicate hands, asked tenderly: "When are you going to make up your new silk dress?"

"Not until your father buys us some house furniture to match the dress," was the astonishing reply.

Records fail to furnish an account of marital discussion or dissension on this matter. The mother spoke to her son her firm resolve. We do know that the dress pattern was never made up. We can but argue from this that the Texas home of Eliza Pinckney Wilson Billingsley was never furnished according to her ideas of completeness.

We wonder, did this fact grieve her? No doubt. She possessed to an unusual degree that quality of the feminine mind that goes far in the regulation of the advance of the race. Without that quality on the part of woman, man would soon lapse, even now, into barbarism. So says an eminent lawyer in our Texas of to-day (1928). Occasionally some man is born who cares to spend his spare time in cleaning house, in keeping his grounds in a little better condition than his neighbor, but such men, as a rule are freaks. On woman must lie the burden of redeeming man from his barbarous tendencies. Eliza, living in her big white house built there in Bastrop for her by the lover of her youth, realized this truth and became all the more determined to hold up her own end of the line. She must have, so she thought, the best of furniture for the house in which she was to spend her own life, in which she was to rear her own children. A dream, maybe, of the old home on Stone river, perhaps, in her lonelier hours a longing to be once more within its hallowed walls, to view the glisten of the mahogany, to feel again the softness of carpets beneath her little feet! Ah, who can say as the days came and went, as the silk, bought in a mistaken idea of love and kindness, lay rotting upon the shelf, who can say just what depths of sorrow that dream and that longing brought to this gentle, sweet-tempered, loving woman! Home! Her own big Texas home with its four rooms upstairs and its five downstairs was precious in her sight. No single service in that home did she ever neglect, but she must listen at times to Clem and his loved helpmate talking of past glories, in their longing to be back "wid ole Massa an' de missis." She, because she was "de missis" in this new home, must stifle in her own heart the longing the negroes voiced without restraint. O! to be once more where ease and luxury and taste and elegance had already appeared as it generally does in the land where men and women are determined to subdue the wilderness! God help all such women, blest as this one was blest with the elevating instinct of home! They must go on in the line they know to be right. God bless all such in their hours of longing!

Eliza's religious life and attitude was just about what one would expect in a woman so devoted to home and its interests. Educated in a college of her day, denied the broader view of life that has come with our own day, unable to discuss any doctrine of baptism or redemption as we would discuss them to-day, her whole life glowed with that love and consideration for others which is the outgrowth of all real religion. Conducting herself with the dignity demanded of a woman who would successfully manage a big home with slaves at her bidding, she yet possessed that inborn beauty of soul that made her grant in all matters of heart and religion the liberty she, herself, demanded. At some time near the beginning of the Civil war, the strife that was to set all slaves free, Dr. Kendrick came into Eliza's neighborhood and there conducted a revival. These services, of a full month's duration, were for white people only. The slaves held their own services,

choosing a time when not needed in the discharge of their
duty to "massa." They seemed to enjoy these services
held for them exclusively better than they enjoyed attendance at the white services where they listened to the
white preacher from the gallery. But on a certain Sunday
afternoon during the revival conducted by Dr. Kendrick,
old Clem, even Clem who had smuggled the love notes into the hand of the fair Eliza, sat in the far end of the arbor
watching and listening to his own "white folks *serbices*."
After several men and women had made the "good confession" old daddy Clem, grown grey and trembling in the
service of those he loved, rose from his seat and asked in
all gentleness if he might make a confession.

Remember, Clem was a slave. At law he had no name
save that of his master. He "owned no foot of land, no
cottage in this wilderness." He stood solely on his merits
as an humble servant of the god he thought he understood.
Wondering perhaps what the attitude of the preacher
might be, Clem, polite by instinct and by training, made
his earnest request.

"Kin I mek de confession?"

Fired with the loving message he would fain deliver, the
minister answered: "Come on brother, make your confession!"

Hurriedly, down the aisle, old Clem walked, his eyes
bent upon the face of the man who had invited him. Great
day for old Clem, old Clem who longed for old Tennessee
and the house on Stone river, for the "massa and de miss-
tis," for when he turned from that altar he met the eyes
of his own "Mis' Liza," and those eyes were brimming
with tears of loving sympathy. Then forgetful of minister
and of time and place, forgetful of battle raging afar in
order that he might be free, old Clem, breaking every law
of order in Divine Worship, looked straight into the face
of his mistress and exclaimed "Mis' Liza, I'se so happy!"

And adds her son who was present, "Mother's own eyes
overflowed with joy."

Simple story, bearing no weight on economic problems,
solving no questions of state or army control, but it presents a sweet, wholesome, authentic picture of the spiritual
relation often existent between the Southern mistress and
her slave.

There could be no better ending to this sketch than a
copy of the closing paragraph of a letter written in 1928
by S. W. Billingsley, a son of Eliza.

"Mother was a woman possessing great will power, not
much to say, well balanced, great patience, gentle and
kind, loved her neighbors and was loved in return. If she
ever had an enemy, I never knew of it. She died at the

age of fifty-eight leaving a heritage of motherly love to her children, fully worthy of the name 'Mother.'   No wonder I cherish and reverence her life!   I could not do anything else and be her son."

Data contributed by—

Mrs. Charles Alford,
Mr. Samuel Wilson Billingsley.

MRS. GEORGE W. SINKS

BORN

JULIA LEE

Along in the spring of 1840, two brothers, Lee by name, came to the young Republic of Texas from the city of Cincinnati. They brought with them two sisters, Lydia, already described in these pages as the wife of Dr. Robertson and Julia the subject of this sketch. The journey, a great thing in the eyes of women of that day, began by boat on the Ohio river, thence on down the Mississippi to the city of New Orleans.

Julia spoke years afterwards of the pleasure of the journey. General Houston was on the boat with his second bride, Margaret Lea. To be with Houston at that time produced a thrill all its own. The horrors of the Alamo and Goliad lingered yet in the minds of everyday folks. The fear of Mexicans was by no means extinct. Indians roamed about the young nation, a little contemptuous at heart over the pitiful Texas army. But San Jacinto had been fought and won. San Jacinto's hero had proven himself worthy in the eyes of all the world, and these newcomers to Texas, spared actual knowledge of the struggles of that little army were just ready to fall under the spell of Houston's personality, a spell that lingered about him throughout all his life. At the last dinner aboard that vessel, General Houston arose and proposed a toast.

"Ladies and Gentlemen: I wish to give a toast, hoping that all may agree with me and with my sentiments also. I drink to the long and vigorous life of the Republic of Texas, to the wisdom of her rulers, both now and in the future, to the success of all finding homes within her borders, to the happiness and content of her citizens, and last but not least, to the beauty and virtue of her daughters."

Still under the spell of this man's magnetism, Julia anchored in Galveston harbor. The temptation to describe Galveston harbor is great, but we must hasten on to tell of the things which attracted Julia most in that wonderful place. There, the water lapping rhythmically against each single little craft, Julia beheld the Texas navy. Small in number, significant in power, but Julia had listened to the magnetic voice of Houston. She had come to feel the quickening power of his own vision for the young republic, and to her the little fleet of vessels was the realization of the big man's dreams.

After a day in Houston, Julia started with her brothers and her sister on the long overland journey to Austin. The brothers established a home there, and then Julia, busy as all women must be in a home in a new country,

found time to take up the studies begun in Cincinnati.
She studied geology and botany, classifying specimens and
pressing flowers. She made scrap books of valuable
clippings, some of them in existence to-day (1929). She
wrote a history of Fayette County and at her death presented this with other valuable papers to the State University. When the bones of Dawson's men and those of the
Mier prisoners were to be buried, she decorated the box
designed to hold them.

But these activities did not in any way interfere with
the discharge of Julia's home duties. She met bravely,
cheerfully, willingly every obligation. Slaves relieved
her of the heavy work, but negroes need always the guiding hand. Julia taught them to card cotton, to spin
thread, to weave it into cloth. She helped them fashion
the cloth thus made into household things and into garments for themselves. She was in short, a capable mistress, looking well to the ways of her household and her
slaves. To her brother she was a great comfort, looking
after his personal wants, a charming, gracious hostess to
his many friends.

On a certain afternoon, not long after Julia became mistress of that log house, she laid by her duties, her studies,
her music, and hied herself away to the home of a friend,
living some distance away, even unto Congress avenue as
it is now known. The usual feminine greetings, plus a bit
of chat ended as it frequently did in the call for a bit of
music on the part of Julia. Nothing loth Julia took up
the guitar, twanged the strings a time or two, twisted a
peg a bit, and then in her sweet low voice, with a certain
amount of shading all her own, Julia began the first stanza
of the old favorite, "Am I Not Fondly Thine Own?"

Into that quiet room, disturbed only by the plaintive
music thus produced, an unknown man rushed, staggering
at last before the astonished women, an arrow through his
body, certain ominous sounds proclaiming the Indians in
hot pursuit. The man, apparently reduced to his last
extremity, gave one glance about the room, realized in that
glance that the house was occupied by defenceless women,
and then curses directed upon his own head fell long and
loud from his quivering lips, for he felt as only man could
feel, that he had unwittingly led the Indians to the place
where the absence of all white men made slaughter so easy.

The young women cared little right then for the curses
the man saw fit to proclaim. They knew only too well
what had happened. Moreover, certain ominous sounds
before mentioned became more ominous. Said sounds demanded action, and quick action, on the part of each and
every individual present. The pioneer woman rarely fails

at such a time to do her part. She often fails to see any just cause for indignation on her part because some one thing has for the moment gone wrong. These women entertained no vindictive thought against this man rushing unannounced into their gentle presence. They were too busy. They were removing the arrow from the blasphemous man's body. They were closing and barricading doors and windows in the hope of protection from the oncoming Indians. On they came, the bloodthirsty savages, their foot-fall audible to the trained ear of the pioneer woman, the man, lying now upon the floor cursing himself the louder with each advancing step, the women, pale and breathless but short of "cuss-words," placing chairs and tables against the doors in what they knew to be a vain hope.

A shot rang out, clear, sharp, incisive, and both men and maidens knew that help had come. Sensing in a way peculiar to pioneer life that something was wrong, a company of men had formed and gone to the rescue. The Indians, realizing the superiority of gunpowder over bows and arrows, took to their heels, following the old trail that lay cross the hill now occupied by the Governor's Mansion.

Julia had presided over her brother's home for some time before the first real romance came into her life. Sought after in that quaint log cabin home, Julia had been too busy over her household duties to give any real thought to would-be lovers about her. She but told herself as each suitor walked away that she was too busy, that her duties were too many to permit of any serious love affair on her part. But Julia was to find that love can laugh at.duties with the same complaisance that love laughs at locksmiths.

Into the little group of males frequenting of an afternoon and evening that log-house parlor walked George Sinks, and for some inexplicable reason Julia immediately forgot her duties. This George Sinks had been born in Rockbridge County, Virginia, but his parents had taken him as a child to their new home in Cincinnati. This young hero, appearing in all the glamour of love's young dream, had lived in that city at the same time in which Julia lived on the farm near by, but some kind providence had kept them apart, had hidden from each the awkwardness of the half-grown child, in order that they might meet in the flush of youth when life for each was at the height of its beauty and its charm. A courtship of several months intervened, a poetic affair as befitted the winning of so dainty a maiden, and in the end young Sinks was successful in his pleading.

The Lees made the very best of preparations for the celebration of the marriage ceremony. It took place according to the custom of the times at home. "Father" Haney, read the service. The wedding supper was served upon a table decorated with wild flowers—flowers the young bride had learned to love through her botany studies, and after that feast was over, the bride was taken to her new home, a log-cabin built in that same city of Austin, just where the Kuntz-Sternenberg Lumber Company does business to-day.

Into this new home, Julia took her household linens, and her books. She took her botanical specimens, her guitar, her maidenish treasures, all a part and parcel of her existence, but she took something else far more valuable than any of these things. She, who had managed her father's home, took with her a wide experience of the duties of the pioneer home-maker, and her husband had occasion many times to bless the hand of that providence that had seen to it that young Julia had been previously trained in the gentle household arts. Six children were born into that home, and the same careful study was given their upbringing that had characterized her always as a woman.

In their advanced age Julia and her husband went to make their home with a son in Giddings. She lived there a number of years, taking much interest in the growth and development of Texas. She became a Daughter of the Republic soon after it was organized. The local chapter in Houston, recognizing the part Julia had played in early Texas days, planned an elaborate meeting in her honor and wrote her to that effect. Julia unexpecedly declined the honor. Her friends, surprised at her action, asked the reason. When she passed away suddenly and quietly a little while thereafter, they had no further complaint to make as to her want of interest. It seemed to them that in this case the coming event had cast its shadow, and the little old lady, beautiful in her old age as she had been beautiful in her youth, had known for some time that the great change was for her close at hand. She died in October of 1904.

Data contributed by—

Mrs. George Roberdeau,
Austin, Texas.

MRS. JOSEPH W. ROBERTSON

BORN

LYDIA LEE

At some time in the year of 1837, Dr. Joseph W. Robertson, born in South Carolina, brought up in that state in ease and plenty, himself already a man of considerable property, this Dr. Robertson put forth with his wife, his children, and his slaves to make a new home in Texas. In any discussion, any comparison of the lives of the men who came thus early to Texas, Dr. R o b e r t s o n fares well. Staunch, true to the spirit and the letter of any obligation he had ever taken upon himself, Dr. Robertson had spent his young manhood preparing himself for the practice of medicine. Did he belong to the school of medicine sometimes designated as the one to believe in hanging and calomel with a third unmentionable ingredient to make the triad complete, your scribe has no right to say. But as she begins this sketch, she thinks somehow with a gentle tenderness of the virile young man, voluntarily placing himself at the call of distress, knowing as he did so that circumstances among prosperous and poor would many times deny him the fee the law allowed. But we are reminded by the actual facts of the matter that the young physician did collect some fees. We know he was already a man of property, and we know just as well that he stood by the right of his inherent manhood, head and shoulders above the common run of folks.

The preparation for his work as a physician and surgeon complete, Dr. Robertson had married back there in old South Carolina, the girl, herself originally from Alabama, and had apparently formed all ties necessary to tie him to that South Carolina home.

But the battle of San Jacinto had been fought and won. News of the new nation thus begun stirred the heart and fired the soul of the young physician. He servered those South Carolina ties, packed his wagons, organized his slaves for the journey, and put forth for the raw, new country, heeding unreservedly its siren call. Just how long that journey took—the journey made now in a few hours—we cannot say, but we do know that Dr. Robertson reached Travis County in the spring of 1837. He settled himself first on a plantation near Webberville, he being the very first physician who had ever made the little settlement his home. When Austin became the capital in 1839, Robertson moved there. When the first congress assembled there, Dr. Robertson was numbered among its members. A just tribute, his election, for Dr. Robertson was a college bred man, a man of good hard sense, a man who could attend to the business at hand calmly, persistently in the midst of any uproar that happened to be about him.

Despite his loving care, despite his physician's skill, in 1840, Dr. Robertson had to see his own wife die. That he suffered keenly in this loss one glance at his tender nature makes sure. But in 1842, he married this Lydia Lee, the lady of whom we now write.

She was the daughter of George Lee, at one time a resident of Cincinnati, Ohio. A beautiful woman, she was a bit reserved, a bit dignified in manner. She with her sister Julia presided over her brother's home in Austin. Her spare time was spent in reading. She read the Bible and the daily papers, and woe be it to any man who undertook even the most casual discussion with Lydia, religious or political, had that man failed to reinforce himself by a few minutes research just before entering the young woman's presence. She read poetry, and she read fiction. Late in her life, her nephew—she had raised him—took on a way of patting Lydia on the head, saying as he patted: "Here's a Congress head. When *you* get in Congress, then they'll do things."

A fit mate, this Lydia, for the young physician, lately bereaved of his wife! A woman sweet and true and fine, mated to a man of like calibre, one who served God and man every day of his life! Ask the old God Hymen, who, according to superstition, instigated the honorable estate of matrimony!

Lydia's marriage to Dr. Robertson took place in the home of her brother-in-law, George W. Sinks, situated at the corner of Sixth and San Antonio streets, and for some time, due perhaps to her brother's widowed state, the newly-weds continued to make their home with him. Just after her marraige, Lydia united with St. David's Episcopal church, but she failed to be a charter member. Dr. Robertson continued to be a member of the Baptist church until his death, but he attended the Episcopal church with his wife, helping the church in all it needed.

In 1848, Dr. Robertson bought a permanent Austin home for his family. He was already possessed of a big farm near Webberville where his slaves were kept busy. When Texas voluntarily gave up her independence in order to become one of the United States of America, Monsieur Saligny, the French minister, must of course return to his native country. This representative of the ever friendly France had built him a home on a high bit of ground, some distance east and south of the hill called Capitol hill. He had brought some necessary hardware from the mother country, the wooden doors, ready to be hung, some glass windows and bolts and locks and keys, but when his days of service were over, Monsieur Saligny felt no desire to burden himself further with the ownership of property in Texas. Dr. Robertson bought the place outright except the furniture and "fixins," bought the land surrounding it to the north and south and east, and thereto he moved his family, his wife and little children, and to this day, the region bounded now by city streets, and cut up into lots and alleys, threaded with telephone and electric light wires, is spoken of by descendants of old Austin folks as Robertson hill.

Into this home of historic value, Lydia moved her belongings, her children, and a slave or two, and that place soon became to her a temple by divine right. Servants to do her every bidding, nay, slaves to anticipate her every want, Lydia found herself busy all day and sometimes far into the night. Eighty years after Lydia moved into that pioneer home, a daughter tells us in ringing tones of the mother's ability in the management of that home. She speaks of her cooking, shows proudly the recipes for fruit cake famous in its day, unrivalled still in this. So much for early impressions.

Perhaps one advantage to be derived from life in a new country lies in the fact that people so living learn that under some circumstances, money is powerless. There was money in plenty in that Robertson home. Strong professionally, possessing in the beginning nice property, Dr. Robertson had little fear that he might fail to keep the wolf from the door. But when it came to little comforts, things, in fact, to which he and his new wife had been accustomed in the land each of his own birth—aye, that was another matter. For instance—the matter of clocks. As if sensing some all-powerful spirit in the thing that ticked on and on without change, the Indians took special delight in destroying all clocks happening to fall beneath their gaze. Money to buy others? Yes, but others meant transportation, the slow-moving oxen the motive power. And cloth! The women could spin the cotton or the wool into thread and weave it into cloth and sew it into garments, but it was at best, a rather rough material. Food, save sugar and coffee and flour, could be brought from the ground, and in most cases, with little labor, thanks to the rich, virgin soil. But man cannot live by bread alone. Neither can woman in the wilderness, and particularly hard she finds such living, if she has hailed from the land of ease and plenty. She longs, and naturally, for the feel of silk beneath her toil-willing fingers. And in company with the silk idea, she longs for a bit of a time when she may laugh with her friends and make merry no matter the dangers lying in wait outside. Lydia Lee Robertson, dignified, attractive and beautiful, must have her friends about her at some time. On one occasion a card game had been planned for a certain evening when news reached the expectant hostess that other friends were coming, too. Welcome, of course. Lydia Lee Robertson lived in pioneer Texas, but where was she to get the table necessary for the extra guests? Frantically, Lydia tried to borrow one. No success whatever! Tables were rare in the raw, new country. In the height of her distress, in walked her husband, an elegant table in his hand, saying as he caught his wife's distressed glance, that a certain Mrs. Wooldridge had desired to sell the table and he bought it thinking she "might like to have it." Not a doubt in the world, everything considered, but that Dr. Robertson was served his favorite pudding at his very next dinner! That same devoted husband gave his wife a fine saddle horse. She recalled the Indians and their malice against clocks, but in a moment of exaltation, believing that the Indians had made their last raid, she traded the horse for a clock, an elegant timepiece, brought to Texas in 1830, and it stands to-day (1928) in the very home in which its old-time tick made sweet music in Lydia's happy ears.

This Lydia Lee Robertson was the mother of ten children. When her husband died in August of 1870, these children ranged in years from six upwards. Some of them no doubt had reached the age of self-support, but when Lydia faced the task of housing those that were already grown, the even greater task of housing and feeding and clothing and educating the younger ones, there must have been times when even her stout heart qualied. But according to the best authority, the authority, in fact of the daughter who always lingered with her, Lydia made a success of it. Left much property and some money, of course, Lydia found out early in the fight that it takes a large amount of ready money to equal the earning power of one good man. But she kept those children in school, and be it remembered, no public schools were at hand to supply the instruction for nothing. She, in addition to the day school, gave each child, even the boys, a chance to learn something of music. She kept them in Sunday School, and she saw to it that each child was suitably clothed before he entered the sanctuary. During the war between the States, Lydia saw her seventeen-year-old son depart for the line of battle, bidding him a bright farewell above a bleeding heart. When she knew to a certainty that the boy had died for his country, she but hid her grief as best she could and went on about her fine, upward way. Her son, George, died in 1900. Two daughters died in their early twenties, but the other children outlived her.

In 1902, Lydia Lee Robertson died beneath the shelter of the home her husband had established for her in 1848. Her body was laid tenderly away in the city cemetery beside her illustrious and devoted husband. Her spirit, strong, brave, tender and true, efficient under any and all circumstances, lingers yet about the home, once blest with her earthly endeavors. Her mantle has indeed fallen upon the daughter who in that shrine of happy domesticity emulates to-day the examples set by her mother. As one stands to-day in the old Robertson home, the place itself reeking with tradition, the house furnished with articles used for two or three generations of one people, somehow in all that old cradle of liberty it is easy to see that the things worth while in women are passed from one generation to another and that this daughter, the owner of that home to-day, our own "Miss Lillie" has preserved for us her own mother's idea of all that was beautiful and noble and good in woman. And may God bless her!

Data contributed by—

    Miss Robertson.

MRS. JOSEPH NAIL

BORN

ALVINA MARTHA WHITE

When we begin to record the events of her life and to comment on the character of Alvina Martha Nail, we must acknowledge first hand that we are ignorant of her own family name. We do know, however, that her people came originally from Holland, were afterwards classed as *Pennsylvania Dutch*, no doubt because of the fact that they followed William Penn from England into Holland and at last to Pennsylvania, the new land in the new country, to be inhabited forever afterwards by Quakers and their descendants. We know that her parents moved to Tennessee, but whether or not this move was made before the birth of the little girl we cannot say. We do know that the little girl was born April 12, 1800, and we know now that she was married March 16, 1817, the bride a slip of a girl, the groom, Joseph Nail, having already attained the age of thirty-seven years.

The circumstances that led to, or the courtship that preceded this marraige must remain matters of conjecture. Just what led Alvina, a young, beautiful, efficient girl to mate with one so much her senior, we cannot say, but we have it on good authority that she was from the beginning a faithful, tender, patient wife, bearing the burdens imposed by the old man's whims, waiting on him, bowing in most instances to his will in important matters. We are told that she was a sweet, Christian woman—her life doubtless held many experiences that were calculated to develop the Christian principles of patience and forbearance—a little woman—it seems easier, somehow, for a little woman to be patient and forbearing—so when her husband suggested, back there in the Tennessee home, that they move to Texas, the little woman, after one heart-breaking, heart-rending sigh, agreed to the idea and proceeded to gather her things together for the long journey.

To agree to that long journey to Texas in that day for any woman was a tragedy. It was the leaving behind of the things women instinctively love. Household comforts, the land "flowing with milk and honey," in this instance represented by vegetables and fruits, by friends and church affiliation, all the things that make life worth living, were hers there in that Tennessee home. But Alvina Martha superintended the packing of her household wares, watched the slaves place the packages aboard the ox-wagons, and then, when the time arrived, took her own place in one of the wagons, and so came with her husband, reaching Texas some time in 1830.

Jospeh Nail settled first in what is now Fayette County,
their place of residence the usual log cabin. Nail provided
some rude accommodations for his slaves, but he soon found
that if he expected to live in Texas, they must have some
form of protection against the Indians. These savages
prowled by night and by day, stealing stock and provisions,
killing when opportunity offered the white man invading
his territory. For this reason, the cabin was converted
into a fort, the negroes trained to stand guard, our Alvina
Martha sometimes taking her own turn in the matter.
Concluding finally that he had best move to another locality
where the Indian trouble would be more easily handled,
Nail had trees cut from the woods, sawed into logs, the
right length, and then dug out to make canoes. In these
crude vessels the Nail family and their slaves were laboriously ferried across the river, moving from there on to the
spot on which the city of Waco now stands. Mr. Nail
built the first house in East Waco, a log cabin with a dirt
floor, but armed and equipped until it became in reality
another fort.

The Indians found Nail in this new location. This
tribe of red men had been expelled from Hood County and
were, therefore, all the more enraged with the white in-
vader. They stole the canoes, they stole the cattle and
the horses. They forced Alvina to stand her turn at
guard just the same. And methinks Alvina questioned
even more bitterly her husband's reason for coming to
Texas.

By this time several children had been born to Mr. Nail
and Alvina, and these little fellows increased of course the
woman's duties. There were seven of them in all, five of
them boys, growing in time to be stalwart men, and two
girls, Elvira and Mary. Frontier life with its limitations,
particularly its want of physicians, made the rearing of
this little brood a stupenduous task, even with the help of
slaves. In the anecdotes told to-day by descendants, some
stress is laid on the two daughters. Mary became the
wife of a man named Renfro, and Elvira married Christopher Clarke. Clarke had been an intimate friend of the
Nails before his marriage to their daughter and had willingly accompanied them from Fayette County on the move
that took them to Waco. But Clarke soon tired of the
frontier life—Waco section was behind Fayette County in
the point of settlement—for Clarke, himself, had come
from a long line of Quaker people. Alvina Nail had been
forced to smother her Quaker dislike for bloodshed, but
Clarke, being of the masculine persuasion, was a bit more
independent. Things looked bad to him, and then his wife,
Mary Nail Clarke, had given him some thrilling pictures

of the struggles of her youth in this Indian matter. She had dwelt on the dangers, particularly to women. She had told him of the days when she must go day after day to the springs for water. She claimed in this telling that the Indians became aware of this duty on the part of the girl, and watched for her coming. Young Mary, quick of eye and ear, detected always the stealthy steps through the bushes, and detected them in time to lie flat upon the ground, there thus hidden by the friendly bushes, to watch and wait her chance to return to the cabin. On one of these excursions, the girl had found a string of beads lost from an Indian moccasin, right in her father's yard. But for all these dangers, they had managed to pull through, none of them ever being scalped or killed. But, remembering these stories, recalling always that the Indians continued to make trouble, even as late as 1856, Christopher Clarke became dissatisfied in this Waco home and decided to go back to Fayette County. The wagons in which he moved his family were guarded across the prairie by a band of white men. Even then, the Indians swung low on the sides of their horses and thus hidden from view, galloped across the prairie in front of them and beside them, but there were so many white men armed with powder and shot that the Indian feared to make an open attack.

Through all these stirring activities, Alvina found time to pursue those feminine accomplishments that help to keep a woman a woman in the midst of distressing conditions. She had slaves in plenty to do her bidding, and she was not slow to bid them, but she was herself a good cook, counting it her privilege to serve her lord and master in this matter of preparing food to his liking. And she was proficient with her needle. Dainty garments for her family and herself, cut from fine linen and from good homespun cloth, were put together without the aid of a sewing machine. Some of the cloth, even, had been woven under her directions. This was true, too, of sheets, towels, even bed-spreads heavily woven, the flowers in the pattern heavily tufted. She made, too, many quilts of dainty patterns, the tulip pattern being a favorite with her. She left samples of these bed-quilts for the delight of future generations, these and pieces of cross-stitch, a thing practically extinct in this part of the world to-day.

And to the wife and mother of to-day enjoying her house equipped even in the country with many conveniences, feeling herself safe because of the protection offered by the law, knowing in her heart that her children may have for their very own the best educational advantages, the best of social advantages, to the wife and mother of to-day, this little figure makes its timid appeal. Denied the education she instinctively craved, surrounded day and night by dangers unspeakable, married to one whose age stood in the way of any real marital felicity for her, putting up with the whims, the exactions of age, struggling to make the most of every single part of her poor daily life, bearing in meekness and in patience, leading beneath her burdens and her cares the sweet, wholesome life of one "who went about doing good!" Aye! And that appeal has had its weight. That appeal has held its own in the fight that has made Texas what she is to-day. That appeal has left its trace on the minds and hearts of many men and women, individuals come through that appeal to be our noble men and women of to-day, and no woman, highly born or low, can ask at the hand of fate a better destiny.

Data contributed by—

Mrs. Edna M. Fergueson,
Austin, Texas.

MRS. GOLDSBY CHILDERS

An account of a stirring Indian fight which took place near Nashville, Texas, in June of 1836 has been submitted for our consideration, and from among the heroes and heroines—for there were women in the little company as well as men—we have selected Mrs. Goldsby Childers as a specimen of womanhood worth study for a little while at least. Of her parentage, of her youth, of her education we know practically nothing. We think of her in the light shed by her descendants as a woman, pure, sweet and undefiled. We picture her passing through the incidents usually found in the life of an attractive woman—a laugh here and a dance there. We even go a bit further that we may find for ourselves some incidents natural to youth and courtship, for we find her spoken of as the wife of Captain Goldsby Childers, one of the few colonists who had taken up lands and had laid plans for a few settlements on Little river and the Leon river, in the tract of land now occupied by Coryell and Bell counties in our own great state.

They had come, Childers and his wife and children, from some other part of our great but new America. Just why they made the move we may never know. We do know that they had known sorrow and hardship and disappointments in the land of their birth. Childers had served in the war of 1812. Captured by the British, he had been taken a prisoner to Canada. Waiting at home for the news that somehow failed to come, Mrs. Childers decided as the days came and went that he was dead, this husband she had loved tenderly, and she felt keenly and rather bitterly the loss thus imposed upon her. She struggled with the thought of the duty stretching out before her, the care of the farm, the up-bringing of the children, the meeting day by day the loneliness, so bitter always to the woman who has once known the joy of a husband's companionship. But she shouldered that burden, went on bravely about her duty as she saw it. She was in no way blind to the importance of that duty, either, or the obligations to young people entrusted by the instincts of nature to her charge. Sometimes the burden assumed startling proportions in her mother eyes, sometimes the spirit of self sacrifice made of them "trifles light as air," but she never looked back, once her decision had been made to carry on unaided the thing she and her husband had planned together.

With her plans well under way, with her children in school as well as they might be kept in that community, with a little of the comfort in her heart that time brings to

us all, she looked toward the door at the sound of a step to
see her husband walking toward her, a wreck of the man
she had sent forth to battle many years before. It would
be hard to imagine that scene, hard to catch even a glimpse
of the emotion stirring in her heart. She looked upon a
man long held in prison, one who had by some means made
his way back to her, and it would seem plausible that
every added line in his pallid face, every scar on his rough-
ened hand might give that woman forever a hatred of
everything grown to life on the Isles of Great Britain.
This seeming on our part may never be answered, but we
do know that something influenced Childers to take himself just as far as possible from any land ever controlled by
Great Britian, and so we find him some years after the
war of 1812 planning to bear a part in a colonization scheme
in Texas. His wife, being a true wife, with, perhaps, an
added tenderness in her heart for him who had suffered,
listened to his schemes, weighed them in her mind, and
then, remembering that separation at her country's call,
she packed her belongings and made ready to accompany
him.

They reached Texas in 1835. The Childers brought
with them to the little settlement on the Leon and Little
rivers, four sons, Robert, Frank, Prior and William, and
four daughters, Catherine, Amanda, Caroline and Elizabeth. Childers planted a few acres in corn in the hope of
providing sustenance for the coming winter, and then because of the trouble brewing with Mexico, these new-
comers abandoned their plantings in order that they might
retreat a little nearer the United States. The victory at
San Jacinto put an end to these Mexican troubles, and
these colonists returned to their homes and their crops and
began life all over again.

Mrs. Childers, the comfort of her family in mind, seeing,
too, that her sons were at work in the fields, saw to it that
each daughter did her share. They were taught to card
and to spin and to weave. They were taught to sew, not
only to make dainty stitches, but to cut and fashion garments for both men and women. They were taught—my
lady of the gas stove take notice—to cook on a fireplace
with a Dutch oven to help out. Just what she managed
for literary education for those children we cannot say,
but we do know that she made every effort to give them the
advantages to be derived from public Christian worship.
She was herself a devout Baptist. She, no doubt, longed
many times in the wilderness for one more hour of worship
in the house of God. She, doubtless, sang the old familiar
hymns as she went about her work, and we are very sure

that her children many times listened as there fell from her devoted lips the winning story of the life of Jesus.

But when it came to this public worship, Mrs. Childers was not satisfied that her children should have only her simple teaching. She had many times felt the uplift that comes from being numbered among the few that may be "gathered together in my name." Feeling this, she was not one to sit down and repine, not one to bewail the thing that might have been. The consequence? The first sermon ever preached within the limits of Bell and Milam Counties was preached by the noble pioneer preacher, Z. N. Morrell in Mrs. Childers home, December 30, 1835. Several years afterwards when Mrs. Childers had moved to Burleson County, her home near Caldwell was again thrown open for religious service, and a Baptist church was there organized and received ever afterward her most ardent support.

Just a little while after that first sermon that was preached in her home and before the organization of that church near Caldwell, the trouble with Mexico assumed threatening proportions, and these troubles were soon felt by these special colonists. Becoming alarmed, they left their crops and their cabins, and they retreated nearer the interior and farther from the Mexicans. After the victory at San Jacinto, they returned to their hastily abandoned homes, full of plans for laying by the corn crop, seeing in this crop sufficient meal to carry them through to the next harvest.

Secure in their relief from Mexican rule and Mexican marauders, all confident in Houston and Lamar, in Burleson and the score and more of men interested in the welfare of Texas and her people, they felt inclined to forget recent outrages, to see only peace and prosperity ahead. On June 3rd of that same year, barely six weeks after the victory of San Jacinto, two couriers rode up from Nashville and informed these families living near the frontier that large hordes of hostile Indians were on the war path and would soon be upon them. These people, freed from their fear of Mexican invasion, protected in a way by the army of the young Republic, knew that with the Indians at hand there was only one thing to be done. The white man thus outnumbered held no slightest chance except in flight.

They took that chance. Captain Childers was an old Indian fighter, had, in fact, commanded a company of men in the Black Hawk war, and he naturally and with little hesitation assumed the command at this time. He sent two men, the Rev. Jasper Crouch and Robert Davidson on ahead. Captain Childers and his wife, our own particular heroine, their four sons and four daughters, John Shackleford, Geo. W. Chapman, Herman Chapman, Mr. Rhodes, Ezekiel Robinson and the two messengers crowded into one wagon drawn by a yoke of oxen, some few of them taking advantage from time to time of the few saddle horses that trailed behind. When the Indians came in sight, Childers placed his men, one each behind a horse, and they stood thus, each man holding a levelled gun at the Indians. That gun in the hands of a white man was rather a persuasive sight in the eye of the Indian. Said white man meant business, so calculated the Indian, and they passed around the white men, circling their way slowly, and drew away neither side having taken a shot. But —just as the Indian had decided that it were better to leave the white man and his gun-powder alone, the quick eye of the leader discovered Crouch and Davidson who had ridden on ahead, estimated that they were thus cut off entirely from their party, fell upon the two men, killed and scalped both of them in full view of the main party who were powerless to help.

The Indian so far had held things pretty much his own way. The lifeless bodies of Crouch and Davidson were clothed, and clothing always conveyed to the Indian a hope that other valuables were hidden by those same clothes. True to his nature, each Indian demanded all for his own, and a fierce quarrel between them ensued. As this Indian quarrel waxed hotter, the white people stole gently away to a grove some four hundred yards distant. The two couriers being well mounted, saw little protection in trees, however thickly they might be scattered over the ground, and said couriers, listening to the Indian wrangle, put their horses at top speed, each fellow determined to save his own scalp. One backward glance as they made a turn in the road made them sure that the whole party had been murdered. Their mistake was natural. They could not take in the whole situation. They could not see that the party, obedient to Childers' orders, had not suffered. Arriving at the grove, the party took the oxen from the wagon, made a barricade of their belongings, crouched down behind them and waited. The Indians galloped about them, shrieking, yelling, seeking in every way to draw the white man's fire. Convinced at last that the white man's indifference was due to the fact that he had plenty of gun-powder stored in those wagons, the Indians kept always a nice one hundred yards between him and the whites, and finally, deeply chagrined, withdrew. The white man's courage and daring, his strategy and his planning had outwitted a cruel foe.

The two deserters—harsh words even to-day—arrived
at Nashville in due time and reported that the entire party,
headed by Childers, had been killed and that they, too, had
escaped, only by a miracle. Perhaps they covered a bit
the ignominy of their own flight. It would have been but
human to do so. They could not cover their confusion
when, after a few hours, the victorious Childers drove his
ox team into Nashville, every soul of the party save Crouch
and Davidson sound and well, their lives being saved by
the strategy and determination of the brave, efficient
leader.

In most trying situations, even in situations providing
thoughts that many times lie too deep for tears, there is
likely to be a little something that excites the God-given
sense of humor. Were it not for this safety valve, man
had never lived through the subduing and the peopling of
the earth. In this fight with the Indians just described,
the trace of humor seems to have centered about
Caroline Childers, one of the young daughters of our
heroine. This miss had reached the mature age of nine
years. As subsequent events proved, she had profited
much from close attendance at her mother's knee. In this
Indian episode, one of the men, O. T. Tyler, being temporarily lame, was forced tò ride a horse in the fight, and behind him on that steed, the captain had placed this young
Caroline, weeping bitter tears, wailing, too, at intervals,
said wailing hushed against the broad back of Tyler, careless of the damage tears might do said Tyler's coat, but
hushing her sobs lest the Indians might hear. These tears
bespeaking her fear of the Indians? Not a bit of it. Young
Caroline had grown accustomed to Indian foolishness. She
was suffering because of the thrift imbibed by inheritance
and association with that mother of hers. Her new sunbonnet, a slatted affair no doubt, had been left behind or
lost in the haste of getting away, and Caroline, thrifty
Caroline, was inconsolable.

Not quite. As before stated she had been placed behind
O. T. Tyler, then a man full grown, and Tyler, a bit
thrifty himself, must have been impressed with the grief of
Caroline over the loss of the sunbonnet. Caroline's mother,
the thrifty Mrs. Childers, was not at hand to offer conso-
lation and comfort. Common charity demanded that
Tyler lend a hand to the weeping damsel. Due in some
measure, no doubt, to the cause of her grief, thrifty cause,
young Tyler ran amuck as men usually run who would
comfort the weeping female. He became enamored of this
one he endeavored to comfort, and fourteen years afterwards, said Tyler and Miss Caroline Childers were married
at old Fort Gates, the necessary license being the first one

ever issued in Bell County.   We look thus a bit ahead of
our story in giving this detail of young Caroline's life, but
in doing so we show just what her mother had meant as a
mother to her children.

And let us go a bit further with young Caroline.   She
lived to see her husband a prosperous man, an honor to his
community, all due in no small measure to her own thrift
and industry.   Tyler became in time the Judge or Chief
Justice of Bell County, and later represented that district
in the Tenth Legislature of Texas.   During that session of
the legislature a fellow member, meeting Tyler in the re-
cess hour or on the street, slapped him on the back saying:
"Tyler, that's a handsome suit you're wearing.   Where
can I get some of the same material for a suit?"

"Sorry," came the ready answer, "but none can be
bought, for my wife spun the thread, wove the cloth and
made the suit."

So had this Caroline felt the power of that wonderful
pioneer life, her own mother Mrs. Goldsby Childers.   She
had inherited her mother's bravery, her spirit of devotion,
her spirit of thrift and energy, and she later transmitted
it to her own children of the third generation, men and
women they are who, to-day, go in and out blameless before the people.   And if that gentle, efficient, pious woman,
struggling with hardship, struggling with care and loneliness, even with heartache—had that woman been given
one glance of the future yet to be, the future grown out of
foundations laid by her own gentle hand—had she been
given but one glance at the future designed for her children
and her children's children, she had passed like Moses
from the earth fully content with God's plan for his people.
Had she been given the glance?   Aye, she had experienced
that glance on the Nebo of her woman's trust and faith,
and she died secure in the joy of the things that were yet
to be.

Data contributed by—

Mrs. R. L. Henry,
Houston, Texas.

MRS. WILLIAM BERRY SMITH
BORN
MARY ANNE ASHMORE

Now we take a step of a hundred miles or so from Bell County up to Milam County, and though we may feel that it is right much of a step, we have but come to look into the home of a so-called neighbor of that same Mrs. Goldsby Childers, none other than Mrs. William Berry Smith. She was born Mary Anne Ashmore, her parents living at the time of her birth in Buncum County, North Carolina. She grew to womanhood in that same county, felt all the flush of love's young dream in the famous old state here-in-before mentioned, married finally William Berry Smith, and when her own son, James Lowry Smith, had reached the age of eleven years, this Mary Anne Ashmore Smith came with her husband and son to Texas, reaching the so-called promised land at some time in 1834.

Some incidents of this woman's history as they are given to us to-day by her descendants, lead us to the conviction that her husband made the move to Texas simply because he saw in the new country unbounded resources, unlimited chances for progress and development. A chance word here and there shows us that the wagons in which they came thither over the long, new trail contained some household articles of no mean value. Then, instead of settling on the head-right granted him by the Mexican government, the husband of this rather remarkable woman postponed using that land until our Mary Anne had been laid in her grave. Other lands were obtained in some way. This obtaining of lands augues funds of some kind brought in some of the covered wagons in their train, and a personal knowledge of the grandson of this same lady leads us still further along the line of belief in funds of some nature safely stored away to meet an emergency. To return to facts, things historically—interested folks must not forget, we know that soon after coming to Texas, William Berry Smith and his wife settled in Milam County, and their first home, the typical log cabin of the day, was about ten miles east of the city of Cameron as it stands to-day.

We know something of this home, but we are not very sure that Mary Anne Ashmore Smith ever gave any definite description of the home she had left in North Carolina. Of its glories, she may have spoken from time to time to the children about her knee, and those children may have caught as she spoke just a shade of longing in her voice, but in full view of the facts of her life, it would be hard to make us believe that she spent any time repining or dreaming, or clamoring for things as they might have been. She was too busy over too many things. She was giving too much of herself to take any time for self-pity. In company with those neighbors, some thirty or forty miles away, she was busy over the food problem for her family— seeing to it that corn and vegetables and potatoes were brought from the ground, keeping an eye, too, on the meat supply, for frontier folks must be fed. Frontier folks must also be clothed, and this woman was busy with the spinning of the thread and the weaving of the thread into cloth, counting it, mayhap, a luxury, the weaving time over, to sit down later in the day, with her thread and needle and scissors that she might spend her spare moments in fashioning the home-spun cloth into garments for herself, her husband and her children.

That spare time, strange as it may seem to us, even the hours allotted for sleep, were crowded full, sometimes, of great anxieties. Think, ye mothers of to-day, even in that very county, crossed to-day by hundreds of wires, that you have but to lift a telephone receiver from its hook at any hour, day or night to have a physician and a good one at the beside of your ailing child in less than thirty minutes! Think of this mother racking her brain before she must decide which of the few drugs brought from home was the drug needed in that particular case! Or working out a plan for some simple application of heat and cold to relieve pain! Think of cut fingers and mashed toes and no antiseptic fluid to aid in the dressing! Think of the stings of insects, the danger of snakes, and woe be unto these pioneer folks, think of the Indians!

There is a temptation to pause right here and look a bit into the Indian's side of this pioneer business. So far as we know the Indians had held the whole of America as his own from generation unto generation. Said Indian had not bothered himself much about his ownership, save to fish in the streams and to hunt in the woods for game, big and little, gathering a few berries and nuts now and then when the latter articles happened to be handy. He had evolved a style of dress suitable to his aboriginal idea of comfort and adornment, and when his wigwam grew filthy, he had ordered his squaw to pack up and move on to a place that was not filthy. He had sacrificed few trees in the forest, for said sacrifice entailed labor, and as for using any fluid that would burn, even when brought from the ground, the sight of such fluid aflame, even in a buzz-wagon had made him take to his heels, believing with all his heart and soul that the Evil One was after him. Each individual Indian then, as we choose to put it, had lived his life in the forest—primeval and had hurt said forrest very little. He had not disturbed the oil asleep beneath its surface, and he had left the upper soil, that immediately beneath his moccasin-covered feet, purely virgin in so much as any effort of his had ever tended to waste its power.

Now into Texas, the domain of this easy-going creature, comes the white man, claiming that he had been given settlement rights by Spain and Mexico. Spain and Mexico were but idle words to these savages. They but heard said words with a grunt—and went fishing. But when the same white man began to fell trees, to dig up woods, in which deer and bear and wild turkeys and wild hogs had flourished for the delight of the Indian huntsman, then Mr. Savage sat up and began to take notice. When the white man hitched horses or oxen to iron things, strangely shaped, and began to thus pull these strange things through the virgin soil, leaving an unsightly furrow behind him, when this white man built unto himself a cabin that kept out the rain, then the Indian began to see that his own place in the country was usurped, and Mr. Indian did about as you or I would have done. He rose in the might of his wrath to resent the intrusion, and many a white man's life paid the penalty imposed by that wrath.

Even the most partisan Indian friend, however, must admit that the Indian might have used more gentle tactics in obtaining his revenge. We grant it, too, remembering, all in a minute that at that time the Indian had heard little of the idea, "Whatsoever ye would that men should do to you, do ye even so to them." The Indian had listened a little to such teachings, for we are told in one of these sketches that Ragsdale had no trouble whatsoever with Indians. A thought, too, of William Penn and his successful barter and covenant with the Indians must give Texas folks a wee bit of a conscience twinge, but these Texas folks dealt with Comanches, and William Penn, mayhap, had failed with his trinkets and his beads, had he endeavored to make covenant with this deadly tribe of aboriginals. Certainly our Texas men and women in pioneer days learned that the Comanche looked upon them with cruel animosity, and we to-day, in our quiet, orderly homes can form little idea of the sufferings of the pioneer mother, her husband forced sometimes to be away from home, thus leaving her and the children at the mercy of these savages.

It is easy to imagine that the maintaining of a guard against the Indian was no small part in frontier life. It is just as easy to imagine the pioneer woman playing her part in this necessary thing. Usually her lord and master saw to it that she was placed with her children in some place of safety while the red man prowled, but her eye more often

than otherwise detected the presence of the enemy before
her husband thought of it. This true of the guarding instinct, it was also true that each Indian raid left her more
efficient in the aid she was to render in time of conflict.
And chief among these aids was the moulding of bullets.

Now this Mary had no doubt heard many times of the
jokes centering about "moulds" which old-time merchants
played now and then on some simple minded darkey—just
any such darkey who happened to be hanging round the
business square when business was dull. In all apparent
seriousness said darkey would be sent to Mr. Jones' place
of business asking for the loan of the "Jew's harp moulds."
Mr. Jones, catching the idea, would declare his own want
of the desired moulds, but would send the darkey to a far
end of town expressing a great hope in Mr. Black's liability
in the "Jew's harp mould" line. This was also true of
calico scales. But Mary's own experience with "moulds"
was one of stern reality. Into an iron ladle, capable of
holding half-a-cup of molten mass, the lead would be
placed, the ladle then be held over a bed of seething coals
until the lead could be poured. This molten lead was
poured into holes in a block of cast iron—the moulds proper,
allowed to harden, knocked out of the mould, the rough
pieces hanging there to trimmed off and thrown back
into the ladle for future use. A crude ammunition from our
point of view—and from the pioneer's, too, maybe, but it
was nevertheless the best he had in time of trouble. And
this moulding of bullets fell often to the woman. Granting without reservation that each raid made the women
more proficient in this bullet-moulding art, some of the
men in that certain county began to feel about 1834 that
things were assuming alarming proportions. Accordingly,
Smith announced that for safety's sake they must move in
nearer the settlement of people.

Mrs. Smith agreed with her husband, and helped him
pack into their one wagon all movable articles of value.
Most of them had been brought from the North Carolina
home and had assumed great value in the wilderness.

Sentiment clung about some of them, too, so they were
carefully packed, the household stuff, as well as the precious ammunition, and all stood ready for departure. Toward afternoon of that last day, up rode a band of Indians,
their manner of approach unmistakably hostile. Smith
drew the women and children into the empty cabin, and
with his wife's help barricaded doors and windows. As
the Indians came within gun-shot, Smith began firing, his
gun being levelled through cracks between the logs that
formed the walls of the cabin. After some few moments
of this fire, Mary observed that her husband's supply of

ammunition was running low. Low !save the mark! and lead and bullet moulds packed in that wagon ready for departure!

Pausing a bit to recall just exactly where these necessary things had been packed in the wagon, Mary, with never a thought of her husband's restraining advice, dashed through the door, out across the yard, arrows whizzing by her, one or two striking her askance on the arm and the shoulder, on to the loaded wagon, to dive deep in the remembered spot for the precious moulds and lead, to return, still running, to the cabin, to begin moulding bullets immediately, her husband hardly aware that she had ever left his side.

The trip on Mary's part to that loaded wagon drew the attention of the Indians thereto. They had begun, perhaps, to feel that the fight with firearms hidden behind logs was a losing game. Accordingly they began inspection of the wagon and the things it contained. Behind that barricaded door, through a crack in the wall, Mary watched that inspection. She knew by previous experience that said inspection would end in destruction. She knew, too, that never in her life would she be able to own again such things as that wagon contained. Something—the feeling of safety since the Indian attention had been perverted from themselves, or more than likely the innate sense of humor present more or less in the makeup of all pioneer people, something gave this Mary a keen interest in the doings of these Indians. She watched them rip up her cherished feather bed, and ye of to-day remember said feathers brought comfort when used on a bedstead that lacked springs. She watched the Indians dance about, the feathers enveloping them as in a mist, clinging to their few rough clothes, settling upon their straight, coal black hair, each separate piece of down delighting apparently the soul of each savage child. Then, O, the savage joy if it! Some enterprising brave discovered a mirror and held it up for all to see. After a careful survey, the Indian looking into the mirror began to realize that the Indian brave before him moved as he moved. A lifted hand—so was the hand before him lifted. A step in the dance, and the figure before him danced a step, too! Antic followed antic in the wake of that innocent dance-step, and before they were well under way, other braves demanded a peep in the magic glass, and each in his turn capered high and yet higher to see if the creature before him could really follow. Taking advantage of this childish glee, Smith managed to wound the leader of the party, and then, maybe, because they were satisfied with their good time, the Indians followed that wounded leader to some other scene of devilment.

But many years after the event occurred, Mary Smith recalled the humorous impression their antics made upon
her, even in her hour of fear, and she repeated the story
many times for the amusement of her own children.

After this episode, the Smith family moved to Washington County in Texas, having lands between Chappell Hill
and Independence. In 1845, not long after the annexation
of Texas to the United States, Mary Smith died in that
home and was buried near there. Soon after her death, Mr.
Smith took up his head-right lands in Bosque County near
Iredell and lived in the town of Iredell until his own death
in 1877. His remains were interred in Iredell.

In his Indian wars and Pioneers of Texas, Brown pays a
glowing tribute to Mary Smith, ending with a prayer that
all such women as Mrs. Smith be thrice honored. He
speaks of her husband as an honest, fearless *Christian man.*
Remembering this, we seem to see the two, this woman and
her husband, taking part in everything worth while in
their sparsely settled community. We feel sure that the
first religious service in Goldsby Childers' home, the first
service ever held in Bell County, received their spiritual
approval, even if denied their actual presence. We know
that they struggled to give their children every advantage
the wilderness seemed determined to deny them, and,
perhaps, after all is said and done, even making all allowance for the fact that every fellow would like to say a
thing in his own way, I say the best thing we can do is to
recall that solemn, earnest prayer of the historian Brown
and add thereto our solemn Amen.

Data contributed by—

Mrs. Frank Andrews,
Houston, Texas.

MRS. W. J. VAUGHN

BORN

MARTHA ANN SPEAKS

For the opening scenes in the life of this tiny, little woman, gentle, cultivated and refined, we must turn back to Alabama, for in that old state, Martha Ann Speaks was born, May 17, 1825. There she grew to womanhood, knowing the comforts, the luxuries, the ease of wealth, receiving the care, the religious training, the education that usually fell into the lives of the daughters of the first men in the community. There, when of suitable age, she united with the Methodist church, and she remained a consistent member all the rest of her life. And there, too, she married W. J. Vaughn, a successful merchant of his day, a man of no little worth, no little importance in his own way in the community. We know very little, if anything, of the courtship that led to that marraige. Refined women of that day had little to say, ever, of their heart experiencies. We know that two children, a boy and a girl, were born of that marriage, back there in that Alabama home, children tenderly watched and cared for, each by its own "black mammy," this "black mammy" glad to serve in any way a mistress so gentle, so considerate, so thoroughly alive to the individual needs of all about her.

Then and there, in the midst of this beautiful life, the seemingly unnecessary misfortune must present itself. In his business as a general merchant of that day and time, Mr. Vaughn bought many bales of cotton. He stored, too, his own cotton, raised by many slaves upon his own broad acres. He sat him down, this was in 1856, as he had many times before sat himself down, to wait the rise in the price of cotton. This time the rise did not come. Instead, the "fleecy staple" dropped and dropped in price until it reached the astonishing price of three cents per pound. Each pound had cost Vaughn more than this to bring it from the ground, and he had paid more per pound for that he had stored. No matter the hope held out when that same staple stood whitening under the Alabama sun, when Northern capitalists and banks demanded pay for goods already consumed, when Southern creditors appeared, too, on the scene, Vaughn had to hold up his empty hands. His money had gone to raise cotton, to purchase cotton, and Vaughn had nothing left but the empty hands herein-before alluded to. The man, struggling with anxiety for his family, struggling with contempt for his own foolish short-sightedness, made some honorable adjustments of his debts and then turned about, ruined financially, to look life again in the face.

From this disastrous experience, Vaughn brought one idea that grew and strengthened through every remaining day of his life. That idea was animosity toward cotton. Like some dishonored queen, stepped down from her high estate, cotton must ever after wear in this man's eyes the crown of disgrace, and as long as he lived, he never allowed another stalk to grow upon a foot of land in his possession. Careless of the criticisms against slavery already rife in New England—where slavery had been a failure financially—Vaughn realized that slavery without cotton was a losing business, an extra expense he had no desire to meet, and every slave save one, even those who had laughed and sung as they chopped their way through the glistening fields of that same cotton, was sold right then and there in old Alabama, and that one was disposed of soon after.

And then Vaughn came to Texas. Financial ruin seems to demand always some change of scene before the victim may start over again. Add to this idea the spirit ever alive in the heart of the American to seek adventure in the new and undeveloped lands about him, and you have in a very few words the reasons for Vaughn's emigration idea. In a new country, his failure unknown, his past experience to help him, in the very change in effort a new country would demand of him, Vaughn saw a healing for his own wounds.

But what of Martha Ann, his wife and the mother of his children? What of the gentle, tender maiden, raised in cultured ease and plenty? What of her in the midst of frontier life and its dangers? No doubt these questions troubled Vaughn no little. No doubt he hesitated in his very love for her to speak the desire trembling in his heart, but he did speak it, carefully, lovingly, and in the end, Martha Ann, being a loyal wife and true, agreed to his plans for them and signified her willingness to come to Texas.

A two-horse wagon was the means of transportation. Into this vehicle the Vaughn's packed the household wares they thought necessary for the new home in the wilderness, sufficient furniture for one room probably,—for transportation, ever the important item, had much to say in the matter—bedding, cooking utensils, clothing, and with their two children put forth for the great adventure into the wilderness. Slowly but surely toward the setting sun, they made their way, fording streams, cutting paths through the hitherto untrod forest, brave, still determined—and hopeful. At the White river in Arkansas they found a boat to take them across. O, the joy thereof! only to have the boat sink midway the stream, losing thereby for these Vaughns the major portion of their household

goods. Near Little Rock, these emigrants encountered
"the chills," that inevitable curse of a swampy country,
and they were "*chill-bound*" there for three months. Up
to-day, every member of the little band, tomorrow all
down, struggling with the shaking, death-like horror, and
then the raging fever that followed. Not ours to discuss
the cause. We but state the simple fact.

But the Vaughns made their way finally to the Cherokee
creek in San Saba County, found no sign of "chills," and
there on the site of an old Indian camp, Vaughn reared his
first Texas home. A log cabin, of course, built, too, with
his own hands, the logs having first come from the trees
felled in the near-by forest. A chimney, built of mud and
sticks and stones in one end, furnished a place for the heat
for comfort and for cooking. Trees, split and hand-planed
into a semblance of boards, formed the rude table. A brass
kettle left by the Indians as they quitted the camp was
used afterwards as an ash bucket. With this domestic
equipment, *Nancy* as she was sometimes called, set about
making a home, but just as she began to put her plans into
operation, her husband became convinced that he could not
get good title to the land. Vaughn, remembering cotton
troubles, had become wary. He would not "squat"—
new-comers take notice—so in the face of this doubt as to
the land title, he decided to move farther on.

This next move brought the Vaughns out into the region
now known as Brown County. Vaughn helped to organize
Brown County as well as San Saba and Menard, and espy-
ing some good land in this section lying north of the Colorado river, he removed his few remaining household effects
thither, his wife and his children, and for four long months,
our Martha Ann lived there in a tent, cooking in the open,
never once complaining, no matter the smoke obedient to
every whim of the wind, choking, blinding at every turn.
Finding again a flaw in the title to the land, Vaughn moved
again, this time settling on Clear creek, a little southwest
of our Brownwood of to-day.

On this new spot, Vaughn built another log house, this
time a double one, that is, a house having two rooms, a
driveway in between, the roof covering the drive as well
as the rooms. It also boasted puncheon floors, logs split
in halves and the straight side up—think of the splinters—
but no windows, save the mark, lest the Indians might take
advantage. Necessary air came through the chinks between the logs, and the wide-mouthed chimney added its
comfort in the matter of ventilation. The one door in
each room was made of rude boards, split from logs and
these boards were fastened into the semblance of doors with
wooden pegs.

Did Martha Speaks Vaughn, lately come from her
luxurious home, waited on by slaves and servants, did she
turn up her proud little nose at these accommodations thus
furnished by her emigrant husband? Not Martha Ann.
The rooms ready for her occupancy, she but turned about
in her woman's way to make a home of it. She placed the
little remnant of furniture to advantage. Each bed
brought from that Alabama home had its trundle bed—
that is the little bed slipped beneath the big bed during the
day to make room, the same bed being pulled out at night
into the middle of the floor for the comfort of the children.
Martha Ann covered each bed with a counterpane, a
snowy white affair woven by Martha, herself, back in
Alabama. White curtains, boasting the same fair hand in
their construction, daintily pulled upon a wire, fell from
the mattress to the floor, thus shutting out by day all view
of the trundle bed. The cooking was done in iron pots on
the fireplace, and Martha Ann, lately mistress of many
slaves, and fully aware of their efficiency, must needs do
all the cooking herself.

These things our little lady met bravely enough. Physical
hardships could be met with physical fortitude, but when
it came to other things, to the subtle, far-reaching, soul-
compelling experiences of life, Martha Ann many times
felt her privations. Educated, cultivated, she longed,
naturally, for association with people of her own kind, but
even more than this, Martha Ann longed for the quiet
hour spent in the house of prayer. Without this sacred
influence she had been forced to bring up her family in the
way she had evolved as best under the circumstances. She
had insisted on a strict observance of the Sabbath. Just
to rest from labor on this day, was not enough for Martha,
so when the Sabbath morning came round, everything
ready in that cabin home for a day of complete rest for its
inmates, even its mistress, she saw to it that the oxen,
Buck and Burl, were yoked or hitched or attached to the
cart, and she and her four children—two little girls had
been born after the removal to Texas—together with the
father, put out for "preachin'." This, with oxen the
motive power, remember, took her some three or four miles
from home, but at the end of the slow journey, Grandpa
Jesse Childers preached long and earnestly to the little
handful gathered together in the Lord's name. The
sermon and simple hymns over, Grandpa Childers, too,
took a place in that cart behind Buck and Burl, and went
for the rest of the day at the home of our Martha Ann and
her husband, and he no doubt derived as much spiritual
strength, as much growth in grace from the hours spent
with Martha in her home as she derived from his two hours

of "preachin'." And then, as if in answer to her one
burning thought in all her hours of prayer, her husband,
even the intrepid Vaughn who had felled logs and fooled
Indians, he professed religion, doubtless in one of those
simple services, and then Martha's religious ideas received heavy reinforcement. Her husband, keenly alive to
his wife's ideas of the Sabbath and its observances, influenced largely in that hour of his stern confession by his
wife's glowing example, promised the Lord that he would
never fish on Sundays, never hunt save to provide his
family with food, and with clear eyes shining in faith, in a
voice vibrant with hope, Martha told again and again as
long as she lived that the Lord, remembering her petition,
sent a deer to her cabin home every Saturday of the world.
Hard on the deer, some wordly critic might make reply,
but that mother's faith went far in the making of our
Texas to-day. That mother's faith caused Martha to
lead family prayer every night of her life, her husband and
her children together with the chance guest gathered about
her, and each prayer, night after night, ended with the
petition, "If we fall into the hands of the savages, let us
all go at once."

And the Indians! Did they ever surprise Martha Ann
and her family? No, but in spite of that nightly prayer
and Martha's faith therein, it is recorded of Martha that
the Indians never surprised them, because as she expressed
it: "we never quit lookin'." Even with this constant
vigilance, however, the Indians would leave tracks in the
yard, usually during the dark of the moon, and horses
would be missing afterwards, or some other simple article
of ranch usefulness.

These simple prowlings ended rather disastrously for
Martha. Two friends, Tankersly and Carmine, both of
them government employees, came one day for a visit at
the Vaughn home. Carmine was a dark man, his hair being very straight and black. Tankersly was of a different
type entirely. His complexion was fair, and his hair,
rather long always and a bit curly was the color of bright
gold. These men had been sent from Comanche to make
some investigations, and this visit to the Vaughn home
came at the close of their work. They made all plans to
leave on a certain morning that they might go on to Comanche and report upon the work just finished. For some
reason the men dreaded the return journey. Even Mrs.
Vaughn felt constrained to speak to them of the reluctance
so unusual in pioneer men in the face of an undertaking.
She watched them off finally, returning slowly to her work.
That day both men were murdered by the Indians. The
bodies were found not far from the Vaughn home. The

hair on Carmine's black head had been disturbed just enough to remove a piece of skin the size of a quarter. Tankersly's golden crown of glory had been removed bodily from the skull, not a shining hair left to remind the mourners of its beauty. Recalling the depression of the men as they left her that morning, Martha Vaughn prepared the bodies in all tenderness for their simple burial. No coffins at hand, she wrapped each body securely, using her own hand-woven, spotless sheets for the covering, and saw to it that the men were decently buried there in her own burying ground.

Some years after this episode, Vaughn moved again, this time to Menard County. He had turned his attention to farming—no cotton, be it remembered—and cattle raising, and he felt the necessity of irrigation. This necessity was amply met in Menard County, and a fine farm came into existence, due to Vaughn's efforts, and many cattle came in time to roam upon his many hills. It was in this home that the Vaughns heard the news of secession. Having parted with his slaves, Vaughn had little to lose in the abolition idea, but for all that, this man who resented cotton and its fickleness, resented, too, the manner in which property, valuable in the eyes of other people, was placed in jeopardy. Just what his part was in the war that followed we are not prepared to say, but he was called from home thereby, and his wife, our Martha, was left to manage the home, to look after the welfare of the children, to manage crops and herds, to dispose of the surplus products as best she could. In addition to this, she worked all day and many times far into the night, carding and spinning and weaving the wool into thread and then into cloth. This cloth was made into clothes for her children, and some of it was sent to help clothe the soldiers who did battle for her in that losing fight. Peace over the land again, a peace brought on by defeat, but, thanks, perhaps, to cotton, a peace that brought little change in the life of Martha. She but kept on at her labors, relieved, of course, by the return of her husband, from many of the heavier burdens, helping in her woman's way to forget the bitterness that must follow always the war of brother against brother.

Martha saw her husband die, there in that Menard County home. Her children had married and gone into homes of their own, but Martha maintained her own home, her own estate, one of the married daughters returning with her own family to bear her company. At some time in 1915, Martha went for a visit to friends or relatives in Sutton County, was taken ill, and died there. Her body was brought back to Menard County and laid beside her husband. We like to think that friends looked to the tender care of that burial, even as she had looked tenderly after the burial of Carmine and Tankersly. We like to think it, for in our hearts we believe that the good deeds done in this life find a ready appreciation in the minds and hearts of those individuals so fortunate as to know about them.

Data contributed by—

Mrs. Rufus Winn.

MRS. JAMES A. WINN

BORN

ELIZABETH HART

Being a little short of data at this moment, it becomes necessary to begin the story of the life of this rather remarkable woman after she had entered into the holy estate of matrimony—even a little further than that—after she had attained unto the proud position of motherhood. This latter named position came to her with the birth of her first child, Rufus Allen Winn, at some time in the year 1839, at a point on the Neches river, just five miles from a beautiful spot on that river known even unto this day as Weiss's bluff. Your scribe is not prepared to say just what may or may not be found to-day in the way of business on this same spot hereinbefore alluded to, but she does know that the holly and the dog-wood, the magnolia and the jasmine flower to perfection, each in its own good season, on this dear old spot, and she further knows that the mists rise from the river to float over sand-bars and alligators, to settle lovingly in the river-side forest, softening into tender beauty the leaves of the oak, the hickory, the ash, even the long stiff straw of the towering pine. The birth of this son, there in that soft forest beauty, was followed by the birth of a daughter who was given the name of Mollie, and there in that land of ease and plenty, these children grew and thrived as all children should thrive who are well born and well bred.

There has been given to us another statement in regard to these children thus born, that wears a tender interest. For some reason, the two children, Rufus and Mollie, were spoken of as the wards of Col. R. C. Doom. What peculiar conditions or relations made this necessary, we do not know. It must be sufficient for our purpose to say that Rufus and Mollie Winn, the children of Elizabeth Hart Winn, grew up under the protection of that most noble and lovable of men. We know, too, that they mingled in the forest round Weiss's bluff with the sons and daughters of Napoleon Weiss. These children, born and trained into efficiency and worth there in that secluded spot, receiving no other education save that which their father gave them, came in time to be the leading business men of East Texas, the one daughter of this Napoleon Weiss being known throughout four counties for her gentle culture and refinement. A little farther up this same river at old Bevilport, nine miles west from Jasper, the county seat, Elizabeth knew Bill and Jim Everitt and their sister Ann, the children all of Stephen H. Everitt whose hand had played its own good part in our Texas Declaration of In-

dependence. These Everitt children shared with Eliza-.
beth Hart and, probably, at the same time, the gentle
guardianship of R. C. Doom, who became in time the
loved and honored step-father of the Everitt children.

Despite the beauty of that forest country, despite the
association with pleasant people, despite the dangers at
that time from all prowlers and marauders, along some
time in the late Sixties, we find Elizabeth Hart Winn with
her husband and children bound for Menard County, expecting there to make them another home. Some strange
fancy, some spirit of adventure, maybe, some irresistible
impulse toward the west had given rise to a desire for
change. In obedience to this desire, all household goods
were loaded into two strong wagons, each to be drawn by
five yoke of oxen, and thus the pilgrimage to their new
home was begun, the distance to be thus covered being a
little more than one hundred and seventy-five miles.

Remember there were no real roads as we call roads to-
day in all the broad domain of Texas. Through that
deep-sanded road, overgrown in many places with vines
and briars and bushes, leaving it hopefully because they
had no idea of the road ahead of them, they travelled their
twelve miles a day in the cool, dark shade, coming out
finally into the prairie country—their land of promise—
and down at last to the bank of the Colorado river. Remember again there were no houses to be seen on that
road—if such it might be called—between the Colorado
river and the San Saba river. In fact the road itself was
little more than a trail, now too narrow for the wagon bed,
now widening out until its general direction was hard to
follow. They crossed Brady creek right where the city of
Brady stands to-day, and being weary, that crossing done,
they made a halt and pitched their tent. For the night
only, so thought our Elizabeth, so anxious was she to reach
her destination.

Now some smart somebody put it into the mouth of some
discerning "cullud gintlemens" to remark that there "wuz
no derpendence ter be placed in de hin' leg uv er mule."
History leads us to believe that in early Texas times the
same thing might have been said of an ox, leaving out the
hind leg idea. An ox, supposedly directed by word of
mouth and supposedly kept on the job by means of a goad,
seems to have been possessed of a way most convenient—
to the ox—of getting lost. Turned out by a grateful
master, after a long hard day, remember said ox travels
twelve miles a day, to graze all through the night, the oxen,
who had plodded apparently weary in body and mind
throughout the long day, seemed always ready when
turned out to take on new life. This new life produced an

astonishing ability to cover the ground—the wagon being absent—and the oxen always neglected to leave any directions behind for the comfort of the forsaken master. On this particular night in which our Elizabeth firmly believed that she was encamped for the night only, there on the site of the future city of Brady, the oxen, once released from the Winn wagon, waiting until dark might be trusted to hide their desertion, took themselves off on a self-planned tour of investigation. They went quietly, too, these beasts of burden, for Winn slumbered on, there in that carefully pitched, carefully guarded tent, ignorant until morning of the dire happening of the night. Just what the deserted master thought when he awoke to the real condition of affairs, just the exact language he used for the expression of that thought, we shall never know. We do know that said master put about immediately to search for the truant beasts, leaving the wife and children in the tent wondering as he left, if he might not find on his return that they, too, had disappeared. And we do know that when the beasts were finally located and persuaded by fair means or foul to return to their labors, several days had passed, precious days when each one held its own significant danger.

The home established by the Winns in Menard County wears the same outline that every other home wore in that early day of western history. The same rude accommodations, the same struggles to provide food and raiment dwelt there in that new abode, but this home, like many others described in these pages, was blessed. Strengthened inside and out, cheered, nay, this home was hallowed by the presence of the woman who controlled its very interest. For months, that home was a tent, and James Winn, the husband and father, must be away gathering cattle, looking after the cattle already gathered, establishing in actual fact the legal title to his many thousands of acres of Texas land. In addition to Indians, the country was overrun with free-booters, with marauders, with ruffians of every description, and no law of any kind restrained such individuals in their desires. Did our Elizabeth scream out her fear, her loneliness? Not a bit of it. That husband gone on his necessary errands, she but stuffed his one extra suit of clothes with grass, put a hat upon the pole that supported it, placed a loaded gun in its arms, strung it up near the tent door and went on cheerfully about her business. Questioned in after years as to the real good thus achieved, she but shook her head a little sadly and then replied with some resignation that, "Anyway, it kept me from being so lonesome." Some other discerning individuals may see in this simple reply a reflection on the character of the beloved husband. Surely, it was a poor kind of a partner whose place might be taken by a sack or suit full of grass, but no such idea ever floated into the mind of Elizabeth. She but stated a simple truth in her simple woman's way, and expected her hearer to take it in the spirit in which it had been uttered.

Along about 1871, James Winn sold a bunch of cattle to Seth Mabry, receiving for them ten thousand dollars in cash. There were no banks in the country, no vaults for safe-keeping, and said money must, therefore, be buried upon the premises. Winn proceeded with this necessary burial, and then went about his business, a little anxious, perhaps, as he rode away from home, comforted, no doubt, by the thought that there were now a few hired men on his premises. Those premises had undergone a change for, remembering the one sale of ten thousand dollars worth, we may be sure that these pioneers had prospered. The tent with its grass-stuffed figure before it had been exchanged for a house. The acres immediately around the house had been converted into a farm, and many hands were busily employed thereon. These field hands were all more or less loyal to Winn and his wife, but it would be rather difficult at any time for any man or any woman to keep the public ignorant of the fact that ten thousand dollars had been paid into one man's hands. To the Indians still roaming the western plains, the money meant little. To the desperate character, white usually, prowling his way through the haunts of men, that money meant much. With Winn away on business, with only hired men to stand between, the marauder saw his way clear. They had but to frighten the hired man, put the woman upon the rack until she told where the money lay buried, then leave her to her own devices.

Men sometimes fail in their calculations as to the conduct of woman under certain pressure, even as folks have been known to fail when depending on the hind leg of a mule. Confident of success, depending on the natural timidity of the woman on guard above that buried treasure, this certain band of marauders conceived the idea of intimidating the men at work in the fields, and to bring about this intimidation, a few well aimed shots must be fired. Not straight at the workman's head—the money-seeker was not anxious to commit murder—but loud enough and often enough to make the woman come clean with the desired secret. So planned the men, their hands itching to begin the task of unearthing that money. But somehow that first shot fired at the men in the fields failed in its mission. Elizabeth Winn heard the shot—her ear was ever open for such things—but somehow the timidity idea failed to materialize. She but seized one of the guns,—stacked as they always were ready for use, shot clean and straight toward the man who had fired the first shot. Another gun from the same stack was fired immediately, and then another, and the thieves paused for breath—and a bit of conference. Deciding at last that a *posse* of men had collected unknown to them and was busy defending the treasure, the thieves moved off, the burial place of the money still a secret.

Through all this pioneer labor and uncertainty and danger, there had remained deep in the heart of Elizabeth certain longings for religious fellowship, religious association with men and women who shared her own religious ideas. This seems to have been denied her in her East Texas home, but once settled in Menard County, she began to fare better in this respect. In 1880, *Brother Tucker*, as she affectionately styled him, preached often at Menardville. Where this man lived permanently, we cannot say. Perhaps it were foolish to even speculate on his place of habitation. He was probably a Methodist *circuit-rider*, all hail thereto! his home wherever God called him for the hour. When that call brought him to Menardville, Brother Tucker made his home with Elizabeth and her family. As the Sabbath morning approached the whole house began to stir. The milking was done by starlight. The breakfast consisting of corn-pone, bacon and coffee was eaten by the glow of the fire on which it had been cooked, and at sun-up, the little company, Brother Tucker included, found itself seated in chairs in the ox-wagon, a wagon guiltless of springs or spring seats, a goodly supply of ammunition piled in the wagon bed, a gun across the knee of every individual capable of handling it, the oxen safely gee-d and haw-d into the open, all bound for church in Menardville where *Brother Tucker* was to preach. "And," says one of her descendants today, "I cannot recall a single instance in which we were late to church."

Along with her devotion to religious service, this same Elizabeth saw to it that her children were spared the dangers that might arise from evil communications. Compelled to live her life in the midst of wickedness and vice, different in a way from the city contaminations of today, having, perhaps, roughness as its chief characteristic, Elizabeth kept her children closely about her, her keen eye ready to detect the first step aside from true manhood and womanhood as she saw it. A little above her kind in her own estimation? Not a bit of it. Granting to every other individual the right to choose his or her companions, Elizabeth but demanded the same right for herself and her children. That the basis of her choice in

this companion matter seemed a bit prudish in the eyes
of some about her, she could not help. If this choice on
her part brought the condemnation of her fellows, she
knew she must bear it. Firm in her purpose, she went
about the business of frontier life as she saw it, and in no
single duty was she ever known to waver.

Those duties were many and varied. Through Indian
fights—and they were many—she bore her own good part.
She stood her ground in defense of home and children,
seeing many other white people, men and women, fall
victims beside her. She went upon errands of mercy,
miles upon miles, sometimes through the night, her gun
across her saddle, and many an Indian fell back before her
steady fire, knowing instinctively at the first shot that a
hand guided by a purpose had held that deadly weapon.
That same capable hand, her solitary journey done and her
gun put aside, soothed many an aching head, her gentler
voice soothed many an aching heart, and her earnest
prayers went with many into the Valley of the Shadow,
many men and many women who had otherwise gone on
into that dread Valley alone and unprepared. And however we may think of it to-day, just what importance we
may attach to the efficacy of prayer, the outward
expression of a devout life, however we may think of it,
she who has placed these facts before us risks the belief
that the prayers of this noble woman saved many lives
from degradation in that wild, uncouth time and place,
and as we close this simple recital of the few bare facts of
the life of Elizabeth Winn, there is, somehow, no disposition on the part of your scribe to deny it.

Data contributed by—

Mrs. Rufus Winn.

MRS. NATHANIEL TOWNSEND
BORN
1. MARIA ROACH   2. ANGELINE TOWNSEND

Women truly fine, truly worthwhile, have many beautiful traits in common. This fact makes story-telling a bit hard, for there lies always close at hand the danger of rushing into the unforgivable sin of repetition. Even as these words snap out from under the typewriter key, your scribe feels sure that they embody an idea already stated, and stated many times. She is very sure that more than once she has explained that the character of the descendant who relates the bare facts of her grandmother's life has a way of spreading her own individuality over things, and such spreading may sometimes woefully cripple the effort to be strictly truthful. In this sketch, for instance, a sketch begun in all earnestness, all determination to tell the truth, your scribe finds herself influenced and dominated to some extent by a certain brave little woman who honored her mother, and no doubt loved her, but one who possessed so deep a veneration for her father that she has given us of her mother only the part of her life that pertained to her husband and his work in which that wife and mother apparently found great joy. That bride of early Texas times may have seen many and grave faults in her young husband. She may have longed as many a young wife has longed to box her husband's jaws, but this daughter born late in the life of that father, had never acknowledged any jaw-slapping necessity, her own dear father the object. When we would know of the life of the mother and its intimate daily happenings, her story comes to us so brimful of *father* and what he had done that it becomes a bit difficult to pick from the romantic story the thread of her mother's own life. In her mind at least her father and mother were as the twain that became as one flesh, and the fate of Texas, mayhap, has rested more than we can ever know on the strength of this idea ground hard into the lives of her pioneer women.

And now for another side of this same trouble! She who tells us this story is so devoid of selfishness, is so far removed from that state of mind or heart that would deny any woman her just due that she tells us freely of her own mother, and—save the mark—of her father's other wife, and both stories are so good that neither can be passed by. So in this one instance we must be pardoned, if in one short sketch, we deal with two women, the women being the successive wives of Nathaniel Townsend, for each woman held her own place, and did her own good part in the life of this Godly man, venerated after so many years by his devoted daughter.

Nathaniel Townsend, the youngest of seven children, was born in Oneida County, New York, June 24, 1804. He grew to manhood there, living the life of the ordinary young man whose people were in comfortable circumstances. When he was about twenty-four years of age, he developed tuberculosis. A change of climate seemed eminently desirable under such circumstances, and his parents persuaded him to make a visit to his oldest brother who had long since married a certain Miss Roach, and had settled permanently in Natches, Mississippi.

Now young Townsend's parents had no idea that in sending his son to a warmer climate, they were sending him as well into matrimony. Surely his mother had no dream of such a thing, seeing as how the mother rather shrinks at the thought of marriage for her son, but truth is truth, and we find young Nathaniel, much improved in health—we hope, we of this late day of hygiene and health ideas, but, at any rate we find him married before very long to Miss Roach, his brother's sister-in-law.

Now the main contributor of the facts in this sketch states that she knows little of that first wife, but, with a striking exhibition of justice and fairness to all, she further states that she must have been a woman "of real pioneer material." A glance at those facts brings from your scribe a ready second, and she proceeds confidently to lay these facts before you.

In 1834, some five years after his marriage to Maria Roach, Nathaniel Townsend made a trip from Natches, Mississippi to St. Louis, Missouri. Nothing unusual in that. Nathaniel Townsend had frequently before made trips to St. Louis, but on this particular one, Townsend fell in with none other than Stephen F. Austin, the intrepid colonizer. In Townsend, Austin saw the making of the real pioneer, and he was not slow to speak the word, not slow to give the thought of emigration, already alive in Townsend's heart, a sudden, solemn boost. We like to think that he reminded Townsend that real health awaited him in the wind-swept plains of Texas. We know that Townsend returned to his Natches home, laid the matter before his wife, already the mother of two children, and she, before very long saw him depart on his visit of exploration to the land described as one of healing by his new friend, Austin. We know that he came on that visit for a brief stay at the little city of Austin, but we know, too, that before he left Texas for Mississippi, he had decided that his permanent home was to be in Texas, at San Felipe, on the Brazos river.

It is a little difficult for us to-day to picture just what this change meant to the wife of Nathaniel Townsend. A similar proposal to a young wife to-day carries little cause for grief. Telegraph, railroads, good dirt roads, automobiles have annihilated distance so that our nation now boasts a certain freedom from the existence of waste places. But she, Maria Roach, born and brought up on that Mississippi plantation, waited on all her life by slaves, living in the height of ease and luxury and splendor that challenged the civilized world; an educated, cultivated woman to leave all signs of education and cultivation, to dwell forever in the land infested by Indians and bears and catamounts, hundreds of miles, perhaps, from any of her kind; to live, moreover, in a land controlled and governed by an alien, and, to her, an inferior people. Surely some other way had been found to satisfy her husband's ambitions!

But no other way appeared. Townsend made all things ready even to the packing into wagons of a nine-thousand-dollar bill of goods such as is sold in a general merchandise store, and his wife, with, perhaps, a slave or two and her two small children, seeing no deliverance at hand, took her place in that wagon, too, and thus began with her husband that journey, which in the eyes of her people was exceedingly foolish.

No incidents of that journey have been recorded, no mention that we can find of the rate of improvement in Townsend's health after he found himself settled within the borders of Texas. We know to a certainty that they found the country in pretty much of an uproar, Mexicans prowling about, instigating peacefully inclined Indians to crime, the deadly Comanche, needing no instigation, making his own deadly visits whenever Indian occasion demanded it. Talk of freedom, of independence from Mexican rule was already in the air, and no doubt many arguments, pro and con, were voiced about the counters of that Townsend general country store. Townsend and his wife listened to all that was said, listened and silently vowed the vow of the patriot.

In March of 1836, probably following the stirring Declaration of Independence and the disastrous battle in the Alamo, Mexicans passing through San Felipe fired the store belonging to Townsend, and the entire stock was burned. Santa Anna later marched through San Felipe and burned the whole town, but owing to the first disaster, the Townsends were probably away from home. In all these stirring national disasters and activities, Townsend served his country in many ways, though his frail health forbade him taking up the life of an active soldier. At the close of the short, sharp struggle, some time in 1837, Townsend was appointed by General Houston to serve as consul at New Orleans, a post he held for two consecutive years. The life at New Orleans must have been a welcome change for the young wife. In the quaint old French city, she must have come again into a life somewhat like the life she had lived in old Mississippi. Many slaves always at hand relieved her again of all onerous burdens, and she felt free to mingle in the gay world about her, some trusty "black mammy" always ready to assume charge of the four children that had come by that time to brighten the Townsend home. But Townsend was not long content in his post of honor. The stirring, western life possible in Texas outweighed in his eyes all the comforts of old New Orleans. Despite his wife's delight in things as they were, when Townsend decided in 1839 that he must return to Texas, even to Austin, his wife hid her regret and accompanied him, all the way, even unto the raw little capital of a raw little nation, bringing her four children with her.

With national affairs resting apparently on a firm foundation, Townsend began to think of establishing himself in business. Owning a body of land adjoining what is now known as Howard's Nursery, Townsend built a home there, and sat himself down for a farmer. His wife aided and abetted him there in that undertaking. About 1841, Townsend bought two lots on Congress avenue in Austin, both situated on the west side of the Avenue between Seventh and Eighth streets. On one of these lots he built a frame building, a pretty large one for its day, and into this building, Townsend brought the first real bill of merchandise ever brought into Austin. Drugs, dry goods, groceries, hardware, boots and shoes, books, harness and ploughs.

Nathaniel sold his muchly mingled stock, and sold it to good advantage. He continued in the business two years or more, but he saw that his wife, cheerful through her pioneer experiences, a loving, tender help-mate in every way, he saw her failing in health and rushed her to New Orleans as a last resort. In that famous old city Maria Roach Townsend died, leaving her husband discouraged, burdened with the care of his four children, practically alone in his misery in the wild, raw country. He struggled on, trying to do his duty and that of the mother, too, but after a bit he sent the children to be with his brothers, then living, the one in New York and the other in Massachusetts. Some three years later, in 1846, after Texas had been admitted to the Union, after Indian troubles had been somewhat reduced, and life looked for him a little brighter, Townsend went back to New England to visit his chidlren.

Some years, be it remembered, had elapsed since Townsend had seen his people. He had grown accustomed to Texas, to the rough and ready manners of her people, the stirring open life of the frontier. He returned to New York, settled hundreds of years before, returned to the land glistening with Dutch thrift and plenty, returned, in short, to find his own people calmly continuing in ·the prosperity he had well-nigh forgotten. He found himself again in elegant homes, surrounded by luxuries, by books and pictures. He mingled with women, the very best of them, clad according to the dictates set for the life of fashionable ease. Townsend took on fresh life and fresh hope and began to feel that he was ready to begin life anew.

Among his numerous cousins, one girl, answering to the name of Angeline Townsend, struck his fancy. Perhaps the strongest argument in favor of the holy estate of matrimony lies in the fact that a man once married is apt to do so again and with less hesitancy apparently than accompanied his first venture. But a look deep into the character of this young cousin striking thus across young Townsend's path leads one to believe that she possessed the certain characteristics of womanhood that are calculated to stir the interest of any ordinary man. She, be it remembered, O, daughter of the South, was a Yankee, born and bred. Accustomed to wealth all her life, brought up, in fact, in an elegant home, Angeline Townsend had been trained to work, to cook, to sew, to spin and to weave. More than this she was a college woman, a student at Williard Seminary at Troy, N. Y. There is no mention of a degree from that institution, but with her other qualifications in mind, it is easy to suppose that this education, once begun, must have been carried to a definite point. At any rate, there was in the light of her eye or the sound of her voice the nameless something that appealed to Townsend, already experienced in matters of the heart, and he, his four children in mind, set about the courtship of the desirable young woman, determined to win. Said courtship, described as most fervent, lasted more than a year—the little Yankee girl must have ample proof of her lover's devotion—but they were married at last on September 11, 1847, and went immediately to New Orleans.

Just what form of business occupied Townsend in the city of New Orleans we are not prepared to say. He lingered there for four years, recuperating, enjoying life, his four children about him, his new wife making a place for herself in their young lives. With the birth of Angeline's own baby, some time in 1850, it seemed that this young wife had inveigled her husband into a belief in New Orleans and its ways and its beliefs forevermore.

But Townsend had lived in Texas.   He had felt the stir
of the new and the wild in his own heart.   He had according
to the old saying, drunk his fill of the waters of the Colorado
river.   He had associated with Houston and Austin and
Burnet, had talked earnestly with them, had shared with
them the vision of things that were yet to be.   To him the
glory of old New Orleans, even the glory of old New York
saturated with family tradition, with the more important
things that had made his young wife desirable in his eyes,
all these began to seem a rather slow and solemn kind of
glory.   The wet, soggy winter made him dream of grass-
covered plains lit with the brilliancy of a winter's sun.
Some of these things put it into the heart of Townsend that
he must return to Texas.

Perfectly plausible, perfectly simple—for Townsend.
But what of his wife, young Angeline Townsend, she who
had been courted twelve months and more with the idea
that her lover had shaken forever the dust of Texas from
his feet?   What of her, energetic, cultivated, college-bred
woman that she was?   What of her opinions and her desires in this matter of taking up life in the wilderness of
Texas?   Just exactly the stand every other worthwhile
woman has taken at this crisis in her life, Angeline Townsend took then.   Her husband, thrown continually with
men of affairs, with men of business, felt it best for them to
move.   His loving care of her could be safely counted on
in Texas as it had been counted on in New Orleans and in
New York.   To her that loving care made up the whole of
life, and when she knew positively that her husband had
set his heart and mind on the venture, she acquiesced in all
his plans with cheerfulness, and fell to with a touching
willingness to further his plans.

The journey, as a journey, was calculated, looked at from
any standpoint, to prove an eye-opener to young Angeline.
The primitive mode of travel—once they were clear the
Mississippi river boats—the fields devoted to cotton culture,
the slaves at work in those fields, the trees draped in moss,
the buffalo, the Indian, all these, entirely new to the little
lady, must have left deep impressions.   They must have
produced, too, in the mind of this female tenderfoot, a
kind of puzzled inquiry as to the why and the wherefore
of the fascination such things had held for her husband.
But she kept such inquiry to herself, nay, she even banished
it from her heart—as much as she could, and went on about
her work, determined to do her part in this strange, new
environment.

Having lived in Austin before, Townsend found himself possessed of a little city property.   This property
consisted in part of the two lots he had used before

on Congress avenue, just north of the Tips building
(1927), and in this same place he again opened a
general merchandise store. He left the matter of a home
to wait for a few months, but he finally selected for this
home a hill crowned by three large live oak trees, a hill
exactly one mile west from the state capitol and a little to
the north. This plot of ground, two blocks in all, was outlined by seventeenth and nineteenth streets on the south
and north, and there beneath the big oaks, Townsend
erected a frame house, and young Angeline set up her
housekeeping.

Remember she was from New York. In that day (1851)
she must have felt the aversion to slavery, so common with
her people. She must have felt, too, the need of servants,
she who had known many in her father's elegant home.
She must have been the victim of contending emotions as
she saw her husband busy erecting small houses about
their own for the use of these slaves, but if she did she made
no complaint. Money there was in plenty, in her own
bureau drawer—she had not come to Texas empty-handed
—but money is sometimes useless in a new country. When
her first baby was expected, she looked about that sparsely,
scantily furnished house and wondered just where a crib
might be obtained, the nearest market New Orleans, and
transportation slow and dangerous. When Uncle Ned, a
negro man, one of the slaves, produced a plausible affair
from a dry-good box, and proudly proved to the expectant
mother that it *would* rock, Angeline was no doubt grateful,
and mayhap Angeline felt for the time at least, that
slavery as an institution might have some redeeming
qualities.

Prosperity came in slow but certain waves to these
Townsends. Frugal in his training, exact in his business
methods, Townsend slowly amassed a fortune in that
Avenue store. In keeping with that fortune, he built a
mansion near the center of that block of ground between
seventeenth and nineteenth streets, and Angeline reigned
there with all the delight of a woman blest with the house-
wifely instinct. Comforts slipped in, as comforts have a
way of slipping where there is money to pay for them despite the limitations of poor transportation. Angeline had
probably the first sewing machine ever brought to Austin.

Meanwhile, Townsend, the efficient husband, was forming some warm friendships in the growing city. Dr. M.
A. Taylor, long and favorable known in the whole of
Travis County, had his office above the Townsend store.
Scores of others might be mentioned, for soon after arriving
in the city, Townsend united with the Daniel Baker church
founded in 1850, thereby establishing himself among the

God-fearing men of his community. Angeline followed in her husband's footsteps in this matter, and in her church relations played ever well her own part. Among the papers still extant we find records of one hundred dollars given as part payment of the church bell purchased by this congregation, and another one hundred dollars given later to the Baptist congregation for the same purpose.

And how unimportant all this seems now. Protestant churches have long since ceased the use of bells in this very city of Austin, and some there be who are inclined to look on the Catholic bell as an enemy to the effort to keep reasonable silence in the face of the noises that naturally arise from the necessary going to and fro in a city. But the simple fact that this man and wife contributed liberally toward the purchase of the bell for the Daniel Baker church, establishes him and his wife among the men and women of his own religious belief. The fact that they contributed as liberally toward the bell for the Baptist church places them at once among the broad-minded people of the community, and little more may be said for anybody. We add to these accounts of the works of this good man, that his wife, Angeline, followed and abetted him in all works, charitable or otherwise, and when we have said this we have placed her, too, among the individuals of whom it may be safely predicted that their children's children may rise up and call them blessed.

Angeline Townsend died on June 6, 1889 at her home in Austin and her remains were interred in the city cemetery.

Data contributed by—

Mrs. Pauline Townsend Culbertson,
Austin, Texas.

MRS. STEPHEN H. DARDIN

BORN
KATHERINE MAYS

With the beginning of this sketch, there comes to the mind of your scribe a vision of a handsome, dignified woman passing down the aisle of the old Methodist church in Austin, her apparel exemplifying her belief in the advice of old Polonious, her manner proclaiming the innate dignity of the real woman.   Her husband, her escort always at this service, bore his part well in that stately passing down, and as before suggested, the little girl who watched them more than fifty years ago has a keen mental vision to-day of the picture they made. They were Stephen H. Dardin and his wife, Katherine Mays Dardin.

Now it were easy enough to turn to state records and find many things about the life of Stephen H. Dardin. Gallant service in the Confederate army, service in Hood's famous brigade, afterward a colonel of Texas troops.   A Confederate Congressman, and a State Comptroller, elected to this last office about 1874.   All this mingles in daily records kept by the state for future reference, and now we turn to look into the life of his wife, she who probably had no small share in bringing about her husband's success, turn to that life to look into it so that the world may some day know a little bit of the part the good wife played.

Mrs. Dardin was born in the old town of Washington, in Arkansas, February 13, 1836.   Her parents were John and Ann Mays, both of Revolutionary ancestry, hailing respectively from Virginia and North Carolina.   They gave the young miss the name of Katherine, and for aught we know, she grew according to the custom of young children, developing there in her Arkansas home the certain physical powers that laid the foundation for physical beauty.   In 1845, John and Ann Mays decided to move to Texas, and of course nine-year-old Katherine had nothing to say.

There was a woeful lack of discussion as to the best way to make the journey to Texas.   The comparative comforts of railway travel and automobile transportation had no place in the thought of those pioneers.   They knew they must come in a horse wagon, a covered one, and perhaps they were so thankful to have horses instead of the slow-going oxen, that the transportation idea seemed great in their eyes.   Tiresome, of course, to my lady of to-day whose Pullman may be trusted to carry her in all privacy over that same stretch of road in less than twenty-four hours!   Tiresome to my lady whose chauffeur at the wheel of her limousine makes the same distance in less than the Pullman!   Maybe so, but in speaking of that journey to her children and her children's children, young Katherine had no such thought. She told of adventures sometimes. She told how they stopped to fish and hunt for the meat necessary on the journey. She told a few Indian stories, now and then, but the little girl, blest with an eye for beauty, managed always in the midst of each recollection to slip in an account of her joy in the flowers that grew by the way. They continued that journey from Arkansas into Texas, down at last to Seguin, and there can be no small doubt that the bluebonnet, the prairie primrose, the dogwood, the magnolia and the jassamine came in for a fair share of childish approbation.

John Mays bought land facing the Guadalupe river—he was too late for the grant of a league and labor—near the town of Seguin. The land soon became a plantation. Mays had brought determination and energy to aid in his pioneer undertakings, a combination hard to defeat, and before many years he became known as a wealthy man, wealthy as men were considered in that day and time. The log house erected for the comfort of his family, save the mark, was a story and a half high. Several children shared that pioneer home, and records have a way of alluding always to the sisters as handsome women. Katherine, by this time dubbed Kate, was probably the handsomest of them all, and one young man visiting in that Seguin home demanded on his return to Kentucky that his newborn sister be called Katherine Mays, giving as his reason that she would then be called after the handsomest woman in Texas. Thus deeply impressed, and he had lived all his life in Kentucky!

In 1854, Katherine Mays became the wife of Joseph L. Evans of San Antonio. Records available fail to speak of the qualifications of this gentleman. We know that there were three children born of this marriage and that some time about 1860, Joseph Evans died, leaving the care of those children to the mother's lone hand.

In the accounts of that young widowhood we find little allusion to struggle. Her own father had probably laid deep the foundation of his own fortune, and Kate in her widowhood profited thereby. We do know that with all the care incident to the bringing up of young children, the young widow after a time found sufficient leisure to mingle in the gay world about her. In 1861 she made a visit to the Governor's mansion in Austin, a guest of Governor Clarke and his family. Word went speedily forth through the little capital of the handsome young widow abiding thus temporarily in the Governor's home. Beauty and charm bring many followers, and before long the young widow was forced to lay aside her grief and mingle in the gay world about her. Many social affairs were given in her honor, affairs attended by both men and women.

One notable event must be cited. While the Legislature was in session—and Mrs. Evans continued her visit—a costume ball was planned and people from far and near were invited. These expected guests ransacked the earth about them in the hope of providing suitable raiment. Old trunks were rifled, and some few story books were unearthed, and fairy tales and tales of ogres, all looked into in order to find themes for the various costumes.

Not so with the handsome young widow! No fairy tale, no imaginary story must form the theme for her own particular setting. Back to history, real history, went this young Kate, to the days when Mark Antony fell a victim to woman's charms, and when she finally appeared in that assemblage it was plain to the most casual glance that she represented Cleopatra. And the representation was all that any history had ever demanded. Her husband's efforts had left her supplied with funds necessary to outward adornment, and the young widow had used them without stint on this occasion. Nature had given her beauty and grace and wit, and we dare say there was nothing lacking to make the picture complete.

Let's keep well in mind the time and place of this gathering.

It has been said by some historians that this city of Austin, made the capital of Texas in 1839, was a unique settlement from the beginning. Selected by certain commissioners as the site for the permanent capitol, it was yet at this time wild frontier. Guards were necessary at all times to protect its inhabitants from the depredations of wild animals and the wilder Indians. But that same little city, its people dreading the coming of the foe, watching at every turn lest they be caught unaware, contained in proportion to the number of its people a degree of refinement, a degree of enlightenment rarely ever found in any city of its size on the American continent. That refinement and that enlightenment had increased as the years came and went. Permanent buildings had been erected. Churches had sprung up, and homes, and when the year 1861 dawned, Texas, being then one of the states of the United States, seemed at the opening of a new era of prosperity.

But war hovered on the horizon. Abolitionists had made their boasts throughout the north. Said boasts had reached the ear of Texas people, and many men and women were arousing to protect property despite the warnings, the advice, the hopes and the prayers of the far-seeing Houston. Men were already too thoroughly aroused. Soldiers of experience were airing their uniforms and testing their rifles, and this certain ball, graced by the presence of the mimic Cleopatra, resounded with the clamor of State's Rights, and the more bitter personal indignation of slave-holding people. But in the heart of Kate Mays Evans, dancing her way to favor in the hearts of old and young, careless, perhaps, of the hope in Houston's heart for adherence on the part of his people to Federal bonds and laws, there began at that ball the second romance of her life.

It has not been stated that she tried any Cleopatra policies in this new love affair. Knowing the outcome of such policies, it seems likely that even while wearing the Cleopatra garb, she preferred to be her own sweet self, for we do know that bowing to him first as Cleopatra must have bowed to all would-be devotees, she retained forever in her train the Senator, Stephen H. Dardin, who saw her first at that ball in her regal capacity. Nor can it be doubted that the Senator touched the heart of this Cleopatra, for we know that they were married after a little bit, in 1862 and left immediately for Virginia where Lieut. Stephen H. Dardin, the happy Mark Antony, triumphing in his love, joined his company in the Fourth Texas Regiment in Hood's famous brigade. Ill health cut short the army services of the Lieutenant, and he was forced to return to Texas. He was made Colonel of Texas Troops and was later a Confederate Congressman.

The life of our leading lady seems to have been a little bare of startling incidents from this point. She moved with her husband in 1896 to Wharton, Texas, to make her home there with her widowed daughter, Mrs. Phillips. Colonel Dardin died in 1912, and then Mrs. Dardin with Mrs. Phillips moved to Dallas.

In this new home, Mrs. Dardin took up life again. Finding a keen interest in her family connection, her daughters and her grand-children, she still found time to give to outside matters. Interested in all forms of educational work, she seldom failed to lend a hand in any cause ever laid before her. She was a Daughter of the Confederacy, a member of the Dallas Forum, and the Dallas Pen Women, and in each she bore a conspicuous part. Beautiful, gracious, she passed her way through the earth her one time and left in the wake of that passing evidences of a beauty of soul not to be denied. She died in the city of Dallas in 1912.

Data contributed by—

> Mrs. Annie Dardin Cruger,
> Dallas, Texas.

MRS. GEORGE ARCHIBALD McDOWELL-BOLLING

BORN

HARRIET ELIZA HAMLIN

At some time in the year 1840, George Archibald Mc-Dowell left the land of his youth, old South Carolina, in order to make a journey to Texas, the little nation then in its own youth and promise down on the Rio Grande. Despite Indians and tales of Mexican butchery as witnessed at the Alamo and at Goliad, McDowell looked over the land as best he might, probably from the back of a bucking mustang, and McDowell, according to his own story, found that land good. We do not know that he made any claims in regard to the flow of milk and honey, but he managed in some way to send word back across the wilderness to the wife of his bosom left in that South Carolina home, and she being a dutiful wife, loving and true, severed her family relations and her friendly ties, and with her children, one of them but three years old, put out on the long journey to join her husband in Texas.

No record remains of the happenings during that journey. Whether this Harriet Eliza McDowell, born Hamlin, came by boat to the coast of Texas and then overland to the point where her husband waited her, or whether she came overland all the way, we do not know. We do know that the journey, however it was made in that day of Indians, of white men unrestrained by any enforcement of law and order, we do know that such a journey for a woman and her children threw a responsibility on the woman few of us to-day would care to assume. And we do further know that this woman made it through, safe and sound, that she joined her husband at Independence in Washington County in about 1843.

One incident of the year spent in that home near Independence throws light on the characters of these certain pioneers. Archibald McDowell taught a school in Independence in 1844. Now that school had lacked adherence, maybe, to the pedagogical rules laid down for us to-day. Nobody, then, had ever discussed nature-study for children, or the methods of Freud, all valuable things in our own day and time. McDowell probably taught that school with his rifle across his knee, but judging that teaching by subsequent events of his life, he fulfilled in every way the idea that the two necessary things to form a school were teacher and pupil, even if they sat each on an end of the same fallen log. All hail the pioneer who came from the mother country equipped in sufficient knowledge of science and art, sufficient knowledge of history and of ethics that he must needs feel the urge to pass on what had blest his own life to the young people growing up around him! And there is no doubt in the mind of all thoughful people in Texas to-day that the few pioneer families living in and around Independence were grateful forever to McDowell for this opportunity offered their children. Inherent in the mind and heart of all Texans to-day is this willingness to make any sacrifice for the sake of the education of their children.

At some time after 1845, McDowell moved with his family to other holdings, this time in Jackson County. They settled on the Caranchua river near the bay of that same name and not far from the old town of Texana. The reason for the move is not quite clear. To be nearer the Gulf was, of course, to be farther removed from the Indians infesting the interior and a little nearer the vessels that occasionally put in at Texas ports. Then, too, they were down where the ocean breeze tempered the winter cold and summer heat, where the tropical beauty met the temperate utility, and methinks the idea of a real home needed both conditions in the eyes of these McDowells. In fact there is evidence of a change of idea in the mind of McDowell. Vague plans of soil culture and its consequent production held his attention. The subduing of the wilderness in reality soon became his ruling idea. He had evolved theories of crops, and he selected this particular spot in Texas as the one best suited for his projects.

For instance, McDowell was among the first few people who cultivated any worthwhile amount of cotton in all the broad domain of Texas. He in company with a few other men, believing that cotton would flourish in that vicinity, imported the seed and went in earnest about the business of its production. There may be men in the south to-day who deplore the fact that cotton was ever imported into Texas. Overlooking the fact that cotton has many times been proclaimed king in Texas, overlooking the simple fact that large fortunes have grown up on foundations laid by the production of the "fleecy staple," this, disgruntled farmers—maybe disappointed would be the better word—can tell you, that cotton takes more work, can promise more and produce less in money than anything ever brought from the ground. Some of these disappointed producers may be tempted to advocate a return to the style of some forty years duration whereby madam, the first lady of the land, clothed now in skin-fitting silk tights and little else, waddled them, to and fro upon the face of the earth, her progress stately and slow, because her under-garments represented some twenty-five pounds dead weight and all of it cotton. But these McDowells lived when cotton was beginning its kingly reign, and they, with slaves in abundance to help with the arduous labor, went about the business, confident, determined and happy.

And they succeeded in the project thus hopefully undertaken. The same devotion, the same adherence to duty that dominated McDowell in the matter of teaching school made the desert immediately under his care "to blossom as the rose." Soil, climatic conditions, both seemed favorable. The negroes worked well under his gentle but firm command, and, as the years came and went, a home, a real home, producing for its master a generous living came into being there on that soft, wind-swept, southern shore. Her husband busy in his own way in field and garden, Harriet Eliza played well her part in the precincts of the home. She saw to it that her women slaves, the more intelligent among them, were taught to spin and weave, and she kept wheels and looms busy. She was, by this time, the mother of several children, and they, with the slaves, must be clothed as well as fed, and not a yard of cloth to be bought nearer than New Orleans, and transportation was slow and uncertain.

With this cotton project fairly well launched, with the home, an outstanding one of its day, well established there in that soft air, with all men on the place—and even the children—keenly efficient through practice in the art of protecting the home from wild animals and a few straggling Indians, with every prospect of a well-regulated frontier life before them, our Harriet had to see her husband die. Miss him? Aye, in the watches of the night, with the rain on the roof, with the call of the beast from the near-by forest to warn her of her danger! Miss him? With his children gathered about her looking to her for guidance, for training, aye, for the very bread they must eat. Perhaps, in each little face raised to her own, she saw something of her husband and lover who had gone on. Perhaps, she felt that in the discharge of that duty, she did her own part and her husband's, too. Perhaps, from all that she found her comfort, her hope in her hour of pain.

In the discharge of this parental duty as she saw it, she became indirectly a help to her neighbors. Recalling the early life and training of her husband, remembering her own early life back in South Carolina, recalling, perhaps, with a gentle sigh, that school conducted by her husband back in Washington County in 1845, she determined that her children must have every possible advantage. No public schools, few private schools existed in Texas in that day, in that locality. Mrs. McDowell employed her own teacher, provided suitable quarters for his labors, and the neighbors' children shared this teacher's instruction with her own.

With her children grown and settled for life, Harriet Eliza became the wife of Robert Bolling. She thus escaped the step usually expected of all widows, a break in house-keeping in order to become one of her daughter's house-hold. With this second companion, she continued her efficient, helpful, hopeful life in the home her energy, her thought had made possible, and there she lived, even after the death of Robert Bolling, lived mistress of her home and her business until she died at the ripe old age of eighty-nine. In fact, this woman doing her part as wife and mother, maintaining her lonely home after her husband was gone, not only for her own comfort, but for the com-fort of those about her, managing her estate including the control of her slaves, was an outstanding figure in her community. Keenly interested in all public affairs, she watched the growth of Texas, studied alike her triumphs and her defeats, made her woman's prophecies for her country's future, enjoying its growth and development over a period of sixty full years.

During those sixty years she saw many sorrows. She buried the father of her children. She buried Robert Bolling, the companion of her later years. She gave two noble sons to the Confederate cause, nor counted the cost too great for the country she loved. She saw the renewal of fellowship beneath the northern states of the United States and the southern. She saw Texas take her place proudly among the other states, even in the production of cotton, the industry she had helped establish. And then she slipped away quietly, the words of the Master ringing its music in her ears, "Well done, thou good and faithful servant, enter now into the joy of thy Lord."

Data contributed by—

Mrs. Frank Andrews.
Houston, Texas.

MRS. WILLIAM ALLEY-McCOY

And now we folks who are inclined to honor in our hearts the pioneer women in Texas, we women denied by custom the right to show our reverence in the bow of an uncovered head, we women-folks must now stand by a little minute in silence, for when we mention Mrs. William Alley, we have taken upon our lips the name of one of the original *Three Hundred*. Added to this honor of being included in that noble company, Mrs. Alley was born in Pennsylvania, the land settled by the disciples of brotherly love. Furthermore, she was born in 1777, her own father, no doubt, at that very time proudly numbered among the patriots who took upon themselves the vows of 1776, proud soldiers, all, who suffered at Valley Forge and gloried at Brandywine. And this little daughter, born in the first trying days of that revolution, in the very heart of the struggling colonies, midst scenes of its worst conflicts and its most signal triumphs, this little girl, inheriting, no doubt, the strength and wisdom of those earlier patriots, came in the fullness of time to play her own good part in that other colonization, that other revolution that in time made of Texas a nation unto itself.

Now it might be well to go back and settle down to some bare facts. Mrs. William Alley, as before suggested, was born in Pennsylvania in 1777. This much has been told us by her proud descendant. The financial, social, religious status, in fact even the name of her parents, has been passed by as a matter of little importance. To this descendant at least, the woman's own personal achievements outclassed anything that might have been Mrs. Alley's by inheritance, and, agreeing with this descendant to some small extent, we, too, must let matters of statistics rest for awhile. The descendant fails even to record Mrs. Alley's maiden name, passes without comment over her courtship and marriage, but tells us simply that Mrs. Alley had gone to make her home in Jefferson City, Missouri, and from that place, along in 1822, she, with her husband, one daughter, five sons, the youngest in his "teens," became numbered among that band of Anglo-Saxon people who waited along the Colorado and the Brazos rivers for Stephen F. Austin to make his treaty with Mexico. Mr. and Mrs. Alley had known Austin intimately back in their Missouri home. He had, in fact, been a frequent visitor beneath their roof, and this wait there in the wilderness was colored and relieved for her by her woman's faith in the man, whose wider vision saw for Texas its day of power and prosperity.

But for all her belief in Austin, all her faith in his ability to adjust matters with the Mexican Government, Mrs.

Alley had her share of frontier hardships to meet. They had received a grant of four and one half leagues of land, situated in what are called to-day Colorado, Fayette, Jackson, Lavaca and Brazoria Counties. For a home they selected the grant on the Colorado river, within three miles of the present town of Columbus. The town called Alleyton, in honor of this couple, stands to-day on the site of that first Texas home. That home was a tent, probably, and into or beneath it Mrs. Alley had them move her few household belongings, brought from old Missouri in a two-horse wagon, and then, being a good woman and true, she turned about to care for her family.

She sat upon herself a mighty task. A husband and five sons, meeting every day at one dinner table presents no small problem to-day to the wife and mother managing that home. Labor and expense stare this wife and mother in the face at every turn. In Mrs. Alley's case, money counted for very little. Things were simply not to be bought, had Mrs. Alley been worth her weight in gold, but husband and sons, alas, must eat, no matter the conditions. The stock of provisions brought from Missouri dwindled despite her careful vigilance. Coffee and sugar soon became memories, pleasing memories, dancing in irony before her dream-dazzled eyes. For one whole year, until corn could be raised and ground into meal, they were without bread. They must needs exist on wild game, and each shot that brought the animals down made our housekeeper sober, for ammunition, too, was getting low, and shots ringing out in the wilderness were signals to the Indians waiting nearby.

In that trying year, before Stephen F. Austin returned to the little colony, Mr. Alley, seeing their meat supply was low, put forth one day in the hope of buffalo meat. His wife watched him go, a certain sinking in her heart. She knew the effort must be made. She knew that no self-respecting man could see his family starve and make no effort to relieve the distress. Holding these facts stubbornly before her, she turned about in the strength born of her few months in the wilderness, and tried to stifle her fears in some simple household labor. When night came on she knew that her fears had been realized. The Karankaway Indians, also intent on procuring buffalo meat, crossed Mr. Alley's path, and his life was the forfeit. The same year, her eldest son, John, was killed during a raid by the Comanches. The next year, her son, Thomas, taking upon himself the responsibilities once shared by his father and brother, went about the business of providing meat. Attracting a *posse* of Indians, he became aware of sinister intentions on the part of the savages, turned to make a retreat, thinking as he turned, no doubt, of that mother waiting him at home. The best way to make that retreat, so thought Thomas, was to swim the river, but Thomas was drowned, unbeknown to his enemy, for his body recovered afterwards had not been scalped.

Grief, more surely than joy, brings out the characters of individuals. The selfish man is more selfish in his grief. The generous man is more generous when the world about him goes wrong. The really earnest individual recognizes in the hour of need the opportunity for the display of his earnestness. When Mrs. Alley found herself bereft of her husband and sons, she saw no occasion for foolish, selfish repining. She did but recognize in her hour of need the opportunity laid before her, and with her daughter and her three remaining sons, she set about the maintenance of her wilderness home, possessed all the while with a patriotic desire to do her own small bit whenever her country should call.

Through all these vicissitudes, Stephen F. Austin had remained her faithful friend. He appointed her oldest remaining son, Rawson Alley, a member of his first electoral assembly convened at San Felipe in 1828, and in that same year Rawson Alley was elected Sindico Procurado of the colony. Mrs. Alley's daughter, known to us as Mrs. Daniels, was the mother of several children, and she maintained her own home near her mother. There is little doubt that this arrangement promised some ease for Mrs. Alley, for the colony was under the firm but gentle control of Austin, her personal friend and—the grandchildren were in daily reach. Mrs. Alley had according to her characteristics covered her grief in her service to her friends and family, and through her labors and her plans through the spinning and the weaving, she began to see some foundation for a hope for a better day.

The fall of 1835 swung round. Mexico, having suffered as a colony of Spain, having at last thrown off the Spanish yoke, failed to see that she in turn abused her own colony, even Texas, stretching from the Rio Grande to the Sabine. A full account of these abuses may be found in the volumes of history written about Texas. We must believe what history says, but sometimes the reasons given for certain conditions are not all of the reasons. Mexico was doubtless brutal in her attitude toward her colonies, but in the absence of brutality or justice, the Anglo-Saxon finds it hard, finds it to say the least, against his inclinations, to bow to the will of any other people. At any rate, it came to the mind and heart of Mrs. Alley that her country, even Texas, was about to go to war. She knew what war meant. She had listened to stories of General Washington and Benjamin Franklin back in her Pennsylvania home. She had, herself, been through the war of 1812, knowing much of the hardships the war entailed upon the young nation. War enough, surely, to last any woman her allotted three score and ten years. No doubt Mrs. Alley thought so, but she was now, alas! a citizen of another nation, a nation facing in quality the same fierce struggle that had begun at Lexington, her people but poorly prepared for the struggle, to end for all that gloriously at Yorktown. Now, in this crisis, what must be her part?

Mrs. Alley looked about her. Her husband and been slain by the Indians. Her two sons had met death in the same fashion. Denied the presence of her remaining sons, she must become again dependent upon her own exertions for food and shelter, for protection against the savages, waiting as she well knew just such a chance. With sickening heart, with glowing smile to hide that sickening heart, she saw her oldest remaining son, Rawson, join the little patriot army. She stifled her thoughts of Mexican treachery, pretending her mother's pride when the gallant son was made captain of a company under brave Ben Milam. At the battle of San Antonio Captain Alley fell, leading his men in battle. The news reached the mother in due time, and her anguish of soul left forever its imprint upon her countenance. The answer she made to that gentle quivering soul was a gentle reminder that she had two more sons to give to Texas. She saw the two sons depart, barely grown, one of them, went back to her household duties, her lips a-tremble, maybe, but her soul still firm.

With these boys really gone, there came to Mrs. Alley the wild story that Houston had been defeated in battle and that the Mexicans were coming in droves, butchering and burning and torturing as they came. She was warned to get beyond the Sabine with all possible haste, and she, having suffered so much, saw nothing else to do. She thought of her daughter, her grandchildren, her household effects, all at the mercy of the worse than savage foe, and to her there seemed no safety in anything save flight.

Easy said, but the boys just sent at her country's call had gone on her last two horses to join the army. The wagon from much stump contact and much miring down in ungraded roads, was, itself, past all thought of use. There remained only the faithful oxen and the "slide."

Now, your scribe has no real knowledge of a "slide" or the manner in which it may be used. Some correlation of idea makes her look upon it as a huge sled, formed of hand-sawed boards, and fastened to the ox-yoke with chains. At any rate, we shall let the matter rest with this idea, for we do know that Mrs. Alley placed her few household possessions, her grandchildren, too, on this so-called slide, and then she and her daughter started out to guide the oxen, to urge them on, the runners of the "slide" sinking inches deep in the sticky mud of that early Texas road. We know that between them, mother and daughter, they maintained that awful journey, picturing the two boys just gone lying dead upon the field of action, picturing their own death, tormented in the end as they knew they would be by the relentless, on-coming, triumphant Mexicans.

At Harrisburg, Mrs. Alley learned part of the truth. It was there explained to her that the news of defeat was false, that it had been spread by marauders in the hope of plunder to be found in all homes thus deserted. She learned to a certainty that Houston had been victorious on the San Jacinto and that her son, Abraham Alley, had been a member of the ill-fated Mier expedition, but had drawn a white bean. She learned, too, that he had played his own good part in that glorious San Jacinto victory, and she, hearing this, felt sure in her woman's way that these boys were to be spared to her for many years to come.

Mrs. Alley made her way slowly back to her home at Alleyton. As Texas, the young nation, began to take on life and form and meaning, she must have felt a justifiable pride in the success of Houston and Austin, and the able coadjutors, for she, too, had made her sacrifices that Texas might be free. She was now in the sixtieth year of her life, her health good, her prospects bright, and she began again in her simple way the task of doing her own good part in the maintainance of a home for the children left her. The daughter, as we already know, was married and living in her own home. Before very long, her son, Abraham married Miss Nancy Millar, but her son, William, remained a bachelor all his life.

Now the convictions that kept William a bachelor all his life were in no way inherited by his active mother. Devoted to her husband and the father of her children, grieved and bitterly, too, that his life must needs be sacrificed to the Indian's insatiate hate, Mrs. Alley, her affairs temporal in good shape, listened to the pleadings of one Thomas McCoy, another of the famous Three Hundred, and before very long after the beginning of said listening, our little lady became this man's wife. Perhaps the marriage lacked the thrill of her first love adventure, but Mrs. Alley-McCoy was spared the degradation of a chair in her daughter's chimney corner, and then, methinks, that as Texas grew and prospered, she found a great joy in living over with this husband of her old age the thrilling things that fell into the lives of the famous *Three Hundred*.

In that home at Alleyton, Mrs. Alley-McCoy passed away, and she was buried by loving hands in the cemetery nearby. No single historic deed recorded in Texas history needs her name to complete its list of participants. No act of special heroism can be laid to her credit. She was a woman, unable to bear arms in defense of her country. She had no right then to cast her ballot in any of the many questions to be decided by the people of the young republic, but her faith and her devotion, her adherence to the truth, shared by those blessed pioneer mothers of another day, was a leading one among the many factors that made for our country's success.

We beg leave, this being true, to end this simple story with an excerpt from a History of Texas written by the Hon. Louis Wortham.

"The Alamo still stands as a monument to remind this generation that men can die bravely in a holy cause, but the women among that little group of pioneers known as the old Three Hundred who were the first to brave the wilds with Stephen F. Austin suffered more for Texas than many a soldier wounded on the battlefield."

Data contributed by—

Mrs. Mannie Coleman,
4440 Walker Ave.,
Houston, Texas.

MRS. EMORY W. ROGERS

BORN

NANCY CHILTON

A fixed belief in the established laws of inheritance sometimes leads us astray. The son of a statesman of renown has been pulled from the gutter in order that he might die some time later in the poor-house. But when a certain descendant tells me that her pioneer grandmother was winsome and dainty and sweet, when I glance, naturally, into the face of the woman making the statement, I am ready to class the gutter-snipe under some stray head of accident, or reversion to type or something else, ready, under the influence of that glance, to believe more firmly than ever in the laws of inheritance. I have been told, you see, that this Nancy Chilton was a little woman, a number one shoe woman, probably in her day boasted an eighteen-inch measurement in the waist, pretty—for want of a better word,—if one might ever in all the world be found—*cute*, and subsequent events in her life proved that with all this irresistible charm, Nancy was blessed with a fund of good, sound sense, and had another fund of good strong will power to bring that fund of sense when occasion demanded it, into instant and efficient play.

Nancy Chilton was born in Alabama, October 18, 1810. Her early home was one of ease and plenty, slaves in abundance to aid our Nancy in all her triumphant girlhood, and there with those same slaves looking with love on "little Missy" in her bridal white, she was married September 19, 1833, to Emory W. Rogers. Three children were born to this young couple, there in that home of ease in old Alabama, and then for some reason best known to folks blest with the pioneer spirit, along about 1838, some five years after their marriage, Mr. and Mrs. Rogers with their three children, the youngest a tiny baby, made the long, perilous, overland journey to Texas, knowing in that day that they were not likely to make the return journey, knowing that there was small chance to ever see again their native land or the friends and loved ones who had made life in that old land so sweet.

Just how long the Rogers family were on the way, we cannot say. No incidents of that journey have been recorded, no record made of the time consumed. We cannot say whether or no any accounts of the tragedies of the Alamo or Goliad, or the glorious victory at San Jacinto had yet reached these emigrants. Neither are we quite sure as to the location of their first home in the infant Republic, but we do know that in 1847 this couple moved to the spot on which the city of Waxahachie is now builded and that they continued to reside there until the time of their death.

In building his home on this particular spot which was part of the head-right granted him by the government, Mr. Rogers became the first settler of Waxahachie. His liberality in the amount of land given the county led to the establishment of the county seat at this place. And just because Mr. Rogers managed in some mysterious way to face that first cabin home on a line running from north-east to south-west, so the streets of Waxahachie to-day take this same line with reference to the compass. This cabin, set in this contrary fashion, was a log house, one room, one door, a chimney made of mud and sticks, and in this place of abode, Nancy stored her few precious belongings, arranged beds and chairs and the one rude table as best she might, and then Miss Nancy began her Texas home-making.

In this business of home-making, Nancy, aided and abetted by her husband, kept a kind of house of entertainment, a primitive hotel, so to speak. No bell-boys answered the impatient summons of the guests, no bell-boy necessity ever arose, for most of the inmates, even the proprietor and his family together with the guests were likely to be crowded within the limits of that one cabin room. Despite such limited quarters, no single word of disparagement of this hotel and its management had ever passed unchallenged in the hearing of old settlers. These settlers boasted proudly that the weary traveller was sure to find there a clean bed and the very best fare the country afforded on our Nancy's table.

But that fare, even on Nancy's table, would seem strange to-day, even to a Texas woman, born and bred. The supply of provisions brought with them from Alabama was scant, transportation to blame, and it early began to disappear. Breadstuffs, sugar and coffee could not be replenished in the wilderness, and our Nancy many times sat her guests down to a meal in which lean venison and the breast of wild turkey formed a substitute for bread. This constant use of flesh food brought disease, for the stomachs even of pioneers, clamored for the starch of vegetables and the other things found in them and in grains. As the spring came on, Nancy had her garden, and Nancy watched prayerfully the growth of potato vines and pumpkins, even squash, anything that might supplement that awful meat diet. The satisfaction, nay, the jubilee that sang aloud in Nancy's heart when that first roasting-ear was ready to boil! The deeper satisfaction when that first corn crop brought from their own Texas land was ripe and ready to be used for bread! This corn before it became meal had to be ground by hand on a tin grater, an endless, hateful job, but it is easy, this grating done, to picture our Nancy in that cabin home, bending above that fireplace, cooking that first Johnny-cake of cornmeal, the first relief from that long subsistence on flesh killed in the wild. And as our Nancy went about that cooking, our Nancy who had laughed her way through her girlhood days, clad in silk and velvet, our Nancy served her Johnny-cake and her new potatoes and her roasting-ears to her family and her guests, clad in a well-fitting gown—of course it fitted well, for she had made it herself, the material used being lindsey, or once in a great while, some gaily printed calico bought at a ruinous price from some peddler happening to stray her way. When Sunday came, a handkerchief was added about the neck and nicer shoes were placed upon the tiny feet, for you shall soon learn that the religious service of the community was always held in Nancy's home. So in addition to the accounts of these creature comforts to be found in our Nancy's home, the traveller, boasting of the "hotel," was likely to add that Nancy, she who as a girl was dainty and cute and sweet, had a kindly manner, a certain womanly sympathy that went far to comfort the weary traveller. And the Major, he who had loved and wooed and won our Nancy, a thorough-going, public-spirited man, gave all help he could to any enterprise, public or private, that came his way. He donated sixty acres of land from his own head-right for the use of Ellis County. He was for many years treasurer of Ellis County, and was afterwards senator from that district. This election (1850) took place in his own cabin home.

The pioneer woman in any part of America had to take thought always for the Indian. Nancy Chilton Rogers had heard back in her Alabama home of the danger from Indians in Texas, had heard of Comanches and their deadly hate. She had, perhaps, listened in the dead of the night for the first stealthy tread about her cabin door. We know that on three separate occasions she bathed and dressed her children for burial, feeling sure that the savage passing by was planning to descend upon them as they waited defenseless in that cabin home. But if the authors of histories of Ellis County, histories already published, were correctly informed, the Indian troubles in that county resolved themselves into little save fear. The savages roaming then through that particular portion of Texas were the Tonkaways. Always more or less peaceably inclined, they were presided over at this particular time by Chief Placidio, a man of exceedingly mild manner, his inheritance being considered. The docile frame of mind had been adopted, perhaps, out of respect to more powerful tribes

of Indians living on the outskirts of the county. Placidio
had recognized the possibility of the moment when he
must flee to his white neighbors for protection against this
powerful enemy, and he wisely considered it best to be-
have himself so far as the white man was concerned. It
has even been stated that Placidio in his old age refused
the offer of the Union Army to fight against the Confederacy, because, he claimed, that in order to do this,
he must fight against the white man in Texas who had always been his friend. True, there were some bloody
atrocities, some real battles, truly horrible in the telling,
right in that neighborhood between the settlers and the
Indians who came looking for buffalo meat, but they were
outside the pale of our Nancy's residence, even beyond the
boundaries of Ellis County. Sometimes news would come
of hostile tribes headed their way, ready to do battle with
the white man and old Placidio, and Nancy would have a
day of terror. Such days had been no harder to bear had
each ended in a massacre, but each day came and went,
and each one brought its own peculiar strength.

These people gathering from time to time in Nancy's
home had their amusements. As soon as there were
sufficient settlers in the county, Nancy had her quiltings,
the women coming for miles to help quilt the articles that
had been pieced together by Nancy from her small scraps
of cloth left from dresses. They would find the quilt
lining already "in" or stretched between the frames, the
cotton laid on the lining, and the design each shining
needle was to follow already laid out. Fun? Think of the talk
four or five women could manage around that suspended
square. Think of the serious discussions, the talk in which
the names of Houston and Lamar must have mingled. Think
of the chatter as to whether or no Texas had best remain
a republic. The love affairs, Heaven help us, the scandal.
And then think of the dinner Nancy served, cooked on that
fireplace. Think of the coffee passed again at four P.M.
with "black cake" or ginger bread. Think of the joy
when the last "roll" of the quilt proved that it was done
and Nancy took it from the frame to make room, folded it
up neatly ready to be finished off at her own leisure with
a daintily run hem.

And in that same cabin home, there were "singing
schools." Let us whisper a word here. We, too, would perhaps be a bit better off did we cling to the old fashion of
meeting together to sing ourselves rather than sit idly by
while some radio artist or some phonograph record attends to
the matter for us. And on the earthern floor of that cabin
or on the dry ground outside, many a dance took place, a
square dance to be sure, the music some negro's Jews-harp

or, maybe, a rare old violin twanged out of all proportion to its value, either or both reinforced by the sympathetic pat of the foot on the part of the happy on-lookers.

It seems that at some time and at some place in the year 1845, Nancy Chilton Rogers professed religion. The sweetness, the beauty, the light that had characterized her before was but deepened and broadened by this experience. From that time forward, her cabin home was ever at the disposal of any minister of the gospel of any denomination who cared to gather together the few souls in the Master's name. In that cabin home, the travelling minister found his rest and his refreshments. This being accomplished and the hour for service having arrived, our Nancy would convert that cabin home into a house of worship. Hungrying herself for the few far-between sermons, Nancy managed to send word here and there throughout the community and the spiritually famished few who gathered there listened earnestly as the faithful missionary of Christ taught the law of life as he understood it. And then, that missionary gone on to another cabin home, miles and miles away, Nancy went back to her work, her cooking, her sewing, her spinning and weaving, the control of her slaves, went back to it all with a deeper tenderness in her heart, a more brilliant radiance transforming her womanly countenance.

Nancy Chilton Rogers was denied the cruel experience of a long widowhood. Her husband died on February 28, 1874, apparently contented to die, evincing a feeling in his heart that life had held for him everything he really desired. Men had honored him, his fellow men with whom he had spent his later life. Comforts, the result of his own efforts, had crept in one by one, to the home sanctified by the presence of the woman he had loved. His children did him honor. What more could any man desire? On the first day of May, 1875, Nancy died, not yet seventy years of age, but having lived a full and happy, a convincing and gallant life. Her going was mourned by many of the settlers of the young nation long grown into a state of the United States, by many of the men and women who had shared with her and her husband and her children the pleasures of that log cabin home. And who among us of to-day, young or old, would dare say just how far into the wide field of usefulness that little woman shed the radiance, the compelling force of life as God had given it to her in the beginning.

Data contributed by—

Mrs. F. L. Hawkins,
Austin, Texas.

MRS. W. B. McCLELLAND

BORN

JULIET LEWIS SMITH

Juliet Lewis Smith, daughter of Brig.-General Smith, an officer doing gallant service in the Revolutionary war, was born at some place in old Virginia at some time in the early eighties of the eighteenth century. Subsequent events in her life lead us to believe that this maiden first opened her eyes in a home of ease and plenty, a home characterized by Virginia customs at their sweetest and best. It is easy to picture her in such a home waited on by slaves who adored her, to picture her directing them, teaching them to spin and to weave, to do many little things as well that were calculated to add to human ease and comfort. Easy, knowing her in her old age, to imagine her living the life of the Virginia belle, her days a-light because of some courtly, powdered-haired patriot, her little feet treading the dance to the *wee sma' hours!* Easy to picture her riding to hounds and the thousand other dainty things Virginia women loved, but fact is fact, and we must here acknowledge that the first real, authentic account of our Juliet brings the astonishing fact that she had married W. B. McClelland somewhere in North Carolina when she was, herself, barely grown, that she lived for some time in Tennessee, and that along in 1846 she came to Texas with her husband, bringing nine children with her.

A woman's life, even her character, is more or less influenced by the man she marries. Failing to escape this influence, Juliet Smith McClelland was exceedingly fortunate in the man she had married. W. B. McClelland was a man of stern integrity, efficient, far-seeing, strict in his business methods, a stay and a comfort to all about him. Just what impulse led him to come to Texas, we cannot say. We do know that deference to his father's wishes held him in the old states long after his ideas of emigration had taken form, and that he continued in his old home until his father's death seemed to remove the last obstacle in the path of his desire. Delayed by his tender consideration, McClelland was denied the joy of participating in San Jacinto, but, perhaps, his own conscience, easy, as it must have been, on the score of filial obedience, made him full amends. We do know that this delay being over, McClelland moved ever afterwards with directness and precision, no dilly-dallying, no holding back in any manner in any of the affairs incident to the establishment of a permanent home in Texas.

But that Texas must first be reached, and from the state of Tennessee. Remember, too, it was more than seventy-

five years ago, years that have been crowded with the
fastest development in the matter of transportation ever
known in a similar period in the history of the world.
There must have been wagons piled high with provisions,
some furniture, and much ammunition, wagons pulled
by horses and oxen. Maybe so, but record boasts the
fact that our Juliet, my dainty lady of old Virginia, rode
the many hundreds of miles intervening between Tennessee
and Texas on horseback, her baby in her arms. The Mc-
Clellands settled in Washington County near Burton, and
Mr. McClelland opened a general merchandise store,
probably in the town of Burton. Into this new country,
a nation in reality just merged into the larger nation to
the north of them, McClelland brought vigorous business
methods. He priced his goods at a fair profit to himself,
yet within easy reach of the pioneers about him. He
dealt with all men coming into his store intent on business
with courtesy and dispatch, but he made it plain in the
very beginning that his store had no room for loungers and
for loafers, that it was maintained strictly as a place for
barter and trade. No swapping of *horse-lies* was to be
done at his store, no political wranglings were to take
place beneath his business roof, and men learned early and
a little thoroughly that it was best always to respect the
merchant's wishes. He encouraged prospective buyers as
behooves a merchant of any day and time, he even *dickered*
a bit as to the price of a yard of calico or a pair of boots,
falling a wee bit sometimes from the first marked price,
but in the end the man succeeded. He laid the foundation
then for the ease and comfort of his old age, and no man
throughout that county ever begrudged him one moment
of that ease.

Along with all this establishment of business, McClelland
was busy with the establishment of a home for his family.
In this last matter, our Juliet had her own way. Loving
her tenderly, realizing the sacrifice the woman had made
that he might satisfy his own desires, McClelland felt that
this wilderness home must be made as far as circumstances
would permit to conform to her own ideas of comfort.
With this idea and the idea of permanence in his mind, he
built this log house entirely of cedar. Even the planks
used in the floor and in the roof were of cedar, and it must
have been a large house for its day, for remember, there
were nine children to be reared beneath its fragrant roof.
Sympathizing with her husband in his ideas of permanency,
giving in her heart a solemn "Amen" to his frequent as-
sertions that this was to be their home for the balance of
their lives, Juliet Smith McClelland set herself about the
business of making that cedar cabin into a real home.

No doubt Juliet had maintained some fine ideas of household management throughout all the years of her married life. Conscientious in an unusual degree in all matters, no home duty had ever slipped by her keen observation. She had, indeed, "looked well to the ways of her house," but in Texas, even in that cedar house, planned in loving care for her, things were very different from anything Juliet had ever known in her other home. There were the slaves, brought, some of them from old Virginia, to do her bidding, to wait upon her in that cedar house, even as they had waited on her in old Virginia. There was no lack of tenderness for her on the part of her husband and the children growing up around her, but Juliet, proud of her Virginia ancestry, proud of her old home and its ease and culture, Juliet, poor child, soon realized that in a new country the pioneer must, himself, bring about and maintain in this raw land some faint imitation of the blessings that had seemed to lie about him, ready for the taking in that old land of ease and plenty. And when Juliet first realized her own share in this side of the pioneer's burden, her heart sank. Culture, education, were, to her certain knowledge, matters of many generations. All these she had known and from them profited. What of the children growing up around her, forgetting in the raw, new country the things of the other dearer, better home?

To feed these children was no small item. To suit the rough pioneer food to tender stomachs required much thought and planning. Negroes standing by ready, nay, anxious to do the cooking, must be trained all over again in this land guiltless of luxuries. Flour, always at a premium, was sometimes missing altogether. Juliet, realizing this, but devised a way of making corn light-bread, a way handed down to many generations of her people who declare that bread made after her own instructions is well-nigh perfect. Then the matter of medicine, first for her own family, later for the community, claimed a large share of her attention. She went about this work in no haphazard fashion. By hook or crook, she procured some medical books, and with much study, learned therefrom the medicinal value of certain roots and herbs. She took her children to the woods with her, in order that they might help her in the work, and as they worked, she explained the value of each thing gathered. She concocted remedies for the stings of centipedes and the bites of snakes, and said remedies were nearly always effective. She made a salve which physicians afterwards declared must be patented in order that it be preserved for the sake of humanity, but Juliet insisted on giving what she had learned to humanity, free of advantage to herself. As a result of this magnanimous idea, the recipe was lost, and man was thereby the loser. She was, too, an exceptionally fine nurse. There being no doctors in the community, she learned early in her residence in Texas to keep herself ready for the call. Many, many times in the dead of night, she mounted her pony and rode through the Indian infested woods to bear some distressed mother company, to relieve her pain, to receive into her own arms the little body that must be bathed and dressed for the first time. She stood by when many an old man or woman, weary with his pilgrimage, laid down his burden, the laying down being all the easier because of her presence and the real aid she was able to offer. Her own children grew up with no other doctor ever being summoned, a hale, hearty set of younsters, their own children profiting in turn by many things handed down from that same school of medicine.

So far so good. Juliet had found herself able always to provide the needs of the body for this prolific brood of young hopefuls, but as they reached out toward maturity, Juliet began to feel that these children must have education. She taught them at her knee as best she could, giving them at the same time word pictures of the ease and culture in old Virginia, and then when the time was ripe, sent them to the Union Hill County School. She watched them through their little love affairs, kept her heart open and ready for all confidences, male or female, and as each child married and went into a home of its own, it was given its portion of the land and slaves. These children settled, for the most part, in that same community, and whenever any perplexity arose, back to Juliet in the cedar log house rushed these youngsters, knowing full well that comfort, maybe, substantial aid, awaited them in that dear presence.

The thought of discussing the religious life of these pioneer women brings to your scribe a strange timidity of spirit. So easy to-day to saunter to the nearest house of worship, to listen there to the eloquent divine trained in all earnestness for his work, the choir also trained in its own helpful service. So easy to pass it all up, if the going necessitates a little skirmish in the daily program. But, when our Juliet found herself safely settled in that cedar house, before even the education of her children had been planned, she had well-formed plans in the back of her mind whereby some idea of formal worship of God must be established in her own community.

She helped gather together that first congregation of the church known to-day as the Christian church in her own community, and when it had become organized, when it had assumed apparently lasting outline, McClelland built a house of worship and presented it to the congregation.

Juliet's hand in it all, no doubt,—a good wife's hand is rarely absent at such times—and then, the church building completed, Juliet, from her own private purse, gave the bell, a sweet-toned necessity in that wilderness—and, save the mark! the chandeliers. Remember, natural gas was still entomed in the bosom of old Mother Earth. Artificial gas was a dream of the "yet-to-be," but this church, before it could be complete in Juliet's eyes, must have chandeliers. Down into her own pocket again, and the desired articles were forthcoming. They were hung, coal oil lamps shedding their soft but feeble radiance from those graceful, carefully hung frames, and to a people lacking experience with electricity, the light was all that could be desired. Certainly, beneath that glow, they were allowed to continue their simple service by night, the prowling Indian giving it a wide berth, lest such a brilliance might prove to be for him the work of some deadly influence.

The war between the States found Juliet and her husband well advanced in years. When Texas seceded and the call came for troops, it seemed to Juliet that she could send her sons forth to battle, but since she could not bear arms herself, there would be little for her to do. She was very much mistaken. Before many days she had turned to her spinning wheel and her loom, had put her remaining slaves to work, and they busied themselves all day and part of the night weaving Confederate Grey cloth that was later made up into suits. Many a passing soldier on his way to and from that doomed army was comforted and fed in Juliet's home, to be sent on his way encouraged, clad in a warm suit of clothes, a suit that replaced his old one of rags. Juliet bore bravely the horrors of reconstruction, the humiliating circumstances allowed uselessly to settle about an already conquered people, but through all its depressing conditions, no thought of deserting the cedar house built for her when she first came to Texas ever entered her determined mind. She died, she and her husband, too, in that same log house planned in loving care for her comfort, and they were buried close by the church they had builded together in their youth, their time of hope and promise.

A descendant writing to-day (1928) of this rather remarkable woman makes use of this expression: "Her heart always went out to the dawn." Mayhap, your scribe misunderstands this expression, we do sometimes fail to see just what is meant by words of tenderness, but under the influence of that expression, I seem to see that mother mounting that horse, see some weeping slave place that baby in her arms, see her turning her back on old Virginia and her girlhood's life, severing home ties to take up her home in the new country. I see and feel all her longing in the face of discomforts in that raw country, her longing for the limpid streams of old Tennessee, the bubbling springs, the holy association, day after day, with women of her own kind, but somehow I seem to see her, her face radiant in all that trail. Again I see her working until the last day of her life, guiding, controlling, directing her children, and her grandchildren. I see her in that house of worship builded by him who had loved her, and somehow, each hymn flitting across her lips, each prayer welling up there in her purified heart seems to have its echo in this day and time. And when I contemplate a certain one of her descendants a strong, brave, efficient woman of her day, entrusted with the control of matters of higher education, when I see another descendant, this time a younger woman, holding her own in the educational world with man, her brother, holding her own, even better, in the world of music, somehow, in looking at these individuals, the same old inheritance idea bobs up. Then the image comes again, the image of that face turned ever to the dawn, the image of that little figure bending far into the night above some bed of pain, and I feel in the presence of its beauty, and reverently, that I stand, for the time, in the presence of holy things.

Data contributed by—

     Mrs. H. J. O'Hair,
     Coleman, Texas.

MRS. A. J. HAMILTON
BORN
MARY JANE BOWEN

The story of this one of our pioneer women, one known personally to the writer, seems for that writer to open with a vision. The vision, clear and altogether distinct, speaks a type of civilization that shall never pass from the earth, for that type is the first and last product of man's onward, upward reach. Details of that type have long since changed to details that may speak a little something gained in that upward reach. Remembering these changes in type—and some of them are startling—we pause a bit to wonder about man's hopes of the upward reach and to argue a bit over the matter. Meanwhile, the vision, careless of types and civilization or anything connected with either idea, trembles on before us, shutting out the present, demanding a bit of expression on our part as to what we may think of the past.

Back yonder in the early part of the nineteenth century, in the happy old state of Alabama, a daughter was born to Judge D. Bowen and his estimable wife, and she was given the name of Mary Jane. In that home, colored with legal lore and a bit of political squabble, Mary grew naturally and easily to womanhood. She followed her mother, probably, about the home, saw to it that slaves worked as they should and that they were cared for in return as they deserved, doing little labor herself—there was small need of it—a typical American girl of her day in a typical American home. Associated with her father, Judge Bowen, in the practice of law was a young man named Andrew Jackson Hamilton, and in the natural, easy course of human events, our Mary Jane became the wife of the young attorney. Then, along about 1843, with her husband and two children beside her, Mary Jane Hamilton made the journey from Alabama to Texas, and thereby hangs the vision.

A question immediately arises. So far no statement has been made that seemed capable of producing a vision. Agreed. There is nothing vision-producing in the simple telling. Hundreds of people had made the trip from Alabama to Texas, but this journey was made in a barouche drawn by two prancing horses, the prance held well in hand by old Henry, the colored coachman, and old Rachel, black as the ace of spades, occupying her place, too, in the famous barouche. Now the dictionary is not necessary for individuals of this generation when it comes to the horse idea—not yet. Slave as a term is understood, too, but when it comes to the word barouche, old Webster is a right nice thing to have around. It is sufficient for our present purpose, however, to state that the *Barouche* was the tip-top notch in things gentile in 1843, and Mrs. Hamilton, more than likely accustomed all her life to this same tip-top idea in all things temporal, saw nothing vision-exciting in her overland trip. She probably lolled a bit on that back seat, sinking back a bit now and then in its wonderous cushions, but accurate accounts of the lady in question incline us to believe that most of the time she held herself firmly erect, taking in the scenery by the way, her sharp eye ready to detect any chance for trouble, her capable, gentle tongue ready to voice any needed advice. No doubt, even in that barouche, attended by Rachel and Henry, Mrs. Hamilton saw many moments of unpleasantness. If so, they passed from her memory. In speaking of that journey, and she many times spoke of it during her long life, she had no complaint to make.

On reaching Texas, the Hamiltons settled first at La Grange. They built a log house there, and made it their home for a little while. Things prospered with them in this place, but Jack Hamilton was not satisfied. He was a college-bred man, and he was a lawyer of no mean ability. He had come originally from the state of New York where he had attained some success, and in Alabama he had lived always in the center of important happenings. No doubt the stories of stirring life in Texas had promised him the activity he craved. He soon realized that in order to take his part in this activity he must live near its center. Accordingly, along about 1844, he moved to Austin, the capital of the Republic. Hamilton opened a law office in this new home immediately, but this did not interfere with his political ambitions. He went almost immediately into the Congress of the Republic. He built for his family domicile a double log house on Third Street and there our heroine set up her first Austin housekeeping.

Judging by the fruits of her efforts in after years, that housekeeping was wonderfully maintained. Mrs. Hamilton never spun, she never wove, she did little real manual labor, but she managed her slaves and her household with firmness and with wisdom. She gave birth to eight children, six of them reaching maturity. With the help of her husband, she saw to it that all children were properly cared for, properly educated.

In her home circle was included one Morgan Hamilton, her brother-in-law. Subsequent events proved how deep and tender were his feelings for our lady, and it might be well at this point to comment a bit upon the character of this man. He had lived in King County, New York, and had been a state senator from that county. Efficient in all matters of life, highly educated, widely cultivated, young Hamilton was no small addition to the coterie of Texas men who labored then over the establishment of the young nation. Faithful in the discharge of all duties, public or otherwise, he fell a victim to the charms of a young widow, Mrs. Marcia P. Chalmers. The widow returned his affection, but the widow was blest with eight children and rather feeble health. On her deathbed, the widow made her mother-anxiety known to Hamilton, and he promised her that the children should never suffer. He kept that promise. He even went a step further. He gave much thought to the moral tendencies of the girls as they grew to womanhood, and woe betide any young woman among them if seen by Morgan Hamilton idling unnecessarily on the streets of Austin.

Despite this sorrow and these responsibiliteis, young Hamilton took his part with his brother, Jack, and his wife, in the city's festivities. The three of them hied themselves one evening, probably at early "candle lighting" to the capitol of Texas, in order to enjoy a *ball*. This capitol was a log cabin, built on the hill now occupied by Austin's City Hall. One room or maybe two, puncheon floor, or maybe good old mother earth, one fiddler or maybe two, the dance went on happily, keenly, Jack Hamilton doing his stunts, cutting a pigeon wing or two, Mary keeping up her own part with her many partners. Morgan Hamilton, too, found many a willing partner, but in the midst of the revelry the cry of "Indians! Indians!!" was raised. Did the dancers scatter in alarm? Not a bit of it. The men whipped out pistols from convenient hip pockets, and the Indians disappeared down the hill, on down Congress avenue, and the dance went on.

Young Morgan Hamilton had an Indian experience that was a bit more thrilling. Out for a walk with Margaret Johnson, afterward the wife of James H. Raymond, the president of the famous old banking institution, Hamilton detected a strange noise. These noises resembled to some extent the clucking of wild turkeys and the grunting of hogs, but the fair Margaret, a winsome lassie at the time, realized with the first sound that she and her gallant escort were about to be surrounded by Indians. There is no record of screams on the part of young Margaret—she may have lacked the screaming instinct—but she did grab young Hamilton around the neck, her arms locking behind him in absolute terror. The idea of arms locking about one's neck conveys a sense of physical discomfort, but Hamilton frequently asserted in after life that the memory of that hug and the joy it brought had kept him a bachelor all his life. These formal festivities, the coming and going of young Morgan Hamilton, interfered with by Indians or peacefully continued, were supplemented in Jack Hamilton's home by hours of chat and relaxation. The log cabin became in time the rendezvous for many men prominent in their day,—Tom Green, Scott Anderson, Dr. Robertson, friend of the family as well as its physician.

Even then, midst the daring, untrammelled life of the new country, Mary Hamilton began to see trouble ahead for them. She had brought two slaves in that *barouche* all the way from her Alabama home, and in the fifteen years following they had here and there without wishing it acquired others. Opposed on general principles to the holding of slaves, Hamilton had endeavored to set his own free. The slaves, ignorant of conditions described in famous Boston literature, refused their freedom. They worked for "massa" and "de missis" gladly—when so inclined and when inclined to lie down and rest there was precious little "massa" could do about it. But "massa" could and would see that no negro ever went hungry, and, somehow, in this instance, the down-trodden slave preferred a full stomach to all the freedom in the world. But the same idea struggling in the mind of Jack Hamilton had swelled to high tide in Boston and in other Eastern communities, and the counter idea of secession was gaining favor in the Southern States. Hamilton and his brother, Morgan, pleaded with the people, voicing their own ideas in the matter. Such pleading was of no avail, save that it brought upon Hamilton the suspicion of his friends and neighbors. Not all of them, to be sure, for many men in his vicinity were agreed with Hamilton, but many of these men, despite their opposition to slavery, followed the banner of Texas throughout the disastrous four years that followed her secession from the Union. Hamilton was not so minded. He stated his opinions bodly and bravely, and then to save his own life took himself to a fastness in the mountains near Austin to await developments.

It is not ours to discuss the moral side of this action. The thought of escape under any conditions brings the idea of cowardice, even, as in this instance, the man had dared to take a stand for what he believed to be right. But the infuriated people who had entrusted Hamilton with honors failed to see any idea of right in the matter. In their eyes the state was supreme, particularly Texas who had once stood alone, and Hamilton had failed the state. It soon became plain to Hamilton and all concerned, that having once escaped, he had best not return to his home. Day after day in that mountain retreat he lived as best he could on berries and roots. A broken leg chained him for days without water.

At home, his wife, our Mary, waited for news of him. Sometimes her heart, heavy with fear, told her that he suffered. Sometimes, and these times were strangley welcome, her heart declared him dead and past all suffering. Added to this racking pain, the social ostracism that can fall mercilessly upon the family of the so-called traitor, came to be Mary's portion. Her home, that new log-cabin on Third street was burned by some so-called rebels, but after a bit the long-drawn out agony was settled. Texas, with other Southern States, had lost the fight. Reconstruction added its horrors to an already horrible condition, but Jack Hamilton was allowed to return to his home and his family. Almost immediately he accepted office at the hands of the foreign element in control—the hated carpet-baggers, and this added a bit of fuel to the flame already threatening our Mary.

This, too, shall pass!

But in the passing such experiences leave their mark. Conscious of the feeling against him, Jack Hamilton went about the business of reordering his life. He had formed some plan of self-restraint that made him sure that he could continue to live among enemies and yet hope to some day be received as one of them. He knew that the first step must be the establishment of a home to take the place of the one burned during the war. For this he selected a community east of Austin. He owned many acres of land there, and the land occupied afterwards by the State cemetery was donated by him to the state for this purpose. In a grove on this land he built a nice home, a big house, two stories high, large rooms upstairs and down, long galleries supported by pillars reaching from the ground floor to the roof, comfortable for all, winter and summer, and there Mary set herself down for some genuine housekeeping.

Her family and friends had met ample entertainment in the log cabin that had served Mary for a home. In the new home the same courtesy, the same satisfaction for the inner man prevailed, but on a larger scale. Where a few men and women had been entertained in the cabin, scores of friends met under the new roof. From that home, Mary saw her children depart, one by one. She suffered there the loss of her husband at some time in the year 1875. With the presence of one daughter, her son-in-law and a grand-daughter, Mary continued to live on in that new home, being herself the sole manager of the estate. In later life she moved into the city of Austin and in her own home there passed away in 1915. Under these conditions, surrounded by youth and its promise, she saw the gradual subsiding of the wave of indignation against her husband, but looking back through the mists of subsequent years to the figure of this woman forever faithful to her trust, we seem to find in her outward demeanor a remnant of reserve, of antagonism, too, a something left by that hard four years when men struggled in a fruitless endeavor to understand each other, in a mistaken idea of what it was to do right. This, too, *shall pass*. Aye, for as the earth moves on in its restless, never-ending march around the sun, events and conditions must change. But does man ever remember the truth intended for him in the catilinism of war? Does he remember it to profit by his memory? Who shall say?

Data contributed by—

Mrs. F. C. Woodburn,
Austin, Texas.

MRS. W. D. ROBERTS

BORN

LOU CONWAY

She isn't very big, and, as the world counts things, she is by no means important—in the eyes of said world—but she trips about the earth to-day, erect, sprightly, her want of weight lost in the sense of her sprightliness, and somehow her friends had lacked the assurance to suggest to her that she lacked importance. In her somewhat limited sphere of human activity she has done her part, and she has done it well. From the vantage ground of age that follows a well spent youth, she looks the world straight in the face, and somehow that look throws a wonderfully dampening influence on him who would dare question her importance. And this individual, by the way, is known to-day (1928) as Mrs. W. D. Roberts.

This name means little to the public. Publicity does not always follow in the path of public service. When public service has been rendered in a time of peace in order to maintain that peace, the chances of oblivion are more pronounced. No thrilling, heroic, heart-crushing events are to be found in the life of this energetic, every-day little woman, but after a close study of the events of her life, after an even closer study of the individual, herself, it seems well to record among our pioneer women in Texas some of the things which befell Mrs. Roberts in the faithful discharge of her duty as the wife of a Texas ranger.

At some time in the late Forties, John Conway, who had married Henrietta Renfro, moved from Illinois to the exceedingly young state of Texas. Just why he came, just where he first settled, we cannot say, but we do know that on September 14, 1849, in Crockett, Texas, a little girl was born to this couple and was given the name of Lou. Judged by present-day standards, we risk the guess that as the years came and went, little Lou became a "likely gal," leaving a few interesting traces behind as she went with her parents, after a bit, to live in Columbus, Texas. Lou, herself, has little to say of her "likely gal" age. She seems to care little for girlhood triumphs—and defeats, for she goes on very primly to tell us that in this incipient city of Columbus she met Mr. Roberts, a frontiersman, employed right then in shipping cattle over the railroad, the railroad, itself, a startling new venture in the wilderness of Texas. She passes silently over the courtship that followed that meeting, passes rather rapidly over anything pertaining to her girlhood and its dreams and its plans, but she does tell us with some show of feeling that she was married to Mr. Roberts in the same city of Columbus on Septem-

ber 13, 1875. No elaborate preparation had been made
for that wedding. Times and conditions in Texas were
not then suitable for display of any kind. Mexican rule
had been thoroughly over-run, slavery had been abolished,
but memories of reconstruction and its horrors lingered
yet in the minds of the people. But, somehow the love in
Lou's heart for her young husband made of the affair a
tenderly beautiful episode. The minister selected for the
ceremony lived at Columbus, but had gone to Osage to
preach on Sunday.

On that Monday morning, he stepped off the train at
Columbus, conscious that he had done his best the day before, but interested right then, most of all, in the performance
of the marriage ceremony that waited him in Columbus.
And this ceremony done in all tenderness and all reverence,
and the newly married pair made their way to the train
the minsiter had quitted, the train that had obligingly
waited until that ceremony could be concluded. Then
the bride and groom being duly settled, the train took up
its slow, smoky, creaking motion direct to Austin. The
couple spent a week in the capital city, a real honeymoon
affair, the even beauty of its every-day happenings disturbed in no way by the memory of slow-going, accommo-
dating railroad trains.

That week in Austin closed for Lou Conway Roberts
the fantasies of girlhood. She took up from that time her
life in real earnest. Just prior to her marriage, her husband had been appointed a captain in the ranger service
in Texas. No war of any kind likely to claim his attention,
but right then, Texas, the home of many upright, determined, honorable men and women, was yet at the mercy
of free-booters and lawlessness, in some sections still
troubled with Indians, and these conditions made it
necessary that men clothed with authority parole the
frontier in order that her people might be protected,
particularly those daringly brave ones who were branching
out in the hope of subduing this special part of the wilderness. With much experience as a soldier to his credit,
being a man of decision and of action, the service made a
distinct gain in the person of Capt. Roberts. Nobody had
ever thought to question this. But we go a bit further.
We dare state that in the person of his little bride, going
forth with her husband into the wilderness, the country
made a distinct gain, in that her presence was all that was
needed to sustain her husband in the arduous labor before him.

They went first to Mason, Texas, and they went in an
ambulance drawn by mules, big, strong, husky fellows,
with rangers in plenty to do the driving. There may be

some among our readers who wonder just why an ambulance
was necessary since no one had as yet been hurt. Just an
added touch of word history. The bride of that day
counted herself lucky to be allowed to ride in the ambulance,
a big three-seated, covered wagon, good springs, swung
high above roots and stumps and boulders, curtains to be
used against the wind and the sun, husky drivers against
whom the mules dared no tricks, and O, ye of romantic
turn of mind, nothing, as this bride puts it, for the travellers
to do "but make love all day." Three days of this travel
brought them from Austin to Mason. The distance is
covered now by automobile in four hours.

In this town of Mason the couple visited for a few days
in the home of Major Holmes. Capt. Roberts, feeling it
necessary to hurry on to his post, left his bride to board a
little while in Mason, while the ranger camp was being
made ready. This, even to trained men, was too much of
a task for one day's accomplishment. Usually, the rangers
piled logs as for a house, up to a height of several feet,
built a mud chimney in one end, and then stretched the tent
proper, upon this foundation. In this case, however, they
found an old log cabin, a chimney in one end, the floor,
measuring twenty by twenty feet, made of rocks, rather
smoothly laid in the soft earth. Covering the rock floor
with gunny sacks for a carpet, they stretched the non-
leakable tent above the walls, sure in their own minds that
the captain's lady would be *snug as a bug in a rug*. They
moved in the few cooking utensils and the stores of food,
a nice bed for the captain and his wife, arranged cots on
the outside for the men—which they promptly discarded
for the ground. And then the captain brought his bride
home to the tent-house-kitchen over which she was supposed to rule. And be it remembered, a cook of the service waited there to do her bidding.

But Mrs. Roberts found plenty to do. A cook in the
tent and no housework at hand, this seems hardly possible.
But the woods immediately about the camp abounded in
game and the streams were full of fish. Taught by the
captain, she soon became proficient in the use of rod and
gun. She learned in a small way to protect herself. Better, however, than any real protection she might have been
to herself, she learned to obey orders.

She learned to sneak back to camp undiscovered when
she caught sight of Indians prowling about, trusting rather
to her ability to sneak than to her use of firearms. During
the Mason County war, a dispute between American
settlers and German ones, Mrs. Roberts carried the sneak
idea further. She hid herself beneath the bed in the day-

time, and she sometimes slept there during the night, for fear the enemy might slip up in an unexpected hour.

In spite of all this, there were gala times in the Roberts camp. The same spirit that prevaded East Texas and the country round about Austin, the sweet spirit of friendliness, a-blossom in all new countries, blest the little wife of the captain, apparently alone in the woods. Women, scattered throughout the county, real Texas pioneer women, some of them, women who had done their own part in the struggles of 'thirty-six came to see the bride, their knitting and sewing much in evidence, and they laughed and they chatted of every conceivable thing. Some of those women were versed in pioneer wisdom. A few of them were fairly well educated. Some of them were related to prominent men of their day, some of them but walked the humble way even unto the end, but in nearly every case the coming to that tent on any pretext was the placing of a foundation for a friendship, destined to last more than fifty years. And that life had its joys. Ever on the *qui vive* lest an Indian band appear, ever a little weary lest a bear or a cat-amount appear, they had yet the courage and the strength necessary for the gala hour. Moreover, this particular company of rangers boasted a rather superior quality of young men—Grooms Lee, L. P. Seiker, Thurlow Weed, and many others now numbered among the prominent men of our state. In their leisure hours, they flocked naturally, these fellows, to the tent of their captain, for they were devoted to him, ready to follow his lead, not blindly, perhaps, but with a devotion that amounted to pretty nearly the same thing. The wilderness limited the number of girls available, there being sometimes only one girl in the community to ten men. When the captain was called away, each girl invited to bear the bereft wife company counted herself fortunate. The men, regretting the small number of women, no matter what the favored maidens thought of this matter of no competition, exerted themselves to be entertaining. Success met these efforts usually. The captain, himself, was no mean violinist, and others among them could sing, could play the horn, the flute or some homemade substitute. No card playing was allowed, but there were foot races and croquet and in-nocent dances, now and then. These activities con-stituted their social life, the participants representing, as a rule, many different classes of individuals. Mrs. Rob-erts, endowed with the qualities of leadership, soon found because of these classes that there would be many oc-casions demanding the use of said qualities. The few cultivated women about her, the few broadminded women, endowed with character but denied educational experience did not compose their entire female world. The same improvident, for want of a better word, the same *shiftless* class of people to be found the world over had a few representatives in that neighborhood. His heart a bit anxious, always for the young wife in her new surroundings, Captain Roberts suggested to her that she take her week's washing to the home of a woman of the shiftless class resident right then in their neighborhood, and ask the woman to do the work for her. Sweet-spirited woman, courteous by instinct, Mrs. Roberts approved her husband's suggestion and put out to obey him, her mind disturbed with no idea of irregularity, no idea of social inequality, no anything calculated to upset the even tenor of the way.

But when she approached the woman recommended by her husband, Mrs. Roberts saw at a glance that something was wrong. No hail-fellow-well-met idea lurked in the mind of the woman recommended. To Mrs. Roberts' pleasant greeting, she answered never a word. She maintained her hunched-over attitude, a thing as expressive as her silence. Feeling at last that to linger longer would be a waste of time, best spent in doing the washing, Mrs. Roberts turned quietly about to leave. Something, mayhap after all that same spirit of friendliness alive in Texas people, even to-day, something got the better of the grouch. The woman called out to Mrs. Roberts to wait, and then the grouch poured out the race-old story of one woman being hurt because the other, living right then in a higher social scale, had not noticed *her* with a visit. And then, her hurt being acknowledged and partially healed by the look in the deep, clear eyes of the young wife, the grouch rose, laid her hand in acceptance upon the bundle of soiled clothes, thrust the other hand deep into her pocket, and drawing out a hunk of tobacco, stretched it generously toward Mrs. Roberts with a deep, slow-drawled, forgiving request: "Hev' er chaw!" History, sometimes lacking in suitable expressions, lapses at this point into silence.

In addition to the people about them, the Roberts enjoyed the care of many pets. Squirrels, dogs, prairie dogs, canary birds, and—mark it down—one cub bear brought in alive from the woods. Said animal fed contentedly and magnanimously from the hand of his gentle mistress. He even learned a trick or two from the soldiers haunting the captain's cabin, but nature asserted herself in due time, and Mr. Bruin, ungrateful for all the care and attention showered upon him, became cross. One exhibition of his increased strength, and Mr. Bruin was turned loose to vent his ire on the woods folks, even on his own kind if he saw fit.

The fishing, too, deserves mention. Plentiful for several months, there came a day when the fish refused to bite in the vicinity of the camp, and Captain Roberts decided that he and his wife would make a trip up the San Saba river, some thirty miles and more from any settlements. They took ten men with them for protection from the Indians. They kept a loaded gun handy, but no Indians appeared.

They fished and they fished, still watchful, but no sign of Indians appeared, except the skeleton of one, found half-buried in a crevice near the river.

But let it not be inferred that this behavior on the part of the Indians right then was evidence that the state had wasted money in the support of Captain Roberts and his ranger company. One glance at the record of the company on duty there just before the captain took charge will shatter any such delusion. Fort Staunton, twenty-six miles away—and miles must be covered then by horses—offered no protection to the inhabitants. Soldiers there in plenty, and brave soldiers, too, but affairs were conducted with so much red tape that the Indian had his own way. Every light of the moon, the savages raided the country, took off all horses and killed every man, woman and child to be found. Realizing the difficulty, Captain Roberts made it plain in the establishment of his camp that more stress was to be laid upon action than upon tape, red or otherwise. In the first battle, ten rangers against ten Indians, one Indian was taken prisoner and six Indians were killed, the chief among the latter number. Vigilance on the part of the new commander soon made it plain to the Indians that this new commander "meant business," and he somehow evolved in his aboriginal way that the captain and his men had best be left alone. This idea held sway in their savage minds during the six years of the captain's service.

And were those years spent thus in the wilderness lost years in the life of Lou Conway Roberts? Did anything in after life compensate her for the time thus wasted, for the loneliness thus endured? Ask anybody who knows her to-day (1928), and the negative answer is sure to be flung back without hesitation. In that tent she read, and some of it was good literature as the world calls it to-day. She had her sewing, and to judge from her appearance to-day, her clothes and those belonging to her husband were never neglected. She embroidered, the finished product exhibited in her tent home or on her own dainty person. She chocheted, too, her nimble fingers flying in and out. She proved, in short, there in that ranger tent that a real woman, influenced to some extent by her surroundings, is yet above them all, for there she plied in her simple, forceful way the gentle arts acquired by the civilized woman, arts whose influence on the development of the race may never be accurately computed.

At the close of this six years of ranger service, captain and Mrs. Roberts went to New Mexico to stay a little while. The little while proved to be thirty years. In this time their son had grown to manhood, had married, and had children of his own. At some time shortly after the son's untimely death, the captain and his wife went to Austin with the son's wife and children and there make their home to-day. And in that home and among the friends she has rapidly formed in that city, Lou Conway Roberts walks her gentle forceful way, showing us

> "—how divine a thing
> A woman may be made."

Data contributed by—

Herself.

MRS. ELI FENN

BORN

SARAH CATHERINE FITZGERALD

The story of the life of the lady whose name heads this sketch has come to us so brimful of glorious happenings in the lives of her many forbears that one is tempted in the reading of it to dwell on the happenings in the lives of the masculine element and to let all thought of woman and her work for the time slip by. So your scribe must be excused if she pulls herself up with a mental jerk, and asserts to her readers that Sarah Catherine Fitzgerald was born on a plantation in Georgia, on August 22, 1797. Her father, David Fitzgerald, a man of Scotch-Irish descent, took part in the Revolutionary war, serving under General Francis Marion, helped Andrew Jackson in his famous fight with the Creek Indians and took part in the war of 1812 against the British.

All very well for our Sarah. A father doing his share at the call of his country leaves a glorious heritage for his daughter. In this case the inherited good was supplemented by the fact that her husband-to-be enjoyed the same reputation. Associated with Fitzgerald in the latter fights was a young soldier named Eli Fenn. He and his father, Willoughby Fenn, had been members of the Milledgeville, Ga., militia. Young Eli had maybe known Sarah all his life, but at a suitable age, he twenty-three and she twenty, Eli woke to the wonder of Sarah's charms. Sarah followed suit, and the wedding took place January 24, 1817. The young couple continued to live with her parents, and were still there when Fitzgerald fell under the magnetic power of Moses Austin and decided to join him in his efforts to colonize Texas with people of the Anglo-Saxon race. The death of Moses Austin failed to check the enthusiasm awakened by this illustrious man. Stephen Austin took up his father's work, and David Fitzgerald, with his family, was forever thereafter numbered among the three hundred famous in Texas history.

There were the usual hardships on that pioneer journey. Across the frontier of Georgia, they met with Indians, became conscious that they were being watched by the aboriginal people, but realized after a bit that the Indians fled at the white man's approach. On the passage across the Gulf—remember there were no railroads to bring them around on land—they encountered storms, had vessels wrecked beneath them, but they finally effected a landing on the Texas coast. David Fitzgerald proceeded then with his son, who had been trained as a civil engineer, to locate the lands that were to be granted him by the Spanish govern-

ment. After much careful investigation the location was
made to suit all parties concerned, and the Spanish officials
met with Fitzgerald and his family to settle the transfer
after their own idea of law and order. Both sides, Spanish
and American, in full dress, met at an appointed spot on
this league and *labor* of land. The Spanish chief of affairs
dug up a bit of land and threw it away. He picked some
wild flowers, kissed them and tossed them aside. There
were a few words spoken in Spanish, and the land including
forest and prairie became the property of Fitzgerald. He
decided almost immediately to make his home on a quarter
of a league, just three miles below the present site of the
town of Richmond, in Fort Bend County.

Eli Fenn and his wife, our Sarah, moved from Georgia
to Mississippi soon after the departure of her family for
Texas. After the passing of time, several years, in fact,
Eli Fenn became uneasy that no word had reached them
from his wife's people. Leaving wife and children in
Mississippi, Fenn made his way to Austin's colony in what
is now Fort Bend County. There he found the Fitzgerald
family. The father of our Sarah had died, but when Eli
returned to his wife he took such glowing accounts of land
that Sarah came back to Texas with him, located in Fort
Bend County and there began the making of her first
Texas home. This was in June of 1833.

They prospered, these Fenns, in this new land. With
Sarah looking after the home, with Fenn busy subduing
the soil, the signs of prosperity peeped forth after a bit in
their pioneer home. Fenn, himself, took part in many a
gallant fight with the Indians, sharing the dangers and the
struggles of a soldier in that little army led by General
Houston. Sarah took part in the famous runaway scrape.
Believing thoroughly the story of defeat, she joined in the
grand disorder of her neighbors, one son accompanying her
in this frantic rush for safety. When the news of victory
finally reached them, Sarah turned back with this son toward home, only to find that the Mexicans had burned a
big shipment of dry goods just purchased for the Fenn
mercantile business. It cost Eli Fenn one-third of a
league of land to pay the wholesale merchants for the
goods bought on time and thus lost through a few days
scamper.

Four years after the victory at San Jacinto, Sarah was
left a widow in the wilderness, her son, John, her only companion. With the first pangs of grief sustained, with her
own emotions under control, Sarah remembered that she
had studied both botany and chemistry. Not the botany
of the gay young sprite, flitting here and there to gather and
press a certain amount of blossoms, but the botany that

led to a real knowledge of plants and their medicinal value. She grew poppies in her garden, distilled them, making in turn some valuable medicines. Some of these were prepared according to directions. Sometimes she compounded medicines according to her own ideas, and before many years, she found herself called upon to visit the sick, to diagnose difficult cases, to serve, in short as any family physician would serve under the same conditions. She finally stood the medical examination and was admitted formally to the practice. She made her professional trips about Fort Bend County on horseback, attended by her maid, Clarissy, the daughter of a faithful old slave who also went with them. Cool of judgment, clear in instructions, brave beyond compare, she met with no obstacles in the path of mercy.

Taken so far with the glory of the woman's work and its significance, we have as yet made no mention of the appearance of Sarah Fenn. She possessed a tall, rather commanding figure, a well formed brow, large hazel eyes, black hair and a fair complexion. She walked the earth in dignity, in graciousness and in truth, and no man failed to yield her his perfect confidence.

Sarah was deeply religious. She had united early in life with the Methodist church, and she read with great delight the literature recommended by its ministers. Baxter's Saints Rest, famous in its own day and the days to follow, was with her a great favorite. She read, too, a book entitled: "A Spiritual Treasury for the Children of God," read it many times for the comfort it brought her in her loneliness. Her home was always open to the ministers of the day, the circuit riders looking upon it as a haven, a refuge. There he found good meals. He found a seat before her cheerful fire, and beneath the pillow on the bed prepared for him he frequently found a gold coin of generous size, securely sealed in an envelope and addressed to himself. This same spirit of Christian helpfulness added its beauty to her presence at the bedside of pain.

From out of an exceedingly interesting mass of detail of the lives of the descendants of this woman, your scribe has selected as a closing thought an incident in the life of Mrs. Fenn's son, John Rutherford Fenn. In 1903, Mr. Fenn numbered among his employees a negro whom he, himself, had reared from childhood, a son-in-law, by the way, of Clarissy, the maid, who had accompanied Mrs. Fenn on her rounds as a physician. He took this negro to the family burial ground, located on the Fitzgerald league of land, and there beside the grave of his mother, Mrs. Eli Fenn, he marked the spot close beside her grave where he wanted his own grave to be made. At his death in 1904,

they complied with this request. His wife died eight
months later and was placed there beside him. They had
lived together fifty-two years. They had lived to see the
skyscrapers of Houston replace the wigwam of the Indian.
They knew that they had done their own part in bringing
about this civilization, and that such women as Mrs. Eli
Fenn had kept pace with her husband in the onward
march. This son of Sarah and his wife told over and over
again that she was a devoted wife, a fond mother, a dutiful
daughter. They claimed that she met each duty grown
out of these relations, day by day, as it came, and no man or
woman, white or black, ever felt for her aught but the
deepest respect.

Such women must leave an impression upon the lives of
all men and women, for all ages to come.

Data contributed by—

Mrs. J. J. McKeever,
Duke, Texas.

MRS. JOHN LINN

BORN

MARGARET DANIELS

The world at large knows of the rivalry existing between Antrim and Cork, counties, both of them, of the Emerald Isle. It has been suggested that fights, pure and simple, have resulted from discussions as to the superiority of one or the other of these two counties. Maybe the fight was all right—a certain amount of rivalry aids man in his onward, upward reach,—but we who have seen matrimony at its best—and its worst, must acknowledge a certain amount of sympathy for this certain lady when we reflect that she, born in Cork County, Ireland, of the good old name of Daniels, emigrated to America to become the bride of John Linn, born in that same Ireland, but alas in Antrim County. We have entertained small hope that marriage, in any case, ever put an end to the delights of controversy. We are not prepared to state that marriage ever aggravated differences already existing between the two contracting parties, so, perhaps, we had best content ourselves with the simple statement that the marriage between John Linn and Margaret Daniels took place according to the rites and ceremonies of the Catholic church, in the city of New Orleans and that it was a marriage worth while from many angles.

With the sea between, with time, too, rolling on, we people in America have some difficulty in obtaining the facts that have to do with this certain Margaret's childhood. We know that she refused throughout all of her life to sit in a rocking chair. In later life she was exceedingly stern in demeanor. In the face of this knowledge, we can imagine little frivolity in the life of this maiden. Even the tender interludes so necessary in the progress of courtship seem a thing afar, but we know to a certainty that John Linn, the gallant knight of Antrim, was very much in love with her. His own birth had taken place in 1798. The French revolution was then in full swing, its horrors reaching at times even unto Ireland. His father, another John Linn, a baronet, identified in no small degree with the patriotic society known as the Irish Brotherhood, must have felt some of the horror of this revolution, for he came to America when our John Linn was only one year old. He established a home for his family at some point in New England or New York, for this one-year-old baby grew to manhood, married and lived for a little while in New York City. Some years after the death of his first wife, John Linn betook himself toward Texas, the country right then demanding attention from all would-be pioneers.

At New Orleans, Linn met our Margaret, and the marriage took place in that city shortly after the meeting.

The date of the marriage was April 23, 1834. The newly-weds took passage at New Orleans in the schooner "Wildcat," headed at the time for Aransas Pass on the Texas Coast. A storm at sea crowded women and children into the cabin until space was at a premium. All provisions save bread and cheese were washed overboard, and the passengers grew thankful after the passing of the days for even this scant provision. To add to their miseries, they ran into the vessel, Cardena, and into their quarters, already crowded beyond comfort, they had to welcome the new passengers, each unhappy pioneer forced the while to make the best of a situation he could in no way modify. They landed at last at a place called Co-paw, and it has been said that Linn afterwards landed the first bill of goods ever brought to Texas at this point.

But trouble came. Cholera appeared among the emigrants, many of them dying therefrom, and John and Margaret decided to move. They went first to Goliad, then to Victoria. John invested in a boat, and put out across the Gulf of Mexico for goods. This stock was later sold about over the young nation at a fair profit. Linn went so far in this business venture as to establish a town of Linnville near the coast. One raid from the Indians wiped this white man's venture from the face of the earth, and John and Margaret with their family returned to Victoria.

But the good old Irish blood triumphed. Neither famine nor cold, sickness, persecution or any one of the many things encountered in the new way dampened the ardor of these people. They helped found the first Catholic church and convent in that neighborhood, and it has been claimed that John Linn gave outright the land on which the two buildings stood. Linn built, too, a home at this place, a frame dwelling, and in this domicile, hallowed by a thousand hopes, they set up their family altar. Some of their fifteen children had already arrived, but as the years drifted on, this couple became aware that additional quarters must be provided. Nothing daunted, they but added room after room, the house gradually spreading itself out like some big mushroom asleep in the sunshine.

Our Margaret ruled this home without interference from her husband. She brought up her children according to her own methods. Those methods lacked much of our modern tenderness toward the youth. On one occasion a young son appeared before his mother, every line in his face showing distress.

"I swallowed a button. What will it do to me?"

One stern look, one silent wonder that offspring of hers might be so simple, and then Margaret made reply:

"Kill you, sir. Go to bed!"

There is nothing extant to-day to prove that any good might come from a corpse going to bed, even in advance. Surely Margaret, who had scorned always the use of the rocking chair, must have seen something worthwhile that might be obtained by the reclining position for the troubled button-swallower, else she had never made the remark. Not Margaret. She moved always according to law and order. We have no information as to the final outcome of her command. We but let it pass with the statement that she controlled her slave women, taught them to spin, to weave, to cook, to help in any way they might be needed, conscious all the while that the men were laboring in turn under her husband, the dearly loved master who directed their efforts in forest and in field.

Things prospered for the Linns under this regime. Both men and women worked willingly under master and mistress so considerate of their own welfare. They seemed to realize that the Linns, demanding much of their servants, gave much in return, and the greatest confidence came to exist between master and slave.

One incident of the life on that plantation is worthy of record. It grew out of the fact that the dearly beloved master could not remain always at home, looking after plantation affairs. National affairs require attention at the hand of just such men, and John Linn found himself in the natural course of events in the Texas Congress, his word being worth much among his fellows. He left instructions with his overseer at home as to the conduct of affairs, and plunged heart and soul into the formation of the new republic, its plans, its laws. Midway an important discussion with colleagues gathered there in Austin, the new capital of a new country, Linn looked up to see a body of colored men approaching. Another look, and he recognized his own men, even the slaves that he had thought busy on that plantation many miles away. These men made their way undaunted before their master. History fails to supply us with the details of the wrongs they there described, but we can imagine the black man giving his master his own side of the difficulty. We can imagine that the Linn blood rose in the might of its Irish wrath, and we fancy the overseer on the Linn plantatian found himself out of employment.

Then our Margaret had a certain pride in her children, despite her stern rebuke to him who would swallow buttons, for no reason but that he did do so. She was particularly proud of her eldest daughter, Honoria Grace. She was

beautiful, gentle, by nature, sweet and refined. She applied herself in the matter of books and with much in-
telligence, and she was, moreover, a musician of no mean
ability. As she grew to womanhood, her every attitude
toward life fulfiling the dreams of her parents, they found
a joy in providing her with the many things they had seen
provided for such Irish lassies across the sea. They
bought her a piano, a big square of course, a thing to be
wondered at in the early Texas days, and right in the front
of the instrument they had a silver plate placed, and the
name of Honoria Grace was thereon engraved.

The fond parents enjoyed the young lady's handling of
the instrument. Even the stern mother relaxed under the
music's witchery. One of her neighbors, noting this relaxation, and not daring to speak of it in Margaret's presence, stated to the neighbors that Margaret was then enjoying the thing that had been denied her in her own
youth. When the Mexicans raided Texas in 1846, the
piano was carried away. Many years later, Edward Linn,
a relative of John Linn, and at that time consul to Mexico,
discovered this piano in the home of a wealthy citizen of the
City of Mexico. The plate had not been removed, and the
instrument occupied its proud position as if no fortune of
war had brought it thither.

John Linn, the husband of Margaret, was himself a man
of no mean ability. As before stated, he had held his own
with the public men of the young republic. A close
student of history could give some interesting details as
to the part he played in such affairs. He was as well a
student, his chief line of endeavor being with matters historical. He was, in fact, the author of a history of Texas,
and he was, in company with most authors, a little proud
of his own handiwork. Now Margaret had probably
been somewhat gratified with her husband's achievements.
We cannot think that the tinkle of the piano under the
fingers of Honoria Grace formed the whole of her enjoyment
of intellectual pursuits, but she began to see after a bit
that her husband was somewhat proud of the book he had
himself written. She found him, time and again, sitting
down to read it, his delight in his own handiwork appearing in this earnest eyes. To Margaret such interest be-
token a weakness, a childishness that needed right then a
stern rebuke. She betook herself on one particular day
to the side of the delighted reader, snatched the book from
his hands, exclaiming as she did so in the might of her
wifely wrath, "Come in here, you vain old man!"

Now we suppose Linn obeyed her. We suppose he left
his comfortable seat on the front porch, just as the button-
swallower went obediently to bed, but there must be no

mistake in this matter of disposition on the part of our Margaret. Any man, any woman reading these lines might gain the idea that Margaret was stern, uncompromising, even cruel to her own husband and children. Circumstances seem to warrant such a belief, but beneath that rigid purpose, beneath that stern idea of right and wrong, there existed a strength of purpose, a purity of purpose, an unselfish devotion to those about her that placed her forever among the women worth while in our own great state. We give you as final authority on this matter of disposition an extract from a letter written by her husband.

"On April 23, 1834, I was married in that city of New Orleans to Miss Margaret C. Daniels of that city, who since that day, through all eventful times, trials, and hardships, in adversity and in prosperity, in sickness and in health, has been to me a true, noble, devoted and loving wife."

Margaret Daniels Linn died at some time in the year 1884.

Data contributed by—

Mrs. R. V. Shelby,
Houston, Texas.

MRS. JOHN CALDWELL

BORN

LUCINDA HAYNIE

In the very beginning of this simple story your scribe is blessed with a vision. A home on Whitis avenue in Austin, in which she, as a child, many times loitered, is the scene of this vision. A gentle old lady, loved and honored by the children about her, revered by the children's mother, the old lady's daughter, is the leading figure. A-down the street, in a *surry* drawn by a beautiful bay horse, comes another lady, attired quietly, but in all elegance, a woman still beautiful despite her fifty years of age, another daughter she is, come on her daily pilgrimage to the home of her sister, avowedly to see the mother of them both. And the two women have many times declared of their mother, separately and together: "She is the sweetest woman in the world, I reckin." The sons-in-law and the friends have been known to declare the same of this rather remarkable woman. Now let's see if sweetness of thought and tenderness of feeling were her only characteristics worth while.

This woman had been most fortunate in her home life, even as a girl. Her father, the Reverend John Haynie, came in time to be known as one of the finest pioneer preachers of the Southern Methodist church. He was chaplain of the last Congress of the Republic of Texas, and her mother, Elizabeth Brooks Haynie, was a woman suited in every way to be the wife of such a man. Our Lucinda was born in Knoxville, Tennessee, December 8, 1809, and passed most of her childhood there. But as she reached out toward her early womanhood—Southern women were inclined to this early reach—she found herself in another locality, even in Alabama, the change due likely to her father's ministerial calling. She found, too, that she had passed through the mysterious process of womanly development. Trained as a musician, a well-read woman, a woman able as long as she lived to keep abreast of the times, she found there in that Alabama home that she had become beautiful. Plump, beautifully formed, glorious eyes, looking straight into eyes bent upon her, refined, dainty, a picture to delight said eyes in every way! She flitted about the parsonage home, her pleasure subdued in some ways to conform to her position as the daughter of a Methodist minister of the gospel, her head, for the most part, held high, for Lucinda did things, despite her sweetness, according to the dictates of her own conscience. Her ministerial father had other interest in life save his labors in the church. He owned lands and a great many slaves, and the luxuries, such as the times afforded, were to be found in our Lucinda's home. She knew little in her girlhood of enforced labor for her, but we risk the guess that she was rarely idle.

Into this life, sweet, innocent, poetic, walked Col. John Caldwell. He was a native of Frankfort, Kentucky, having been born there at some time in the year 1805. He had come to Alabama, however, from Nashville, Tennessee, had established himself in the practice of law, and before very long it became apparent that our Lucinda had given him all of her love. They were married in 1827. They lived on there in Alabama, in her father's home, and then in 1831 there came for our Lucinda the great change.

This change was nothing more nor less than the fact that her husband had caught the Texas fever. He had heard of Austin and of Houston, of Lamar, of many other men well equipped for life who had left the old states for the wilderness. He had heard of the lands, wild, rich, virgin soil to be had, all of it for the asking, and Caldwell must see for himself. He suggested to his wife that she wait in the comfort of her father's house until he might spy out the land. Lucinda was of another mind. Her personal inclination, her idea of wifely duty and devotion precluded any idea of separation from her gallant husband. Distressed, perhaps, that his ideas of life had suggested this change for them, she bade her relatives and friends good-bye and departed for Texas. The journey was long and tedious, now by boat, now by wagon, over rough roads and smooth. At some time during that journey, on a slowly moving river craft her little baby was born and died. The boat was stopped long enough to lay the little body beneath the trees, and then Lucinda, saddened, but by no means dismayed, felt the boat glide on again, leaving the little body behind them.

They stopped first in Matagorda County, Texas. After a bit they moved to Jackson County, to locate finally on a tract of land in Bastrop and Travis Counties. Col. Caldwell bought land certificates that called for seven leagues of land from Hosea Antonio Nevarro, land stretching from Onion creek near Austin to Bastrop County, and on this land, answering in every way to the wildest of Caldwell's dreams, Lucinda settled down with her husband.

Now what could any man do with seven leagues of land? What could any woman do, the wife of that man, as her own share in the subjugation of that soil? A descendant to-day will tell you that they kept a great deal of the land, will speak vaguely of the hope of oil thereon, but in the young womanhood of our Lucinda the land was sold at times, some of it for a song. It was even given away, in the hope of bringing neighbors to settle about them in order that all hands might be a little safer. Safer? Fear in Texas, where even the land was to be had for the asking. Aye, the Indian, deadly, treacherous foe to all newcomers, was about. Close questioning, however, reveals the fact that the Indian did no more serious damage to the Caldwell home than to steal horses and chickens and the like. They were, in fact, termed *friendly Indians*, but in the coming of the friendly idea, the Indian had not laid by his thieving propensity, and the white man's hen house and his hog pen and his corral must suffer the consequences. Our Lucinda heard of real atrocities committed by these savages, heard it from her husband and the many men wandering their way, and she had been duly warned. Her husband had set a boundary line, a certain stream of water called a "branch," beyond which she must never wander alone. Lucinda, independent as well as sweet, dared disobey one day. She was out on horseback, her little baby in her arms. An unusual noise fell on her ear, and Lucinda made it back to boundaries with more dispatch than dignity.

The Caldwells established themselves finally at a point on the Colorado river, some eighteen miles below Austin. They built there a double log house, set up their few household wares, and then Lucinda felt that her real work had begun. They had brought five slaves with them to Texas. Of these slaves, Uncle Fred and Aunt Melinda had just been married, were in fact a little jealous of their position as *bride and groom*, but they were none the less eager to help in that home building. There were many interruptions in the process, of course. There came the Texas revolution, short, but intense. Col. Caldwell, too busy to practice his legal profession in this wild land, was ever consulted by the makers of the new nation as to some point at law. He sympathized with the revolutionists, and put off to join the little patriot army. Lucinda followed him to the gate, to the horse block, and there spoke her farewell. With Caldwell safely away, she dropped herself down upon the block and gave way to tears. An old man found her there directly.

"Sister Caldwell"—he, too, was a Methodist—"what you cryin' about?"

"Mr. Caldwell's gone to join that army, and I am afraid he'll get killed." More tears.

"Well," contempt in his tone, "he ain't dead yet?" What ye cryin' for? Don't bid the devil 'good morning' till yer meet him."

Uncouth, well intended, commonplace words, but the latent heroism in our Lucinda rose to grasp the idea, and she took up her work and went on. Caldwell, in reality, was detailed by Houston to warn settlers of the Mexicans and their chance invasion, and when he returned to the army, the battle of San Jacinto had been won, and Caldwell's chance to die for his country had been materially lessened. A Mexican invasion in 1842 forced Caldwell to move his family into Bastrop, but, with these things quieted, Caldwell returned to his holdings near Austin and established his permanent home.

He built a large two-storied frame house, its rooms spacious, its halls airy and cool, its doors ever open to the guest passing that way. It became known throughout Central and West Texas as the White House. Houston, Austin, Wharton, Burnet, Lamar, Henderson, the Methodist minister, the minister of Baptist pursuasion, stopped there over night, sometimes for consultation with Caldwell, sometimes for the joy, the comfort, pure and simple, to be found in our Lucinda's home.

And to our Lucinda must be given full credit for the comfort of the home. John Caldwell must be away much of his time. He was a member of the third Texas Congress. He influenced a hitherto squabbling committee to select the present site as the Texas capital, pointing out the many advantages to be found in a city that rested on its seventy hills. His personal business, thriving and growing, demanded his personal attention. Lucinda, therefore, must carry on much of her home life without him.

Her children, eight in all, had begun to come. Her slaves, the five of them brought to Texas in the beginning, had multiplied. They had bought others, and Lucinda realized that they must be taught, if they were to be worth anything to the master. She took the women as her share of the burden. She kept them about her, teaching them, correcting them, looking after them. She had looms set up for the weaving of cloth, and the place began to resemble a factory. She taught the women to do practical sewing, and she held regular cooking classes for their instruction. It has been said by a grateful descendant that no little pickaninny was ever born on all that plantation that Lucinda was not present at the birth, or immediately thereafter, to see that it was properly cared for, to see that the mother was looked after. In short, our sweet-tempered Lucinda worked with her husband and without him in that stupendous labor of subduing their own little part of the wilderness. They brought from the ground the foundation of a big fortune that blesses the center of Texas to-day, and John Caldwell had no disposition to deny that Lucinda's labor, dainty, beautiful Lucinda, held no small share therein.

Again your scribe reminds you that pioneer women in Texas had their own good times. In Lucinda's home, with slaves trained and willing to provide luscious foods and plain foods, the entertainment of her women friends often took the form of a quilting party. The quilt already in the frame—Lucinda had pieced it from scraps left from the children's clothes—the neighbors gathered, coming in some instances fifteen miles a muleback if no horse were handy, and there they vied with each other in the beauty of their stitches. One woman of the neighborhood, falling short of the proficiency of their standards was, sometimes, with all tact and graciousness, given something else to do, lest her straggling stitches mar the beauty of the finished product. Failing in the use of tact, the woman must sometimes be allowed to work on, the owner of the quilt later laboriously removing the crooked stitches and substituting therefor her own infinitesimal ones. About that quilt they gossiped, they exchanged ideas that had to do with policies, policies governmental, domestic, religious, everything that played a part in their lives. Then the pioneer woman had her church affiliation. In Lucinda's case, the work was done under the guidance of the Methodist pioneer ministers, brave, intrepid souls who labored according to their lights to subdue the heathen nearest at hand. She remained a staunch Methodist all her life, brave little daughter of a Methodist minister, holding her own always in life's battles.

The war of seccession hit Lucinda hard. Slaveholding to her had ever been an honorable institution. They had used their slaves, had profited by them, but they had cared for them, and no man, woman, or child on their premises had ever been abused. John Caldwell, with his wife, made every effort to retain their slaves as any man would retain valuable property. They went into the fight, helping, encouraging, sending their sons to do battle for the cause. When the Texas State Treasury became empty, John Caldwell, aided again by Lucinda, loaned the state a quarter of millions dollars in gold. He took as security for these loans bonds which to this day have never been redeemed. The failure of the Confederacy broke John Caldwell's heart. He never regained the vigor, the poise, the intrepid bravery that had characterized his life.

Not so Lucinda. Bowed to the earth, face to face with the problem of life without the slaves she had controlled and nourished and enjoyed, face to face with the daily problems such a change must bring, she but held her head a bit higher. The spirit that made her in her youth go a little bit further than the boundary set for her safety, sustained her in her trials. Her children married and gone, into homes of their own, her slaves set free, Lucinda knew after her husband's death in the early seventies that it was best for her to make her home with one of her daughters. She lived for ten years in Austin in the home of her daughter, Mrs. J. H. Pope. Later she selected the home of Mrs. R. T. Hill—because Mrs. Hill was any dearer to her mother heart? Not a whit. She selected the Hill home, because Mr. Hill, one of her beloved sons-in-law, must be often away from home on business. Sweet, I grant you, but the vision of the dainty little woman, guiding, guarding her children, guiding, guarding, protecting her slaves, the vision of the woman standing shoulder to shoulder with her pioneer husband speaks, too, of a force, a determination, a breadth and depth of character that must have had for its foundation a sense of beauty, of infinite holiness which we in some way have come to call God.

Lucinda Haynie Caldwell died in the home of her daughter, Mrs. R. T. Hill, on December 30, 1895.

Data contributed by—

Mrs. Annie Hill Snyder,
Austin, Texas.

MRS. WILLIAM SIMPSON WALLACE-BURLESON

BORN

MARY ANN O'CONNELL

The descendants of this certain Ann have failed to liken her charms to those of the famous Irish lass whose
"brow was like the snae-drift,
and we have no record of their even suggesting that her
"throat is like the swan's,"
but we do know from these descendants that this certain Mary Ann O'Connell was born in O'Connell Castle in Limerick County, Ireland, about the year 1822 or '23, and that she was sister to four stalwart brothers, John, Thomas, William and Maurice, all older than she, all so closely attached to this young princess of the house of O'Connell as to make it necessary to give a bit of the history of these boys in order to really understand the place of Mary Ann in the scheme of things.

We know little of the Castle O'Connell in Ireland. A kind of a halo rests about such an edifice when pictured by the ordinary American of to-day. A certain flavor of romance lingers over most things, even remotely connected with the Emerald Isle, but in this instance, some defect must have appeared in the life of these high-born Irishmen, for about 1832 A. D., we find the brothers, all four of them, leaving Ireland in a bunch, determined to make a home for themselves and their sister, somewhere in the New World, far across the rolling water. They left the little Mary Ann in a private school in Ireland, where her every wish was anticipated by the numerous attendants, took passage in one of the slow-going vessels of the day, landing in the course of time at Savannah, in Georgia. From this point they made their way to Birmingham. Cotton as a foundation for business struck their fancy, and they soon controlled an immense business of this character, both in Birmingham and in Mobile. They did a general merchandise business as well as dealing in cotton, and they owned, after a time, large plantations and many slaves.

The money panic of 1837 crippled these operations. Extensive cotton culture and the general merchandise idea that obtained then in the south in the United States demanded much borrowed money for its successful operation. The money was not to be had, and O'Connell creditors could not wait. The usual sacrifice of their fields, of a large part of their slaves, and of much personal property was made, and then the brothers decided in the face of this disaster that they must move to Texas. They felt that sufficient funds could be raked from the ruins to meet the expenses of the trip, and they felt as well that in a new country, under new conditions, the fortune could be made all over again.

But what of Mary Ann in her private school in Ireland? The changes in fortune for her brothers meant that funds for that elegant life in that elegant school were no longer forthcoming. This thought, perhaps, brought its own bitterness to the hearts of those brothers, particularly the oldest one, but even he bowed at last to the inevitable. Fully decided at last on the move to Texas, John O'Connell made the long journey back to Ireland in order that he might safely bring his young sister to their home in Birmingham. This attention, connected with other outstanding features, robbed the coming of the young woman of any traces of poverty as we see it to-day. She was elegantly attired, and she was attended by a maid and a governess. No doubt these women did well their part in caring for this girl, bereft in her youth of both her parents, but we are indebted to *Aunt Eliza*, the slave woman never sold by the O'Connells, for the most accurate accounts of young Ann.

Aunt Eliza, with a number of slaves, came with the O'Connells when they settled in Bastrop. This brother, John, indulging Ann in every way, built, of course, a suitable house for her reception, but *Aunt Eliza* has remained provokingly silent about it. We do know, for Aunt Eliza has told us, that John O'Connell operated the first carriage ever brought to Bastrop. It was a primeval affair, drawn by four big horses, with a coal-black negro driver for the horses on a lofty seat and a number of outriders to open gates, to help prize wheels from the mud, to run any errands "Massa" might desire when stopping here and there through the country. "Massa," himself, the much-loved brother John, matched in point of grooming the carriage surroundings, for he had brought his "purple and fine linens" from old Alabama, and he did not scruple to use it in the new country. He wore his silk hat, his elegant clothing, just whenever the fancy struck him, and *Aunt Eliza*, watching him one day as he stepped into his waiting carriage, snorted forth in great disdain:

"Dis here wild country ain't no count fur folks lak dem."

Maybe so. Maybe the elegant carriage would soon be splashed with mud from the ungraded road, maybe that dishonored carriage was but a symbol of the many things her "folks" were destined to endure in this wild, new country. But for all that seeming incongruity, *Aunt Eliza* knew she had to endure it, and *Aunt Eliza* but turned herself about and made the best of it.

For you see, there was Mary Ann, the young "Missis." Aunt Eliza in after life described this individual as small of stature, plump of build, brown eyes, Irish complexion at its sweetest and best, reddish brown hair, alight over her smooth brow where it waved and curled back in a line of singular beauty. And she possessed other charms beside her beauty, for she was well educated, was a Catholic maiden, born and bred, and she was a fine pianist. *Aunt Eliza*, with some wisdom and much discernment, reminded us that she was brought to Bastrop to keep house for her brothers about 1840, a time in the history of Texas when girls were scarce and therefore in much demand. And *Aunt Eliza* further declared that the men flocked into this home, ruled by the beautiful maiden from the Emerald Isle—flocked in such numbers that the shy young maiden became uncomfortable at times and fled for protection to the shelter of *Aunt Eliza's* ample bosom.

Romance rarely fails to appear under these conditions. This time it came in the person of William Simpson Wallace. He was classed as a fine young man, tall and a little spare of built, a sight to delight the womanly eye. He had served his country wisely and well. He had taken part in the battle of Brussy, Salado and Plum creek. He had commanded a company of Texans, numbering fifteen, marching against a body of Mexicans under command of Gen. Flores and numbering one hundred and fifty. In the engagement, Flores, confident of victory, ran out in front of his men, claiming a wild desire to have a personal hand in the death of Wallace, only to meet death himself, a death inflicted by the hand of Wallace. Valuable papers and much booty had been recovered from the invaders, and President Lamar had ordered the sword of Flores presented to the successful commander of the Texan forces. This made of Wallace no small hero in the eyes of his little world, and from all accounts his looks, his manners justified the hero worship. Passing back and forth through the streets of Bastrop, his eye fell upon Miss Mary Ann O'Connell, in the most casual way, but after that first glance there was little of the casual left in the intercourse of the two young people. Wallace made no attempt to hide from his people the infatuation awakened by his association with the fair young damsel. He openly paid Aunt Mary, his negro slave, the sum of one dollar "to do up his best ruffled shirt," because, according to Aunt Mary's stories, "he wuz goin' ter see Mis' Mary." Just how long the courtship continued, just how many dollars Aunt Mary earned in the ruffled-shirt laundry business, we can never say, but we know that they were married afterwards in the hotel at Bastrop, the company dancing after the ceremony the better part of the night, the bride and groom taking their own good part in the revelry.

The Wallace couple then went to housekeeping in Bastrop, probably in their own home, but we have no records of any day or time when our Mary Ann had to use the spinning wheel or the loom or the needle. Slaves in plenty seemed to meet all these demands, leaving for Mary Ann's dainty hands a bit of cross-stitch now and then as it happened to strike her fancy. She kept up her music in a way, and her reading, and then close upon the heels of each other, her four children were born, only one of the number being a girl.

Her husband, being a surveyor by profession, decided that it were better for him to move from Bastrop out nearer the frontier. He took up land on Onion creek, not far from the city of Austin, some of it being in the possession of his descendants to-day (1928). In 1842, he moved his family to this place. With everything once more cozily settled, Wallace set off for a surveying trip, no uneasiness in his mind, seeing that his wife and children were well guarded by faithful slaves, both men and women. Day after day passed, each bringing the home-coming of Wallace a bit nearer. But one morning, from the porch of that house builded in a most beautiful valley, upon the crest of the ridge enclosing the valley, Mary Ann spied a company of Indians coming rather hastily toward her. At the first glance she estimated the number at one hundred and fifty, and from the head-dress of the Indian leading the party our Mary Ann was very sure that they were deadly Comanches on the warpath.

What of it? Her faithful slaves, led by Uncle Dan, had been taught to guard her, some of them being adept with both gun and pistol. She had but to turn to give the alarm. Alas! for that turning! Negro eyes, too, had detected the advance of Indians, and negroes, enjoying in a small way the use of gun and pistol, had possessed more faith in their heels and had not scorned to use them. Pell-mell, caring not a whit that the mistress was thus deserted, the negroes made for the woods. With sinking heart, Mary Ann, conscious of the slave desertion, watched the steady approach of the Indians. Thankful that her older children were away for the day, Ann snatched her baby from its cradle, and with one impulsive, determined idea of saving her little life at any risk, she placed the still sleeping child in a trunk, closed down the lid and sat down upon it.

"Mis' Mary, I's here."

The voice came slowly, softly, little more than a whisper, from the front door, and Mary Ann looked up into the face of old Uncle Dan, its dusky hue grown ashen in his fright. Reaching out one trembling white hand for the black one extended her way, Mary Ann turned to watch through the window the swift approach of the enemy.

And Mary Ann saw some strange proceedings. Viewed at close range, the individuals, seen first upon the crest of land surrounding that valley, lost a bit of the savage aspect. Two of them left their horses, slowly, deliberately, made their way to the front door of the house and knocked. With a courage born of that fervent negro handclasp, Ann answered the knock, and to her intense surprise, the Indians asked pleasantly for something to eat. Ann thought of her kitchen—thought of how very far short its supply would go toward feeding one hundred and fifty Indians— and her heart died within her. Then, as if in answer to prayer, she thought of some cattle in the *corral* nearby. She made the Indians understand that they might kill as many as they wanted, and to her moment's relief the men went back to the other Indians.

Ann soon realized that the savages had taken her at her word. With Uncle Dan close beside her, her baby, relieved from her trunk cradle, and asleep upon her breast, Ann watched the proceedings through the half-shut windows. She saw one big beef fall, a victim to the Indian arrow, watched breathlessly the rather primitive butchering, the still more primitive preparation of the meat after it was butchered. How long would it take to kill enough meat to satisfy them all? How many beeves—O, God, how little she really cared how many they killed? Their hunger appeased, and their spirits up, what might she not expect at their cruel hands?

The sun went down crimsoning the west, painting the trees and shrubs and blossoms on that beautiful ridge and in the heart of that peaceful valley, but Ann cared naught for either beauty. The sun rose again, to show the Indians still encamped in front of the house. The long day made it clear that they had killed more beeves. Once more the night and again the dawning! Three days in all, and then the savages quietly made off having eaten only five beeves in all, but having rifled completely the pumpkin patch. And the slaves, fleeing for their lives before the advance of the savage foe, came back to Mary Ann with no apology to make, came back to breast the mute inquiry in Miss Mary Ann's eyes and the contempt of old Uncle Dan, by no means mute, by all means scornful and everready.

In 1848, William Simpson Wallace died. Struggling under the blow, Mary Ann continued her lonely life, full to the brim of plantation responsibilities, full of family cares, upholding as best she might the principles by which her plantation had ever been governed. Not far removed

from her lived John Burleson, himself bereft of a help-mate
and possessed of many grown children. To Burleson, the
loneliness, even when surrounded by his family of grown
children, was unspeakable. At a dance at Hornsby's
Bend, John Burleson met our young widow. To him the
Irish beauty, the sweet Irish shyness, the accomplishments
that follow so often a wise use of money, blended to make
of Mrs. Wallace a thing to be desired. He danced with
her once, and yet once again, and before they separated
that night, it was understood that Mr. Burleson was to
make a visit to the plantation on Onion creek. He knew
that the widow lived there in a nice new house which
Wallace had built for her, all the work of construction being done while he and Mary Ann were on a visit to the old
home in Tennessee. Curiosity, to see the new house, of
course—men are always interested in home building—but
that visit was followed by many others, friend Burleson
counting it little less than nothing that he must ford or
swim Onion creek in order to reach his lady-love. Creek
or no creek, the wooing prospered, and the day and hour
and place—the bride's own home—were chosen for the
wedding.

As that day of all days approached, the rain began to
fall. Not showers from a few passing clouds, but a steady
downpour, reaching the torrent stage ever and anon, a
rain often experienced in this portion of Texas. Valuable
to fields and to stock and to gardens, aye, but Burleson was
interested right then in a ride of ten miles or so that must
be taken across a road guiltless of grading and of gravel,
a road that inconsiderately included a crossing of Onion
creek. In her own home, all ready for the proposed
wedding, Mrs. Wallace watched the rainfall and wondered
herself as to the outcome. A little uneasy in her mind,
rather a little sober over the prospect of the marriage, the
mixing together of familes, the holding to its best the
marriage relation, each side having laid a loved partner in
the grave, Mary Ann listened to the insistent patter of the
rain throughout the day. Different members of the household—there were many friends gathered there—looked at
the bride in her gloom, but dared not suggest that Mr.
Burleson could not be expected to reach the house that
night. Finally Aunt Eliza approached her mistress, suffering herself in the gloom of the loved countenance—and
speaking low, suggested that Mr. Burleson could not come,
could not possibly get across the creek running at full tide
at every point between them. The prospective bride
heard the suggestion through, turned again to listen to the
downpour upon the roof, and then said slowly but firmly:
"If I do not marry him tonight, I shall never marry him."

Aunt Eliza went about the house spreading this saying of her mistress. She could read, as did all those present, the sense of neglect struggling to life in Miss Mary's tender, sensitive heart, and they wondered and they wondered. But not long after the hour appointed, Burleson appeared, drenched to the skin, his horse having been forced to swim the rushing torrent, his heart full of concern lest his lady-love had been worried, for all that a determined, ardent wooer, and after a time allowed the groom for preparation, the wedding went on. The rain continued, but after the ceremony the gaiety came out strong, as it always does when folks outwit the elements in the pursuit of pleasure.

The bride of that stormy night was not destined to comfort her husband for many years. Always a dainty, delicately formed woman, strengthened through her wife-hood and her motherhood by the constant watchfulness of her husbands and her brothers, she began soon after this second marriage to droop, and on December 7, 1857, she passed away. Denied the fullness of life as the years come and go, denied the right to bring up the children she had given being, she yet escaped in her early death one of the horrors lurking even then on the horizon. She was spared the anguish of Civil war, the horrors of reconstruction. She was spared the pain of parting with the family servants trained to do her bidding. She was spared the breaking of ties between mistress and slave. All these things considered, these things connected in our thought with her beauty, her tenderness, her delicate up-bringing, all these things lead us many years afterwards to close this simple story of her life with the thought that

"He doeth all things well."

Data contributed by—

Mrs. Maud Wallace McDonald,
Austin, Texas.

MRS. HARRY HULME SEVIER

CLARA DRISCOLL

A slow-witted fellow once sat him down to read Webster s unabridged dictionary. Tradition says he finished the reading, but tradition tells us, also, that the fellow described his reading matter as "somewhat disconnected." So far, nobody had ever undertaken to disabuse his mind of the disconnected idea. But for all this fault, and we acknowledge it is a grievous fault usually in any volume, the book referred to has a way of clearing the mists from a clouded brain. It even has a way of relieving the mind of a preconceived idea of the meaning of a word. For example:

When we think of our pioneer women in Texas, it is to immediately visualize a patient, efficient, determined somebody, ruling her own log cabin, caring for her husband and children, outwitting Indians and bears and wildcats, working early and late, in most cases in the fear and admonition of the Lord, a saintly figure of another day and time, whose memory brings to most of us a sigh of fervent thanksgiving, dashed with a hint of tears. But the famous unabridged dictionary defines a pioneer as one *who goes before.* There is an added line of explanation—*as into the wilderness, preparing the way for others to follow.* In accordance with this comprehensive definition, in spite of circumstances widely different in her life, we feel that we have a right to include in this list of pioneer women in Texas the present efficient president of the Daughters of the Republic of Texas, Clara Driscoll Sevier.

This well-known woman never in all her life endured a real physical hardship. From her cradle to the present day she has known the comfort that comes from a wise use of money. Born on a Texas ranch, the descendant of a San Jacinto hero, the recipient of her father's care and bounty, the recipient of her brother's love and devotion, she has developed into a state of womanly existence, even as a flower in suitable surroundings attains unto its beauty and its bloom. Thoroughly educated in good schools, both in America and abroad, she has attained a polish and a poise that mark her as one among women wherever and whenever she appears. In her happy married life, in her happy home life, she, as a type of women, speaks much for the women of old who laid full and deep the first foundations of Texas history.

Granted all this, the beauty, the poise, the bloom, but according to old Webster, the pioneer must *go before*, must suffer for the sake of those who follow, must lead on into

the wilderness. Well and good. We stand firm on our
first statement. Step back a few decades and look into
public happenings in Texas. A little further back to the
days when the Spanish priests, in an honest effort to Chris-
tianize the Indians, built a chain of missions in Texas,
some of them near the bank of the San Antonio river.
They were not many, Concepcion, San Jose for example,
but not far from the bank of that beautiful winding San
Antonio river, they built the Alamo, a small structure as
structures go to-day, a wonder in the day of its building
in the eyes of those simple savages. Look even to-day at
the walls of that chapel, seeing as you look the fatal day
when Bowie and Crockett and Travis died there, their
lives a sacrifice that roused the world about them to bitter
resentment, a sacrifice that led in a short time to the
victory at San Jacinto. So far, so good. History has set
its seal on the heroic past. We talk glibly to-day of the
Alamo and of San Jacinto, even the children know all
about it, but in our own day and time, far removed from
pioneer troubles and crosses, the Alamo, the scene of our
State's greatest tragedy, was again the center of interest
in another battle that must be staged and won.

From the little Mexican settlement, the rude adobe
houses clustered about the old mission of the Alamo, San
Antonio had grown to be a city. Changes in government,
development in idea, had brought Northern and Western
capitalists to dwell in the quaint old place. No matter
the crooked, narrow streets, the filth of Mexican quarters,
homes deserving the name sprang into being, and business
houses followed suit. Commercial interests crowded the
Alamo Plaza even unto the very walls of the sacred old
church. Hotels, a warehouse used for government supplies, stores joined it on every side. Men and women
almost forgot that the squat little adobe building held any
significance for anybody. Seeing the advantage of a
business maintained on the very spot, money was offered
for the edifice and the adjoining building erected in the
fifties, and the deed was ready, but not signed.

Texas had spent little time and less money in the preservation of historic spots. Youthful nations are rarely
ever concerned with this preservation idea. Battlefields
and heroes' graves called for money it seemed best to spend
in some other way. Appeals to the Legislature in behalf
of these spots of interest were looked upon by that body
as the handiwork of the sentimentally rash. And time
passed on, the walls of the Alamo in danger. Then stepped
forth our brave pioneer. No young woman just attained
unto her majority, just come into possession of her private
fortune, had ever before held any such idea. No young

girl, beautiful and accomplished, had ever before concerned herself with musty old churches, too dilapidated for use, too ugly in their decay to deserve existence in a land of promise. No young girl had ever cared that her native state had grown careless of the heroes whose blood had sanctified the Alamo's walls, and she, this pioneer among women, must have felt her own isolation as she stepped forward, check in hand, ready to purchase for her very own the property, standing then in jeopardy. She went further. She made it plain in that first business interview that the property was to be held as a shrine for the state, that the land adjoining the building was to be cleared until the plaza at that corner resembled as nearly as possible the plaza of 1836.

The title to the property duly settled, the triumphant young woman ready to embark upon her plans of restoration and clearance, and then the storm broke. People arose from unexpected places, declaring as they arose that the adjoining building, bearing over its door the date of 1856, was a part of the Alamo proper and must not be destroyed. Before the state body of Daughters of the Republic of Texas, Miss Driscoll appeared with pictures and with plans, and there told the story of her earnest desire to restore the Alamo to its original proportions. Insurgents, seeing in her plans a destruction of a real part of the sacred shrine, had many discouraging—and discourteous things to say of her plans. Sustained at last by the state body of the Daughters of the Republic of Texas, Miss Driscoll appeared before the State Legislature, laid her plans before them, explaining each and every contemplated step—on her own property, be it remembered, explaining every step with that deftness, that polish, that comes to individuals who have studied long and earnestly, individuals who have acquired in that study the ability to give heart and soul to any project they may undertake. In the end this pioneer woman won her suit, won the right to tear modern buildings from the land immediately surrounding the Alamo, and the Alamo stands to-day as it stood in 1836, its recovered grounds and hallowed walls a fitting monument to this one women who dared to blaze the trail in this new work for women.

Not very long after this question was settled, not long after Miss Driscoll was graciously granted the right to spend her own time and money in the preservation of this shrine, this patriotic woman became the wife of Henry Hulme Sevier. After much travel abroad and on our own continent she went with her husband to Austin and established there, her home. She selected for this home the point of land once selected by Stephen F. Austin, for the

same purpose, a point standing high on the bank of the
Colorado river, but washed, too, on the eastern slope by
the waters of Taylor's Slough, right at the foot of Mt.
Bonnell. Into this home, Laguna Gloria, aided by her
able and willing husband, Mrs. Sevier put no small amount
of money, allowing full sway to her own taste in architec-
ture and in decoration, a taste acquired in long years of
study and travel, both at home and abroad. Rising, a
turret of limestone amid the unfading green of the cedar-
crowned hills, this house shelters for the hour many a
happy, pleasure seeking friend, many an earnest seeker
for truth, many a statesman in need of a little relaxation,
while the grounds about the house, grounds sloping to the
water's edge, speak the owner's love of beauty in vine and
shrub and blossom.

In this hospitality side of her life, Mrs. Sevier has seemed
to take the place in Austin made vacant by the death of
Miss Julia Pease. "Miss Julia," the daughter of a Texas
governor, maintained the home of her youth, long after her
father and her mother had passed away. The rare old
house amid its oaks and its cedars, some little distance
west from Shoal creek, a one-time boundary of the city of
Austin, was in its day the scene of just such activity as
characterizes Laguna Gloria. Denied any great amount of
physical beauty, Miss Julia possessed a charm of manner,
a beauty of feeling, aided both by a fund by no means
small of good hard sense that set her a bit apart from other
women. Educated by a careful father, able according to
the old darky's account "ter step off er parcel uv ground
same ez er man," she was yet joyous, full of life and hope,
the center in her youth of gay crowds of young folks, no
small amount of the male persuasion being included. Returning from a horseback ride with these young people
at an hour a bit unseemly in the eyes of her painstaking
mother, "Miss Julia" must take a scolding. Her sister,
already married, would on such occasions exclaim: "Give
it to her, mamma," while the darky, supposed to be in
bed and asleep, would creep within hearing distance in a
vain hope to help the beloved "Miss Julia" if she only
dared.

Miss Julia lived, unmarried herself, to raise the children of that very sister who took her mother's part in the
filial battle. Of them she made noble men and women.
She managed in all success a large estate. She helped all
charities deserving of help, and no individual in any kind
of distress ever went to her without gaining help in some
form or another. There be many in Austin who pass the
old, red brick house among the cedars wishing as they pass
that Julia might again bless its precincts with her gracious

presence.   And then, winding on a bit farther beneath the
cedars and the oaks, over roads newly graded, clean and
smooth, across those verdant hills, these Austin folk reach
Laguna Gloria.   A little while beneath its hospitable roof,
and for these people things take on a better pace.   Beneath its roof the same old life under Miss Julia seems to
have been born anew.

With these womanly traits of character, Mrs. Sevier
has combined within her personality an unusual amount
of business sense.   Trusting the well-beloved brother in
most business matters, she has been selected at his death
to take that brother's place on the board of directors of
one of our prominent state banks.   She is the author of
two books—one "Under the Shadow of the Alamo," being
a series of stories colored with the life of San Antonio and
its people as she knew it.   No worthwhile charity ever
appeals to her in vain.   President in reality for many
years of the Daughters of the Republic of Texas—throughout, in fact, most of Mrs. Fisher's term of office, president
in reality now of this same body, she has ever presided over
the meetings of this organization with courtesy, with ease,
with fairness for all, with dispatch, all these attributes
blending together to make of her the finest woman presiding officer in the state of Texas.

MRS. CLEMENT CLINTON DYER

BORN

SARAH STAFFORD

At some time during the eighties in the seventeen hundreds, as years have been notated on the face of the earth —say about 1784, in North Carolina, a little daughter was born to William Stafford and his wife. Because of some particular grandmother who had borne the name, or because maybe, of some veneration for the patriarch Abraham and his dearly beloved wife, the little daughter was called Sarah. She came into the world to find herself the object of every kind of loving care, for she was surrounded by relatives and by slaves, all anxious to serve her, there in that North Carolina home. She grew up, even as the first Sarah grew up, into such astonishing beauty that any husband had been tempted as that first Abraham was tempted to pass his young wife for his sister lest some man, conscious of her charms, had resorted to murder in order to clear the track of his own desires. Lacking as yet the husband, Sarah, herself, gave little thought to her beauty. She went about her simple girlhood's life, happy, contented, looking life full in the face as one would naturally look who expected much.

Beautiful or otherwise, looking life still in the face without thought of fear, when our Sarah reached her fifteenth year there in the land of her birth, a great change came in the current of her daily life. Her father, than whom in Sarah's eyes no greater man had ever lived, had been taken with the idea of moving to a new country. He had heard of Texas and of Stephen F. Austin. He had heard of boundless plains and powerful rivers, of forests and of prairies, of land, rich, virgin land in unlimited quantities waiting the colonizer who might have it for nothing. We must confess, too, that William Stafford possessed his share of the desire for adventure, that he possessed, too, a certain weariness of things that might be expected always to stay "put," and so, on hearing of that first colony brought by Austin to settle in Texas, Stafford felt that he must obey the call of the new and the untried and try his own hand in the new country. Accompanied by his wife and many slaves, with several children and our Sarah among them, William Stafford reached Texas in her very early days, took up his grant of land in what is now Fort Bend County near the town of Richmond and there settled himself and his family, expecting and succeeding in his expectations of finding adventure in plenty, labor in plenty, and food also in plenty as a result of that labor.

And there was his daughter, Sarah. Appreciating the worth of material comforts, this Sarah spent much time in thought of elevating things, in the perusal of the few books brought with them on that journey from the North Carolina home, and in thinking of them after they were perused. She was too, a pretty girl—no apologies to that Hebrew Sarah—small of frame, but throughout her life there was a flash to her eye and a poise in her manner and a crispness in her voice that spoke the born commander. A goodly quality in woman, and we to-day acknowledge it.

But, before Sarah could reach Texas, she encountered the experience that changes the real woman from a born commander to a real follower. She met her first love— she was only fifteen years old—and as fate would have it, this lover proved to be a man of her own kind, a man worthy in every way of our Sarah, though it be a little hard to have to say so. This lover boasted the name of Clement Clinton Dyer, and he had come from good pioneer stock, his people having been numbered among the intrepid colonizers of Tennessee. Failing to possess the soldier qualifications to any great degree, Dyer was a man of no mean intellectual attainment. Despite his youth— he was barely twenty-one—he had studied law and had practiced some in Tennessee. He, too, had heard of Texas and had dreamed of living there. In fact the love for Sarah was the last thing needed to make young Dyer desert his childhood home for Texas.

Now things are a bit misty as to the arrangements for that wedding. No parental objection of course, but remember they had met on the way. The love passages between them had been interrupted by balking teams and slowly moving oxen becoming surly, and the many things incident to a pioneer journey. But they stopped finally at Natchitoches, in Louisiana, and were married. If they had flowers for the ceremony, they were picked in the fragrant forest. We are very sure there was no ice cream. They may have had to wait several hours while the priest or the circuit rider swam a swollen stream or two in order to perform the ceremony, but it was a marriage, nevertheless, of two determined young people, and the fruits thereof changed ever afterwards the current of the little world about them. They came immediately after the wedding to Texas, went to live in San Felipe, and in that bridal abode, some two years later, their first son was born.

We have every reason to believe that Dyer succeeded in the practice of his profession. That any legal work might exist in a country so new seems a bit strange, but it is a matter of record that Dyer practiced law in many places.

He had to travel about—on horseback of course, from place to place to look after the interests of these scattered clients—his life ever in danger from the Indians. Later, he became judge of a district composed of many counties, and this necessitated more horseback travel, and just as much danger from the Indians. But we are not writing particularly of this young lawyer. We are concerned with his wife, Sarah, and speak of him only because his success or his failure must mar or make her happiness. Before he had attained unto his legal success, in fact, as we have before stated, shortly after their first child was born, Sarah went with her husband to live on that Fort Bend County plantation, and there, according to the best of references, Sarah exercised her ability to control, for from that time forward, life, for the Dyers, was maintained on a large scale.

We doubt if this plantation home might have held its own with Mount Vernon or with Monticello from an architectural standpoint. The furniture, too, might have been crude, but this home in which our cherished Sarah was to live, and die, held every bodily comfort procurable in the wilderness, every comfort ever designed by the heart of woman for the pleasure of those dependent upon her. For you see, Sarah managed this home. There were slaves, increasing in number as the years went by, and Sarah looked out for their comfort, too, and their general welfare, seeing to it at the same time that each slave gave just return for her attention in efficient service. Horses, cattle, sheep, chickens increased in numbers, too, suggesting at times a scale beyond Sarah's control, but Sarah only doubled her efforts and made the scale double in proportion.

"She made her peach preserves," so states a descendant, "in a washpot, out in the yard, and woe betide any negro woman who stirred them so as to break one of the delicately pared quarters." She superintended as well "hog-killing and sausage making," looked after the placing of the meat in the "smokehouse," and he who has eaten of the bacon she prepared will as yet testify to its tastiness. Then, sure that each slave woman not needed in the field had some suitable employment, certain in her own mind that none were being abused and none neglected, Sarah sat her down, drew her children about her and taught them much of the learning and widsom that had been taught her in the Carolina home. A bit of Latin, a bit of English, some mathematics, too, and she taught the girls to piece quilts, to spin and to weave and to make their own clothes and clothes for the slaves. When these children arrived at suitable age, she sent them where more suitable instruction from more widely informed instructors might improve on her own Latin and mathematics, for Sarah believed much in the worth of being trained for the battle of life.

How commonplace all this reads to-day.   All mothers now believe in education for their children.   But the ward school lies within a few blocks, the kindergarten even closer.   The high school is at the most, ten blocks away. There, too, is the university and many affiliated schools, the vision of our forefathers, but at that day and time Sarah knew deep down in her woman's heart that despite her many and varied home interests, she must be to her children kindergarten, grammar and high school, and be it said to her everlasting glory, Sarah met every requirement.

To trace the influence of this Sarah through her day and time, and afterwards it might be well to look for a bit into the character of her children, those children grown up about her, children listening to the learned advice of a good father, drawing, however, from an energetic, capable mother, the spirit to do and dare, the spirit to investigate and to go ahead.

One of her sons lived on a ranch situated where the town of Rosenberg now stands, and he made it pay.   Another son, inheriting much of his mother's quickness of mind, loved mechanics.   On Brushy creek not far from Round Rock, Texas, he installed a water mill to grind meal and wheat, said to be the first mill of its kind in Williamson County.   He, like his level-headed mother, believed in a machine to do the work.   He possessed himself of the latest inventions in reapers and mowers, and, no doubt, when the machine turned out per minute the work of several men per hour, he felt that the eyes of his mother were upon him, that her mechanic-loving heart gave a solemn *Amen* to everything he did in that line.   His own descendants regret, and many times, that this son of Sarah's failed to live long enough to own and drive an automobile, for they knew that Sarah's son had enjoyed every humming throb of the engine.   We go further.   We wish Sarah, herself, capable, black-eyed, progressive Sarah, had been granted the joy of the turn of the steering wheel, the gentle tap of the foot on the feed, the all-compelling pressure of brakes that control in an instant a machine so powerful, so apparently omnipotent.   We know that to Sarah the experience had been worth while.

Another of Sarah's sons married a sister of Mr. S. M. Swenson, who was afterwards known as a successful banker on Wall street.   Mr. Swenson was in Texas about this time, himself, and seems to have been pleased with his sister's marriage, for we know that he later gave the young husband four hundred acres of good farming land in order to have him settle near the little city of Austin. When the war between the States became imminent, Swenson, opposed to slavery, opposed to secession, being withal a man of decided opinions, feeling because of those opinions a stranger in a distressed land, Swenson drifted to New Orleans and finally to the city of New York where he soon established himself in business.

Into this woman's busy, frontier life, Indians intruded but once. To be sure they prowled about the plantation, and Dyer had to call upon slaves to mount some kind of steed that they might give chase, but to Sarah, these events were more or less like the hogs breaking by mistake into the goober patch—when the goobers were nearly dry—or into the potatoes all ready for the digging. To Sarah, such events were to pioneer life like the famous fleas given by the merciful hand of the Almighty to the dog just to "keep him from worrying about being a dog." Such foolish, inefficient, stolid creatures could never harm her. So thought our Sarah, when she first set eyes on Texas and Indians. But there came a time in Sarah's life, and pretty soon after she reached Texas, that changed her mind on the Indian idea a little.

She was in her cabin alone save for her first baby, who was then an infant. She was expecting no trouble—she was busy of course—when a company of Indians walked boldy through the gate, up to the house, through even the open cabin door to stand at last, and defiantly before an astonished Sarah. They bent down, one by one, to look at Sarah. Then each looked up, eyed the room, and then one stalwart savage, more diabolical than the others in appearance, stepped to the baby's crib, seized the child and made off with it. Another Indian seized Sarah, another drew her down to her chair. Then, sure in their minds that the thief and the pack were well away, Sarah's captors released her and joined their fleeing confederates.

One pause, one look at that empty cradle, one weak moment in which to tell herself that it was of no earthly use, and then Sarah grabbed her bonnet, mounted her horse and put out behind the cloud of dust that spoke plainly the way of the Indian flight. On and on, urging her horse, keeping the dust in sight, reaching finally the camp the Indians were hastily making for the night.

I doubt if this camp and its occupants ran true to the accepted form of Indians and their domicile. I doubt the presence of the becoming, feather trimmed war bonnet on the head of the chief. To my mind, having seen a few real live Indians in their native lair, these early Texas Indians were a bunch of dirty, brown, small-eyed, stolid people. The camp they had pitched for the night was, as I see it, in keeping with their dirty, shiftless lives, and the food they were about to cook must be cooked in a dirty, greasy pot, or else, half-way heated before a smouldering fire. Maybe so, but when Sarah reached that camp, when she slipped from the back of her trusty horse, she found that camp a place beautiful, for on a pile of dirty blankets, her baby had fallen asleep, and one quick glance was enough to assure her that it was as yet unharmed.

Then Sarah rose to the might of her power. She doubted not that power. She forgot that she was as yet a young woman, that experience of this kind had never before come her way. All the learning obtained in her Carolina home, all the subtle charm grown out of her intensive womanhood, all the persuasive ability acquired in the management of her father's slaves came trooping to her aid. She stood brave and firm and true before the savages. She argued with them gently. She made them promises. She prayed, she even wept, keeping in mind that little sleeping child, keeping in mind his possible fate, a thing more horrible right then to her than her own t h r e a t e n e d desolation. In the end the child was restored to her, was even handed to her a bit tenderly by a man who seemed amused at her anguish (to him papooses were of so little importance) and so far as we know this was the glorious ending of the only trouble Sarah ever had with the Indians.

On that plantation in Fort Bend County, Sarah Stafford Dyer rounded out her life. Her husband, her youthful lover and companion, died. Her children, as we have seen, scattered into homes of their own. Bereft of her slaves by the mandates of a triumphant party, Sarah pursued her own way about her own plantation, managing it in every particular, and making it pay. She was found dead one day in her chair. She who had helped so many, she who had asked so little help in return, had died as she had lived, and those who looked into that placid face after death felt that even in her going she had scorned to be a burden to anybody. Let the tender memory of that beautiful life hover about us, a blessing in our time of joy, a comfort in our hour of pain.

Data contributed by

> Mrs. Starkey Duncan,
> Austin, Texas.

MRS. CASEY ASKEW

BORN

ELIZABETH GARRISON

Some forty years and more ago, a certain woman living in Travis County, Texas, gave a description of the life she had led on her husband's farm, a description replete with stories of hunting and fishing, with a bit of time spent now and then seeing that the negroes did their work in the broad fields devoted to the growing of cotton. She summed the description up with these words. "We made money, yes, but it was such an idle life for us." When the story, grown out of the experiences of this certain Mrs. Askew, has been laid in full before you, when you recall that she lived on her husband's farm back in the pioneer days of our own Texas, your scribe believes that you will immediately take issue with this woman and her comment on farm life. It will seem to you impossible that anybody might think, even for an infinitesimal length of time, that life on a farm could ever be an idle life. We are very sure that Mrs. Casey Askew failed during the whole of her life to wring her hands one single time because she had nothing to do. This security of mind anent our heroine brings the thought that idleness of life on a farm or idleness of life in a city depends entirely on the characteristics and qualifications of the individual who leads such life. Were the individual busily inclined by nature, no matter the presence of slaves, work in plenty might be depended upon to bob up, worthwhile work, leaving its trace for many years upon many generations of people. A careful study of this woman's life, its plans, its hopes, its dreams, its fulfillments, will lead the unbiased student to agree that idle people may be idle in the city as well as in country, and *vice versa*—to the everlasting good of the human race.

Elizabeth Garrison Askew was born in Tennessee in the year 1825, her father being Samuel Jones Garrison, her mother having been born Emily Evans. When Elizabeth reached her nineteenth year — in 1844, her parents forsook the peace and plenty of old Tennessee for the newer, wilder, broader country of Texas, the young republic existent then for some eight years down on the Rio Grande. Denied, perhaps, any personal knowledge of D a v i d Crockett, they had heard of his sacrificial death. They had known of Houston, certainly of his wide family connection there in their first home, and Texas appealed to the Garrisons in a most enticing fashion. In the end, they yielded to the appeal and proceeded to get themselves ready for the journey and the move.

So far, so good. If Samuel Garrison and his wife saw
fit to give up the civilization of the older state for the sake
of the roughness in the new, all well and good. Life had
bound them irretrievably together. No hardship could ever
alter the fact that they had each other, that they leaned
on each other in times of battle and in times of peace.
But what of their young lady daughter? What of Elizabeth already wedded to beauty and refinement and to
art? What might she expect in this new life in the little
republic, shaky yet upon its foundations, a possible
victim for Mexican treachery despite the horror of Goliad
and the glory of San Jacinto? Experience seems to whisper
to folks now beyond their prime that this Elizabeth was in
for a hard, stern battle with herself. But records fail to
accord with that whisper. Record fails to acknowledge
any hesitancy on the part of our Elizabeth, for we find her
in 1844 in the historical old town of Marshall, and, save
the mark, busily teaching in the Female Institute of that
place.

Crude, her efforts, perhaps, in matters pedagogical as
such matters are administered to-day, but there our
Elizabeth gave the best of her knowledge to the young
ladies attending that institute. She taught them to paint,
to reproduce the color in flowers, she, herself, so admired.
She taught them to model in wax and in plaster. Some
real artist, straying her way in this early Texas time, had
doubtless found fault with the work of Elizabeth. Certainly we know that it never quite satisfied her own ideals
of beauty, but we, to-day, hazard a guess that the young
women crowded about Elizabeth in that art class, young
women, denied in the wilderness as Elizabeth had been
denied, the beauties following hard on the heels of civilization, we hazard a big guess that those women watched
the nimble fingers of that teacher at work in plaster and
wax with a newer and better thought of life in their minds,
because she had unconsciously explained to them some of
the grandeur of the world lying close about. From these
moulded figures in wax and in plaster some influence has
doubtless spread about through our great Texas that shall
yet produce the great artist, the product, solely of our
Texas.

And then, just because she was a woman, and capable,
being a woman, of turning her hand to many things,
Elizabeth dropped at times the wax and the plaster and
taught these young ladies how to embroider. Failing in
the artistic as the world calls it to-day, some of them must
have lacked the talent—these pupils had yet a chance to
learn something of beauty in the use of the needle. Some
great author of twenty years ago burst forth on one oc-

casion with an envious observation that woman could find
unlimited comfort in sewing. Maybe so. Maybe the
thing that chained her hard and fast before the coming of
the sewing machine became for her daughter, in good time,
a pleasure and a pastime. Maybe at that time woman
did enjoy sitting down to a quiet hour of rolling and
whipping and hemstitching and briar stitching, maybe
she did love in the good old days to make her own particular John some neat hand-tucked shirts. Maybe she
did love to think in that quiet hour of the joy she, herself,
must feel when she could at last look into the as yet unborn face and know that its little body was clothed in the
product of her own hands. But wait a minute! We are
to talk of Elizabeth Garrison, busy with her class in the
Female Institute at Marshall, and these things take us a
little ahead of our story.

Not much, not very far ahead. In this same town of
Marshall, soon after her arrival, Elizabeth met Casey
Askew. Nothing particularly startling in that. Elizabeth had met many men in her time, and some of them,
maybe, had boasted as well an Irish name. But Askew
was at the time postmaster at Marshall, a man of some
importance. He was, as well, publisher of the Harrison
County Times, one of the oldest newspapers in Texas.
We have no doubt he was altogether great in Elizabeth's
eyes, for they were soon married there in Marshall, and
their first home was there, and there on December 17,
1845, their son Henry Garrison Askew was born. Other
children followed him in time—there were four in all—
and each child as it came brought a new responsibility.
Each responsibility was met, fully met, despite the fact
that these young parents were not annoyed with a surplus
of funds. They had few slaves to help in household
duties, so Elizabeth must cook and sew and spin and
weave. She went without hesitation to the work thus
laid out before her, and her family failed to lack at any
time any of the intangible comforts that must fall from a
woman's facile hand.

In the fall of 1855, the Askew family moved to the
"turnpike place," three miles distant from Sulphur Springs,
in Hopkins County. There Elizabeth took up again her
domestic activity. She helped, too, in the care of a kind
of toll bridge across the river, and she entertained many
times the traveller seeking a good night's rest. No neighbor, and it had been hard to set a boundary for her neighborhood, ever came for her at a time of distress and failed
to receive her help. She was a devoted and consistent
member of the Baptist church, doing her part in every way
as long as she lived.

But through all these absorbing things of time and sense, Elizabeth found time to enjoy her passionate love of the beautiful. The yard about her home, sloping down to that toll bridge, was a bower of beauty. Roses, myrtle, jasmine, mingled with the forest flowers of the community, transplanted and watched and worked by the devoted Elizabeth, doubled their beauty in grateful acknowledgment. She gloried in each added shrub that took on life after its transplanting, for it seemed thus to say to her that it came gladly from the forest primeval to make its home with her. She loved, too, the beauty of wild animals, loved the bright plumed birds and the gay singers. She frowned upon any who dared kill these forest folks, a frown transmitted to a male descendant who has never eaten flesh food since he was told as a child that the life of the animal must first be taken before its body is fit for food. Her papers speak of a flock of paroquets seen one time near that Texas home, and from the minute description contained therein, we must believe she was not mistaken in her classification.

A descendant speaking of her to-day (1928) uses these words: "She was quiet, not caring much for the outside world, but ever ready to help her neighbors in distress." Remembering her devotion to duty, remembering her care of her family and her home, remembering her nimble fingers in plaster and in wax, remembering her love of beauty under any and all circumstances, we can but feel that this sentence expresses much. Ready always to help a neighbor in distress, but caring little for the outside world. Easy this to understand. She had small need for the outside world, for deep in her own heart and mind and soul she carried a world of her own, and this world was in itself more than sufficient.

Data contributed by—

Mrs. James McLaughlin,
Austin, Texas.

MRS. ROBERT RICE

BORN

MARTHA LYNN

An interview with a worthwhile grandson of a noble woman brings a peculiar pleasure. Said man invariably hesitates to speak of that grandmother. He even assures the person desiring the information that he knows nothing of importance about her, but this worthwhile fellow may be depended upon to bring forth at last some tender things, some beautiful things, that make the every-day work of an every-day woman beautiful in the minds of folks. He may omit some of the things the grand-daughter had gladly given place—there are limitations of sex despite the nineteenth amendment—but this pleasure hereinbefore alluded to is due to the fact that for the time being we are looking into the life of an individual through the eyes of one who remembers her tenderness rather than her strength.

Now for a few facts. Martha Lynn was born in Kentucky. Her father had taken his full share in the pioneer settlement of Virginia, and her mother's people had probably done the same. They had emigrated, however, from Virginia to Kentucky, and there, in 1828, their daughter, our Martha Lynn, was born. We know little of the youth of the maiden, save that she grew up in a home of ease and plenty, a home of culture, surrounded always by people of like calibre. Her menfolks stood well before the world, one cousin, Lynn Boyd, being at one time Speaker of the House of Representatives of the United States. We have an idea that she was beautiful, and, remembering again that grandson and his comments, we judge that she must have possessed a nature passing sweet. And then we know that along in 1844, in Alabama, whither they had again emigrated, she met and married Robert Rice, himself a native of Virginia.

Almost immediately after that marriage, Robert Rice and his wife, our Martha, moved to Texas. No harrowing stories of bankruptcy, no broken health, no tragic family matters lent their influence in the matter of moving. In their first home, Rice had been a successful planter, an even more successful man of business, had owned slaves and had known how to make them worth while. The wife of such a man, our Martha had for her very own every social advantage, every social joy. But Texas, already an established government, a government built up by men who had been from the first determined and undaunted, offered to Rice and his wife large tracts of virgin land, and in that land, unbounded chance for growth and development. They went about the move deliberately, packing all valuables, looking, in fact, toward a home in Texas that must be in keeping with the home they were about to leave. They brought their books, their silver, their china and glass. They brought their furniture, some of it in use to-day (1929) and elegant in the eyes even of the most casual beholder. They packed these precious household things in wagons and set forth in all confidence for their new field of action.

Rice settled first in Burnet County. Realizing after a bit that the county, though beautiful, failed to favor his plans, he moved his family and belongings, first to Austin, the capital of the Republic, and then to Bastrop. The neighborhood surrounding this young settlement was an outstanding one in early Texas times. Any schoolboy can tell you that. Bare of the glitter of life necessary to us to-day, denied electric lights, gas, and sewerage, this place rejoiced then in the fundamental attributes of a social center. The latter term is used advisedly. The social whirl, sometimes despised by folks not included, plays a part in the development of men and women. We have, however, no desire to place upon some pinnacle the extremes of gaiety and foolishness. When we claim that Bastrop was at that time a social center, we mean that it was the home of the learned men, some few, and the home of beautiful women, of busy men, lots of them, bringing the substance from the earth and from the vast herds wandering here and there over its prairies. We mean that the Rices found there the best of men and women, and that they gladly took their rightful place among them. There were the families of Hubbard, Trigg, Higgins, Young, Nicholson, Garwood, Hill, McGehee, the heads of said families adept in the arts necessary to the subduing of a new country, even more adept in the arts that smooth over the rough places of life, that keep up the onward march of civilization.

Of course, the first step for any man on reaching this community was the building of a house. Rice decided upon a two-story house, to be built of logs and weatherboarded, two rooms downstairs and two above, with large halls upper and lower. The kitchen was detached from the house, O, relic of slavery, lest the noise in the kitchen, the chatter of the pickaninnies might offend "de white folks" at meal time. The kitchen was, in time, connected with the house by a covered porch, and the house entire is standing to-day. Into this home in that early day, the Rices moved their elegant belongings brought from old Kentucky, and then they began life in earnest.

The children came in time. Many people the world over come in time to regret the birth of their children, and the world commends their regret. The mothers and fathers of children look with envy upon the childless woman following her husband to and fro upon the earth. They know little of the empty arms, of the void beneath that childless woman's smile, but there has never been since the beginning of the world any sorrow quite comparable to that of the woman denied her motherhood. Incompetent, maybe, she had proven herself for its exacting office, but nothing in that woman's eyes quite takes the place. Perhaps Martha Lynn Rice sensed some of this truth far in the night when her babies showed a ruthless disregard of the mother's right to slumber. Perhaps such sensing kept her serene beneath her mental cares. We like to hazard a guess that joy in one of her daughters repaid her for every night of watchfulness beneath the roof of that log-cabin home.

This daughter bore the name of Julia. Born about the time Texas was admitted to the United States, she grew and thrived as Texas grew, her beauty at times surpassing even our Martha's dreams for her daughter. She was trained, too, by her mother and her black *mammy*, Phyllis, into the manners and the ways of a perfect lady, and as she stood at last in the crown of her womanhood, she had readily passed muster in any court in Europe or any capital in America. An old likeness shows her face beautiful in outline, hair parted exactly mid-way her brow, her eyes, wide apart, looking straight at the world as if no secret had ever troubled her young heart. The elegant dress is cut low in the neck, its edge outlined with a beautiful lace bertha. Her hands with fingers delicately pointed are encased in black lace mitts, and they lie easily in her lap. Her wide flowing skirt worn over an immense hoop is settled about her, hiding her feet, and the waist line of that skirt boasted eighteen full inches in length.

Julia loved life, loved it from many angles. Her laugh rang true and sweet and clear. Song slipped from her lips as she fluttered about her father's house, as she went to and fro in that worthwhile neighborhood, some anxious swain always in attendance. She visited many times in the Caldwell home, this house having been built in 1835 on the edge of Bastrop County. She spent many a happy week-end with friends in the McDowell home, and when the evening fell, there would be dancing to the tune of some efficient negro fiddler, some square dances, a Virginia reel, and now and then a little bit of waltzing.

All innocent enough in your eyes and mine, innocent enough in the eyes of Martha watching her daughter and her friends whiling away the hours, but there were people in Texas in those days not so liberal in their ideas when it came to matters of amusement. Foremost among these were the Methodist ministers, brave men, wandering about the new nation, carrying their own part in the burden of civilization, upright, fearless, honorable men, burning with the desire to impress the world with religion as they had been impressed, as they had seen and felt its glory and its power. In this immediate vicinity there were, from time to time, Josiah Whipple and James Ferguson. There was I. G. John, afterwards famous as the editor of the Texas Christian Advocate. These men found themselves frequently in the Rice home. They looked on young Julia in her innocent glee, and they felt as they looked that they had come upon one dangerously near the day of destruction. They made every effort to crush from young Julia all desire to dance, or to mingle with those who did dance. Failing in their attempts, they appealed to Julia's mother, our Martha. Record fails us here. Martha no doubt made some suitable reply, some reply not calculated to offend the priestly office, but Martha managed to let Julia know simply that in her eyes the dance was all right. Sustained by this wise mother, Julia tripped her way onward, unharmed, serene in her sweet womanliness.

Then there was novel reading. We wonder sometimes if the early Texas ministers among the Methodists had read many novels. We wonder if they had ever heard of Kenilworth and the beautiful Amy. The love between David Copperfield and Steerforth, the beautiful picture of Agnes had not then been given to the world, but there must have been other stories. We wonder, as that minister listened to marriage vows spoken by young people under his own direction, if he thought nothing of the love between men and women that must inevitably precede those marriage vows, if they be honorably spoken. Wondering aside, the pious men of early Texas, Methodist, Baptist, Presbyterian, looked upon novel reading as the giving way to the suggestion of the devil, a lasting personal harm to the reader and to the individuals scattered about him.

Martha and her husband, even their daughter, Julia, loving light and joy and life, had affilliated with the Methodist Church. They helped build a big church in their community as early as 1850. They helped establish a church school, but Martha did not sympathize with the Methodist idea of continual prayer, and, Saints defend us, Martha could see nothing wrong in the perusal of a novel. Being of a mature mind, being a little above the age commonly ascribed to discretion, Martha bowed somewhat to the ministerial demand in the novel reading matter, but Martha knew, even as she bowed, that the daughter

Julia was reading the precious books dealing with love and its devious ways.

And how could young Julia withstand that temptation? Her son, a white-headed man to-day, a man who has enjoyed the confidence of his state and the nation at large, will look you calmly in the eye and tell you that he enjoys reading again and again the works of Augusta Evans Wilson, calling them over by name, St. Elmo, Beulah, Infelice. He will tell you that it is impossible to find an early edition of any one of these novels that is not bethumbed, showing constant use. He agrees with your scribe that no such woman as Edna Earl ever lived on the earth. He agrees that no woman ever boasted the blue black hair and the eyes "blue as the border of a clematis," that belonged respectively to Regina Orme and Irene Huntingdon. And then he and your scribe again agree that any one of the books from the pen of this author can be trusted to soothe the mind, to produce a kind of self-satisfaction that is a good sleep producer after a hard day's work. He reminds your scribe that Mrs. Wilson was a Texas girl by birth, that her life in Alabama began after she was about grown, and then your scribe cheerfully states that she sympathizes with Martha Lynn Rice in her attitude toward novel reading.

No matter the ban on novel reading, the great romance came to Julia in all its force and power. Perhaps the ministers who knew of the novel reading had rejoiced in an "I told you so." Julia herself probably forgot all about novels in the face of the romance she was living herself, for her young lover, Andrew Jackson Batts, was in every way worthy of her. The courtship proceeded along the usual lines, having its required number of heartaches and joys and sorrows. The wedding was celebrated in the usual plantation style as became the wedding of a daughter of a successful planter. Friends gathered from all quarters of the state anxious for a share in the festivities, and we hope a little surreptitiously that there was some dancing during the evening. Aye, for the night of life fell soon enough upon them!

Texas seceded from the Union in 1861. The young husband, Andrew Jackson Batts, went forth at the first call for soldiers in the war that followed and served during the entire conflict. The community of Bastrop was of course spared all noise of battle, all raids of soldiers, all thieving at the hands of desperadoes following always in the wake of battle. Distance from the scene made this possible, but the women waiting at home the return of the defeated soldiers knew that they faced a change in conditions, the like of which had never before visited any nation on the earth. Tales of outrages against slaves (and what man would abuse a fine animal he hoped to use?) had found ready credence in the north. In the natural order of events, these women waiting at home had been justified in the fear that the slaves might turn against them in lawful retribution. To be perfectly accurate few slaves had known abuse, and the Southern woman, dependent right then on her slaves for protection, found that kindness lives on, that every attention she had ever shown her black folks had left its mark on the minds of her trustworthy slaves, and that they in turn, controlled those less worthy in motive.

There was, however, a disturbing element in this Bastrop community. During the war of secession some foreigners, residents in Texas since 1850, hid out in the hills. They returned when the coast was clear, their eyes wide open, looking for some exhibition of authority, of cruelty on the part of the Southern man toward his old slaves. The Southern man, conscious of the wide-opened eyes, made no sign, but he withdrew himself, his family and his servants—all of them ex-slaves—unto himself. Public schools had just been established, but the people of Rice's class founded for their own use a school known as Excelsior college.   When the state returned to Democratic control, and the *carpet bagger* and the foreigner of the watchful eye had disappeared, the college was discontinued.

Troubled a bit, perhaps, by these conditions, Martha Lynn Rice made a visit to Virginia with her husband shortly after the war. She no doubt enjoyed the short stay among relatives and friends, but she returned before long to Texas to die. Her daughter, Julia Rice Batts, continued to make her home in Bastrop County. With that young husband who had departed soon after the marriage for the horrors of war, with the lover of her youth sobered but in no way daunted by those horrors, Julia established there a home, in which they lived prosperous and happy throughout a long life together. She lived to see reconstruction pass, lived through the depressing period when white men were forced to take the iron-clad oath in order to save their homes and their property. She lived to see her own children grown and to know that they were an honor to their country. She died in 1926, having spent her life of more than eighty years in Texas.

Data contributed by—

Judge R. L. Batts,
Austin, Texas.

MRS. WILLIAM HARRISON COULSON

BORN

MARTHA ELEANOR SIMS

Way back, not far from the beginning of things in America, in fact, near the year 1800, in the four-year old state of Tennessee, we find a physician of no mean ability answering to the name of Elisha Sims. We further find that this man owned Elk Springs, a few bubbling fountains of purity drifting down through the earth from the mountains to ripple and sparkle in the shade of the glen below. Recognizing the power of water suitably applied to the physical organization, Dr. Sims had built cottages about the springs, and in these cottages he frequently installed his patients, that they might have the proper surroundings while following his medical advice. Thither came young men interested in the study of medicine, and there beneath the guidance of this practical physician, they read as he would have them read, all that learned men had had to say of the divine art of healing. These young men later attended medical college, some at Philadelphia, some at New Orleans.

On November 28, 1818, a daughter was born to Sims and his muchly deserving wife. If Sims felt in the birth of this female that the Lord had dealt harshly with him, he kept such feeling from the outside world. He may have felt, even at her birth, some pride in this wee lassie. Subsequent events proved that he even then demanded much of her in his heart.

Eleanor grew up there in her Presbyterian home, doubtless in the fear and admonition of the Lord, her parents anxious that she be educated as befitted a young woman of her day and station in life. She was sent to a young lady's school at McMinnville, Tennessee. She went home thinking her school days done, looking as women will look to the glad day when she could enter her own home, its reigning mistress, but glad to run light and free just a bit before settling down to life's real duties. Perhaps she "got gay," just a little bit. We do know that her painstaking father heard her say one day: "I don't know where it's at," and our young lady was dispatched forthwith and immediately back to college for another degree.

Just what that other degree meant to her we cannot say. We know that she had drifted into a way of attending the lectures delivered by her father in the Elk Springs school. Somehow, we cannot place that added term of school away from home in keeping with her study under her father in company with those young men, hoping to be physicians. We have an idea that in this second school she learned only

womanly things.   Not caring to start any argument as to
the character of study suitable for woman, we pass on with
the statement that Eleanor pursued the gentle art of
music, playing her own accompaniments to her melodious
rendering of Annie Laurie and the like.   Touched with
his daughter's ability in this line, Dr. Sims determined to
buy a piano.

How simple a thing such a purchase is to-day.   A few
words over the telephone settles the matter, delivery
following in a few hours.   Not so, the piano belonging to
our Martha Eleanor.   To old Boston town in Massa-
chussetts, Dr. Sims sent for the instrument.   It had been
made in London, England at 79 Cornhill, had been shipped
in a slow-going sailing vessel across the Atlantic, to Boston.
From Boston to Norfolk, Virginia it was brought by boat,
from Norfolk to the home of Dr. Sims' in an ox-wagon,
the team being driven by Dr. Sims body-servant, who
answered, we think, to the name of Jim.

Set up at last in the Sims front room, the little instrument became an object of wonder to the pioneer people
about.   Some five and one-half octaves in length of key-
board, about thirty inches wide and fifty-four inches in
length of body, the instrument boasted for some reason
six richly carved legs.   In addition, there was another
downward attachment of wood which bore the pedal, a
thing bearing the shape of my lady's slipper.   The instrument had brass strings, and was felted with buckskin.
The case was rosewood, ornamented with a line of brass,
studded at intervals with brass rosettes around the four
sides.

It would be impossible to speak accurately to-day of the
tone of the instrument, for pressure upon the yellow keys
brings only a thump.   That same pressure is likely to release a bit of ivory, for time, always good to a violin, has
no respect for a piano.   To put it short, the thing from
the standpoint of a pianist of to-day is decidedly in-
adequate.   There can, however, be no shadow of a doubt
that the instrument was a delight to our Martha Eleanor.
Among the young men studying medicine with her father
there was a young German who gladly undertook to instruct Martha Eleanor further in the use of the instrument.
How much she learned of Beethoven and Mendelsshon,
and other musicians dear to the heart of her Teutonic
master, we shall never be able to say.   We do know that
she sang a Scotch air to perfection, and it is easy for us
who have been privileged to view that first Texas piano
in its home in the museum at Austin, to picture her there
beneath her father's roof, singing to her own tinkling accompaniment, a few medical students forgetting now and

then heartbeats and temperatures and matters of digestion in the beauty of her song.

But these things cannot make up the whole of the life of woman. Man must appear and demand a hand in things. This time he came in the person of a Scotch-Irishman, answering to the name of Coulson. Regular of feature, neat in his dress, attractive in manner, but a little man, alas! a disappointment always in the eyes of woman. Her father, a large man, joined Eleanor in this regret. Indeed, he went further in his attitude toward the would-be lover. He dared to speak, even to Eleanor of the matter.

"Why do you want that ugly little man?" he demanded.

Eleanor made no reply—girls rarely answered back in those days, particularly when the father spoke. There was nothing left for Eleanor to do but go off and cry, and Eleanor did it.

But Eleanor married her William Harrison Coulson, despite her father's comments as to size, and she and her husband made a home in an adjacent county in Tennessee, living there some twenty years. During those years seven children were born to Eleanor (let us hope some of the sons attained sufficient height to please an exacting grandfather) and then in 1858, the Coulsons decided to move to Texas.

For what reason? They lived on a plantation that included many acres of fine land. The home, standing in a grove of chestnuts, trimmed up above the house's upper windows, was a frame house, but it boasted a stone foundation, outside porches—and listen, good people, these porches were built entirely of marble. There were twelve rooms in all in the house, the woodwork being maple of the finest grain. The furniture was elegant, some of it having come straight from Scotland. There was an elegant four-poster bed among the stuff from Scotland. In 1812 the mother of William Harrison Coulson had decided to make a counterpane to be held against the glad day of little William's marriage. Twenty-six years later this counterpane was used on this same four-poster bed.

Suppose we stop a minute to think about the counterpane. The mother of this William Harrison possessed no small amount of pioneer spirit herself. She superintended the planting of the cotton, watched the little pickaninnies hoe it, chop it, watched it grow to perfection as cotton will sometimes grow, watched the little pickaninnies pick it from the stalks and then when night had come, the little pickaninnies gathered round the "missis" fire and laboriously picked the seeds by hand from the precious white fleece. Shades of the cotton gin, take notice! Then the slave women on the premises wove the spun thread into the counterpane designed for this William Harrison, and in this way it came at last to adorn the four-poster bed in that Tennessee home.

From all this elegance, the Coulsons decided to move to Texas. It had been suggested that Coulson returned from one of his trips to Texas and the west to find that his private fortune had become much involved, owing to the fact that he had gone on the note of a brother-in-law. He had always boasted that he would never sell a slave. Recalling his boast on the part of her husband, our Eleanor had a plan to offer. She declared that if Coulson would promise never to go on the bond of another man, she would go with him to Texas. The promise was readily given and the journey begun.

Let us get a clear idea of the method of that journey. There was the barouche, designed of course for the comfort of Eleanor, drawn by four fine horses. There were sixty teams, some ox-teams we think, and there were some fifty and more slaves who walked along the way, hopping a ride now and then behind somebody, for a short distance. The once despised Coulson rode horseback, and Jess, his body servant, must have done likewise. We know that Jess in his old age boasted many times after this fashion. "I dun toted Tobe (Henry Coulson) frum Tennersee ter Mis'ouri en frum Mis'ouri back ter Tennersee." So we imagine old Jess must have been close behind his master on this journey to Texas.

Old Jess as a character is worthy of notice. For instance:
"How old are you, Uncle Jess?"

"I wuz twenty-one y'rs ole de y'er James K. Polk run fer Prisident."

To your scribe has been stated that for each of his five slaves, a slave owner was allowed an extra vote. This accounts for old Jess's knowledge of the election of James K. Polk, for he insisted that his master encouraged his negroes to mingle freely with white men at the polls on election day.

But to return to our story. That journey on the part of the Coulsons to the new land of Texas consumed many years in point of time. They stopped in camp as long as three weeks at a time. By and by other families joined them, the caravan headed in full for Texas. Two children were born to these people on the way. Some of the families stopped at Waxahachie, Texas, but the Coulsons continued their way to Bastrop, reaching there about 1858, on a December day, bright and sunshiny, followed by a day of snow and ice.

In this vicinity the Coulsons settled on a thousand acres of land, obtained, probably by purchase, since they were too late for the colonial grant. Some of the land remains in the family to-day (1929). There Coulson busied himself managing the clearing and laying out of the place, becoming in time a land agent, managing under Martinez the sale of leagues of land with the same assurance that we might manage the disposition of a corresponding number of acres. He dealt a bit in political issues, his time therefore pretty well taken up outside his home.

And what of Eleanor? In her log cabin home she established herself, her children, her books, her furniture, her china and her beloved piano. She went in and out seeing to the comfort of her family and her slaves, superintending the education of her children, careful, no doubt, to have them omit always the offensive preposition at the end of the sentence. But she found time every day to play the little piano, her children gathering about her to yield unconsciously to the refining influence of the tender harmony. Mayhap, she sometimes felt guilty in thus squandering the precious minutes.

For this reason, Eleanor had brought to Texas the knowledge of medicine obtained in her girlish way at her father's school for young men. The long, wandering journey to Texas had furnished many opportunities for her to show her skill in applying that knowledge, and before long Eleanor and those about her began to see that no small amount of her time was to be thus taken up. Far into the night, a weary night for her, too, maybe, old Uncle Jess would knock upon her door.

"What is it, Jess?"

"Well—well—Ole' Miss, Clarice is mighty sick."

Through the sleet and the rain, through the heat or the cold, "Ole Miss" must take herself a full eighth of a mile to the negro quarters in the hope of relieving Clarice of pain caused no doubt by too much indulgence in "taters en backbones." Another time, a little baby in a neighboring home might be nigh unto death, the mother in anguish until Mrs. Coulson could appear upon the scene. Failing to despise animals, she one day made Uncle Jess cut open the body of a horse that had died with a disease called "botts" in order that she might study the disease firsthand. We shall not bother ourselves now to provoke a quarrel with veterinary science, but it is stated on apparently good authority that Eleanor found the cause of this disease and evolved a use of chloroform for its cure. Successful with her own animals, she allowed Uncle Jess to pursue her methods on an animal belonging to a neighbor, Judge Garrett, and Uncle Jess sported thereafter an elegant

silk handkerchief considered always by his colored mind
as adequate return of his veterinary services.

This labor soon brought Eleanor a reputation throughout the country.   Called many times in consultation
with Dr. Sayers, the father of our famous Joseph D.
Sayers, she became in all save title a family physician.   Dr.
Sayers in his own quaint, determined way, frequently declared that he had rather practice with Eleanor than any
other physician in Texas.   In fact, he appeared many
times astride his dependable nag, to halt at Eleanor's door
and demand a consultation.   Seeing the advance of age in
the doctor's face and figure, Billy Sayers, living then in
Seguin, Texas, decided that the doctor must have a buggy.
Procuring the vehicle, he harnessed the doctor's horse
thereto and suggested that he start forth in ease   and
comfort on his excursions with Eleanor.   But the doctor
had a mind of his own.   He refused the buggy because,
Heaven help us, there was no place for the saddle.

But this life of strain began to tell on Eleanor, even before she had reached her fortieth year.   Her husband,
active in politics, fond of any form of social activity, was
away from home a great deal, leaving farm matters in
Eleanor's hands.   She superintended the planting and
harvesting of crops.   She had Uncle Jess in potato harvest
—or digging to be strictly Texas—hitch up the carriage, put
a rocking chair in it, and then at the back of the field, a
mile or so from the house, she would sit all day measuring
potatoes for sale.   She helped, too, in public matters.
With Coulson's aid she engineered the sale of land for a
schoolhouse, the building to be used, too, as a church with
the cemetery about it.

Bowed down at last by her work, Martha Eleanor took
to her bed.   For eight long months Dr. Sayers made the
ten-mile horseback journey three times a week in the hope
of rendering some aid to his one-time efficient helper.
She lived through the Civil war, lived to see her slaves, unconscious of any abuse, given their freedom, lived to know the
desolation following hard on defeat.   Then she passed away
at forty-seven years of age, and her body, frail little house
of clay for its noble tenant, was the first to be laid in the
cemetery acquired largely by her own efforts.

Data contributed by—

    Miss Oneita Coulson,
    Austin, Texas.

MRS. GARRET H. GOWAN

BORN

MARY E. LYLES

There lies before me as I begin to write, some four pages of clearly written manuscript, the work of a woman who claims the honor of full fourscore years. Contemplation of these pages brings—among other things—a sneaking wonder as to my own ability at fourscore years. A thought of the work immediately ahead of me brings me mercifully back to the present. Comparisons, usually odious, slip into the background where they belong. I sit me down a bit encouraged—all because of the slipping —in the thought of the effort I am about to put forth. This effort shall be concerned entirely with the idea of giving to folks a picture of the life of Mrs. G. H. Gowan, at present a resident of Fort Worth, a city of our own dear Texas.

As we have before intimated, she was born in 1849, on June the ninth. The birth took place in Macon, Mississippi, her father being John Tharp Lyles, and her mother Julia A. Lyles, born Davis. She tells us simply that she was educated at the Zeb Gathright Female Seminary in Summerville, Mississippi, and then, as if her girlhood life held no other matters worth recording, she states that on May 16, 1866, she was married to Garret Gowan. This young man had been her schoolmate, even up to the days of the female seminary idea, was at the time of the marriage just past twenty-one years of age. He had worn the Confederate grey throughout the whole of that disastrous struggle. The marriage took place near Raleigh, in Smith County, Mississippi, the officiating minister being Rev. Frank Sharbrough. Four days after this ceremony, the young couple started for Texas.

To get into the present-day mind an idea of that move on the part of these enterprising young people requires some careful consideration. They were leaving a country that had suffered greatly from the fall of the Confederacy. They had grown up, waited upon and loved and watched by slaves. They had played with those slaves, had controlled them and had loved them. They had suffered in the effort to maintain that relation between the white man and the black, only to bow in defeat before a stronger power. They must have felt that life in Mississippi, denied the co-operation of slaves was, to say the least, impracticable. They must have seen in Texas, a bit removed from the horrors of reconstruction, a promised land of no mean beauty. Surely carpet-bag rule had never penetrated its virgin precincts. So much for the buoyancy of youth, and its belief in the glory of the land "a little farther on."

The Gowans took train at Lake Station, Mississippi, headed for Vicksburg. In this last city they stopped at the famous S. S. Prentiss Hotel, hard by the Mississippi river, there to wait the coming of the Madam Ruth, the finest boat then afloat on the famous old avenue of travel. Fine. Another generation may poo-hoo the elegance claimed for the Mississippi steamer. Said generation may even class such boats with antiques and foolishness, but some there are among us to-day who still cling to the halo idea of this certain Madam Ruth. Perhaps she took two or three times the number of days now spent in covering the distance. What cared this young bridal couple? The cabins were elegant, the cuisine beyond criticism. There was music on deck, and dancing in the moonlight. There was, in short, every possible inducement to make people— young people—forget the tragedy of war, the even greater tragedy of reconstruction. Up the Arkansas river, after a time, aboard the Linnie Down, they steamed their way to Little Rock, and there they were joined by Mr. Gowan's sister and her husband, they, themselves, bound for Texas.

From this point no more elegance of travel awaited the Gowans. The dance in the moonlight, the elegant cuisine, the light and the laughter were laid aside, for our bride must now take her place in an old Illinois wagon, the motive power, oxen, four of them, stolid, slow-going, dependable creatures. And the bride knew that they must have at night the blue sky for shelter, or the beat of the wind and the rain against the wagon sheet, and that many days and many nights must thus be spent on the way. Tiresome? Perhaps, but all thought of tediousness was overshadowed in the wonder as to what the Indians might have to say to the invaders of his land. They knew they must pass through a corner of Indian territory, as the home of the savages was then called. Tales dealing with Comanches had reached the Gowans in their Mississippi home. When they reached Hot Springs, a place that had suffered dreadfully from the ravages of war, the desolation plus the Indian tales, made it seem desirable to make some plan of protection for themselves against the Indians.

Disguise was the first step in this protection. The bride and her elegant groom packed away the clothes they had worn on the moon-lit steamer deck. Mrs. Gowan tells us that she donned a calico dress and a sunbonnet, that Mr. Gowan put on a homemade suit and homemade shoes. No bank in the wilderness, each traveller must be his own bank. Hence, beneath the simple homemade clothes, our bride and groom wore round their waists belts made of feather ticking, each belt crowded full of twenty-dollar gold pieces.

Said disguise must have proven all powerful, for we note next that these young people, after a stop of a few months in Ellis County, Texas, moved on to Navarro County. From George David of Milford in that county, Mr. Gowan purchased the famous U D brand of cattle, giving four and one-half dollars per head, cash. A trip through that portion of Texas to-day would reveal few conditions existent in the county when Mr. Gowan bought that brand. There were then no well-kept fields of cotton, no corn glistening in the spring sunshine. A little wheat, enough to make bread for a few folks, maybe, but on the hills and in the valleys, over the wind-swept plains and beneath the sheltering mesquite, thousands upon thousands of cattle roamed, no fences to limit the wandering, no guard to protect the cattle, save the unwritten law respecting a man's brand, and the law of the range that dealt summarily with him who might in some weak moment over-step that unwritten law. Wolves, coyotes, battled at times with the powerful longhorn, but said longhorn had a way of coming out ahead. Truly, he roamed a thousand hills, monarch of all he surveyed, only a cowboy to suggest now and then the better way to pastures new and waters limpid and sweet.

But Mr. Gowan was of a progressive turn of mind. He had acquired with his cattle some sheep and hogs. He began to see the benefits to be derived from some control, some limitation set about the antics of his straying herds. The result? Mr. Gowan built the first wire fence to be built in all that country.

It would be hard to imagine the wife of this progressive man sitting with folded hands, begging to be amused. We know even to-day when there is much talk of contagion, that industry is of itself contagious. But, the contagion idea was in this case by no means necessary. It had been born in the blood of this young woman. Children came early into the home, and children under any circumstances mean work for somebody. Food of the character Mrs. Gowan preferred to set before her family was sometimes hard to obtain, and with her husband busy continuously on the range, this food-providing task fell largely on the wife at home. Then, too, our little lady taught school.

We are proud many times of the provisions our forefathers made for our common schools and our University of higher learning. Many of those men we know had enjoyed the real college education, but there is, just the same, much evidence of the influence of the mother of our colonial time in this matter of education. She dreamed above the one pot on her fireplace of the days when her children should reap the blessings of mental training, and the dreams of women are, to say the least, large factors in determining the mind of man. This wife and mother went beyond that dream. Lacking the schoolhouse, the desk, the blackboard, Mrs. Gowan taught the first country school in that community, the point being about four miles north of Dresden in Navarro County. She had probably never heard the famous old definition of a school, a thing whose necessary elements consisted of teacher and pupil, even if they must sit during recitation on the same hollow log. That definition—and who would question it?—avoids any mention of the teacher's recompense. True to this ideal, our teacher worked without certificate, without contract. She knew that the parents of her pupils had no money. True to her pioneer spirit, she took in payment for her pedagogical efforts, calves, lumber, pottery, even a big longhorn or two when a parent was particularly well pleased. And to this day no man or woman has ever heard this true disciple of pedagogy complain that she failed to receive her just reward.

We are not prepared to say that Mr. Gowan shared the sentiments of the Texas man, who some years ago left his holdings of many years standing because the settlement of men within twenty miles of him threatened to crowd him to the detriment of his business, as well as his family interests. We do know that when the farms became thick about him, Mr. Gowan decided that he must move, newer and better range for his cattle being his idea. To the Indian Territory he went, and there he waited four years in the vain hope of seeing the land become a state of the United States. Failing to realize this hope, Mr. Gowan and his wife came back to Texas, settling this time in Clay County on the east fork of the little Wichita river. This claim took in old Camp Witchita in the shadow of Lookout Mountain. The Indians had been recently moved from this part of Texas, and governmental authority promised protection to the white man, should the red man return bent upon mischief. With all respect due Federal ability, men and women who had once witnessed the power of the red man and suffered from it, could not lay aside all at once the fear of the Indian raid.

This fear, however, failed to keep the Gowans from going about the business of "making a home." They hauled from Sherman the so-called "box lumber" for the house, but the sills and sleepers were hewn from large logs, probably cut from the nearby woods, this ranch being bordered by the ridge of upper cross timber. The chimney was built of unpolished rocks, a club-ax being the solitary tool,

with Gowan and his wife the stonemasons and helpers and
timekeepers and everything else usually considered
necessary to a job of this kind. They placed the rock,
then piled in the mortar by hand, said mortar freezing
many times in the process. More than fifty years old, the
house stands intact to-day (1929). It belongs to two sons
of that brave woman who helped in the construction of
its chimney. The pastures about the house are dotted
with white-faced cattle, in all a thriving business concern,
a tribute in itself to the sterling qualities of the woman who
helped lay the foundation. In the home of a daughter
there is a pair of vases which were given Mrs. Gowan in
the days of that foundation-laying in return for weaving a
wagon sheet for an aunt who was preparing to move to
Texas. During the Civil war, Mrs. Gowan spun and wove
a mixture of cotton and wool cloth from which she made
her father a dress suit. And then these little labor items
being recorded, our lady tells us naively that she has
celebrated both her silver and her golden wedding days,
and that on May 16th, 1929, she had been married to
Garrett Gowan, the sweetheart of her youth, full sixty-
three years.

In prosperity, in comfort, independent of the world
about them, they sit together, the boy who wore the grey,
and the sweetheart of his youth, watching the sun a-down
the western slope. Beautiful picture, too beautiful, perhaps, to allow utilitarian thought to intrude, but your
scribe wishes to hazard a statement. She realizes that
said statement may bring upon her an avalanche of protest
and denial, maybe, a bit of proof, now and then, that she
is wrong. But—no family in which the mother has stood
shoulder to shoulder with her husband, no family in which
the mother has been willing and able to work efficiently
with her hands has ever come to want. No woman willing
to work with her hands has ever languished in her old age,
a burden on individuals bound to her by ties of blood. As
foundation for my rash statement, I ask you to re-read
with me a bit of what this lady has to say of her present
life and its joy.

"'Twas my pleasure to visit there (the ranch house) this
summer." Two sons still have part of the ranch land in
pasture, now covered with white-faced cattle. "I enjoyed the beautiful scenery, beautiful in extreme, and I
remarked to our oldest son: 'You boys have one of the best
and prettiest ranches in the state. I am hoping you will
always keep same.' "

Recall that first ranch home still standing. Recall that
chimney built in loving companionship, the woman willing
and ready and able to do her part. Picture that woman

as you recall it standing in her girlhood before the loom, dancing in the moonlight, struggling as a wife in the school-room, handling in all dexterity the mortar that froze as it settled in nook and crevice between those uneven stones. Picture all this, I say, and then take issue with me if you dare.

Data contributed by—

Mrs. G. H. Gowan,
2300 Sixth Avenue,
Fort Worth, Texas.

MRS. EDWIN WALLER

BORN

JULIET M. DeSHIELDS

The would-be historian soon realizes that circumstances have a large influence over the lives of individuals. When it comes to ascertaining real facts about folks, even our own folks, this idea of circumstantial influence looms large. Right now, for instance, we would like to study the life of an interesting woman at close range, a woman married to an interesting man, but this circumstantial idea hereinbefore alluded to blocks the way. The woman's own daughters are dead. Morover, they died in their young womanhood before they had had time to give to their children the intimate details of their own grandmother's life. But, by looking here and there, by piecing out a bit, from some well established facts, we have gained what we consider a pretty clear idea of the life of Juliet DeShields, who came in time to be the wife of Edwin Waller, a man closely allied with Texas and her welfare from the very beginning.

We cannot say exactly when Juliet was born. We know on the best authority that she was educated in the east, a bit more thoroughly, perhaps, than was the usual woman of her day. She studied music, too, and remembering a certain graceful descendant, we hazard a guess that she was adept at the tripping of the "light, fantastic toe." She visited many times in Washington, where her beauty and her wit made her a great favorite in the first circles of society. Then before she was twenty years of age, she married Judge Edwin Waller. To quote a descendant of to-day: "She stood valiantly by his side during the early struggles of Texas."

We have drifted into a way of saying that women stand by in the undertakings brave men perform, and a question has popped up as to the exact meaning of the expression. Just what good or what harm can come to man from a woman's presence, if that man be in the pursuit of a great idea, a great achievement? Leaving out all questions as to equality of sex, as to rights and privileges, arguing the thing pro and con, just what is the truth of the old idea that woman is a helper, a support in man's busy life? There have been great men in the world, solitary souls who accomplished great things, who never felt the need of somebody at hand to urge on, to hold back, to strengthen and to soothe. But we are concerned with every-day men, men who have been the backbone of our nation from the beginning, and in their lives as we have seen and known them we have found much evidence in proof of the value of woman in the onward march of things.

Now, let's look into the case of Juliet DeShields Waller. She had married Judge Waller before she was twenty years of age. They had established a plantation home known as Waller Glen, in Waller County. With our beautiful Juliet for mistress, the house speedily became the scene of gracious hospitality, many of the grand old men of that period being entertained there on a lavish scale. In those rooms, built perhaps of logs, the talk ran high of Texas and the indignities she must suffer at the hands of Mexico. Men there argued as to ways and means, and it was finally left for Judge Waller and William Wharton to commit the first overt act of defiance against Mexican authority. With a bit of thought, maybe, of the Boston Tea Party, staged some sixty years before in old New England, these men ran the blockade at Velasco. This bit of audacity all but cost Waller and Wharton their lives, but it proved to the world that Texans were imbued with a commendable love of liberty. This act of disobedience fired the spark of revolution already existent in the hearts of the Texas folks, and things then and there began to take on a turn. Waller bore his part in that revolution as a soldier and as a statesman. He was a farmer and a signer of the Texas Declaration of Independence, and he was in time the Postmaster-General of the new republic.

When President Lamar came to Austin to take charge of the government, Waller made the address of welcome. In his work as a public surveyor, he laid out the city of Austin. He had probably been one of the men who selected the exact spot for the state capitol. He had glimpsed old Mt. Bonnell, blue and solemn, in the distance, head and shoulders above the other hills sloping down to the banks of the Colorado river. More than this they took in the "gully" between hills, a depression that sloped from another hill a mile from the river, a hill just high enough to make a fine place for a capitol building. We like to think that right then those men set aside the section upon section of land to be given one day in exchange for the granite building, just as real to those men of vision as it is for us who behold it to-day, its noble proportions, its beautiful outline speaking in all sincerity of the men who visioned it.

Any good Texas history will give you these details. We do not deny any of them. In fact there is a great sense of satisfaction in speaking of the men-folks attending those early congresses and conventions. We are all proud to claim descent from such folks. We want to know, though, just what it meant to be the wife of a prominent Texas man, left at home during the days of the republic.

Now our Juliet lived at Waller Glen. She had her children and her friends to bear her company. She had slaves to do her bidding. Easy all of it until one remembers that slaves must be directed and controlled. They must sometimes form as well the sole defense of the white woman and her children, but they must sometimes be corrected in the course of their work if "Massa" might hope to feed them and his family. To bring this about, overseers were necessary. The word *overseer* suggests something unpleasant. It suggests some implacable tyrant, watching at every turn and corner, lest some workman neglect his job. Necessary, no doubt, but our Juliet, sensing the disagreeable factor in the idea, made of herself an overseer of overseers. At one time, a "peg-legged" negro was shot—not fatally—for some stupendous act of folly. All right and proper, according to alien ideas of daily happenings on Southern farms at that time, but in this instance, the overseer the next day received his "walking papers" from the hand of an irate mistress.

Aside from any womanly feeling of sympathy, Juliet understood the real value of her slaves. She understood their dependence upon her for bread and she understood their idea of loyalty to her.

To-day one wonders a little that women dared lean upon such an idea of protection, but your scribe is yet to be told of any Southern slave failing his mistress in time of danger, no matter how much he may have listened to the talk of aliens anxious to uplift the down-trodden people. But with all due respect to the faithfulness and the sagacity of slaves, our Juliet in time of danger possessed something within herself that proved a greater defense than any devotion or sagacity ever supplied by any slave in any clime, under any conditions.

For instance: Judge Waller was away, busy with national affairs. Juliet at home with her little children, on a certain day when there were guests in the house, saw a band of Mexicans approaching. The Mexicans of this class represented to Juliet the scum of the earth. In the presence of such individuals she could hear the battlecry as they scaled the walls of the Alamo, butchering right and left. She could see in each brown face a replica of the men who had murdered the Texans at Goliad. And here in her own home, her children about her, her guests, helpless women themselves whiling away a few hours snatched from the endless round of work, here she must meet the men face to face.

Juliet failed to do the natural thing. She failed to scream out to her guests to flee for their lives. She failed to order her children into hiding. Summoning all the poise, all the charm acquired in her young life in Washington, re-calling the strength, the bravery of her absent husband, Juliet stepped out to meet the captain of the little band, a little pale, maybe, but all fear hidden beneath her smile. She greeted the leader of that band graciously. That leader, struck by her beauty, by her graciousness of manner, stood abashed before her, his big, heavy hat in his ugly, brown hand. Another smile, another assurance of welcome from this lady of the manor, and the leader gave a few signals for departure, having done no harm whatsoever. As the day waned, Juliet lost a bit of her faith in her own powers. She began to fear that the men might overcome the temporary embarrassment and return more determined than ever. She took her family to the home of the Hills, and she learned upon her husband's return that the Mexi-cans had made another attempt on her property and had done considerable damage. This episode failed to end her trouble with Mexicans. She was called upon many times to exercise her gentle manner and her gracious smile in order to preserve her home and the lives of her little chil-dren.

But she made it through. In addition to managing the farm and caring for and directing slaves, she was the mother of thirteen children. Now your scribe has had some experience in the professional world, in the business world, too, and she has made a small study of the political world and its business, but in summing up this woman's life she wants to remind her readers that no business on earth, no profession, no calling, requires quite as much at the hand of an individual as that of being a mother. Laws of wages and time, etc., can be enacted for every other type of labor but the mother knows no law, no time limit, no rest. And a mother in the wilderness!

Now somebody objects that Waller's Glen lacked much of being any part of the wilderness. Refinement and culture, education and good hard sense had made of it a paradise for those who dwelt there, but no electric light waited the pressure of the button. No telephone hung upon the wall to help summon the police in time of danger, to signal the fire department, to call the doctor in time of illness. The doctor, once notified, could not reach his patient on the back of his most spirited mount until many hours had elapsed. Schools were practically unknown. Little children, if they were taught at all, must be taught at the mother's knee. But we repeat, our Juliet made it through. She stood by her husband at every turn of their lives. She left in the history of her state traces of her graciousness and her charm. Her children unto the third and fourth generations rise up and call her blessed. And what woman among women could ask more at the hands of fate?

Data contributed by—

Mrs. Byrd Cuney Wray,
Dublin, Texas.

MRS. STEPHEN WILLIAMS

BORN

JEAN BLACK

A great many people in the United States of America and, maybe in England, rejoice in the name of Williams. Common sense would demand an explanation of its popularity. Curiosity might take the same attitude. Curiosity might demand investigation of the history of the name, its origin, its real meaning, its future, and so on. Right now for want of time, we must pass such ideas by. We must announce that our next character under discussion, a woman sweet and true and fine, willingly, because of her love for a man, took on the common, oft-repeated name, and never, so far as we can learn, did she regret taking the step.

This woman was the daughter of Edward Black. At her birth, there on the plantation in Georgia, she was given the name of Jean. She grew to womanhood in that same home, waited upon by slaves, trained and developed by careful parents, educated after the manner of the times, educators in a new country being limited both as to number and ability. As she grew to womanhood, the inherent characteristics of the female developed, and she became a great belle in her own little social world. Quick to see, to feel the truth under any and all circumstances, she failed to exaggerate the gallant words, the impassioned glances of the first few men crossing her path, but along about 1805 she fell in with Stephen Williams, even Stephen of the common name, Stephen whose father had been an officer in the Revolutionary war, and before many months, she cheerfully resigned the protestations of many lovers in order to accept the vows of one.

Marriage under any conditions must produce changes in the life of the ordinary woman. No matter how faithfully she has played her part as a daughter in her father's house, no matter how well her mother may have trained her, when the woman first assumes charge of her own home, life becomes full of absorbing duties calling for patience, for evenness of temper, lightness of soul, and many other assets not yet accorded suitable names for the use of the general public. All these changes Jean met, dealing successfully with each as it came. Children were born to her, boys and girls, and Jean lived on in her Georgia home, perfectly contented after the manner of good wives and mothers.

And then for some reason, Jean's husband decided that he must move to Texas. Imagine—if you can—the dismay of the wife already settled in her home when her husband first presents the idea of a move. Add to that imagining the fact that said move must land her at last in the raw, new country called Texas, a country infested with Indians and snakes and Mexicans, and some few other horrors not worth mentioning. Imagine the dismay of her friends, her relatives. Imagine the wife's quiet obedience to her husband's wishes, her solemn preparations for departure.

Remember, she was to be separated from her girlhood friends and associates, the dearest friends a woman ever makes. She was to leave father and mother and brothers and sisters and the old house in which she had been born, the other house, too, in which she had begun her married life. More than all this, she was to leave behind her oldest son that he might finish his education at the University where he had then been a student for two years. But—she was to stand shoulder to shoulder with her husband. That meant, to her, that she must play her part in the new undertaking. She must help establish the new home, the new business, and to Jean Black Williams that was enough. She packed their clothes, she packed their furniture, her china and her glassware, her houshold linens, some of it very fine, and then after a good-bye to the boy to be left behind, she, with her husband and children and some twenty slaves, began the solemn journey.

This must have been early in the year 1833. Stephen Williams received a grant of land and settled on Mill's creek, close to old Washington-on-the-Brazos. He built for his residence a big log house, another log house served as a kitchen, each house boasting a chimney of no mean proportions. In the fireplace in the kitchen chimney hung the big pots on cranes, and clustered around on the stones beneath were the skillets and griddles, the latter ready for the hoe-cake and pone bread, all made of corn meal. For the slaves, smaller cabins were built around that first large one, and then master and slaves set about the clearing of the land, the ploughing and the sowing. Jean, then, with the women slaves to help her, began to make of that cabin her woman's temple.

There were trials, there were tribulations, but there were joys, too, in the new home. The children began to see new things in the woods, in the prairies, and, after a few heartbreaking attacks of homesickness, Jean began to get on very well. She began to look forward to the homecoming of the son left in college, and hope, as usual, ligthened the load. But, when the winter came on, her husband fell a prey to pneumonia. Jean beside his bed constantly, felt many a pang as she looked into his fever-tinged face, as she listened to his cough, ominous throughout the night.

To add to her dismay, her husband informed her that certain important papers must be sent immediately to Georgia.

Well and good! Mail them, I hear you say? On what, may I ask? Flying machines, trains, even horse conveyances, none of them were at hand. Williams, himself too sick for the journey, there was nothing left for them but to send the oldest boy remaining at home on the journey, and that son at that time boasted the mature age of eight years. The boy, William Williams by name, enthusiastic, fond of adventure, enjoying the prospect of a long ride, trained as well in perfect obedience, felt no misgivings over the matter. He probably bragged a bit to the little negroes as to his importance. It may be, even, that his black mammy had to *take him down a peg or two*, but picture that mother's dismay! Feel for her as she packed his clothes in the saddle-bags, as she listened to the instructions given the boy by his suffering father!

Those instructions in themselves were unique. The father outlined the way, mile by mile, certain farm houses along the way to be his stopping places. If the boy reached the house designated as his next stop in the middle of the day, he was told to wait there until the next morning. Williams, no doubt, hoped to keep up in his own mind with the traveller. He must have had an idea that he would feel some comfort in saying to himself: "Tonight, William stops with so and so." In the boy's pocket, he placed a way bill that explained who he was and why he was travelling thus alone, asking that he be given every consideration.

Alive to the importance of the matter, young Williams started off. Day by day he made his journey, presented his note at each successive house along the road, meeting with kindness, with consideration at the hand of men and women, glad, all, to help him along the way. They questioned him at the far end of the journey as to Texas, and like most boys—and some grown folks living in the vast domain even today—William let his enthusiasm lead him now and then beyond the limits of truth. Seated one night on the porch of a plantation home, spinning his childish yarns, thinking no doubt of mother, troubled with the memory of his father's cough, the boy became aware, all in an instant, that something was about to happen. The stars twinkling down on them, just as they had always twinkled in the wilds of Texas, took on a new aspect. They grew glum in manner, and then, as if tired of the eternal job of smiling by night on a troublesome old world, the stars began to fall, to shower, to settle down on the very bosom of old Mother Earth, and for the space of several very tense moments, moments in which the night had suddenly turned to day, it seemed to our young Williams that everything must be at an end.

Above the tumult in the child's heart rose the clamor, the howl from the negro quarters.

"De day uv judgmint hab cum!"

The doors of hell had opened wide to receive each recreant son of Ham—and some daughters, not to mention a few white folks thrown in for good measure! Nothing but repentance and confession plus the grace "uv de Lord," might avail at such a moment.

"I stole massa's hosses for er ride, jes' las' nite."

"I stole de taters en de aigs."

On and on these confessions, the tumult increasing with every speck that seemed to fall. Only a minute or two at best—the old earth wastes little time passing through the tail of a comet—then silence took the place of the moan of repentance. And the little boy, far away from home and mother on his strange errand! Maybe he failed to say much, but we wager a guess that he watched the stars the next night at the same hour wondering what might be expected. But the child completed his journey, delivered his business papers, transacted his own little personal business (we hope he bought himself a new knife or some marbles or something) and then turned his face homeward. He declared ever afterwards that he had little to do on the homeward journey. After each stop, he mounted his horse, gave him the bridle, and the horse brought them both home over the same long road without missing a bend or a curve. And was his mother, our Jean, glad to see him?

There has been ever a foregone conclusion that Indianin Texas were a menace to the white man. When a des scendant of our Jean makes a contrary statement we picture at once some kindness on the part of our lady, some inborn grace that gave her ready access to the savage heart. Truth demands that we give some space in this article to the real reason. The Indians in the Williams neighborhood viewed the planter's undertaking with some plans all their own, and the Indians made some few advances. By this time, Jean's son, William J. Williams, the college man, had taken his place in the home. Sighting the son's size, and the play of the muscles in his big arms, the Indian advances were coy, a bit subtle, some pretense being shown toward friendliness.

Two young men cannot be long together without some form of pitched battle. The Indian is not behind his white brother in this matter of scuffle. So, just to test matters, Mr. Red Man precipitates a crash with young

Williams. To his intense surprise, young Williams, fresh from college, threw the Indian in the first round. Back again the Indian came, only to meet defeat at the hands of pale-faced college man. A little wiser—and a good deal sadder, the Indian took himself off. Stephen Williams looked for all kinds of raids that night. He loaded his shotgun and he primed his pistol, and he crowded his children close about him. On the morrow, the Indian did appear, and he brought with him three chiefs, all ready for the fray. Young Williams, his mother watching from the door, downed the first two with little trouble. The third came on, a glint in his eye that boded Indian methods, but young Williams gave little thought to the glint. True to form, the Indian tried some few tricks not allowed in the game, but Williams, quick as a flash, "busted him on the ground," so his young descendants claim—no explanation following for the comfort of female minds—and never again, in the life of the Williams family did an Indian trouble them. They passed many times in the road, of course, but they let Jean's hens and chickens severely alone.

A little later, the Indians appealed to Charles Tate, a brother-in-law of Stephen Williams, in time of trouble, a little like a child might appeal to his mother. They brought to Tate a boy suffering with *dropsy* as it was then called, the body already swollen to enormous size. Tate had never studied medicine, save as every pioneer learns medicine and law at the hand of experience, but he proceeded in this instance to *tap* the boy and had the satisfaction of seeing the body gradually assume its normal size. From that day forward the Indians looked upon Charles Tate as a marvel of power and goodness. A little knowledge, tempered with patience, coupled with a certain amount of strength to stand one's own ground availed much with this savage tribe, and Tate, Williams and his wife, Jean, reaped many a rich harvest thereby.

Jean Williams in this Texas home raised five children, three sons and two daughters. One son, only eighteen years of age, burned with a desire to vote for General Houston. His father explained the law and its penalty. The son put it by obediently, being a son of Jean, too, but the idea would come back. One day later, the idea was voiced in a group of men, all friends of the elder Williams. One man asked if the boy wanted to vote for Houston. The young man answered in the affirmative and eagerly enough. Williams suggested to his son that if he voted he must bear arms in defense of his country. The friend, taking in the size and muscles of the young fellow, declared that he would be physically able. The Indians, no doubt, had agreed, believing that strength is likely to run in families, and there could be little doubt that the ardent admirer of Sam Houston lacked little in inclination. Young Williams cast his eighteen-year-old vote for his beloved commander, and there is no doubt he followed the old warrior whenever his country called him.

Jean Williams was a member of the Baptist church, but she attended religious services whenever and wherever they were held. Once a year she went to the arbor meeting, similar to camp meeting of the Methodist church, and she frequently travelled in a wagon the necessary twenty miles in order to hear "preaching" at the home of a neighbor.

Jean was a busy woman at home. She had the cotton cloth made on her own looms. She made cloth, too, from wool sheared from the backs of her own sheep. Her slave women, under her directions, wove blankets from the wool, a rather rough article, to be accurate, but exceedingly warm. And when William N. Williams announced in 1852 that he was to marry Miss Miller, the daughter of another pioneer in Fayette County, his mother had the slaves weave the cloth for his wedding suit, superintended the dyeing of it, and then a negro woman, an efficient seamstress among his mother's slaves, made the suit under Jean's directions.

"I am not saying it was a good-looking suit," remarks Jean's grandson to-day, "but he got married in it all right."

Our Jean Williams died at some time during the days of the republic of Texas, and was buried in Fayette County. Her husband having served in the war of 1812, lived on, but found himself unfit for service in the war with Mexico in 1846. Hard to believe him unfit, he who in youth had measured six feet, two inches in his stockings, who had weighed 240 pounds and was yet not fat, but life must take its toll, He died at home during this war, a son absent in the army. but some of his children about him. They buried him for some reason by torchlight in the very dead of the night. This weird ceremonial took place just a little while after Jean had been buried. The thought of that burial has its own note of pathos. Under the cloud of war, at the end of a useful life, at the end of a happy life together, the two, the husband and wife, were laid in their graves in Fayette County. Then the thought of the happy life they lived, of the love ever existent between them, crowds out the pathetic thought following that weird funeral at the dead of night, and we see only the beauty in the story of this simple woman's life well lived.

Data contributed by—

    Mr. Estill Williams,
    Austin, Texas.

MRS. THOMAS RADFORD BOLLING

BORN

MARY PLEASANTS CARTER

When we begin this sketch of Mrs. Thomas Redford Bolling we are conscious that the date of her coming to Texas is a little late. Having set as the limit of pioneer things in Texas the year of 1845, having set such a date our very own selves, we demand the right to stretch the limit a bit now and then. We are a bit particular, we admit in the stretching idea, but we feel justified in including Mrs. Bolling in our pioneer women, for she is inseparably linked with the early times in Texas, "befo' de wah" times, and from our own point of view her life held many things really worth while, things worth remembering in our effort to catch a glimpse of Texas women of another day as they really were.

From an ancestral standpoint, Mary Pleasants Carter fared well. Through Rosamond the Fair she was descended in a straight line from King Edward III of England, but somewhere in the line she had crossed blood with the Quakers. One grandfather in the line boasting Quaker blood in his veins departed a bit from the teaching of his church in that in the new land of America he owned slaves and many of them. His church demanded that he conform with non-slave holding ideas, but said grandfather preferred his "niggers" to his church. It is not ours to discuss the attitude of this grandfather. We mention the matter only because it may be depended upon to explain some otherwise inexplicable strain in the character of our Mary. In the same spirit we state that she was a grand-daughter of Gov. John Pleasants of Virginia and that she was closley related to King Carter, known all over old Virginia in its proudest of many proud days. She was born in 1802 on her father's plantation in Goochland County, Virginia, her father being James Carter and her mother Sarah Logan Carter. James Carter, by the way, as a young man, won the medal for oratory at Williams and Mary College. He was often called the Patrick Henry of the war of 1812.

The same regime famous through Virginia and the other Southern States held sway in this Virginia home. Slaves tilled the soil and looked after the gardens and the stock, and material comforts of all kinds were ever at hand. Amid these surroundings, Mary grew up, cared for as a princess, taught to work as became the lady of a noble house. Before she had reached her tenth year she had become proficient with her needle, and the sampler—useless thing maybe in its day, is to-day a silent witness to the

fact that every stitch, even at that tender age of the
seamstress, was carefully and accurately placed. A little
older in years, and our young miss was sent to a girl's
school in Staunton, Virginia. Your scribe can remember
a day when many young women yearned in their inmost
hearts for a finishing year at some school in Staunton. Our
Mary may have felt this yearning in the beginning, she
may have imbibed much useful knowledge there, but in
after life she would never countenance the idea of such
education for her own daughters. Perhaps the co-educational idea was strong in her own mind even then. Perhaps she felt intuitively, and her Quaker blood had helped
in this idea, that if men and women were to live together
as equals they must share the same educational advantages.
Perhaps, she felt, too, that the heyday of youth was the
best time for men and women to be together in order that
they might understand the mysteries of human companionship.

But for all her attitude in this co-educational matter,
her own life was not lacking in the association of the sexes
which must form after all life's greatest joy. In her own
neighborhood, lived Thomas R. Bolling. His social life, his
financial situation the same as Mary's, they had played
together all their lives, had grown up believing in the same
institutions, the same religion, the same belief in things
political. His people were the Bollings of Center Hill,
Petersburg, Virginia. They were, in short, rich in lands,
planted in cotton and tobacco. He afterwards served in
the same Legislature in Alabama with General Sam Houston, and he was ever a close friend of the old commander.
They were married, then, our Mary and her lover,
Thomas Radford Bolling, and two years later emigrated
to Alabama.

In that home Mary showed her wonderful executive
ability. She directed the slave women who made the
cloth from cotton and wool grown on the premises. She
directed the women who did the cooking, the preserving.
She directed the negro men in the cutting up of the beef,
and we have no slighest doubt that the sausage made on
the premises bore gallant testimony to the taste of "de
missus" in "hog killin' time." At one time Bolling was called
in the settlement of an estate to go to Virginia. He knew
the journey, on horseback of course, and the business together would keep him from home full six weeks. Did he
fear rack and ruin in his absence? Not our Thomas. He
had known and loved our Mary too well, too fondly. When
he did at last come in sight of his home at the end of that
journey, he hardly knew the place. Mary had made the
negroes collect oyster shells and make them into white-

wash. She had seen to it that every cabin, every chicken-coop, every stable had received its own liberal coating of white, and Thomas, laying his arms tenderly about her, declared to her a little reverently that she was the greatest woman in the world.

And now what had all this to do with Texas and her pioneer folks? Patient, just a minute, please. In 1837, just after Sam Houston and his army had settled things at San Jacinto, Bolling made a horseback journey to Texas. It had come to him, probably through some of Sam Houston's people and through his close friend, William H. Jack, that the young nation was on the upward move, and Bolling had come to see for himself. He visited Bastrop and its vicinity. He met there the cultured people who had come voluntarily from the older states. He caught, perhaps, some glimpse of the possibilities in the great nation with land to be had for the asking. But— Bolling had heard, too, of Indians. He had sensed the fight between the aboriginal man and the man who would claim his territory, and Bolling had decided that Alabama, possessing a few Indians of its own, but Indians more at peace with the world than the Comanches ever were, was the best place for a man's family.

The call of the new and the untried is hard to resist. Bolling had left the old country to wander about the new. He had studied the possibilities of both from every angle. The years slipped by, the thought of Texas failing to slip from Bolling's mind. Their many children, adopted and otherwise, gradually left them. When the last daughter married and announced after a bit that she and her husband, Thomas Cowles Shearer, were coming to Texas, the old Texas idea received much impetus. In the end the call of the new won out, and Thomas Bolling and his wife Mary moved to Texas.

We have no record of the attitude of Mary toward this moving. She had brought into the world ten children and had raised with them six orphans. As before stated these children had left them for the estate of matrimony. If she thought her time had come to settle down in idleness after her long years of work there has been no record of it. With that same spirit of wifely devotion that does help the world to move, she superintended the packing of her household wares with the same executive ability that had been displayed in watching the cutting up of the beef. She had packed every rare piece of china, every wonderful old portrait, some of the latter having been made by well-known artists. She watched the packing of her elegant furniture, her silver—and her sampler. Special attention was given the packing of the books and family papers.

and then they put out for Galveston, the *summun bonum* then of everything in Texas, the entrance and the outlet of all important merchandise.   In Galveston they rented one big house built on colonial lines, and there they set up their household wares.

The Civil war came on within a few months.   To escape the dangers incident to life on the sea coast, after the fall of Galveston, the women and children were moved into Houston on the mainland, but when peace came, the Bollings went back to Galveston and there established on a scale commensurate with their Alabama-Virginia home their first real Texas one. Many folks in Texas to-day (1929), speak of that Galveston home.   After the horrors of war were a bit forgotten, after the Southern people realized that slavery had carried its obligations as well as its comforts, after they knew that the negroes of that generation were to serve as well as servants paid by the month as they had served as slaves—minus the obligation to care for them on the part of "massa," life on the old island began to run true to form.   Prosperity followed the efforts of the defeated people, and the Bolling home in the city by the sea became famous for its hospitality.

Mary, a woman of exquisite poise, made no objections to her husband's demands in the matter of entertaining. The woman who could run a plantation in the absence of her husband felt no dismay at the thought of an unexpected guest, and it became generally known that the best the country afforded in brains, in culture, in experience was to be met about her table.   Questions of state, of religion, legal tangles were all discussed about that board, our Mary able to bear in all of them no mean part.   Men less fortunate in education, but men worth while on their own endeavor mingled there with the more fortunate ones, Mary making it plain that the simple man, though worthy, was equal in her eyes with the man for whom much had been done.   There was Big Foot Wallace, and there was Rip Ford, both of them from Virginia, all of them Indian fighters in their day.   They hung about Bolling, Bolling enjoying them through their very difference in the matter of culture.   In this man's home, in the presence of his children's children, the old men told their yarns, dealing in the main with Indians and Mexicans.   Other children gathered there, and with our Mary's grandchildren sat willingly at the feet of the old warriors and learned their Texas history first hand.   These children listened to Isadore LeClere, in command right then of a company of soldiers, as he told of fights with Indians.   He claimed in the telling that every Texas man shared everything else he had with any Texas man—except his coffee.   That

liquid enjoyed a distinction, a notoriety that set it apart.
The pot in which it was brewed rarely got cold in the
average Texas home. It hung, too, over the camp fire,
always warm, always ready for each man a *certain number*
of times a day. LeClere learned—mysteriously—that one
of his men had taken to slipping in for an extra swallow of
the precious fluid. He bided his time until certain of this
selfish fellow's plans. He made no move to intercept him
in the act of taking that extra drink, but when that fellow
had emptied his tin cup, poured full of the reviving liquid,
LeClere calmly pulled an Indian scalp from the pot.
An Indian scalp from the standpoint of richness might
take the place of cream, but these men had not preferred
it. The one-time thieving man was thereafter satisfied
with his own share of the coffee, and his soldier brothers
were glad to follow his example.

Then Big Foot Wallace would give in grand style the
story of the Alamo. Prancing back and forth, his big
hands upraised, he could picture the men and women
huddled in the old church. He could tell with pathetic
beauty the story of the little child born in the Alamo during the fight. The children would listen to the story,
tears running down their cheeks. As if delighted with his
success as a story teller, Wallace would turn at once to
the glory of San Jacinto. He would dwell on Houston and
his skill in the leadership of men, of his prowess in battle,
and then after a vivid description of the firing of the little
Texas cannon would come the forceful account of the
Mexican plea: "Me no Alamo! Me no Goliad!"

Perhaps the Bollings regretted that they had no share
in the winning of Texas independence. We acknowledge
the possibility of such a regret, but they made it possible
for their grandchildren and other men's grandchildren to
learn of men who had borne the brunt of its battles, to
share in this way the heritage of children more fortunate.
Even as these Bollings raised their adopted children to
noble men and women, so they upheld through life the
glory of the country they had adopted, and such upholding
is never lost in the rough and tumble of development.

Mary Bolling died at the home of her son-in-law in
Galveston, at the age of seventy-six years. Her lover-
husband had gone on some time before. The last conscious act of his life had been the laying of a mantle about
our Mary's shoulders lest she suffer in the wind. Under
the blow of his sudden death—and who can question its
power?—she maintained the poise that had characterized
her through life. Forced into a railway journey with her
grand-daughter, her own feet crippled with rheumatism,
she watched her son-in-law fasten a Masonic pin on the

bosom of the little girl. A sweet thought, no doubt, one that helped in a way, but our Mary even in her old age possessed within herself the thing that outweighs emblems in the minds of men. Her own forceful loveliness, her own womanliness, brought her always the attention of men happening to be about her, and Mary throughout that journey lived the life of a queen.

So she passed through the earth, brave, tender, efficient, and the path of her passing is even for us of to-day passing sweet.

Data contributed by—

Mrs. George F. Pendexter,
Austin, Texas.

MRS. JAMES MONROE DANIELS

BORN

MARY ANN GREEN

At some time prior to the year 1836 a man named Green came with his wife from Tennessee to live in Texas. We have no right to say that General Houston and his coming to Texas had in any way influenced these young people, that he had ever suggested to them to exchange the well settled state of Tennessee for the wild one of Texas, but we do know that Green came to Texas at that time, that he took up land according to the colonization scheme, that he with his wife and slaves made of that land a plantation that held its own with any of its day. At the breaking out of war between Texas and Mexico, this Green became a scout in the little Texas army, and he related many stories of San Jacinto and of the events that preceded that famous day. Among other things he claimed always, that scouts had little trouble tracking the Mexican army, for the steady fire of cigarettes pointed their way, even in the dead of the night.

His part in this battle of San Jacinto done, Green retired with his wife to the upper part of East Texas. In December of 1840 they retired for some reason into the famous old stone fort at Nacogdoches, and there on December 6th, of that year a little daughter was born to them and given the wholesome, Texas-flavored name of Mary Ann. Two brothers, Newton and Art, with many other brothers and sisters, made up the family.

There is a peculiar pleasure in discussing the lives of women who differ radically from one's self on some one fundamental thing. This Mary Ann Green, efficient, sweet-tempered, strong-minded woman, had come from a family given to the Catholic faith. Her own mother had been a Catholic before her. Her uncles, her mother's brothers, had supplied funds to build the chapel at Nacogdoches, and to-day a cousin of Mary Ann's, Mary Burch, is Mother Superior at the Urseline convent in Galveston. Arriving at suitable age, therefore, our Mary Ann was placed in the convent then situated in Nacogdoches in order that she might be educated, and some there be to-day who willingly testify to its thoroughness.

From that school life Mary Ann returned to her father's plantation, not to work, for slaves in plenty waited to do her bidding. Not to be idle, we likewise assure you, for Mary Ann was past grand master of the needle. She made also exquisite tatting, and there is in existence to-day, a bedspread made by Mary Ann on knitting needles, the whole thing being made of diamond-shaped sections, knitted in raised design, put together and then bordered all around with fringe many inches deep. She made her own clothes, too, and helped about the family sewing.

But these labors failed to keep Mary Ann at home. She succeeded with her needle because she did most things well that she undertook. She was not given as a rule to the things that interest women, usually. She preferred the great outdoors and the sports to be found there. Simple matter this preference with the woods round Nacogdoches spread out for her pleasure. Holly, oak, pine, magnolia, hickory and beech crowded her very home door. She tramped the woods with her brothers. She rode horseback, too, and she was a good shot. We hazard the guess that she found a beauty in the woods, a solemnity, a something that made up a good part of her inner life. She learned there to find redeeming qualities in the Indians, and they loved her. As a child she played with the Indian children, teaching them and being taught in return. To her own grandchildren she sang the songs she learned from these strange playfellows, and the little Indians, no doubt, carried the memory of the little white maiden throughout their own lives. Perhaps she neglected some household duties—she did not like housework—but her slave women waited at home to do everything possible for so sweet a "missus," and Mary Ann's life felt not the slightest shadow of unhappiness.

And then, contrary to all ideas of law and order, of suitability of mind and purpose, when Mary Ann had reached seventeen years of age, she married a man named Armstrong, a dapper, orderly fellow who suffered agony if one pin stood crooked in the cushion on the bureau. No amount of suggestion from this overly clean husband changed Mary Ann's ideas on the subject. He came home one day to find the floor about his wife's chair littered with threads recently pulled from linen. Mary Ann knew the threads had no business on the floor at the hour of her husband's return home. She knew that wifely consideration demanded her attention thereto. But the work had been fascinating, and the time had flown, and the husband came in a bit too soon. She made no move to clear away the litter. Mr. Armstrong laid hold on the broom, and without one word, the slaves probably looking on, cleaned up the mess. Mary Ann was furious, but somewhere Mary Ann had learned to hold her tongue, and Mary Ann put said knowledge into stern action. We cannot say that the incident broke the little lady from throwing threads pulled from linen on the floor, but we have our suspicions. At another time, between the births of her two children, Mary Ann took a notion in the summer time that she must

have some spareribs of pork. Her husband replied that
it was too warm to kill pigs. Again our Mary Ann grew
furious, and this time she acted accordingly. She went to
the pen and killed the pig herself. As far as record sspeak
in the matter, the husband felt this to be a time in which
he had best have nothing at all to say. Not very long
after this incident, Mr. Armstrong died, leaving Mary Ann
alone on her plantation save for her slaves and her two
little children.

With that unexpected death casting its shadow, with the
work of maintaining the plantation home as Armstrong
had planned it staring her in the face, with the thought of
the children to be trained and fed, Mary Ann felt herself
unfit for the task. But her efforts brought results. Some
noble men and women descended from her little group,
and we of to-day have little right to discuss the ways and
means.

About a year after her husband's death Mary Ann put
forth for a walk in her beloved woods. According to her
own story, she went forth to think, to form some plans for
her daily life, her lonely woman's life burdened with the
care of two children. She felt right then her own responsibility in the matter, her own desire to do the best
for each child dependent upon her, and opportunities at
that time in Texas were exceedingly limited. Even in the
woods, surrounded by every possible beauty, Mary Ann's
courage had failed her a bit. She dropped down on a fallen
log and the failure of her courage was written upon her
countenance.

Now that countenance was beautiful. Every line in her
face had fulfilled its youthful promise. Marriage, the
birth of her children, the death of her husband, had left
tracks not to be denied, but the tenderness in her own
heart had sweetened, had glorified her in every way for
the eye of man. She must have formed there upon that
log in the woods, the soft East Texas air about her, she
must have formed in every way a picture not to be denied.

The necessary observer of the picture appeared in due
time. This observer answered to the name of Daniels.
He was rated a highly educated man in his day. He had
studied both medicine and law, but he leaned toward the
latter for a profession. He could write poetry, reams of
it, our Mary Ann Green Armstrong in sight, and this he
proceeded to do at every opportunity. Moreover, he had
enjoyed practice in the lover's art. Some years before he
had married a Miss Fitzgerald from Columbus, and two
children had been born to them. The wife had been dead
about one year at the time of this romantic meeting in the
woods, and before very long, love had its way, and his

children and her children watched the two of them pay
their marriage vows to each other.

Life moved on gently as it moves for folks who do their
share.   Daniels opened a law office in Columbus, did well
at the practice, and the four children in the home welcomed
each in its turn four more children born of this second
marriage.   The oldest of the four children became in time
the partner of Sidney Porter in the paper known as the
Rolling Stone.   After many sorrows and tribulations, this
Sidney Porter became known to the world as O'Henry,
which, by the way, is another story.

Mary Ann may have put some more linen threads on the
floor, but if so Daniels had nothing to say.   Mayhap our
beautiful lady had learned that discarded threads had best
be thrown immediately into the fire.   At any rate it was
apparent to all concerned that Mary Ann was living the
happiest life she had ever known, the life of a loved and
honored wife who loves and honors her husband in return.

The sheriff appeared one day in the office of Daniels in
Austin and told him that the notorious gang of robbers and
desperadoes, headed by Jesse James, had appeared in
Lampasas and that he was wanted to go along with the
party made up to take the outlaw.   Daniels, being patriotic,
had no alternative, and he shouldered his gun, sent a message
to Mary Ann in their home at Fiskville, six miles away, and
joined the posse.

They found their man in a Lampasas saloon, his gang
gathered about him.   The gang filled all requirements of
the outlaw idea, even in that wild time.   They had selected,
too, for their stopping place the most suitable haunt in the
world, the old-fashioned saloon where wine and beer and
whiskey were sold unrestrainedly, where gambling raged
day and night, where women of questionable morals were
ever at hand to add to the horror.   Fully aware that a
reward had been offered for him, dead or alive, James began shooting at the party as they appeared, his men
following suit.   To the surprise of all concerned, the bar-
tender entered the ranks of the gang, and Daniels was
killed by a bullet from this man's gun.

And what of that wife, our adoring Mary Ann?   On that
farm near Fiskville, with the three sets of children, she
waited   the   homecoming   of   her   lover-husband.   The
telegram containing the news of his death was relayed
through Austin, reaching her at the cow-pen, in the act
of milking.   She read the short, incisive message—and
fainted, for the first time in her life.   As long as she lived
afterwards nobody ever sent her another telegram.

But Mary Ann must take up her life again.   Her children needed her and within herself, the woman had some

MRS. HERMANN LUNGKWITZ

BORN

ELSIE PETRI

In a neat little cottage nestled beneath the century old oaks at the head of the deep ravine just east of Shoal creek and reaching toward it, with palms and ferns a-flourish about the immaculate yard—in this cottage dwells a daughter of the only early Texas artist brought to our notice—so far. She ranks among women as one of keen insight, level judgment, stern in her adherence to the right, but possessed as well of a heart full of tender mercy and loving kindness. Her father's pictures adorn the walls of her little house, real pictures, betraying the master hand, and the woman sits her down beneath them to tell us, not of the artist himself, but of the wife of the artist, her own mother.

We are glad to include this sketch among our pioneer women in Texas. Married life as a rule entitles women to honorable mention. This woman's life entitled her, maybe, to a little more. It brought her into daily association with a keen-sighted man, one quick to catch the shades of color, the dance of the sunlight on the wall and on the water— one just as quick to catch other forms and shadow and shortcomings, just as intense in the latter catching as if they too, must be reproduced upon canvas. Not an easy place to fill, I hear you say, and then I remind you that she was the only woman in Texas prior to 1860 who occupied this honorable, uneasy position.

Mrs. Lungkwitz, known in her youth as one of the four beautiful Petri sisters, was born in Dresden, Saxony, April 23, 1823. The home was a beautiful three-storied house, and the four girls with their brothers brought thereto the young folks of the neighborhood, and all over Saxony for that matter. There were balls and banquets. There were elegant clothes and jewels, for Petri had prospered in the world, and he was not inclined to deny his children the fruit of his labor. One son, the youngest brother of our Elsie, Richard Petri, was an artist. He had studied at the Kunst Academy of Fine Arts under the famous Ludwig Richter. During the course of this study he formed an intimate acquaintance with a fellow artist, a man much older than himself, and together they sketched and they talked art, planning for a future for each that was to be full of all manner of delights. Richard invited his sister Elsie to the art exhibit. Elsie must of course meet her brother's friend, this Mr. Hermann Lungkwitz.

Now beauty, female or otherwise, is supposed to entice men. When the certain individual man under question happens to be a strong, virile man, possessed with all other qualifications of the ability to see, to analyze beauty in women, when such an individual comes into the presence of real beauty, then all kinds of delightful things are sure to take place. The meeting of the beautiful Elsie with her brother's artist companion ran true to form. Love's young dream began in earnest, and the young people were married shortly afterwards, at some time in the year 1850.

Troubles began to deepen soon after this marriage. Remember the revolution in Saxony had taken place in the year 1848. The men inciting this revolution were earnest and honest in their efforts and purposes. They had begged the king for some form of municipal rights, some form of representation in the government of Saxony. He had refused all pleas, all demands, all suggestions. When the dissatisfied people rose against him, the king of Saxony called on the king of Prussia to aid him and the revolution was a failure.

Now Lungkwitz had been numbered among the revolutionists. He had dreamed with other men of the life in a free nation, governed by a free people who made their own laws and executed them. They had grown tired, too, of the eternal warfare, planned and executed for the gratification of the king's vanity. Therefore, some two years after the failure of that revolution, we find our Elsie married to her artist lover and ready to sail for America, even for Texas.

Now why had they felt called to come to Texas? They were living in Germany, even in the city of Dresden, famous for its culture, its ease, its plenty. They had known all the comforts brought by civilization. Did they value these things so little that they were ready to give them up for a whim? Far from it. They felt in their hearts, they even declared to each other that they sought in the new country the political, religious freedom that had been denied them in the old. Affairs in Texas had been painted for them in glowing terms, in colors rich and rare, as some of Lungkwitz's own canvases. They had believed every glorious story of the rich, new land, a state in the United States to be sure, but one in which men met on terms of equality, where men saw to it that no man ever dared oppress his fellow. Romantic? Aye, even for these Saxony seekers after truth.

It is easy to imagine the conditions that met these people. They lived, Lungkwitz and Petri brothers, for a little while at New Braunfels. There it became plain to the young artists that they might not live by their work unless they persuaded other men to believe in its value. Lungkwitz and Petri made trips to San Antonio, walking all the way, in the hope of selling some pictures there. They felt sure that they must find some educated people in the city who would appreciate their work. They did sell some pictures, and they made drawings of San Antonio and Fredericksburg which were sent to Dresden to be lithographed.

Shortly after this trip the Lungkwitz and Petri families moved to Fredericksburg. They built there a big log house, two rooms and a hall with a kitchen and smokehouse close by, and then our Elsie and her sisters, they who had lived in ease and plenty in Dresden, they must turn their attention to the control of the house, to the milking of the cows, and other menial tasks, for these emigrants had brought no slaves with them. And the men, even Lungkwitz and Petri, who had dreamed all their lives of artistic things, must plough and sow and reap into barns that they and others might be fed. Elsie watched them at such labor, resentfully, perhaps, remembering her husband's talent, but Elsie had her fund of common sense.

To her the idea of bread was real, and she bowed before it. But she managed as the days came and went, days full of labor for her and all the colony, to incite her artist-husband to take up his work again. She managed to make days for him when he might be free to see and feel the beauty lying prodigally about him. She even dared criticise his work—he claimed afterwards that she was ever his best critic—and life by and by began to lighten. They organized singing societies, ringing out the lusty, martial airs of the Germany they had left behind. They met together socially, they learned to know each other's wants, each other's dreams.

Six children were born to Elsie. She watched them grow, thinking doubtless in the wilderness of the home in which she had grown to womanhood. She gave them the best of herself, dreaming of the future as it must be for those children, dreams just like those which warm and strengthen the heart of motherhood to-day.

The war following secession broke into this peaceful life. The necessary restrictions, the necessary sacrifices of war soon appeared. Blockade on the coast placed coffee and sugar at a premium. Accustomed to the afternoon coffee at gatherings of women, they parched corn and other grains and concocted a make-believe beverage. On Sundays they added twelve grains of the precious coffee, in honor of the day, in honor, too, of the demand for the old-time flavor. Previous to this war, the Indians had given them no trouble. They had, if anything, been too friendly. They had appeared in the homes from time to time, glad to exchange fresh meat for bread and other delicacies. The war incited them to treachery. They stole the white man's horses, and when the man went to look for his property, trouble nearly always ensued. Some men were killed outright in the effort to recover the animals, and the fear in the hearts of the women may be imagined.

But this trouble passed. Reconstruction meant little to people who had never owned slaves. Gradually the tide of life swung back, and Elsie saw the peaceful home life resumed. They moved shortly thereafter to San Antonio, and there she saw her husband take up his artistic work again. She watched the picture of the "Enchanted Rock" in Llano County take on form. She criticised the painting of Bear Mountain, near Fredericksburg. She spoke her mind until the painted granite took on the pink, grey hue of the Texas stone. She watched him picture the Indian crossing on the Guadalupe river near Comfort, having again her say as to the light and shadows on the everlasting green of the oaks. These artistic criticisms done, our Elsie could then sit her down and read and knit at the same time, two occupations she enjoyed. She was also an expert needle woman, making her stitches firm and even and fine, as some work extant to-day will show.

A question as to her religious attitude brings the suggestion that in the emigration to America these people had left behind some of their religious enthusiasm. They were protestants in Germany, and in the Texas home, the Protestant minister made a long journey to the home in order to christen the first-born son. All neighbors were invited to this christening. But the distances were great, and the ministers few, and they gradually gave up the idea of public worship. But we hazard a guess that this wife, loving her home, her brothers and sisters, idealizing her husband and his work, leading her own children in paths best for their untried feet, we hazard a guess that this tender, beautiful woman had inculcated in her inner consciousness that lasting beauty of life and heart and soul that made of her a true disciple of Him who went about doing good.

She died in 1880, just fifty-seven years of age. Perhaps life in the wilderness of Texas had been too much for her. Perhaps the trying position of wife to her artistic lover had been a bit too keen. Perhaps—but Elise had never allowed it said in her presence, brave, tender, patient wife of him who has left behind much work full of beauty and of power.

Data contributed by—

    Mrs. Jacob Bickler,
    Austin, Texas.

MRS. ISAAC VAN ZANDT

BORN

FRANCES LIPSCOMB

After the first careful reading of the happenings in the life of Mrs. Isaac Van Zandt, a collection of happenings given, in part, by herself, your scribe laid the paper aside slowly, even reverently, for she had felt all at once that she had thoughtlessly intruded upon sacred things. From out that mass of details, details of unlimited value to the student of Texas history, there had emerged the figure of a woman, barely thirty years of age, the one-time wife of a man strong in this world, powerful in his time, the mother, even then, of five children, and left alone, a widow in the wilderness. To-day, many women face that burden of widowed mother-hood, face it bravely, and in a measure cheerfully, face it successfully, too, hiding from family and friends the des-olation that widowhood has brought. To-day, be it re-membered, no Indian lurks about, no jealous Mexican watches the doings of his imported neighbor, and the wilderness of Texas has long since blossomed into beauty and power. These things being true, that strangely, solitary figure of a woman represents to him who would see a forceful something well-nigh beyond our understand-ing of to-day.

But now, suppose we forget for the time this impressive little figure and proceed in all seriousness to learn something of our heroine's life. The daughter of William and Ann Day Lipscomb, our Frances was born March 4th, 1816, in Louisa County, Virginia. When Frances had reached her twelfth year, she moved with her parents to Salem, Frank-lin County, Tennessee. In this new home, Frances grew to womanhood, fair and sweet, we take it, though she leaves this for us to say, for in December of 1833, she became the bride of Isaac Van Zandt. Van Zandt was some three years older than his bride, a man of some education, a man of much brain power as subsequent events proved, and Frances faced this marriage venture with little thought in her heart save that success would crown their united efforts.

Young folks rarely succeed in life's battle if denied this faith in themselves. Said faith is indeed a tower of strength and all kinds of pillars of fire throughout the rainy, desolate night. Sometimes, even the faith fails to see the real result, fails to make the world see the matter as each would have it see, but not often. In this case faith and a few other virtues did each their perfect work—but not immediately. We find that Isaac Van Zandt and our Frances moved to Mississippi after some two or three years of married life, that Van Zandt engaged there in some form of mercantile business, and in 1837, lost in the venture, everything he had previously accumulated. Still, and we depend on the words of Frances herself, she did not lose her faith in her husband and lover, nor yet in her own bright self, and when her husband suggested midst their trials that they move to Texas, our Frances grasped the idea at once and eagerly. Her husband had spent the twelve months elapsing since his mercantile failure in the study of law, and had made a business trip to Texas. He no doubt returned from that trip with much to say of Texas, for he was under the lure of the new and the beautiful country in which lands were to be had for the asking and the whole world seemed there to be laid at the feet of the energetic. So with her husband and two children—babies two and four years of age—Frances stepped happily onto the boat at Memphis, slipped thus down the Mississippi river to Natches, then up Red river to Natchitoches, across to old Fort Sabine, still happy, for, to quote her own words, "Texas was to me the land of promise."

Fort Sabine, a collection of some fifty houses, had been abandoned, but the water there was good, and many people stopped there on the way. Several months our Frances must remain there, waiting with her husband for some money from a former partner, which money never came. Frances stood the privations well enough, but her husband, never very strong, was often very ill. The burden must fall of course on the wife. In this fort Frances traded her best dress for five bushels of corn and the next best for a bottle of medicine.

At last, a bit weary of the foolish wait in old Fort Sabine, a wait made anxious by fears of Indians—which by the way were never realized—the Van Zandts traded the small amount of furniture they had brought from Mississippi for transportation to the part of Texas now known as Harrison County. There they set themselves down in a log cabin of one room, an unfinished cabin, too, knowing that they had two neighbors only, each of them living within a mile, but the distance to the post office from this palatial abode stretched to some fourteen miles.

Of the many things incident to life in this cabin, when Frances Van Zandt came to tell the story, she seemed determined to stress one thing above all others. Stating that it was many times necessary for her husband to be away from home, she gives one the idea that her few neighbors were ever ready to help her in every possible way.

"If we had no meat, we felt no hesitancy in going to a neighbor for it—if he had any. To the first wedding to which I was invited in Texas, I carried the dress in which

the bride was married, and the plates from which we ate
the wedding dinner." This same idea held good in the
fight with the Indians. Men divided themselves into
squads in the days of the republic in Texas in order that
they might keep a sharp lookout for Indians. One day a
man came to Van Zandt, explained that his turn had come
in the Indian defense, so to speak, but that he every moment
expected a new baby in his little cabin home. Without
question, without parley as to price, Van Zandt immediately
and willingly took the man's place. In return for this
gracious service, the man so relieved gave Van Zandt a
beef. Said animal was killed, the meat divided between
the neighbors, and then our Isaac, not to be outdone in
thrift, either by men or women, tanned the hide, made a
shoe-last of a sapling, and enjoyed for the next year or so
a pair of comfortable, homemade shoes. With a saw and
a drawing knife for tools, Van Zandt made a crib for the
baby that arrived in his own family, soon after he moved
to Harrison County.

This home in Harrison County, so it seems to your scribe,
was the scene of many events of importance. Our young
people took charge in 1842, but before that event in family
history could materialize the place had to be reached. The
way of that reach was across some swollen streams, and
one day, that family load found itself beside a stream so
angry, so restless, so brimful, that to undertake to ford
it had been foolish. The wagon-bed was, therefore, taken
to pieces, formed into a raft, and the people thereon floated
safely over. But, O, shades of hunger! As the chicken
coop with its inmates was lifted from the bank toward this
newly made raft, some of them escaped. Frances' heart
sank down, and then down, for Frances had some sensible
idea of the food question in Texas. She knew from long
experience that a chicken is likely to be a law unto himself,
but then the meat problem in early Texas was likely to be
a law, too. Judge of her delight, when the morning finally
smiled upon them, to find that in the night the chickens
had flown across the stream in search of their old mistress.
Maybe, now maybe, remember, the chicken had found
himself unable to forget the hand that had fed him.

But these people found themselves at home at last in one
large room, the very first home they owned in Texas, and
this was in 1842. They professed to be mightily pleased
with the cabin, because, forsooth, it boasted a puncheon
floor. This cabin had been sturdily built, too, for it is
standing to-day (1928), but our Frances has left statements
to the effect that the cabin was so loosely constructed that
the Texas wind, utterly careless of the comfort of human
beings, frequently blew the cover from the beds in this

cabin home, and that, too, when the only possible point of entry was the cracks between the logs. Maybe so, maybe comforts were lacking, but within those hallowed walls, the Texas homestead law was conceived. Later, its author, Isaac Van Zandt, left that cabin for his work in Washington, and no man matching brains with Van Zandt from Texas ever cared that his home had boasted a puncheon floor, and the wind entered with ease the chinks in its walls. And Frances, the wife left at home, the husband as he left fully confident that she might run things to his satisfaction! Was her satisfaction complete? Hardly. No ordinary woman could be satisfied under such conditions, but this woman lived in the glory of the day yet to come. Meantime, she spent few months repining. She taught herself in that cabin home to eat bear meat. There she made another woman a dress, taking in payment for the labor a hatchet. There she traded a bunch of peafowl feathers to two Indians (the only Indians by the way, that she ever saw in Texas) for a ham of venison. There she found comfort in a bunch of hogs asleep beneath the house, for she knew that the hogs might be depended upon in her husband's absence to raise an alarm if intruders came her way. She spun the cotton and the wool into thread, and then wove it into cloth. She made the cloth into clothes, the sewing all done by hand. She made her husband an overcoat from a wool blanket, carded the remaining scraps into thread, and knit the thread into comfortable socks for that same beloved husband.

Now suppose we look a bit into the political life of Van Zandt. It was about 1840, that said life took on form and meaning. The man had just returned from a three months' business trip to Mississippi, was sick in bed with malarial fever when Bailey Anderson appeared, and stated to the man just recovering from a chill, probably, that the only way in which they might hope to defeat an undesirable candidate for a seat in the Texas Congress was to see that Van Zandt ran against him. There was no little anxiety over the matter, so declared Anderson, for Texas, a proud republic before the world, was at heart still afraid of Mexico. The results? Isaac Van Zandt, but one year resident of the little republic—no, the young republic, was elected to its Congress.

In the notes placed before your scribe, Frances has left a clear, concise statement of her husband's political attitude. She states that her husband's first speech in Congress was made in opposition to Mr. Houston's bill to sell the Cherokee Indian lands. Mr. Houston made short reply to the speech, saying only that the young man reminded him of the goat that jumped so high it broke its

city life as it came to her notice. She lived to see, right there in that same city, the birth of her one hundred and fourth descendant. Thirty-six of these descendants were members, with Frances, of the First Christian church of Fort Worth. Christian union was a ruling passion with Francis, and she frequently exclaimed: "No book but the Bible, no name but Christian, no creed but Christ."

For thirty-one years a widow in the wilderness, her little children in the beginning, crowded about her. Until some of them could reach the age suitable for work, Frances must supply their every need. Then it was that Frances realized fully the existence of the thing she, herself, classed as the best thing to be found in a new country, the spirit of loving helpfulness existent between all peoples. She realized then, even more fully, that a woman, when the need arises, can meet any obligation, bear any burden, endure any pain. She continued to trade corn for cloth when it was necessary, and she made many short cuts, and, maybe, sometimes yearned a bit for the "flesh-pots of Egypt," but our Frances made it through to ease and plenty, to peace and prosperity.

Once in the latter end of her life, the peaceful end, she fell ill, only to recover her health and strength, even to the astonishment of her own physician. When he found her one morning, free from fever and free from pain, he stood, looking a bit nonplused if the truth were told, stood there quietly looking down into the determined face smiling back at him from the pillow. Faith in his own skill had been tried, almost to the limit. According to all laws established by all schools of medicine, her life should have ended in the night. But there she lay, careless of his lack of hope for her, there she lay a little weak, perhaps, but otherwise ready in every way to take up the battle again.

And that physician, a man honest to the core, forgetful that his own skill might have played a good part—that man turned from that bed exclaiming: "Plague take these old Texans! They can stand anything."

Data contributed by—

    Mrs. Ida Van Zandt Jarvis,
    Fort Worth, Texas.